Pay Dirt

The Business of Professional Team Sports

James Quirk and Rodney D. Fort

D0068188

Princeton University Press

Princeton · New Jersey

Library of Congress Cataloging-in-Publication Data
Quirk, James P.
Pay dirt : the business of professional team sports / James Quirk
and Rodney D. Fort
p. cm.
Includes bibliographical references and index.
ISBN 0-691-04255-1
ISBN 0-691-01574-0 (pbk.)
1. Professional sports—Economic aspects—United States.
I. Fort, Rodney D. II. Title.
GV716.Q57 1992 338.4'3796—dc20 92-15349

This book has been composed in Trump by
Pine Tree Composition, Inc.

Princeton University Press books are printed on acid-free paper
and meet the guidelines for permanence and durability of
the Committee on Production Guidelines for Book Longevity
of the Council on Library Resources

Second printing, and first paperback printing,
with an update by the authors, 1997

Printed in the United States of America

3 5 7 9 10 8 6 4

To Shirl and Leslie

Contents

List of Illustrations

Plates

Following page 332

1. Chris von der Ahe
2. John Montgomery Ward
3. Charles Comiskey and Ban Johnson
4. Judge Kenesaw Mountain Landis
5. Colonel Jacob Ruppert, Miller Huggins, and Frank Chance
6. Red Grange and C. C. Pyle
7. Babe Ruth and Jacob Ruppert
8. Stan Kostka
9. Bill Veeck
10. Ben Lindheimer, Dud DeGroot, and Harry M. Thayer
11. Branch Rickey, Burt Shotton, and Leo Durocher
12. Walter O'Malley
13. George Halas
14. Red Auerbach and Fred Schaus
15. Pete Rozelle
16. Al Davis
17. Gary Davidson and George Mikan
18. Marvin Miller
19. Ed Garvey
20. George Steinbrenner

Figures

List of Illustrations

List of Tables

List of Tables

List of Tables

Update
(for the paperback edition)

THE mid 1990s' years since this book first came out, the Clinton years, were "the best of times, and the worst of times" for professional team sports. How else to describe a period in which, for all sports except strike-ravished major league baseball, payments for television rights continued to skyrocket, carrying along with them ever-increasing player salaries, team profits, and franchise values? According to *Financial World*, in 1996 an average NFL team was worth $174 million; an average NBA team, $127 million; an average major league baseball team, $115 million; and an average NHL team, $74 million. Multimillion-dollar contracts in all sports have become commonplace, and superstar players such as Michael Jordan have become so well known and so salable that they can earn much more from commercials and endorsements than from their player salaries. Even team owners such as Jerry Jones and George Steinbrenner have their own TV commercial careers.

But this has been the worst of times as well. How else to describe a period that included a bitter baseball strike and the cancellation of the 1994 World Series, Los Angeles losing both of its NFL teams to much smaller markets, and Art Modell deserting arguably the most loyal fans in football for greener pastures in Baltimore? And how else to describe a time when newspapers began to carry a special feature on the sports pages, "sports jurisprudence," bringing fans up-to-date on the latest illicit activities (including barroom brawling and DWIs, substance abuse, dealing in drugs and wife battering, among other misdemeanors and felonies) of well-known athletes, stars, and superstars?

The premise of this book, certainly not a novel one, is that the key to understanding modern-day pro team sports is to follow the money trail, wherever it leads. If there are still any lingering doubts about this, the events of the past three or four years should banish them. The behavior of leagues, team owners, and players is best understood in terms of simple economic self-interest, and increasingly, if there's a conflict with outsiders, the rule is "the public be damned."

When the NFL's TV contracts came up for renewal in 1994, CBS, which had televised league games since the advent of national broadcasts in 1962, submitted a bid of $1 billion for coverage of the next three years of NFC games. Their bid was topped by Fox's bid of $1.6 billion, as Fox tried to turn the Big Three (CBS, NBC, and ABC) into the Big Four. Thirty-two years of close cooperation by CBS with the NFL went down the drain, as the NFL made the obvious economic choice of following its self-interest and dropping CBS for Fox. To put things in context, data on the history of the market value of TV rights for pro team sports appears in the Data Supplement to this book.

In Milwaukee, Bud Selig was something of a hometown hero because of his 1970 success in bringing the bankrupt Seattle Pilots to town as the Brewers, to replace the departed Milwaukee Braves. Selig himself had been a vocal critic of the "carpetbaggers" who bought and moved the Braves in the mid 1960s, but that was history. After botching up an attempt to bring the union to heel in his job as acting commissioner of baseball in the mid 1990s, Selig announced to the good citizens of Wisconsin that he would move the Brewers, as the carpetbaggers had moved the Braves thirty years earlier, unless there was an infusion of a cool $160 million (or maybe $210 million) in public money for a new stadium to replace County Stadium. If some other city was willing to pony up the money for a stadium, how could anyone argue with the economic logic of squeezing as much as possible out of the hometown and state? What in the world should loyalty to one's hometown fans have to do with an owner's decision?

The Seattle Mariners got the message from their (acting) commissioner, and parlayed a similar blackmailing threat into an agreement for a new stadium to open in 1998. Following a publicly financed bailout of the Target Center and the Minnesota Timberwolves, Twins owner Carl Pohlad announced that he was unhappy with attendance at the Humphrey Metrodome, and would have to consider his options if plans were not begun for a new state-of-the-art, baseball-only facility in the Twin Cities. The Metrodome was only 14 years old, but apparently the rate of obsolescence of stadiums had increased, especially since the construction of the successful big-bucks facilities in Toronto, Baltimore, and Cleveland. In 1995, to buttress Pohlad's argument about bad attendance, the Twins held a fire sale of high-priced players, and set a team record for ERA ineptness, ending in the AL cellar and drawing the proverbial flies.

In fairness, we should commend the other Metrodome tenant, the Vikings, who had threatened to leave 16 years earlier if a new stadium (the Metrodome) had not been built. The Vikings announced that they were quite happy with the Metrodome as a facility; all they wanted was to solidify their ties to the Twin Cities by taking over the revenues earned by the stadium. In today's climate, that counts as a major concession by a team.

Back in Seattle, the Seahawks tried as hard as they could to make the not-entirely-convincing argument that earthquake dangers in Seattle made it necessary for them to move to southern California (!). But the NFL stood up for principle on this proposed move. However, it was not the somewhat flawed nature of Ken Behring's argument, but the fact that there was a big payday awaiting the owners on the arrival of a new expansion team into the recently vacated Los Angeles and Orange counties that got the backs of the other NFL owners up. This was the kind of principle that the owners truly did understand, something to take a stand on.

It is still too early to tell for sure—fans have a history of dedication to players and teams far above and beyond the call of duty—but the mid 1990s might mark the beginning of the end of the extended love affair between fans and pro team sports. One of the interesting and significant straws in the wind is a recall election that took place in Wisconsin in June 1996. The state senator who was subjected to recall had switched his vote to one in favor of a new stadium for the Brewers, allowing that bill to pass the state senate by just one vote. The bill increased the sales tax on residents in his district and was met with strong objections. For the first time in Wisconsin history, a sitting state senator lost a recall vote, and it happened purely and simply on the basis of the sports stadium issue.

The love affair of fans with pro sports began somewhere in the late 1960s to mid 1970s, and has carried on for over 20 years. In hindsight, it appears that the love fest grew out of a combination of technological and demographic factors. The rise of television as an entertainment medium and the TV-friendly nature of team sports combined to make the emerging baby boomer generation, the first generation to be raised on TV, the dominant targeted market for advertisers. Pro team sports piggybacked on these underlying factors to become the big, booming, profitable business—for owners and players alike—that we see today.

There is no lack of irony in the current situation in pro sports. The single most important factor in the marketing of pro sports is the identification of fans with "their" home teams. Substantial sums have been invested over time by teams and leagues to establish just such fan identification and loyalty. But these long term investments in goodwill are eroded by the short term profit-motivated actions of team owners. Fans are beginning to discover the unpleasant fact that loyalty in pro team sports is definitely a one-way street. If an owner is unhappy with the current stadium contract, or if there are sweeter deals elsewhere, the record of the past few years makes it clear that a team stays in a city only at the owner's sufferance. There is no such thing as a "city's" team or a "fan's" team—a pro sports team is strictly and unequivocally the "owner's" team. In the short run, the owner might be able to use his or her leverage to extract more money out of a local government, but in the long run, costs are potentially disastrous for a sports league. Fans with no sense of identification or loyalty to a team will desert a losing team like rats leaving a sinking ship, and half the teams in any league are going to have losing records each year.

In the past, leagues exercised a modicum of control (not much control, admittedly, but some) over the movement of member teams. The NFL's lack of interest in short-circuiting Art Modell's move stems in part from the impact of the financial penalties the league suffered in the antitrust case arising from its refusal to sanction the Raiders' move from Oakland to L.A. (The Raiders have now deserted Los Angeles for a return to Oakland.) But there are other long term factors at work. Traditionally, owners settled their disputes within the league; appeals to the courts were true rarities. Tradition, however, is a thing of the past, reflecting the simple fact that teams have become so expensive and have so much potential prestige and dollar value that owners are no longer willing to accept, willy-nilly, the rules of the league when their interests are threatened.

The problems created by resorting to the court system are not trivial. Court cases expose the dirty linen of teams and leagues as well as financial facts that owners prefer to keep private, possibly leading to a souring of public relations. Ultimately, the true nightmare of owners, namely, regulation of the industry or actions by the Department of Justice to enforce the antitrust laws against leagues, might result. The checkered history of sports and antitrust laws is covered in Chapter 5.

The size of the stakes involved on the part of owners has also led to the decline in the powers and prestige of league commissioners—in fact, baseball has managed to get along, if that is the correct phrase for it, without a commissioner since the untimely death of Bart Giamatti in 1993. League commissioners have always represented the owners against the world; that is, against Congress, players, cities, television networks, the IRS—all the potential enemies. But commissioners have also acted to promote the interest of the league when it has come into conflict with the interest of individual owners. It is this aspect of the commissioner's role that has eroded as the dollars involved in sports have grown. As the power of the commissioner declines, there are fewer restraints on the actions of individual team owners, and teams are free to pursue strategies that benefit themselves—even when they are at the expense of other team owners or of the league as a whole.

The erosion of fan loyalty to teams and to players has been exacerbated by disputes between owners and player unions. During strikes and lockouts, which occur with predictable regularity in sports, releases by owners paint players as overpaid, arrogant, and selfish. Fans can identify with this portrait because it is descriptive of only too many players. Still, from an owner's point of view, this method of defense is not really a terribly smart way to entice fans into the stadium or arena once the strike or lockout is over. The public relations battles between players and owners, coupled with public reports of high player salaries and owners' blackmailing threats, have led to a situation where it is a toss-up whether fans dislike players or owners more. That they dislike both groups is not a matter in dispute. There is a growing realization among fans that player-owner labor disputes are just battles between two wealthy insider groups to decide which side gets more of the spoils that the much less wealthy fans provide from the outside. Is it any wonder that the general public attitude is "a pox on both your houses"?

In the mid 1990s, the big issue in labor disputes was the salary cap; that is, placing both a floor and a ceiling on the amount that any team could spend on salaries. Owners argued that a salary cap was essential if "competitive balance" was to be preserved in a league, and essential for the very survival of small-town teams as well. The NBA instituted a salary cap in 1983, and in terms of attendance, TV revenues, profits, salaries, and public acceptance, has had its most successful years since. The other leagues have pointed to the success of the NBA to justify introducing a salary cap in their sports. Interestingly, data on salaries show that because of various provisos and exceptions to the rules, the NBA salary cap did not result in equalizing salary payments among teams, as advertised by league owners. Nor has there been an increase in competitive balance under the salary cap. In fact, league championships have been even more highly concentrated since the cap came into effect. The evidence suggests that the success of the NBA was due in part to the general increase in interest in sports during the 1980s, and in part to the very popular superstars who came on the scene during the period, such as Bird, Magic, and Michael. The latest NBA contract provides for a "hard" cap, which is supposed to close the loopholes. Based on past experience, though, don't bet too much that the Bulls will be spending the same as the Timberwolves.

In 1994, following a long string of losing and expensive antitrust suits involving its players' association (par for the course for the NFL when dealing with the NFLPA), the NFL put its version of the salary cap in place, arguing that this was an essential step in preserving competitive balance in the NFL. A year later, Commissioner Tagliabue announced that, despite the salary cap, competitive balance was still such a problem that it could only be solved if smaller cities built new stadiums with more luxury boxes and funneled more stadium revenue to teams. So much for the argument that the salary cap would eliminate the NFL's competitive balance problems.

But it was the baseball owners, the true dinosaurs in labor relations in sports, who made the salary cap an absolute article of faith: there was to be a salary cap or no baseball, period. The sport could not survive without a cap. The frustration of the owners is understandable—they had a lifetime batting average of around .115 in dealing with the union, and they had to figure on hitting a homerun, winning a strike/lockout, sometime, for Pete's sake! Unfortunately for Bud Selig and his fellow owners, this was not the time. After losing roughly $800 million in revenues (and about $300 million in profits), and after canceling the 1994 World Series, the owners finally faced facts and backed down from their non-negotiable support of the cap. The economics of competitive balance are discussed in Chapter 7.

The baseball situation is interesting because of the antitrust exemption that baseball enjoys. In the other sports, owners really need unions. They need them because the kinds of restrictions they want to impose on their labor markets (for example, rules with respect to college drafts) would be violations of the antitrust laws if not for the nonstatutory labor exemption. This exemption applies to agreements between an employer and a union, so long as the provisions of the labor contract are arrived at by arms-length negotiations and have minimal effects on third parties. But baseball is exempt from antitrust, so it has no need for the labor exemption, leaving the owners free to pursue the disastrous course they have followed ever since Marvin Miller was hired as head of the baseball players' association in the late 1960s. The attitude has been one of treating the labor negotiations process as a way to break the back of the union. Hope seems to spring eternal among the owners, but perhaps the 1994 fiasco opened enough eyes to scuttle this strategy in the future.

Within player unions, problematic changes are taking place as well. In many ways, pro team sports reflects the same kinds of tensions and pressures that affect the rest of the society. It is well known that, in the broader society, the gulf between the haves and the have-nots keeps growing. The same is true with respect to sports salaries, as is documented in Chapter 6. Not only have superstar salaries gone up dramatically over the past twenty years, but the percentage of total salaries that superstar salaries occupy has gone up almost as dramatically.

Before the free-agency era, it was legitimate to talk about the reserve clause as owners' exploitation of players as a group. Player unions were organized in the 1960s and early 1970s as a joint effort among players of varying skill and earning power levels to offset the monopoly power of owners. Today, conflicts between journeymen players, earning the league minimum, and the multimillion-dollar-salaried superstars are a fact of life. One striking example from the recent past is a group of superstar NBA players' attempt to derail the collective bargaining agreement that was reached by the NBA and its players' association in 1995. Certainly there will be a push in the future for union activities directed more toward higher minimum salaries and greater fringe benefits, and less toward maintaining or improving the bargaining power of a select group of superstars. Among other things, the salary cap acts to heighten the tensions between star players and other players—every extra dollar spent on a superstar means that much less for the rest of the roster. The potential of salary caps to create problems within the union is one of the reasons that player unions have opposed the cap so vigorously. Additionally, internal squabbles within player associations have the potential for further eroding fan loyalties to players.

It is particularly ironic that pro team sports sells vigorous competition on the playing field, while their growing public relations and substantive problems arise almost entirely from the fact that pro sports leagues are monopolized cartels. As long as pro sports was only a marginally profitable enterprise—the state of the industry as a whole up to around the 1960s—the problems stemming from monopoly were also marginal, excluding their effects on players. But when pro sports became big business, the problems arising from monopoly power became big, too.

It seems a long time ago now, but it was only forty years ago that local governments simply were not players in the pro team sports game. Partly, this was because of the ethos of the times; local governments weren't supposed to be in the business of subsidizing private enterprises. But added to this was the limited political clout of the sport constituency, which typically did not include the local establishment.

As pro sports franchises increased in both monetary value and prestige, owners, as economically rational cartel members, "naturally" took advantage of their privileged position in the market for franchises. Chapter 4 details the record of public stadium and arena contracts in pro sports, ending with a rough estimate of the annual subsidies provided by local governments to pro sports teams through these contracts, circa 1990. The estimated annual subsidy (in 1990 dollars) was around $500 million per year. But the past few years have signaled a move toward a much higher level of subsidies, as the new stadiums coming on line move up the $250–$350 million bracket. Combined with these increased construction costs are hyped-up sweetheart stadium contracts, such as those negotiated by the Rams with St. Louis or by Art Modell with Baltimore.

The ability of teams to extract large subsidies from local governments stems entirely from the monopoly power wielded by sports leagues. If there were several competing leagues in a sport, simple profit incentives would lead toward expansion of leagues into any city that could profitably support a team, and blackmailing threats would be a thing of the past. There would be no incentives, such as those that exist at present, to leave a few potentially profitable locations without teams, as threats to the local government. Issues of franchise location and rival leagues are discussed in Chapters 8 and 9.

Competition among rival leagues in a sport would also work to eliminate the troubles associated with the lack of competitive balance that is due to differences in drawing power among league cities. One of the main sources of competitive balance problems is the veto power exercised by teams located in the megalopolis markets to restrict entry into their territories. With several competing leagues in existence, New York and Los Angeles would be supplied with as many teams as they could support profitably, and the differences in revenue potential between New York and Kansas City or Cincinnati would be drastically reduced. Chapter 7 details the empirical record of successes by big city versus small city teams, under a monopoly league organization.

With the competitive balance problem solved through competition for franchise sites among several rival leagues, the arguments for devices such as the reserve clause, salary caps, luxury taxes, and the like also become irrelevant. A movement to a completely free competitive labor market becomes inevitable and makes simple economic common sense.

It might be thought that replacing the present monopoly league structure by several rival leagues in a sport would result in even further increases in player salaries, with more teams bidding for scarce playing talent. But this ignores the fact that the present day level of player salaries reflects the ability of players to generate revenue for an owner, in a monopolized setting. In a competitive pro sports environment, teams and leagues would be competing with one another for TV coverage, franchise sites, and fans. Inevitably, competition, as compared to a monopoly setting, would reduce the revenues that teams earn, and just as inevitably, this would be reflected in lower, not higher, player salaries.

Similarly, with lower revenues and more competition for fans, profits for teams would decline. This would lead to lower values for franchises, since the value of a franchise depends in large part on expected future income of the team. Chapter 2 and the appendix on franchise ownership provide a considerable amount of historical information on the value of franchises in the various sports, indicating that, in the past, investment in a sports team has been remarkably lucrative, indeed. The high rate of return on investments by owners, as reflected in the escalation of franchise values in all sports over past years, also can be attributed to the monopoly power exercised by leagues historically.

What competition accomplishes in any industry, and what it would accomplish in pro team sports, if it were implemented, is to transfer power from the insiders, owners and players, to the outsiders, fans and taxpayers. The present regime, in which decisions affecting fans and taxpayers are made by the members of the league cartel that controls the sport, would be replaced by one in which competitive market incentives would determine outcomes, such as where franchises would be located, TV coverage, arena rental contracts, and ticket prices. Monopolies such as present-day sports leagues increase profits by restricting the output of whatever it is they are producing. Competition would expand the number of franchises in a sport and increase overall TV coverage, while reducing ticket prices and tax-payer subsidies of teams. Dating as far back as Adam Smith's 1776 *Wealth of Nations*, economists have recognized the power of competitive markets to allocate resources efficiently. An infusion of competition into the sports industry would essentially resolve all of the outstanding problems in sports, as, unfortunately, almost no other approach will. As indicated in Chapters 8 and 9, the incentives for collusion in pro team sports are so great that, absent rigorous and creative enforcement of the antitrust laws (which has been missing in the past), a monopoly structure in sports is a foregone conclusion. From a public policy point of view, we recommend a suggestion first advanced by Professor Steve Ross: break up the existing leagues in each sport into independent competing leagues, applying the antitrust laws to enforce among leagues as vigorous competition in the boardroom as the present monopoly leagues provide on the playing field.

Preface

THIS is the first volume of a projected two-volume study of the economics of the professional team sports business in the United States. This volume looks at the history of the reserve clause, the salary determination process in baseball, competitive balance in sports leagues, the market for franchises, tax sheltering, arenas and stadiums, and rival leagues. The second volume, by Rod Fort and Roger Noll, will examine the baseball arbitration process, salary determination in the National Basketball Association, player unions, the demand for sports, exploitation, and a number of other issues not covered in the present volume.

This book has been written with a general audience in mind—fans, players, player agents, general managers, owners, and sportswriters. There is a bare minimum of economic jargon, and no mathematics (except in some brief technical appendices, which are there only for economists and can be skipped by everyone else without losing anything of substance).

League histories, team statistics, anecdotes about players and owners, and sports lore and traditions are a central part of the appeal of pro team sports, and we have relied heavily on these in the organization and writing of the book.

There are many individuals who contributed generously of their time and expertise in providing information and suggestions, too many to list here. But we especially want to thank Gerry Scully and Stan Engerman for reviewing an earlier draft of the manuscript. We also want to thank Joe Horrigan of the Professional Football Hall of Fame, Joe O'Brien of the Naismith Memorial Basketball Hall of Fame, Wayne Wilson of the Amateur Athletic Foundation, Bill Lester of the Metrodome, and Roger Noll for their assistance, along with Rubin Saposnik, Pat Pahl, Rich Hill, Phil Porter, and Andy Zimbalist. We had help from the Government Division of the U.S. Bureau of the Census, and the staffs of UCSD Library, the USD Law Library, the Hill Library of St. Paul, and the University of Minnesota have been most helpful. The Special Collections division of the UCLA library generously supplied photos for the book, as did the Archives of the University of Minnesota, the Basketball Hall of Fame, and the National Baseball Hall of Fame. Lyn

Grossman did an outstanding job of copyediting the manuscript under severe time pressures. Molan Chun Goldstein not only managed the production process with skill and patience, but made other suggestions that improved the book. Christopher Brest translated our crude sketches into the figures for the book, and my multi-talented daughter, Colleen Stone, shot the picture for the cover. The enthusiastic support of my other multi-talented kids—Mary Quirk, Janice Ratliff, Jill Powell, and Tom Quirk—has been a great help, too. I'd like to thank Quent Quirk and his son Jim for their technical help. Jack Repcheck of Princeton University Press was the individual who first raised the idea of this book, four years ago. He has provided all the encouragement and assistance that anyone could possibly hope for, and was a major factor in getting this book completed. Rod Fort is the author of Chapter Six and its technical appendix, and I am responsible for the other chapters. Neither of us could have done this without the tender loving care of our wives—Shirley Quirk and Leslie Fort—and we want to let them know we really appreciate it.

Jim Quirk
Grantsburg, Wis.
April 1992

Chapter 1

Introduction

A S THE STORY goes, in the late 1950s, just a few years before he died, Ty Cobb was interviewed by a young reporter. The reporter was interested in Cobb's views on the pitching "pheenoms" of the day—Billy Pierce, Early Wynn, Whitey Ford, Don Drysdale, Warren Spahn, Robin Roberts, and the like. He asked Cobb what he thought he would hit against modern-day pitching. Cobb thought for a few seconds and then said, "Oh, about .300." The reporter knew that Cobb held the lifetime batting record in baseball at .367, and he was surprised. "Only .300?" he asked. "Well," said Cobb, "You have to remember that I'm almost 70 years old."

For Ty Cobb and those of his generation, the golden age of baseball was not the post-World War II years. It was the dead ball era that ended in 1920, an era when the ball came into the plate brown with tobacco juice and so scuffed up that it could almost do tricks on its own, when relief pitchers were unknown and when hit-and-run plays and base stealing and coming into second base with your spikes up were more important factors in winning ball games than home runs. Today, for most of us in the over-the-hill gang, sportswriters have made a convincing case that the golden age of sports was the roaring twenties—the time of Babe Ruth, Red Grange, Nat Holman, Jack Dempsey, Bobby Jones, Bill Tilden, and Knute Rockne—when bigger-than-life heroes seemed to dominate every sport. More recently, at least one book (Robert Creamer's *Baseball in '41*) has appeared arguing that 1941 was the greatest year in the history of baseball, with Ted Williams batting .406, Joe DiMaggio setting the consecutive game hitting record at 56 games, and the Dodgers and Yankees meeting in the first of their memorable matchups in the World Series.

But all of this relates to the golden age of sports on the playing field. Our concern in this book is with a different aspect of sports, namely, the business side of professional team sports, the bottom line for owners and players alike. For the pro team sports businesss, the good old days, the golden age, was not a time in the distant past; it was the Reagan and Bush years—the 1980s and early 1990s—when, as never before, pro team sports became big business.

How big a business are we talking about? In July 1991, *Financial World* estimated the annual revenue of major league baseball teams at $1.35 billion, the National Football League (NFL) at $1.31 billion, the National Basketball Association (NBA) at $606 million, and the National Hockey League (NHL) at $465 million, for a total of a little over $3.7 billion in revenue for the four major pro team sports in the United States. Tables 1.1 through 1.4 on the next four pages give the *Financial World* estimates of operating income and team values for all teams in the American League (AL), National League (NL), the NFL, the NBA, and the NHL, as of 1991. According to these estimates, major league baseball teams earn about $185 million in annual profits before interest payments (operating income), NFL teams earn $248 million, NBA teams earn $129 million, and NHL teams earn $63 million, for a grand total for all major professional sports leagues combined of $625 million in operating income per year. Major league baseball teams were estimated to be worth about $120 million each, NFL teams were worth an average of $132 million, NBA teams were valued at around $70 million each, and NHL teams had an estimated average value of about $44 million. The total market value of all teams in the five major sports leagues—AL, NL, NFL, NBA, and NHL—was estimated by *Financial World* at just under $10 billion in mid-1991. Pro team sports truly has become a booming and highly profitable big business enterprise.

It wasn't always this way, of course. In the not-too-distant past, excluding major league baseball, the typical pro sports team was a mom-and-pop operation that barely broke even or, most often, lost some money for the team's owners. In fact, it's hard to overstate just how much the pro team sports business has changed over time, and certainly how much it has changed since the pre-World War II years. A few examples from the history of the NFL might make the point. Back in 1929, Chris O'Brien, the longtime owner of the NFL Chicago Cardinals, decided that he had lost as much money as he could afford, and he put his team on the market. George Halas, owner of the much more successful crosstown rival Chicago Bears, wanted to have a friendly face at the Cardinals. He tells in his autobiography, *Halas by Halas*, of talking his friend, David Jones, into buying the Cardinals: "I promised him that if the losses continued, I would absorb 40 percent; if there were a profit, I would take none of it" (p. 135).

Somehow, it's hard to imagine, say, Al Davis or Victor Kiam—or any other NFL owner of the 1990s, for that matter—making a commitment like this to a new owner of an NFL franchise, even a close friend. To

Table 1.1

Estimated Operating Income and Team Values, Major League Baseball, 1991
(millions of dollars)

	Operating Income	Team Value
AMERICAN LEAGUE		
New York Yankees	24.5	225
Baltimore Orioles	9.6	200
Boston Red Sox	12.3	180
Toronto Blue Jays	13.9	178
Chicago White Sox	8.8	125
Kansas City Royals	−9.8	122
Oakland Athletics	12.4	116
California Angels	8.7	102
Texas Rangers	9.1	101
Detroit Tigers	5.1	84
Minnesota Twins	0.6	81
Milwaukee Brewers	3.9	81
Cleveland Indians	−6.8	75
Seattle Mariners	−3.1	71
AL totals	89.2	1,741
NATIONAL LEAGUE		
New York Mets	15.8	200
Los Angeles Dodgers	7.6	200
Philadelphia Phillies	11.1	130
St. Louis Cardinals	10.5	128
Chicago Cubs	9.2	125
San Francisco Giants	9.0	105
Cincinnati Reds	11.0	102
San Diego Padres	8.5	99
Houston Astros	−2.0	92
Pittsburgh Pirates	−0.7	82
Atlanta Braves	7.8	74
Montreal Expos	6.4	74
NL totals	94.2	1,411

Source: Financial World, July 9, 1991.

put things in context, the Bears had a fairly good year in 1930, and ended up making a cool $1,696; a badly managed team in the NFL today easily could drop $5 million or more in a year. (Estimated losses of the New England Patriots in 1989 and in 1990 were approximately $5 million per year.) Moreover, Halas regarded his promise as just a generous gesture of one friend to another. Today, if an offer like Halas's were made by one

Table 1.2
Estimated Operating Income and Team Values, NFL, 1991
(millions of dollars)

	Operating Income	Team Value
Miami	12.5	205
Green Bay	5.5	200
Dallas	15.2	180
San Francisco	5.2	150
New York Giants	11.6	150
Cleveland	10.4	145
Philadelphia	7.9	141
Los Angeles Rams	11.4	135
Los Angeles Raiders	10.6	135
Seattle	4.6	130
Chicago	11.6	126
Buffalo	10.5	125
Washington	10.5	125
New York Jets	8.9	125
Cincinnati	8.8	125
New Orleans	9.5	124
Kansas City	8.7	122
Phoenix	10.7	120
Houston	6.0	119
Minnesota	9.2	119
Indianapolis	8.9	116
Detroit	8.9	116
Tampa Bay	8.8	114
Pittsburgh	4.5	114
San Diego	4.4	113
Denver	9.1	113
Atlanta	9.9	112
New England	4.0	100
NFL Totals	247.8	3,699

Source: *Financial World*, July 9, 1991.

owner to another and it became public, the resulting scandal might well cause both owners to lose their franchises. Apropos of this, charges that the Yankees and Kansas City Athletics were a little too close to each other led to a congressional investigation in the late 1950s.

To take another example, in 1932, the Bears tied with the Portsmouth Spartans—yes, Portsmouth (1930 population 30,000) actually had an NFL team in those days—for the NFL title. A playoff game for the

Table 1.3
Estimated Operating Income and Team Values, NBA, 1991
(millions of dollars)

	Operating Income	Team Value
Los Angeles Lakers	30.2	200
Boston	8.8	180
Detroit	23.3	150
Chicago	7.3	100
New York	3.4	100
Phoenix	3.9	99
Philadelphia	4.1	75
Cleveland	6.1	61
Orlando	9.2	61
Portland	1.4	60
Charlotte	6.4	59
Miami	7.5	59
Houston	3.3	58
Dallas	2.7	54
Atlanta	1.2	53
Milwaukee	4.3	53
Minnesota	4.7	51
Golden State	1.1	51
Sacramento	5.2	49
San Antonio	0.3	47
Utah	0.9	45
Los Angeles Clippers	1.1	43
New Jersey	1.8	43
Denver	−1.8	41
Washington	−2.4	38
Seattle	−1.8	37
Indiana	−3.5	33
NBA totals	128.7	1,900

Source: Financial World, July 9, 1991.

league championship was held in Chicago in December on a day when there was so much snow on the ground that the game was moved inside, to be played in Chicago Stadium, the home arena of the NHL Chicago Blackhawks. The Bears won the game, 7–0, on the rarest of trick plays, a one-yard fourth down touchdown pass from Bronko Nagurski (!) to Red Grange. But another item of interest concerning the game is that Portsmouth had to play the game without its star runner, passer, and kicker, Dutch Clark. Clark wasn't injured; his problem was that

Table 1.4
Estimated Operating Income and Team Values, NHL, 1991
(millions of dollars)

	Operating Income	Team Value
Montreal	4.9	60
Boston	9.3	57
New York Rangers	4.8	54
Calgary	3.2	52
New York Islanders	10.3	52
Edmonton	3.7	52
Hartford	4.1	45
Toronto	3.4	45
Quebec	0.0	45
Los Angeles	1.7	45
Chicago	6.7	45
Detroit	4.6	44
Philadelphia	2.2	43
Vancouver	0.9	42
Pittsburgh	0.6	42
Washington	1.7	38
Buffalo	4.4	37
New Jersey	0.8	35
St. Louis	0.7	32
Winnipeg	− 0.4	30
Minnesota	− 4.9	30
NHL Totals	62.7	925

Source: Financial World, July 9, 1991.

playing in the NFL was just a sideline to his regular job as basketball coach at Colorado College. Clark's schedule hadn't allowed for a post-season championship playoff game. The basketball season was under way by the time of the game, and Clark had coaching obligations in Colorado, so the Spartans played without their franchise player and lost.

A very similar case arose in 1941, when Art Rooney hired Buff Donelli to coach his struggling family enterprise, the NFL Pittsburgh Steelers. Donelli also held the jobs of athletic director and head football coach at Duquesne, a college powerhouse in those days (best in the East in 1939 and again in 1941, with undefeated records in both years). NFL Commissioner Elmer Layden required Donelli to give up his title as coach at Duquesne, but Buff continued to be the de facto coach there.

Donelli would coach the Steelers in the morning, and would move across town to coach his Dukes in the afternoon. Midway through the season, Duquesne had a game in California on Saturday against St. Mary's, and the Steelers had an NFL league game on Sunday. Given a choice between his two job responsibilities, Donelli opted to take the train west with his college team and let his assistant handle the Steelers' game. That was too much for Layden, who forced Rooney to fire Donelli, possibly the first and certainly the last person to hold a full time college head coaching job at the same time he was moonlighting as an NFL head coach.[1]

Donelli was hired by the Steelers at a time when major college teams, such as Notre Dame, Michigan, and Minnesota, were drawing 50,000 fans and more to their games, while NFL teams were lucky to average 25,000. The only pro sport that most of the public knew anything at all about before World War II was baseball, even though the NFL had been around for 20 years, and the NHL for 25. All sports, including pro team sports, languished during World War II, and then there was a miniboom in public interest in pro sports between 1946 and 1950, as the veterans came home. After an adjustment period, attendance began increasing again during the 1950s and 1960s, and really began to take off for most pro sports leagues from the mid- to late 1970s on. Figures 1.1 through 1.5 show league attendance for the AL, NL, NFL, NBA, and the NHL, for various periods up to the 1990 or 1990/91 season.

From Figures 1.1 and 1.2, we can see that the NL outpaced the AL in attendance growth in the 1950s and 1960s, due partly to the NL's lead in racial integration, with rising black NL stars such as Willie Mays, Roy Campanella, Roberto Clemente, and Willie Stargell, and due partly to new stadiums built for NL teams in the 1960s. In the late 1970s, it was the AL with the rapid growth in attendance, with Toronto and Seattle coming in as expansion teams, and with a crop of new or rebuilt stadiums in AL towns. Both leagues had a boom in attendance in the 1980s, as baseball came to be regarded by the public as one of the best entertainment buys around.

---

[1]Another factor in Donelli's firing might have been Pittsburgh's 1–9–1 record, the worst in the NFL East in 1941. And, in Donelli's defense, missing a game wasn't all that new for college coaches. Back in 1926, Knute Rockne was writing a syndicated column while acting as head football coach of Notre Dame. One Saturday, when the Irish were playing a much weaker opponent, Rockne skipped the game to report on the Army-Navy game for his readers, handing over the coaching job to one of his assistants. The story wouldn't be so memorable were it not for the fact that Notre Dame got thoroughly whipped, 19–0, by Carnegie Tech, that underrated opponent, in one of the most stunning upsets in Notre Dame history. Rockne showed up for the rest of the Notre Dame games during his remaining years with the school.

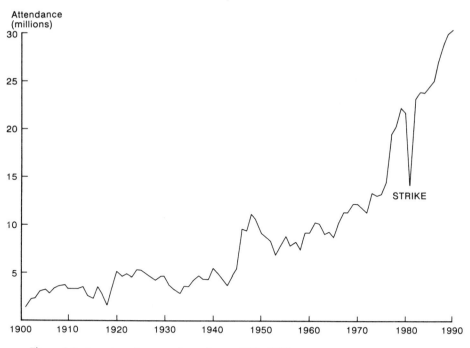

Figure 1.1 American League, Attendance, 1901–1990

Figure 1.3 on page 10 shows the steady growth in attendance in the NFL from 1950 through the late 1960s, and then the surge in attendance in the 1970s following the NFL-AFL merger. League expansion (from 12 teams in 1959 to 28 teams in 1976), lengthening the league season (from 12 games in 1960 to 16 games in 1978), and new, larger stadiums, all played a role in attendance growth. Attendance has been flat since about 1980, because of stadium capacity limits coupled with a conservative NFL policy on league expansion.

Figure 1.4 on page 11 charts the runaway success story of the 1980s— the NBA. The NBA weathered a rough period in the 1970s, when it was involved in an interleague war with the ABA and also lost an important antitrust case, but everything has been coming up roses for NBA owners since about 1980, including some spectacularly successful expansion franchises. In recent years, attendance in the NBA has been increasing at 11 percent per year, an explosive growth rate.

Figure 1.5 on page 12 shows attendance growth in the NHL. Attendance had its boom period in the late 1960s and early 1970s, when the NHL tripled its membership. The league might have expanded too rapidly, however, because there was a falling off in total attendance in the mid-1970s that was only offset when the NHL took in the remnants of

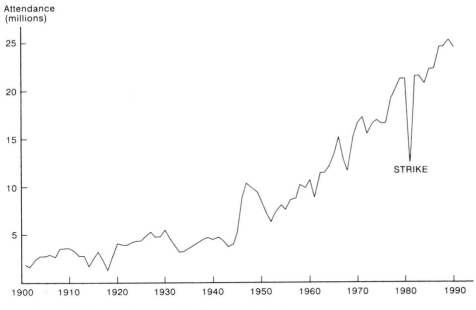

Figure 1.2 National League, Attendance, 1901–1990

the WHA in 1979. Attendance has been growing at a slow but steady pace in the 1980s and early 1990s.

As recently as 1980, NBA teams had an average attendance of about 10,000 per game. By 1990, the average was up to 15,000, and more than half the league had virtual season-long sellouts. In the AL, teams averaged 1.5 million in home attendance in 1980, and by 1990, the average was up to 1.9 million. The NL average went up from 1.75 million in 1980 to just over 2.0 million in 1990. In 1960, the average NFL team drew around 260,000 for the season (roughly 43,000 per game); by 1970, the average was up to 367,000 (52,000 per game), and by 1980, it was 478,000 (60,000 per game). Attendance has remained close to that figure since that time. The NHL has a long tradition of sold-out arenas—there aren't that many hockey fans, but they are all fanatics! In 1960, the average NHL team drew 386,000 fans (11,000 per game); by 1970, it was 518,000 (13,300 per game); and that increased to 536,000 (13,400 per game) in 1980, and to 636,000 (15,900 per game) in the 1990/91 season.

And then there is television. Back in 1950, when the coaxial cable and network TV were still a few years off, the NFL Los Angeles Rams signed on with a local sponsor for one of the early attempts to make some money from televising sports contests. The Rams' contract called for the televising of six home games to viewers in the Los Angeles area, with the sponsor agreeing to make up any loss at the gate. The Rams had averaged

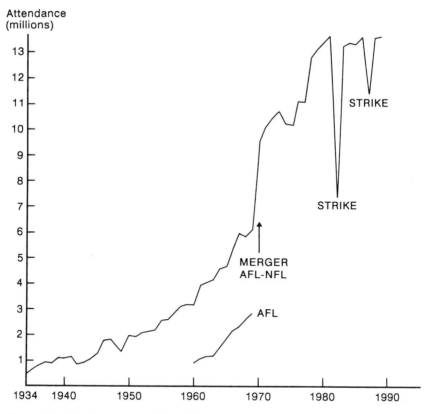

Figure 1.3 NFL, Attendance, 1934–1990

$75,000 per game in gate receipts in 1949. There were two home games in 1950 that were not televised, and they averaged $77,000 at the gate. The six games that were televised brought in an average of only $42,000. The sponsor was stuck with a bill for $198,000 in payments for gate losses, and had no interest in renewing the contract for 1951.

Actually, there had been an earlier TV experiment in the NFL, with pretty much the same results. The Philadelphia Eagles put all their home games on local TV in 1948, and watched attendance drop from 217,000 in 1947 to 155,000 in 1948. This occurred despite the fact that 1948 was the year in which the Eagles won their very first NFL championship. The NFL concluded from these happenings that TV should be viewed as a problem rather than an opportunity. NFL owners passed restrictive league rules on televising of games into the home territories of teams that led to a federal antitrust suit against the league (*United States v. NFL*, 116 F. Supp. 319 (E.D. Pa. 1953), 196 F. Supp. 445 (E.D. Pa. 1961)).

Attendance (000)

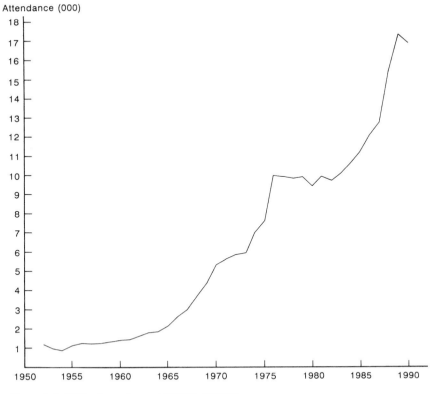

Figure 1.4 NBA, Attendance, 1952/53–1990/91

In 1962, after Congress had passed antitrust exemptions for league-wide TV contracts, and under the new leadership of Commissioner Pete Rozelle, the NFL signed its first network TV contracts, with CBS and NBC, for a total of $5.8 million per year (the AFL had a $2 million contract with ABC). By 1970, when the AFL and NFL had merged, the NFL was earning $49 million per year from TV, a sum that increased to $167 million in 1980. Pete Rozelle's popularity with NFL owners was based to a large extent on his success in negotiating those ever-larger TV contracts.

But it was in the 1980s and early 1990s that TV really came into its own as a dominant source of revenue for pro sports leagues. *Financial World* estimated that in 1991, TV (and radio) accounted for about 25 percent of NHL revenues, 30 percent of NBA revenues, almost 50 percent of AL and NL revenues, and 60 percent of NFL revenues. In 1991, the NFL earned $940 million from its contracts with CBS, NBC, ABC, TNT, and ESPN, and local contracts (for a total of $34 million per NFL team); major league baseball received $615 million—$363 million from

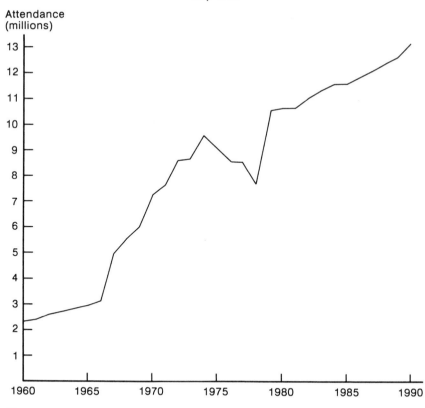

Figure 1.5 NHL, Attendance, 1960/61–1990/91

network contracts and $252 million from local radio and TV, for an average of $24 million per major league team; and the NBA earned $219 million from its NBC and TNT contracts, plus $104 million from local contracts, around $12 million per team. Only the NHL was left out so far as (U.S.) network TV is concerned, earning only $5.5 million in the 1991/92 season.

Figures 1.6 through 1.8 show the growth in TV revenues over time for major league baseball (AL and NL combined), the NFL, and the NBA. (Detailed historical information on TV revenues in pro team sports is provided in the data supplement.) Network contracts signed in the late 1980s pushed TV income for major league baseball, the NFL, and the NBA, to levels unimaginable just a few years earlier. Competition among the networks and cable systems had made sports broadcasting so expensive that the profit picture of an entire network could hinge on the success of its sports TV contracts, as illustrated by the problems CBS faced in 1990 and 1991 because of its major league baseball contract. (In

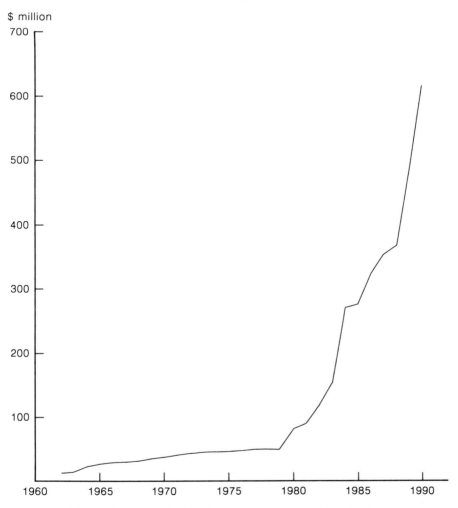

$ million

Figure 1.6 Major League Baseball, TV and Radio Revenues, 1962–1990

the third quarter of 1991, CBS announced a quarterly loss of $169 million, much of which was attributed to its baseball contract.) By early 1992, widespread reports in the business press indicated that network bids on the next baseball TV contract (beginning in the 1994 season) would be for substantially less money, and there were even rumors of a prospective drop in bids for future NFL network TV contracts as well.

With pro sports teams riding a wave of fan popularity, player salaries have been going through the roof as well. In the 1950s, average baseball salaries were around $15,000. By the early 1970s, before free agency came to baseball, average salaries had been boosted to around $40,000.

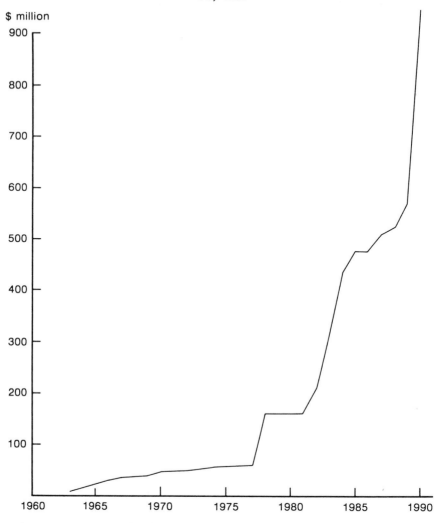

Figure 1.7 NFL, TV and Radio Revenues, 1962–1990

In 1980, after four years of free agency, the average had increased to around $115,000.

In 1991, the average baseball salary was $851,000. Baseball salaries increased by almost 650 percent between 1980 and 1991, almost matching the percentage increase in TV and radio income over that time period. Average franchise values in baseball also rose by about 700 percent during the 1980s.

While baseball salaries have gotten much of the publicity, player salaries are up in the other sports as well. In 1990, the average NBA salary

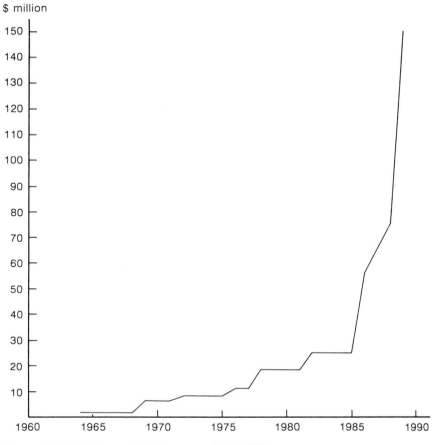

Figure 1.8 NBA, Network TV Revenues, 1962–1990

was $925,000, the average NFL salary was $300,000, and the average NHL salary was $240,000. Things don't get any better than this for owners and players alike in the pro team sports industry.

As exhilarating as the fabulously high player salaries, team profits, and rates of escalation of franchise values are for players and owners, they do raise some questions for those of us who are on the paying rather than on the receiving side of all this money. There is no doubt that pro team sports is providing an enthusiastic public with a quality product, and that pro team sports leagues do a superior job of promoting and marketing their products—the market success of pro team sports is convincing evidence of this.

The questions concerning pro team sports relate instead to the monopoly status of pro sports leagues, and the role of this monopoly power in extracting bucks from the rest of us. After all is said and done, the high incomes earned by players and by owners in sports are largely, if not almost exclusively, monopoly rents. Treating the AL and NL as a single entity (major league baseball), there is currently monopoly control of each of the four pro team sports of baseball, football, basketball, and hockey, as there has been over most of the histories of the sports. Through exclusive territorial franchises, leagues provide each member team with a local monopoly in the sport, giving it special bargaining power in its dealings with local radio and TV stations, with the municipally owned stadium or arena in its city, and even with the ticket-buying public. The league is a monopolist in its negotiations with competing network and cable TV systems, in contracting for national TV coverage of its sport. Players with highly specialized skills have their own element of monopoly power to wield in negotiations with management.

Economic theory argues that individuals or organizations with monopoly power use it to increase their incomes at the expense of the rest of the society; the theory also argues that monopoly power leads to a misallocation of resources in the society, in that too little of the monopolized commodity is produced. In the case of pro team sports, monopoly power can lead to fewer cities having professional franchises than are capable of supporting them, to higher ticket prices for games than under competition, to restrictions on TV coverage, and to lower rentals being paid for the use of municipally owned sports facilities, than would occur under competition. To the extent that the monopoly power of owners has historically provided them with bargaining advantages in dealing with players (this is in the pre-free agency days), we would also find a disproportionate share of the monopoly rents in a league going to owners rather than to players. The wielding of monopoly power by team owners would, of course, be reflected in the prices that teams sell for in the franchise market.

Currently, we are going through one of the most interesting eras in the economic history of pro team sports, in that something approaching free agency has characterized labor markets in both baseball and basketball since the mid-1970s. This represents a radical change from the traditional player reservation system based on the reserve clause, and has eliminated much of the monopsony bargaining power of owners in those sports. Predictably, free agency has been followed by soaring player salaries, as monopoly rents have been transferred from owners to players. But free agency raises other issues as well, especially those relating to the preservation of competitive balance in sports leagues, a long-standing bone of contention between players and owners.

We will be examining these and a number of other related issues in this book. In Chapter 2, we look into what is undoubtedly the most important money payoff from team ownership, namely, capital gains in the form of escalation in franchise values. Not only is this of interest for its own sake, but data on franchise price escalation also offer some clues to the profitability of pro team sports, that is, how much of the monopoly rents of the industry are captured by owners. Because almost all pro sports teams are closely held corporations or limited partnerships, there is no legal requirement for teams to make public their profit and loss statements. A rare exception is the publicly traded Boston Celtics, but for other teams, franchise price escalation can be used as an imperfect proxy in assessing profitability. Along the way, the chapter also delves into turnover rates of franchises and tenure of ownership, and how these have changed over time. We also look into the sustainability of the current rates of franchise price escalation in sports.

In Chapters 3 and 4, two important sources of public subsidies to pro team sports are explored. Chapter 3 is concerned with the tax-sheltering aspects of team ownership. As the discussion there makes clear, tax sheltering was a major economic factor in pro team sports between 1950 and the mid-1970s, but recent changes in the tax laws have reduced its importance substantially. Still, if the moves under way in 1992 to reduce capital gains tax rates succeed, the tax shelter could once again become a moving force in pro team sports. Beyond this, an understanding of how the shelter works certainly helps in making sense of the economic history of pro team sports in the early post-World War II era. During those days, owners could pocket impressive after-tax income payoffs from teams that barely broke even, or actually lost money.

Chapter 4 examines in some detail a major source of monopoly rents for sports teams—subsidized rental arrangements with publicly owned stadiums or arenas. The data presented there document the change that took place between the early 1950s and the present, with publicly owned sports facilities replacing the previously team-owned facilities. Something on the order of $3.0 billion was invested between 1950 and 1990 by cities and states in stadiums and arenas used by major league pro sports teams. Details of the stadium contracts are presented for most publicly operated facilities. A very rough estimate of the size of the annual subsidy provided by cities and states to tenants of publicly owned stadiums and arenas (most of which goes to pro sports teams) is on the order of $500 million per year. There also is a brief discussion of problems with coming up with believable measures of the benefits that teams or stadiums provide to their host cities.

Chapters 5 through 7 look into the division of monopoly rents between owners and players. The history of the player reservation system and related antitrust cases is taken up in Chapter 5. Chapter 6 deals with the elementary economics of the player labor market, and contrasts the outcomes under a reserve clause system with those under free agency. In particular, the role of free agency in increasing player salaries is spelled out. The relationship between ticket prices and player salaries is explained. A model of salary determination for baseball players is developed in the chapter, and the model is used to provide evidence of collusion by owners in the 1986 free agent market, and to identify the root cause of salary escalation in the late 1980s. The effect of free agency on the distribution of income among players is also explored. As it turns out, in baseball, a disproportionate share of the benefits of free agency flow to star players as compared with run-of-the-mill players. Chapter 7 looks at the competitive balance problem, reviews the record of pro sports leagues with respect to competitive balance, and examines in detail the contention that restrictions on the player labor market are needed to preserve competitive balance in pro sports. Briefly, an examination of the profit incentives under free agency and under a reservation system leads to the conclusion that free agency would have no effect at all on competitive balance in a sports league, and empirical results from free agency in baseball and basketball agree completely with this conclusion.

The final two chapters of the book, Chapter 8 and Chapter 9, go over the history of rival leagues in sports. Entry into a monopolized industry is the way in which market forces can be brought to bear to limit monopoly power, and this applies as well to pro team sports as to other industries. The histories of these rival leagues, most now long defunct, have antiquarian interest to sports fans for their own sakes, but they also show how entry and the threat of entry have acted to force expansion on the dominant league, and have limited monopoly power in other ways as well. The question as to why rival leagues get organized and interleague wars get fought, is an interesting one, and is discussed and documented in detail in the chapters.

Some of the questions examined in this book are mainly quantitative in nature, and some are mainly theoretical. When theoretical issues are involved, verbal and occasionally graphical arguments are presented for the conclusions arrived at. Quantitative questions are addressed by brute force data accumulation, or, in some cases, by simple statistical hypothesis testing, using whatever data are available. But in either case, an effort has been made throughout the book to lay out the historical setting in which the problem arose, and, as much as possible, to document its development over time. Taking this approach can be a major help in understanding the issues involved—besides, it's more fun dealing with actual real-life confrontations involving specific teams and owners and players, than taking a purely abstract and hypothetical approach. But unearthing the team and league histories and other elements of a data base to back up this approach turned out to be something of a challenge. The data supplement presents some of the series developed for the book, a first attempt at establishing a data base for the economic history of pro team sports. These include franchise ownership histories for teams in all major league sports leagues, attendance records, and TV revenues for sports leagues. Other data series appear or are summarized in tables in the main text of the book.

The fundamental framework used here to analyze the business of pro team sports is mainstream microeconomics, which is solidly based on the notion of self-interest-motivated behavior by individuals and organizations, operating in a market environment.

The importance of economic incentives for owners and players in the pro team sports business is a fact of life long recognized by fans and insiders alike, who have views on such matters that range all over the map. Earl Weaver, the great Baltimore manager, once said, "I get sick of hearing about the poor owners. Baseball owners today are happier than pigs in slop. They're making money hand over fist" (Adler 1986).

But the money doesn't come free. Owners have to deal with players like Don Sutton, the longtime pitcher of the Dodgers and assorted other teams, a free spirit who made the famous remark, "I'm the most loyal player money can buy" (Adler 1986). And owners have to deal with players like potential Hall of Famer Rickey Henderson of the Oakland A's, who try to renegotiate long-term multimillions-per-year contracts after they have had a good year and discover that some other players are making more than they are.

And it is not just players who try to renegotiate contracts. Managers of city-owned arenas and stadiums are only too familiar with team owners who try to renegotiate long-term stadium or arena rental agreements after a bad year (and sometimes even after a good year). These are the same owners who issue annual or semi-annual threats to leave the city for some other town offering an even sweeter rental deal.

While the economist's fundamental notion that "markets work" is something that has been gaining rather widespread support everywhere in the world, especially in the last decade or so, economists and the economic way of thinking have not been without their detractors. As early as the 1790s (Adam Smith's *Wealth of Nations* was only 20 years old!), Edmund Burke, the father of modern conservatism, wrote, "The age of chivalry is gone; that of the sophists, economists and calculators has succeeded it." Modern-day critics talk about the need for a one-armed economist, someone who can't say "on the one hand . . . and then on the other hand. . . ." And *Readers Digest* (July 1991) got into the act of badmouthing economists by reporting on Albert Einstein's arrival in heaven, with a story that goes something like this: The first person he meets says, "Dr. Einstein, I have an IQ of 190." Einstein smiles, and says, "Wonderful, we can discuss general field theory." A second person comes up to say, "Dr. Einstein, I have an IQ of 150." Einstein smiles again, and says, "We will have long conversations on special forms of nonlinear second-order partial differential equations." The third person arrives and says, "Dr. Einstein, I have an IQ of 85." Once again, Einstein smiles with delight, and says, "Wonderful to meet you. And what do you think is going to happen to interest rates over the next six months?"

It is well known that students who have taken a college course in economics almost invariably have evil memories of the course. Economics 101 is recalled as being dull, oppressively theoretical and hypothetical, and jargon-laden. To add to the misery, there were all those graphs to remember. And the application of economic principles to the real world seemed to involve near-impenetrable obscurities. But things don't have to be that way, and we certainly have tried to make sure that they are not that way in this book. Throughout the book, we have striven for the same simplicity and clarity of presentation of economic principles that was achieved by the late great Casey Stengel, the "old professor," in his classic appearance before a congressional committee looking into the economics of sports in the late 1950s. Casey's performance merits an extended quote:

SENATOR KEFAUVER: Mr. Stengel, are you prepared to answer particularly why baseball wants this bill [exempting baseball from the antitrust laws] passed?

MR. STENGEL: Well, I would have to say at the present time, I think that baseball has advanced in this respect for the player help. That is an amazing statement for me to make, because you can retire with an annuity at 50 and what organization in America allows you to retire at 50 and receive money?

I want to further state that I am not a ballplayer, that is, put into that pension fund committee. At my age, and I have been in baseball, well, I will say I am possibly the oldest man who is working in baseball. I would say that when they start an annuity for the ballplayers to better their conditions, it should have been done, and I think it has been done.

I think it should be the way they have done it, which is a very good thing.

The reason they possibly did not take the managers in at that time was because radio and television or the income to ball clubs was not large enough that you could have put it in a pension plan.

Now I am not a member of the pension plan. You have young men here who are, who represent the ball clubs.

They represent them as players and since I am not a member and don't receive pension from a fund which you think, my goodness, he ought to be declared in that too but I would say that it is a great thing for the ballplayers.

That is one thing I will say for the ballplayers they have an advanced pension fund. I should think it was gained by radio and television or you could not have enough money to pay anything of that type.

Now the second thing about baseball that I think is very interesting to the public or to all of us that it is the owner's own fault if he does not improve his club, along with the officials in the ball club and the players.

Now what causes that?

If I am going to go on the road and we are a traveling ball club and you know the cost of transportation now—we travel sometimes with three pullman coaches, the New York Yankees and remember I am just a salaried man and do not own stock in the New York Yankees, I found out that traveling with the New York Yankees on the road and all, that it is the best, and we have broken records in Washington this year, we have broken them in every city but New York and we have lost two clubs that have gone out of the city of New York.

Of course we have had some bad weather, I would say that they are mad at us in Chicago, we fill the parks.

They have come out to see good material. I will say they are mad at us in Kansas City, but we broke their attendance record.

Now on the road we only get possibly 27 cents. I am not positive of these figures, as I am not an official.

If you go back 15 years or if I owned stock in the club I would give them to you.

SENATOR KEFAUVER: Mr. Stengel, I am not sure that I made my question clear. (Laughter)

MR. STENGEL: Yes sir. Well that is all right. I am not sure I am going to answer yours perfectly either. (Laughter)[2]

Later, after Casey had finished, the Yankees' superstar, Mickey Mantle, had his turn before the committee:

[2]*Organized Professional Team Sports: Hearings before the Senate Committee on the Judiciary,* 86th Cong., 1st sess., 1959. 11–24

SENATOR KEFAUVER: Mr. Mantle, do you have any observations with reference to the applicability of the antitrust laws to baseball?

MR. MANTLE: My views are just about the same as Casey's. (Laughter)[3]

How can we top that? Our views are just about the same as Casey's, too.

[3]Ibid.

Chapter 2

The Market for Sports Franchises

BACK in the days of the Roman Empire, it was traditional for wealthy senators to spend enormous sums of money to put on games and circuses for the general public, thereby acquiring great prestige in an early display of something akin to Thorstein Veblen's "conspicuous consumption." More recently, public morality has been less sympathetic to shows in which Christians are thrown to the lions, and wealthy, public-spirited individuals have turned instead to providing financial support for universities, libraries, art museums, and hospitals—and there are even some who have funded the modern equivalent of the Roman circus, by purchasing a professional sports team.

Actually, the analogy was closer back when team sports had not yet quite made it into the big business category. In the 1930 and 1940s, a standard joke among the owners of sports franchises went something like this: "Do you know how to make a small fortune? Start with a big fortune and buy a sports team." This might have been a little self-serving, but in fact there was more than a grain of truth in the story. It was not uncommon for wealthy individuals to take on the ownership of a sports team as a civic duty, expecting to lose some money in the process, but gaining some favorable publicity. Notable examples often cited were the Cubs' owner, Phil Wrigley, Cincinnati's Powell Crosley, Cleveland's Alva Bradley, and Tom Yawkey of the Boston Red Sox.

That was back in the good old days. By the 1980s, franchises had become so expensive that even the wealthiest of owners—Carl Pohlad of the Minnesota Twins, or Ted Turner of the Atlanta Braves and Atlanta Hawks, for example—would find it difficult to treat the ownership of a franchise simply as a hobby, but instead would be moved by economic common sense to look upon it much as they would regard any other investment. In 1961, Joan Payson headed a syndicate of wealthy New Yorkers who purchased the New York Mets expansion franchise from the National League for $2 million. Mrs. Payson was an avid and knowledgeable baseball fan, and buying the Mets fulfilled a lifelong ambition. Earlier, as a minority stockholder of the New York Giants, she had tried unsuccessfully to buy the team from Horace Stoneham to keep it in New York. In 1975, Mrs. Payson died, and ownership of the club passed on to her husband and children. In 1980, the Payson heirs sold the Mets to Doubleday and Co., the book publishers, for $21 million. Six years later, Doubleday was involved in a takeover, one provision of which required that Doubleday divest itself of ownership of the Mets. The team was sold to Nelson Doubleday and Fred Wilpon for a cool $100 million.

Joan Payson was a very wealthy woman, and the $2 million purchase price of the Mets in 1961 might well have been regarded by her as a "pin money" investment, but the money involved in the 1986 sale is so large that it is clear that the new owners can ignore bottom-line considerations only at their extreme peril. The idea of being in the business only for the fun of owning a baseball team is probably pretty much a thing of the past.

The history of the Mets points up something else that is going on in the franchise market as well. Between 1961 and 1980, the $2 million original investment in the Mets appreciated in market value by $19 million, representing an annual rate of increase of almost 12 percent per year. This rate of return on total capital is over and above any profits that the Mets earned from the day-to-day operations of the team. Moreover, most sports teams are highly leveraged, using lots of borrowed money, so that the return on equity of franchise price escalation is much higher than the return on total invested capital. In hindsight, the purchase of the Mets franchise certainly turned out to be a highly profitable investment for the Payson family. And then, between 1980 and 1986, the new owner, Doubleday and Co., enjoyed an escalation in the market value of the Mets of 26 percent per year, which certainly produced a truly spectacular rate of return on equity capital.

There is quite a bit of evidence to indicate that the Mets' experience during the 1980s is not all that different from the experience of other franchises, not only in baseball, but in the other major league team sports as well. The day when owning a major league sports franchise was a financial burden borne by the owner for the public good is certainly a thing of the past, although you wouldn't know it from the statements of some owners, especially when it is time to negotiate a new rental agreement with a publicly owned stadium. The fact of the matter is that there is an interesting amount of money to be made simply from the escalation of franchise prices. To paraphrase the late senator from Illinois, Everett Dirksen, "a hundred million here and a hundred million there, and the first thing you know, you're talking about real money." Franchise prices have been increasing so fast that this raises the question as to whether the recent rate of increase in franchise values can be sustained over time, or whether we might be witnessing a "bubble" in the franchise market.

In this chapter we will be looking at the market for sports franchises, the ownership history of teams in the various sports, and franchise prices. The bulk of the chapter recounts in some detail relevant data on the franchise market. The final sections of the chapter summarize the economist's theory of asset prices and apply it to the sports franchise market. Ownership histories for all franchises in the major pro team sports leagues can be found in the data supplement.

The Market for Baseball Franchises

Table 2.1 gives a summary view of the rate of activity in the franchise market for baseball, by decade, from 1901 through 1990. The kinds of activities that are summarized are the creation of new franchises through league expansion; abandonment or cancellation of franchises when teams go out of business; franchise moves when teams transfer from one city to another; and sales of existing franchises.

Looking at the data for baseball, one of the surprising things is that the rate of turnover of franchises (sales plus abandonments of franchises per franchise-year) was actually higher during the period 1901–1920 than during any comparable later period, for both the AL and NL. This casts some doubt on the notion that old-time owners were paragons of civic virtue who were deeply concerned with the long-term interests of their teams, in contrast to the supposedly short-sighted go-go owners of the present day. Certainly there were some striking examples of long-term ownership dating back to the early days of baseball—the Comiskey family, which owned the Chicago White Sox from the beginning of the American League in 1901 until 1959; Clark Griffith and his nephew Calvin, with 72 years of ownership of the Washington Senators/Minnesota Twins; Charles Stoneham and son Horace, with 58 years of ownership of the New York/San Francisco Giants; and the Ebbets family's 46 years with the Brooklyn Dodgers. But for the "typical" (median) franchise owner back in the 1901–1920 period, ownership tenure averaged about 6.5 years, as compared to an average tenure of about 11 years as of 1990, as is indicated in Table 2.1. The typical present-day owner actually owns a club almost twice as long as did the typical owner back in the first decades of the century.

Moreover, there are present-day owners with records of longevity that

Table 2.1

Activity in the Baseball Franchise Market by Decade, 1901–1990

	1901–1909	1910–1919	1920–1929	1930–1939	1940–1949	1950–1959	1960–1969	1970–1979	1980–1990	1901–1990
AMERICAN LEAGUE										
(1) Franchise sales	7	9	2	3	5	6	7	8	9	56
(2) Expansion franchises							4	2		6
(3) Franchise moves	2					2	2	2		8
(4) Abandoned franchises										0
(5) Franchise years	72	80	80	80	80	80	100	126	154	852
Turnover ratio: [(1) + (4)] ÷ (5)	.097	.113	.025	.038	.063	.075	.070	.063	.058	.066
NATIONAL LEAGUE										
(1) Franchise sales	9	8	3	2	7	1	3	5	7	45
(2) Expansion franchises							4			4
(3) Franchise moves					3	1				4
(4) Abandoned franchises										0
(5) Franchise years	72	80	80	80	80	80	98	120	132	798
Turnover ratio: [(1) + (4)] ÷ (5)	.125	.100	.038	.025	.088	.013	.031	.042	.053	.056
Median tenure of ownership (years) at end of decade (years)[a]										
American League	7.0	5.5	13.0	18.0	24.5	11.0	9.5	8.0	10.5	
National League	7.5	6.0	11.0	21.0	6.5	16.5	24.5	12.5	11.5	

Sources: New York Times, Sporting News, and other books and publications.

[a]Expansion teams excluded in decade when they enter league.

come close to the best of those of the early years—Walter and, later, his son, Peter O'Malley, have owned the Brooklyn/L.A. Dodgers since 1945; Anheuser-Busch and Gussie Busch and his family heirs have held title to the Cardinals since 1953; and California (Gene Autry), Toronto (La-Batt's Breweries), and Kansas City (Ewing Kaufman) have been one-owner franchises over their entire team histories.

The period of greatest stability of combined ownership and location of franchises in baseball was between 1920 and 1950. The golden decade of the 1920s was a bonanza for most teams, which tended to promote the holding of franchises, and during the 1930s the market for franchises was so depressed that four of the five sales that took place involved teams that were on the verge of bankruptcy. There was a flurry of sales in both leagues immediately after World War II, but for the AL, the median tenure of ownership peaked around 1950; for the NL, the peak occurred around 1970. After the move of two teams in the first years of the American League (Milwaukee to St. Louis after the 1901 season, and Baltimore to New York after the 1902 season), there were no moves of franchises in either the AL or NL until the Boston Braves moved to Milwaukee in 1953. Moreover, expansion of the major leagues didn't occur until 1961 (1962 in the NL), under the threat posed by the Continental League. Beyond that, baseball has had an unbroken record (since 1901) of preserving existing franchises—franchises have been moved from city to city, but no franchise in the past 90 years has been abandoned.

There are striking differences in the histories of the various franchises with respect to stability of ownership. The teams with the most ownership turnover in their histories are the NL Boston/Milwaukee/Atlanta Braves and the AL Cleveland Indians and Milwaukee Brewers/St. Louis Browns/Baltimore Orioles, each with 11 different owners over its history (10 franchise sales). Among the non-expansion teams, those with fewest ownership changes in the AL are the Washington Senators/Minnesota Twins and the Philadelphia/Kansas City/Oakland Athletics, both with only four different owners. In the NL, it is the Dodgers, with only three different owners, followed by the Giants and the Pirates, each with four different owners over their histories since 1901.

All of this raises the question as to what factors explain the timing of sales of franchises in baseball. In particular is the typical pattern one in which teams are sold at the top of the market, when they are making big profits and winning pennants, or is it instead when they are doing badly on the field or even going bankrupt? Has there been any tendency for the pattern to change over time?

There have been some classic cases of teams being sold because the owner was going broke, either because of losses of the team or because of losses suffered in other investments of the owner. In the National League, the Boston Braves were teetering on the brink of bankruptcy in 1935, when owner Emil Fuchs sold the team to its main creditor, Charles Adams. The team was back in trouble again in 1941 when ownership was transferred to a syndicate headed by Bob Quinn. In 1933 the Cincinnati Reds made it to last place, owner Sidney Weil went broke, and the team was taken over by the Central Trust Compnay, which sold it a year later to Powell Crosley. The Philadelphia Phillies went belly-up in 1943, after a decade of undercapitalized ownership by Mrs. May Nugent and her son, Gerald P. Nugent. There was a rather unusual history associated with this ownership. Mrs. Nugent had been the secretary of the club under owner William Baker. When Baker died in 1930, he left part of his stock to Mrs. Nugent and part to his wife. When Baker's widow died in 1933, she left her stock to Mrs. Nugent as well. The only assets owned by the Nugents were their Phillies shares. The NL took over the Phillies from the Nugents in 1943 when the team couldn't pay its bills, sold the club to a syndicate headed by William Cox, and then got the team back shortly thereafter when Cox was thrown out of baseball by the commissioner, Judge Landis, for betting on games. Bob Carpenter finally took on the burden of the Phillies from the Cox syndicate. More recently, the San Diego Padres were sold in 1973 by owner C. Arnholdt Smith after he was indicted for tax evasion, and in 1976, the Houston Astros' owner Roy Hofheinz went broke, and the team was taken over by his main creditors, GE Credit Corporation and the Ford Motor Credit Corporation, who sold the Astros a couple of years later to a syndicate headed by John McMullen.

The AL has had a somewhat less spectacular history of bankruptcies and other legal problems. In 1916, Charles Somers, who had provided the funds to finance half of the original AL franchises, went broke and was forced to sell his team, the Cleveland Indians. Harry Frazee's financial problems led first to the sale of a number of star players on the Boston Red Sox and finally to sale of the team itself, in 1923. The Red Sox were bankrupt again under the team's new owners, Bob Quinn and Mrs. Palmer Winslow, when Tom Yawkey came in to take over the franchise. Finally, another undercapitalized franchise was the Seattle Pilots under Dewey Soriano; after only one year of operation as an expansion team, the bankrupt Pilots franchise was sold in 1970 to Bud Selig, who moved the team to Milwaukee as the new Milwaukee Brewers (the original Brewers team had played only the 1901 season in the AL before moving to St. Louis).

At the other extreme, it might make good economic sense for an owner to unload a franchise when it is at its peak, say, just after winning a pennant. There are a few instances of this. In the AL, the Boston Red Sox team was sold four times—in 1903, 1904, 1912, and 1916—during championship years; the St. Louis Browns franchise was sold in 1945 after its one and only pennant-winning year; and the New York Yankees was sold by Dan Topping and Del Webb to CBS in 1964 after it won the 1963 pennant (and then went on to win the 1964 pennant as well). The last team to be sold during a pennant-winning year was in 1979, when Jerry Hoffberger sold the Baltimore Orioles to Edward B. Williams.

As might be expected, much more common has been the sale of cellar teams. In the NL, sales of cellar teams include the Cubs (1981), Cincinnati (1933, 1934), and Pittsburgh (1985); in the AL, they include Boston

(1923), Washington (1903), Philadelphia (1954), Kansas City (1960), and the new Washington Senators team (1963).

Team Historical Graphs

Immediately following this chapter, team performance graphs are presented for all baseball teams, from 1901 (or date of entry into the league) through 1990. Figure 2.A gives AL graphs, and Figure 2.B gives NL graphs. These graphs show the W/L histories of each team over this period, and home attendance over the same period. In addition, the graphs for the sixteen original teams in the AL and NL show profits for each team over the periods 1920–1950 and 1952–1956. The performance graphs also identify the dates of franchise sales for each team, and the dates when new stadiums opened.

There are a couple of general comments that can be made about the relationships shown on the performance graphs. First, team W/L records for most teams tend to follow a cyclical pattern, with periods of sustained winning teams followed by periods of sustained losers. There aren't many cases of overnight successes or flops in the graphs—it takes time to build a winning team, and winning teams ultimately deteriorate into losers. The 1991 season marked the first time in the modern (post-1901) era in which a cellar team from the previous year won a divisional title or pennant in the next year; stretching probabilities, two teams managed to accomplish this in 1991—the Twins and the Braves. Second, team attendance records exhibit cycles linked closely to the W/L percentage cycles, but in addition, for most teams, there is a strong upward trend in attendance over time. The upward trend has become particularly pronounced in the decade of the 1980s. Third, in some cases, new stadiums have had a spectacular impact on attendance, both in the short run and in the long run, although there are wide variations among teams. Finally, the graphs display profits by team for the period 1920 through 1956 (excluding 1951), based on data collected in two congressional hearings held in the 1950s. Comparable comprehensive profit data are not available for any other years. Profits follow the same general cyclical pattern as that of the W/L percentage and attendance, except that the swings in profits (at least over the 1920–1956 period) are much more pronounced than are swings of the other series.

Using the information contained in the performance graphs, over the period 1901–1990, 53 percent of NL sales were of teams that had losing seasons on the field as of the year of the sale, and 54 percent of AL sales were of losing teams. The same general conclusion holds when we look at the lifetime average W/L percentages of teams and franchise sales: 54

percent of the NL sales occurred when a team had a W/L percent below its lifetime average and 57 percent of AL sales occurred with teams below their lifetime averages. Thus, in baseball, teams have been more likely to be sold when doing poorly than when doing well, but the difference is not a striking one.

Finally, in the decades of the 1970s and 1980s, 59 percent of the sales involved teams with losing W/L records, and in the period from 1901 through 1919, 58 percent of the sales involved winning teams. Thus there is a tilt to the historical record—the earliest sales were more likely to be of winning teams than is the case with the sales in the recent past.

The Market for NBA Basketball Franchises

Table 2.2 summarizes the record of activity in the franchise market for the NBA. The NBA has had a much more tumultuous history than that of organized baseball, and this is reflected in the data shown in Table 2.2. In particular, the turnover ratios for the NBA have consistently been far above those for either the AL or the NL, averaging about 70 percent higher than the baseball ratios over the history of the NBA. Similarly, the median tenure of ownership in the NBA averages out to only about two-thirds that of the baseball leagues. Up until the recent past, basketball teams have turned over, on average, about every six and

Table 2.2
Activity in the NBA Franchise Market by Decade, 1946–1990

	1946–1949	1950–1959	1960–1969	1970–1979	1980–1990	1946–1990
(1) Franchise sales	—	6	9	23	20	58
(2) Expansion franchises	11	—	6	5	5	27
(3) Franchise moves	—	4	5	6	2	17
(4) Abandoned franchises	5	9	—	—	—	14
(5) Franchise years	48	88	103	201	236	676
Turnover ratio:						
[(1) + (4)] ÷ (5)	.104	.107	.087	.114	.085	.107
Median tenure of ownership at end of decade (years)[a]		7.0	6.0	6.5	8.0	

Sources: As in table 2.1.
[a]Expansion teams excluded in decade in which team enters NBA.

a half years. There are indications, however, that the NBA is quieting down, with median ownership tenure up to eight years as of 1990, and with the lowest turnover ratio in its history during the 1980–1990 period. Among other things, this might reflect the shift in tax advantages to buy-and-hold over buy-and-sell ownership strategies, as discussed in Chapter 3.

The NBA came into existence as the merger of the Basketball Association of America (BAA) and the National Basketball League (NBL) in 1949, after the four best teams in the NBL had jumped to the BAA in the previous year. In this merger, the BAA had the arenas and the marketing areas—the big cities of the East—and the NBL had the players—by and large, performing in small Midwestern towns. In particular, the NBA had the dominant player of the early years of pro basketball, George Mikan. There is some harsh economic reality in the fact that of the 10 teams of the NBL that joined the NBA, five (Anderson Packers, Denver Nuggets, Sheboygan Redskins, Waterloo Hawks, and Indianapolis Jets) had their franchises canceled, four after just one year in the NBA. The remaining five NBL teams all subsequently moved to new cities (Minneapolis Lakers to Los Angeles; Ft. Wayne Pistons to Detroit; Rochester Royals to Cincinnati, then to Kansas City, then to Sacramento; Tri Cities Hawks to Milwaukee, then to St. Louis, and then to Atlanta; and the Syracuse Nationals to Philadelphia, where they were renamed the 76ers). Moreover, of the original ten teams in the BAA, only the Boston Celtics, the Philadelphia Warriors (later San Francisco and then Golden State Warriors) and the New York Knicks survived beyond the 1950 season. The Chicago Stags, Cleveland Rebels, Detroit Falcons, Pittsburgh Ironmen, Providence Steamrollers, St. Louis Bombers, Toronto Huskies, and the original version of the Washington Capitols, all charter members of the BAA, had dropped out of the league before the 1950–1951 season was completed. In 1954, the original Baltimore Bullets also dropped out of the NBA. The Bullets had been added to the BAA as the lone expansion team from another early competitor of the BAA, the American Basketball League. The Bullets franchise was the last one to be abandoned by the NBA, although franchise moves continued to occur with some regularity right into the 1980s.

As is the case in baseball, there are noticeable differences in the stability of ownership among the various NBA franchises. Leading the pack is the New York Knicks, which has been owned and operated by the Madison Square Garden Corporation since the BAA began operations in 1946. Among the other long-time teams, the Fort Wayne/Detroit Pistons team has had only three owners, and the Tri Cities/Milwaukee/St. Louis/Atlanta Hawks and the Philadelphia/San Francisco/Golden State Warriors have had four owners in their histories. The team with the most checkered ownership history might come as something of a surprise. It is the Boston Celtics, with 10 owners in 45 years. The story is interesting enough to merit detailed treatment later in this chapter.

In 53 percent of the franchise sales in NBA history, the sale occurred when the team was experiencing a losing season; and in 55 percent of the cases, the franchise sale occurred at a time when the team's W/L record was below its lifetime average. The 14 abandoned franchises during the first nine years of operation of the NBA in most cases effectively represented bankruptcy cases, and in addition, one sale of the Boston Celtics (1972) occurred when the owner, Transnational Corporation, went broke, and defaulted on its payments to the previous owner, Ballantine Brewing. There have been several instances of teams being sold during or immediately after a championship year—Boston in 1965, 1968, 1975, and 1983 and Los Angeles in 1979. Cellar teams that were sold or disbanded in the same year include Pittsburgh (1947), Providence (1949), Washington (1950), Philadelphia (1953), Baltimore (1954), Minneapolis (1957), New Jersey Nets (1978), Houston (1982), and Indiana (1983).

Generally speaking, the record here is very similar to that of baseball—over the history of the NBA, it has been more likely that cellar teams will be sold (or abandoned) than that championship teams will be sold, and it is more likely that a team with a losing record will be sold than one with a winning record, but again the difference is not striking. Fifty-five percent of the franchise sales during the decades of the seventies and eighties involved teams with losing records, slightly higher than the 53 percent that holds for the entire NBA history; as in the case of baseball, there is a slight tilt toward a higher relative frequency of winning teams' being sold early in the history of the NBA than in later years.

The Market for NFL Franchises

Table 2.3 gives the record of activity in the franchise market for the NFL over its history from 1920 through 1990. The first formative phase of the NFL (1920–1932) was a hectic one, with a majority of the member teams going broke and/or abandoning their franchises during this period. By the time that divisional play was established in 1933, with a stripped-down league membership of 10 teams (it had been as high as 22 in the mid-1920s), the worst was over. Since the 1950s, the NFL has had the most stable ownership in team sports, as is indicated by the

Table 2.3
Activity in the NFL Franchise Market by Decade, 1920–1990

	1920–1929	1930–1939	1940–1949	1950–1959	1960–1969	1970–1979	1980–1990	1920–1990
(1) Franchise sales	10	8	7	2	4	5	9	45
(2) Expansion franchises	27	4	1	4	4	12	—	52
(3) Franchise moves	4	5	2	—	1	1	3	16
(4) Abandoned franchises	29	6	1	2	—	—	—	38
(5) Franchise years	167	98	99	121	150	268	308	1211
Turnover ratio: $[(1) + (4)] \div (5)$	.234	.143	.081	.033	.027	.019	.029	.069
Median tenure of ownership at end of decade (years)[a]		7.0	13.0	19.0	28.0	18.0	25.0	

Sources: As in table 2.1.
[a]Expansion teams excluded in decade team enters NFL.

low turnover ratios and by the median tenure of ownership data, up to 25 years as of the end of 1990.

The grand old man of the NFL was, of course, George Halas, who was one of the individuals most instrumental in organizing the original American Professional Football Association in 1920, which then became the National Football League in 1922. Ownership of the Chicago Bears by Halas and then by his daughter, Virginia McCaskey (since 1983), spans the entire history of the NFL. The second-longest ownership tenure is that of the nonprofit Green Bay Football Corporation, which has operated the Green Bay Packers since 1923, when Curly Lambeau, the original franchise owner, went broke and the corporation took over the team. The Mara family has controlled the New York Giants since the team came into the NFL in 1925; Charles Bidwill, his widow, and then his son, Bill Bidwill, have owned the Chicago/St.Louis/Phoenix Cardinals since 1932; and Art Rooney and then his son, Dan, have owned the Pittsburgh Steelers for all but six months of the team's history, beginning when the team entered the league in 1933. Other teams with highly stable ownership histories are Atlanta (Rankin Smith), Buffalo (Ralph Wilson), Cincinnati (Paul Brown and son, and others), Houston (Bud Adams), Kansas City (Lamar Hunt), Miami (Joe Robbie and heirs), and Tampa Bay (Hugh Culverhouse), all of which have had no turnover of ownership in the lifetime history of the team. The most volatile franchise in terms of ownership tenure is the Frankford Yellow

Jackets/Philadelphia Eagles (eight owners since Frankford entered the NFL in 1924). Another team with a colorful and varied ownership history, to be detailed below, is the Washington Redskins.

The list of teams that abandoned their NFL franchises, mainly during the 1920s, is a long one, but it is worthwhile taking the space for the list just to bring back for recall these almost completely forgotten early NFL teams. The list includes the following: Akron Indians (earlier the Pros), Baltimore Colts, Boston Bulldogs (earlier the Pottsville Maroons), Brooklyn Lions, Brooklyn Tigers (earlier the Dayton Triangles and Brooklyn Dodgers), Buffalo Rangers (earlier the All-Americans, and the Bisons), Canton Bulldogs, Chicago Tigers, Cincinnati Celts, Cleveland Bulldogs (earlier the Cleveland Indians), Columbus Tigers (earlier the Columbus Panhandles), Dallas Texans, Detroit Heralds, Detroit Panthers, Evansville Crimson Giants, Hammond Pros, Hartford Blues, Kansas City Cowboys (earlier the Blues), Kenosha Maroons (earlier the Toledo Maroons), Los Angeles Buccaneers, Louisville Colonels (earlier the Brecks), Milwaukee Badgers, Minneapolis Red Jackets (earlier the Marines), Muncie Flyers, New York Bulldogs (earlier the Boston Yanks), New York Yankees, Oorang Indians, Providence Steam Roller, Racine Tornadoes (earlier the Legion), Rochester Jeffersons, Rock Island Independents, St. Louis All Stars, St. Louis Gunners (earlier the Cincinnati Reds), Tonawanda Kardex, and the Washington Senators.

All of these abandoned their franchises in the 1920s except for the Minneapolis Red Jackets (1931), St. Louis Gunners (1935), Brooklyn Tigers (1946), New York Bulldogs (1950), Baltimore Colts (1951), and Dallas Texans (1952). (The Colts came back into the league in 1953 as a replacement for the Texans.) As a reading of the rest of the list indicates, most of the teams going under in the 1920s were from small Midwestern towns. Even some of the exceptions are misleading. For example, the Los Angeles Buccaneers fielded a team in the NFL during the 1926 season, but the team had its home base in Chicago, and played all of its games on the road. The early NFL was just a loose confederation of local club teams, who typically played many non-league games along with their NFL schedule. In the early 1920s, the league membership fee was $1,000, but it is unlikely that any teams actually paid this fee. Instead, any organization with 11 warm bodies and a place to play had a good chance of being accepted for NFL membership. League rules were changed to eliminate almost all small-town teams after the 1926 season, Green Bay being the only small town team to survive into the modern era.

Other than the abandoned franchises that were canceled by the NFL, bankruptcy was a factor in the following NFL franchise sales: Dayton Triangles, which went broke in 1930, with the team franchise being purchased from the NFL by Bill Dwyer and John Depler to relocate the team in Brooklyn as the Brooklyn Dodgers; Portsmouth Spartans, bankrupt after the 1933 season, with the franchise sold to George Richards, who moved the team to Detroit as the Detroit Lions; Frankford Yellowjackets, bankrupt midway in the 1931 season, taken over by the NFL, with the franchise purchased from the league in 1933 by Bert Bell and Lud Wray to form the Philadelphia Eagles; Cincinnati Reds, broke midway in the 1934 season, with their franchise sold to the St. Louis Gunners, who finished out the season and then had their franchise canceled before the 1935 season; and the Newark Tornadoes, broke after the 1930 season.

Teams sold in the year in which they won an NFL championship begin with the Decatur Staleys, which was moved to Chicago in 1921 by co-owners George Halas and Dutch Sternaman as the Chicago Staleys. The team played for one year under the old name (for a $5,000 fee) and won the NFL title, before the name was changed to the Chicago Bears. In 1923, the Canton Bulldogs won the NFL title. After the season, the team was sold to Cleveland Indians' (NFL) owner Sam Deutsch, who transferred most of the players to his Cleveland team, and renamed it the Cleveland Bulldogs. Cleveland then went on to win the 1924 title. The Philadelphia Eagles won the NFL title in 1948 and lost $80,000. Owner Alex Thompson sold the club in 1949 to a syndicate headed by Jerry Wolman, and the Eagles went on to win the NFL title in 1949 as well.

One other unusual sale of a winning team should be mentioned. In 1928, the Detroit Wolverines ended in third place in their first year in the NFL, with a team featuring ex-University of Michigan great Benny Friedman. Tim Mara, owner of the New York Giants, was well aware of the drawing appeal of a Jewish football star in New York, and bought the Wolverine franchise simply to acquire Friedman for the Giants. The Wolverines' franchise was then canceled, and Friedman went on to a highly successful NFL career in New York.

In contrast to baseball and the NBA, franchise sales in the NFL have overwhelmingly involved losing teams, with 68 percent of the sales being of teams with losing records in year of sale; and 74 percent of sales occurring during years when the team's W/L record was below its lifetime average.

NHL Hockey

Table 2.4 presents data on activity in the NHL franchise market from 1917, the first year of operation of the NHL, through 1990. During the

Table 2.4
Activity in the NHL Franchise Market by Decade, 1917–1990

	1917–1919	1920–1929	1930–1939	1940–1949	1950–1959	1960–1969	1970–1979	1980–1990	1917–1990
(1) Franchise sales	—	6	4	2	2	4	21	11	50
(2) Expansion franchises	—	6	—	—	—	6	10	—	22
(3) Franchise moves	—	2	2	—	—	—	2	2	8
(4) Abandoned franchises	1	—	3	1	—	—	1	—	6
(5) Franchise years	11	69	84	62	60	78	171	229	764
Turnover ratio: [(1) + (4)] ÷ (5)	.091	.087	.083	.048	.033	.051	.129	.048	.073
Median tenure of ownership at end of decade (years)[a]		4.5	5.0	14.5	20.0	21.0	4.0	12.0	

Sources: As in table 2.1.
[a]Expansion teams excluded in decade team enters NHL.

first seven years of its existence, the NHL was purely a Canadian league, operating with only three or four teams (for most years, Montreal, Ottawa, Toronto, and Hamilton). Beginning in 1924, the NHL added a second team in Montreal, the Montreal Maroons, and expanded into the United States, adding the Boston Bruins and moving the Hamilton Tigers to New York as the New York Americans. The New York Rangers, Detroit Cougars (later Red Wings), Chicago Blackhawks, and Pittsburgh Pirates were added in 1926. Gradually, marginal franchises went under, and by 1942, the league was back down to six teams— Montreal, Toronto, Boston, Detroit, Chicago, and New York—and the NHL remained a six-team league until it expanded once again in 1967. The stability of the league during the period between 1940 and the late 1960s is indicated in the table, with the median tenure of ownership peaking around 1970.

During the 1970s, the turnover ratio skyrocketed, reflecting the continuing expansion of the NHL and the less stable ownership pattern of the expansion franchises, and median ownership tenure was down to only four years. By the late 1980s, things had quieted down considerably in the NHL franchise market, and median tenure of ownership was beginning to recover towards its levels in the 1950s and 1960s. As of the 1980s, NHL hockey had a turnover ratio roughly comparable to that of baseball, with ownership much more stable than the NBA, but nowhere near as stable as the NFL.

Going back to the earliest years of the NHL, there has been a tradition of ownership of teams by the arena corporation owning the facility in which the team plays. The Montreal Maroons came into the league in 1924 as the representative of the just-completed Montreal Forum, built and owned by Donat Raymond and Thomas Strachan. In 1939, despite a successful playing history, the Maroons were in financial trouble, and petitioned the league to move to St. Louis, a move that was denied by the NHL. The Maroons franchise was then canceled, and Donat Raymond bought control of the Canadiens. Major Conn Smythe, the owner of the Toronto Maple Leafs, built his own facility, Maple Leaf Garden, which opened in 1931. The New York Rangers were and are the entry of the Madison Square Garden Corporation. Abe Pollin owns both the Washington Capitols and Capitol Center, and George and Gordon Gund owned the Richfield Coliseum when the Cleveland Barons played there in the mid-1970s.

One of the most bizarre links between arena coporations and NHL teams occurred during the late 1940s and early 1950s, at a time when, as noted above, the NHL consisted of six teams: New York, Chicago, Detroit, Boston, Toronto, and Montreal. In 1933, James Norris and Arthur Wirtz bought the Detroit franchise and Olympic Stadium. In the early 1940s, Norris became the leading stockholder in the Madison Square Garden Corporation, the owner of the Rangers, in effect becoming an owner of two of the six teams in the league. And, in 1945, Norris and Wirtz were the silent partners who funded a syndicate that purchased Chicago Stadium, which owned its major tenant, the Chicago Blackhawks. Thus, for a period of time, Norris controlled half of the six teams in the NHL. This was strictly in violation of league rules, but in a congressional hearing into antitrust problems with sports, league president Clarence Campbell argued that if Norris had not taken over the Blackhawks, the franchise would have gone under. In 1952, the Red Wings franchise was purchased from Norris and Wirtz by a syndicate headed by Norris's son, Bruce, and including his daughters, Marguerite Riker and Eleanor Kneible, and later Norris and Wirtz divested themselves of their holdings in the Madison Square Garden Corporation, following an antitrust case brought by the federal government.

The New York Rangers team has been owned by the Madison Square Garden Corporation since the team entered the league in 1925. Other than the Montreal Canadiens (with seven different owners since 1917), the remaining long-term franchises have had very stable ownership histories: Chicago Blackhawks, three owners; Detroit Red Wings, three owners; Toronto Maple Leafs, four owners; Boston Bruins, five owners. Among the expansion teams, Buffalo (Seymour and Northrup Knox), Philadelphia (Ed Snider), and Washington (Abe Pollin) have been one-owner franchises. The most volatile franchises have been the Atlanta/ Calgary Flames (five owners since 1972) and the Oakland Seals/California Golden Seals/Cleveland Barons (six owners in its 11 year history).

Teams sold in a championship year include Montreal (1957, 1964, 1970), and Toronto (1961). The great hard luck story concerning franchise sales is that of Roy L. M. Boe, who had the misfortune to go broke in 1979, just before his team, the New York Islanders, put together a string of four straight Stanley Cup championships. In the bankruptcy proceedings in 1979, the Islanders were auctioned off to a syndicate headed by John Pickett, who had been a minority stockholder in Boe's syndicate. Sales of cellar teams include Quebec (1920), to be moved to Hamilton, Montreal Canadiens (1935), Ottawa (1934), to be moved to St. Louis (Eagles), California (1974), and Colorado (1978, 1981).

In the NHL, the link between franchise sales and performance is much the same as with baseball and the NBA. 59 percent of the franchise sales have been of teams with losing W/L records in year of sale, and 55 percent involved teams with W/L records in year of sale below their lifetime W/L averages. In the 1970s and 1980s, 55 percent of franchise sales were of teams with losing W/L records, and during the 1920s and 1930s, 50 percent of the sales involved teams with losing records; thus the tilt is slightly in the direction of a larger fraction of sales involving losing teams in the recent past as compared to earlier years.

The Franchise Markets: A Summary

Table 2.5 summarizes the information from the previous tables, giving comparisons among the five sports leagues. The NFL displays the most stable ownership picture, from World War II on, with the NBA having the highest turnover ratios for franchises and the lowest median tenure of ownership. Except for the decade of the 1970s, when the league was involved in a rapid expansion phase along with an interleague war with the WHA, the NHL has had a record of turnovers and ownership tenure comparable to that of the two baseball leagues.

Owners and the "Forbes 400"

In the early days of baseball, several owners came "up through the ranks", moving up from being players to becoming owners—Connie Mack, Clark Griffith, Charles Comiskey, John McGraw, Al Spalding, John Montgomery Ward. These and a number of other owners in pro sports made their living from their teams in those days, and their mod-

Table 2.5
The Franchise Markets: A Summary, 1901–1990

	1901– 1909	1910– 1919	1920– 1929	1930– 1939	1940– 1949	1950– 1959	1960– 1969	1970– 1979	1980– 1990	1901– 1990
TURNOVER RATIO										
AL	.097	.113	.025	.038	.063	.075	.070	.063	.058	.066
NL	.125	.100	.038	.025	.088	.013	.031	.042	.053	.056
NBA					.104	.170	.087	.114	.085	.107
NFL			.234	.143	.081	.033	.027	.019	.029	.069
NHL		.091	.087	.083	.048	.033	.051	.129	.048	.073
MEDIAN TENURE OF OWNERSHIP										
AL	7.0	5.5	13.0	18.0	24.5	11.0	9.5	8.0	10.5	
NL	7.5	6.0	11.0	21.0	6.5	16.5	24.5	12.5	11.5	
NBA						7.0	6.0	6.5	8.0	
NFL				7.0	13.0	19.0	28.0	18.0	25.0	
NHL			4.5	5.0	14.5	20.0	21.0	4.0	12.5	

est wealth holdings made them vulnerable to swings in the business cycle, and to swings in their clubs' fortunes.

Things are a little different nowadays. Table 2.6 lists owners of major league sports teams who made the Forbes 400 roll of the 400 richest individuals in the country in 1990. It is not a short list; 22 owners of sports teams had estimated wealth holdings of $300 million or more, and several others, on the Forbes list, including Edgar Bronfman ($1.9 billion, Montreal Canadiens), William Wrigley ($565 million, Cubs), Joan Kroc ($920 million, Padres), and George Argyros ($290 million, Mariners), are recent ex-owners. These are the superrich, the owners who, if they wished, could certainly spend themselves into championships, almost regardless of league rules. How have their teams done?

There are a couple of gold-plated success stories—the San Francisco 49ers, under Edward DeBartolo, Jr., has a W/L record of .587, and four Super Bowl championships. Jack Kent Cooke's Redskins have the best long-term W/L record (.648) of any of the teams owned by the superrich, and three Super Bowl victories to boot. Another sparkling long-term W/L record is the .620 posted by the Boston Bruins, who have also won one Stanley Cup championship under the ownership of Jeremy Jacobs.

Those are the success stories. There are also some duds. The worst of the lot is the Tampa Bay Bucs, who have a W/L record of .304 over the 17-year period 1974–1990, under the ownership of Hugh Culverhouse. As of 1990, the Atlanta Braves have a .442 record under Ted Turner's ownership since 1976; the Jets' W/L record is .421 under owner Leon Hess, somewhat worse than the Lions' .450 under owner William

Table 2.6

Track Records of Owners of Sports Teams Making the Forbes 400 List, 1990

Owner	Estimated Wealth (millions of dollars)	Team	Purchase Date	W/L Record[a]
Ted Arison	2,100	Miami (NBA)	1988	.264
Laurence Tisch	1,500	N.Y. Giants (NFL)	1991	—
Edward DeBartolo, Sr.,		Pittsburgh (NHL)	1978	.440
and Edward DeBartolo, Jr.	1,400	San Francisco (NFL)	1977	.587
Ted Turner	1,300	Atlanta Braves (NL)	1976	.442
		Atlanta Hawks (NBA)	1977	.540
Paul Allen	1,200	Portland (NBA)	1988	.654
Jack Kent Cooke	1,100	Washington (NFL)	1979	.648
Edward Gaylord	1,000	Texas (AL)[b]		
Ewing Kaufman	835	Kansas City (AL)	1968	.521
William Davidson	725	Detroit (NBA)	1974	.516
Carl Pohlad	680	Minnesota (AL)	1984	.493
		Minnesota (NFL)[b]		
Leon Hess	650	N.Y. Jets (NFL)	1976	.450
William Ford	610	Detroit (NFL)	1963	.441
Alex Spanos	600	San Diego (NFL)	1984	.407
Tom Monaghan	550	Detroit (AL)	1983	.534
Jeremy Jacobs	550	Boston (NHL)	1975	.620
Robert Lurie	500	San Francisco (NL)	1976	.494
Richard Jacobs	500	Cleveland (AL)	1986	.461
Hugh Culverhouse	305	Tampa Bay (NFL)	1974	.304
Fritz Dixon	300	Philadelphia (NL)[b]		
Kenneth Behring	300	Seattle (NFL)	1988	.521
Gene Autry	300	California (AL)	1960	.470
Overall weighted average				.489

Sources: Forbes Magazine, October 22, 1990, and league guides.
[a]W/L record from date of purchase through 1990 (1990/91) season.
[b]Minority owner.

Ford; and there is the .407 W/L mark of the Chargers since Alex Spanos took over the team in 1984. Finally, there is the other DeBartolo story—the Pittsburgh Penguins under Edward DeBartolo, Sr.—a W/L record of .440 between 1978 and 1990. The senior DeBartolo decided to sell the team after its first stunningly successful season (1990/91) when the Penguins won the Stanley Cup.

Averaged over all cases, the W/L percentage of teams under the ownership of the superrich turns out to be a less than impressive .489. This should put to rest at least some of the fears that wealthy owners will be so consumed by a desire to win that they will destroy the competitive balance of sports. You don't get on the Forbes list by throwing away your money, and there is scant evidence that the superrich owners act differently as owners of sports teams than they do in their other occupations. The Edward DeBartolo, Jr./49er case turns out to be an aberration. On the other hand, it might be that the improved record of sports in recent years, so far as ownership tenure and franchise turnover is concerned, reflects in part the fact that rich owners today are under less pressure to sell during bad times than were the more modestly wealthy owners of the past.

Some Detailed Franchise Histories

Team ownership histories compiled for this book represent a revision and extension of the franchise histories developed in Davis and Quirk (1974b). There were various sources used to compile this information, including the *New York Times*, *Sporting News*, *Sports Inc.*, *Sports Illustrated*, official encyclopedias of the various sports, league registers and guides, memoirs of owners and players, congressional hearings, and team and league histories. While there certainly are reliability problems concerning details of franchise transactions (especially concerning franchise prices), there are reasons to believe that they generally don't apply in the identification of the syndicates involved in franchise transfers. (An exception is in cases such as the Norris-Wirtz secret ownership of the Chicago Blackhawks, however.) With these caveats, we give the ownership histories for several leading teams in the various sports.

Duluth Eskimos/Washington Redskins

The story of the Redskins begins in the icy reaches of northern Minnesota, at the head of the lakes in Duluth. The Duluth Kelleys were a well-known semipro team for years before joining the NFL for the 1923 season, regularly trouncing the leading teams from St. Paul and Minneapolis, including the Minneapolis Marines. The team was coached by tackle Dan Williams, who was also a co-owner of the team, and the team starred halfback Joey Sternaman, the younger brother of Dutch Sternaman, co-owner of the Chicago Bears. The Kelleys went 4–3–0 in the 1923 NFL standings, and then compiled a 5–1–0 NFL record in 1924, to end up in fourth place in an 18-team league. The team ran into troubles in 1925, losing its only three NFL games, and early in 1926, Williams and his co-owners decided to get out of the football business.

They sold the team to the club treasurer, Ole Haugsrud, for $1, and Haugsrud changed the name of the team to the Duluth Eskimos.

The year 1926 was a critical one for the NFL, because it was facing its first competition, the American Football League, organized by Red Grange and his manager, C. C. Pyle. (See the discussion in Chapter 9.) Ole Haugsrud was instrumental in helping the NFL to weather out the 1926 season. After becoming owner of the Duluth team, Haugsrud got in touch with an ex-high school player from the Duluth area, who had just finished a spectacular career as a college fullback. The player was Ernie Nevers, a two-time All American at Stanford. Haugsrud signed Nevers to a personal services contract, and built the Eskimos' offense around him. Nevers turned out to be one of the greatest players in the history of the NFL, and almost as much of a drawing card as Grange himself. The Eskimos ended the 1926 season with an official NFL record of 6–5–3, and they were among the best-drawing teams on the road in the league. After the season was over, the Eskimos hit the exhibition trail, and ended up playing 29 games (2 at home and 27 on the road!) before calling it quits for the year.

The AFL folded after the 1926 season, with Grange's New York Yankees moving to the NFL. While most small-town NFL teams turned in their franchises before the 1927 season under the new rules set up by NFL president Joe Carr, designed to eliminate the weakest franchises in the league (including the requirement that league teams post a $2,000 performance bond), the Eskimos stayed in the league. Even with Nevers in the lineup, an all-pro as he was in every year he was in the NFL, Duluth had a bad year, ending up with a record of 1–8–0, 11th in a 12-team league. The team suspended operations for the 1928 season. Ole Haugsrud was out of football, and so was Ernie Nevers, because of that personal services contract he had signed in 1926. Nevers spent part of his time out of football in 1928 as he had during the summers of 1926 and 1927, pitching for the St. Louis Browns, ending up with a lifetime 6–12 mark, and he also acted as an assistant football coach at his alma mater, Stanford.

The NFL wanted Nevers back, and in 1929, a buyer was found for the Duluth franchise. Ole Haugsrud sold the franchise for $2,000 to Edwin Simandl, who moved the team to Orange, New Jersey, for the 1929 season. Haugsrud then took a job as general manager of the Chicago Cardinals, bringing Ernie Nevers with him to that team, where Nevers played out his career, retiring after the 1931 season. George Halas, for one, never forgot what Ole Haugsrud had done for the NFL, and when Haugsrud sold the Eskimos franchise, Halas promised Haugsrud that the next time the NFL added a team in Minnesota, he would be a co-owner. When the Vikings came into the league in 1961, Haugsrud put up

$60,000 of the $600,000 expansion fee, and became a 10 percent owner of one of the most successful franchises in the NFL.

Simandl's Orange Tornadoes didn't do all that badly on the playing field in 1929 (3–4–4) but they didn't draw, and the team was moved to Newark for the 1930 season, where they ended up last with a record of 1–10–1. The franchise was forfeited to the league, which put it up for bids. No bids were received before the 1931 season, so the franchise was suspended for one year.

At this point, there is some ambiguity in the historical record as to what happened to the old Duluth franchise. Joe Horrigan, curator of the NFL Hall of Fame, reports that there are no league records specifically identifying this franchise from 1931 on, and he argues that the franchise was probably just canceled after the 1931 season. On the other hand, in his taped reminiscing at the Hall of Fame, Ole Haugsrud, who was still in the league with the Cardinals in 1931, claimed that the Duluth franchise was the one the league finally sold in 1932. Rosenthal (1981) also agrees with this.

In any case, buyers came along in 1932 to put up a fee of $7,500 or thereabout (although the precise dollar amount is a matter of dispute) for a franchise that might have been the original Eskimo franchise. The buyers were members of a syndicate that included George Marshall, whose main business was operating a laundry in Washington, D.C., and who had taken a bath with a pro basketball team in the original American Basketball League in the mid-1920s. The franchise was assigned to Boston, and the team was named the Boston Braves. The Braves ended up with a respectable 1932 record of 4–4–2, but the team lost $46,000, and part of the syndicate pulled out, leaving Marshall as the majority owner. He renamed the team the Boston Redskins.

In 1936, the Redskins faced in-town competition from the Boston Shamrocks, who won the league championship in the rival American Football League (the second of this name). The Redskins also were winners, ending up with the Eastern division title in the NFL. The championship game, with the Packers, was scheduled for Boston. However, during the season, the Redskins had barely outdrawn the Shamrocks, posting a per-game attendance of only 8,500. Marshall was furious about the lack of fan support, and moved the championship game to New York, where the Packers beat the Redskins for the title. After the 1936 season, Marshall moved the team to Washington, where it became the Washington Redskins.

The year 1937 was the second year of the player draft in the NFL, and Marshall hit the jackpot, ending up with a true franchise player, Sammy Baugh. Baugh quarterbacked the Redskins for the next 15 years, throwing for 188 touchdowns, 21,996 yards, and ended with a lifetime completion precentage of 56.5 percent. Baugh still holds the NFL lifetime record as a punter, with an average of 44.9 yards per kick.

During the late 1930s and early 1940s, the Redskins dominated the NFL East as the Bears dominated the West. After World War II, the franchise went into decline. Its problems on the field were compounded by competition at the gate from the Baltimore Colts, who had moved into the NFL from the All American Football Conference in 1950. In the mid-1950s, Marshall sold 25 percent of the Redskins to radio announcer Harry Wismer. In 1960, Wismer financed his purchase of the New York Titans (later Jets) franchise in the newly formed American Football League by selling his holdings in the Redskins to Jack Kent Cooke, for $350,000. In 1962, Edward B. Williams, the Redskins attorney, purchased 3 percent of the club to join Cooke (23 percent), Leo Dorsey (12 percent), Milton King (11 percent), and Marshall (51 percent) as co-owners. In 1969, Marshall died and left his shares to a foundation, disinheriting his children. Court cases following this eventually led to the purchase of all the Marshall holdings by Pro Football, Inc., the Redskins' corporate shell, with Cooke the majority stockholder. In 1972, 24 percent of the outstanding shares were purchased for $3 million and retired; in 1974, 32 percent of the outstanding shares were purchased for $5,720,000 and retired. By the early 1980s, Jack Kent Cooke had become the sole owner of the Redskins, at a total outlay estimated by *Sports Inc.* at approximately $15 million over the period 1960–1988.

Boston Celtics

The Boston Celtics team was a charter member of the Basketball Association of America at its founding in 1946, owned and operated by the Boston Garden Corporation. In 1951, after five successive years of losses, the team was sold by the corporation to its president, Walter Brown, for $2,500. Later in the year, Brown sold a half-interest in the Celtics to Lou Pieri for $50,000. While the team had been losing money, the decision had already been made that would make its future golden, when Red Auerbach was hired as coach. Once George Mikan had retired and the Mineapolis Lakers were in a decline, the Celtics began the unbelievable stretch of nine straight NBA championships (1957–1965).

In 1964, near the end of the Celtics' unbroken string of league championships, Brown died, and control of the team passed to Pieri and Brown's widow. In 1965, the team was sold for $3 million to the Ruppert Knickerbocker Corporation, headed by Marvin Kratter and Jack Waldron. Three years later, the team was sold again, this time for $6 million, to Ballantine Brewing Co.

After Ballantine was taken over by Investors Funding Co., there was another sale of the Celtics, in 1971, to Transnational Communications, Inc., for $6 million. Transnational was a firm organized by three ex-jocks (Whitey Ford, Dick Lynch, and Pat Sumner), with minority holdings by Seymour and Northrup Knox. Apparently, the major owners were better athletes than managers. The firm had bought the Oakland Seals franchise in 1969, and then had bailed out in 1970 after the team had defaulted on its league debts, selling the Seals to Charlie Finley. The story with the Celtics was more of the same. By 1972, Transnational was behind in its payments to Ballantine for the team, and the franchise once more reverted to Ballantine, which was again looking for a buyer.

In early 1972, for payment of a $50,000 fee, Irv Levin and Harold Lipton obtained an option to buy the Celtics from Ballantine for $4 million. But when Levin and Lipton attempted to exercise their option, they were turned down by the NBA. The league argued that because Levin and Lipton were both executives in the National General Corporation, a firm whose president was Sam Schulman, owner of the Seattle SuperSonics, there would be potential conflict of interest problems. Following their turndown, Levin and Lipton looked around for someone to sell their option to, and found a willing buyer in Bob Schmertz, a New Jersey contractor who was a part-owner of the Portland Trail Blazers, and of the World Hockey Association New England Whalers, and who later became the owner of the New York Stars of the World Football League. Schmertz bought the option from Levin and Lipton for $50,000, exercised it, and paid $4 million to become the next in this long string of owners of the Celtics.

The plot thickens at this point. Levin and Lipton brought an antitrust suit against the NBA because of the action blackballing them as potential owners (*Levin v. National Basketball Association*, 385 F. Supp. 149 (S.D.N.Y. 1974)). This suit was thrown out of court, on the ground that there was no violation of the antitrust laws in the action of the NBA.

In 1974, the two brought suit against Schmertz, claiming that at the time that Schmertz purchased the Celtics option from them, he had made an oral agreement to pay them an additional $100,000 when he had successfully exercised the option, and also had agreed to sell Levin and Lipton a 50 percent interest in the Celtics for $2 million within a year from the time he purchased the club. As the noted legal scholar Sam Goldwyn, once said, "An oral agreement isn't worth the paper it's written on." But in this case, Levin and Lipton had an eyewitness to the agreement, who turned out to be none other than Sam Schulman. Levin and Lipton won their case against Schmertz, who sold them half the team for $2 million in early 1975. This time, the NBA board of governors agreed to accept Levin and Lipton as owners, reversing their earlier decision. Later that year, Schmertz was indicted for bribery of New Jersey officials in connection with a building contract, but before the case came to trial, he died of a brain tumor. His widow then sold the remaining Schmertz share of the Celtics to Levin and Lipton.

Three years later, after a couple of bad years for Boston, the team was traded by Levin and Lipton to John Y. Brown, of Kentucky Fried Chicken fame, and Harry Mangurian, for their ownership of the Buffalo Braves. Levin and Lipton took several starting players from Boston with them as part of the deal. Having acquired the Buffalo franchise, they immediately moved the team to San Diego, where it became the San Diego Clippers, which they sold to Donald Sterling for $13.5 million in 1981, the team ultimately ending up in Los Angeles as the L.A. Clippers.

In 1979, Harry Mangurian acquired sole ownership of the Celtics from Brown, and the Celtics had their second-in-a-row bad season. It was so bad, in fact, that the Celtics had one of the top draft choices for the year, and, with the legendary luck of the Irish, ended up, of course, with none other than Larry Bird and more future NBA championships. But Mangurian was unhappy with the rental agreement the club had with the antiquated Boston Garden, and sold the team in 1983 for $15 million to Allen H. Cohen, Don F. Gaston, and Paul DuPee.

The last chapter of the Celtics franchise history is a particularly intriguing one. In 1986, the Celtics went public. Cohen, Gaston, and DuPee offered a 40 percent interest in the club in the form of 2.6 million shares of stock, which were sold at a price of $18.50 per share. Using some elementary arithmetic, this means that the implicit market value of the entire team at time of public stock sale was approximately $120 million.

In 1990, a partnership formed by the Celtics bought TV station WFXT (channel 29) and radio station WEEI (AM 590), and will air their games on these stations until at least the year 2000. Stockholders of the Celtics have the right to become members of this partnership as well.

Summary statistics on the finances of the Celtics over the period 1986–1990 are as follows:

	1986	1987	1988	1989	1990	1991
Earnings (millions of dollars)	$3.58	$6.5	$10.34	$12.22	$8.0	$10.97
Earnings per share	$0.55	$1.00	$ 1.59	$ 1.88	$1.23	$ 1.69
Price range	(15–18)	(10–16)	(11–15)	(13–19)	(14–19)	(16–20)

The market value of the team (based on the midpoint between high and low stock prices over the year) went from $120 million in 1986 to $84.5

million in 1987 and 1988, $104 million in 1989, $107.5 million in 1990, and $117 million in 1991.

To find out how the Celtics are doing in the NBA, check the sports section of your local paper. To find out how the Celtics are doing at the till, check the New York Stock Exchange listing in the business section of your paper.

Milwaukee Brewers/St. Louis Browns/ Baltimore Orioles

The most successful team in the AL over the past 30 years has been the Baltimore Orioles, with an average lifetime W/L percent of .537, and six AL pennants. This can be viewed as divine justice, given the history of the franchise before it arrived in Baltimore, or perhaps more or less compelling evidence for that good old standby, the law of averages. On the other hand, maybe we should give credit where credit is due, to Earl Weaver, rated by Scully (1989) as one of the greatest managers in the history of baseball, and to that magnificent pitching staff he put together.

The story begins in Milwaukee, where the Milwaukee Brewers played as a charter member of the AL in 1901. At the end of the first AL season, Henry Killilea, the Brewers' owner, sold the team for $50,000 to a syndicate headed by Robert Lee Hedges, who moved it to St. Louis as the St. Louis Browns. (Killilea then moved on to Boston, where he bought the Red Sox and then sold the team a year later.) The Browns quickly became a perennial second-division team, saved at the gate only by the fact that their in-town NL rivals, the Cardinals, were even worse.

In 1914, the Federal League began operating as a competitor to organized baseball, and fielded a third major league team in St. Louis, owned by Phil Ball and Otto Stifel. In 1915, an out-of-court settlement was reached in an antitrust case filed by the Federal League against organized baseball. As part of that settlement, Ball was allowed to purchase the Browns for $525,000, with the AL putting up $50,000 of the purchase price. The Browns had some modest success on the field in the early years under Ball, primarily because of the hitting of George Sisler, acquired in 1915. But by the early 1930s, St. Louis was becoming not only a surefire second-division team but a competitor for the permanent last-place position. In 1933, Phil Ball died, and in 1936 the Ball heirs sold the Browns to Don Barnes and Bill De Witt for $325,000.

During the war years, things turned around for the team, and the Browns won their only AL pennant in 1944, losing to the Cardinals in the World Series. With somewhat unseemly haste, the Barnes syndicate unloaded the team in 1945, selling it to Richard Muckerman for $1,443,000. Muckerman also purchased title to Sportsman's Park for $500,000. Four years later, the team was back deep in the second division, and Bill De Witt and his brother purchased 56 percent of the team and stadium for $1 million (implicit value of team + stadium = $1,786,000). They held the team only two years. In 1951, Bill Veeck headed a syndicate that purchased 58 percent of the team and stadium from the De Witts for $1,400,000 (implicit value of team + stadium = $2,413,000). Later, the syndicate acquired an additional 21 percent of the team and stadium.

Veeck has recounted the story of his days in St. Louis in his fascinating autobiography, *Veeck as in Wreck*. After losing $396,000 in 1952, Veeck asked for league permission to move the team to Baltimore. Veeck was turned down twice, first after the 1952 season, and then again after the 1953 season (when he dropped another $706,000). After the second turndown, he sold the team for $2,475,000 to a Baltimore syndicate headed by Clarence Miles, and sold the stadium for $850,000 to the St. Louis Cardinals, who had been tenants of the Browns in Sportsman's Park. The AL then reversed itself and voted to permit the Browns to move to Baltimore, where the name was changed to the Baltimore Orioles.

The team began improving almost immediately, and by the early 1960s had become a pennant contender. In 1965, the team was sold for an unknown price to Jerry Hoffberger. Hoffberger was the owner during the greatest years of the franchise, winning AL pennants in 1966, 1969, 1970, and 1971. In 1979, the Orioles again won the pennant and Hoffberger sold 80 percent of the team to Edward Bennett Williams for $10,500,000 (implicit price of team = $13,000,000), retaining a 20 percent interest for himself. The decade of the '80s was one long downhill slide for the Orioles, which bottomed out in 1988 when the team set an all-time AL record for most consecutive losses at the beginning of the season. Williams died in 1988 and the team was sold by Williams' heirs for $70 million to a syndicate headed by Eli Jacobs.

Cleveland Barons

Thus far, our franchise histories have all been success stories, at least in terms of escalating franchise values, but there have been one or two clinkers, even in the booming franchise market of recent years. A case in point is the Cleveland Barons of the NHL. This team began operations in Oakland as the Oakland Seals, one of six expansion teams taken in by the NHL in 1967. Owners Barry Van Gerbig and George Fleharty paid $2 million for the franchise. In 1967–1968, Oakland came in last in the league, but it improved to eighth (in a 12-team league) in 1968–1969. That was to be the banner season for the franchise, which then proceeded to end up last in its division seven of the next nine years.

However, this was all in the future in 1969, when the team was sold for $4,500,000 to the same Transnational Corporation that was mentioned earlier in connection with the Celtics. Within a year, the team was in default on its bills, and Transnational sold the Seals for $4.5 million to the owner of the Oakland Athletics AL team, Charlie Finley. Finley renamed the team the California Golden Seals, and stayed with the team for four lean years. Finally, in 1974, Finley sold the team to the NHL for a price between $4.5 and $6 million, and the league operated the franchise for a year while it looked around for another buyer.

In 1975, the team was sold for an unknown price to Mel Swig, who moved the team to Cleveland in 1976, renaming the team the Cleveland Barons. The move didn't do much good, and in 1977 the team was broke again. Swig sold the team for $5.3 million to George and Gordon Gund, superrich owners of the Richfield Arena and the NBA Cleveland Cavaliers. The Gunds operated the team for one year, losing a reported $3 million, and in 1978 negotiated a merger of the Cleveland franchise with the Minnesota North Stars franchise, with Cleveland going out of business. The Gunds took over ownership of the Minnesota North Stars, and held that team until 1990, when, in a complicated cash and player deal, the North Stars were purchased for $31.5 million, first by Howard Baldwin and Morris Belzberg, and then resold to Norman Green. The Gunds moved on from their unsuccessful hockey franchises in Cleveland and the Twin Cities, to a new expansion franchise in San Jose, which began play (with a lot of the best young players from the North Star system) in the 1991/92 season. In a roundabout kind of way, it was *déjà vu* all over again; the last remnants of the Oakland Seals were coming back to the Bay area, with high hopes for a better shake than the last time around.

Franchise Prices

Sports franchises are assets that generate a cash flow for the owner (which might be negative, of course) through after-tax profits from the regular season schedule of games and from playoffs. In addition, an owner earns capital gains (which again could be negative) from appreciation (or depreciation) in the price of the franchise between the time it is bought and the time it is sold. As has been pointed out earlier, profit data are not available for pro sports teams, except for a few isolated instances. Here we look instead at the capital gains aspect of team ownership. Data are presented for the AL, NL, NBA, and NFL. There is insufficient information available to warrant presenting a history of franchise prices in the NHL.

In Table 2.7, data on franchise prices are presented for all present-day teams in the AL and NL. As noted above, franchise prices are those reported in a variety of sources, ranging from the *New York Times* to the personal memoirs of owners, managers, and sportswriters, and hence the data range from highly reliable to highly speculative.

For both the AL and NL, the franchise price history of each team is given, covering all sales for which price information is available. Sales of teams where no price information is available are excluded from the table. The table includes some imputed franchise price information not associated with a change in ownership of a team, as in the occasional case where a minority block of stock changes hands at a reported price, which is blown up proportionally to obtain an imputed value for the team. The data cover approximately 100 observations of franchise prices in baseball between 1901 and 1990.

The table provides data on the average annual rate of increase in the franchise price, caculated in two different ways: rate of increase to the next sale, and rate of increase to the final sale. The figure reported in the "to the next sale" column gives the average annual rate of increase in the franchise price between the date of this sale and the date of the next sale for which price information is available. It represents the average annual rate of return on initial invested capital (in the form of capital gains) from holding the franchise to the next sale date reported. The figure reported in the "to the final sale" column gives the average annual rate of increase in the franchise price between this date and the date of the last sale for which franchise price information is available for the team. It gives the average annual rate of return on initial invested capital (in the form of capital gains) that would have been earned if an individual had bought the team at this date and then held the team until the last sale date reported in the table.

For example, in the case of the Atlanta (Boston/Milwaukee) Braves, the team was sold in 1906 for $75,000, sold again for $114,000 in 1910, sold many more times, and finally sold (to Ted Turner) for $11 million in 1976. The average annual rate of increase in the franchise price between 1906 and 1910 was 10.5 percent; the average annual rate of increase in the franchise price between 1906 and 1976 was 4.8 percent. The rates of increase shown in the table assume continuous compounding, which is roughly equivalent to daily compounding, and which leads to a lower rate of increase than if, say, annual compounding had been used.

Table 2.7
Average Annual Rates of Increase in Franchise Prices, Baseball

Team	Year	Franchise Price	Avg. Annual Rate of Increase To Next Sale	To Final Sale
NATIONAL LEAGUE				
Boston/Milwaukee/				
Atlanta	1906	$ 75,000	10.5%	7.1%
	1910	114,000	49.5	6.9
	1911	187,000	9.5	6.4
	1919	400,000	5.6	5.8
	1923	500,000	−12.6	5.8
	1925	388,000	−1.8	6.6
	1935	325,000	13.9	8.6
	1941	750,000	0.0	7.7
	1944	750,000	10.6	8.4
	1964	6,200,000	4.8	4.8
	1976	11,000,000	—	—
Chicago	1905	105,000	15.6	6.9
	1915	500,000	5.6	5.6
	1981	20,500,000	—	—
Cincinnati	1902	146,000	7.8	6.0
	1929	1,200,000	4.2	4.8
	1966	20,500,000	—	—
Houston	1960	2,000,000	11.4	11.4
	1979	17,900,000	—	—
Brooklyn/Los Angeles	1912	200,000	6.1	8.0
	1944	1,388,000	7.8	19.8
	1945	1,500,000	20.6	20.6
	1950	4,200,000	—	—
Montreal	1968	10,000,000	—	—
N.Y. Mets	1960	2,000,000	11.8	15.0
	1980	21,000,000	26.0	26.0
	1986	100,000,000	—	—
Philadelphia	1903	200,000	9.3	6.4
	1909	350,000	0.4	6.2
	1943	400,000	11.4	11.4
	1981	30,175,000	—	—
St. Louis	1917	375,000	5.7	6.4
	1947	2,100,000	23.0	9.7
	1949	3,330,000	3.0	3.0
	1953	3,750,000	—	—
San Diego	1968	10,000,000	3.0	10.6
	1974	12,000,000	10.8	10.8
	1990	75,000,000	—	—

(continued)

Table 2.7 (cont.)
Average Annual Rates of Increase in Franchise Prices, Baseball

Team	Year	Franchise Price	Avg. Annual Rate of Increase	
			To Next Sale	To Final Sale
NATIONAL LEAGUE				
N.Y. Giants/				
San Francisco	1903	125,000	16.7	5.9
	1919	1,820,000	2.7	2.9
	1976	8,500,000	16.3	16.3
	1977	10,000,000	—	—
AMERICAN LEAGUE				
Milwaukee/St. Louis/				
Baltimore	1902	50,000	18.1	8.4
	1915	525,000	−2.3	6.7
	1936	325,000	16.6	10.3
	1945	1,443,000	−2.9	9.0
	1949	1,286,000	15.0	10.2
	1951	1,736,000	17.8	10.0
	1953	2,475,000	6.4	9.5
	1979	13,000,000	18.7	18.7
	1988	70,000,000	—	—
California	1960	2,000,000	—	—
Chicago	1959	5,000,000	22.2	6.3
	1961	7,800,000	2.3	4.7
	1975	10,700,000	10.4	10.4
	1981	20,000,000	—	—
Cleveland	1916	500,000	6.3	5.4
	1927	1,000,000	−13.9	5.2
	1932	500,000	8.3	7.6
	1946	1,600,000	14.9	7.2
	1949	2,500,000	6.6	6.2
	1956	3,960,000	7.0	6.0
	1966	8,000,000	4.2	4.2
	1972	10,300,000	—	—
Detroit	1903	50,000	17.6	8.6
	1920	1,000,000	4.6	6.2
	1935	2,000,000	4.8	6.7
	1956	5,500,000	8.2	8.2
	1983	50,000,000	—	—
Kansas City Royals	1968	5,350,000	9.4	9.4
	1983	22,000,000	—	—

(continued)

Table 2.7 (cont.)
Average Annual Rates of Increase in Franchise Prices, Baseball

Team	Year	Franchise Price	Avg. Annual Rate of Increase	
			To Next Sale	To Final Sale
AMERICAN LEAGUE				
Washington/				
Minnesota	1912	270,000	4.2	6.6
	1919	363,000	6.9	6.9
	1984	32,000,000	—	—
Seattle/Milwaukee	1968	5,350,000	35.1	35.1
	1970	10,800,000	—	—
Baltimore/				
N.Y. Yankees	1903	18,000	28.2	9.0
	1914	400,000	25.2	5.5
	1922	3,000,000	−0.2	2.4
	1945	2,880,000	27.6	4.4
	1948	6,600,000	8.7	4.7
	1964	14,000,000	−3.7	−3.7
	1973	10,000,000	—	—
Philadelphia/				
Kansas City/				
Oakland	1950	1,910,000	4.6	6.3
	1954	2,300,000	8.4	6.6
	1960	3,800,000	6.0	6.0
	1980	12,700,000	—	—
Seattle	1976	7,000,000	12.4	18.3
	1981	13,000,000	22.1	22.1
	1989	76,000,000	—	—
Washington/Texas	1960	3,000,000	17.0	11.3
	1963	5,000,000	12.3	10.7
	1969	10,440,000	6.1	10.2
	1970	11,100,000	10.4	10.4
	1989	80,000,000	—	—

Sources: As in table 2.1.

There are stories behind almost all of the sales that are reported in the table. Consider the case of the Brooklyn/Los Angeles Dodgers. The 1912 franchise price of $200,000 identifies the sale by Charles Ebbets of a 50 percent interest in the Dodgers to the McKeever brothers, Ed and Steve, for $100,000, because of Ebbets' need to obtain the money required to complete construction of Ebbets Field. Ebbets died in 1925, and Ed McKeever died a week later. Control of the Dodgers was now in the hands of the Ebbets and McKeever heirs (including the surviving McKeever brother, Steve), and they couldn't stand each other. For the next 13 years, the two factions, each owning exactly 50 percent of the team, disagreed about everything. It got so bad that the National League stepped in to appoint an arbiter for the team so that there would be a Dodger vote recorded on the major issues facing the league. (More recently, something similar happened with the NFL New York Giants when Wellington Mara and Tim Mara each controlled exactly 50 percent of the team; general manager George Young made team decisions because of the all-out war between the two Mara groups.)

By 1938, the Dodgers were head over heels in debt to the banks, and in a desperation move, a new general manager, Larry McPhail, was brought in to run the team. McPhail did such a great job that four years later, the team was completely out of debt, and over the remaining sixteen years in Brooklyn, the Dodgers dominated the NL, on the field and at the box office. It was in 1942 that the Dodgers made two more front office decisions, hiring Branch Rickey to replace McPhail, who had gone into the service, and hiring Walter O'Malley as the lawyer for the club.

In 1944, the McKeever heirs put up their 25 percent share of the team for sale, and O'Malley, Branch Rickey, and John Smith bought the shares, for $347,000. A year later, the Ebbets heirs sold their 50 percent interest for $750,000 to the trio. In 1950, Smith died and O'Malley and Smith's widow decided to force Rickey out of the team, first by firing him as general manager, and second by offering to buy Rickey's 25 percent interest in the club for what he had paid for it in 1944 and 1945, that is, $360,000. After long negotiations, Rickey sold out instead for $1,025,000, which represented an impressive 20.6 percent annual rate of return on his investment in the years since he bought into the team. With the move of the team to Los Angeles, it became what Roger Noll once described as "baseball's version of the U.S. mint." And it all started with the purchase of an undervalued franchise at the end of World War II.

But if the Dodgers were a steal, what about the Yankees? In 1922, Jacob Ruppert bought out his partner, Colonel Tillinghast Huston, for $1.5 million, and became the sole owner of the team. Ruppert died in 1939 and left the team to his two nieces and a friend. The ladies decided to sell the team in 1945, and found a buyer in the form of a syndicate consisting of Larry McPhail (just back from the service), Del Webb, and Dan Topping. The Yankees (including Yankee Stadium, built in 1922 for $2.5 million) sold for just $2.88 million. McPhail was again a great general manager and the Yankees were winning under the new ownership team, but he was not easy to get along with, and in 1948, Webb and Topping bought out McPhail's one-third interest in the team for

$2.2 million. The (imputed) market value of the team had increased from $2.88 million to $6.6 million in just three years, a rate of increase of 27.8 percent per year, as indicated in Table 2.7. There is no doubt that the Yankees were grossly underpriced in 1945.

But this is not the end of the Yankee saga. Webb and Topping sold Yankee Stadium in 1953 for $6.5 million, still retaining ownership of the team itself. The buyer of the stadium was Arnold Johnson, who would later become the owner of the Kansas City Athletics, the team that under his leadership supplied the Yankees with a steady stream of players during the 1950s, including among others Roger Maris. The Yankees were sold in 1964 to CBS for $14 million. Taking into account the income generated by the stadium sale as well as the sale of the team, the rate of return earned on initial invested capital from capital gains alone between 1948 and 1964 was 8.7 percent.

CBS managed to run the Yankees into the ground, and in 1973 unloaded the team for $10 million, $4 million less than had been paid for the team in 1964. The new owner was a syndicate headed by George Steinbrenner, and included Mike Burke, who had been an executive with CBS. Even at the time, there was amazement at the price the Yankees sold for. To put things in context, the bankrupt Seattle Pilots sold for $10.8 million in 1970, the floundering Washington Senators/Texas Rangers sold for $11.1 million in 1970, and the NL sold expansion franchises to Montreal and San Diego for $10 million in 1968. There was a stockholder suit by a disgruntled CBS stockholder who thought CBS had been taken to the cleaners and/or there was some funny business afoot. But the suit failed, and that was the end of things. In 1988, after the Yankees had negotiated a $45 million per year deal for cable televising of the team's games, the *Wall Street Journal* estimated the market value of the Yankees at $250 million.

Beyond the anecdotes, what can be said about the general pattern of franchise prices in baseball? Table 2.8 presents a summary of the information contained in Table 2.7 with respect to average rates of increase in franchise prices. In part A, the average rate of increase to next sale is shown, cross-classified by decade of sale and decade of next sale. Generally speaking, what part A shows is that franchises were relatively undervalued in the 1901–1919 period, and relatively overvalued in the 1920s (from hindsight). Moreover, the table indicates that the rate of escalation of franchise prices increased substantially in the 1980s. In part B, the average rate of increase to the final sale is cross-classified by decade of sale and by decade of final sale. Weighted averages of rate of returns are used, with the weight being the number of years between sales. The overall average rate of increase of franchise prices over the

Table 2.8
Annual Rates of Increase in Franchise Prices,
Weighted Average over All Teams, Baseball, 1901–1990

| | Average Annual Rate of Increase to Next Sale | | | | | | | | |
| | Date of Next Sale | | | | | | | | |
Date of Sale	1901–1909	1910–1919	1920–1929	1930–1939	1940–1949	1950–1959	1960–1969	1970–1979	1980–1990
1901–1909	9.3	18.7	11.6	—	3.8	—	—	—	—
1910–1919		9.7	14.3	−2.3	5.9	—	—	2.7	6.2
1920–1929			−12.6	−0.6	−0.2	—	4.2	—	—
1930–1939				—	12.0	4.8	—	—	—
1940–1949					10.6	10.6	8.0	—	8.5
1950–1959						9.0	13.8	6.4	8.2
1960–1969							12.6	6.8	9.1
1970–1979								16.3	12.5
1980–1990									23.5

| | Average Annual Rate of Increase from First to Final Sale | | | | |
| | Date of Final Sale | | | | |
Date of First Sale	1950–1959	1960–1969	1970–1979	1980–1990	Overall Average
1901–1909	—	6.0	7.3	7.3	7.2
1910–1919	7.2	—	5.4	6.6	6.6
1920–1929	—	—	—	—	—
1930–1939	—	—	—	—	—
1940–1949	—	—	—	—	—
1950–1959	—	—	—	6.3	6.3
1960–1969		—	12.7	11.6	11.9
1970–1979			—	18.3	18.3
1980–1990					—
Overall avg.	7.2	6.0	7.4	7.9	7.5

entire period is 7.5 percent per year, with a much larger rate of increase in the decade of the 1980s.

To put this in context, the "rule of 70" might be helpful. The rule of 70 says that if you want to find out to a close approximation how many years it takes for your money to double at any interest rate, you simply divide the interest rate into 70. Thus at an interest rate of 10 percent, it takes 7 years to double your money; at an interest rate of 5 percent, it takes 14 years. The overall average rate of increase of franchise prices of 7.5 percent means that over the past 90 years, franchise prices have doubled about every 9 years. For franchises that were sold in the 1970s and then sold again in the 1980s, on average it took about 5.5 years to double, and for the two franchises (the Mets and the Rangers) sold twice in the 1980s, on average it took only a little less than 3 years to double in price.

Table 2.9 gives the history of franchise prices for teams in the NBA. Data are much less complete for the NBA than for baseball, with only 44 data points shown in the table, and many data points are simply the expansion fee paid by the owners. For most franchises, one average rate of increase in franchise price is available, or, in some cases, none at all. Sales of the Boston Celtics alone account for almost 20 percent of the data points.

While this limits the reliability of the results, still there are some general comments that seem to be in order concerning the NBA, based on the data shown in Table 2.10. First, the average rate of increase of franchise prices in the NBA is considerably higher than that of baseball, with the exception only of the decade of the 1970s. The 1970s were an almost unmitigated disaster for the NBA, involving the final years of the battle with the ABA, the rise of the players union, the loss of the *Robertson* case, and a period of operation of the league under court supervision. The 1980s saw a complete reversal of this.

Overall, the average annual rate of increase in franchise prices for NBA teams from 1950 to the present runs around 16 percent, roughly twice that of baseball over its history. Using the rule of 70, this means that, for a typical NBA team, its franchise price doubled every 4.5 years. Moreover, of the 14 teams for which first and last price data are available, 9 had average annual rates of increase between 11 and 19 percent, with 3 below and 2 above these limits, and with a median of 14.6 percent. The discrepancy between the average annual rates of increase of franchise prices in the NBA and in baseball is greatest in the case of teams purchased in the early years of the NBA (1950–1970). In the decade of the 1970s, the rate of increase in franchise prices in the NBA was roughly comparable to that of baseball, while in the 1980s, the NBA had a higher rate of growth than that of baseball.

Table 2.11 presents the franchise price histories of NFL teams. Only 53 data points are available, but at least there are price estimates for the most recent sales of NFL teams. Among the interesting stories concerning NFL franchise sales prices is that of the Los Angeles Rams. The Rams came into existence in 1936 as the Cleveland Rams, a member of the American Football League II. The team entered the NFL as an expansion team in 1937, paying a $10,000 fee.

In 1941, owner Homer Marshman sold the Rams to Dan Reeves and

Pay Dirt

Table 2.9
Average Annual Rates of Increase in Franchise Prices, NBA

Team	Year	Franchise Price	Avg. Annual Rate of Increase	
			To Next Sale	To Final Sale
Tri-Cities/Milwaukee/				
St. Louis/Atlanta	1968	$3,500,000	8.1%	8.1%
	1977	7,270,000	—	—
Boston	1951	100,000	24.3	20.3
	1965	3,000,000	23.1	17.6
	1968	6,000,000	0.0	16.6
	1970	6,000,000	−20.3	18.7
	1972	4,000,000	14.7	24.3
	1983	15,000,000	69.3	69.3
	1986	120,000,000	—	—
Charlotte	1988	32,500,000	—	—
Chicago	1966	1,250,000	23.1	13.6
	1972	5,100,000	9.0	9.0
	1985	16,430,000	—	—
Cleveland	1970	3,700,000	6.4	6.4
	1980	7,000,000	—	—
Dallas	1980	12,000,000	—	—
Denver	1985	19,000,000	31.0	31.0
	1989	65,000,000	—	—
Detroit	1974	7,100,000	—	—
Golden State	1962	850,000	—	—
San Diego/Houston	1967	1,750,000	29.1	12.2
	1971	5,600,000	−51.5	6.1
	1973	2,000,000	18.9	18.9
	1982	11,000,000	—	—
Buffalo/San Diego/				
Los Angeles	1970	3,700,000	11.4	11.4
	1981	13,000,000	—	—
Minneapolis/				
L.A. Lakers	1957	150,000	43.8	43.8
	1965	5,000,000	—	—
Miami	1988	32,500,000	—	—
Milwaukee	1968	2,000,000	12.4	12.4
	1985	16,500,000	—	—
Minnesota	1989	32,500,000	—	—
Orlando	1989	32,500,000	—	—
Syracuse/				
Philadelphia 76ers	1963	500,000	17.7	17.7
	1981	12,000,000	—	—
Phoenix	1968	2,000,000	16.9	16.9
	1987	50,000,000	—	—

(continued)

58

Table 2.9 (cont.)
Average Annual Rates of Increase in Franchise Prices, NBA

			Avg. Annual Rate of Increase	
Team	Year	Franchise Price	To Next Sale	To Final Sale
Portland	1970	3,700,000	16.3	16.3
	1988	70,000,000	—	—
Rochester/Cincinnati/ Kansas City/ Sacramento	1958	225,000	—	—
Seattle	1967	1,750,000	14.6	14.6
	1984	21,000,000	—	—
New Orleans/Utah	1974	6,150,000	9.6	9.6
	1984	16,000,000	—	—

Sources: As in table 2.1.

Table 2.10
Annual Rates of Increase in Franchise Prices,
Weighted Average over All Teams, NBA

Average Annual Rate of Increase to Next Sale

Date of Next Sale

Date of Sale	1950– 1959	1960– 1969	1970– 1979	1980– 1990
1950–1959	—	31.4	—	—
1960–1969		23.1	15.6	15.5
1970–1979			−35.9	12.3
1980–1990				50.2

Average Annual Rate of Increase from First to Final Sale

Date of Final Sale

Date of First Sale	1950– 1959	1960– 1969	1970– 1979	1980– 1990	Overall Average
1950–1959	—	43.8	—	20.3	24.7
1960–1969		—	8.1	15.2	15.0
1970–1979			—	13.4	13.4
1980–1990				50.2	50.2
Overall avg.	—	43.8	8.1	16.1	16.5

Table 2.11
Average Annual Rates of Increase in Franchise Prices, NFL

Team	Year	Franchise Price	Avg. Annual Rate of Increase	
			To Next Sale	To Final Sale
Atlanta	1965	$ 7,723,000	—	—
Chicago Bears	1931	76,000	—	—
Cleveland	1953	600,000	23.5%	19.1%
	1961	3,925,000	10.6	10.6
	1965	6,000,000	—	—
Dallas	1960	600,000	19.2	18.1
	1984	60,000,000	11.5	11.5
	1988	95,000,000	—	—
Denver	1984	70,500,000	—	—
Portsmouth/Detroit	1934	21,500	39.1	19.3
	1940	225,000	− 2.4	14.0
	1948	185,000	23.2	22.2
	1963	6,000,000	8.0	8.0
	1964	6,500,000	—	—
Green Bay	1922	250	—	—
Baltimore/ Indianapolis	1948	180,000	− 42.7	18.6
	1951	50,000	32.1	27.3
	1964	3,226,000	19.6	19.6
	1972	15,500,000	—	—
Cleveland/L.A. Rams	1937	10,000	63.1	21.5
	1941	125,000	− 100.0	16.2
	1947	6	93.2	59.0
	1962	7,100,000	9.8	9.8
	1972	19,000,000	—	—
Minnesota	1960	600,000	18.0	18.0
	1985	54,300,000	—	—
New England	1988	85,000,000	—	—
New Orleans	1966	8,500,000	11.1	11.1
	1985	70,200,000	—	—
N.Y. Giants	1925	500	19.1	19.1
	1991	150,000,000	—	—
Frankford/ Philadelphia	1933	2,500	38.8	19.6
	1936	8,000	26.5	18.5
	1949	250,000	21.5	15.6
	1963	5,050,000	19.4	11.8
	1969	16,155,000	8.9	8.9
	1985	67,500,000	—	—

(continued)

Table 2.11 (cont.)
Average Annual Rates of Increase in Franchise Prices, NFL

Team	Year	Franchise Price	Avg. Annual Rate of Increase To Next Sale	To Final Sale
Chicago/St. Louis/				
Phoenix	1929	12,500	46.3	16.2
	1932	50,000	13.9	13.9
	1972	13,000,000	—	—
Pittsburgh	1933	2,500	59.9	59.9
	1940	165,000	—	—
San Diego	1982	40,000,000	34.7	34.7
	1984	80,000,000	—	—
San Francisco	1977	18,200,000	—	—
Seattle	1974	16,000,000	11.5	11.5
	1988	80,000,000	—	—
Tampa Bay	1974	16,000,000	—	—
Duluth/Orange/				
Newark/Boston/				
Washington	1926	1	253.4	34.8
	1929	2,000	44.1	20.2
	1932	7,500	18.7	18.5
	1960	1,400,000	18.1	18.2
	1972	12,350,000	18.4	18.4
	1974	17,820,000	—	—

Sources: As in table 2.1.

his partner Fred Levy for $100,000. World War II wasn't kind to the NFL—most of the players were in the service, and a lot of the fans were as well. Reeves went into the service himself, and the Rams shut down completely for the 1943 season, the year that Philadelphia and Pittsburgh combined forces as the Steagles. (The next year, it was Pittsburgh and the Chicago Cardinals fielding a joint team, nicknamed the Carpitts—record, 0–10–0.) Reeves came back out of service in 1945, put together an NFL championship team (9–1–0), and lost $50,000. When the All American Football Conference announced that it was fielding a team in Cleveland coached by Paul Brown and starring Otto Graham, Reeves decided it was time to go, and persuaded his fellow NFL owners to allow him to move the team to Los Angeles as the Los Angeles Rams. (Part of the persuasion involved the Rams picking up the transportation cost for other teams to the West Coast.)

There was AAFC competition in L.A. as well in the form of the Los

Angeles Dons, owned by Ben Lindheimer and actor Don Ameche. After taking a big loss in 1946, Reeves decided to bring in some outside capital, and sold two-thirds of the team to his old partner, Fred Levy, and three wealthy local businessmen, Ed Pauley, Harold Pauley, and Hal Seley. The price to the four was $1 each, and for that price they got to share in the losses of the Rams. In 1948, the Rams lost $250,000.

But that was the bottom of the barrel. The next year, the AAFC went under, the Rams were the only major league pro game in town, and southern California was beginning the population and business boom that has continued largely unabated since that time. In 1953, Harold Pauley died, and Bob Hope bought up his $16\frac{2}{3}$ percent of the team. By 1962, there were disputes among the owners, and Reeves wanted more freedom of action. By mutual agreement, a sealed-bid auction was set up under which the high bidder would get the team and would pay off the other owners. Reeves was the high bidder at $7.2 million. He paid the other four owners their $4.8 million by selling shares in a new holding company, which was assigned ownership of the Rams, with Reeves holding 51 percent control of the holding company.

In 1971, Reeves died, and in 1972, the Reeves estate sold the Rams for $19 million to Robert Irsay. Irsay in effect was acting on behalf of Carroll Rosenbloom, owner of the Baltimore Colts. After buying the Rams, Irsay exchanged the team with Rosenbloom for the Colts, with Rosenbloom making a side payment of between $3 and $4 million in cash. In 1979, Rosenbloom drowned, and his widow was given 70 percent control of the team, with his children left the remaining 30 percent. In 1980, his widow, Georgia Frontierre, reorganized the Rams, buying up the minority interest held by the children to become the sole owner of the Rams.

The rise in price of the Rams franchise from $10,000 in 1937 to $19 million in 1972 represented an average annual rate of increase of 21.5 percent (doubling about every 3.25 years). As Table 2.12 shows, this was about average for all the NFL teams for which we have price data—overall, the average rate of increase between first and last sales of NFL franchises was 20.4 percent. The rate of increase from one sale to the next was highest in the early years of the league, but of course this has to be weighed against the teams that went broke during the early years.

From the tables, we conclude that, on average, over their league histories, baseball franchise prices have been increasing at an annual rate of about 8 percent per year, NBA basketball franchises at about 16 percent per year, and NFL franchises at about 20 percent per year. Baseball and NFL franchise prices were increasing at around 20 percent per year during the 1980s, while NBA franchises were increasing at a faster rate, around 30 percent per year, during the 1980s. There is insufficient infor-

Table 2.12
Annual Rate of Increase in Franchise Prices,
Weighted Average over All Teams, NFL

| | Average Annual Rate of Increase to Next Sale | | | | | | |
| | | | | Date of Next Sale | | | |
Date of Sale	1920–1929	1930–1939	1940–1949	1950–1959	1960–1969	1970–1979	1980–1990
1920–1929	253.4	33.6	—	—	—	—	—
1930–1939		38.8	38.8	—	18.1	13.9	—
1940–1949			−70.8	−42.7	34.6	—	—
1950–1959				—	23.5	—	—
1960–1969					10.6	18.7	14.7
1970–1979						18.4	11.5
1980–1990							19.2

| | Average Annual Rate of Increase from First to Final Sale | | | | | |
| | | | Date of Final Sale | | | |
Date of First Sale	1940–1949	1950–1959	1960–1969	1970–1979	1980–1990	Overall Avg.
1920–1929	—	—	—	25.2	—	25.2
1930–1939	59.9	—	19.3	21.5	19.6	25.5
1940–1949	—	—	—	18.6	—	18.6
1950–1959		—	19.1	—	—	19.1
1960–1969			—	—	16.2	16.2
1970–1979				—	11.5	11.5
1980–1990					34.7	34.7
Overall avg.	59.9	—	19.2	21.8	17.2	20.4

mation about prices of NHL franchises to arrive at any reliable conclusions about the rate of franchise price inflation in that league.

Another way to see what has been happening to franchise prices is to graph the franchise price time paths for each of the sports. (When two or more sales occur in a year, the price shown is the average of those prices.) This involves some problems of noncomparability, because no distinctions are made in the graphs between big-city and small-city franchises, despite obvious differences in their market values, especially in baseball and basketball. Figures 2.1, 2.2, and 2.3, show the franchise time paths for the three sports using a semilog graph. A semilog graph is one that leads to a straight line graph for a constant rate of increase in franchise price per year, with the slope of the line being the annual rate of increase of price.

Figure 2.1 displays the rapid rate of increases in franchise prices in baseball in the early decades of the century. The outlier in 1922 is the sale of the Yankees, as is the outlier in 1948. The depressed nature of the franchise market in the 1930s shows up as well, with the outlier here being the sale of the Detroit Tigers in 1935, the only franchise sale of the decade that didn't involve a bankrupt team. The 1940s through the early 1950s was a period when prices increased rapidly to more or less reestablish the long-term trend that had been interrupted by the Depression.

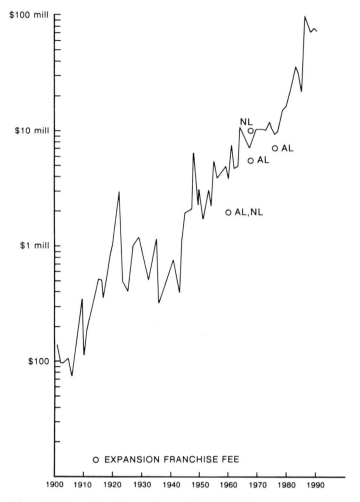

Figure 2.1 Franchise Prices, Baseball, 1901–1990

In 1960, the AL and NL each added two teams, at bargain prices, as indicated by the circles on the graph. Expansion teams should sell for less than established teams, in part because of the organizational expenses that have to be incurred in order to get the expansion team off the ground, and in part because, typically, expansion teams are located in weaker drawing areas than are established teams. But the $2 million fee for the Mets, Astros, Senators, and Angels was only about half of the going market price for a franchise in 1960, perhaps because of a deliberate attempt on the part of organized baseball to forestall Branch Rickey's proposed Continental League. Expansion in 1968 in the AL involved a price about one-third below the market price of an established franchise ($5.5 million versus about $8 million for established teams), but the NL charged the owners of the new Montreal and San Diego expansion franchises even more than the market price of established teams ($10 million versus $8 million). In 1976, again the AL charged about 70 percent of the price of an established franchise for its two expansion franchises in Seattle and Toronto.

One predictable effect of expansion, from simple demand and supply considerations, is to lower the rate of increase in the price of existing franchises. As the graph indicates, the period from the mid-1960s through the mid-1970s was one of stability of franchise prices in baseball at about the $10 million level, as the 10 expansion franchises of the two leagues were absorbed. From about 1976 on, franchise prices have been increasing at a rate comparable to that of the period from 1910 to 1920, the fastest rate of growth in the history of the sport.

Figure 2.2 shows the escalation in prices of NBA franchises between 1950 and 1990. (ABA franchises are excluded from the graph prior to the merger of the ABA and NBA in 1976.) The steep increase in franchise prices between 1950 and 1965 can be thought of as an explanation in part for the emergence of the ABA as a rival league, as the profit potential from capital gains in franchise prices became apparent to outside investors. The NBA acted to combat the ABA by expanding its own stable of teams, and, as with baseball, the early expansion fees were bargain basement prices, half or less of the going price of existing franchises in the mid-1960s. Expansion within the NBA and the existence of a rival league slowed the rate of growth of franchise prices between 1965 and the late 1970s. After the merger agreement in 1976 and the new revenue-sharing labor agreement, franchise prices took off again from 1980 on, at a rate comparable to that of the 1950–1965 period. The Dallas expansion franchise entered the league in 1980 at an expansion fee of $12 million, which was almost twice the going rate for existing teams. But it is an indication of just how explosive the escalation of NBA franchise prices has been since 1980 that the Dallas expansion

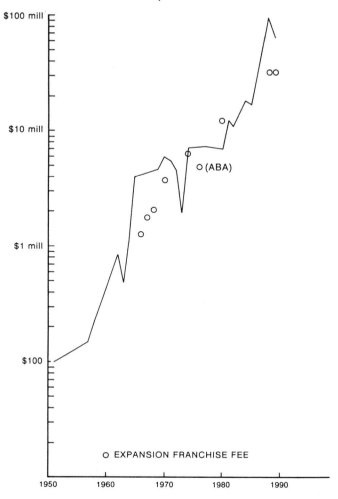

Figure 2.2 Franchise Prices, NBA, 1950–1990

price of $12 million now looks like a steal. The same appears to be true of the expansion teams (Orlando, Miami, Charlotte, Minnesota) of the late 1980s—at $32.5 million per team, the owners were paying less than half the going price of an NBA franchise at the turn of the decade.

Figure 2.3 graphs the NFL franchise price history, charting a record of growth in franchise prices that has been much more stable and predictable than that of either baseball or NBA basketball. The periods with retarded growth rates are the 1930s, because of the Depression; the 1940s, because of the AAFC; and the period between about 1965 and 1975, when the AFL was being absorbed into the NFL, along with other

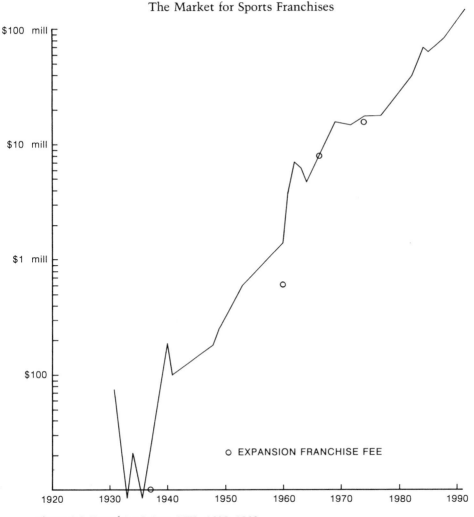

Figure 2.3 Franchise Prices, NFL, 1920–1990

expansion franchises. Since 1975, NFL franchise prices have been increasing at the historical rate of around 20 percent per year.

The Economics of Franchise Markets:
A World of Certainty

There is a rather well-developed theory of asset markets in economics that should help to shed some light on the franchise price data that we have been discussing thus far in this chapter. In particular, microeconomic theory provides explanations as to how the time path of price of any asset (including a sports team franchise) is determined by market forces, and it even provides simplified formulas for calculating the predicted market price of any asset, depending upon the circumstances holding in the specific market.

Suppose we begin with the simplest possible situation, one in which there is complete certainty as to the future income that a franchise will provide and as to the price of the franchise at all future times. In addition, suppose that anyone can borrow or lend as much as he or she wants at the going rate of interest of i percent per year, compounded annually. In this simple situation, microeconomics provides a correspondingly simple answer to the question What price will a franchise (or any other asset) sell for? The answer is that under these conditions, any asset will sell for a price equal to the present value, PV, of the cash flows that the asset generates. And how does one calculate PV? Let $y(t)$ denote the cash flow generated by the asset t years into the future. Then PV is given by the formula

$$PV = y(1)/(1 + i) + y(2)/(1 + i)^2 + \ldots + y(t)/(1 + i)^t + \ldots .$$

To illustrate, if the interest rate is 10 percent per year ($i = 0.1$), and an asset pays out $110 at the end of the first year and nothing thereafter, then the market price of the asset will be $PV = \$110/(1.1) = \$100$. Why is this the market price? If the market price were less than $100, say, $95, then anyone could borrow $95 at an interest rate of 10 percent, buy the asset, wait a year, and receive $110 in income. The interest on $95 for one year is $9.50, so all that has to be paid back to the lender at the end of the year is $95 + $9.50 = $104.50. There is a clear profit of $5.50 = $110 − $104.50 on the deal. At any price less than $100, any investor can make a sure profit by borrowing the money to buy the asset, and then use the cash flow from the asset at the end of the year to pay off the loan with interest and pocket the difference between this and the cash flow.

If the price were greater than $100, say, $105, then anyone owning the asset can make a sure profit by selling the asset. If the owner sells the asset, he or she can invest the $105 at 10 percent interest and, at the end of the year, receive $10.50 in interest plus the $105 principal back, for a total of $115.50, whereas holding the asset only generates a cash flow of $110 at the end of the year. Pressure by owners to sell the asset if the price is above $100, and pressure by investors to buy the asset if the price is below $100 will force the market price of the asset to $100. The same kind of argument applies to the later terms in the expression for present value, PV, when an asset generates cash flows for several or more years into the future.

Given that under conditions of certainty as to future cash flows, any asset sells in the market for its present value, the question that then arises is When, if ever, will we see the price of an asset increase over time as franchise prices have in the graphs above? Using the same kind of arguments that establish that under conditions of certainty as to the future, the market price of an asset equals its present value, the following can be proved:

First, in a world of certainty, all assets will sell at prices such that investment in the asset will earn the investor the same rate of return, namely, the market rate of interest, i.

Second, in a world of certainty, an asset will go up in price in any year in which the cash flow the asset earns is less than the amount that could be earned by selling the asset and investing the proceeds at the market rate of interest.

Third, in a world of certainty, if the cash flow an asset earns increases over time at a rate of r percent per year (r less than i), then the market price of the asset will also increase by r percent per year.

Fourth, in a world of certainty, the only time that an asset can increase in price at a rate greater than the market rate of interest (i percent), is when the current cash flow from the asset is negative. (Of course, there must be positive cash flows coming in future years if the asset is to have a positive price.)

Fifth, in a world of certainty, no asset can increase in price over time continuously at a rate that exceeds the market rate of interest.

We are particularly interested in the fifth proposition, which follows from the fourth. To see why the fourth must hold, suppose that we know that an asset will increase in price this year at a rate higher than the market rate of interest. If the cash flow from the asset is positive, then we can make a riskless profit by borrowing the price of the asset (at the market rate of interest), using the money to buy the asset, hold it for one year, and then sell it. At the end of the year, the escalation in the price of the asset will by itself more than pay for the interest on the loan, and so any positive cash flow is just gravy, adding to the riskless profits from the investment. Investors will bid up the current price of the asset in this situation, up to the point where the prospective escalation in market price of the asset plus the cash flow from the asset will yield a rate of return on investment equal to the market rate of interest. Hence, it follows that if the price of an asset increases at a rate faster than the market rate of interest, the cash flow from the asset must be negative.

Applying this to the fifth proposition, the only case in which an asset can continuously increase in price at a rate faster than the rate of interest is a case in which the cash flow from the asset each year is negative.

But an asset with a negative cash flow each year would not have a positive price, since its market price equals its present value, which will be negative.

Turning now to the pro franchise market, the first question that must be raised is the appropriate rate of interest that applies to this market. Since we do not have access to the books of the teams or the personal financial ledgers of the owners, we cannot use the actual rates at which capital (debt and equity) were raised to purchase teams. A natural starting point for the choice of a market rate of interest to evaluate investments in sports teams is the rate of return earned on industrial stock investments. Table 2.13 uses the Standard and Poor index of industrial stock prices together with the Moody dividend yield series to construct a decade-by-decade market rate of interest to apply to the analysis of franchise prices.

The average annual rate of return on industrial common stocks from 1901 through 1990 is 9.8 percent, equal to a 5 percent annual rate of escalation in stock prices plus a 4.8 percent rate of dividend yield (dividends per share/average share price). The average rate of return over the 1920–1990 period (applicable to the time span of the NFL) is 10.3 percent, and the average rate of return over the 1950–1990 period (the time span of the NBA) is 11.4 percent.

The financial history of baseball since 1901 has been a relatively sta-

Table 2.13
Average Annual Rate of Return on Industrial Common Stocks
by Decade, 1901–1990

Decade	Avg. Annual Rate of Stock Price Rise	Avg. Annual Dividend Yield	Avg. Annual Rate of Return
1901–1909	2.3%	4.9%	7.2%
1910–1919	2.6	6.0	8.6
1920–1929	9.3	5.5	14.8
1930–1939	−4.3	4.0	−0.3
1940–1949	5.4	5.4	10.8
1950–1959	11.8	4.9	16.7
1960–1969	4.3	3.1	7.4
1970–1979	3.9	3.8	7.7
1980–1990	10.1	3.9	14.0
Avg.	5.0	4.8	9.8
Avg. 1920–1990	5.7	4.6	10.3
Avg. 1950–1990	7.5	3.9	11.4

Sources: Stock price rise from Standard and Poor industrial common stock index; dividend yields from Moody's dividend yield on industrial common stocks.

ble one. In particular, no baseball team has gone out of business in all the years since 1901. This suggests that over this period, a typical industrial stock (or even a portfolio of industrial stocks) has been, if anything, a riskier investment than a major league baseball team; thus the 9.8 percent rate of return (1901–1990) shown in Table 2.13 would not be a bad choice for a discount rate in evaluating baseball franchises.

In the cases of the NFL and the NBA, a distinction has to be drawn between the early formative years of these leagues, and later years. Between 1920 and 1933, roughly three out of every four teams in the NFL went out of business, and the league lost another 20 percent of its members between 1945 and 1952. The early years of the NBA (1946–1952) were even worse. Both the NFL and NBA were really hobby-type activities until late in the histories of these leagues. Investment in NFL franchises was definitely highly speculative up to the late 1950s, and NBA franchises were in the same category at least until the late 1960s. This means that in the formative periods of the NBA and the NFL, the average annual return on industrial stocks understates the appropriate discount (interest) rate to use in evaluating franchise prices. It is only in the later years (1960s on for the NFL, 1970s on for the NBA) that the return on industrial stocks becomes a relevant measure to use in evaluating franchise price escalation in these leagues.

The other thing to emphasize is that the data presented here on price escalation are for the teams that survived, so if we "averaged" out the rates of return on initial investment over all teams, including those that went out of business, the average rate of return would be a lot less than shown in our tables. Again, this applies particularly to rates of return on investments that date back into the formative years of the two leagues.

Admittedly, the assumption that future cash flows are known with certainty is highly unrealistic in the case of sports franchises, but there are still some insights provided by the certainty case. In fact, during the early years of the NBA and NFL, almost all teams lost money from their current operations. As we have seen, the Cleveland Rams lost $50,000 in their championship year of 1945, and the Philadelphia Eagles lost $80,000 in winning the NFL championship in 1948, so it is highly likely that teams with poorer records lost money as well. There is confirmation of this in the large number of teams that dropped out of the NFL in the pre-World War II era, and in the large number of teams that dropped out of the BAA and/or NBA up to the mid-1950s. The certainty model applied to the early years of either league thus would forecast franchise price increases at a rate higher than the interest rate, in order to compensate owners for negative cash flows in the present, while awaiting the contemplated positive cash flows in future years.

But the certainty model doesn't offer much in the way of help in understanding the explosion in franchise prices in all leagues since the mid-1970s, since for much of the period since then, almost all teams in the major sports leagues have been profitable. It is necessary to add some elements of uncertainty to the picture to see how it might be possible for well-functioning markets to generate a pattern of franchise price increases that go on at a rate higher than the rate of interest, as in the period since the mid-1970s.

The Economics of Franchise Markets: Uncertainty

In particular, the so-called Bayesian model of uncertainty introduces a way of thinking about asset markets that might be relevant to understanding the recent rise in franchise prices. In the Bayesian approach, the realistic assumption is made that individuals, such as team owners or outside investors, are uncertain as to what the future cash flows of a team are going to be. They have certain subjective beliefs about how probable alternative time paths of cash flows might be, but those beliefs are tentative and subject to change on the basis of the actual observed cash flows that a team generates. Over time, as more and more information is obtained in the form of realized cash flows, beliefs are revised ("updated") and uncertainty is reduced.

An economically "rational" decisionmaker will use a rule for updating his or her beliefs that is known as *Bayes's rule*, which need not be dealt with in detail here. What is important about Bayes's rule for us is that revisions of belief on the basis of observed outcomes are "damped" by the beliefs held prior to observing the outcomes. For example, suppose an individual is unsure as to whether a coin is fair, but his or her best guess is that it is fair. The coin is tossed once, and a head appears. Under Bayes's rule, this will move the beliefs slightly in the direction of an unfair coin with a higher probability of heads than tails. If a head appears again on the second toss, the beliefs are revised a little more in the direction of an unfair coin. After 10 tosses, suppose that 7 heads have appeared. Then the updated belief as to the probability of a head according to Bayes's rule will be some value between 1/2 (fair coin), the original or prior belief, and 7/10 (the observed fraction of heads). The more observations, the less weight attaches to the prior belief and the more to the observations, in determining the updated belief as to the probability of heads. This is the way that Bayes's rule works.

Next consider the following scenario. The franchise market for a sport has been stable for some time, with cash flows increasing over time at a constant rate (less than the rate of interest) and with franchise prices increasing at the same rate, as follows from the third proposition of the certainty model (discussed above). For concreteness, assume that the interest rate is 10 percent per year and that cash flows are increasing at 5 percent per year; thus, under certainty as to future cash flows, the franchise price is increasing at 5 percent per year as well.

Now asssume a change is introduced into the market, for example, the emergence of cable TV as a profitable alternative to network telecasting of league games. Suppose that cable TV is so lucrative that teams find their cash flows increasing at a rate that, varies about an average value of 7.5 percent per year. The important point is that initially owners do not know what this new average rate of increase is, but instead will revise their beliefs over time on the basis of observed cash flows under the new situation.

Team owners go into the new situation uncertain as to what the future holds, but with skepticism based on previous experiences with cable TV. Thus to begin with, they assume that cash flows will continue to expand at about the old rate of 5 percent per year. But then information begins to come in of larger than expected cable revenues and audience, so, under Bayes's rule, there is a gradual revision of beliefs, damped especially in the earlier years by prior beliefs. As more and more information becomes available, owners and outside investors finally realize that the new situation is one in which cash flows will be increasing at 7.5 percent per year into the indefinite future, and the price path of the franchise then adjusts to this revised belief. In other words, the adjusted time path of franchise price will increase at 7.5 percent per year to match the rate of increase per year in cash flow.

Suppose that the cash flow in the current period is $100. Then it can be shown that with an interest rate of 10 percent per year and a rate of growth of cash flow of 5 percent per year, under certainty, the market price of the asset today would be $2,000 = $100/(.10 − .05), and the asset would increase in price at the rate of 5 percent per year. In the new situation, with a rate of growth of cash flow of 7.5 percent per year, the revised market price of the asset today would be $4,000 = $100/(.10 − .075), and the price of the asset would increase at 7.5 percent per year. The situation is as shown in Figure 2.4. $PV_0(t)$ denotes the time path of the price of the asset with a 5 percent rate of growth in cash flows, and $PV_1(t)$ denotes the time path of the price of the asset with a 7.5 percent rate of growth in cash flows.

We illustrate the impact on the franchise price time path, under the Bayesian approach, with gradual revision of beliefs on the basis of observed cash flows, by the curve line with arrows. For the case shown in the graph, it takes about 14 years for the market to fully adjust to the new situation. The important thing to note is that during the adjustment process under Bayesian updating, the price of the asset increases

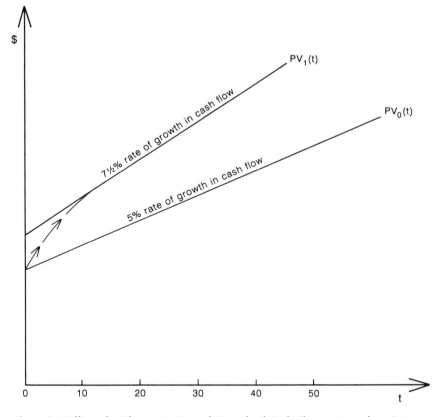

Figure 2.4 Effect of a Change in Rate of Growth of Cash Flow on Franchise Price

not only more rapidly than under the 5 percent case, but more rapidly than under the 7.5 percent case. Given a 14-year adjustment time as in the graph, the average rate of increase in the asset price over the adjustment period is 12.5 percent per year. The shorter is the adjustment time; the larger is the average rate of increase in the asset price during the adjustment period.

Thus we have identified a factor that might well be relevant in explaining the high rates of growth in franchise prices during the period since 1975. This would be the adjustment of prices in the franchise market to a new situation involving higher rates of increase in cash flows, resulting in part from the emergence of cable TV and in part from a change in public tastes, a shift in market demand, in favor of pro team sports. As we have seen, during the adjustment period, there is a market escalation of franchise prices, with rates of increase that could be higher than the going interest rate. The critical thing to note about this, however, is that unless there are new, unforeseen developments that will lead to even higher rates of increase in cash flow, the present situation is only temporary. As the period of Bayesian adjustment comes to an end, franchise prices would then resume a time path with a rate of increase determined by the rate of increase in expected cash flows, rather than by the higher rate characteristic of the adjustment period.

Thus there are explanations for the historical pattern of increases in franchise prices that are consistent with well-behaved markets and rational investors and owners. To briefly recap, the rapid rate of increase in franchise prices in the early years of the NFL and NBA occurred when cash flows were negative; in effect, owners who survived were investing in good will for their franchises, with the payoff to come in the future. As we have seen, when the current cash flow is negative, the market price of an asset can increase faster than the rate of interest, even under conditions of certainty as to future cash flows. Moreover, we are only observing the success stories; since the many teams that failed in the NBA and NFL are not included in our data set, averaged over all investments in these leagues, the observed rates of return might not be out of line with a 10 percent plus rate of return. Moreover, over the period between 1975 and the present, there have been developments in sports that promise more rapid increases in cash flows for teams than previously. The period of adjustment of franchise markets to this new situation is associated with temporarily high rates of increase in franchise prices, and this might well be a correct characterization of what has been going on since 1975.

The Economics of Franchise Markets: Bubbles

Another possibility, of course, is that the sports franchise market is experiencing a bubble. By a bubble, we mean a situation in which the current price of an asset is determined by what investors expect the future price of the asset to be, rather than by the expected cash flows from ownership of the asset. For example, in the 1970s, in part because of lenient lending policies by government agencies, farmers bid up the price of agricultural land year after year even though net revenues per acre and rental rates were constant or falling. Agricultural land appeared to be a "good investment," not because you could make money by buying land and farming it, but because you could make money by buying it and reselling it later at a higher price. For half a dozen years, agricultural land kept increasing in price, and the typical pattern of a bubble developed—that is, whenever an individual sells during a bubble, it is always too early, and whenever an individual buys, whatever the price, it turns out in hindsight to have been a "steal." As with all bubbles, the agricultural land bubble burst in the late 1970s and early 1980s, and land prices tumbled to levels at or below those consistent with the actual net revenue potential from farming the land. Thousands of farmers, mainly the young and inexperienced, were unable to make loan payments contracted to buy land while the bubble was expanding, and went bankrupt.

Bubbles are regarded by economists as something of an oddity, even though they have been able to generate bubbles in an experimental setting, and even though economists are well aware of the famous historical instances in which bubbles have occurred, for example, the tulip bubble in Holland in the early 1700s. About the only thing economists know for sure about bubbles is that finally they always burst. The problem is that there is nothing in microeconomics that tells us when a bubble is going to burst, or that even tells us the signs that signal that the bubble is about to burst. From a theoretical point of view, what is fascinating about bubbles is an inherent contradiction between the thinking of the individuals participating in a bubble market and the logic of markets themselves.

For example, consider the market for southern California real estate. During the 1980s, an almost surefire way of making money was to buy residential property in southern California, and hold it for a few years before selling it and pocketing a huge profit. A situation developed in which the purchase of a home was regarded not so much as the purchase of housing services but instead as investment in an asset that would more or less inevitably appreciate in price at 20 or 30 percent (or more) per year. But once individuals begin to believe that it is more or less certain that houses will go up in price by, say, 30 percent per year, this increases the current price of houses as investors flock into the market to buy this desirable asset. As the current price of houses goes up, this makes it less and less likely that expectations will be realized, since future housing prices have to escalate to meet the anticipated 30 percent increase over current prices. And, as current housing prices increase, this increases the profits of building more houses today, which tends to lower the current and future prices of existing homes.

All of this underlies the idea that bubbles always burst. Finally the contradictions between expectations of investors and the logic of markets explodes the bubble, and prices readjust to a level linked to the present value of cash flows. Returning to franchise markets, the two leading competing explanations for price rises of the period since 1975 are (1) Bayesian adjustment to an unexpected increase in cash flows from team operations and (2) a bubble in the franchise markets. In order to come up with a definitive answer, we would need detailed data on profits, which are simply not available.

What we do know, however, is that whether the current franchise market is experiencing a bubble or is in the process of adjusting to a new equilibrium reflecting a higher rate of growth in profits for professional sports, in either case the current rates of escalation of franchise prices should be a temporary phenomenon. Either the bubble will burst at some point, or updated information on prospective profitability will be incorporated into franchise prices, lowering the rate of escalation to something consistent with a market rate of interest in the 10 percent plus range.

Figure 2A W/L Percentages, Attendance, Profits, and Team Sales, American League, 1901–1990

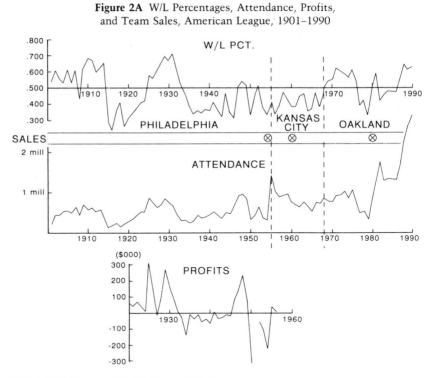

Philadelphia/Kansas City/Oakland Athletics

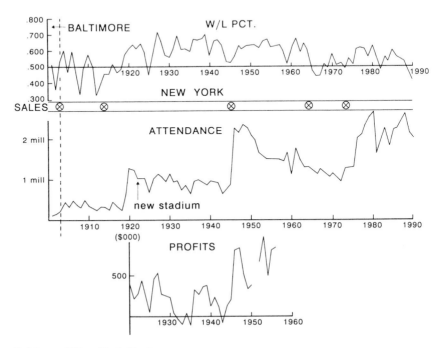

Baltimore I/New York Yankees

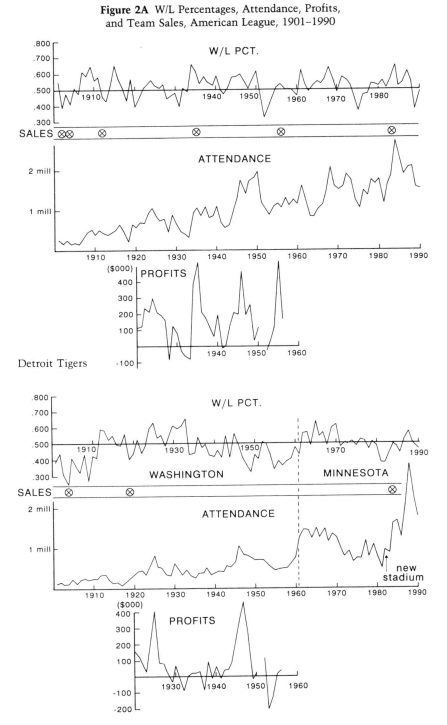

Figure 2A W/L Percentages, Attendance, Profits, and Team Sales, American League, 1901–1990

Detroit Tigers

Washington Senators I/Minnesota Twins

Figure 2A W/L Percentages, Attendance, Profits,
and Team Sales, American League, 1901–1990

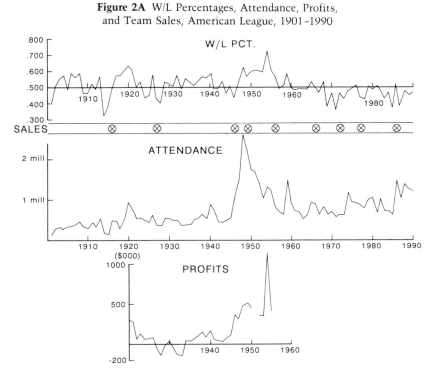

Cleveland Indians

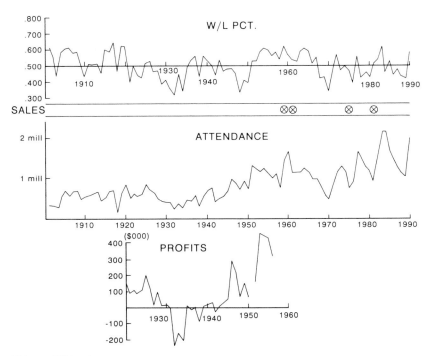

Chicago White Sox

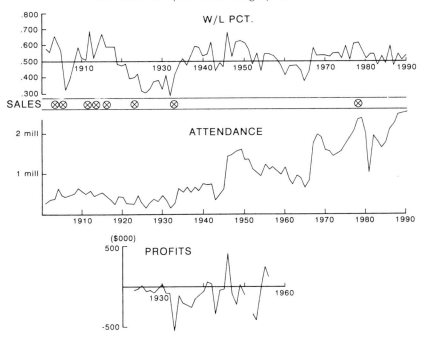

Figure 2A W/L Percentages, Attendance, Profits, and Team Sales, American League, 1901–1990

Boston Red Sox

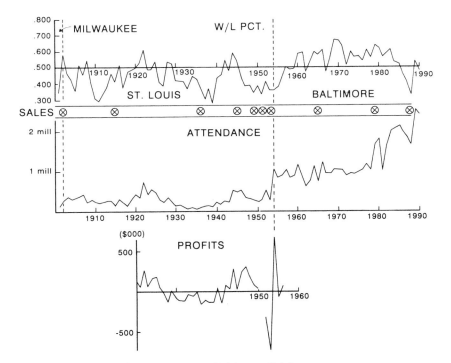

Milwaukee Brewers I/St. Louis Browns/Baltimore Orioles

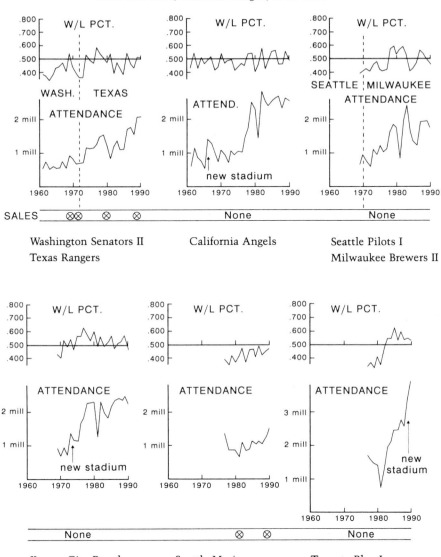

Figure 2A W/L Percentages, Attendance, Profits, and Team Sales, American League, 1901–1990

Figure 2B W/L Percentages, Attendance, Profits, and Team Sales, National League, 1901–1990

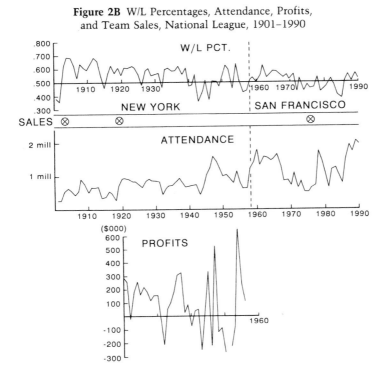

New York/San Francisco Giants

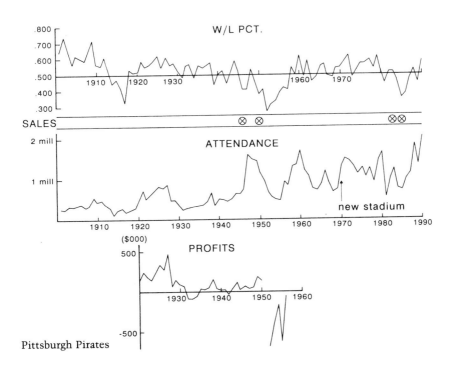

Pittsburgh Pirates

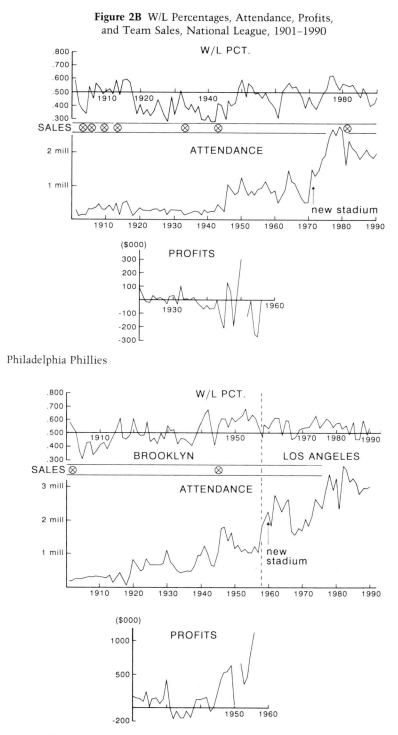

Figure 2B W/L Percentages, Attendance, Profits, and Team Sales, National League, 1901–1990

W/L PCT.

SALES

ATTENDANCE

new stadium

($000) PROFITS

Philadelphia Phillies

W/L PCT.

BROOKLYN   LOS ANGELES

SALES

ATTENDANCE

new stadium

($000) PROFITS

Brooklyn/Los Angeles Dodgers

Figure 2B W/L Percentages, Attendance, Profits, and Team Sales, National League, 1901–1990

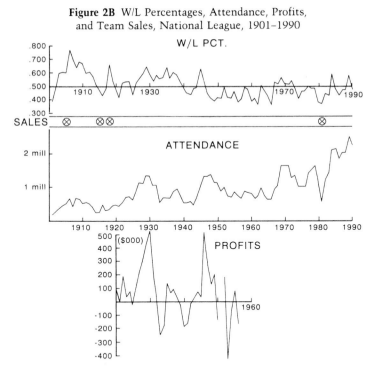

Chicago Cubs

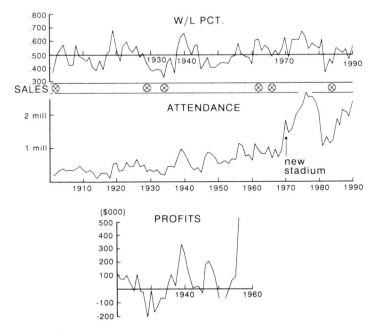

Cincinnati Reds

Figure 2B W/L Percentages, Attendance, Profits, and Team Sales, National League, 1901–1990

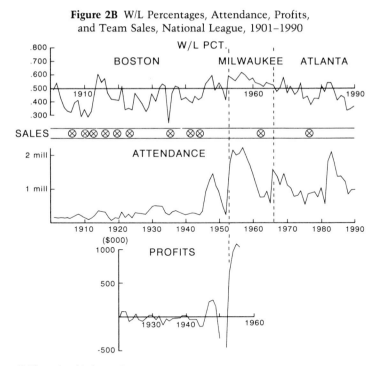

Boston/Milwaukee/Atlanta Braves

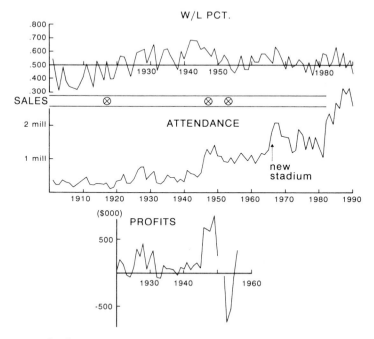

St. Louis Cardinals

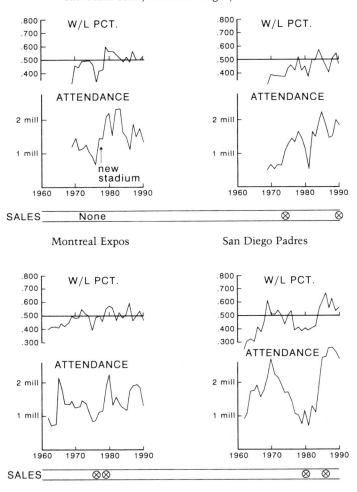

Montreal Expos   San Diego Padres

Houston Astros   New York Mets

Chapter 3

Taxes, Taxes, and
More Taxes

Look, we play the Star Spangled Banner before every game—you want us to pay income taxes too?

—**Bill Veeck**
The Hustler's Handbook

O N SUNDAY, August 19, 1951, one Eddie Gaedel went into the baseball record books with a walk in his only time at bat, in the most celebrated of the outrageous actions of baseball's greatest owner-promoter, William Veeck, Jr. At the time, Bill Veeck owned the St. Louis Browns, then resting in seventh place in the American League. As a promotion stunt for Falstaff Brewery, radio sponsor of the Browns games, Veeck put on a birthday party for the brewery between games in a doubleheader against the Tigers, the last-place AL team. The feature of the party was a huge birthday cake, which was carted out to the pitcher's mound. After the candles were lit, a tiny figure burst from the cake, dressed in a Browns uniform, and the emcee then announced that this was a birthday present from Falstaff to Zack Taylor, the hard-pressed St. Louis manager—what else but a "new Brownie" for the team!

There was some polite applause and laughter, and then the second game began. In the bottom of the first inning, the Browns came to bat, and there was an announcement of a pinch hitter for the leadoff hitter. Bouncing out of the dugout came the "new Brownie" from the birthday stunt—Eddie Gaedel, a three-foot-six midget, carrying a kid's bat, and with the number "1/8" on the back of his jersey. The Tigers' manager, Red Rolfe, suppressing a wide grin, came onto the field to raise a loud and vocal protest, but Taylor had in his hand the official AL player contract that Gaedel had signed the day before, along with proof that a copy of the contract had been mailed to Will Harridge, AL president, as required by AL rules. (The rules were changed to require actual league approval of contracts before a player is eligible after this memorable event.)

After some consultation and much soul-searching, the umpire allowed the game to proceed, and Gaedel dug in. He was walked on four pitches, all over his head. Gaedel ran down to first base, to be replaced by a pinch runner, and his baseball career was over. For the rest of his life, Veeck was first and foremost known as the owner who had pulled the midget gag. And, for the rest of his life, Eddie Gaedel, who died in 1961, waited (in vain) for Bill Veeck to call him to resume his major league career once again.

Bill Veeck did a lot of funny and irreverent things as an owner, but he also was responsible for some important innovations in the economics of baseball, many of which are discussed in Gerald Eskenazi's book, *Bill Veeck: A Baseball Legend*. He had a solid baseball background, having been raised as the son of William Veeck, Sr., president of the Chicago Cubs during some of the team's better years, from 1917 through 1933. As a kid, Bill was a gofer for the Cubs, and after the death of his father, he learned the business with the Cubs from the ground up, doing everything from working the concession stands to scouting players. In 1941, at the age of 28, and with not much more than a couple of bucks in his pocket, Veeck became the owner of the Milwaukee Brewers of the American Association. He took an eighth-place team that was on the financial ropes (it was the carry-forward tax losses that made it so attractive an investment for the group that financed Veeck), and turned it into a pennant winner and the best drawing card in the league in just one year.

Veeck spent World War II in the Marines, where he received the leg wound that was to cause him problems for the rest of his life. When he returned to baseball, he put together a group of investors with the audacious plan (several years before Jackie Robinson came up with the Dodgers) to buy the bankrupt Philadelphia Phillies and stock the team with players from the Negro leagues. He talked to Judge Landis about this scheme, and the Phillies were quickly sold to another group.

In 1946, Veeck headed a syndicate that bought the Cleveland Indians of the AL. He put on fireworks shows, had midgets racing toy cars around the park, introduced Bat Day into baseball, and had special promotions for every conceivable group of fans. The Indians had an attendance of 558,182 in 1945, outdrawn by every other team in the league except for Philadelphia and St. Louis, and Veeck turned Cleveland into the hottest thing in baseball. He signed the second black player to reach the majors, and the first in the American League, Larry Doby. Later Veeck was roundly criticized by the old guard in baseball for his publicity gimmick in signing up the immortal Satchel Paige, who proceeded to show everybody that there was more than a little life left in the old man yet. In 1948, Cleveland won the AL pennant and then the World Series, with a team starring Lou Boudreau, Joe Gordon, Doby, Gene Beardon, and Bob Feller. The Indians drew 2,620,627 in Municipal Stadium, an AL record that held for 32 years, until the Yankees drew 2,627,417 in 1980.

Veeck sold out after the 1949 season, to have his leg amputated. For the rest of his life, he stomped around on a wooden leg, which gave him almost as many problems as his bad leg had. In 1951, after the first of many repair jobs on his damaged stump, he was back in baseball as the owner of the St. Louis Browns, a woefully weak franchise. Besides the midget caper, Veeck organized one Browns game as "Grandstand Manager's Day," a chance for the fans to act as managers. For the game, Zack Taylor was retired to the stands, and a vote of the crowd during the game decided such weighty matters as whether the infield should play back for a double play or play in, whether to pitch to a batter or put him on base, and whether to go for a sacrifice or hit away.

With his weak-drawing franchise, Veeck pushed for local TV revenue sharing in the AL, with no success. Suggestions like this did succeed in rousing the wrath of the Yankees, however, a team that Veeck loved to hate, during all his years in baseball. When Gussie Busch bought the in-town rival Cardinals, Veeck tried to get permission from the AL to move the Browns, first to Milwaukee and then to Baltimore. Given that no major league team had moved in 47 years, this was one more revolutionary Veeck idea. It was the threat of a move to Milwaukee posed by Veeck that caused the Boston Braves to move there themselves after the 1953 season, but Veeck had alienated so many owners in the AL that they turned him down twice on his own request to move to Baltimore. Once he had sold the team to a group of Baltimore businessmen, the AL approved the move of the Browns unanimously.

Following his stint with the Browns, Veeck joined with Conrad Hilton and Henry Crown in an attempt to buy the struggling Philadelphia Athletics to move them to Los Angeles. Instead, partly because of pressure brought to bear by the Yankees, the Athletics were sold to Arnold Johnson, who had earlier bought Yankee Stadium from the Yankees, and the Athletics were moved to Kansas City. Veeck then formed a syndicate to buy the Detroit Tigers from Spike Briggs, only to be outbid by another group. Veeck reports that he and Crown had one other "running project—conversational only" to buy the Cubs from Phil Wrigley, but again nothing came of this.

In 1958, Veeck bought the Chicago White Sox, and brought his traveling circus to Comiskey Park. He had fireworks shows after every game, introduced the exploding scoreboard, and had the great good sense to rehire Al Lopez as manager. In 1959, the Go-Go Sox won the first pennant for the team since the infamous Black Sox of 1919, with Louie Aparicio and Nellie Fox performing spectacular feats as Chicago nickel-and-dimed the opposition—and especially the Yankees—to death. Once again, health problems surfaced, and Veeck sold the team in 1961.

Veeck's last foray into baseball came in 1975, when he overcame some deeply ingrained opposition from AL owners to once again become the owner of the White Sox. This violated one of his maxims—never go back to a place where you've already done your stuff—and this time the Veeck magic didn't work so well on the field or at the box office either. But Veeck did stir things up by hiring Larry Doby as manager for one season, only the second black (after Frank Robinson) to get a managing job. In 1981, Veeck sold out for the last time, and he spent much of the final years of his life back where he had started, in the bleachers in Wrigley Field, talking it up with the old-time fans of the Cubs.

Without any question, the best books that have been written by an insider about the business aspects of baseball are two by Bill Veeck (with Ed Linn): *Veeck as in Wreck* and *The Hustler's Handbook*. Among other things, in these books Veeck tells of how he came across an idea that completely changed the economics of team ownership, not just in baseball, but in all team sports. The boom in franchise prices, league expansions, and the creation of rival leagues in team sports in the post–World War II period are all beholden to Veeck's idea of converting team ownership into a tax-shelter. From the late 1940s through the mid-1970s, tax avoidance was a dominating factor in the economics of team sports. Court cases in the early 1970s led to changes in 1976 in the tax code dealing with contract writeoffs, which, together with changes in general tax rates, substantially reduced the tax-sheltering possibilities from purchase of a franchise. The passage of the Tax Reform Act of 1986 effectively eliminated most (but not quite all) of the remaining tax-sheltering aspects of team ownership, as it did for just about every other tax shelter. But, for over 25 years, tax avoidance thanks to Bill Veeck was a big part of the professional sports picture, and tax sheltering still plays a role in the team franchise market. Moreover, if the capital gains tax is repealed or substantially lowered, the Veeck tax shelter will be back in business again, so knowledge of how the tax shelter works is not simply an exercise in ancient history.

The idea came up when Veeck was operating the Cleveland Indians, just after World War II. Veeck put it this way: "I had always been struck by a basic inconsistency in the way we carried our players on the books. When you buy a ball club, you list your whole roster of players as a cash item, which means you cannot depreciate them. And yet, if you buy a player at any time thereafter, you carry him as an expense item, which means that you can write him off immediately just as you would write off paper clips, stationery or any other business expense" (*Veeck as in Wreck*, p. 340). The IRS first ruled that cash purchases of players could be written off as an expense item in 1935 in a case involving the Pittsburgh Pirates. Veeck was referring to this rule. The IRS changed the rules with respect to cash purchases of players in 1967; since that time, such purchases have to be written off over the expected useful playing lifetime of the player.

Having already purchased two baseball teams, Veeck was interested in the implications of the IRS treatment of player contracts for someone purchasing a team. When a team is purchased, in effect, the new owner acquires a collection of assets. And what assets does a team possess? Most of the assets are intangibles—the team's franchise and territorial rights, its right to share in the revenue from the national TV and radio contracts of the league, its right to sell TV and radio rights to its home games, its stadium contract, its rights to concession income, its right to draft players in the free agent draft, its rights under the waiver rules, the goodwill the team has developed over its stay in the city, and the rights to the services of the players the team has under contract. A team also owns some equipment and office furniture, and the rare team actually owns its own stadium; but the bulk of the typical team's assets consist of intangibles. The problem with most intangible assets is that they are not depreciable for tax purposes—they have no determinable lifetime or no ascertainable value, they don't wear out, and they don't have to be replaced—or if they are ruled depreciable, it is only over a very lengthy period, 20 years or more. But thanks to that IRS ruling back in 1935, player contracts are different.

The conniving genius of Bill Veeck saw that there was nothing in the tax code to stop a new owner who took over a team, from reorganizing the team as a new business (partnership or corporation), and then assigning most of the purchase price of the team to the player contracts the team owns. Organizing as a new business was crucial, because if the owners did not reorganize, then, under the tax code, the new owners would be bound by the book values assigned to player contracts by the previous owners, who had already expensed their acquisitions of players, so that the book value of contracts would be negligible. Veeck saw that player contracts acquired by the new organization could be treated as depreciable assets, which means that after reorganization and assigning a value to the player contracts acquired, the new team could now deduct from its income a (noncash) player contract depreciation cost, to reduce its income for tax purposes.

Originally, Veeck had hoped to talk the IRS into permitting a new owner to expense the player contracts immediately, to create a big tax loss carryover for the team, which could be used to reduce future taxable income, but the IRS instead required that the amount assigned to player contracts be depreciated over the expected useful playing lifetimes of the players acquired. An average playing career in baseball is around five years, so a reasonable length of time to depreciate the player contracts would be five years. (In practice, the IRS actually accepted depreciation periods as short as two and one-half years for some teams.) At the end of the five years, the player contracts would be completely written off, and now the team would find itself subject to taxes on its entire income, of course. But at the end of five years, the team can be sold to someone else, who then proceeds to do the same thing and writes off most of his or her purchase price over five years as well. If each succeeding owner sells out when the tax advantages are exhausted, there is no end to the tax sheltering associated with the franchise.

There is no doubt that that was a stroke of pure genius on the part of Veeck, but there are a couple of important qualifications to his philosopher's stone for the owners. In order to reorganize the team as a new business (and thus to revalue the assets held by the team in favor of player contracts), by law the new owner must acquire a substantial fraction of the ownership interest of the old team. The minimum fraction required by law varies from state to state, but generally, around 75 or 80 percent of the team's ownership must be acquired by the new owner. Moreover, there is the nagging problem of inconsistency between the previous owner's book value of the player contracts and the new owner's assignment of value to the contracts. This didn't create many complications back when Veeck invented the tax shelter, but it grew into a problem later on, when owners who had exploited the tax shelter sold to new owners who also wanted to use the team as a tax shelter. We will return to this problem of "recapture of excess depreciation" later. And, of course, there is the problem of justifying to the IRS the value that is assigned to player contracts by the new owner. This led to some of the most interesting mental gymnastics by owners and league officials once the tax shelter became a central part of each league's operations. Moreover, because each individual player contract had to be valued separately and depreciated separately, keeping track of the allowable depreciation on contracts of a changing list of players added substantially to the bookkeeping aspects of team ownership.

A Hypothetical Example

To illustrate how the Veeck tax shelter idea works, let's return to the era in which the idea first came up. Consider the case of a hypothetical baseball team that is purchased in 1950 for $3 million, an average price for that era. The new owner acquires 100 percent of the shares of the corporation that previously owned the team, and sets up a new corporation. This new corporation is registered with the IRS as a *subchapter S* corporation, again a typical way of setting up corporate ownership in sports teams in the 1950s. A subchapter S corporation is like any run-of-the-mill corporation—in particular, the owners of the corporation have limited liability for corporate debts—but one special feature characterizes subchapter S corporations: income earned by a subchapter S corporation flows directly to the owners of the corporation. Since any income earned by a corporation is subject to the corporate income tax (with a flat 52 percent rate in the 1950s), and since any income of the corporation flowing to owners is subject to the personal income tax (with a maximum effective rate of around 72 percent at the time), this sounds like a disadvantage to the owners. And, in fact, if the corporation were expected to actually show a positive profit, organizing as a subchapter S corporation would be a disadvantage. But, if the owners expect the corporation to show a loss (for tax purposes), then, as we shall see, the subchapter S form has some important tax advantages to the owners.

In any case, with the corporation set up, financed, say, 70 percent by stock and 30 percent by bank loans, as a part of this reorganization, the new owners revalue the assets held by the team to assign, say, 90 percent of the value of the team to the player contracts; 90 percent of $3 million is $2.7 million, and dividing this by five gives a contract writeoff of $540,000 per year for five years. (Intangible assets such as player contracts are not eligible for accelerated depreciation—only straight line depreciation is permitted under the tax code.) Finally, on average, cash flow from team operations over the next five years is taken to be $200,000 per year, typical for the period.

Figure 3.1 gives balance sheets and income statements for the team over the first five years of operation following the purchase by the new owners. The beginning balance sheet (as of the purchase date of January 1, 1950) indicates that total assets of the team are equal to $3 million, divided between player contracts ($2.7 million) and other assets ($300,000). The team has bank loans outstanding of $900,000, with ownership equity of $2.7 million; thus, just as the accounting books say, the balance sheet balances, with assets equal to liabilities plus equity.

The income statement for the year of 1950 shows a $200,000 cash flow from operations of the team. The team reduces this income by the writeoff of player contracts of $540,000, so that the income before taxes reported to the IRS is −$340,000. The negative income (for tax pur-

Figure 3.1 Financial History of Hypothetical Baseball Team, 1950–1954

1950. New owner takes over.

Beginning Balance Sheet, January 1, 1950 ($000)				Income Statement, 1950 ($000)	
ASSETS:		LIABILITIES:		Cash flow from operations	$200
Contracts	$2,700	Loans	$ 900	Less: contract depreciation	– 540
Other	300	Equity	2,100	Income before taxes	– 340
Total	$3,000	Total	$3,000	After-tax cash flow	$444.8

Balance Sheet, January 1, 1951				Income Statement, 1951 (same as 1950)
ASSETS:		LIABILITIES:		
Contracts	$2,160	Loans	$ 900	
Other	300	Equity	1,560	
Total	$2,460	Total	$2,460	

Balance Sheet, January 1, 1952				Income Statement, 1952 (same as 1950)
ASSETS:		LIABILITIES:		
Contracts	$1,620	Loans	$ 900	
Other	300	Equity	1,020	
Total	$1,920	Total	$1,920	

Balance Sheet, January 1, 1953				Income Statement, 1953 (same as 1950)
ASSETS:		LIABILITIES:		
Contracts	$1,080	Loans	$ 900	
Other	300	Equity	480	
Total	$1,380	Total	$1,380	

Balance Sheet, January 1, 1954				Income Statement, 1954 (same as 1950)
ASSETS:		LIABILITIES:		
Contracts	$ 540	Loans	$ 900	
Other	300	Equity	– 60	
Total	$ 840	Total	$ 840	

Balance Sheet, January 1, 1955			
ASSETS:		LIABILITIES:	
Contracts	$ 0	Loans	$ 900
Other	300	Equity	– 600
Total	$ 300	Total	$ 300

poses) provides the explanation of why the team was organized as a subchapter S corporation. As a subchapter S corporation, the (negative) income of the team flows directly to the owners of the team. The owners are wealthy individuals, who are assumed to be in the 72 percent personal income marginal tax bracket. The owners can use the $340,000 loss for the team to reduce their personal income for tax purposes by that amount. This saves them 72 percent of $340,000, or $244,800, in personal income tax payments. Thus the after-tax cash flow that the owners earn from their investment in the team for the year of 1950 is $444,800 = $200,000 cash flow from team operations plus $244,800 savings on personal income taxes on outside personal income. This is a tidy sum, especially from a business that is showing a $340,000 loss on its books.

The second balance sheet shows the financial status of the team at the beginning of its second year of operation. Player contracts have been depreciated by $540,000, so on the asset side, the contracts show up with a value of $2,160,000. There have been no changes in "other assets" or in "bank loans," so the decrease in the value of the player contracts shows up as a decrease in ownership equity.

The income statement for 1951 is identical to that for 1950, so the owners capture an after-tax cash flow of $444,800 from the team once again, and this continues on for the first five years of the team's operations, as long as player contracts are being written off. So far as the balance sheet is concerned, each year there is a further erosion of the player contract asset account to reflect contract depreciation, and a corresponding decrease in ownership equity.

Looking just at the financial statements of the team over the period 1950 through 1954, what comes through is every sign of an unmitigated financial catastrophe. Each year the team shows a loss of $340,000, and the value of the assets owned by the team continues to fall over time, with ownership equity actually becoming negative by 1954. Under normal circumstances, the team would be a prime candidate for the bankruptcy court, and the bank certainly would have called in its loans long before the equity account went negative.

This is only the appearance, of course. In fact, given average quality management, our hypothetical team will be every bit as alive and well financially, and every bit as talented on the playing field, on January 1, 1955, with its book value of $300,000 in assets and $600,000 negative equity position, as it was with its book value of $3 million in assets and $2.1 million of equity, when it was purchased five years earlier. The reason is that the IRS permits the team to write off as current expenses its scouting costs, farm club costs in the form of losses of minor league affiliates, salaries of players, and waiver and drafting expenses. Thus, other than signing bonuses and purchases of players for cash, the team can write off as current expenses all the costs that are incurred by the team to replenish its stock of players; and the IRS also permits the team to capitalize and write off over a period of years signing bonuses and purchases of players from other teams. All such out-of-pocket costs have already been deducted from income in arriving at the $200,000 annual net cash flow from operating the team. Assuming that we began with a team of average talent, and given only average management skill, the team will find itself in 1955 with about as much (and perhaps more) playing talent as it began with in 1950. The balance sheet and the income statement simply lie in describing the financial health of the team, as they do with the typical tax shelter operation.

In connection with this, it should be noted that as the original players acquired by the team retire or are traded, new players come on board. If a new player is acquired through a cash purchase of his contract from another team, the team purchasing the contract writes off this cash purchase over the expected useful playing lifetime of the player, in the form of contract depreciation. Similarly, if a player is traded to another team, any remaining unused depreciation goes with the player as well, so the team losing the player loses his unused depreciation as well, which now can be used by the team acquiring the player. For players who are acquired through the draft or through minor league farm clubs, acquisition costs are written off as a normal cost of doing business, so no depreciation account arises in these cases (except for signing bonuses). If a player retires or is placed on the inactive list before his expected playing lifetime expires, the team is allowed to write off any remaining unused depreciation on the player against income in the year the player retires. Thus, over time, trades, retirements, and player sales and purchases will result in changes in the amount of depreciation that a team is permitted to charge under IRS rules, but the basic principles involved are as described in our simplified example. In particular, after five years or so of operation of the team, most if not all of the opportunities for exploiting the tax shelter through contract depreciation write-offs will be gone for the owners of the team.

Reduced to its fundamentals, the Veeck tax shelter works because under the scheme, costs of replacing players are (at a minimum!) double-counted. In our example, the team starts with a group of players with a certain market value—certainly nowhere near as much as the assigned book value of $2.7 million, but for simplicity, let's make the assumption that they are actually worth $2.7 million. Given that players have an average playing lifetime of around five years, this means that in order to maintain the level of skill of the team, there will have to be an expenditure of about $540,000 per year to acquire (through the draft, the waiver system, the farm system, or purchases of established players) the talent needed to keep the team on an even keel. Except for the relatively minor expenditures for signing bonuses and cash purchases of players, these outlays can be written off immediately against cash receipts to determine the net income for tax purposes. (This is the "cash flow from operations" number in Table 3.1.)

What the Veeck tax shelter does is to add to this annual deductible cash cost of $540,000 an additional annual deductible non-cash player contract depreciation writeoff of $540,000, over the five-year period. The whole point of any depreciation allowance is to allow a business to accumulate the funds needed to replace the capital assets that wear out in the normal course of generating the current income of the business. But there is no need to accumulate these funds in a business such as baseball, where the costs of replacing players are already considered allowable expenses against income (again excepting signing bonuses and cash purchases of players, which are instead written off over a period of years). This is true whether the value assigned to player contracts is $2.7 million, as in our example, or $27—in neither case is there any economic justification for permitting player contract depreciation to be an allowable deduction against income for tax purposes, given that the out-of-pocket costs for replacing players are already allowable deductions. The IRS simply made a mistake when it bought Veeck's notion that player contracts acquired when buying a team should be treated as a depreciable asset.

We have said that, at a minimum, the cost of replacing players is double-counted. Since player contracts are the single most important team asset to qualify for short-term depreciation writeoffs, owners will, of course, assign as much of the purchase price of the team as possible to player contracts. In practice, the typical team writes off in depreciation much more than the annual cost of replacing the players who were acquired when the team was purchased. Hence the cost of replacing players is typically more than double-counted under the Veeck tax shelter.

The True Economic Value of Player Contracts

In connection with this, a relevant question to ask is this: What in fact is the true economic value of the player contracts owned by a team? The economist's answer goes something like this. If there is an active, freely competitive market in sales of players for cash, then the best source of information on the value of player contracts would be the dollar amounts that change hands when player contracts are bought and sold in this market. However, for reasons discussed in Chapter 7, some relating to (what else!) taxes, there are incentives for owners to avoid cash sales of players, and instead to engage in bilateral and multilateral trades of players for players, or in trades of players for draft rights.

In the absence of an active cash market in player contracts, we are reduced to estimating the value of player contracts on the basis of what, in principle, such contracts should be worth to a team. An owner acquiring a player contract is acquiring an asset that has value to the extent that it generates a stream of profits for the team. In this sense, a player contract is no different from any other asset. Using this approach, we can calculate the value to a team of a particular player's contract as follows. We estimate the number of years that the player will be committed to the team under the contract. (Under the traditional reserve/option clause system, this would be the expected useful playing lifetime of the player; under a complete free agency system, the player would be committed only for one year, unless he voluntarily signs a multi-year contract.) For each year the player is committed to the team, we calculate the increase in revenue for the team that the player generates for the team. (This is the player's *marginal revenue product*, or *MRP*, one of the few items of economic jargon that will appear in the book.) We deduct from this the player's salary. The difference between the two is the increase in profits for the year to the team from acquiring the player. We then use a market discount rate, say, the rate of return on industrial common stock, to discount future years' profits to the present, to determine how much those future profits are worth today. The present value of the additional profits the player will generate for the team is then the maximum amount the team would be willing to pay for the player, which is the player's true economic value to the team.

A few points should be noted about this. As sports moves towards more free agency, players are committed to teams for shorter periods than under the old-time reserve system. In and of itself, this reduces the value of player contracts to a team, because there are fewer years of profits to earn from the player contract. Another factor reducing the value of the player contract under free agency is that player salaries go up under free agency, and the higher are player salaries (other things being equal), the less player contracts are worth to teams, because the added profits from acquiring the player decrease. In fact, if there were complete free agency, with competitive markets for players, and ignoring informational problems, player contracts would have zero value, or close to it, since players would find that their salaries would be bid up to their MRPs (or close to them). In any case, to the extent that player contracts are valued on the books of a team at any amount over the present value of the added profits that can be earned from owning the contract, they are overstated.

One final point should be made concerning the value to be assigned to player contracts. The revenues that players generate for a team depend, of course, on the territorial rights of the team, which help determine the gate receipts of the team and the television income that the team earns. The salaries that are paid to players are affected by the waiver and drafting rights of the team. Both from a theoretical and from a practical point of view, there is no way to separate out the specific value of player contracts from the value of the territorial rights and the other rights acquired by a team as a member of a league.

The Hypothetical Example Again

But we are not done with our hypothetical example as yet. As the team enters 1955, all the player contracts are now written off. One possibility for the owners is to sell the team. We will examine the consequences of this later. Another possibility is for the owners to continue to operate the team. In this case, it appears that the IRS will recoup on the owners' original decision to operate as a subchapter S corporation, because from 1955 on, assuming an ongoing cash flow from operations of $200,000, and with no contract depreciation, the income of the team will be subject to the personal income tax rate of 72 percent, generating a tax of $144,000, much greater than the corporate income tax of only 52 percent, or $104,000.

Right? Wrong. The tax code conveniently provides that once in the lifetime of a subchapter S corporation, the owners may change the status to that of a regular corporation. The owners will, of course, exercise this option, and beginning on January 1, 1955, the team will operate as an ordinary corporation. The team will continue to operate this way until it is sold, paying $104,000 each year in taxes, and generating $96,000 per year in after-tax income, which will be reinvested in the team, and hence will not be subject to the personal income tax. Because, at the time (1955), the corporate tax rate (52 percent) was less than the personal income tax rate of the owner (72 percent), operating as a regular corporation had tax advantages over operating as a partnership, although later on in time, changes in the tax laws reversed this advantage, so that most teams today are organized as limited partnerships.

The other alternative as we reach 1955 is for the owners to sell the team. Assuming average management, the team should be worth as much in 1955 as it was in 1950, so let's assume that the teams sells once again for $3 million. The new owners are now free to reorganize the team, just as the old owners did, and in that reorganization, assign, say, $2.7 million of the value of the team to player contracts, and begin the depreciation process all over again. Are there any problems here?

One problem is that the old owners have completely written off the player contracts they acquired on January 1, 1950. Ignoring replacement player contracts acquired through cash purchases, player contracts on the books of the team as of January 1, 1950, carry a value of zero dollars, but the new owners are going to claim that the contracts really are worth $2,700,000. They both can't be right, can they? Well, for years, the answer of the IRS was, "Sure, they can"; the IRS either ignored the inconsistency or bought the owners' argument that the inconsistency arose from causes that did not affect the excess depreciation issue.

Why does it make any difference? Consider this. If the old owners admit that the "true" value of the player contracts they possess is $2.7 million, then it appears that there has been "excess depreciation" that has been charged over the previous five years—the old owners have written off more depreciation of player contracts than has actually occurred. When the IRS recaptures excess depreciation from a taxpayer, it does so at the normal income tax rate. In effect, in this case, assuming a final value of player contracts of $2.7 million, the IRS would go back and recalculate the tax liability of the old owners of the team as if no contract depreciation had taken place during any of the five years. For a subchapter S corporation, the result would be disastrous, because then for each year of our example, the team would have shown a $200,000 profit rather than a $340,000 loss, so that the owners would have owed $144,000 in personal income taxes per year, as compared to the net annual *savings* of $244,800 (a *negative* tax of $244,800) per year in personal income taxes under the Veeck scheme.

However, the problem for the IRS in attempting to recapture excess depreciation is that most, if not all, of the players originally acquired by the old owners in 1950 have either retired or been traded away by 1955. The old owners can argue with some logic that those players really did "wear out" over the five-year period, so that no excess depreciation occurred. What they have in 1955 is an entirely new set of players, most acquired through their minor league system or through trades, so any arguments concerning the original group of players are irrelevant in assessing the issue of excess depreciation. This argument turned out to be persuasive, to the IRS at least—there are few, if any, documented cases of substantive amounts of back taxes that were collected from sports teams because of recapture of excess depreciation of player contracts.

Assuming that no excess depreciation is recaptured by the IRS, the tax situation of the old owners at time of sale is this. They are selling the team for $3 million, but the book value of the team (the "basis") is just $300,000. Under the tax code, the old owners have to pay a capital gains tax on the difference between the sales price of the team and the basis (assuming no excess depreciation). During the 1950s, for wealthy owners, the capital gains tax was around 35 percent, so the owners would pay the government 35 percent of $2.7 million, or $945,000, in capital gains tax, and the net (after-tax) proceeds from the sale would be $2,055,000 ($3 million minus $945,000) in capital gains tax.

This gives us another way to view the Veeck tax shelter. What it does is to permit the owner of a team to convert ordinary income into capital gains income, and to delay the payment of the capital gains tax on this income until the team is sold. This means that the value of the tax shelter to an owner depends in part on the difference between the ordinary income tax rate and the capital gains rate. In the 1950s, the ordinary income tax rate for wealthy individuals was roughly twice that of the capital gains tax rate (72 percent versus 35 percent). In the early 1980s, the top personal income tax rate was reduced to around 50 percent, with the capital gains rate reduced to around 20 percent. In the Tax Reform Act of 1986, the capital gains rate became the same as the personal income tax rate, at 28 percent (for wealthy individuals), which further reduced the value of the tax shelter.

Table 3.1 shows the flow of after-tax income that is generated from purchase of the team in 1950 for $3 million, operation as a subchapter S corporation for five years, and resale of the team in 1955 for $3 mil-

Table 3.1
After-Tax Earnings from Hypothetical Baseball Team
Purchased January 1, 1950, and Sold January 1, 1955

Year	Investment	After-Tax Cash Flow
1950	$3,000,000	$444,800
1951	—	444,800
1952	—	444,800
1953	—	444,800
1954	—	$2,499,800[a]

Note: The internal rate of return i on investment in the hypothetical baseball team can be calculated as follows. With the tax shelter, $0 = -\$3,000,000 + 444,800/(1 + i) + 444,800/(1 + i)^2 + 444,800/(1 + i)^3 + 444,800/(1 + i)^4 + 2,499,800/(1 + i)^5$. Solving, i is approximately equal to 0.10 (10 percent). Without the tax shelter, $i = (0.48)$ ($200,000) / ($3,000,000) = 0.032 (3.2 percent).

[a]Equal to $444,800 after-tax cash flow from operation of team for year of 1954, plus $2,055,000 received from sale of team for $3,000,000, less capital gains tax of $945,000.

lion, with no recapture of excess depreciation, given the tax rates of that era. It is assumed that income is received at the end of each year, and that the team is sold at the end of 1954, this accounting for the $2,499,800 of cash flow for 1954.

Table 3.1 also calculates the internal after-tax rate of return i on investment in the team, which turns out to be roughly 10 percent. (The internal rate of return is that rate which, if used as a discount rate, sets the present value of the stream of income from an investment—including purchase as negative income—equal to zero.) This rate should be contrasted with the after-tax internal rate of return that would be earned by buying the team for $3 million, and operating it into the indefinite future (perpetual ownership) as a regular corporation (with a 52 percent tax rate on the annual $200,000 cash flow), without benefit of the Veeck tax shelter. As shown in Table 3.1, this leads to an after-tax internal rate of return on the original $3 million investment of only 3.2 percent. Thus in our example, the Veeck tax shelter roughly triples the after-tax rate of return for an owner.

Use of the Tax Shelter

The first time the tax shelter was used was in 1949, when Bill Veeck's syndicate sold the Cleveland Indians for $2.5 million to a syndicate headed by Ellis Ryan and Hank Greenberg. The IRS took the bait—hook, line, and sinker—and agreed that the new owners could write off a portion of the purchase price of the team as depreciation of the player contracts, and the world changed for sports team owners. As indicated by our example, the potential advantages to a new owner from the tax shelter are substantial. Thus, once the idea of the tax shelter had been approved by the IRS, it is reasonable to assume that every new owner who could took advantage of the shelter. Because most teams are operated as closely held corporations or limited partnerships, data to confirm this are not generally available. However, in 1972, at congressional hearings into the proposed merger of the NBA and ABA, data were collected under congressional subpoena by Roger Noll and Ben Okner relative to the tax shelter, covering all teams in those leagues operating in 1971. The data are shown in Table 3.2, which is taken from Okner (1974b).

The data show that essentially all teams took at least some advantage of the tax shelter—7 of the 10 ABA teams for which data were available assigned a part of the purchase price of the team to player contracts, the portion ranging from 47 percent to 95 percent; and 16 of the 18 NBA teams assigned a portion of the purchase price of the team to player

Table 3.2

Assignment of Value of Team to Franchise and to Player Contracts,
Basketball Teams Operating in 1971

| Team | Assignment of Value (thousands of dollars) | | | Player Contracts as % of Total |
	Franchise	Player Contracts	Total	
AMERICAN BASKETBALL ASSOCIATION				
A1	250	—	250	0.0
A2	100	885	985	89.8
A3	—	—	—	—
A4	15	280	295	94.9
A5	200	1,350	1,550	87.1
A6	172	280	452	61.9
A7	20	—	20	0.0
A8	—	—	—	—
A9	425	375	800	46.6
A10	255	—	255	0.0
A11	6	100	106	94.3
ABA	1,443	3,270	5,319	69.4
NATIONAL BASKETBALL ASSOCIATION				
N1	250	250	500	50.0
N2	1,100	4,500	5,600	80.4
N3	1,035	4,140	5,175	80.0
N4	400	3,200	3,600	88.9
N5	400	3,037	3,437	88.4
N6	50	1,200	1,250	96.0
N7	416	600	1,016	59.1
N8	200	478	678	70.5
N9	465	3,170	3,635	87.2
N10	101	1,056	1,157	91.3
N11	100	—	100	0.0
N12	180	1,727	1,907	90.6
N13	331	3,166	3,496	90.5
N14	25	—	25	0.0
N15	50	2,990	3,040	98.4
N16	—	23	23	100.0
N17	150	1,284	1,434	89.5
NBA	5,253	30,821	36,073	85.4

Source: Statement of Roger G. Noll and Benjamin A. Okner, in *Professional Basketball: Hearings before the Subcommittee on Antitrust and Monopoly of the Senate Committee on the Judiciary*, 92d Cong., 2d sess. 1972, pt. 2, 1000.

contracts, with the portion ranging from 50 percent to 100 percent. On average, ABA teams assigned 69.4 percent of the purchase price of a team to player contracts, and NBA teams assigned 85.4 percent to player contracts. While the specific teams are not identified, it seems reasonable to conclude that the teams not taking advantage of the tax shelter were teams that could not do so. For example, in the NBA in 1971, the Detroit Pistons were owned by Fred Zollner, who had originally founded the team way back in the 1930s (as the Fort Wayne Zollners), when the tax shelter was not available; and the New York Knicks were still owned by the Madison Square Garden Corporation, which had founded the team in 1946, again, before the tax shelter was invented by Bill Veeck. Because it would take a sale of the team, with reorganization and assignment of value to player contracts, to use the tax shelter, neither the Pistons nor the Knicks would have been eligible to use the shelter by 1971. (The Pistons were sold in 1974, and presumably the new owners used the tax shelter at that time.) In the ABA, the Denver Nuggets, the Indiana Pacers, and the Kentucky Colonels all were owned by the same individuals who had purchased them when the ABA was organized, under circumstances that made it impossible for them to assign any portion of the purchase price to player contracts, since the ABA did not hold title to any player contracts at the time.

Table 3.2 simply confirms what economic intuition suggests, namely, that any new owner purchasing a sports team from roughly 1950 on would make use of the Veeck tax shelter, which was a legal way to operate, and highly remunerative to boot.

During the 1950s and 1960s, there are no indications that sports teams encountered any problems with the IRS in connection with the tax shelter, and, as Table 3.1 indicates, owners were assigning the great bulk of the purchase price of teams to player contracts. This was as true in the other sports as in baseball. For example, Veeck reports in *The Hustler's Handbook* that when the Bartholomay syndicate purchased the Milwaukee Braves in 1962 for $6,218,480, the new owners assigned $50,000 to the franchise, and $6,168,400 as the value of the player contracts acquired, which represented 99.19 percent of the value of the team. The contracts were written off over 10 years, an unusually long writeoff period.

Court Cases Involving the Tax Shelter

It took until the early 1970s before the IRS finally began to look with some suspicion at what was going on in sports. In 1974, in what appears to be the first serious attempt by the IRS to limit or eliminate the Veeck tax shelter, the IRS disallowed the contract writeoff of two minority owners of the Atlanta Falcons, E. Cody Laird and his wife, Joanne H. Laird. The Lairds sued, resulting in the most important court case dealing with the tax shelter, *Laird v. United States*, 391 F. Supp. 655 (N.D. Ga. 1975). *Laird* was to be a test case. Commissioner Alexander of the IRS reported in 1976 that there were 130 contract depreciation cases pending when *Laird* came to trial, including cases involving the Kansas City Royals, the Miami Dolphins, the Seattle Supersonics, the Philadelphia Flyers, and the Kansas City Athletics.

The facts that came out in the *Laird* trial are these. The Atlanta Falcons entered the NFL in 1966 as an expansion team, paying $8.5 million to enter the league. Ownership of the team was vested in a subchapter S corporation under the name of Five Smiths, Inc. Rankin Smith was the major stockholder of Five Smiths, owning 64 percent of the shares, with the Lairds owning 6 percent. The $8.5 million price for the team was divvied up as follows. The NFL sold the team its NFL franchise for $50,000, and $727,086 of the purchase price was deferred interest due the league, resulting from the fact that the team was allowed to pay the league its money over several years into the future. The $50,000 franchise fee was paid for the various privileges accorded the Falcons as a new member of the NFL, including its exclusive territorial rights to Atlanta. Among those privileges was the right to share equally with other NFL teams in the national TV contract of the NFL, a contract that was paying each team $1,248,000 for the 1966 season. (The Falcons were to begin play in the 1967 season.) It was in part the discrepancy between the $50,000 franchise fee and the $1.2 million to be earned in TV income from possession of the franchise in just one year that got the attention of the IRS.

The remainder of the $8.5 million expansion fee, namely, $7,722,914.04 (90.9 percent), was allocated to the player contracts acquired by the Falcons in the expansion draft. In the first round of the expansion draft, each existing NFL team was allowed to freeze 29 players from its 42-player roster, and Atlanta was allowed (required!) to pick one player per team from each existing team's remaining 13 non-protected players. Thus each existing team was allowed to exempt its starting lineups (offensive and defensive) and its kickers, plus several additional players. There were two more rounds of the expansion draft, with existing teams allowed to protect additional players in the later rounds. The Falcons ended up acquiring 42 players from the 14 existing NFL teams (3 from each team), most of the drafted players being older players in the twilight of their careers, or younger players considered of less promise than the players protected by existing teams in the draft.

Dividing $7,722,914 by 42 yields an average "cost" per player of $183,879, and a payment of $551,637 to each of the existing 14 teams in the league. The Falcons listed $7,722,914 as the value of the player contracts on the team's balance sheet, and opted to write off the player contracts over a 5.25-year period (five years and three months), yielding an annual player contract writeoff of $1,471,031 for the first 5.25 years the team operated.

The Falcons were very successful at the gate. In the first two years the team was in the league, the net cash flow from team operations (cash receipts less cash outlays) came close to $1 million per year: $964,702 in 1967 and $889,984 in 1968. After deducting the player contract writeoff, these were turned into tax losses of $506,329 in 1967 and $581,047 in 1968. Making the conservative assumption that the owners of the Falcons were in the 50 percent personal income tax bracket, this means that the team was generating an after-tax cash flow of around $1,175,000 per year (net cash flow from operations plus 50 percent of book loss).

The IRS originally cut the valuation of player contracts from $7,722,914 to $1,050,000, but at the trial, the IRS took the position that the correct amount to allocate to player contracts was zero. The IRS argued that Five Smiths had purchased a "bundle of inextricably intertwined assets whose values were so interrelated that they were not capable of separate valuation, and, thus, are not eligible for the depreciation deduction." Judge Frank Hooper rejected the IRS argument, and ruled instead that it was possible to arrive at a figure that represented the value of the player contracts purchased by the team, and that such player contracts were depreciable.

The lawyers for the Lairds argued two positions: (1) the $7,722,914 valuation assigned to player contracts was a valid estimate of the value of the contracts; and (2) if the court rejected this, then $4.3 million should be assigned to the share of the national television contract acquired by the team, and the remainder to player contracts, with the TV contract to be written off over a four-year period.

To justify the Falcons' first position—the $7.7 million valuation of player contracts—various experts were brought in by the lawyers for the Lairds, including Jim Finks, at the time the general manager of the Chicago Bears, and Tex Schramm, then general manager of the Dallas Cowboys. Finks estimated the value of the 42 players at $6,825,000, and Schramm came up with a figure of $7.3 million. These valuations applied to a group of players of whom 7 were released before the 1967 season and were not claimed by any team (at a $100 waiver price), 4 others were claimed on waivers, 1 went on injured reserve, 2 were traded to other teams, 3 were placed on Atlanta's reserve list, and the remaining 25 made the Atlanta team (18 were regular starters in 1967); 19 players were around for the 1968 season, and 8 remained for the 1969 season. Finks and Schramm found it somewhat difficult to explain how it could be that a player drafted in the spring had a value of around $180,000, but by the fall was not worth the $100 waiver fee, as was true of seven of the drafted players—or was just worth the $100 fee, as was true of four more. With the team's expensive lineup, Atlanta came in seventh in the Eastern conference in 1966, with a record of 3–11–0, had the worst record in the NFL in 1968 (1–12–1), and tied for the worst record in the NFL in 1969 (2–12–0).

In the face of this expert testimony, Judge Hooper rejected the first position. He accepted the $4.3 million valuation of the TV contract, but then held that because the Falcons would share in the revenue from any renewal of the contract into perpetuity, the TV contract had no determinable lifetime and hence was not depreciable. This view of the non-depreciable nature of TV contracts has been followed in several other cases, including *McCarthy v. United States*, 807 F.2d 1306 (1986), a case in which the New York Yankees' depreciation of the local and national baseball TV contracts was disallowed.

Judge Hooper decided to allocate $50,000 of the purchase price to the franchise, $727,086 of the purchase price to deferred interest, $4,277,043 to the nondepreciable TV contract, $3,035,000 to player contracts (depreciable over 5.25 years), and $410,871 to other nondepreciable rights acquired in the purchase. Judge Hooper's decision must have had something Solomon-like about it, because both the government and the Lairds appealed the decision, which was upheld in the Federal Circuit Court of Appeals in 1977.

At about the same time as the Falcons case, the IRS took out after the Seattle SuperSonics (see *First Northwest Industries of America, Inc. v. Commissioner of Internal Revenue*, 649 F.2d 707 (9th Cir. 1981)). The SuperSonics had come into the NBA in 1967 as an expansion team, paying a $1,750,000 fee to the league. The NBA charged Sam Schulman and Gene Klein, owners of the SuperSonics, $150,000 for their NBA franchise, and $1,600,000 was allocated to player contracts, which were written off over five years. In the 1971 Senate hearings on basketball, the income statements and balance sheets of the SuperSonics for their first two years of operation (1967/68, 1968/69) were shown. The Super-Sonics used a fiscal year ending on May 31. Summary balance sheets for the team for May 31, 1968, and May 31, 1969, are shown in the accompanying table.

Taxes, Taxes, and More Taxes

Seattle SuperSonics Balance Sheets (thousands of dollars)

	Income Statements	
	Year Ending May 31, 1968	Year Ending May 31, 1969
ASSETS		
Current assets	96	332
Fixed assets	10	212
League franchise	150	150
Player contracts	964	767
Other assets	262	716
Total assets	1,376	1,633
LIABILITIES		
Current liabilities	712	555
Fixed liabilities	800	550
Total liabilities	1,512	1,633
Ownership equity	− 136	527

	Income Statements	
	Year Ending May 31, 1968	Year Ending May 31, 1969
Revenue	924	992
Operating expenses	818	886
Interest expense	58	51
Earnings before amortization	46	55
Amortization of player contracts	322	276
Net loss	− 276	− 219

Source: *Professional Basketball: Hearings before the Senate Committee on the Judiciary*, 92d Cong., 1st sess., 1971, 360–363.

The increase in ownership equity shown on the balance sheet for May 31, 1969, arose because after the 1968 fiscal year, Sam Schulman, the owner of the SuperSonics, converted the firm from a subchapter S corporation to a regular corporation, and sold shares (very successfully) to the general public, while retaining a controlling interest in the team in his own hands. Funds received by the corporation from the stock sale account for the increase in ownership equity between 1968 and 1969, during a period when the corporation was showing a book loss.

According to the financial statements, the SuperSonics generated a net cash flow of $46,000 in fiscal year 1968, and $55,000 in fiscal year 1969, while showing losses for tax purposes of $276,000 in 1968 and $219,000 in 1969. In the SuperSonics' financial report, the president, Sam Schulman, informed his stockholders that the net loss figures shown for the team had to be taken with a grain of salt:

> You will note that our financial report discloses a loss of $219,000 from the period covering June 1, 1968 to May 31, 1969. In fact, this figure is misleading, since the Seattle SuperSonics Corporation showed earnings of $46,734 before amortization of player contracts for the 1967–68 season and earnings of $55,133 before amortization of players contracts for the 1968–69 season.
> . . . I know of no business as fascinating, rewarding and stimulating as that of professional sports. You share that fascination, reward and stimulation with me as shareholders in the Seattle Super-Sonics.

The trial court apparently decided that while it had no objection to the fascination and stimulation of owning an NBA team, it did object to the reward. The court rejected the $1.6 million allocation by the SuperSonics to player contracts. Instead, the court allocated $250,000 of the expansion fee of $1.75 million to the right to share in the proceeds from the 1968 NBA expansion, and reduced the allocation to player contracts to $500,000. Both of these allocations were held to be depreciable, but the remaining $1 million was held to be nondepreciable. On appeal, the trial court was upheld.

These cases represented victories of a sort for the IRS, because the valuations originally assigned to player contracts by the teams were reduced greatly by the court. On the other hand, the court bought into the proposition that it was legitimate to assign a portion of the cost of a team to the player contracts the team obtained, and to depreciate this over the useful playing lifetimes of the players involved.

In one case, however, the IRS lost on all counts (see *Allen H. Selig v. United States*, 565 F. Supp. 524 (E.D. Wis. 1983), *aff'd*, 740 F.2d. 572 (7th Cir. 1984)). This case involved the purchase of the Seattle Pilots AL club by Bud Selig in 1970, who then moved the team to Milwaukee as the Milwaukee Brewers. Selig was the majority owner of the Milwaukee Brewers Baseball Club, Inc., a subchapter S corporation organized to obtain a new team for the city, after the Braves left town in 1966. Selig bought the Pilots for $10.8 million, of which $10.2 million (94.44 percent) was assigned to the player contracts, with $100,000 assigned to miscellaneous supplies and equipment, and $500,000 for the franchise. The IRS disallowed the player contract depreciation, arguing that no contract depreciation should be allowed. Selig paid his taxes and sued the IRS for recovery.

This case had one difference from the Falcons and Supersonics cases in that Selig had purchased an existing team, rather than an expansion franchise. The Pilots had come into the AL as an expansion team in 1969, owned by Pacific Northwest Sports, Inc., a subchapter S corporation headed by Dewey Soriano, with major stockholder William Daley. Pacific Northwest paid $5,350,000 to the AL for the team, in addition to agreeing to forgo its share of national TV or radio revenues for three years, and agreeing to contribute 2 percent of gate receipts to the league office for three years. The AL assigned $100,000 of the purchase price of the team to the franchise, and $5,250,000 to 30 player contracts to be acquired by the Pilots in an expansion draft, with each player chosen priced at $175,000.

Predictably, the Pilots ended up in last place in the AL Western division in 1969, with a record of 64 wins and 98 losses, 33 games out of first place, and 4 games out of next-to-last place. Seattle drew only 677,944 to the team's minor league park. The Pilots were teetering on the verge of bankruptcy after their first season, when Selig bought the team.

One of the problems for the court was to determine how it was possible that the players owned by the Pilots could increase in value from $5,250,000 in October 1968 (at the time of the expansion draft) to $10.2 million a year and six months later, when Selig bought the team, especially given the evidence on the playing field of the marginal character of the talent on the team, and the evidence at the box office of the marginal drawing potential of the team. (In connection with this, if you were the owner of an AL team, you might want to ask how it was possible for the league to so underestimate the market value of an expansion franchise when it set a price of only $5,350,000 for the Seattle franchise in 1968, given that the team would sell for $10.2 million 18 months later!)

Perhaps it was that the roster had improved in the year and a half? Well, there was an improvement—in 1970, the Milwaukee Brewers ended up with a record of 65 and 97, a full one game better than the team's record at Seattle. The Brewers did draw 933,607, a lot better than in 1969, but by 1971, attendance was back down to 731,531, as the Brewers moved up to 69 and 92. It would be hard to make a case for a doubling of the value of the player contracts on this record—but the court made it.

The most charitable thing that can be said about the court decisions (trial and appeal) in this case is that it is not just in basketball that there is a "home court" advantage. The *Selig* case was tried in the U.S. dis-

111

trict court in Wisconsin, which held for Bud Selig and the Brewers on all counts, and the appeals court sustained the lower court, after the case was appealed by the IRS. Among other things, the lower court judge in the case argued in approving fashion that the Veeck tax shelter was somehow designed into the tax laws in order to help the poverty-stricken sports team owners: "The tax laws help baseball clubs survive despite their unprofitability. The tax laws permit owners to write off (deduct) the cost of the player contracts that they purchase and to write off as an expense the cost of developing new players. This in effect enables the owners to double up on expenses (that is, tax deductions) during the first five years of operation (that is, the period of amortization)" (p. 528). Thus, it appears that the judge was saying that having once made the mistake of allowing depreciation of player contracts in team purchase, the IRS was condemned to keep making the same mistake ad infinitum. The court's position in effect meant giving the store to the owner; the only issue left to resolve was how expensive a store the owner was going to get, that is, how much were the player contracts really worth?

The Brewers presented the testimony of expert witnesses to back up the $10.2 million valuation figure. The witnesses were Frank Lane, longtime baseball executive with the White Sox, Indians, and other clubs; Cedric Tallis of the Royals and the Yankees; and Marvin Milkes and Bobby Mattick. Milkes and Mattick were front-office executives with the Brewers, and had held similar jobs with the Pilots, so their testimony was rightly regarded by the judge as lacking somewhat in objectivity. But after Lane had appraised the roster, he was appointed general manager of the Brewers, which did not affect his believability, in the view of the judge. The judge also thought that Tallis could be quite objective, even though the Royals were currently involved in a dispute with the IRS over precisely the same issue of overvaluation of player contracts.

In any case, the Brewers had assigned a value of $10.2 million to the player contracts before obtaining the appraisals of Lane and Tallis, who knew going in what figure Selig had set on the contracts. Lane ended up valuing the contracts at $10,351,000, and Tallis valued them at $10,358,000. The trial judge developed an involved argument concerning the difference between the player market and the market for clubs to justify accepting the $10.2 million figure. The decision of the appeals court, which upheld the lower court on all counts, is one of those rare legal opinions that is actually fun to read for its own sake, whatever its merits in terms of economics. The decision ends as follows:

> "Oh! somewhere in this favored land
> the sun is shining bright;

The band is playing somewhere, and
somewhere hearts are light.
And somewhere men are laughing, and
somewhere children shout;
But there is no joy in Mudville—
mighty Casey has Struck Out.

There should be joy somewhere in Milwaukee—the district court's judgment is affirmed.

Changes in the Tax Laws

As the cases involving the Falcons, the Supersonics, and the Brewers wound their way through the courts, the Congress also got into the act of imposing some limits on the Veeck tax shelter. Hearings were held in 1976 on a number of proposals to change the existing law, and the Congress ended up enacting two basic changes in the tax code relating to sports teams. First, the code was changed to include a presumption that not more than 50 percent of the purchase price of a team can be allocated to player contracts, unless it is specifically established that a higher percentage is justified. Second, in the sale of a team, when player contracts are sold, the value assigned to any contract by the new owner cannot exceed the basis (book value) for that contract on the books of the old owner plus the gain (if any) recognized by the old owner in selling the contract. Thus, if a contract were on the books of the old owner at $100,000 and if the old owner claimed that at the time of sale of the team, the contract was worth $100,000, then the new owner could only assign a value of $100,000 to the contract. The new owner could assign a value, say, of $250,000 to the contract only if the old owner paid the taxes due (including recapture of excess depreciation, if present) on the $150,000 difference between the book value and the value assigned to the contract by the new owner.

The provision limiting the valuation assigned to player contracts to 50 percent of the value of a team was an important substantive change, since, as we have seen, owners had been assigning a much higher fraction of the purchase price to player contracts up to that time. The second change is more cosmetic, despite its intent. It appears to correct the abuse of differing valuations for player contracts between the seller and the buyer of a team, to provide the basis for the IRS to recapture excess depreciation on contracts that have been depreciated by the old owner and revalued upward by the new owner in the course of the purchase of a team. Any such gains recognized by the old owner would then be subject to normal income taxes.

But the provision has teeth only with respect to contracts where depreciation has occurred, and not to the contracts of those players who have been acquired since the team was purchased, through the usual process of college or free agent draft, minor league training, and calling up to the major league roster. For such contracts, the gain recognized by the old owner results only in a capital gains tax, rather than taxation at the normal income tax rate. In particular, if the old owner holds the team long enough so that all of the players originally acquired when the team was purchased have retired or been traded, the change in the tax law will have no effect on the tax liability of the old owner at time of sale—the owner will only be subject to the capital gains tax, and not to recapture of excess depreciation at the normal income tax rate. Moreover, this provision of the tax law can be bypassed simply by assigning the increase in value of player contracts to those contracts that have not been depreciated. Since there is no objective market measure of the value of most player contracts, based on a previous cash sale of the contract, it is difficult for the IRS to overturn the appraisal value of a contract as submitted by a team. Thus, the 1976 changes did impose some limits on tax sheltering by sports teams, especially by the 50 percent provision, so the barn door wasn't as wide open as before, but they certainly didn't close down tax sheltering completely.

What was ultimately even more important in eating away at the value of the tax shelter over time was a general reduction in normal income tax rates on wealthy individuals and changes in the capital gains tax rates. The process of reducing income tax rates for the wealthy reached its culmination in the Tax Reform Act of 1986. The primary objective of the Tax Reform Act of 1986 was to drastically reduce the role of tax incentives in directing investment decisions in the U.S. economy. Along with reducing marginal income tax rates on wealthy individuals, one of the most important steps taken in that direction was eliminating the difference between the normal income tax rate and the capital gains tax rate. Since 1986, the marginal normal income tax and capital gains tax rates for wealthy individuals have both been set at the same level of 28 percent. (The 1990 tax law changes enacted as part of the budget compromise deal did open a small gap between normal income tax rates and capital gains rates for some wealthy individuals, but the effect so far as tax sheltering is concerned is minimal.) As we shall see, this change had the effect of reducing the tax advantages of buy-and-sell ownership strategies relative to buy-and-hold strategies. Buy-and-sell strategies had been fostered by the tax rate structure in the early years of the Veeck tax shelter. Moreover, with the capital gains and normal income tax rates equal at 28 percent, the issue of recapture of excess depreciation basically goes away, since excess depreciation is taxed at the same rate as capital gains.

The Value of the Tax Shelter

The Veeck tax shelter increases the after-tax income that can be derived from ownership of a sports team. The forces of supply and demand operating in the franchise market work to capitalize this higher after-tax income into the price of the team so that the market prices of sports teams will tend to reflect the tax-sheltering advantages from team ownership. This raises the general question of how much the Veeck tax shelter was worth to owners, what impact the tax shelter had on the turnover of franchises, and how much the market prices of sports teams have been affected by the tax shelter. Before turning to empirical information concerning this, it is of interest to see what microeconomic theory tells us about the value of the Veeck tax shelter. There are good reasons why the theory can't generate an exact answer that you can bet the weekly paycheck on, but at least we can get a feeling for the "order of magnitude" effects on owners and on franchise prices.

A technical appendix to this chapter (following Chapter 9) presents formulas that permit the calculation of hypothetical valuations of the tax shelter, under various simplifying assumptions about the pattern of ownership of a team, about tax rates, and about the way in which the tax shelter is used. Among the simplifications built into the formulas is the assumption that buyers and sellers of teams take the present pattern of tax rates as continuing unchanged into the indefinite future; that the future path of income from the team is known with certainty, as is the future price of the team; and that owners act as if they were certain that the present IRS treatment of the tax shelter will continue unchanged into the indefinite future. In all cases, it is assumed that the team is operated either as a subchapter S corporation or limited partnership during the contract writeoff period, and as a limited partnership or ordinary corporation after that period, whichever is most advantageous in terms of tax status.

The formulas in the appendix are used to construct the numerical examples shown in Figure 3.2, covering the situation that prevailed in 1991. In Figure 3.2, we consider a team with a net cash flow from operations of $1 million in year 0, say, 1990. We use the tax rates and tax code provisions that applied in 1991, based on the Tax Reform Act of 1986, to look at three different scenarios. Scenario A is one in which a team is owned in perpetuity by an individual who makes no use of the tax shelter, so the owner simply pays normal income taxes on the net

Figure 3.2 Value of the Tax Shelter after the 1986 Tax Reform Act

I. Constant cash flow from operations.

A. No tax shelter. Value of team = $7,200,000.

Year	Cash Flow from Operations	Contract Depreciation	Taxable Income	Tax	After-Tax Cash Flow
1	$1,000,000	0	$1,000,000	$280,000	$720,000
ff.	1,000,000	0	1,000,000	280,000	720,000

B. Tax shelter: Buy-and-hold. Value of team = $8,090,000.

Year	Cash Flow from Operations	Contract Depreciation	Taxable Income	Tax	After-Tax Cash Flow
1	$1,000,000	$809,000	$191,000	$53,500	$946,500
5	1,000,000	809,000	191,000	53,500	946,500
ff.	1,000,000	0	$1,000,000	$280,000	720,000

C. Tax shelter: Buy-and-sell. Value of team = $7,695,000.

Year	Cash Flow from Operations	Contract Depreciation	Taxable Income	Tax	After-Tax Cash Flow
1	$1,000,000	$769,500	$230,500	$64,540	$935,460
5	1,000,000	769,500	230,500	64,540	935,460
Sale	$7,695,000	—	$3,847,500	$1,077,000	$6,618,000

II. Seven percent annual rate of growth in cash flow from operations.

A. No Tax shelter. Value of team = $24,000,000.

Year	Cash Flow from Operations	Contract Depreciation	Taxable Income	Tax	After-Tax Cash Flow
1	$1,070,000	0	$1,070,000	$300,000	$770,000
2	1,145,000	0	1,145,000	321,000	824,000
3	1,225,000	0	1,225,000	343,000	882,000
4	1,311,000	0	1,311,000	367,000	944,000
5	1,403,000	0	1,403,000	393,000	1,010,000

Value of team at end of year 5 = $33,672,000.

B. Tax shelter: Buy-and-hold. Value of team = $26,966,000.

Year	Cash Flow from Operations	Contract Depreciation	Taxable Income	Tax	After-Tax Cash Flow
1	$1,070,000	$2,697,000	−$1,627,000	−$456,000	$1,526,000
2	$1,145,000	$2,697,000	−1,552,000	−435,000	1,580,000
3	$1,225,000	$2,697,000	−1,472,000	−412,000	1,637,000
4	$1,311,000	$2,697,000	−1,386,000	−388,000	1,699,000
5	$1,403,000	$2,697,000	−1,294,000	−362,000	1,765,000

Value of team at end of year 5 = $33,672,000.

C. Tax shelter: Buy-and-sell. Value of team = $17,928,000.

Year	Cash Flow from Operations	Contract Depreciation	Taxable Income	Tax	After-Tax Cash Flow
1	$1,070,000	$1,793,000	−$723,000	−$202,000	$1,272,000
2	$1,145,000	$1,793,000	−648,000	−181,000	1,326,000
3	$1,225,000	$1,793,000	−568,000	−159,000	1,384,000
4	$1,311,000	$1,793,000	−482,000	−135,000	1,446,000
5	$1,403,000	$1,793,000	−390,000	−109,000	1,512,000

Value of team at end of year 5 = $25,153,000.
Net to owner after selling and paying capital gains tax = $20,620,000.

cash flow from operations of the team. Scenario B is one in which a new owner makes full use of the tax shelter for a five-year writeoff period, and then continues to own the team into perpetuity, a buy-and-hold scenario. Scenario C is one in which a new owner makes full use of the tax shelter for a five-year writeoff period, and then sells it to someone else, who does the same thing, a buy-and-sell scenario.

We should note that scenario C is much more of an idealized view of the franchise market than are the other two scenarios. Under scenarios A and B, the owner's decision (along with those of the IRS) determine the time path of after-tax income that will be earned by the team. Under scenario C, in contrast, the payoff to any owner depends crucially on how much the next owner will be willing to pay for the team. Scenario C is an extreme "rational expectations" scenario, in the sense that each owner in turn expects that the next owner will be willing to pay the maximum full value of all future after-tax benefits from owning the team, to be obtained by selling it after the tax advantages are exhausted. Scenario C is best viewed as a way to estimate the maximimium payoffs that could occur from a buy-and-sell strategy, rather than as an estimate of what the actual market price of a team employing the tax shelter might be.

The first section of Figure 3.2 considers the case of a constant net cash flow from team operations of $1 million per year into the indefinite future. It is assumed that the market discounts after-tax income for the team at a 10 percent rate. The normal income tax and capital gains tax rates are equal to 28 percent, and the maximum allocation of the team price to player contracts is 50 percent.

Under scenario A, the market value of the team, the price that any investor would have to pay for the team, is $7.2 million. This arises because the team earns $720,000 per year in after-tax income, ad infinitum. Investing $7.2 million in a team that earns $720,000 per year in after-tax income generates an after-tax rate of return of 10 percent, which explains the price of the team when no use is made of the tax shelter. Given that other investments yield a 10 percent after-tax rate of return, no owner would sell a team yielding $720,000 per year in after-tax income for less than $7.2 million, and no investor would pay more for it than that. The market price of the team would be $7.2 million.

Under scenario B, the buy-and-hold scenario, the market value of the team is $8,090,000. With a maximum 50 percent allocation of the purchase price to player contracts, and with a five-year writeoff period, the owner can write off $809,000 per year of contract depreciation. This reduces the taxable income of the team from $1 million to $191,000, resulting in a tax of $53,500 per year (as compared to the $280,000 tax bill in scenario A). For five years, the team generates an after-tax cash flow of $946,500 per year. At the end of five years, the tax shelter has been exhausted, so from then on, the after-tax cash flow from the team is the same as under scenario A, $720,000 per year. The team earns an additional $226,500 of after-tax income for each of the first five years after the team is purchased, and this translates into an addition of $890,000 in the value of the team.

Under scenario C, the purchaser of the team assigns 50 percent of the purchase price to player contracts, writes them off for five years, and then sells the team to a new owner, who does the same. Interestingly, the value of the team under this scenario, while greater than in scenario A, the no tax shelter case, is less than in the buy-and-hold case. The reason for this is that under scenario B, the owner avoids paying capital gains taxes to the government, by the simple expedient of not selling the team and thus not realizing any capital gains. The buy-and-sell strategy of scenario C loses out to the buy-and-hold strategy because of all the capital gains taxes that each successive owner has to pay.

The situation is even more extreme when we look at the valuation of a team whose income is growing over time. In the second section of Figure 3.2, the assumption is made that the net cash flow from operations increases by 7 percent per year. All of the other assumptions remain unchanged.

A team operating with perpetual ownership without the tax shelter would have a market value of $24 million given a base (year 0) cash flow from operations of $1 million and a 7 percent rate of growth per year in that cash flow. The market value of the team would increase by 7 percent per year as well. Under scenario B, a buy-and-hold strategy employing the tax shelter would result in an initial value of $26,966,000, with the value of the team rising (at 7 percent per year) to $33,672,000 by the end of year 5.

A buy-and-sell strategy using the tax shelter would have an initial market value of only $17,928,000, even less than the value of a team operated without the tax shelter (but held by one owner in perpetuity). The reason that things are so turned upside down in the case of a growing cash flow from operations is, once again, the workings of the capital gains tax. With cash flow increasing each year, the value of the team increases each year whether or not the tax shelter is employed. The problem for a buy-and-sell strategy is that each five years, the owner must pay the government not only the capital gains tax that arose from the use of the tax shelter, but also the capital gains tax on the increase in the value of the team due to the rising cash flow from operations. The combination of the two makes selling a team so expensive an operation (in terms of tax costs) that the no tax shelter/perpetual ownership option is actually worth more than the after-tax income stream associated with the buy-and-sell strategy.

The numerical examples of Figure 3.2 are based on the tax rates adopted in the Tax Reform Act of 1986, with the tax code changes that were adopted in 1976. Figure 3.3 presents some comparisons with the situation in earlier periods.

In Figure 3.3, we compare the three scenarios, A, B, and C, under the tax rates and tax code prevailing, first, in the early to mid-1950s; second, during the late 1970s and early 1980s; and finally, after the changes adopted in 1986. The no tax shelter/perpetual ownership case is taken as the base for comparison, so the figures shown in the table are team values as multipliers of that case.

In the case of a constant stream of income, Figure 3.3 shows that between 1950 and the mid-1950s, a buy-and-hold strategy using the tax shelter would roughly double the value of the team, while a buy-and-sell strategy (once the tax shelter is exhausted) would lead to a fivefold increase in the value of the team. This bias in favor of fast turnovers of franchises during this period reflects the high personal income tax rates (72 percent maximum) relative to capital gains tax rates (35 percent) for the period, and the high fraction of the value of the team assigned to player contracts (90 percent is used in the figure).

The period from the late 1970s up to 1986 was one in which it is assumed that only 50 percent of the value of a team gets assigned to player contracts, while the personal income tax rate is taken to be 50 percent and the capital gains tax rate is 20 percent. The tax shelter adds 25 percent to the value of a team under a buy-and-hold strategy, and about 55 percent under a buy-and-sell strategy, in the constant cash flow case. Thus, the incentive for quick turnover of teams was reduced substantially, relative to the earlier period.

Figure 3.3 Value of the Tax Shelter Relative to the No Tax Shelter, Perpetual Ownership Case, Various Periods, 1950–1990

Period	Constant Cash Flows from Operations			7% Growth Rate in Cash Flows from Operations		
	No Tax Shelter	Buy-and-Hold	Buy-and-Sell	No Tax Shelter	Buy-and-Hold	Buy-and-Sell
1950 to mid-1950s	1.0	2.04	5.18	1.0	2.04	*
Late 1970s to 1986	1.0	1.25	1.54	1.0	1.25	7.58
After 1986	1.0	1.12	1.07	1.0	1.12	.75

Note: Asterisk indicates that value is limited only by amount of outside income available to owner for tax sheltering.

After 1986, as we have seen from the earlier example in Figure 3.2, the buy-and-hold strategy actually makes more sense from the point of view of tax avoidance than does the quick turnover strategy. Moreover, the value of the tax shelter has been reduced to only a 12 percent advantage over the no tax shelter/perpetual ownership scenario, again assuming a constant cash flow from operations of the team.

The second section of the figure gives the effects of the tax shelter in a world in which the cash flow from operations is increasing at 7 percent per year. The numbers in the buy-and-hold column are unchanged from the constant cash flow case—the percentagewise advantages of the tax shelter are not affected by the rate of growth of cash flow form operations.

In contrast, in the earliest period, covering the early to mid-1950s, the buy-and-sell strategy was so productive of after-tax income that the only limit imposed on the value of this approach arises from the amount of outside income available for tax sheltering. Even after the 1976 change in the tax code, reducing the allocation to player contracts to 50 percent, buy-and-sell maintains a substantial advantage over the buy-and-hold strategy. The 1986 change completely reversed the earlier situations, with the capital gains tax acting to wipe out the payoffs from the buy-and-sell approach.

As noted earlier, the uncertainties inherent in team operations, and in tax rates and the tax shelter itself, mean that the precise figures shown in Figure 3.3 should be taken with a grain of salt. What they do show, however, is that the incentives for rapid turnover of franchises decreased following the tax code changes of 1976, and even more so, following the changes in 1986. Moreover, the figures certainly indicate that the provision of the Tax Reform Act of 1986 that equated the normal income tax rate and the capital gains tax rate reduced the importance of the tax shelter to owners to something that accounts for only a relatively minor fraction of the value of a franchise. After 1986, it is no longer true that sports teams should be viewed as "primarily" tax shelters—they are tax shelters, but the tax shelter accounts for only a little more than 10 percent of the value of the team.

The Record of Sports Leagues and the Tax Shelter

The history of the Veeck tax shelter suggests that franchise prices should have increased in the 1950s due to the higher after-tax return that could be earned from buying a team, and, as we have seen, there were incentives working in the direction of faster turnovers of teams in the period from 1950 through at least the mid-1970s, while the incentives to buy-and-hold were encouraged by the 1986 Tax Reform Act. What do the histories of the various leagues indicate about this?

Table 3.3 presents data on franchise sales for the four major team sports by decade from 1940 through 1990. With the exception of the NFL, all of the sports show an increased turnover rate measured by team sales/franchise year in the 1960s, relative to earlier periods, and they also show a dropping off of team sales activities in the 1970s and 1980s. In a general way, the record matches the developments in the tax shelter, changes in the tax rates, and changes in the tax code. In

Table 3.3
Franchise Sales, Including Expansion Franchises,
by Sports League, and Decade, 1940–1990

	1940–1949	1950–1959	1960–1969	1970–1979	1980–1990
BASEBALL					
Franchise sales	12	7	18	15	16
Existing	12	7	10	13	16
Expansion	—	—	8	2	—
Franchise years	160	160	198	246	286
Sales/franchise years	.075	.044	.090	.061	.056
NATIONAL BASKETBALL ASSOCIATION					
Franchise sales		6	15	28	25
Existing		6	9	23	20
Expansion		—	6	5	5
Franchise years		88	103	201	236
Sales/franchise years		.068	.146	.139	.106
NATIONAL FOOTBALL LEAGUE					
Franchise sales	8	6	8	1	9
Existing	7	2	4	5	9
Expansion	1	4	4	12	—
Franchise years	99	121	150	268	308
Sales/franchise years	.081	.050	.053	.063	.029
NATIONAL HOCKEY LEAGUE					
Franchise sales	2	2	10	31	11
Existing	2	2	4	21	11
Expansion	—	—	6	10	—
Franchise years	62	60	78	171	229
Sales/franchise years	.032	.033	.128	.181	.048

Sources: As in table 2.1.

particular, one way in which leagues exploited the tax shelter in the earlier years was by taking in expansion teams, which become better buys for prospective purchasers once the government had taken on much of the profit risk through the tax shelter.

Table 3.4 gives some rough estimates of trends in team prices by sport and decade between 1940 and 1990. There are so many factors at work affecting team prices that it is difficult to isolate the effects of the Veeck tax shelter, especially given that we do not have access to profit data for teams of this period. While the baseball data show roughly a doubling of franchise prices in the 1950s as compared to the 1940s, and NFL football data show a tripling of prices, certainly inflation, shifts in public tastes with respect to sports, national TV coverage of the major sports leagues, and other factors played roles every bit as important as that of the tax shelter in escalating franchise prices.

In a world in which there were perfect certainty that the tax shelter invented by Bill Veeck would persist into the indefinite future without challenge in the courts or in the Congress, franchise prices would have shown an immediate and abrupt escalation as soon as the tax shelter was known to investors. Under these conditions, we would expect the market prices of sports teams to rise to the point where all of the future after-tax benefits of the tax shelter would already be reflected in the prices of teams. What this means is that, despite the existence of the tax shelter, individuals buying teams after this point in time would not experience any "bonanza" in the form of higher than ordinary after-tax returns on their investments. Instead, the prices of teams would have been pushed so high that investors taking full advantage of all tax-

Table 3.4
Average Mid-Decade Franchise Prices, by League and Decade, 1940–1990

	1940– 1949	1950– 1959	1960– 1969	1970– 1979	1980– 1990
BASEBALL					
Avg. franchise price ($000)	$2,000	$4,000	$7,500	$11,000	$40,000
% change from previous decade		+100%	+87.5%	+46.6%	+263.6%
NATIONAL BASKETBALL LEAGUE					
Avg. franchise price ($000)		$250	$1,500	$6,500	$22,000
% change from previous decade			+500%	+333%	+238%
NATIONAL FOOTBALL LEAGUE					
Avg. franchise price ($000)	$200	$600	$5,000	$24,000	$70,000
% change from previous decade		+200%	+733%	+380%	+192%

Sources: As in table 2.1.

sheltering possibilities from team ownership would just earn a market rate of after-tax return on their investments.

There are several reasons why the market for sports teams didn't work that way. It took some time for investors to learn about the best way to exploit this tax shelter, and in particular, to discover how much of the purchase price of a team could be assigned to player contracts without getting a reaction from the IRS. More important, there was (in hindsight, justified!) uncertainty during the 1950s and 1960s on the part of investors, as to how long the IRS, the Congress, and the courts would permit the tax shelter to operate unchallenged. Among other things, the uncertainty posed by this in and of itself tended to encourage quick resale of franchises. It might well be that the court cases of the 1970s were on balance encouraging to owners, even though the valuations assigned to player contracts were cut in several cases, simply because the cases established that the courts were willing to accept the principle underlying the tax shelter. In connection with this, it should be emphasized that if efforts to cut capital gains taxes turn out to be successful in the future, the tax shelter will once again become an important aspect of team prices.

Concluding Remarks

In the congressional hearings in 1975, looking into revisions of the tax code to limit the benefits that owners could earn from the Veeck tax shelter, Commissioner Bowie Kuhn of baseball argued strenuously that baseball is not a tax shelter. As evidence of this, he noted the long tenure of ownership of many clubs, the number of teams that had been organized as ordinary corporations, and the long-term investments that had been made by owners in farm clubs and other activities. What his evidence showed was that baseball was not *just* a tax shelter—the game had been around for 100 years and would continue to be around whether or not the government closed all the tax loopholes that owners were benefiting from. But to deny that baseball, and the other team sports, have received special tax-sheltering treatment under IRS rules regarding player contract depreciation is to play footloose with the truth.

As we have seen in this chapter, after 40 years of the tax shelter, changes in the tax rules in the 1970s and 1980s have led to a major downsizing of its importance to sports, and this is a good thing, from the point of view of economics. The economy works best when investments are made on the basis of the market-determined rates of return that investments can earn, rather than on the basis of administratively determined tax breaks. This applies as much to sports as to any other industry.

The final irony of the tax shelter should be noted. Bill Veeck put lots of after-tax money in the pockets of owners who bought into teams from 1950 on. But Bill didn't use the shelter when he bought the Cleveland Indians in 1946—he hadn't invented it yet. And when he bought the St. Louis Browns in 1951, his syndicate was so short of money that it wasn't able to buy up the 75 percent control of the team needed to reorganize as a new corporation, so he couldn't use the shelter there. Then, when Veeck bought the White Sox in 1959, he bought into a family feud between Chuck Comiskey and his sister, Dorothy Rigney. Veeck's group offered to pay a premium to obtain Chuck's 46 percent of the team to go along with Mrs. Rigney's 54 percent, but it was no deal, and so once again, Veeck was not able to reorganize the team and revalue the player contracts. It was only in his last purchase of the White Sox in 1976 that Veeck finally made some use of the shelter, but by this time, of course, changes in the tax code and in tax rates had eliminated a lot of the tax advantages.

Moreover, because tax breaks tend to be capitalized into the price of assets, Veeck had created a monster of sorts. As he himself noted, the tax shelter he thought up is particularly attractive to very wealthy individuals. Because the price of a sports team tends to reflect the capitalized value of its after-tax earning potential to the best-paying prospective purchasers, Veeck found that the tax shelter he had invented was pricing middle-income hustlers like himself out of the market. It is sad to relate that the day when a guy like Bill Veeck could pick up a team like the Indians or the Browns for a song, and turn things around for the fans of some cellar team, is long gone—and in part because of Veeck's ingenious tax shelter.

Chapter 4

Stadiums and Arenas

THE TRUE sports fan not only reveres the memory of great players and great teams—he or she can wax poetic about the charms of the great and the not-so-great stadiums of the past as well. For the old-time Giants fan, there was the Polo Grounds, with its short foul lines, where a lucky pop fly could be a home run, and a monstrous drive to center could be just another out for Willie Mays. Brooklyn fans had Ebbets Field, one of the class of expensive brick and concrete stadiums built back in the pre-World War I days when $750,000 really meant a lot of money, with short power alleys and with the fans right on top of the action everywhere in the park. In downtown Philly right into the late 1930s, there was the elderly Baker Bowl, with the shortest right field fence in the majors, where a visiting outfielder easily could play a 270-foot fly ball off the fence into a triple. And in the western stretches of the state was the Pirates' Forbes Field, with its outfield like a huge pasture, although there was some cheating in later years in the form of Kiner's Korner (*née* Greenberg Garden) in left field. In fact, just about every one of the old ballparks had some distinctive feature that was exploited to the full in the player roster of the home team, and that made it an adventure and a challenge for any visiting team that played in the park.

Unfortunately, there are fewer and fewer stadiums in use today that legitimately can be described as memorable. With the passing of the original Comiskey Park after the 1990 season, and with Tiger Stadium scheduled for replacement, the only old-time baseball parks that are still classic favorites are Fenway Park, Wrigley Field, and, of course Yankee Stadium. Fenway Park was built way back in 1912, is cozy and compact, like a small-town park, seemingly is always packed with fans, and features the Green Monster out in left field. Wrigley Field was originally built for the Federal League Chicago Whales in 1914, and then was dressed up by those ivied outfield walls that Bill Veeck installed in the late 1930s. The park and Cubs fans were dragged, kicking and

screaming, into the era of nighttime baseball only in the late 1980s—
Phil Wrigley must be turning over in his grave! Yankee Stadium, the
"house that Ruth built," was one of the last built of the old stadiums.
It dates back to 1922, when it was constructed for the outlandish price
of $2.5 million—and then was refurbished in 1975 by the city of New
York for a mere $106 million or so more. With its vast outfield and
the monuments in center field (now off the playing field, though), the
Stadium is as awe inspiring today as it was when the Yankees really
had a "murderers' row" lineup.

Inevitably, ball parks age and deteriorate, and eventually the time
comes when it is a lot cheaper to tear down the old park and replace it
than to upgrade and modernize it. And it isn't only the deterioration of
the stadium that matters. In recounting the history of Shibe Park (Connie Mack Stadium), Kuklick (1991) points out the central role that the
deterioration of the neighborhood about the park played in the decision
to abandon it in 1971.

The old ball parks might have become decrepit and uncomfortable,
but they certainly had individuality. The wave of stadium building between 1960 and 1990 produced, in contrast, nondescript "cookie cut-
ter" clones, to use Michael Benson's (1989) phrase, parks that look
pretty much the same whether they are located in San Diego (Jack Murphy Stadium), or in Philadelphia (Veterans Stadium), or in New York
(Shea Stadium)—or in Los Angeles, where Dodger Stadium set the pattern that was followed in the rest of the country.

The new stadiums are, by and large, designed to be multi-purpose,
with football as much in mind as baseball, so they have much larger
seating capacities than did the earlier parks. Of more importance from
our point of view, with only a couple of notable exceptions—Dodger
Stadium, Joe Robbie Stadium, the Rangers' Arlington Stadium, and the
Patriots' Schaefer/Sullivan/Foxboro Stadium—the new stadiums are
publicly owned. (Most new arenas are also publicly owned, the exceptions of those built in the 1980s being ARCO Arena in Sacramento,
owned by the NBA Kings; the Palace of Auburn Hills, owned by the
Detroit Pistons; and the Timberwolves' Target Center, which opened
for play in the 1990/91 season.) And, while the new stadiums are much
more comfortable than the earlier parks, there is an impersonal quality
to them. The fact is that the stadiums themselves, save for Kansas
City's Royals Stadium, the new Skydome in Toronto, and Baltimore's
fabulous Camden Yards, are pretty boring.

But our main interest, of course, is with the economics of stadiums
and arenas and not with the esthetics. We want to examine the changing ownership status of stadiums and arenas, the role of stadiums in
the movement of franchises among cities, and the extent to which

teams are subsidized through favorable rental agreements with publicly owned stadiums. We begin our examination of these questions by looking at the current list of stadiums and arenas used by major league sports teams.

Current Lineup of Stadiums and Arenas

Table 4.1 lists the stadiums and arenas that were in use by major league sports teams during the 1991 season (1990/91 season for the NBA and NHL). The table identifies the ownership status (public/private), the date the stadium or arena opened for play, the seating capacity as of the 1991 season, and the use of the stadium or arena by major league sports teams (single or multiple major league use).

Table 4.2 summarizes the characteristics of the stadiums and arenas for each league in terms of ownership status, age, capacity, and use. The American League has the oldest collection of stadiums of any major sports league. In 1991, 6 of the 14 parks dated back to the 1950s or earlier, including the venerable Fenway Park (1912), Cleveland Stadium (1931), Tiger Stadium (1912), and Yankee Stadium (1922). The National League had a surge in attendance during the 1960s and early 1970s, accounted for in part by the stadiums that were built in the 1960s. Wrigley Field is the only NL park that dates back to before the 1960s. The old-timers in the NFL are Soldier Field (1929), the L.A. Coliseum (1922), Denver's Mile High Stadium (1948), and Cleveland Stadium (1931). In the NBA, Boston Garden (1928) is the oldest arena, with Chicago Stadium (1929) a close second. The NHL has a number of older arenas, with the classic Montreal Forum (1924) and Toronto's Maple Leaf Garden (1931) heading a list of old-timers that includes Chicago Stadium and the Boston Garden, along with the Colisee du Quebec (1940), Buffalo's Memorial Arena (1939), and the St. Louis Arena (1927).

What Table 4.2 shows is that as of 1991, stadiums and arenas in use by major league sports teams were overwhelmingly publicly owned—65 of the 84 stadiums and arenas in use (77 percent) were publicly owned. Stadiums are more likely to be publicly owned than arenas—37 of the 44 stadiums in use (84 percent) were publicly owned, while 28 of the 40 arenas (70 percent) were publicly owned. Stadiums are expected to last 40 years or more, and arenas not quite so long. The median age of stadiums in use as of 1991 was 25 years in the AL, 25 years in the NL, and 23 years in the NFL. The median age of arenas was 17 years in the NBA, and 23 years in the NHL. Of the six multiple-use stadiums in the AL, the Metrodome and the Kingdome are football stadiums used for baseball, while the others were designed originally for baseball. In the

Table 4.1
Stadiums and Arenas of Teams In Professional Sports, 1991

Team	Stadium/Arena	Public/ Private	Capacity	Opened	Use
NATIONAL BASKETBALL ASSOCIATION					
L.A. Clippers	L.A. Sports Arena	Public	15,561	1959	Sgl
Phoenix	Arizona Vets Memorial Coliseum	Public	14,461	1964	Sgl
L.A. Lakers	Great Western Forum	Private	17,505	1967	Mlt
Golden State	Oakland-Alameda County Coliseum	Public	15,025	1966	Sgl
Sacramento	ARCO Sports Arena	Private	16,440	1987	Sgl
Denver	McNichols Arena	Public	16,700	1975	Sgl
Miami	Miami Arena	Public	15,500	1988	Sgl
Orlando	Orlando Arena	Public	14,412	1988	Sgl
Atlanta	The Omni	Public	17,000	1972	Sgl
Chicago	Chicago Stadium	Private	17,458	1929	Mlt
Indiana	Market Square Arena	Public	17,300	1973	Sgl
Washington	Capital Centre	Private	18,000	1973	Mlt
Boston	Boston Garden	Private	15,509	1928	Mlt
Detroit	Palace of Auburn Hills	Private	19,259	1988	Sgl
N.Y. Knicks	Madison Square Garden	Private	19,212	1968	Mlt
New Jersey	Byrne Meadowlands	Public	20,149	1981	Mlt
Charlotte	Charlotte Coliseum	Public	23,300	1985	Sgl
Cleveland	Richfield Coliseum	Private	20,000	1974	Sgl
Portland	Portland Memorial Coliseum	Public	12,600	1960	Sgl
Philadelphia	The Spectrum	Public	17,973	1967	Mlt
Dallas	Reunion Arena	Public	17,000	1980	Sgl
Houston	The Summit	Public	15,964	1975	Sgl
San Antonio	HemisFair	Public	16,000	1968	Sgl
Utah	Salt Palace Arena	Public	13,078	1969	Sgl
Seattle	Seattle Center Coliseum	Public	14,229	1962	Sgl
Milwaukee	Bradley Center	Public	18,600	1988	Sgl
Minnesota	Target Center	Private	18,200	1990	Sgl
NATIONAL HOCKEY LEAGUE					
Boston	Boston Garden	Private	15,000	1928	Mlt
Los Angeles	Great Western Forum	Private	16,000	1967	Mlt
Hartford	Veterans Memorial Arena	Public	16,500	1975	Sgl
Chicago	Chicago Stadium	Private	17,317	1929	Mlt
Washington	Capital Centre	Private	17,000	1973	Mlt
Detroit	Joe Louis Arena	Public	20,666	1979	Sgl
Minnesota	Met Center	Public	15,200	1966	Sgl
St. Louis	St. Louis Arena	Public	17,700	1927	Sgl
New Jersey	Byrne Meadowlands	Public	19,000	1981	Mlt
Buffalo	Buffalo Memorial Arena	Public	18,000	1939	Sgl

(continued)

Table 4.1 (cont.)
Stadiums and Arenas of Teams In Professional Sports, 1991

Team	Stadium/Arena	Public/ Private	Capacity	Opened	Use
NATIONAL HOCKEY LEAGUE					
N.Y. Rangers	Madison Square Garden	Private	19,000	1968	Mlt
N.Y. Islanders	Nassau Veterans Memorial Coliseum	Public	16,200	1972	Sgl
Philadelphia	The Spectrum	Public	17,400	1967	Mlt
Pittsburgh	Civic Arena	Public	16,025	1961	Sgl
Calgary	Olympic Saddledome	Public	21,500	1981	Sgl
Edmonton	Edmonton Northlands	Public	17,309	1974	Sgl
Vancouver	Pacific Coliseum	Public	16,200	1966	Sgl
Winnipeg	Winnipeg Arena	Public	17,000	1952	Sgl
Toronto	Maple Leaf Garden	Private	16,316	1931	Sgl
Montreal	Forum	Private	18,300	1924	Sgl
Quebec	Colisée du Quebec	Public	15,300	1940	Sgl
NATIONAL LEAGUE					
Atlanta	Atlanta-Fulton County Stadium	Public	53,043	1964	Mlt
Chicago	Wrigley Field	Private	37,741	1914	Sgl
Cincinnati	Riverfront Stadium	Public	51,786	1970	Mlt
Houston	Astrodome	Public	45,011	1965	Mlt
Los Angeles	Dodger Stadium	Private	56,000	1962	Sgl
Montreal	Stade Olympique	Public	59,149	1977	Mlt
N.Y. Mets	Shea Stadium	Public	55,101	1964	Sgl
Philadelphia	Veterans Stadium	Public	56,581	1971	Mlt
Pittsburgh	Three Rivers Stadium	Public	50,235	1970	Mlt
St. Louis	Busch Memorial Stadium	Private	53,029	1966	Sgl
San Diego	Jack Murphy Stadium	Public	59,192	1967	Mlt
San Francisco	Candlestick Park	Public	59,083	1960	Mlt
AMERICAN LEAGUE					
Baltimore	Memorial Stadium	Public	54,076	1950	Sgl
Boston	Fenway Park	Private	33,583	1912	Sgl
California	Anaheim Stadium	Public	65,158	1966	Mlt
Chicago	Comiskey Park	Public	44,702	1991	Sgl
Cleveland	Municipal Stadium	Public	77,797	1931	Mlt
Detroit	Tiger Stadium	Public	54,220	1912	Sgl
Kansas City	Royals Stadium	Public	40,762	1973	Sgl
Milwaukee	County Stadium	Public	53,192	1950	Mlt
Minnesota	Metrodome	Public	55,122	1982	Mlt
New York	Yankee Stadium	Public	55,101	1922	Sgl
Oakland	Oakland-Alameda County Coliseum	Public	48,621	1966	Mlt
Seattle	Kingdome	Public	59,438	1976	Mlt
Texas	Arlington Stadium	Private	43,508	1964	Sgl
Toronto	Skydome	Public[a]	49,500	1989	Mlt

(continued)

Table 4.1 (cont.)
Stadiums and Arenas of Teams In Professional Sports, 1991

Team	Stadium/Arena	Public/ Private	Capacity	Opened	Use
NATIONAL FOOTBALL LEAGUE					
San Diego	Jack Murphy Stadium	Public	60,750	1967	Mlt
Phoenix	Sun Devil Stadium	Public	73,248	1958	Sgl
L.A. Rams	Anaheim Stadium	Public	67,000	1966	Mlt
L.A. Raiders	L.A. Coliseum	Public	92,514	1922	Sgl
San Francisco	Candlestick Park	Public	62,000	1960	Mlt
Denver	Mile High Stadium	Public	76,123	1948	Sgl
Washington	RFK Memorial Stadium	Public	57,497	1961	Sgl
Miami	Joe Robbie Stadium	Private	75,000	1987	Sgl
Tampa Bay	Tampa Stadium	Public	74,317	1966	Sgl
Atlanta	Atlanta-Fulton County Coliseum	Public	60,700	1964	Mlt
Chicago	Soldier Field	Public	67,000	1929	Sgl
Indianapolis	Hoosier Dome	Public	61,000	1984	Sgl
New Orleans	Superdome	Public	72,968	1975	Sgl
New England	Foxboro Stadium	Private	60,000	1970	Sgl
Detroit	Pontiac Silverdome	Public	80,635	1975	Sgl
Minnesota	Metrodome	Public	63,500	1982	Mlt
Kansas City	Arrowhead Stadium	Public	78,097	1972	Sgl
N.Y. Jets	Giants Stadium	Public	77,000	1976	Mlt
N.Y. Giants	Giants Stadium	Public	77,000	1976	Mlt
Buffalo	Rich Stadium	Public	80,290	1973	Sgl
Cincinnati	Riverfront Stadium	Public	59,755	1970	Mlt
Cleveland	Municipal Stadium	Public	80,032	1931	Mlt
Philadelphia	Veterans Stadium	Public	66,943	1971	Mlt
Pittsburgh	Three Rivers Stadium	Public	60,000	1971	Mlt
Houston	Astrodome	Public	70,000	1965	Mlt
Dallas	Texas Stadium	Public	73,855	1971	Sgl
Seattle	Kingdome	Public	70,000	1976	Mlt
Green Bay	Lambeau Field	Public	59,000	1957	Sgl
	County Stadium	Public	56,531	1950	Mlt

Sources: League guides, team media guides, and other publications.
[a]Skydome sold to private interests in early 1992.

NL, all of the multiple-use parks were originally designed for baseball. Capacity expansions since original design, however, have altered the character of a number of the stadiums, including Jack Murphy Stadium, Candlestick Park, and Anaheim Stadium, in favor of football at the expense of baseball viewing.

Table 4.2
Characteristics of Stadiums and Arenas In Use, 1991

	No.	Public	Private	80s	70s	60s	Older	Capacity			Use	
								Minimum	Maximum	Median	Sgl	Mlt
AL	14	12	2	3	2	3	6	33,583	77,797	53,669	7	7
NL	12	9	3	0	4	7	1	37,741	59,192	54,072	4	8
NFL	28	26	2	2	10	9	7	56,531	92,514	70,000	17	11
NBA	26	17	9	8	6	9	3	12,600	24,000	16,850	20	6
NHL	20	13	7	2	5	6	7	15,200	21,500	17,000	14	6

Sources: As in Table 4.1.

Note: Stadiums or arenas listed as opened in the 1980s include those opened in 1990 or 1991.

Changes in Stadiums and Arenas over Time

Changes in the stadium/arena market are among the most important factors that have improved the profitability of pro sports teams over time. In the era just after World War II, most major league teams in all sports played in privately owned stadiums or arenas. Most NFL teams played in baseball parks that were owned by baseball teams; and among major league baseball teams, only Cleveland played in a publicly owned stadium. NHL teams played in privately owned arenas, and about half of the NBA teams also played in privately owned arenas.

The stadiums and arenas were a lot smaller than those in use now. The NBA Fort Wayne Zollner Pistons played on a high school court, and several of the small-town NBA teams fit their schedules around those of the colleges whose arenas they were using. Moreover, the NBA was something of a traveling circus during its earlier years, frequently drumming up trade by scheduling regular league games in hotbeds of basketball interest, such as Bismarck, North Dakota, or Dubuque, Iowa.

NFL teams scheduled their games to avoid conflicts with their baseball landlords. Those were the days of natural grass playing fields, of course, when using a baseball field for football created major maintenance problems. Traditionally, the Bears didn't start their home season in Wrigley Field until the Cubs' season was over, and the NFL Giants also had late home season openings in the Polo Grounds. To compensate (and to take advantage of the weather), the Packers always began their NFL season with three or four home games in a row, going on the road for late season games.

By way of contrast with the situation in 1991, Table 4.3 lists the stadi-

Table 4.3
Stadiums and Arenas of Major League Teams, 1950

Team	Stadium	Public/Private	Capacity	Use
NATIONAL BASKETBALL ASSOCIATION				
Baltimore	Baltimore Coliseum	Private	4,500	Sgl
Boston	Boston Garden	Private	15,509	Mlt
New York	Madison Square Garden	Private	18,000	Mlt
Philadelphia	Convention Hall	Public	12,000	Sgl
Syracuse	Fair Grounds Coliseum	Public	7,500	Sgl
Washington	Uline Arena	Private	13,000	Sgl
Minneapolis	Minneapolis Auditorium	Public	10,000	Sgl
Rochester	Edgerton Park Arena	Public	5,000	Sgl
Fort Wayne	North Side High School	Public	3,800	Sgl
Indianapolis	Butler Field House	Private	17,000	Sgl
Tri-Cities	Wheaton Field House	Private	6,000	Sgl
NATIONAL HOCKEY LEAGUE				
Detroit	Olympia Stadium	Private	12,500	Sgl
Chicago	Chicago Stadium	Private	16,666	Sgl
Boston	Boston Garden	Private	13,500	Mlt
Montreal	The Forum	Private	13,201	Sgl
Toronto	Maple Leaf Garden	Private	12,586	Sgl
New York	Madison Square Garden	Private	15,284	Mlt
AMERICAN LEAGUE				
Boston	Fenway Park	Private	27,000	Sgl
Cleveland	Municipal Stadium	Public	77,797	Mlt
Detroit	Briggs Stadium	Private	54,220	Mlt
Chicago	Comiskey Park	Private	44,492	Mlt
New York	Yankee Stadium	Private	55,987	Mlt
Washington	Griffith Stadium	Private	27,400	Mlt
St. Louis	Sportsman's Park	Private	30,500	Mlt
Philadelphia	Shibe Park	Private	33,608	Mlt
NATIONAL LEAGUE				
Brooklyn	Ebbets Field	Private	31,497	Sgl
New York	Polo Grounds	Private	55,987	Mlt
St. Louis	Sportsman's Park	Private	30,500	Mlt
Boston	Braves Field	Private	40,000	Sgl
Philadelphia	Shibe Park	Private	33,608	Mlt
Cincinnati	Crosley Field	Private	29,488	Sgl
Pittsburgh	Forbes Field	Private	35,000	Mlt
Chicago	Wrigley Field	Private	37,741	Mlt
NATIONAL FOOTBALL LEAGUE				
Cleveland	Municipal Stadium	Public	80,032	Mlt
N.Y. Giants	Polo Grounds	Private	55,987	Mlt
N.Y. Yankees	Yankee Stadium	Private	67,000	Mlt

(continued)

Table 4.3 (cont.)
Stadiums and Arenas of Major League Teams, 1950

Team	Stadium	Public/Private	Capacity	Use
NATIONAL FOOTBALL LEAGUE				
Philadelphia	Shibe Park	Private	33,608	Mlt
Chicago Cardinals	Comiskey Park	Private	44,492	Mlt
Chicago Bears	Wrigley Field	Private	37,741	Mlt
Washington	Griffith Park	Private	27,400	Mlt
Los Angeles	L.A. Memorial Coliseum	Public	102,000	Sgl
Detroit	Briggs Stadium	Private	50,000	Mlt
Green Bay	City Stadium	Public	20,000	Sgl
	State Fair Park, Milwaukee	Public	32,500	Sgl
Baltimore	Memorial Stadium	Public	31,000	Sgl
San Francisco	Kezar Stadium	Public	60,000	Sgl

Sources: As in table 4.1.

ums and arenas used by major league teams in 1950. Table 4.4 summarizes the changes over time in the mix of private and public stadiums and arenas, and in the sizes of stadiums and arenas, between 1950 and 1991.

Table 4.4 shows that there was a rather steady increase in public ownership of stadiums and arenas for all leagues between 1950 and 1980. Then, in the 1980s, the St. Louis Cardinals bought title to the previously city-owned Busch Stadium, the Texas Rangers bought Arlington Stadium from the city (for the bargain price of $17.8 million), and, as noted above, the Detroit Pistons, Sacramento Kings, and Minnesota Timberwolves of the NBA built new privately owned arenas for their teams, while the Miami Dolphins of the NFL moved from the publicly

Table 4.4
Stadium and Arena Characteristics at Beginning of Decade
by Pro Sports Leagues, 1950–1991

League	Percentage Public					Median Capacity				
	1950	1960	1970	1980	1991	1950	1960	1970	1980	1991
AL	12	37	75	86	86	39,050	45,246	46,313	50,906	53,669
NL	0	50	67	83	75	34,304	35,370	48,880	54,072	54,072
NBA	46	62	71	76	65	10,000	11,219	12,800	16,000	16,850
NHL	0	0	42	52	65	13,350	15,907	16,485	17,000	16,867
NFL	36	60	81	96	93	47,246	47,300	59,327	68,500	70,000

owned Orange Bowl to the team-owned Joe Robbie Stadium. It is certainly too early to conclude that this signals a trend away from public ownership of stadiums and arena. In particular, in 1990, the city of Chicago bought old-time Comiskey Park from its private owners, in order to demolish the park at the end of the season to provide a parking lot for the new (publicly owned) Comiskey Park across the road, and Baltimore's publicly owned Camden Yards opened for the 1992 baseball season. However, the seemingly inevitable move toward complete public ownership of stadiums and arenas is no longer quite as inevitable as it appeared as recently as the 1970s.

Table 4.4 shows a steady increase in average (median) capacities of arenas and stadiums for all leagues since 1950 as well. But there are built-in limits on future increases in capacity. The problems of providing good sight lines for fans, and locating a maximal number of seats in optimal viewing positions, lead to natural limits on stadium and arena capacities, limits that differ among the various sports. A convincing argument can be made that the very worst stadium used by a major league baseball team in the modern era was a pretty good football stadium, the Los Angles Coliseum, which was the home of the Dodgers for their first four seasons in L.A. Those were the years when Wally Moon became a home run threat with his fly balls into the ever-so-close left field stands, which featured a foul pole just 251 feet from home plate. Benson (1989) reports that in 1958, the Dodgers' first year in the Coliseum, there were 182 homers into the left field stands, and just 11 anywhere else in the park, and things didn't change much in the next three years. The Coliseum had a seating capacity for baseball of 93,600, but both the Dodgers and their fans heaved a sigh of relief when the team moved to a legitimate ballpark in 1962, when Dodger Stadium, with a capacity of 56,000, opened. Several NBA teams—the SuperSonics, the Pistons, the New Orleans Jazz, and the Minnesota Timberwolves—have played in domed stadiums with seating capacities for basketball ranging from the mid-20,000s to 35,000 (Timberwolves in 1989/90). All of these teams abandoned their high-capacity arenas as soon as more conventional lower-capacity alternatives were available.

Stadium Construction, 1960–1990

When Lou Perini moved the Boston Braves to Milwaukee in 1953, one of the big attractions for him was the publicly owned County Stadium, built in 1950 for the Packers and the minor league Brewers. Baltimore built Memorial Stadium for the Colts in 1950, and this provided a home for the St. Louis Browns in 1954, when they became the new Baltimore

Orioles. In 1955, Kansas City bought up the minor league Blues' stadium as part of the deal under which Arnold Johnson, owner of the Philadelphia Athletics and the Blues stadium, moved the Athletics from Philadelphia to Kansas City. By the end of the 1950s, it had become an accepted fact of life in baseball that any city that wanted an expansion franchise or wanted to attract an existing team, would have to provide a stadium (at favorable rental terms) as part of the bargain.

Teams at the old established locations put a reverse spin on this, threatening to leave for greener pastures (that is, pastures piled higher with greenbacks). if their cities didn't build stadiums for them, too. Any thought that these were idle threats was forever put to rest when, after several years of increasingly vocal lobbying for a new stadium, Walter O'Malley pulled the Brooklyn Dodgers out of town in 1957, and took Horace Stoneham and the New York Giants along with him. Earlier moves had involved teams loaded with red ink, but the Dodgers were the most successful team in baseball, from a bottom line point of view—Brooklyn had accounted for 47 percent of the profits of the NL over the decade before the team moved. But the Dodgers moved, nonetheless, and while the city of Los Angeles didn't build a stadium for the team, O'Malley was given title to one of the prime pieces of near-downtown real estate as location for Dodger Stadium.

Mayors and city managers got the point. Beginning about 1960, local governments began to invest in stadiums to replace the older facilities owned by existing major league teams, in order to keep the teams in town. Table 4.5 gives a breakdown of the pattern of construction of

Table 4.5
Stadium and Arena Construction by Decade, 1960–1990

	1960–1969		1970–1979		1980–1990	
	No.	Capacity	No.	Capacity	No.	Capacity
AL	3	127,569	2	100,200	2	104,622
NL	7	349,240	4	217,751	—	—
NFL	10	556,244	10	678,139	3	195,755
NBA	9	140,083	6	104,964	8	143,660
NHL	6	99,825	4	71,425	2	40,500
Total stadiums	14	703,403	12	718,901	4	245,555
Total arenas	12	187,508	9	159,439	9	165,160
Total	26	890,551	21	878,340	13	410,715

Sources: As in table 4.1.
Note: Totals exclude double counting.

stadiums and arenas by decades from 1960 on. Included in the table are all stadiums and arenas constructed during the 1960–1990 period for any team that was a member of one of the five major leagues during that period.

To put these numbers in context, the total capacities of the various leagues as of the 1990 season were as follows: AL (14), 734,570; NL (12), 635,951; NFL (28), 1,935,755; NBA (27), 473,235; NHL (21), 362,933. Roughly, about 50 percent of AL capacity was built between 1960 and 1991, along with 60 percent of NHL capacity, 80 percent of NFL capacity, 85 percent of NBA capacity, and 95 percent of NL capacity.

Estimates of construction costs are not available for all stadiums and arenas built since 1960. However, on the basis of the data collected for this book (see the discussion later in this chapter), it appears that construction spending on new stadiums and arenas for major league teams in baseball, football, basketball, and hockey (most of it by local governments) was approximately $500 million in the decade of the 1960s, about $1.5 billion in the 1970s, and about $1.5 billion in the 1980s.

The decline in numbers of projects and capacity, decade by decade, shown in Table 4.5, and the flattening out of construction expenditures could be interpreted to suggest a slowing down in the 1990s in the construction boom for stadiums and arenas. This might be misleading. As of 1991, the following projects were on the planning board or already under construction: a $70,000,000 downtown arena seating 18,000 for the Phoenix Suns; an $85,000,000 Anaheim Arena seating 22,000 to attract NBA and/or NHL teams; a new ARCO baseball park for Sacramento; the 72,000-seating-capacity Georgia Dome to house the Atlanta Falcons; a $95,000,000, 22,000-seating-capacity facility to replace Chicago Stadium, to house the Bulls and the Blackhawks; a $150,000,000, 19,500-seating-capacity arena to replace Boston Garden, and provide a new home for the Celtics and Bruins; the $65,000,000, 18,000-seating-capacity Knickerbocker Arena in Albany, looking for an NHL team; a new $150,000,000 stadium to replace Soldier Field for the Chicago Bears; the $60,000,000, 20,000-seating-capacity Memphis Pyramid sports and entertainment complex; a $100,000,000 domed stadium for San Antonio, looking for an NFL expansion team; the innovative stadium at Camden Yards seating 46,000 for the Baltimore Orioles; and a $120 million stadium for Milwaukee to replace County Stadium, seating 50,000 for Brewers' baseball and 60,000 for Packers' football. In addition, Cleveland voters have approved a bond issue to finance a new stadium for the Browns and Indians, coupled with construction of an arena to attract an NHL team, and St. Louis voters have approved a multimillion-dollar convention complex that could be converted into a 70,000-seating-capacity stadium for an NFL team to replace the Chicago/St. Louis/ Phoenix Cardinals.

There are expansion plans for all five sports leagues. In fact, there is every indication that the boom in the sports business will carry with it a boom in stadium and arena construction well into the 1990s.

Impact of New Stadiums on Attendance and Performance

Major league teams in all leagues put enormous pressure on local governments to finance the building of new stadiums and arenas over the post-war years, and the pressure is continuing into the 1990s. An important payoff to teams is the increase in attendance that occurs at new stadiums, with accompanying increases in revenue and profits for teams housed in the new stadiums. To illustrate the impact of the new stadiums, Table 4.6 shows the changes in attendance associated with

Table 4.6
Attendance and New Stadiums, Baseball, 1960–1982

| | Year Stadium Opened | Five-Year Average Attendance (thousands) | | | League Average Change |
		Pre-Stadium	Post-Stadium	Change	
NATIONAL LEAGUE					
Cincinnati	1970	894	1,820	+926	+ 70
Houston	1965	790[a]	1,625	+835	+ 58
Los Angeles	1962	1,996	2,539	+543	+104
Montreal	1977	993	1,793[b]	+800	+323
N.Y. Mets	1964	1,002[a]	1,756	+753	+ 40
Philadelphia	1971	766	1,610	+844	+ 60
Pittsburgh	1970	895	1,340	+445	+ 6
St. Louis	1966	1,074	1,825	+751	+ 31
San Francisco	1960	1,348[a]	1,571	+223	− 2
AMERICAN LEAGUE					
California	1966	779	1,116	+337	+ 74
Kansas City	1973	804[a]	1,441	+637	+178
Minnesota	1982	947[b]	1,257	+310	+217
Overall avg.		1,017	1,641	+624	+ 96

Sources: League guides.

[a]Four years for Los Angeles and Kansas City, three years for Houston, and two years for the Mets and San Francisco.

[b]Excludes strike year of 1981.

the twelve new baseball stadiums that came on line between 1960 and 1982, and compares these changes with changes in average attendance per league team over the same periods.

On average for baseball teams, moving into a new stadium increased attendance by 62 percent—over 600,000 per year—during the first five years a team was in a new stadium, as compared to the previous five-year period. In contrast, on a comparable basis, average attendance for all league teams increased only 96,000 per year, and in every case listed in the table, the team moving into a new stadium showed a higher average attendance increase than did the league as a whole. The best results occurred in the cases of teams playing in stadiums that were obviously too small and/or too old—Houston, which moved from its temporary home in Colts Stadium (32,000 capacity) to the glamorous Astrodome; Cincinnati, which abandoned a tiny and rather decrepit Crosley Field (29,488 capacity) for Riverfront Stadium; and Philadelphia, which moved from old-time Connie Mack Stadium (Shibe Park) (33,608 capacity) to Veterans Stadium. The poorest results involved the Giants (the problems with Candlestick Park were discovered by the fans early on); the Angels, who suffered for years from that image as the second team in town; and the Twins, who moved from a great outdoor baseball stadium (the Met) to a domed football stadium that was marginal for baseball. When the Metrodome first opened, there was a theory that because of the dome and because part of the stadium was below ground level, it would be so cool inside that no air conditioning would be needed. It took only one hot, humid game to dispel this quaint notion, but it took a year for the Metropolitan Stadium Commission to come up with the $10 million to install air conditioning, and somewhat longer for the once-bitten, twice-wary fans to return to the stadium.

Part of the increase in attendance associated with the new baseball stadiums was due to the curiosity of fans, coming as much to see the new park as to see the team. And part of it reflects the fact that teams play better in a new stadium. Table 4.7 gives the won-lost performance records associated with the stadium moves shown in Table 4.6.

Table 4.7 shows that, on average, teams improved their W/L records over a five-year period by 35 points after moving into a new stadium. This amounts to winning five and one-half games more per year in the new stadium, which would involve moving up one or more places in the standings. A part of the explanation for the improvements shown in Table 4.7 is that four of the twelve teams involved—the Mets, the Astros, the Angels, and the Royals—were recent expansion teams, who would naturally improve over time through the draft. But even allowing for this, Table 4.7 still shows that most established teams who made a move to a new stadium increased their won-lost percentages.

Table 4.7
Effect of New Stadium on W/L Performance, Baseball, 1960–1982

	Year Stadium Opens	Five-Year Average W/L Percentage		
		Pre-Stadium	Post-Stadium	Change
NATIONAL LEAGUE				
Cincinnati	1970	.528	.590	+ 22
Houston	1965	.405[a]	.443	+ 38
Los Angeles	1962	.534[a]	.582	+ 48
Montreal	1977	.453	.528	+ 75
N.Y. Mets	1964	.283[a]	.375	+ 92
Philadelphia	1971	.474	.451	− 23
Pittsburgh	1970	.532	.549	+ 17
St. Louis	1966	.537	.549	+ 12
San Francisco	1960	.529[a]	.558	+ 29
AMERICAN LEAGUE				
California	1966	.474	.480	+ 6
Kansas City	1973	.462	.553	+ 91
Minnesota	1982	.466	.443	− 23
Overall avg.				+ 35

Sources: League guides.

[a]Four years for Los Angeles and Kansas City, three years for Houston, and two years for the Mets and San Francisco.

An economic argument can be made for improved performance at a new stadium, which goes something like this. A new stadium will tend to improve the drawing potential of a team, for a given roster of players. As makes sense intuitively (and from economic theory—see Chapter 7), the stronger the drawing potential of a team, the more a profit-maximizing team finds it worthwhile to spend in improving the caliber of the team. In effect, a new stadium converts a small-town market, such as Kansas City, into a market that is not quite so small as before, and the profit incentives this creates lead predictably to the team's acquiring higher-quality players, producing a better performance on the playing field, as indicated in Table 4.7.

Attendance and Stadium Capacity

The spectacular increases in attendance that occurred in baseball when new stadiums were opened cannot be extrapolated to the other sports. One of the unique characteristics of baseball is that teams rarely sell out their stadiums—in fact, in 1990, the only teams to sell out with any regularity were the Boston Red Sox and the Toronto Blue Jays, with the Cubs and the Athletics having the most success of the other clubs. Fenway Park (capacity 33,583) has the lowest seating capacity in the majors, with Wrigley Field (capacity 37,741) just behind, and the Blue Jays had just moved into the Skydome, where they were setting attendance records that might never be approached anywhere except in the Skydome.

In the other leagues, sellouts are the rule rather than the exception. For the non-baseball leagues, capacity is an effective constraint for most teams, and increases in attendance when a new facility opens, such as those displayed in Table 4.6, simply aren't in the cards, because new stadiums or arenas almost never boost capacity by as much as 60 percent. On the other hand, a new stadium or arena can increase profits substantially even when attendance does not increase a lot, through higher ticket prices at the new facility.

Table 4.8 gives the sellouts during the 1990 season (1989/90 for the NBA and NHL) for all major league teams, where a sellout is defined as attendance at a game that exceeds 90 percent of capacity. In baseball, only Boston and Toronto sold out a majority of their games. In the NHL, 16 of the 21 teams sold out more than three quarters of their home games, and only for Minnesota, New Jersey, the New York Islanders, and Winnipeg could a fan find tickets freely available for most games.

In the late 1970s and early 1980s, a number of NBA franchises were on the ropes. That situation had completely turned around by 1990. In the NBA, 14 of the 26 teams had virtual season-long sellouts in the 1989/90 season. These included the best teams in the league—the Celtics, the Lakers, the Pistons, the Bulls, the Jazz, the Trail Blazers, and the Spurs—but they also included some woefully weak teams, such as the Sacramento Kings, Miami, and Charlotte. And one team for which the sellout figures were misleading was the new Minnesota Timberwolves. Playing in the Metrodome, with a listed capacity of 35,000, the Timberwolves only sold out six times during the season, but still managed to set an all-time NBA attendance record in their first year in the league. The problem teams in the league, so far as attendance is concerned, were the New Jersey Nets, Washington Bullets, and L.A. Clippers.

In the NFL, only two teams had important attendance problems in the 1990 season—the New England Patriots and the Phoenix Cardinals, although Tampa Bay and Atlanta both were showing some weakness in season ticket sales.

All of this raises the question of why it is that in baseball, almost all teams have tickets available for all games, and in the other sports, most

Table 4.8
Sellouts 1989/90 and 1990 (percentage of all games)

AL and NL	%	NHL	%	NBA	%	NFL	%
AL		Boston	100	Atlanta	42	Atlanta	38
Baltimore	2	Buffalo	90	Boston	100	Buffalo	100
Boston	75	Calgary	95	Charlotte	100	Chicago	62
Calfornia	0	Chicago	80	Chicago	100	Cincinnati	100
Chicago	11	Detroit	100	Cleveland	32	Cleveland	75
Cleveland	0	Edmonton	95	Dallas	100	Dallas	0
Detroit	0	Hartford	45	Denver	32	Denver	75
Kansas City	14	Los Angeles	88	Detroit	100	Detroit	12
Milwaukee	2	Minnesota	22	Houston	98	Green Bay	88
Minnesota	1	Montreal	78	Indiana	23	Houston	0
N.Y. Yankees	1	New Jersey	38	L.A. Clippers	28	Indianapolis	62
Oakland	21	N.Y. Islanders	30	L.A. Lakers	98	Kansas City	62
Seattle	2	N.Y. Rangers	95	Miami	100	L.A. Rams	50
Texas	10	Philadelphia	100	Minnesota	15	L.A. Raiders	0
Toronto	86	Pittsburgh	100	New Jersey	15	Miami	38
NL		Quebec	100	New York	95	Minnesota	50
Atlanta	0	St. Louis	35	Orlando	100	New England	12
Chicago	33	Toronto	100	Philadelphia	24	New Orleans	75
Cincinnati	5	Vancouver	85	Phoenix	100	N.Y. Jets	12
Houston	0	Washington	100	Portland	100	N.Y. Giants	88
Los Angeles	0	Winnipeg	28	Sacramento	100	Philadelphia	100
Montreal	0			San Antonio	68	Phoenix	12
N.Y. Mets	0			Seattle	51	Pittsburgh	62
Philadelphia	2			Utah	100	San Diego	25
Pittsburgh	9			Washington	20	San Francisco	100
St. Louis	1					Seattle	0
San Diego	1					Tampa Bay	38
San Francisco	1					Washington	100

Sources: Game summaries, *Sporting News; New York Times.*
Notes: Sellout is defined as 90 percent of capacity or more. NBA and NHL figures for 1989/90 season; AL, NL, and NFL figures are for 1990 season. NFL figures exclude no-shows.

teams sell out all their games. Consider a profit-oriented team playing in a stadium or arena with a seating capacity denoted by K. The team faces a demand for tickets, as shown in the first panel of Figure 4.1. For simplicity, we assume the demand for tickets to be a simple straight line, which is labeled D. The demand curve, D, tells us, for any ticket price p, the number of tickets, t, that the team can sell. As indicated by the demand curve, D, the lower the ticket price, the more tickets the team can sell.

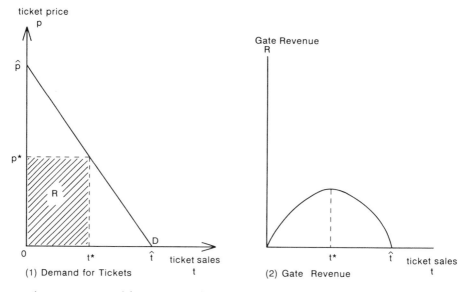

Figure 4.1 Demand for Tickets and Gate Revenues

Gate receipts revenue for the team equals the price per ticket, p, times the number of tickets sold, t. Graphically, this means that for any ticket price p and associated ticket sales t, revenue is equal to the area of a rectangle with vertical distance p and horizontal distance t. A revenue triangle is shaded in for $p = p^*$ and $t = t^*$. At a ticket price of zero, revenue will be zero, and at a ticket price of $\hat{p}$ (where D touches the price axis), revenue is zero as well. In panel 2 of Figure 4.1, revenue is graphed against tickets sold. By sketching in the revenue rectangles in the first panel, it can be verified that for a straight line demand curve, D, revenue is a maximum at the midpoint of the demand curve, D, at a ticket price of p^* and attendance (ticket sales) of t^*.

Suppose that the team operates under a rental agreement under which it pays a fixed percentage of gate receipts as rent for use of the stadium. Then, for a given roster of players, it is easy to verify that the team maximizes its profits by maximizing its gate revenue.

In Figure 4.2, the effect of stadium capacity on the choice of the ticket price and on attendance is shown. In the first panel, the stadium capacity, K, exceeds t^*. A team operated to maximize profits would choose a ticket price of p^*, sell t^* tickets, and would not sell out. In the second panel, stadium capacity is less than t^*. In this case, stadium capacity acts as an effective constraint on the team's choices. The team would prefer to set the ticket price lower and increase attendance (and revenue), but it doesn't have enough seats to accommodate a larger crowd. Hence, the team sets its ticket price at p^{**}, and sells K tickets, where K is the capacity of the stadium.

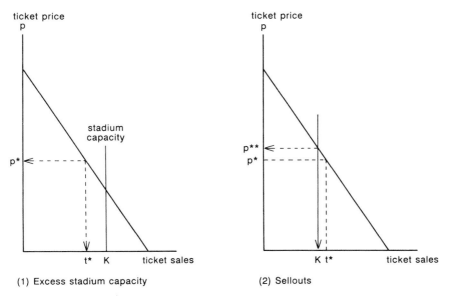

Figure 4.2 Effect of Stadium Capacity on Attendance and Ticket Price

Note that in the first panel, where there is excess stadium capacity, while decreasing the ticket price would increase attendance, the team would earn less revenue in that case. The team is already operating at the ticket price-attendance combination that maximizes its revenue. In the second case, if capacity were increased, the team could increase its revenue by lowering the ticket price. In neither case could the team gain by increasing its ticket price.

There are good reasons to believe that baseball teams are in the situation of the first panel in Figure 4.2, with "excess" stadium capacity, while the other sports are in the situation of the second panel. One reason for excess capacity of baseball stadiums is that most teams play in multiple-use stadiums, with capacity designed for football rather than baseball. When a stadium is designed specifically for baseball, as in the case of Royals Stadium or the new Comiskey Park, capacity is restricted, in order to bring the fans as close to the action on the field as possible. It appears that the ideal size of a stadium built solely for baseball is at or below the 45,000-capacity level, and this is simply inadequate for football. The consequence is that as cities have moved to multiple-use stadiums to save on construction cost, baseball teams have ended up in stadiums that are built too big for baseball. Another reason for the low number of sellouts in baseball is the length of the playing season—81 games are a lot harder to sell out than, say, 8, as in the NFL.

In any case, the point of all this is that attendance at sports contests reflects deliberate decisionmaking on the part of team management in setting ticket prices, together with the limitations, if any, imposed by stadium capacities. A reasonable presumption is that the observed ticket prices and attendance figures for pro sports teams are the best-informed guesses of management as to the combination that maximizes team revenue, subject to stadium capacity constraints.

Finally, a related question is this: how large a seating capacity should be built into a new stadium or arena, from the point of view of economic efficiency? The basic economics are pretty straightforward. Increasing the capacity of a proposed facility by, say, 1,000 seats has a more or less predictable effect on the construction cost of the facility. That additional construction cost would be economically justified if the revenue to be derived from the added seats more than covers the added construction cost. Since revenues will be earned over the entire lifetime of the facility, we have to discount such prospective revenues, year by year, back to the present to make them comparable with the addition to current construction cost, using a discount rate that reflects the cost of capital. Thus, if adding 1,000 seats increases construction cost by $1 million, and if we expect to sell out those seats 10 times per year at a ticket cost of $20 per seat, each added seat will generate $200,000 per year in added revenue. (For simplicity, we ignore any spillover effects of the added seating on revenues from other seats, say, due to changes in sight lines or in aisle spacing, and so forth.) Using a 10 percent discount rate, $200,000 per year over a 40-year stadium life is worth between $1.9 and $2.0 million today, so adding the seats would make economic sense.

When stadiums or arenas are built by team owners, presumably they will take into account just such calculations in making capacity decisions, so privately owned stadiums can be taken as the models against which publicly financed stadiums can be measured. The problem with publicly financed stadiums or arenas is that typically teams play a major role in making capacity and other stadium construction decisions, without being responsible for construction costs. This leads to "gold plating" of publicly financed facilities, including the construction of stadiums and arenas with excess capacities, relative to what would have been built under private financing. The consequences show up in the construction costs of publicly owned stadiums, to be discussed later in the chapter.

Stadium Rental Contracts

Making the move from an old, privately owned stadium to a new public stadium has the possibility of improving a team's profitability not only by increasing its attendance and revenue (and its performance, as indicated in Table 4.7), but also by decreasing its costs as well, through favorable rental agreements with the manager of the stadium. The fundamental fact of life concerning stadiums and arenas is that once they are built, they are fixed in place, while the teams that use them are potentially mobile. This puts an enormous bargaining advantage in the hands of teams playing in publicly owned stadiums. Teams can exploit their threat of leaving a city to wring out of the manager of the stadium rental agreements that leave the city pretty much holding the bag. A team can argue, persuasively, that the city should be willing to provide subsidized rental terms because of the income and jobs that the team generates for other businesses—hotels, restaurants, bars, downtown shops—by out-of-towners who are drawn into the city to see major league sports. This provides the political justification for rental contracts that often allocate as much of the costs of operating the stadium as possible to the city, and as much of the revenues from stadium operations as possible to the team.

By keeping franchises scarce relative to the demand for them by cities, leagues create an environment in which cities compete with one another for franchises. Competitive bidding by cities produces pressures to reduce rental rates in all cities to the lowest rates being offered by any city. As noted earlier, there are enough instances of teams pulling up and leaving, even from successful situations, that cities must treat threats to move as real. Just in the 1980s, the NFL has seen the move by the Raiders from Oakland to Los Angeles, the strange midnight move of the Colts from Baltimore to Indianapolis, and Bill Bidwill's move of the hapless Cardinals from St. Louis to Phoenix. The moves of the Raiders and the Colts occurred despite long histories of sellouts and financial and playing success.

In September 1985, the IAAM (International Association of Auditorium Managers) conducted a survey of its members as to the terms of the rental contracts between stadiums and arenas and professional sports teams. Tables 4.9, 4.11, 4.12, and 4.13 summarize the results of this survey, updated to reflect more recent contract terms as reported by the IAAM, *Amusement Business,* or *Sports Inc.,* when such information was available. Certain teams are not covered by the survey, including some teams playing in privately owned stadiums whose managers did not want to divulge contract information to the public, and some teams playing in publicly owned stadiums that they manage and operate under contracts with a city.

Looking first at the baseball information in Table 4.9, most rental agreements between teams and stadiums provide for a rental based on admission receipts, with the percentage varying between the zero-rent contract renegotiated (down from 7.5 percent) by Carl Pohlad for his

Table 4.9
Stadium Contracts, Baseball

Team	Stadium	Public/ Private	Admission Tax	Lease Date and Length	Escape Clause
Baltimore	Memorial Stadium	Public	10%	1990/2 yrs.	No
California	Anaheim Stadium	Public	No	1981/21 yrs.	No
Cleveland	Municipal Stadium	Public	Yes	1974/10 yrs.	Yes
Detroit	Tiger Stadium	Public	—	1978/30 yrs.	No
Milwaukee	County Stadium	Public	No	1970/25 yrs.	No
Minnesota	Metrodome	Public	10%	1989/10 yrs.	Yes
Oakland	Oakland-Alameda County Coliseum	Public	No	1980/14 yrs.	Yes
Seattle	Kingdome	Public	No	1985/3 yrs.	Yes
Toronto	Exhibition Stadium	Public	Yes	1976/15 yrs.	Yes
Atlanta	Atlanta-Fulton County Stadium	Public	No	1964/25 yrs.	No
Cincinnati	Riverfront Stadium	Public	Yes	1967/40 yrs.	No
Houston	Astrodome	Public	Yes	1962/40 yrs.	Yes
Montreal	Olympic Park Stadium	Public	Yes	1984/3 yrs.	No
Philadelphia	Veterans Stadium	Public	Yes	1966/30 yrs.	No
Pittsburgh	Three Rivers Stadium	Public	Yes	1970/40 yrs.	Yes
St. Louis	Busch Memorial Stadium	Private	Yes	1965/30 yrs.	No
San Diego	Jack Murphy Stadium	Public	—	1969/20 yrs.	No
San Francisco	Candlestick Park	Public	Yes	1958/35 yrs.	No

Team	Stadium Percentage				Rental Arrangements
	Food	Parking	Luxury Boxes	Other Concessions	
Baltimore	0	0	0	0	50% of team net operating income; averaged $1.5 million over 1980s[a]
California	90	50	—	—	7.5% of gate on first 2 million attendance, 10% over 2 million
Cleveland	80	100	0	17.5	8% of gate
Detroit	0	0	None	0	Rent ranges from $150,000 to $400,000 per year, on attendance[b]
Milwaukee	—	100	None	10	5% of gate, 1–1.5 million; 7.5%, 1.5–2 million; 10% over 2 million
Minnesota	10	100	See NFL	0	Zero rent
Oakland	40	62	None	0	5% of gate up to 1.45 million, rising to 8% over 1.9 million
Seattle	37	100	7	0	7% of gate to 1 million, 10% over 1 million

(*continued*)

Table 4.9 (cont.)
Stadium Contracts, Baseball

Team		Stadium Percentage			Rental Arrangements
	Food	Parking	Luxury Boxes	Other Concessions	
Toronto	38	100	100	0	7.5% of gate to 1.5 million, 10% over 1.5 million
Atlanta	42	100	0	0	5% of gate
Cincinnati	30	100	0	10	7.5% of gate
Houston	100	100	—	—	11.2% of gate
Montreal	—	100	100	0	6.5% of gate to 1 million; rising to 9.5% over 1.8 million
Philadelphia	64	100	40	0	10% of gate
Pittsburgh	30	100	100	0	10% of after-tax gate
St. Louis	0	100	0	0	7% to 10% of gate
San Diego	50	88	100	0	8% of gate
San Francisco	0	100	0	0	5% of gate

Sources: IAAM Professional Sports Lease Survey, September 1985; *Sports Inc.,* January 30, 1989, 49.
[a]In 1990 agreement, city allowed team to charge $2 million of interest as an operating expense.
[b]Team pays for stadium maintenance, estimated at $600,000 to $700,000 per year.

Minnesota Twins in 1989 (just after the Twins had set an attendance record for the AL!), through the favorable low contracts of 5 percent for Atlanta and San Francisco, up to the steepest rental contract, the 11.5 percent paid by the Astros to the Astrodome. (In fairness, it should be noted that there is a 10 percent ticket tax on Twins tickets, with all of the revenue from the tax being earmarked as income for the Metropolitan Stadium Commission, which operates the Metrodome and leases out Met Center to the North Stars.) Many of the rental agreements provide for a sliding percentage scale, increasing as receipts increase. The Detroit Tigers have a contract with the city under which the team pays a rent that varies between $150,000 and $400,000 per year, depending on attendance. This would be less than half the rent paid, say, by Atlanta or San Francisco. However, the Tigers also pay for maintenance and repair of Tiger Stadium, at a cost of around $700,000 per year, increasing their out-of-pocket stadium expenses to between $850,000 to $1.1 million per year, which is still a better than average deal for the team, offset, of course, by the age, location, and condition of the stadium.

Baltimore is the only team in major league sports that paid a stadium rental based on the profitability of the team. Under its contract with Memorial Stadium, the Orioles' rent was pegged at 50 percent of the club's net operating income (operating revenue minus operating costs). Over the decade of the 1980s, the Orioles' rent averaged out at a reported $1.5 million per year. The Orioles were sold in 1989, and the new owners took on a heavy debt burden to purchase the club under a leveraged buyout. When the stadium contract was renegotiated in 1990, the city agreed to permit the team to charge $2 million per year of interest as an operating cost, thus effectively decreasing the team's rent by $1 million per year, only partially offset by other changes in the contract.

The typical pattern of stadium contracts in baseball is one in which the stadium gets most or all of the revenue from parking, teams get most or all of the revenue from the sale of programs and novelties, and food and drink revenues are split, with between one-third and one-half going to the stadium and the rest to the team. There are a few cases in which luxury box revenues are captured by the stadium (Toronto, Montreal, Pittsburgh, and San Diego), but generally such revenues go mainly to the team, which often incurs the expense of building the boxes.

Concession revenues can be large, especially in the case of stadiums with large parking lots, and divvying up this income can be as much a bone of contention in contract talks as the rental rate. For example, Anaheim Stadium can generate up to $80,000 in parking revenue per game, and the Astrodome can bring in up to $75,000 per game. At the other extreme, the Metrodome has only a handful of parking slots, accounting for less than $4,000 in revenue per game. Non-parking concessions can be large as well. Table 4.10 gives non-parking concession sales for 15 teams in the major leagues, for 1988. Spending on food and beverages, novelties and souvenirs, and "other" (mainly banqueting services) averaged out to $5.91 per person attending a baseball game, a figure not too far below the average ticket cost for that period. Concession income available for sharing between the team and the stadium would be much less than this, of course, because the cost of supplying concessions has to be deducted from the gross sales figure.

Interestingly, only about half of the baseball stadium contracts provided an escape clause under which the team can abrogate the contract and leave the city if it draws less than some predetermined attendance for several years in a row. And most of the stadium contracts are for relatively long terms, although the more recent contracts tend to be for shorter lease terms than the earlier contracts.

Teams not covered by Table 4.9 include the Cubs, the Dodgers, the White Sox, and the Red Sox, all of whom played in privately owned

Table 4.10
Concession Sales, Selected Baseball Teams, 1988 (all figures in thousands)

Team	Attendance	Food and Beverages	Novelty Sales	Other Sales	Total Sales	Per Person Sales
AMERICAN LEAGUE						
Baltimore	1,835	$7,248	$923	$303	$8,474	$5.57
Boston	2,465	12,058	1,793	1,304	15,154	6.91
California	2,400	10,087	1,307	1,205	12,599	6.70
Chicago	1,116	6,253	—	62	6,315	6.34
Cleveland	1,411	5,569	881	517	6,967	5.13
Minnesota	3,031	11,243	—	—	11,243	3.71
New York	2,600	15,200	3,000	1,800	20,000	8.89
Seattle	1,022	2,913	564	785	4,261	4.59
NATIONAL LEAGUE						
Atlanta	1,061	$4,064	$ —	$124	$4,188	$4.94
Chicago	2,089	11,353	2,195	693	14,241	6.71
Cincinnati	2,482	9,830	1,669	243	11,742	5.17
Houston	2,116	8,417	1,074	1,340	10,832	5.60
New York	3,048	17,900	4,860	2,690	25,450	8.35
Philadelphia	1,990	8,311	1,275	1,921	11,506	5.44
Pittsburgh	1,875	8,147	1,265	—	9,412	4.57
Average	1,996	9,404	1,773	1,065	11,805	5.91

Source: IAAM Baseball Survey of Concession Sales.

stadiums. In addition, the Mets, the Royals, the Tigers, and the Yankees operate and manage the publicly owned stadiums in which they play, and they will not supply data on stadium operations. However, conversations with officials involved in supervising the Kansas City stadiums indicate that the total payments made by the Royals per year (presumably including rent and concession and parking sharing) is around $1 million, which would make the Royals' contract one of the better contracts for baseball teams.

NFL stadium contracts are more uniform than the baseball contracts, with most teams paying between 8 and 10 percent of admission receipts in rent, as indicated in Table 4.11. There are a couple of outliers here, however. The Indianapolis Colts pay only $25,000 per game (amounting to $200,000 for an eight-game season, plus $50,000 for two exhibition games), which works out to less than 2 percent of admission receipts— one reason that the Colts found it so easy to make the move to Indianapolis. Another outlier is the contract of the New Orleans Saints, who are charged only 5 percent of admission receipts, roughly half of the average rental in the NFL. The Superdome sweetened the Saints' con-

Table 4.11
Stadium Contracts, NFL

Team	Stadium	Public/ Private	Admission Tax	Lease Date and Length	Escape Clause
Atlanta	Atlanta-Fulton County Stadium	Public	—	1965/25 yrs.	No
Cincinnati	Riverfront Stadium	Public	Yes	1970/37 yrs.	No
Cleveland	Municipal Stadium	Public	Yes	1984/14 yrs.	Yes
Dallas	Texas Stadium	Public	—	1968/40 yrs.	No
Denver	Mile High Stadium	Public	Yes	1977/30 yrs.	No
Detroit	Pontiac Silverdome	Public	No	1975/30 yrs.	No
Houston	Astrodome	Public	Yes	1987/10 yrs.	No
Indianapolis	Hoosier Dome	Public	No	1984/20 yrs.	No
L.A. Raiders	L.A. Coliseum	Public	No	1982/10 yrs.	Yes
L.A. Rams	Anaheim Stadium	Public	No	1980/35 yrs.	No
Minnesota	Metrodome	Public	10%	1982/30 yrs.	No
New Orleans	Superdome	Public	Yes	1975/30 yrs.	No
Pittsburgh	Three Rivers Stadium	Public	Yes	1969/40 yrs.	Yes
San Diego	Jack Murphy Stadium	Public	Yes	1967/35 yrs.	Yes
Tampa Bay	Tampa Stadium	Public	No	1976/20 yrs.	No
Seattle	Kingdome	Public	Yes	1976/20 yrs.	Yes
Washington	RFK Stadium	Public	Yes	1960/30 yrs.	No
Chicago	Soldier Field	Public	—	ends 1999	—
Buffalo	Rich Stadium	Public	—	ends 1998	No
Green Bay	Lambeau Field	Public	—	ends 2004	No
N.Y. Giants	Giants Stadium	Public	—	1976/30 yrs.	Yes
N.Y. Jets	Giants Stadium	Public	—	1978/30 yrs.	Yes
Philadelphia	Veterans Stadium	Public	Yes	ends 2011	No
Kansas City	Arrowhead Stadium	Public	—	ends 1995	No
San Francisco	Candlestick Park	Public	—	ends 2008	No
New England	Foxboro Stadium	Private	—	ends 2001	No

			Stadium Percentage		
Team	Food	Parking	Luxury Boxes	Other Concessions	Rental Arrangement
Atlanta	100	100	10	50	10% of gate
Cincinnati	30	100	0	10	10% of gate
Cleveland	47	100	92	17.5	8% of gate
Dallas	84	100	0	100	8% of gate
Denver	100	100	8	0	8% of gate
Detroit	100	100	100	50	7% of gate
Houston[a]	50	70	0	—	9.5% of gate

(continued)

Table 4.11 (cont.)
Stadium Contracts, NFL

	Stadium Percentage				
Team	Food	Parking	Luxury Boxes	Other Concessions	Rental Arrangement
Indianapolis	100	100	58	0	$25,000/game
L.A. Raiders	83	None	None	—	8% of gate
L.A. Rams	55	50	20	0	7.5% of gate
Minnesota	90	100	—[b]	0	9.5% of gate
New Orleans	—	0	0	0	5% of gate
Pittsburgh	70	100	100	0	10% of gate
San Diego	90	84	0	0	8% of gate
Tampa Bay	—	—	20	0	$63,000/game
Seattle	70	100	55	0	10% of gate
Washington	100	100	None	0	12% of gate
Chicago	100	100	None	100	12% of gate
Buffalo	50	50	0	50	15% of gate
Green Bay	0	90	0	0	$150,000/year
N.Y. Giants	75	75	—	0	15% of gate
N.Y. Jets	75	75	—	0	15% of gate
Philadelphia	85	100	90	0	10% of gate
Kansas City	55	5	5	0	$500,000/year
San Francisco	50	42	20	0	10% of gate
New England	100	100	100	0	$1.2 million/year

Sources: IAAM Professional Sports Lease Survey, September 1985; *Sports Inc.*, January 30, 1989, 49.
[a]Team gets $1.05/person minimum as concession share.
[b]Metrodome gets $1 million/year, 1992–1996, $1.3 million/year thereafter.

tract substantially by assigning all of the parking revenue of the Super-dome (roughly $25,000 per game) to the Saints, who also get to keep all of the luxury box receipts as well, and much of the food and drink revenue. Since the Hoosier Dome keeps all parking revenues and 58 percent of the luxury box revenues, it is a tossup as to whether the Saints or the Colts have the best stadium contract, but there is no question that these two teams are the ones that have been most successful in their negotiations with their host cities. Other teams with favorable contracts are Tampa Bay, which pays $63,000 per game for use of the 72,000-seating-capacity Tampa Stadium, and gets to keep 80 percent of the luxury box revenues as well; the Kansas City Chiefs, who pay a flat $500,000 rental per year for Arrowhead Stadium, which they manage and operate (although there are indications that concession and parking revenue sharing brings the Chiefs' total payment to the city up to around $1 million per year); and the Green Bay Packers, who pay a rent of $150,000 per year (plus operating and maintenance costs of around $175,000 per year) for their four games in Green Bay. In contrast, the typical NFL team paid a stadium rental in 1990 of between $125,000 and $175,000 per league game. From the point of view of the team, the worst stadium contracts in the NFL are those of the Jets and the Giants at Giant Stadium (15 percent of gate receipts) and the Bills' contract at Rich Stadium, which also charges 15 percent. (However, Rich Stadium is operated by the Bills, so the actual cost to the team might be over-stated in the rental rate.) The Redskins also have a poor contract from their point of view, paying 12 percent of receipts in a relatively small stadium with no luxury boxes, and with RFK taking parking and food and drink revenues as well.

Except for Three Rivers Stadium, the Pontiac Silverdome, and the Hoosier Dome, luxury box revenues, when they exist, go to the team rather than the stadium. (Minnesota's Metrodome receives about 25–30 percent of the luxury box revenues from the Vikings, who built and own the boxes.) Luxury boxes are particularly desirable to NFL teams, because box rentals are not subject to the 60–40 gate-sharing arrange-ment of the NFL. As in the case of baseball, stadiums generally take parking revenues (the Superdome is a rare exception) and teams take program and novelty revenues. Stadium contracts tend to be long term, 20 years or more, and escape clauses are the exception rather than the rule.

Table 4.12 gives arena contract terms for NBA teams. In contrast to the NFL, rental terms in the NBA vary all over the map. At one extreme is the quintessential sweetheart contract possessed by the Charlotte Hornets, who will pay $1 per game as rent for the first five years of the team's existence, and then will pay a rent that varies between 4 and 8 percent of admission receipts, depending on attendance. At the other extreme is the Houston Rockets, who are charged a rent of 15 percent of admission receipts. Since the typical NBA game in or around 1990 drew from $200,000 to $300,000, a rental of 8 percent would amount to around $20,000 per game or $820,000 per year. This appears to be about an average rental for NBA teams, with Charlotte, Golden State, the L.A. Clippers, Milwaukee, Orlando, San Antonio, and Utah substantially be-low this level and with Houston and Phoenix significantly above the average. The expansion Minnesota Timberwolves operated in 1989/90 under a one-year, no-rent contract with the Metrodome, but, as with other Metrodome tenants, a 10 percent ticket tax is collected by the Metrodome, which acts as an effective 10 percent rental fee. The pat-tern of NBA contracts is one in which the arena gets parking revenues

Table 4.12
Arena Contracts, NBA

Team	Arena	Public/ Private	Admission Tax	Lease Date and Length	Escape Clause
Charlotte	Charlotte Coliseum	Public	—	1988/5 yrs.	—
Cleveland	Richfield Coliseum	Private	No	1989/1 yrs.	—
Dallas	Reunion Arena	Public	—	1980/12 yrs.	No
Denver	McNichols Arena	Public	10%	1986/17 yrs.	Yes
Golden State	Oakland-Alameda County Coliseum	Public	No	1986/5 yrs.	—
Houston	The Summit	Public	—	1987/5 yrs.	No
L.A. Clippers	L.A. Sports Arena	Public	Yes	1984/5 yrs.	—
L.A. Lakers	Forum	Private	Yes	—	No
Miami	Miami Arena	Public	—	1988/10 yrs.	—
Milwaukee	Mecca Arena	Public	—	1985/2 yrs.	Yes
Orlando	Orlando Arena	Public	—	1989/10 yrs.	—
Philadelphia	Spectrum	Public	Yes	1967/20 yrs.	No
Phoenix	Arizona Veterans Memorial Coliseum	Public	Yes	1981/12 yrs.	—
Portland	Portland Memorial Coliseum	Public	No	1986/10 yrs.	Yes
San Antonio	HemisFair	Public	No	1987/10 yrs.	No
Seattle	Seattle Center Coliseum	Public	Yes	1985/10 yrs.	Yes
Utah	Salt Palace	Public	Yes	1985/14 yrs.	Yes
Minnesota	Metrodome	Public	10%	1989/1 yr.	Yes

Team	Arena Percentage				Rental Arrangements
	Food	Parking	Luxury Boxes	Other Concessions	
Charlotte	100	100	—	100	$1/game, years 1–5; rent goes to 4–8% after year 10, based on gate
Cleveland	100	100	—	100	10% of gate (team owns arena)
Dallas	100	100	100	0	8% of gate
Denver	100	100	100	0	City is guaranteed $1,083,000 per year by team
Golden State	Sliding scale based on attendance				$41,000/year minimum; 6.5% of gate over 287,672 attendance
Houston	100	100	0	100	15% of gate
L.A. Clippers	50	100	—	50	$3,000/game

(continued)

Table 4.12 (cont.)
Arena Contracts, NBA

			Arena Percentage		
Team	Food	Parking	Luxury Boxes	Other Concessions	Rental Arrangements
L.A. Lakers	100	100	None	—	12.5% of gate (team owns arena)
Miami	53.5	100	$12,500 per box	0	$575,000/year, first 5 years; $600,000/year after that
Milwaukee	32	74–80	None	74–80	$4,400/game, 1986/87; rent free, 1987/88
Orlando	50	100	—	50	$7,000 minimum per game
Philadelphia	100	100	100	20	12.5% of gate
Phoenix	100	100	None	0	10% of gate
Portland	Team gets first $510,000; 50/50 split after that				$10,200/game
San Antonio	15	0	None	15	$205,000/year
Seattle	100	100	None	$5,000/year	8.5% of gate
Utah	50	85	None	0	7% of gate to $142,857; 3.5% above that
Minnesota	65	0	0	65	No rent

Sources: IAAM Professional Sports Lease Survey, September 1985; *Sports Inc.,* January 30, 1989, 49.

(which are much smaller than for baseball or football stadiums), most of the food and drink revenues, and most luxury box revenues, with the team getting program and novelty revenues.

Much less information is available concerning NHL teams. Table 4.13 shows that rental rates vary from the no-rent arrangement of the Pittsburgh Penguins (under a 99-year contract!) up to the 15 percent rental paid by the Philadelphia Flyers. The Minnesota North Stars, Winnipeg Jets, and Hartford Whalers have relatively low-cost rental contracts. The data in Table 4.13 indicate that the typical NHL contract called for roughly a 10 percent rate, which works out to around $25,000 to $30,00 per game, or roughly $1.1 million per year. The NHL pattern is one in which the arena takes food and drink and parking revenues and shares in luxury box revenues.

Stadium Finances:
Construction Costs of Stadiums

Michael Benson's authoritative monograph on baseball parks, *Ballparks of North America*, recounts in detail the stories of the parks used by all

Table 4.13
Arena Contracts, NHL

Team	Arena	Public/ Private	Admission Tax	Lease Date and Length	Escape Clause
Calgary	Saddledome	Public	No	1983/20 yrs.	No
Edmonton	Northlands Coliseum	Public	No	1984/5 yrs.	—
Hartford	Civic Center	Public	No	1982/10 yrs.	—
L.A. Kings	Forum	Private	Yes	—	—
Minnesota	Met Center	Public	Yes	1985/25 yrs.	Yes
Philadelphia	Spectrum	Public	Yes	1967/30 yrs.	No
Pittsburgh	Civic Center	Public	Yes	1979/99 yrs.	Yes
Quebec	Quebec Coliseum	Public	Yes	1980/10 yrs.	No
Vancouver	Pacific Coliseum	Public	No	1983/19 yrs.	Yes
Winnipeg	Winnipeg Arena	Public	Yes	1979/8 yrs.	No

Team	Arena Percentage				Rental Arrangements
	Food	Parking	Luxury Boxes	Other Concessions	
Calgary	100	100	50	0	$800,000 minimum per season
Edmonton	100	100	None	0	—
Hartford	100	None	0	20	0% on first $6 million; 5% of gate on $6–$7 million; 10% on over $7 million
L.A. Kings	100	100	None	—	12.5% of gate (team owns arena)
Minnesota			2% of gross receipts for rent		
Philadelphia	100	100	50	—	15% of gate
Pittsburgh	100	100	40	100	No rent
Quebec	—	—	100	0	8% on first $6 million; 10% on anything over $6 million
Vancouver	100	100	15	0	10% of gate
Winnipeg	100	100	100	0	6% of gate, $462,000 minimum

Sources: IAAM Professional Sports Lease Survey, September 1985; Sports Inc., January 30, 1989, 49.

of the major league teams over their history. The story of the Dodgers is more or less typical. Back in 1883, the Brooklyn Trolley Dodgers of the American Association built Washington Park, a wooden structure that seated 2,500 fans, for $30,000. The Brooklyn Superbas of the NL used Washington Park in 1890 and 1891, and then moved to Eastern Park, where they paid $7,500 per year rent. In 1898, owner Charles Ebbets talked two of the local streetcar companies into sharing the $60,000 cost of building a new Washington Park. The park was upgraded in 1908 for an additional $22,000, and ended up with a seating capacity of around 16,000, although many more could be squeezed into standing-room-only locations. The Dodgers played at Washington Park until 1913, when Ebbets Field was constructed at a cost of $750,000. The original seating capacity of 18,000 was expanded over the years, to a level of 31,497 in 1957. The expense of building Ebbets Field was so great that Charles Ebbets was forced to sell half the team in 1913 (to the McKeever brothers) in order to obtain the money to complete the park. Ebbets Field was the home of the Dodgers for the rest of their days in Brooklyn, although Walter O'Malley did schedule a handful of games at Roosevelt Stadium in Jersey City in 1956 and 1957, when he was feuding with the city fathers about a new publicly financed stadium for the team.

The Dodgers went west in 1958, and played in the L.A. Coliseum for four years. In 1962, Dodger Stadium opened, with a construction cost of $23 million, and a seating capacity of 56,000, on land donated to the Dodgers by the city, and the Dodgers have played there ever since, to great artistic and financial success.

Baseball stadiums were fairly simple, cheap, and impermanent wooden structures into the early 1900s. The growth of attendance following the AL-NL war (1901/02) generated a demand for larger structures, and team owners were looking for ways to avoid the costs of fires and accidental collapses that plagued the wooden stands. As Kuklick (1991) points out, a technological innovation came along just after the turn of the century to revolutionize heavy construction, and in particular to revolutionize the stadium construction business. This was the invention of reinforced concrete, with fireproofing qualities, durability, and strength that made possible the construction of much larger stadiums.

There was a veritable boom of stadium construction between 1909 and 1915, when 10 of the 16 major league teams replaced their wooden stadiums with spanking-new brick, steel, and reinforced concrete affairs, most costing between $250,000 and $750,000 each. This was the era that produced Braves Field (1915), Ebbets Field (1913), Wrigley Field (1914), Crosley Field (1912), Forbes Field (1909), Fenway Park (1912), Comiskey Park (1910), Tiger Stadium (1912), Shibe Park (1909), and Cleveland's League Park (1910). In the 1920s, the only new park to be built was Yankee Stadium (1922), although Sportsman's Park (1876) was completely refurbished in 1925 by the Browns, at a cost of half a million dollars. Cleveland's Municipal Stadium opened in 1932, costing almost $3 million, but it was so huge that the Indians continued to use League Park for most games right up to World War II, moving to Municipal Stadium only on holidays or other special occasions.

No stadiums were built for major league sports teams during the Depression, other than Municipal Stadium. In 1950, Milwaukee's County Stadium opened as a part-time playing field for the Green Bay Packers, and in 1953, the Boston Braves moved to Milwaukee as a second tenant at the facility. It was also in 1950 that Baltimore built its publicly owned Memorial Stadium for use by the NFL Baltimore Colts, at a cost of $6.5 million. In 1954, the St. Louis Browns/Baltimore Orioles moved into the stadium.

By the mid-1950s, most major league stadiums were 40 years old, near their life expectancies, and attendance was more than double what it had been when most of the parks were built. Moreover, the parks had been built in an era when fans came to the games in streetcars, and these had pretty much been displaced by the private automobile by 1955. To complicate things, the population was moving to the suburbs, while the stadiums were in mid-downtown, most with few, if any, parking spaces available, and in deteriorating neighborhoods.

Thus, the stage was set for the stadium-building boom that began in the 1960s, and has continued up to the present. A central ingredient was a simple replacement cycle—the 1960s produced a stadium-building boom as a kind of echo of the earlier boom during the 1909–1915 period, as those earlier stadiums all reached retirement age at about the same time. It was also during the 1960s that professional football came into its own as a spectator sport, drawing crowds on a par with the big college football teams. This radically changed the stadium design problem, and added to the demand for new facilities.

The stadiums that were built from the 1960s on were a lot more expensive than the stadiums they replaced. During the 1960s, Dodger Stadium (1962) was typical, costing $23 million; Shea Stadium (1964) ran $24 million, Busch Stadium (1966) cost $25 million, Anaheim Stadium (1966) cost $24 million, and Jack Murphy Stadium (1967) cost $26 million. The expensive stadiums for the 1960s were Candlestick Park (1960), at $32 million, and the Astrodome (1965), the first domed park, at $38 million. Atlanta-Fulton County Coliseum (1964) was the bargain, costing $18 million.

The stadiums built in the 1909–1915 period averaged out at about $500,000 each, while those built in the 1960s ran about $25 million each. Based on the *Engineering News-Record* index of construction costs, inflation in the construction industry increased costs in the 1960s to about 11 times their levels in 1915, so that a stadium costing $500,000 in 1915 dollars would have cost about $5.5 million in 1965 dollars. The high price tags of the stadiums built in the 1960s reflected much more than inflation of construction costs. The new stadiums were much larger inside and outside, typically encompassed additional acres of parking space, and were considerably more elaborate and elegant facilities than the parks they replaced.

In the 1970s, costs of stadiums went up another notch to the $50 million and above range. Three Rivers Stadium (1970) and Veterans Stadium (1971) came in at $50 million each, Riverfront Stadium (1970) cost $45 million, and the Pontiac Silverdome (1975) cost $56 million. Kansas City's Arrowhead Stadium (1972) cost $53 million, Giants Stadium (1976) came in at $68 million, and the Kingdome (1977) cost $67 million.

There were two steals—Rich Stadium (1973), built for $22 million, and the Patriots Schaefer/Sullivan/Foxboro Stadium (1970), a 60,000-seating-capacity facility that cost a miniscule $6.7 million. Interestingly, both of these parks were built by the same contractor. The Patriots' stadium was a throwback to the stadiums of the far-distant past, a bare bones edifice that was built with private rather than public money, and with infinite care taken to keep costs to a minimum and to exploit every opportunity to pass along to someone else any costs that simply had to be paid. Among other things, the name of the stadium was leased to the Schaefer Co., the stadium scoreboard was acquired for free under another leasing arrangement providing advertising privileges in the stadium for the donor, and the original artificial turf was donated by a company trying to break into the stadium supply field. The cost containment story of the stadium should be studied by anyone who thinks that the free enterprise system and private incentives can't work to keep costs down.

There were some true financial horror stories in the 1970s as well, all involving publicly funded stadiums. The first was the Louisiana Superdome (1975), which was a classic case of a construction project where political interference led to a situation in which costs got completely out of control. The initial cost estimate of the Superdome was in the $40 million range, and the final cost was at or near $168 million. A second involved the refurbishing of Yankee Stadium, undertaken by the city of New York to keep the AL Yankees in town. This project had an original cost estimate of $23 million, and ran up a bill of $106 million by the time it was finished. However, as scandalous as the problems of the Superdome and Yankee Stadium were, they were dwarfed by what happened in Montreal when labor problems and tight delivery schedules required for the 1976 Olympics pushed the price of the Stade Olympique (1976) to an incredible $770 million in Canadian dollars, roughly U.S. $620 million.

On average, stadium costs rose from about $25 milion per stadium in the 1960s, to around $55 million per stadium in the 1970s. This increase corresponds rather closely to the inflation in general construction costs over that period.

Four stadiums were built in the 1980s—the Metrodome (1982), built for a "bargain price" of $62 million (including the $10 million air conditioning add-on) under a unique labor-management cost control accord; the Hoosier Dome (1984), for $77 million; Joe Robbie Stadium (1987), for $100 million; and the Toronto Skydome (1989), with a complex of associated hotels, restaurants, and shops that brought the price tag to $532 million in Canadian dollars. Construction costs doubled between 1975 and 1987; thus, once again, inflation accounts for most of the rise in price between the construction of, say, the $68 million Giants Stadium (1976) and the $100 million Joe Robbie Stadium (1987).

As noted earlier, a number of stadiums were in the planning stages or under construction in the early 1990s, with price tags mainly in the $125 million and up range.

Much less information is available concerning the construction costs of arenas. The older generation of arenas, built for hockey and general entertainment, came on line in the 1920s. This included the old Madison Square Garden in New York City (1925), the Montreal Forum (1924), Detroit's Olympia Stadium, Boston Garden (1928), and Chicago Stadium (1929). The cost of Chicago Stadium was $7 million, and Olympia Stadium cost $2.5 million. In the 1930s, Maple Leaf Garden (1931) opened (cost $1.2 million), and Buffalo built its Memorial Arena (1939) for its minor league hockey team.

The first of the post-war arenas to be built for major league hockey and/or basketball teams was the $5.9 million L.A. Sports Arena (1959), which smoothed the way for Bob Short's move of the Lakers from Minneapolis to Los Angeles after the 1959/60 season. Jack Kent Cooke's fight with Los Angeles County over rental terms at the Sports Arena led to his building the L.A. Forum (1967), at a cost of $16.7 million. Other major arenas built in the 1960s include the Oakland-Alameda County Coliseum Arena (1966), which housed ABA and NHL teams, the rebuilt Madison Square Garden (1968) which, with associated office space, cost $133 million, Portland's Memorial Coliseum (1960), San Antonio's HemisFair (1968), the $17 million Salt Palace Arena (1969), the Seattle Center Coliseum (1962), the Twin Cities' Met Center (1966), the Spectrum in Philadelphia (1967), Pittsburgh's innovative and expensive ($22 million) Civic Arena (1961), and Vancouver's Pacific Coliseum (1966).

In the 1970s, the privately financed Richfield Coliseum (1974) and the Capital Centre (1973) opened. Public facilities included the Omni (1972) in Atlanta, Denver's McNichols Arena (1975), the Indianapolis Market Square Arena (1973), the Summit (1975), Hartford's Memorial

Arena (1975), Joe Louis Arena (1979), and the Edmonton Northlands (1974). The Richfield Coliseum complex cost $45 million, the Omni cost $17 million, McNichols Arena came in at $13 million, and Joe Louis Arena had a $27 million construction cost.

In the 1980s, two privately financed arenas opened—the ARCO Sports Arena (1987) in Sacramento; and the Palace of Auburn Hills (1988), which cost $70 million. Public facilities included the Miami Arena (1988), for $50 million, the Orlando Arena complex (1988), for $110 million, New Jersey's Byrne Meadowlands Arena (1981), built for $85 million, Milwaukee's Bradley Center (1988) for $53 million, and the Charlotte Coliseum (1985), at $55 million. The Timberwolves' Target Center Arena opened in 1990, with a construction cost of around $93 million. Clearly the escalation in stadium building costs has carried over into arena construction as well.

Table 4.14 presents data on original construction cost for stadiums and arenas in use by major league teams during the 1990 season (1989/90 for NBA and NHL teams), where available, as well as data on costs of earlier stadiums. Data are shown in current dollars (as of the date of construction) and also, for comparative purposes, in 1989 dollars, based on the *Engineering News-Record* index of general construction costs to adjust for inflation. In addition, cost estimates for major refurbishments and enlargements of stadiums are shown, where available.

Stadium Finances— Operating Revenues and Costs

Publicly owned stadiums and arenas are operated under a variety of management arrangements. In some cases, the city or the state sets up a commission that manages and operates the facility, and the team is simply a tenant. This is the case, for example, with the Metrodome in Minneapolis, operated by the Metropolitan Stadium Commission, with 1991/92 tenants consisting of the AL Minnesota Twins, the NFL Minnesota Vikings, and the NCAA Minnesota Gophers. In recent years, an increasingly common setup has been one in which the locality hires a stadium management corporation, such as Spectacor, to act as its agent in operating the facility and in dealing with the team and other users of the facility. The L.A. Coliseum and Sports Arena are managed in this way, as are Three Rivers Stadium and the Pittsburgh Civic Center. Another common management arrangement is one in which the city or state owns the facility, but the team manages and operates the facility under a rental and/or revenue-sharing agreement, with the team re-

Table 4.14
Stadium and Arena Construction Costs in Current and 1989 Dollars,
Selected Stadiums and Arenas (thousands of dollars)

Facility	Year Opened	Cost Current Dollars	Cost 1989 Dollars
Baker Bowl	1894	120	—
Hilltop Park, N.Y.	1903	75	—
Forbes Field	1909	2,000	—
Shibe Park	1909	368	—
Comiskey Park	1910	750	—
Crosley Field	1912	225	—
Tiger Stadium	1912	500	—
Ebbets Field	1913	750	—
Wrigley Field	1914	250	—
Yankee Stadium	1922	2,500	64,000
L.A. Coliseum	1922	955	24,000
K.C. Municipal Stadium	1923	400	8,300
Sportsman's Park (refurb.)	1925	500	10,900
Wrigley Field, L.A.	1925	1,100	23,900
Comiskey Park (refurb.)	1926	1,000	21,700
Olympic Arena, Detroit	1927	2,500	54,300
Soldier Field	1929	7,900	171,700
Seals Stadium, Seattle	1931	600	15,000
L.A. Coliseum (refurb.)	1931	951	23,800
Maple Leaf Garden	1931	1,200	30,000
Cleveland Municipal Stadium	1931	3,000	75,000
Exhibition Stadium, Toronto	1947	3,000	15,000
Baltimore Memorial Stadium	1950	6,500	57,000
Braves Field (sale)	1952	450	3,500
Sportsman's Park (sale)	1953	800	6,000
K.C. Municipal Stadium (sale)	1955	650	4,400
Met Stadium, Bloomington	1956–1961	8,500	50,300
Lambeau Field	1957	969	6,000
L.A. Sports Arena	1959	5,000	24,000
Candlestick Park	1960	32,000	174,800
Pittsburgh Civic Arena	1961	22,000	99,100
Colt Stadium, Houston	1962	2,000	10,300
Dodger Stadium	1962	23,000	118,600
Arlington Stadium	1964	19,000	51,100
Atlanta-Fulton County Coliseum	1964	18,000	86,500
Shea Stadium	1964	24,000	115,400
Astrodome	1965	38,000	175,900

(continued)

161

Table 4.14 (cont.)
Stadium and Arena Construction Costs in Current and 1989 Dollars,
Selected Stadiums and Arenas (thousands of dollars)

		Cost	
Facility	Year Opened	Current Dollars	1989 Dollars
Busch Memorial Stadium	1966	25,000	110,100
Anaheim Stadium	1966	24,000	105,700
Jack Murphy Stadium	1967	26,000	109,200
L.A. Forum	1967	16,700	70,100
Cleveland Municipal Stadium (refurb.)	1967	5,000	21,100
Madison Square Garden	1968	133,000	517,500
Mile High Stadium (sale)	1968	1,800	7,000
Mile High Stadium (refurb.)	1968	3,000	11,700
Salt Palace	1969	17,000	60,000
Riverfront Stadium	1970	45,000	146,600
Three Rivers Stadium	1970	50,000	162,900
Foxboro Stadium	1970	6,700	21,800
Texas Stadium	1971	25,000	73,300
Veterans Stadium	1971	50,000	146,600
Candlestick Park (refurb.)	1971	16,500	48,400
Arrowhead Stadium	1972	53,000	155,400
Nassau Veterans Coliseum	1972	28,000	82,100
The Omni	1972	17,000	45,300
Rich Stadium	1973	22,000	52,300
Royals Stadium	1973	47,000	111,600
Richfield Coliseum	1974	45,000	98,300
Cleveland Municipal Stadium (refurb.)	1974	3,600	7,900
Pontiac Silverdome	1975	56,000	114,300
Louisiana Superdome	1975	168,000	342,900
Yankee Stadium (refurb.)	1975	106,000	216,300
McNichols Sports Arena	1975	13,000	26,500
Exhibition Park (refurb.)	1976	17,800	33,300
Giants Stadium	1976	68,000	127,100
Kingdome	1976	67,000	125,200
Stade Olympique, Montreal	1977	620,000	1,069,000
Mile High Stadium (refurb.)	1977	25,000	43,100
Joe Louis Arena	1979	26,500	39,600
Soldier Field (refurb.)	1980	30,000	41,800
Byrne Meadowlands Arena	1981	85,000	108,400
Metrodome	1982	62,000	68,800
Arlington Park (refurb.)	1983	3,000	3,300
Hoosier Dome	1984	77,000	81,700
Charlotte Coliseum	1985	55,000	57,800

(continued)

Table 4.14 (cont.)
Stadium and Arena Construction Costs in Current and 1989 Dollars,
Selected Stadiums and Arenas (thousands of dollars)

| | | Cost | |
| | | | |
Facility	Year Opened	Current Dollars	1989 Dollars
St. Louis Arena (sale)	1986	15,000	15,400
Joe Robbie Stadium	1987	100,000	105,000
Miami Arena	1988	50,000	51,000
Orlando Arena	1988	110,000	112,000
Palace of Auburn Hills	1988	70,000	71,000
Bradley Center	1988	53,000	54,000
Astrodome (refurb.)	1989	60,000	60,000
Skydome	1989	532,000	532,000
Target Center	1990	93,000	90,000

Sources: New York Times, Amusement Business, team media guides, and other
publications.
Note: Conversion to 1989 dollars not included for years before 1922.

sponsible for the booking schedule of the facility, and often taking care
of maintenance and repairs. The Met Center in Bloomington, housing
the NHL Minnesota North Stars, operates in this fashion, as do Arrowhead and Royals stadiums in Kansas City, Tiger Stadium, Market
Square Arena, Lambeau Field, and a host of other facilities.

Financial data on stadium operations are scattered, even for those stadiums that are publicly owned, and for a number of publicly owned
stadiums and arenas, no published data are available. In doing the research for this book, a mail survey of stadium/arena finances was conducted of all publicly owned stadiums and arenas housing teams in one
or more of the five major sports leagues. About half of the facilities
failed to respond to the mail survey, and about half of those that did
respond refused to divulge information on the grounds of confidential-
ity. Data were obtained in the survey, however, for 17 stadiums and
arenas for the 1989 fiscal year. These data were supplemented by data
on stadiums and arenas appearing in the budget reports of cities and
states owning the facilities, using the library of the Government Division of the U.S. Bureau of the Census in Suitland, Maryland. These data
are roughly comparable with the data obtained in the survey, except
that in certain cases, data were available only for years earlier than
1989. Table 4.15 presents a summary of data on operating revenue and
expenses for 39 publicly owned stadiums and arenas.

Table 4.15

Operating Revenue, Operating Expenses, and Net Operating Income, Selected Stadiums and Arenas, ca. 1989 (thousands of dollars)

Facility and Team	Fiscal Year	Operating Revenue					Total Operating Revenue	Operating Expenses	Net Operating Income
		Rent	Luxury Boxes	Parking	Concessions	Other			
Reunion Arena (Dallas NBA)	1988	2,238	0	1,212	2,072	746	6,268	2,890	3,377
Riverfront Stadium (Cincinnati NFL, NL)	1989	—	—	—	—	—	5,510	5,392	118
Anaheim Stadium (Los Angeles NFL, Calif. AL)	1989	6,945	0	—	3,292	2,514	12,751	7,146	5,605
Superdome (New Orleans, NFL)	1989	3,804	1,259	2,139	1,593	1,265	10,060	17,983	−7,922
Hoosier Dome (Indianapolis NFL) and Market Square Arena (Ind. NBA)	1989	2,142	1,831	657	2,740	2,760	10,103	11,203	−1,100
Portland Coliseum (NBA)	1989	1,939	0	981	723	1,206	4,849	4,220	629
Kingdome (Seattle NFL)	1989	3,439	0	1,786	1,612	454	7,291	5,756	1,535
L.A. Coliseum (Raiders NFL)	1989	2,636	0	0	1,613	0	4,249	3,574	675
L.A. Sports Arena (Clippers NBA)	1989	1,354	0	0	1,709	0	3,064	2,130	934
County Stadium (Milwaukee AL, Green Bay NFL)	1988	—	—	—	—	—	3,746	3,755	−10
MECCA (Milwaukee NBA)	1988	1,189	0	—	885	1,186	3,269	4,104	−834
Metrodome (Minnesota AL, NFL, NBA)	1989	2,376	0	788	3,056	4,857	10,952	5,398	5,554
Met Center (Minnesota NHL)	1989	125	0	0	0	0	125	0	125
Giants Stadium (NY Giants, Jets NFL)	1989	—	—	—	—	—	30,228	25,078	5,150
Byrne Meadowlands Arena (N.J. NBA, NHL)	1989	—	—	—	—	—	36,003	33,462	2,541
Orlando Arena (NBA)	1989	1,406	0	408	1,608	496	3,920	3,792	128
Buffalo Arena (NHL)	1989	1,183	0	0	433	164	1,680	1,561	119
Charlotte Coliseum (NBA)	1989	440	0	1,155	3,626	743	5,964	2,332	3,632
Astrodome (Houston, NL, NFL)	1989	912	0	0	0	0	912	0	912

Stadium	Year								
Oakland Coliseum (NFL, Golden State NBA)	1989	—	—	—	—	—	12,650	9,587	3,063
Candlestick Park (San Francisco NL, NFL)	1989	1,992	0	0	0	0	1,992	1,893	99
Jack Murphy Stadium (San Diego NL, NFL)	1988	2,917	0	2,036	784	128	5,865	5,929	-64
Mile High Stadium (Denver NFL)	1989	—	—	—	—	—	102	0	102
McNichols Arena (Denver NBA)	1989	—	—	—	—	—	239	1,038	-799
Miami Arena	1988	—	—	—	—	—	454	465	-11
Atlanta-Fulton County Coliseum (NL, NFL)	1989	—	—	—	—	—	8,058	9,536	-1,478
Omni (Atlanta NBA)	1989	1,130	0	0	0	0	1,130	0	1,130
Veterans Stadium (Philadelphia NL, NFL)	1989	1,871	0	390	2,872	2,005	7,138	—	—
Seattle Center (NBA)	1987	—	—	—	—	—	10,389	14,356	-3,967
RFK Stadium (Washington NFL)	1989	—	—	—	—	—	6,855	1,925	4,930
Lambeau Field (Green Bay NFL)	1989	150	0	0	0	0	150	0	150
Soldier Field (Chicago NFL)	1988	3,725	0	0	0	0	3,725	—	—
Arrowhead Stadium (Kansas City NFL) and Royals Stadium (Kansas City AL)	1987	—	—	—	—	—	3,063	464	2,599
Texas Stadium (Dallas NFL)	1988	988	0	0	0	0	988	0	988
Pontiac Silverdome (Detroit NFL)	1989	—	—	—	—	—	6,594	6,389	205
Salt Palace (Utah NBA)	1989	—	—	—	—	—	5,112	5,751	-639

Sources: Stadium annual financial reports, and files of the Government Division, Bureau of the Census.

Data are shown for operating revenues, broken down (where available) into rental payments, luxury box revenues, concessions, parking, and other. Excluded from operating revenues are non-operating items, such as interest income and non-recurring payments, such as the award received by the L.A. Coliseum as compensation in the antitrust suit it won against the NFL. Revenues shown are those received by the stadium or arena, exclusive of any amounts representing shares of parking and concessions or luxury box revenues received by the team.

Operating expenses are those variable costs, mainly labor, management, and supplies, incurred in operating the facility. Excluded from operating expenses are depreciation and amortization of buildings and equipment, expenditures on items of capital equipment, and interest on outstanding bonds and notes.

Operating revenue less operating expenses gives net operating income, the amount by which operating revenue exceeds the variable costs of operating the facility. When net operating income is negative, as it is for 10 of the 39 facilities, this means that the facility would generate smaller losses by shutting down completely than by remaining in operation. Under any circumstances—whether operating or shut down—there are fixed costs of interest on outstanding bonds to be paid, and depreciation of the facility due to aging goes on as well. With a negative operating income for a stadium or arena, the city must ante up not only the interest payment on outstanding bonds, but also enough cash to cover the operating loss of the facility.

Because accounting procedures differ from city to city, there are some problems of comparability in the data shown in Table 4.15. Still, there is some internal consistency between the net operating income figures shown, and the terms of stadium contracts discussed earlier. In particular, the success stories shown in Table 4.15 are Anaheim Stadium (net operating income of $5,605,000), the Metrodome ($5,554,000), Giants Stadium ($5,150,000), and RFK Stadium ($4,930,000), with Reunion Arena, Byrne Meadowlands Arena, Charlotte Coliseum, and Oakland-Alameda County Coliseum showing net operating income in the $2.5 million to $3.5 million range. As noted earlier, Giants Stadium has the highest rental terms (15 percent of gross) charged NFL teams, and it is the only stadium in the country that houses two NFL teams, the Jets and the Giants, both of which have an almost unbroken record of sellouts in the stadium. The Metrodome was the only stadium in the country to host three major league sports teams in 1989—the Vikings, the Twins, and the Timberwolves—and the Timberwolves set an NBA attendance record, the Vikings had virtual sellouts of their eight regular season games, and the Twins were still on an attendance roll dating back to the 1987 season. In addition, the Metrodome hosted one of the quarterfinals of the NCAA basketball tournament in 1989. While the Metrodome shows a modest $2,376,000 rental income figure, an additional $4,207,000 (included in "other operating revenue") is derived from the 10 percent ticket tax, which increased the effective rental income for the Metrodome to $6,583,000. Anaheim Stadium hosts the Rams and the Angels, two success stories at the gate. Rental income under the Angels' contract is particularly responsive to attendance, with the rent increasing from 7.5 percent to 10 percent on attendance over 2 million. In 1989, the Angels accounted for 55 percent of stadium revenues, the Rams for 21 percent, and other activities for the remaining 24 percent. RFK Stadium is something of an oddity among the successful stadiums, in that only one major league team, the Redskins, uses the stadium. As noted earlier, the Redskins' contract is one of the costliest (from the point of view of the team) in the NFL, and this is one factor in RFK's high net operating income figure. It might also be the case, however, that there are operating and maintenance costs for the stadium that show up elsewhere in the budget of the District of Columbia, because the operating expenses appear to be out of line with those of other stadiums hosting NFL teams.

At the other extreme from the "success" stories are the stadiums and arenas showing negative operating income. Leading this list is the Louisiana Superdome (−$7,922,000), followed by the Seattle Center (−$3,967,000), Atlanta-Fulton County Coliseum (−$1,478,000), and the Hoosier Dome/Market Square Arena complex (−$1,100,000), with the Milwaukee MECCA, Denver's McNichols Arena, and the Salt Palace of Salt Lake City also showing relatively large operating losses.

The Superdome has only the Saints as a major league tenant, and its giveaway contract (outlined earlier) more or less ensures that the facility will take a bath on its main tenant. Atlanta has had weak-drawing NFL and NL teams for several years, and the Braves' contract in particular is highly favorable to the team. However, there is some ambiguity in the budget data shown for Atlanta, since the city of Atlanta groups together the Coliseum and the zoo in a single budget category, and it might be that the deficit shown reflects zoo operations rather than losses at the stadium. The Hoosier Dome is operating under a sweetheart contract with the Colts, negotiated when the team was being seduced away from Baltimore, so the existence of a deficit is not surprising. The remaining cases involve arenas hosting NBA teams, all of which are drawing well. The MECCA operated under a no-rent contract with the Bucks in 1988, which might help to explain the deficit shown. But it should be emphasized that, while stadiums have few clients other than sports teams, arenas offer a diverse range of other attractions such as rock concerts, plays, conventions, and the like, so that the deficits shown for arenas might be due in part to subsidization of non-sports activities.

Estimates of Subsidies to Teams by Publicly Owned Stadiums

In the financial reports of many public stadiums and arenas, there is a tendency to equate a positive level of net operating income with successful operation of the facility. In almost all cases, fixed costs, including depreciation and amortization of buildings and equipment, are ignored completely. As with other governmental units, municipal governments typically conduct their accounting and structure their budgets on the basis of cash inflows and outflows only, and this can produce a distorted picture of the true economic status of a stadium or arena.

The appropriate model to use in evaluating the operation of a publicly owned stadium or arena is the model of a privately owned, profit-oriented facility. Tenants of a publicly owned stadium or arena are being subsidized if they are not being charged rental fees equal to what they would pay in a competitive market to a private owner operating the facility so as to earn a market rate of return on the owner's investment.

In a competitive market under long-run equilibrium conditions, the owner of a stadium or arena would be able to charge tenants rental fees sufficient to cover operating expenses plus depreciation and amortization of buildings and equipment plus profits representing a market rate of return on invested capital. Moreover, since a private owner would have to pay property taxes on the facility, the fees charged users would have to cover property taxes as well.

Finally, in a competitive market, what matters is not the historical cost of an asset but its replacement cost. Depreciation expenses and return on invested capital are calculated on the basis of the market value of an asset, which, in a competitive market under long-run equilibrium conditions, will be equal to the replacement cost of the asset. Competitive markets in assets are forward looking in the sense that from the point of view of any potential buyer or seller of an asset, the only thing that matters is what income the asset will yield in the future, and what the current cost of construction of the asset (its replacement cost) is.

Since there is no active market in public facilities, we do not have price bids by investors for the facilities to use as estimates of the value or replacement cost of a facility. A second-best approach would involve putting together a time profile of past investment expenditures on the facility, beginning with the initial construction cost and continuing through expenditures on updates, improvements, expansions, and refurbishments of the facility. These expenditures would then be adjusted for inflation. (Throughout this chapter, we have used a 1989 base so that expenditures would be converted into 1989 dollars, using the *Engineering News-Record* construction cost index.) Finally, each successive inflation-adjusted investment expenditure would be depreciated through time, using a standard 40-year lifetime expectancy. The resulting figure would give a fairly good approximation to the 1989 market value (replacement cost) of the facility.

Information on the time profile of investments in stadiums and arenas is not generally available, so a much cruder method (an adjusted original cost method) has been used for most facilities to come up with lower-bound estimates of subsidies provided by publicly owned stadiums and arenas. Under an adjusted original cost method, the only investment in the facility that is taken into account is the original construction cost of the facility, adjusted for inflation. Data on original construction costs are available for a number of facilities (see Table 4.14), while subsequent investments for most facilities are difficult to track. (In a case such as the Astrodome, where cost information on major refurbishments was available, original cost was adjusted to take this into account.) By using an original construction cost basis, depreciation, return on capital, and property taxes are underestimated, since these figures do not reflect the higher replacement cost of a facility due to investments during the operating life of the facility.

In Table 4.16, subsidy estimates are shown for a number of the facilities for which net operating revenue information is available. The approach that has been taken is this. For each facility shown in Table 4.16, the construction cost in 1989 dollars calculated in Table 4.15 has been used as the basis for calculating replacement cost. Facilities are assumed to have 40-year lives, and depreciation is calculated on a straight line basis, so the depreciation figures shown in Table 4.16 are 2.5 percent (1/40th) of the construction cost (in 1989 dollars) of the facility. Facilities over 40 years old, and lacking information on refurbishment cost are excluded from the table.

The replacement cost of any facility is assumed to be the original cost plus refurbishment cost, if available, less accumulated depreciation, adjusted to 1989 dollars. Thus, a facility 20 years old with no refurbishment expenses would have a replacement cost equal to 50 percent of its original construction cost in 1989 dollars. The "return on capital" column gives the annual payment needed to generate a 10 percent rate

Table 4.16
Estimates of Subsidies for Stadiums and Arenas, with an Inflation-Adjusted
Original Cost Basis, ca. 1989 (thousands of dollars)

| Facility | Net Operating Income | Original Cost Basis (1989 Dollars) | | | |
		Depreciation	Return on Capital	Property Tax	Subsidy
Riverfront Stadium	118	3,700	7,300	1,466	$12,348
Anaheim Stadium	5,605	2,640	4,228	845	2,108
Superdome	−7,922	8,572	21,400	4,280	42,174
Hoosier Dome and Market Square Arena	−1,100	2,043	6,945	1,389	11,477
Kingdome	1,535	3,130	8,138	1,628	11,361
L.A. Sports Arena	934	725	600	120	511
Metrodome	5,554	1,720	5,504	1,101	2,771
Giants Stadium	5,150	3,175	8,579	1,716	8,320
Byrne Meadowlands Arena	2,541	2,710	8,370	1,674	10,213
Orlando Arena	128	2,800	10,920	2,184	15,800
Charlotte Coliseum	3,632	1,445	5,202	1,040	4,055
Astrodome[a]	912	5,900	12,600	2,520	20,108
Candlestick Park[a]	99	5,580	6,910	1,362	13,753
Jack Murphy Stadium	−64	2,730	4,641	928	8,363
Mile High Stadium[a]	102	1,545	3,907	781	6,131
McNichols Arena	−799	662	1,656	331	3,448
Miami Arena	−11	1,275	4,925	985	7,196
Atlanta-Fulton County Coliseum	−1,478	2,160	3,243	649	7,530
Omni	1,130	1,125	2,475	495	2,965
Rich Stadium	0	1,325	3,050	610	4,985
Lambeau Field	150	153	155	31	189
Arrowhead Stadium	2,599	3,885	8,547	1,709	11,452
Texas Stadium	988	1,825	3,795	759	5,391
Pontiac Silverdome	205	2,857	7,144	1,429	11,225
Salt Palace	−639	1,500	3,000	600	5,729

[a]*Includes refurbishment since original construction.*

of return on replacement cost. Under public ownership, bonds can be issued to pay for stadiums, at interest rates below those paid by private businesses, in part because of the lower riskiness of municipal bonds, and in part because of the exemption of municipal bond interest from federal income taxes. But use of a municipality's borrowing power to fund a stadium is in itself a subsidy to stadium tenants, so it is the rate of return earned in private markets rather than the municipal bond market that is relevant in estimating subsidies. Here, a 10 percent rate is used, because extensive empirical work by Stockfish (1967) indicates that the average pre-tax real corporate rate of return for the U.S. economy has been at or about this level for an extended period of time.

Finally, property taxes were estimated at 2 percent of the assessed (replacement cost) value of a facility. This is a very rough estimate of something that varies a good deal from city to city, but that does not account for a substantial portion of the subsidy in any case.

For any facility shown in Table 4.16, the amount of the annual estimated subsidy provided by the facility is equal to the net operating income of the facility less depreciation, less return on capital, and less property tax. The estimated subsidy is thus the amount by which revenues fall short of covering all the costs that would have been incurred if the facility were operated by a private owner.

Because we have included fixed costs and return to capital as charges against a facility, the subsidy estimates shown in Table 4.16 indicate that almost all facilities are operated to subsidize their sports team tenants, and most by sizable amounts. In particular, of the "success stories" identified earlier, three of those four stadiums with large positive net operating income figures—Anaheim Stadium, Giants Stadium, and the Metrodome—show subsidies to tenants from operations, with Giants Stadium subsidizing the Jets and Giants to the tune of over $8 million per year. There are six facilities—Riverfront Stadium, Superdome, Kingdome, Byrne Meadowlands Arena, Astrodome, and Pontiac Silverdome—showing subsidies of over $10 million per year, with the Superdome showing a horrendous $43 million annual subsidy.

All this being said, the point that has to be kept in mind is that these figures *underestimate* the amounts of subsidies provided by the stadiums and arenas, because data were not available for all investments in the facilities subsequent to original construction. The facilities shown in Table 4.16 for which subsidy estimates have been calculated represent only about one-third of the publicly owned stadiums and arenas housing major league teams. The subsidy estimates for these facilities underestimate the true level of subsidies, as noted above. Estimated subsidies for the facilities shown in Table 4.16 sum to around $170 million for the year of 1989. While these facilities are in no sense at all a random sample from the set of publicly owned stadiums and arenas, if the data here reported are in fact typical of publicly owned arenas and stadiums in general, then such facilities housing major league sports teams would have been providing around $500 million in subsidies to tenants in 1989.

It should be pointed out that it is not only sports teams and their owners who are subsidized by current rental practices in publicly owned stadiums and arenas. There are tenants other than the teams, and these are undoubtedly subsidized just as the teams are. Moreover, a part of the subsidy is passed on by the team to ticket buyers, since the team is competing with lots of other entertainment attractions in the city for recreation dollars. This being said, it is still clear that subsidies to sports teams by publicly owned stadiums and arenas represent substantial amounts of money. In an era in which local governments are under intense budgetary pressures, this raises the question of whether it is possible to find an economic justification for stadium subsidies of $500 million per year.

Value of a Facility or Team to a City

The large sums that cities expend on stadiums and arenas built primarily for pro sports teams is prima facie evidence that public officials, and presumably the general public, think that professional sports teams are valuable assets for a city. There is no question but that sports teams can play a role in bringing together diverse groups in a city through a common identification with the city's team, can enhance the quality of life of the city, and can help to establish a city's reputation as "big league." The payoffs from these can be important, although hard to quantify in dollar terms.

When a proposal is made to build a publicly financed facility for a pro sports team, it is usual to hear these benefits stressed, together with some more "hard-nosed" arguments to the effect that the facility will provide measurable benefits to the city, far in excess of any costs the city incurs in building the stadium or arena to attract or to keep a major league sports team. It is this that we want to look into a little more closely.

To begin with, construction of a stadium or arena will provide jobs for workers in the city, and income for contractors and materials suppliers. Then, once the facility is opened, pro sports teams housed in the facility will provide benefits for a city through expenditures by the team and by the fans attending team games, generating sales and income for businesses located in the city and jobs for workers in the city, and resulting in additional tax revenues for the city itself.

The procedure that is used to estimate the economic benefits provided by a team or facility is first to estimate the direct expenditures by the team for goods and services it purchases in the city, and then to add to this expenditures by fans on goods and services (other than game tickets) purchased in the city, together with expenditures by players on purchases of goods and services in the city. The resulting sum is the amount of direct expenditure benefits to the city provided by the team.

But of course firms and workers in the city who earn incomes from these direct expenditures in turn spend a portion of these incomes on goods and services purchased in the city, and this continues on through successive rounds of expenditures. These are the indirect expenditures benefits of the team. A multiplier must be applied to direct expenditures to determine the total expenditures benefit (direct plus indirect) engendered by a team or a facility. The size of the multiplier depends on the marginal propensity to consume (on purchase of goods and services in the city) of city residents, that is, the fraction of additional income received that is spent on purchases of goods and services in the city by recipients of income. Estimates vary as to the size of this multiplier, but commonly, a figure of from 1.5 to 3 is used as the indirect expenditures multiplier. With an indirect expenditures multiplier of 1.5, the total expenditure benefits for a city arising from a sports team are 2.5 times the amount of direct expenditure benefits; that is, total expenditures equals direct expenditures plus indirect expenditures, where indirect expenditures are 1.5 times direct expenditures.

Using this procedure, one consulting firm in 1987 estimated the prospective total (direct and indirect) benefits of the Minnesota Timberwolves and their new arena to the city of Minneapolis at about $25 million per year, with tax revenues to the city increasing by about $3 million per year. Baade (1987) cites a 1979 estimate of the economic impact of the Pittsburgh Pirates on the city of Pittsburgh at $33 million per year, while at about the same time, the Steelers were estimated to provide $11 million of expenditures benefits to Pittsburgh. Oakland city officials claimed a loss of $30 million per year of direct expenditures due to the departure of the Raiders (*U.S. News and World Report,* May 21, 1984)—and a whopping $100 million per year in indirect benefits. By way of extreme contrasts, Baade notes a published estimate of $500 million per year as the expenditure benefits provided to Philadelphia by its professional sports teams (Eagles, Phillies, 76ers, Flyers) in 1983; and another study cited in the *Wall Street Journal* found that the economic impact of the Baltimore Colts just before their move to Indianapolis in 1984 was a meager $200,000 per year. In contrast, just after the Colts left for Indianapolis, some Maryland officials estimated the total benefits of the Colts to the city of Baltimore at $30 million per year (Johnson 1985), while a study at about the same time produced for the city of Indianapolis came up with an estimate of $21 million per year as the expenditure impact of the Colts on the Indianapolis economy. And a 1984 study for the state of Maryland estimated the annual benefits to the state from the Baltimore Orioles at $94 million.

In 1984, it was estimated that the Minnesota Twins pumped $30 million into the Twin Cities economy, while a 1985 study reported that the Cincinnati Reds accounted for $55 million in annual expenditure benefits. A study by a faculty member of the University of New Orleans came up with an estimate that the Superdome provided $900 million in direct and indirect expenditure benefits in the first 10 years of its operation. In 1988, when the Phoenix Suns were lobbying for a new downtown arena, one study estimated the economic impact of the proposed $70 million arena to be from $2 billion to $3.5 billion over a 30-year period, or around $80 million per year. A University of North Carolina economist estimated in 1986 that the Charlotte Hornets would add $184 million to the Charlotte economy over a five-year period (around $40 million per year), and said in 1988 that he had underestimated the actual impact. Finally, Toronto's half-billion-dollar Skydome was expected to produce $450 million in Canadian dollars in expenditure benefits for Toronto the very first year after it opened, and directly and indirectly to account for 17,000 jobs in the Toronto area.

In the face of these widely varying estimates of expenditures benefits from a new stadium or from hosting a team, the correct attitude is one of skepticism. It is hard enough to estimate the prospective cost of a major facility such as a stadium or arena (for example, the Timberwolves' Target Center had a 1987 estimate of $45 million and opened in 1990 after incurring a construction cost of $93 million), but estimating the expenditure benefits to a city of a team or a facility involves a significantly higher order of difficulty. Moreover, in the case of cost estimates at least we can check after the fact to see how far off the estimate was—and be appropriately impressed by just how inexact (and downward biased) construction cost estimates really were (see, for example, Quirk and Terasawa 1986). In the case of benefit estimates, as a practical matter there is no way to verify or falsify estimates empirically, because of the difficulty of separating out the effects of a team or a stadium from all the other activities that are going on in a city. Moreover, benefits from a facility or a team are spread through the entire city economy and at best represent only a miniscule fraction of the total economy of the city.

There is also a basic procedural problem with expenditures benefits estimates that should be noted. Direct expenditures estimates are constructed by surveying fans at ballparks to find out what they spend on hotels, restaurants, and other goods and services in the city when they come to see a game. The total dollar amount they report spending is then taken as the estimate of the direct expenditures benefit to the city. The difficulty is that fans have only limited amounts of money available to spend on recreational and leisure time activities. Any money spent on attending a sports event means there is less available to spend on alternatives, such as movies, plays, concerts, VCR rentals, and the like. And decreases in spending on these other activities produce direct and indirect expenditures losses for city businesses to offset in part or in whole any expenditures benefits associated with the team or the facility. Procedurally correct estimates of expenditures benefits for sports teams should incorporate estimates of expenditures substitutions that take place, and should correct expenditures benefits for such substitutions. Unfortunately, it is even more difficult to verify expenditures substitution estimates than it is to verify expenditures benefits estimates.

One of the fascinating things about the rosy projections that are made of the impact of a new stadium or arena on a city is that, as we have already seen, most existing publicly owned stadiums and arenas do not cover their fixed and variable costs. If these facilities are going to generate so much income for city businesses, it seems strange that they generate so little income themselves that they must be subsidized by city taxpayers. And it is also strange, in the face of the optimistic estimates of expenditures benefits, that more stadiums and arenas aren't built by teams and other private entrepreneurs. Admittedly, direct and indirect expenditures on goods and services, such as restaurants and hotels, can't be captured by a team or facility owner. But if, as in the case of Phoenix, a $70 million arena is expected to increase income for residents of the city by over $80 million per year, it would seem that some sort of sharing arrangement could be worked out under which, say, the city shares its increased tax revenues (resulting from the arena) with the team, with the team building the stadium, and taking the up-front risks. While there have been one or two joint public-private facility ventures discussed, they all involve substantial residual public sector risk taking. There isn't much evidence of the "put your money where your mouth is" variety that teams give any more credence to the high-side projections of expenditures benefits than skeptical economists do.

There have been some attempts made to determine from the historical record whether substantial expenditures benefits have been generated by new stadiums or new teams, as promised by their partisans. Baade (1987) did a study of expenditures benefits of stadiums and sports teams by examining the pattern of growth in income over time of cities, before and after a team or a facility was acquired by the city. Baade studied nine cities: Buffalo, Cincinnati, Denver, Detroit, Miami, New Orleans, San Diego, Seattle, and Tampa Bay. In each of these cities, there was construction of a new stadium or arena (or rehabilitation of an old stadium or arena) or a move of a team into the city at some time between 1965 and 1983. For four cities (Cincinnati, Denver, Detroit, and Seattle), construction of a stadium or move of a sports team to the city was followed by an increase in the rate of growth of income for the city. For the remaining five cities, there was no discernible change in the rate of growth of income for the city following acquisition of the facility or team.

Of course, there are a lot of factors at work other than sports teams and sports facilities, and they all affect the rate of growth of income of a city. Baade attempted to partially account for this by comparing the rate of growth of income for cities in his study with the rate of growth for the region (for example, state) in which the city was located. What he found was that in seven of the nine cities in his study, move of a team into the city or construction of a stadium in the city was followed by a *reduction* of the city's share of regional (for example, state) income. As noted above, because of the many factors impacting income growth in cities, and because of the minor role teams and stadiums play in the city economy, statistical results such as this are, of course, not conclusive evidence against the existence of susbstantial expenditures benefits, but at least they do raise questions concerning this.

Other attempts to measure the actual expenditures benefits associated with teams or stadiums have generally come up with comparable negative results. In the face of the estimated $94 million expenditures benefit of the Baltimore Orioles in 1984 cited earlier, Johnson (1985) found financial benefits to the city in excess of direct expenditures on the Colts and the Orioles by the city in only four of the seven years in his study. Rosentraub and Nunn (1978) studied the Arlington, Texas, and Irving, Texas, publicly owned stadiums, and determined that there was no significant difference in the rates of income growth for these cities and other towns and cities in the same locality. This suggests that it is difficult for cities funding stadiums to capture whatever benefits occur because of the stadium. Instead, whatever benefits are generated by a stadium tend to be spread over an entire region. For what it is worth, Arlington made the decision to sell its stadium to the Texas Rangers in 1988, and is no longer in the stadium business.

It might well be that the most important benefit that a team provides for a city is as a common identification symbol, something that brings the citizens of the city together, especially during those exhilarating times when the city has a World Series champion, or a Super Bowl winner. It is next to impossible to quantify this aspect of the benefits of a team, but this does not mean that the benefits don't exist. It can be argued that recognition of this role for a pro sports team is what really underlies the large subsidies that cities have provided for sports teams, rather than the more mundane (and, as we have seen, almost as elusive to measure) expenditures benefits.

Case Study:
A Stadium That Didn't Get Built

We conclude this chapter by recounting an instance in which a team threatened to leave a city if a new stadium didn't get built, whereupon the city's leaders investigated the costs and benefits of a new stadium, and then took the politically courageous step of rejecting the stadium. It would be nice to report that showing some political courage paid off, but in the go-go sports world of the 1980s, the teams held all the trump cards, and in this case, the team left town, and there were major political costs to pay. Three years later, city voters approved a multimillion-dollar bond issue to build the stadium that had been rejected earlier, with the hope of attracting an expansion team into town.

The city involved was St. Louis, and the team was the NFL Cardinals. The Cardinals are the oldest professional football team in the country, having been around since the 1890s. The team has been owned by the Bidwill family since the early 1930s. Up until 1960, the Cardinals were the second team in Chicago, playing in the shadow of the Bears. The team was moved to St. Louis in 1960, and had some good seasons during the Don Coryell/Jim Hart years, but then sank into a more or less permanent non-contender status, and in effect became the second team in town, playing in the shadow of the baseball Cardinals.

Both Cardinals teams played in Busch Stadium, which had a seating capacity for football of about 56,000. The Stadium was originally publicly financed and operated, but in the mid-1980s, Gussie Busch, owner of the baseball Cardinals, bought the stadium from the city. Between 1976 and 1988, the Cardinals average per-game attendance was 48,000, one of the lowest in the NFL. In 1985, Bill Bidwill, owner of the football Cardinals, announced that he was unhappy with Busch Stadium, and was looking at alternatives. One alternative was construction of a new stadium for football in St. Louis, with the Cardinals staying town. The other alternative was moving the Cardinals to another city.

Bidwill argued that Busch Stadium was too small for NFL football (it was the smallest stadium in the league), and he also objected to the sale of beer in the stadium. With Anheuser-Busch as owner of the stadium, it was going to be hard to change that rule. The capacity argument was a rather strange one, since the Cardinals had not sold out in Busch Stadium for several years.

Two groups formed to promote the building of a stadium to keep the Cardinals in town. One envisaged a stadium to be located in the western reaches of St. Louis county on the river flats, and to be privately owned. This was the Riverdome proposal. While Riverdome was to be privately owned, $120 million of the $150 million construction cost was to be covered by bonds issued by the city or county. The second proposal was also for a covered stadium, but with a solid rather than a fabric roof. This stadium was to be located next to the downtown Cervantes Convention Center, and was to be owned and operated by the city of St. Louis. Both stadiums had seating capacities of 70,000.

Engineering estimates were prepared of construction costs, prospective rental income, and facility operating costs. Riverdome came in with a projected net operating income of almost $10 million per year, and the downtown facility showed a projected net operating income of $7 million per year. After deducting interest expenses on facility bonds, Riverdome showed a net operating surplus of $2 million per year, and the downtown facility showed a net operating deficit of around $5 million per year.

What is interesting about these engineering estimates is that both facilities were projected to have net operating income figures that exceeded the net operating income of all the stadiums and arenas surveyed in Table 4.15. Moreover, the St. Louis facilities were to accomplish this with only one guaranteed major league tenant, since the baseball Cardinals were quite happy with Busch Stadium. The engineering estimates projected either an NHL team (the Blues) or an NBA team (expansion) as well as the NFL Cardinals, but the match between a domed stadium and basketball and/or hockey has not been a good one.

In particular, if a comparison is made between the actual operating experience of a domed stadium, such as the Metrodome (with both the Twins and the Vikings as tenants), and the proposed St. Louis stadiums, it is of interest that the Metrodome shows a net operating income considerably less than the amounts projected for either of the proposed St. Louis stadiums.

When the engineering estimates were revised downward to reflect a little more reality, it turned out that the downtown stadium could be expected to cost the city in the neighborhood of $10 million per year, while Riverdome would cost around $5 million, the difference reflecting more parking income at Riverdome, and private versus public ownership.

After an intense public debate, the mayor of St. Louis rejected both proposals in favor of a proposal to refurbish Busch Stadium by adding luxury boxes and extra seating capacity. Bill Bidwill rejected this as inadequate. Given court decisions in the Oakland Raiders case, the NFL then raised only token opposition to Bill Bidwill's request to move the Cardinals to Phoenix, where the honeymoon lasted just long enough for Phoenix fans to find out how much the Cardinals were going to charge for tickets. Once again the team is playing to sparse crowds, and with middling playing success. St. Louis is looking for a replacement team, and has voted approval of funding of the downtown stadium proposal that had been rejected three years earlier.

Chapter 5

The Reserve Clause and Antitrust Laws

WE TURN next to the division of the monopoly rents in pro team sports between owners and players. Back in the 1960s and earlier, before player unions and before free agency, things were a lot simpler for everyone involved in professional team sports. The rules were straightforward: the owner, the general manager, and the coach decided among themselves what was good for the team and what was good for the players, and they then informed the players, who went along with this or else. There is a famous story, told by Jerry Kramer in *Instant Replay*, about Vince Lombardi during the years when he ran the Packers in his combined role as coach and general manager. Jim Ringo, the Packers' outstanding center, supposedly came to Lombardi's office to negotiate his salary for the next year, was admitted to the coach's office, and then announced to Lombardi that his agent, who was in the outer room, would do his negotiating for him. Lombardi asked Ringo to step out of his office for a few minutes. When Ringo was called back in, he asked Lombardi if he could bring his agent in with him. Lombardi said, "Don't bother—you've just been traded to the Eagles."

In a later interview, Jim Ringo denied the details of the story (see Stuart Leuthner's *Iron Men*), but Ringo *was* traded to the Eagles after he asked Lombardi for a raise. In any case, there is no doubt that player agents were not welcome in Lombardi's Packer organization, and any player who would even think of hiring an agent didn't belong in the Pack. Later on, after the NFL Players Association was formed, it would be player reps and other strong union supporters who would be traded away from the hard-line NFL teams. Many of these ended up with George Allen, at the Rams and at the Redskins; Allen always considered them the brightest and most highly motivated players in the league, and built some first-class teams around these discards.

The power that teams in all the pro leagues exercised in negotiations with players back in those years rested on the player reservation system—the reserve (or option) clause, player waiver rules, and the college or rookie draft. The pro team sports industry has developed its own highly distinctive set of business rules over its history, dealing with everything from territorial rights to the powers of league commissioners. But the single most important—and most controversial—business rule that pro team sports leagues have operated under is the player reservation system based on the reserve clause. The reserve clause was first introduced over a hundred years ago in baseball, and then was adopted later in various forms by all the other major team sports leagues. Chapter 6 examines the effect of the player reservation system (and free agency) on player salaries, and Chapter 7 goes in some detail into the argument that the reserve clause is needed in team sports to preserve competitive balance in a league. But before getting into this tricky question, the present chapter traces the history of the reserve clause and the player reservation system from its beginnings back in the nineteenth century.[1] Along the way, we'll also review the related murky and equally controversial court decisions that have been handed down regarding the antitrust status of pro team sports leagues. The story begins in the earliest days of that hoary and hallowed institution, the National League.

The Reserve Clause: Early History[1]

In 1876, when the National League opened for business, the market for players was an economist's dream—free as the proverbial breeze. Players signed one-year contracts with a team, and were free to negotiate with other teams for succeeding seasons at any time, even during the playing season. Owners and players operated in an almost completely unrestricted competitive market. The National League had supplanted an earlier league, the National Association of Professional Baseball Players, organized in 1871. The NA operated under a rule prohibiting players from signing with another team during the playing season. The NA went out of business at the end of the 1875 season, after William Hulbert, owner of the Chicago NA team, broke the NA rules by raiding the championship Boston team during the 1875 season, signing four of Boston's star players—Al Spalding, Cal McVey, Deacon White, and Ross Barnes—for the 1876 season. These were not just any run-of-the-mill players—the *Bill James Historical Baseball Abstract* (1986) lists all four

[1]This section is drawn from Seymour (1960) and Voight (1983).

players on its National Association All Star Team (1871–1875), and lists White and Barnes on its National League All Star Team (1876–1879). To avoid returning the Boston players as required under NA rules, Hulbert pulled his Chicago team out of the NA and then joined with seven other owners from the NA (incredibly including the Boston owners!) to form the NL. The fortified Chicago team proceeded to take the first (1876) NL pennant.

It took only two seasons for the NL to revert to the old NA rules. Beginning in 1878, players were prohibited from signing with another team until October 1, after the playing season had ended. Among the owners who voted for this rule to restrict player negotiating rights was the individual charged with enforcing it, none other than the same William Hulbert, who had by then added the job of NL president to his duties as owner of the Chicago White Stockings. This was the first tentative step in a series of moves by NL owners aimed at lowering player salary costs by restricting competitive bidding by owners for player services. Taken together, these moves ultimately converted the original "free as a breeze" market for player services into a market that was locked up as tight as a drum.

The true stroke of genius in this direction—the reserve clause—had its genesis at the 1879 meetings of the NL in Buffalo, based on a suggestion by Arthur Soden, one of the owners of the Boston team. Owners were well aware that an important source of their cost problems was the salaries paid out to a limited number of superstar players, the players that every owner wanted to bid on. At the Buffalo meeting, NL owners reached a secret agreement on the Soden proposal under which each team was allowed to "reserve" five of its players, by excluding them from the end-of-season player market. The owners agreed that they would not negotiate with or employ any of the players reserved by another team and that they would not play games against any team that used a player reserved by another team. Teams would thus have exclusive bargaining rights with respect to their five reserved players.

With this primitive reservation system in place, player salaries were cut for the 1880 season, and, for the first time, most NL teams began to make money. The reservation system was also used with a vengeance to discipline players. In one striking case, Charles Wesley Jones of Boston refused to play for the team until he was paid $378 in back salary owed him by the team. Owner Soden placed Jones on the Boston reserve list and then suspended him, so that Jones was blacklisted by the NL, being out of baseball for two years.

During the 1880s, there was action galore on the business side of major league baseball. Two rival leagues were organized—the American Association in 1882, and the Union Association in 1884—with accompanying interleague wars that temporarily bid up player salaries. The AA survived its one-year war with the NL, and became an equal partner with the NL, while the UA went under after just one season. By the end of the decade, organized baseball, as represented by the NL and AA, had tight control of player salaries, with a well-developed player reservation system firmly in place, and with all players subject to the system.

Up until 1887, there was no formal "reserve clause" in the standard player's contract; instead, the contract contained a provision stating that the player agreed to abide by the constitution and bylaws of organized baseball, which incorporated the reservation system. When players protested about being bound by a changing set of rules over which they had no control and often no direct knowledge, the owners decided to add a reservation clause to the contract. In its 1889 version, the clause read as follows:

> It is further understood and agreed that the party of the first part [the team] shall have the right to "reserve" the said party of the second part [the player] for the season next ensuing . . . [subject to the condition that] the said party of the second part shall not be reserved at a salary less than that [paid in the present season]. . . .

The interpretation placed on this clause by owners was that of a perpetual option on the player's services, for his playing lifetime in the sport, and this was backed up by the agreement of other owners not to hire players who were on the reserve lists of other teams.

During the late 1880s, baseball attendance was booming, with most teams in both the AA and the NL profitable, while players remained profoundly unhappy with the reservation system. In 1890, the ongoing conflict between owners and players led to the single most revolutionary event in the business history of baseball, the formation of the Players League. The Players League was a league of cooperatives formed by the players themselves together with a group of outside investors. Each of the eight PL teams was run by a board consisting of an equal number of players and owners. Players were signed by teams to three-year contracts with no reserve clause (players were free agents after three years), with salaries fixed at the levels the players had earned in 1889. Team revenues were assigned first to non-salary operating expenses, and then to player salaries. Profits were shared between owners and players.

During its brief (one-year) history, the new league was spectacularly successful in recruiting star players from the AA and NL. Almost all the star players in baseball joined the PL. However, there were legal challenges. The leading case involved catcher Buck Ewing, one of the greatest players of his era, who jumped his New York Giants (NL) contract to move to the New York PL team. In *Metropolitan Exhibition*

Co. v. Ewing, 43 F. 198, 202 (S.D.N.Y. 1890), a federal district court ruled that the reserve clause in Ewing's contract, as interpreted by the owners, was unenforceable, in part because of its vagueness. The court also ruled that the reserve clause, in its 1889 version, was simply a one-year option, applicable only to the next season, and not a perpetually renewable option. And the court ruled that the reserve clause only gave the team first negotiating rights with the player, not a claim on the player's services for the next season: "In a legal sense, it [the reserve clause] is merely a contract to make a contract, if the parties agree." This setback to owners led to one of the many rewrites of the reserve clause in attempts to find something that the courts would enforce, and that would maintain the owners' bargaining power. The victory for players was only a temporary one; the PL went out of existence after the 1890 season, and, by 1892, the NL was operating as a 12-team monopoly league, after a one-year war with the AA, with the old reservation system still in place.

The Reserve Clause, 1900–1970

The next spate of cases testing the enforceability of the reserve clause came in connection with the National League-American League war of 1901–1902, during which the outlaw AL signed over 100 NL players to contracts, with most courts ruling against enforcement of the reserve clause in NL contracts. The most famous case, however, was one in which the NL prevailed. It involved the legendary Hall of Famer Napoleon Lajoie, one of the greatest second basemen of all time, with a lifetime batting average of .339. Lajoie jumped from the Philadelphia NL team to Connie Mack's Philadelphia AL team in 1901, batting .422 in that banner year. In 1902, the NL obtained an injunction in the Pennsylvania state courts prohibiting Lajoie from playing in the state for any team other than the Phillies. The AL countered this by engineering a trade, sending Lajoie to Cleveland, where he was so productive and so popular that during his years with Cleveland, the team's nickname was the Naps. During 1902, when Cleveland was playing the Athletics in Philadelphia, Lajoie took a vacation at nearby Atlantic City.

At the end of the AL-NL war in 1903, both leagues agreed to abide by each other's player contracts, and agreed to honor the reserve clauses of all teams. Among the players who had jumped their reserve clause contracts during the AL-NL war were Clark Griffith, a star pitcher who moved from the Chicago NL team to Charles Comiskey's Chicago AL team, and who was later owner of the Washington Senators, and John McGraw, who moved from the St. Louis NL team to the Baltimore AL

Orioles, and later became a part-owner of the New York Giants. Other players who had jumped reserve clauses and later became owners include Connie Mack, who jumped from the Washington NL team to the Buffalo PL team in 1890; Charles Comiskey, who jumped from the St. Louis AA team to the Chicago PL team in 1890; and John Montgomery Ward, part-owner of the Braves before World War I, who organized the PL and jumped from the New York NL team to the Brooklyn PL team in 1890. All of these individuals later, as owners, became defenders of the reservation system. In fact, the former firebrand, John Montgomery Ward, actually ended up as the lawyer for the National League, charged with defending all those rules he had fought so vigorously against back in 1890.

The Federal League war of 1914–1915 provoked further legal confrontations involving the reserve clause, and, once again, the courts generally ruled against its enforceability (see, e.g, *Weegham v. Killefer*, 215 F. 289 (6th Cir. 1915); and *American League Baseball Club v. Chase*, 86 Misc. 441, 149 N.Y.S. 6 (1914)). For a time during the war, the AL and NL dropped the reserve clause from player contracts in favor of simple three-year contracts. Once the war was over, however, the reserve clause was once again reinstated in the standard player contract.

What was new about the Federal League war was the first filing of an antitrust case against organized baseball. The Federal League filed this suit in 1914, in the court of Judge Kenesaw Mountain Landis. Landis's court was chosen deliberately by Federal League owners in their filing of the case, because of Landis's reputation as a staunch foe of the "trusts," based on the million-dollar fine (later overturned on appeal) he had assessed against Standard Oil in an earlier case. However, as it turned out, Landis viewed the baseball "trust" in a much more benign way. Landis held up the Federal League case for almost a year in order to encourage a compromise agreement between the parties, a friendly gesture that later played a pivotal role in his selection as the first commissioner of baseball. Ultimately a settlement was reached between organized baseball (AL and NL) and seven of the eight FL teams, under which the FL teams agreed to drop the antitrust case, with the FL going out of business. One team, the FL Baltimore Terrapins, refused to accept the settlement terms, and pursued its case in the courts.

Baltimore sued for damages of $80,000 (which were automatically tripled under the Sherman Act), and won its case in the trial court. The decision was reversed on appeal, with the court ruling that baseball was not interstate commerce in the sense of the commerce clause of the Constitution, and hence was not subject to the Sherman Act. Baltimore then appealed to the Supreme Court, which upheld the appeals court decision (*Federal Baseball Club of Baltimore, Inc. v. National League of Professional Baseball Clubs*, 259 U.S. 200 (1922)). Justice Holmes handed down the unanimous decision for the Court, ruling as follows:

> The business is giving exhibitions of baseball, which are purely state affairs. It is true that . . . competitions must be arranged between clubs from different cities and States. But the fact that in order to give exhibitions the Leagues must induce free persons to cross state lines and must arrange and pay for their doing so is not enough to change the character of the business. . . . As is put by the defendants, personal effort, not related to production, is not a subject of commerce. That which in its consummation is not commerce does not become commerce among the States because the transportation that we have mentioned takes place.
>
> . . . If we are right the plaintiff's business is to be described in the same way and the restrictions by contract that prevented the plaintiff from getting players to break their bargains and the other conduct charged against the defendants were not an interference with commerce among the States.

This was to become a highly controversial ruling. Within 20 years, the Court's expansion of the scope of the commerce clause negated essentially every substantive point that was made in the Holmes decision. Notwithstanding, organized baseball had received the exemption from the antitrust laws that remains in force up to the present day.

As it appeared in baseball contracts from around the 1920s into the 1950s, the reserve clause read as follows:

> [I]f, prior to March 1, . . . the player and the club have not agreed upon the terms of such contract [for the next playing season], then on or before ten days after said March 1, the club shall have the right to renew this contract for the period of one year on the same terms, except that the amount payable to the player shall be such as the club shall fix in said notice. . . .

Whatever an outside observer might think about the economic implications of the reserve clause or its equity, still, from a professional point of view, it's hard not to marvel at the subtle, convoluted, and diabolical legal mind that put this beauty together. When a player signs a contract with a team for the first time, he is accepting all terms of the contract, including this clause. But signing the contract for this year also binds the player for the next year, so long as the club submits a contract to the player before March 11, whether the player signs the new contract or not; and, having been under contract for the second year, the contract (including the reserve clause) gets renewed by the team for the third and each succeeding year simply by meeting the March 11 deadline for submitting a contract to the player.

The interpretation placed on the reserve clause by organized baseball for almost a hundred years was that the player signing a contract containing the reserve clause is bound to the team for his entire playing career, or to any other team that purchases the contract from the previous owner. Under this interpretation, the reserve clause in a baseball player's contract gives the club a perpetual option on the services of the player. (As will be spelled out below, in later years, the NFL, NHL, and NBA adopted more modest interpretations of their versions of the reserve clause.)

There was a nice, if somewhat lopsided, balancing of obligations between the player and the team involved in the standard baseball contract. On the one hand, the player signing the contract bound himself to the team for the rest of his playing career; on the other hand, the team was obligated to give the player a full 10 days' notice before voiding the contract by firing him. (In fairness, the 10 days' notice requirement held only from 1887 to 1947; since 1947, major league teams have been required to give 30 days' notice before dropping a player.) The inherent inequity in obligations of the two parties under the reserve clause has been the major factor in the reluctance of the courts to enforce the clause in disputes between owners and players, or between owners of teams in rival leagues.

But the shaky legal status of the reserve clause becomes relevant only when player contracts end up in the courts, for example, when there are competing claims by two or more teams to a player, and this typically occurs only when there are rival leagues in a sport (not always, however, as in the cases involving George McGinnis and Julius Erving in the NBA in the mid-1970s, or in the Scott Perry case in organized baseball in 1918). An essential element of all of the existing league rules is an agreement among the teams in the league to respect the reserve clause contracts of other teams in the league. Thus the mere fact that the perpetual option version of the reserve clause is generally unenforceable in the courts did not prevent baseball teams from enforcing it within organized baseball from 1879 until 1976. Moreover, the Supreme Court's decision in *Federal Baseball* had cut the legs from under any attempt by the players themselves to fight the reserve clause in the courts as a violation of the antitrust laws.

By the early 1920s, the NHL and NFL had adopted business rule structures patterned closely on that of organized baseball, including the reserve clause. Among the memorabilia at the Pro Football Hall of Fame in Canton, Ohio, is an NFL Uniform Player's Contract between the Toledo Maroons and S.V. Peabody, signed on September 30, 1922. The relevant clauses of that contract read as follows:

> 8. Any time prior to August 1, 1923, by written notice to the Player, the Club may renew this contract for the term of that year, except that the salary rate shall be such as the parties may then agree upon, or, in default of agreement, such as the Club may fix. . . .
>
> 11. The reservation of the Club of the valuable right to fix the salary rate for the succeeding year and the promise of the Player not to play during said year otherwise than with the Club, have been taken into consideration in determining the salary specified herein and the undertaking by the Club to pay said salary is the consideration for both the reservation and the promise.

The NHL standard player's contract also followed this pattern, as did player contracts in the American Basketball League of the 1920s and early 1930s. For all practical purposes, the other team sports leagues simply borrowed from organized baseball the business devices, such as the reserve clause, that had already been shown to work to keep costs down, and that acted to promote profitability and survival of the league.

The NFL was responsible for an innovation that widened the set of restrictions on player negotiations when, in 1936, football owners introduced a college draft. Originally, NFL rules allowed any team to negotiate with any college player who had exhausted his college playing eligibility. Then, in 1925, the Bears signed Red Grange one day after his college season had ended, and played Grange in the Bears' last two NFL games of the season. College coaches raised a storm of protest, and NFL rules were changed in 1926 to provide that college players could be signed only after their class had graduated. The Bears were fined $1,000 in 1930 for their midseason signing of "Jumping Joe" Savoldi, one of Rockne's star players, after Savoldi was expelled from Notre Dame for breaking the school's rule against married students. George Halas argued, to no avail, that the rule against signing college players shouldn't apply to a player expelled from his school. But, while the NFL continued to ban negotiations with players still in college, once a player's class had graduated, any NFL team could negotiate with him.

Then, after the 1934 season, a bidding war erupted between Dan Topping's Brooklyn Dodgers and Bert Bell's Philadelphia Eagles, for the services of Stan Kostka, the hard-driving fullback on Bernie Bierman's 1934 Minnesota Golden Gopher national championship team. After the smoke had cleared, Kostka had signed with the Dodgers for the almost unheard-of salary of $5,000 (as much as the premiere player of the league, Bronko Nagurski, was earning with the Bears). At the next meeting of the league, Bell proposed a reverse-order-of-finish college draft, which has been a part of the NFL rules since that time. (For a period after World War II, at the behest of the front-running Chicago Bears and Washington Redskins, the NFL had a "bonus draft," under which the first choice in the draft was assigned by lot, after which the regular draft began. The bonus draft went on for the 12 years needed for each NFL team to win the honor, and was dropped thereafter.)

Whatever the benefits of the college draft in equalizing playing strengths among teams (see Chapter 7 for a discussion), the college draft certainly acted to lower bonuses and salaries paid to players entering pro football. Thus it is not surprising that the NBA incorporated a player draft into its business rules, soon after it was organized. Baseball and hockey didn't adopt a rookie free agent draft until much later, because these two sports had a history of developing players through the minor leagues rather than through the colleges, and because of opposition to the draft by the strongest teams. Baseball finally introduced a rookie free agent (high school and college player) draft in 1965, and the NHL introduced a draft shortly thereafter.

To return to our story, the next testing of the reserve clause in the courts came after World War II, when another rival baseball league surfaced. In 1949, Danny Gardella sued organized baseball under the Sherman Act, for damages suffered when he was blacklisted by Commissioner Happy Chandler after jumping his contract with the New York Giants to play in the Mexican League. Gardella's suit was dismissed by the trial court on the basis of the antitrust exemption of *Federal Baseball*, and Gardella appealed the ruling. In a split decision, the appeals court reversed the ruling of the trial court (*Gardella v. Chandler*, 172 F.2d 402 (2d Cir. 1949)).

Ruling for the majority of the appeals court, Judge Learned Hand argued that the economic environment of baseball had changed drastically since the 1922 ruling of the Supreme Court. In particular, the importance of radio and television as a source of income to teams rendered organized baseball a matter of interstate commerce in the 1940s, whatever its status at the time of the *Federal Baseball* case. In a concurring opinion, Judge Frank went further in condemning the reserve clause: "[Assuming . . . the truth of the statements in the complaint], we have here a monopoly which, in its effect on ball-players like the plaintiff, possesses characteristics shockingly repugnant to moral principles that, at least since the War Between the States, have been basic in America, as shown by the Thirteenth Amendment to the Constitution, condemning 'involuntary servitude'. . . ."

Organized baseball did not appeal the decision, and instead settled the Gardella case out of court. Then, four years later, baseball was in the courts again, this time being sued under the antitrust laws by a minor league player in the New York Yankees chain, who was black-listed when he refused to report to the club he was assigned to. Once again, baseball won in the trial court, and this time the decision was eventually appealed to the Supreme Court (*Toolson v. New York Yan-kees*, 346 U.S. 356 (1953)). The majority opinion of the Court upheld the earlier *Federal Baseball* case, pointing out:

> Congress has had the ruling [*Federal Baseball*] under consideration [since that time] but has not seen fit to bring such business under these laws by legislation having prospective effect. The business has thus been left for thirty years to develop, on the understanding that it was not subject to existing antitrust legislation. . . . We think that if there are evils in this field which now warrant application to it of the antitrust laws it should be by legislation. Without reexamination of the underlying issues, the judgments below are affirmed, . . . so far as that decision determines that Congress had no intention of including the business of baseball within the scope of the federal antitrust laws.

Justices Burton and Reed dissented, agreeing with Judge Learned Hand's earlier view that baseball was clearly engaged in interstate commerce, and that *Federal Baseball* should be overturned.

Next, it was the NFL's turn to appear in court to defend itself from antitrust charges (*Radovich v. National Football League*, 352 U.S. 445 (1957)). George Radovich, an all-pro guard with the Detroit Lions before World War II, returned from military service to play with the Lions in 1945. In 1946, his father in Los Angeles was ill, and Radovich asked the Lions to trade him to the Rams. When the Lions refused, Radovich joined the Los Angeles Dons of the All American Football Conference and played with the Dons for the 1946 and 1947 seasons. He retired from pro football after the 1947 season, and applied for a job as coach with the San Francisco Clippers in the Pacific Coast League, which had affiliations with the NFL. The NFL informed the Pacific Coast League that Radovich was on the NFL blacklist and that the PCL would suffer severe penalties if Radovich were hired. Radovich did not get the coaching job, and he sued the NFL.

When Radovich went into court, his case was dismissed on the ground that the NFL, like organized baseball, was exempted from the antitrust laws, on the basis of the *Federal Baseball* and *Toolson* decisions. The case was appealed to the Supreme Court. Justice Clark handed down the majority decision, which reversed the trial court, holding professional football subject to the antitrust laws, despite the admitted fact that "professional football has embraced the same techniques which existed in baseball at the time of the former [*Federal Baseball* and *Toolson*] decisions."

Clark made no bones about the anomalous nature of the earlier baseball decisions: "If this ruling is unrealistic, inconsistent, or illogical, it is sufficient to answer, aside from the distinctions between the businesses [of football and baseball], that were we considering the question of baseball for the first time upon a clean slate we would have no doubts. But *Federal Baseball* held the business of baseball outside the scope of the Act. No other business claiming the coverage of those cases has such an adjudication." Dissenting opinions were filed by Justices Frankfurter, Harlan, and Brennan, all of whom felt that, correctly applied, *stare decisis* would imply that team sports businesses, such as the NFL, that have employed the same business rules as organized baseball should also be covered by the umbrella of exemption extended to baseball by the earlier decisions.

Even before the *Radovich* decision was handed down by the Supreme Court, the NFL had modified its version of the reserve clause to convert it into a (one-year) "option" clause. Thus a copy of the 1950 standard player's contract of star halfback Bill Dudley of the Washington Redskins contains the following language: "On or before the date of expiration of this contract, the Club may, upon notice in writing to the Player, renew this contract for a further term until the first day of May following such expiration on the same terms, including rate of compensation to the Player, as are provided by this contract, except that after such renewal this contract shall not include a further option to the Club to renew the contract. . . ."

In the early 1950s, one of the few NFL players to test the new option clause of the NFL contract was Bud Grant. Grant had had a spectacular multi-sport career at the University of Minnesota, and played with the Minneapolis Lakers of the NBA during the 1950/51 season. He also signed with the NFL Philadelphia Eagles, and starred with them in 1951 and 1952, playing out his option during 1952. Despite the fact that he was one of the league's best ends, he could find no NFL team (other than the Eagles) that would offer him a contract, and he moved to the Canadian Football League in 1953, first as a player and later as a coach, finally returning to the NFL in 1967 as the highly successful coach of the Minnesota Vikings. Another player who tested the option clause was George Ratterman of the New York Yanks, who played out his option in 1950. Ratterman got no offers from NFL teams, and signed with Montreal of the CFL. Ratterman was then sued by the NFL, and settled out of court by returning to the Yanks and being assessed a $2,000 fine.

There is no record of any NFL player who had played out his option getting an offer from another team until 1963, when Carroll Rosenbloom, owner of the Baltimore Colts, signed free agent R. C. Owens, who had played out his option with the 49ers. Rosenbloom had thereby violated a "gentlemen's agreement not to sign free agents" (Harris 1986, 182). NFL owners reacted to the signing by adopting at their next meeting what has come to be known as the Rozelle rule. Under the rule, if a team signed a player who had played out his option, and if the signing team and the previous owning team could not agree as to compensation, the commissioner of the NFL (Pete Rozelle at the time) decided on an appropriate compensation for the team losing the player, from the roster of the team signing the free agent. In practice, Rozelle's choices of compensation were designedly so severe on the team signing a free agent that when negotiations between teams failed, teams were unwilling to undertake the risk of having Rozelle determine the compensation. Thus, in *Mackey v. NFL*, 543 F.2d 606 (1976), it was reported that between 1963 and 1974, 176 players played out their options. Of these, only 34 signed with other teams, and there were only four cases in which the rule was applied, with Rozelle determining the compensation involved.

During the 1960s, the Congress passed legislation exempting league-wide television contracts in all team sports from the antitrust laws, and exempting the merger of the AFL and NFL from antitrust as well. Otherwise, the paradoxical situation of a complete exemption of baseball from the antitrust laws while other team sports were subject to them continued. In 1966, when the Milwaukee Braves were being spirited out of town to Atlanta by their new owners, the state of Wisconsin sued the team under its own state antitrust law, only to find the courts ruling (and being upheld by the Supreme Court) that, so far as baseball was concerned, the federal government had preempted the field, so that baseball's antitrust exemption applied to state laws as well as to federal laws (*State v. Milwaukee Braves, Inc.*, 385 U.S. 990 (1966)). Later cases established the preeminence of federal antitrust laws over state laws for the other team sports (see, e.g., *Robertson v. NBA*, 389 F. Supp. 867 (S.D.N.Y. 1975), aff'd, 556 F.2d 682 (2d Cir. 1977).

A few years after the Wisconsin decision, Judge Friendly commented on the strange antitrust status of professional sports as follows: "We freely acknowledge our belief that *Federal Baseball* was not one of Mr. Justice Holmes' happiest days, that the rationale of *Toolson* is extremely dubious and that, to use the Supreme Court's own adjectives, the distinction between baseball and the other professional sports is 'unrealistic', 'inconsistent', and 'illogical'. . . . While we should not fall out of our chairs with surprise at the news that *Federal Baseball* and *Toolson* have been overruled, we are not all certain the Court is ready to give them a happy despatch" (*Salerno v. American League*, 429 F.2d 1003, 1005 (1970)).

At one congressional hearing on pro sports, Ted Turner, owner of the NL Atlanta Braves and NBA Atlanta Hawks, as well as the owner of the Turner TV network, was queried about the justification for an antitrust treatment of baseball different from that of the other sports. Asked if there were any significant differences between baseball, say, and football, and, with tongue firmly in cheek, he replied, "Well, football is played in the fall, and it uses a different shaped ball."

Bill Veeck had a few biting comments about the situation as well, although his interpretation of *Federal Baseball* and *Toolson* certainly leaves something to be desired:

> It is no secret that baseball has been engaged in a highly successful rear-guard action against being placed under the restrictions of the antitrust law, ever since that delightful day in 1922 when the Supreme Court granted us an exemption on the grounds that baseball was "not a commercial enterprise."
>
> Of course not. Baseball, like loan sharking, is a humanitarian enterprise. (*The Hustler's Handbook*, p. 75)

It is only since the early 1970s that the player reserve system has been subjected to major changes. The impetus for those changes has been the emergence of strong and active players' unions in all the pro team sports, with rival leagues also playing a secondary role. Prior to the 1970s, individual players were reluctant to file antitrust suits against teams or leagues, even in the sports other than baseball, because even if a player won his suit, trial delays and league sanctions would ensure that he would sacrifice his playing career. The existence of unions made it possible to file what were in effect class action antitrust suits attacking the player reservation system; owners couldn't blacklist the entire union membership. While the developments in the different sports all parallel one another, it is convenient to consider the history since the early 1970s of each sport separately.

The Reserve Clause in
the 1970s and 1980s: Baseball

The most dramatic changes in the reserve system have occurred in baseball, where, in the past, the reserve clause had its strictest interpretation as a perpetual option on the player's services. Changes in the player reservation system that have taken place in baseball since the early

1970s are due almost exclusively to the actions of the Major League Players Association under Marvin Miller.

Miller's leadership was critical in turning the MLPA into an effective bargaining unit. In 1964, at Senate hearings into a law designed to provide protection for all sports from antitrust prosecution, two player representatives of the MLPA testified. When asked whether the reserve clause was needed in baseball, pitcher Bob Friend of Pittsburgh replied, "I think the players realize that for the best interests of baseball, and naturally to promote the game, that the reserve clause is essential." Bob Allison, outfielder with the Twins, added, "I feel the same."

Judge Robert Cannon, the lawyer for the players association, then chimed in, "If I might, Senator, preface my remarks by repeating the words of Gene Woodling . . . 'we have it so good we don't know what to ask for next.' I think this sums up the thinking of the average major league ballplayer today" (*Professional Sports Antitrust Bill—1964* 42) Shortly thereafter, Cannon was replaced by Miller. One thing is for sure—Robert Cannon was no Marvin Miller.

Once Marvin Miller had taken over the MLPA, things began to happen. Miller gives his version of the story in his autobiography, *A Whole Different Ball Game*, while Bowie Kuhn sees things from a different perspective in his *Hardball: The Education of a Baseball Commissioner*. Briefly, from the point of view of the players at least, the mid-1970s to early-1980s were "Star Wars," and the mid-1980s looked more like "The Empire Strikes Back," until the collusion rulings near the end of the 1980s put the players back in the driver's seat.

The 1970s opened inauspiciously enough for baseball players with the Curt Flood case, filed in January, 1970. Curt Flood was an all-star outfielder for the St. Louis Cardinals (seven gold gloves, lifetime batting average of .293), who was traded to the Philadelphia Phillies in 1969, and refused to report. He requested free agency to negotiate his own deal with NL teams, was refused, and filed suit under the Sherman Act. In 1971, his contract was traded to the Washington Senators, and Flood reported, played a few games, and then retired from baseball, but continued his legal actions, supported by the MLPA. Flood lost at the trial level when the trial court ruled that *Federal Baseball* and *Toolson* exempted baseball from the antitrust laws. He lost also at the appeals level, and the Supreme Court upheld the lower courts on final appeal (*Flood v. Kuhn*, 407 U.S. 258 (1971)).

Justice Blackmun wrote the majority opinion, stating:

1. Professional baseball is a business and it is engaged in interstate commerce.

2. With its reserve system enjoying exemption from the federal

antitrust laws, baseball is, in a very distinct sense, an exception and an anomaly. *Federal Baseball* and *Toolson* have become an aberration confined to baseball. . . .

4. Other professional sports operating interstate, football, boxing, basketball, and, presumably, hockey and golf—are not so exempt.

Justice Blackmun concluded:

Accordingly, we adhere once again to *Federal Baseball* and *Toolson*, and to their application to professional baseball. We adhere also to *International Boxing* and *Radovich* and to their respective applications to professional boxing and professional football. If there is any inconsistency or illogic in all this, it is an inconsistency and illogic of long standing that is to be remedied by the Congress and not by this Court. . . . Under these circumstances, there is merit in consistency even though some might claim that beneath that consistency is a layer of inconsistency.

Justice Douglas, who had voted with the majority in the *Toolson* case, dissented in this case, stating: "While I joined the Court's opinion in *Toolson* . . . I have lived to regret it; and I would now correct what I believe to be its fundamental error."

Justice Marshall also dissented, but pointed out that the emergence of collective bargaining in baseball (and the other team sports) could drastically change the legal status of the reservation system, because of the long-established practice of exempting certain areas of collective bargaining from application of the antitrust laws. In fact, issues involving collective bargaining and the reservation system have been at the forefront of developments since *Flood*.

The *New York Times* (June 23, 1972) took the following editorial position on the Court's ruling in *Flood*:

Everything about the Supreme Court's renewed finding that baseball, alone among the professional sports, is exempt from the antitrust laws bespeaks that captivity to "foolish consistency" which Emerson deplored. . . . The only basis for a judge-made monopoly status of baseball is that the Supreme Court made a mistake the first time it considered the case fifty years ago and now feels obligated to keep on making the same mistake because Congress does not act to repeal the exemption it never ordered.

There was a player strike over the reserve clause during spring training in 1972, and expectations that a strike might occur in 1973 as well. In handing down the *Flood* decision, the Supreme Court had suggested that labor-management negotiations might settle the issue of player contract terms, and bargaining over free agency occurred during the 1972 season.

Spring training in 1973 was delayed by negotiations. Finally, on March 1, 1973, a three-year contract was signed, with no change in the reserve system. However, the new contract contained a provision for the arbitration of salary disputes, providing that any player with two or more years of major league service could submit his salary for arbitration to a three-member arbitration board, one member appointed by management, one member appointed by the union, and one independent member. The board was required to choose either the salary level submitted by the owner or that submitted by the player.

The arbitration procedure produced a real bombshell in the December 1975 arbitrations, when Andy Messersmith of the Dodgers and Dave McNally of the Expos asked to be declared free agents after having played the 1975 season without signing their contracts. They argued that the reserve clause was simply a one-year option clause, as in football and basketball, and that playing for one year without a contract fulfilled their obligations.

On December 23, 1975, the independent arbitrator, Peter Seitz, ruled that Messersmith and McNally were free agents. Immediately after announcement of the ruling, Seitz was fired by the owners, who appealed Seitz's ruling in the federal courts. The trial judge, Judge Oliver, suggested that collective bargaining was the correct arena for deciding the issue, rather than the courts: "The track record of the parties would indicate that they might even seek some sort of review in the United Nations." In February 1976, the Seitz ruling was upheld, and in March, it was upheld on appeal, whereupon the owners finally gave up.

Major concessions were reached in collective bargaining in the spring of 1976, after a 15-day lockout during spring training. The agreement provided that any player refusing to sign his 1976 contract would be a free agent after the 1976 season and any player signing for 1976 but playing out his option in 1977 would be a free agent after the 1977 season. Any player becoming a free agent would be subject to a "free agent draft." Following the 1977 season, under any contract signed from then on, a player with six years of major league service could become a free agent simply by notifying the club after the season was over, and any player with five years' service could demand a trade, subject to certain limitations.

Free agency became an important factor in baseball player markets in the late 1970s, with the Yankees and the Angels being the most notable successful bidders for free agents, and with the Twins and the Athletics the most prominent losers. Owners were predictably unhappy with the escalation of player salaries, because player salaries did increase rapidly, more than doubling on average between 1976 and 1979.

On December 31, 1979, the labor contract expired, and the owners announced that they would seek an end to salary arbitration, and a change in the free agency rules to provide for Rozelle rule-like compensation to a team losing a free agent by the team acquiring the free agent. Negotiations continued during the spring, with a strike only barely averted, under an agreement to set up a player-owner committee to study free agency and arbitration issues, and to report back in January 1981. During the 1980 season, the owners prepared for a strike by setting aside 2 percent of gate receipts for a strike fund, and using part of this money to purchase strike insurance from Lloyds of London. Under the policy, after a 12-day grace period, the insurance paid $100,000 for each game canceled because of the strike up to a maximum of 500 games ($50 million).

When no agreement was reached by the committee, negotiations resumed and continued during the early part of the 1981 season. Negotiations were finally abandoned on June 10, 1981, and a strike began on the next day, the first in-season strike in the history of organized baseball, and one that lasted 50 days. The strike was settled on August 1, just after the owners' strike insurance ran out. The agreement reached to settle the strike was on terms remarkably close to those suggested before the strike by Marvin Miller. The major change that was introduced into the free agency system was to permit some strictly limited compensation for outstanding free agents, in the form of players on major league rosters. The arbitration system was left essentially unchanged, and the contract was to run until the end of 1984.

By 1984, there were owner claims in the newspapers that baseball as a whole was losing near $100 million per year. The issue of the financial viability of baseball became central to the negotiations between players and owners, and, under National Labor Relations Board rules, for the first time, baseball opened up its books to the union. Book losses for 1984 were first reported at $36 million, and then scaled down to $27 million by an independent auditor hired by the owners. The union claimed that excessive executive payrolls and shifts of revenues from teams to parent corporations could lead to a reduction of losses to as little as $9 million for the year.

In the spring of 1985, there was another baseball strike. This time the owners had no strike insurance (Lloyd's of London had learned its lesson), and the strike lasted exactly one day. Settlement was on terms close to those of the 1981 agreement, except that the players agreed to a requirement of three years of major league service for a player before he was eligible for arbitration, and compensation was changed so that only amateur draft choices could be used for compensation. The old free agent draft was replaced by one in which any team could negotiate with any free agent, with the team owning the player required to agree to arbitration to retain its negotiation rights, when the player requested arbitration.

Problems began arising even in the first year of the new agreement. At the end of the 1985 season, 62 players filed for free agency, and not one of them received an offer from any team other than the team he had played for during the 1985 season. The players' union filed a grievance charging collusion on the part of the owners. Midway in the grievance proceedings, the owners attempted to fire the arbitrator, Thomas Roberts. This led to a further grievance hearing, at which Roberts was reinstated as arbitrator of the collusion hearing. Following the 1986 season, only a handful of free agents received offers from outside teams, and the union filed a second unfair labor practice charge against the owners.

In September 1987, arbitrator Roberts ruled that the owners had in fact colluded in the free agent market following the 1985 season. Seven players were awarded free agency under Roberts's ruling. Later rulings held that there was collusion after the 1986 season as well, and 13 additional players were granted free agency. Among other things, the collusion hearings revealed that owners were exchanging information with one another as to the salary bids they were making to retain players who had opted for free agency. One prominent case where information was exchanged was that of Andre Dawson, who was paid $1.5 million by Montreal in 1986, and then was signed by the Cubs for $500,000 (plus bonuses that added $200,000 more) for the 1987 season, and was one of the few free agents who actually moved. Finally, in 1990, the arbitrators ruled that baseball owners would have to pay players $280 million in the way of damages because of their collusive actions following the 1985 and 1986 seasons. This roughly matched reported profits of all baseball teams for the 1989 season. Near the end of 1990, both the owners and the union agreed to the damage settlement.

In March 1990, following a lockout during spring training, a new three-year labor agreement was signed in baseball. The agreement continued free agency and the arbitration system, with minor changes. It also provided that the union would receive triple damages if owners were found guilty of colluding again. Finally, a study commission was set up to investigate a plan of revenue sharing based on the NBA model, an approach that had been raised as a bargaining issue by management before the lockout.

The Reserve Clause in
the 1970s and 1980s: Football

Player salaries in football increased dramatically during the 1970s and 1980s, reflecting strong growth in gate and TV revenues for the league, player successes in several court cases in the early and mid-1970s, and the impact of two short-lived rival leagues. On the other hand, the decision on the part of the NFL Players Association to go for short-term rather than long-term objectives in its negotiations left the basic reservation and player control system of the NFL pretty much intact, at a time when baseball and basketball were moving toward freer competitive labor markets.

The NFL Players Association has been one of the least successful of the major player unions, in part because of the short playing careers in football relative to the other sports, and in part because of the "team" nature of football, where coaches are more important and superstars less important than in the other team sports. Moreover, the NFL's institutional structure—particularly its rules promoting equalization of revenues among teams—has made it the most unified and effective owner organization in sports.

The decade of the 1970s began with a player strike that ended just before the 1970 All Star game. The NFL and NFLPA signed a four-year contract, the first collective bargaining agreement in the history of the NFL. The agreement contained no provisions at all relating to the player reservation sytem, the college draft, or the Rozelle rule.

In March 1972, Joe Kapp brought an antitrust suit against the NFL (*Kapp v. NFL*, 390 F. Supp. 73 (N.D. Cal. 1974)). Kapp had signed a three-year, $600,000 contract with the New England Patriots in 1970 after playing out his option with the Minnesota Vikings, where he had been voted the MVP of the NFL. At his insistence, Kapp's Patriots contract did not include the option (reserve) clause. While Kapp played during 1970 under this contract, in 1971 he was informed by the league that he would not be permitted to play in the future unless he signed a standard NFL contract including the option clause. Kapp refused and did not play during 1971 (or any subsequent year).

In 1974, Judge Sweigert ruled that the NFL contract and player reserve system were "patently unreasonable and illegal," in holding that Kapp had established that there had been antitrust violations in his case. Judge Sweigert went on to state that the Rozelle rule "is unreasonable under any legal test and there is no genuine issue to require or justify a trial (other than to establish damages)." In April 1976, there was a surprise ending to the *Kapp* case, when a jury ruled that despite the actions of the NFL, which included abrogating a two-year contract paying $200,000 per year, Kapp was not entitled to any damages. The jury decision was upheld on appeal.

While the *Kapp* case must have brought chills to the spines of NFL owners, in fact the most significant legal suit of the 1970s involving football was a class action suit filed in federal court in Minneapolis in 1972, by 32 players, headed by John Mackey, president of the NFLPA (*Mackey v. NFL*, 543 F.2d 606 (1976)). The suit asked triple damages for losses in income suffered by players due to the operation of the option clause and the Rozelle rule.

The trial court ruled that the Rozelle rule was a per se violation of the Sherman Act, and specifically rejected the NFL argument that the Rozelle rule was protected from the antitrust laws because it was an agreement that been negotiated through collective bargaining. The appeals court rejected the per se conclusion, but found that the Rozelle rule was an unreasonable restraint of trade; and the court concurred that there had not been meaningful arm's-length negotiations concerning the rule during collective bargaining and hence it was not exempt from application of the antitrust laws.

In its ruling, the appeals court spelled out the test for an exemption from the antitrust laws based on the argument that the relevant practices had been negotiated in a collective bargaining agreement:

> First, the labor policy favoring collective bargaining may potentially be given pre-eminence over the antitrust laws where the restraint on trade primarily *affects the parties* to the collective bargaining agreement.... Second, federal labor policy is implicated sufficiently to prevail only where the agreement sought to be exempted concerns a *mandatory subject of collective bargaining.* ... Finally, the policy favoring collective bargaining is furthered to the degree necessary to override the antitrust laws only where the agreement sought to be exempted is the *product of bona fide arm's-length bargaining.* ... (quoted in Nelson 1980) (Nelson's italics)

The court ruled that the final element was lacking in the NFL's defense; hence it ruled for the players.

In evaluating the case, the appeals court agreed with the finding of the trial court that

> the Rozelle Rule significantly deters clubs from negotiating with and signing free agents; that it acts as a substantial deterrent to players playing out their options and becoming free agents; that it significantly decreases players' bargaining power in contract negotiations; that players are thus denied the right to sell their services

in a free and open market; that as a result, the salaries paid by each club are lower than if competitive bidding were allowed to prevail; and that absent the Rozelle Rule, there would be increased movement in interstate commerce of players from one club to another.

Following that verdict, bargaining between the NFL and the Players Association resulted in an agreement and out-of-court settlement of *Mackey*, under which the NFL agreed to pay $15.8 million in damages to players who had been under contract during the 1972–1975 period. There were increases in contributions to the player pension fund and increases in the league minimum wage. The union got the checkoff of union dues, and a change in the Rozelle rule—instead of compensation choice by the Commissioner, the compensation to be paid for a free agent would be determined by his salary in the previous year, ranging from no compensation for a player earning $47,000 or less to two first-round draft choices for a player earning over $200,000 per year. Over time, as new labor agreements were signed, the dollar categories were adjusted, but there was no change in the basic principle governing compensation.

In the event, the new compensation rules turned out to be even more restrictive than the old Rozelle rule. Between 1977 and 1988, on average, each year from 125 to 150 players announced as free agents, but in that 12-year stretch, only 3 players actually moved from one team to another under the new compensation rules—Norm Thompson, who moved from the Cardinals to the Colts in 1977, Wilber Marshall, who moved from the Bears to the Redskins in 1988, and John Dutton, who moved from the Colts to the Cowboys in 1979.

A year after the *Mackey* decision, a federal court ruled that the NFL's college draft was an unreasonable restraint of trade, attacking another underpinning of the NFL reservation system (*James McCoy (Yazoo) Smith v. Pro Football, Inc.*, 593 F.2d 1173 (D.D.C. 1978)).

In July 1979, John Dutton of the Colts announced that he was an unrestricted free agent after playing out his option during the 1978 season. The NFL rejected this argument, and Dutton and the NFLPA filed a grievance with the NLRB. By mid-October, Dutton had signed with the Cowboys, who agreed to compensate the Colts according to the schedule negotiated in 1977, and Dutton dropped his grievance against the NFL, but the union carried the case on. In May 1980, in a significant decision, the federal arbitrator ruled for the NFL on the ground that free agency rules were now a part of the negotiated settlement between the NFLPA and the NFL, including the compensation scheme, and that individual players were bound by the agreement.

When time came for renewal of the labor agreement in 1982, Ed Garvey, head of the NFLPA, was making public his argument that the gate and TV sharing rules of the NFL made it impossible for a competitive free agent market to develop. Garvey presented his proposal for a contract that would specify minimum salary levels based on position and seniority, to be funded by a payment to the union of 55 percent of the gross revenues of the NFL. Garvey illustrated his argument concerning the nonviability of a free agent market in the NFL by the case of star running back Walter Payton of the Bears, who opted for free agency after the 1981 season, and received no offers from any team other than the Bears.

Negotiations between owners and players broke down, and on September 21, 1982, the first in-season strike in NFL history began, to continue until November 17, the longest strike (57 days) in team sports history in the United States. The strike was settled by the players' once again trading off an agreement to continue the existing free agency and compensation rules for short-term gains in pension payments and severance pay.

In 1987, it was time for contract negotiations in the NFL again, and, once again, free agency was the basic issue. The union was pressing for complete free agency after four years of service, with right of first refusal for players with less than four years' service. Management demanded a continuation of the compensation system already in place. Once again, there was a strike, this time for 24 days. This strike was unique in that teams continued to play out their regular season schedule, using a collection of minor league, amateur, and retired players, along with those regular players who had crossed the picket lines.

Three weeks after going out, the NFLPA called off its strike, and announced that with the breaking off of negotiations, it would return to the courts to attempt to obtain free agency through application of the antitrust laws, abandoning the collective bargaining approach. The collective bargaining agreement expired in February 1988, and shortly thereafter, a case was filed in federal court in Minneapolis, seeking an injunction against continuation of the NFL's player reservation system, and asking for free agency for 280 members of the NFLPA. In July 1988, Judge Doty ruled against the NFLPA, holding that an injunction was inappropiate and that the issue of free agency might better be addressed through collective bargaining than through the courts. He did say, however, that he believed there was a good chance that the NFLPA would prevail at a trial of the case on its merits. The trial court's decision was upheld on appeal.

In February 1989, the NFL announced a modified free agency plan, as a rearguard action against the union's antitrust suit. Under the plan, teams were allowed to "reserve" roughly 65 percent of the players they had under contract, with the remaining 35 percent being granted complete free agency. A number of moves of "Plan B" free agents occurred before the 1989 season, and the plan was continued into the 1990 and 1991 seasons as well.

In November 1989, the NFLPA announced that it was decertifying itself as the bargaining agent for NFL players. NFL owners denounced this as a ploy that was being used in an attempt to evade the labor exemption applicable in antitrust cases. A surprise development in the NFLPA case still under litigation was an announcement in 1990 by the Justice Department that the government agreed with the NFLPA position that the nonstatutory labor exemption should not automatically apply simply because the issues in question had been subjects of bargaining in the past. Trial of the NFLPA case was scheduled for Minneapolis in the spring of 1992. Meanwhile, there were reports in the press that NFL owners were discussing among themselves introduction of a revenue-sharing arrangement with a salary cap, based on the NBA model, in an attempt to bring the union back to the bargaining table.

The Reserve Clause in the 1970s and 1980s: Basketball

Traditionally, basketball's reserve clause has been interpreted as a one-year option clause, as in the case of football. And, as with football, signing of a free agent involved compensation a la the Rozelle rule. The emergence of the ABA in 1967 as a competitor to the NBA led to interleague bidding wars both in the veteran player market and in the market for college players. Basketball players were thus the first of the pro team sports athletes to see salary levels skyrocketing. And pro basketball has been a full employment program for lawyers as well—basketball has been the most litigious of all pro team sports.

Competition between the ABA and NBA during the late 1960s had eaten into profits for teams in both leagues, so that by early 1970, merger talks had begun between the two leagues. In April 1970, the National Basketball Association Players Association filed an antitrust suit (*Robertson v. NBA*, 389 F. Supp. 867 (S.D.N.Y. 1975), 556 F.2d 682 (2d Cir. 1977)) to block any merger agreement and asked that merger talks be prohibited. A preliminary injunction was issued, banning an ABA-NBA merger, but permitting talks for the sole purpose of petitioning the Congress for antitrust exemption legislation (with respect to a merger).

While the *Robertson* case was in the courts, a second case was filed involving the NBA's college draft. The individual involved was All Star player Spencer Haywood. Haywood had signed with Denver of the ABA after his sophomore year in college. He played one year with Denver and then sat out one year, claiming that Denver had breached its contract with him. He then signed as a free agent with Seattle of the NBA. The NBA refused to permit Haywood to play, because his college class had not graduated. This led to a three-sided case involving Denver, Seattle, and the NBA (*Haywood v. NBA*, 401 U.S. 1204, 1205 (1971)). At the appeal court level, it was ruled that while Denver had no rights to Haywood, he could not play for Seattle either. This decision was reversed by the Supreme Court, which in effect voided the class-graduation aspect of NBA college draft rules, in permitting Seattle to play Haywood.

In June 1971, the NBA formally abandoned its rule preventing the signing of a college player before his class had graduated, and replaced it with provisions for "hardship" cases. This allowed any player to request to be included in the draft if it would involve undue hardship to wait a full four years before turning professional. Beginning in 1975, any player who requested inclusion was automatically included in the draft list.

In March 1973, a three-year contract was signed between the NBA and the NBAPA, the first labor agreement in the history of the NBA. In January 1974, as merger talks ground to a halt, the ABA announced that it was reviving its antitrust suit against the NBA. Both the NBA and the NBAPA had made public announcements opposing a merger.

Later in the year, Judge Carter, who was hearing the *Robertson* case, announced that the stalled ABA-NBA merger talks could not proceed until an agreement was reached with the NBAPA concerning the player reserve system. In February 1973, Judge Carter handed down his ruling in *Robertson*, holding that "[the] player draft, uniform player contract, and reserve clause were analogous to devices which were *per se* violative of the antitrust laws," and continued his injunction against a merger. The decision was appealed by the NBA, while plans were made by the union to sue for damages under the Sherman Act.

In May 1975, George McGinnis of the Indiana Pacers of the ABA filed an antitrust suit against the NBA. McGinnis had decided to jump from the ABA to the NBA. NBA draft rights to McGinnis were held by Philadelphia, but McGinnis had signed instead with the Knicks, so there were disputes within the NBA involved, as well as between the NBA and the ABA. The case was incorporated into the *Robertson* case. A similar internal dispute arose with respect to Julius Erving, who was drafted by the Milwaukee Bucks of the NBA, but who signed instead with the Atlanta Hawks of the NBA. The Hawks then proceeded to sell

Erving (for $400,000) to the New York Nets of the ABA. Larry O'Brien, Commissioner of the NBA, ruled that the Knicks' contract with Mc-Ginnis was invalid, and fined the Knicks a first-round draft choice for tampering; and O'Brien fined Atlanta $400,000 for its actions in the Erving case.

Judge Carter's courtroom became even more crowded in November 1975, when the ABA Players Association filed an antitrust suit against the ABA to prevent it from merging with the NBA, thus joining the NBAPA, the NBA, McGinnis, etc., as parties to the *Robertson* case. Finally, to complete the picture, a late arrival was Wilt Chamberlain, who was also suing the NBA. Chamberlain had jumped his NBA contract to move to the ABA. His old NBA team, the Lakers, sought to enjoin him from his move and won in arbitration. Chamberlain sat out the 1973/74 and 1974/75 seasons, and then attempted to sign with an NBA team for the 1975/76 season, only to find himself faced with a group boycott. Chamberlain already owned most of the NBA scoring records. He now had added a further record: "He claims to be the only NBA player ever to 'sit out' his option year with his old team and then to attempt to negotiate with another team." (footnote, *Robertson*, p. 687)

In February 1976, an out-of-court settlement of *Robertson* was announced. The NBA compensation form of the option clause was dropped, beginning with the 1980 season. Moreover, the option clause was to be removed from player contracts, after the 1976 season. Beginning with the 1980 season, players were to be free agents, subject only to the right of first refusal by the team last owning a player's contract. The college draft rules were changed, beginning with the 1976 draft, to provide that any drafted player would have to be signed by the team within a year, or the player would be returned to the draft pool for the succeeding year.

Settlement of *Robertson* led to the suggestion by Judge Carter that the ABA and NBA settle their antitrust case out of court as well. In August 1977, a merger agreement was reached between the ABA and NBA that met with the approval of the court and the union, and the two leagues merged.

In 1977, the appeals court ruled on *Robertson*, affirming the judgments of the lower court, and affirming the agreements that were reached to settle the case out of court.

Expansion of the NBA to accommodate the ABA teams taken in by the merger, coupled with changes in the reserve system, led to financial problems for the NBA, especially for small-city teams. An Arthur Andersen audit showed overall NBA losses at $13 million for the 1979/80 season, with 17 of 23 teams showing losses in the 1980/81 season. Small-city teams were asking for gate sharing and sharing of local TV revenues, leading to a meeting in New York by the big-city teams—Lakers, Knicks, Nets, 76ers, Celtics, and Bulls—to present a united front against any change in the sharing rules. These teams represented a blocking coalition under the league rule requiring a three-fourths' majority vote to change the sharing rules.

On April 1, 1983, a truly innovative labor agreement was signed, aimed at solving the league's financial problems within a modified free agency format. The agreement included a guaranteed revenue-sharing provision, under which the players were guaranteed a minimum of 53 percent of the gross revenues of the league (regular season gate receipts plus local and national TV and radio revenues, plus net pre- and post-season gate revenues). The contract also established salary floors and salary caps per team. Each team's salary cap was set equal to 53 percent of league gross revenue divided by the number of teams, while the salary floor was set at around 90 percent of the salary cap. No team could have a salary bill less than the floor, and teams could exceed the salary cap only under restrictive conditions, for example, if such higher expenditures were needed in order to match offers (in the free agent market) by other teams for veteran players of the team, or to maintain existing salaries of players. The original salary cap (for 1984/85) was set at $3.8 million, and the cap has climbed over time, to around $12 million for the 1990/91 season. Free agency rules have remained unchanged. Teams above the salary cap at the time of the agreement were allowed to continue exceeding the cap so long as present players remained on the roster, with adjustments occurring as players retired. Finally, a provision was made for compensation of weak teams by payments by strong teams, when financial problems developed.

The labor agreement expired in 1987. Players asked for an elimination of salary caps, the right of first refusal, and the player draft. Bargaining broke down in October, and the union decided to file suit against the NBA, rather than strike. In 1989, an agreement was reached between the NBAPA and the NBA, which continued the basic revenue-sharing arrangement, and which remains in force in 1992.

The Reserve Clause in the 1970s and 1980s: Hockey

During the 1960s, the NHL was in as strong a position relative to its players as was organized baseball—there were no competitive leagues, and the reserve clause in hockey contracts was interpreted as a perpetual option clause. There were, however, some indications that troubles were brewing for NHL owners. In 1969, a Canadian federal government task force recommended abolishing the reserve clause in the NHL. Clarence Campbell, president of the NHL, responded: "No professional sport can operate successfully without the reserve clause. There is strong reason for rejecting the playing-out-an-option formula, and that is that the public demands absolute integrity on the part of those that play." Three years later, in defending its contract provisions in an antitrust suit filed by the World Hockey Association, the NHL argued that its reserve clause gave a team only a three-year option on a player's services.

In 1972, Gary Davidson, who had earlier been the promoter and organizer of the ABA, announced the formation of the World Hockey Association. WHA owners agreed to follow the practice of honoring NHL contracts, exclusive of reserve clause provisions, and proceeded to hire NHL players who had completed the terms of their existing contracts. Among the star NHL players signed by the WHA were Bobby Hull, Derek Sanderson, Gerry Cheevers, and Bill Flett.

In state courts, there was the usual mix of court decisions supporting and rejecting the validity of the reserve clause. The most important case was that involving Bobby Hull, who had received $1 million in cash plus a multi-year contract (financed by all teams in the WHA) to play with the Winnipeg Jets of the WHA. In an Illinois state court, Hull was enjoined from playing in the state except for the Chicago Blackhawks.

Seven cases involving the signing of NHL players to WHA contracts were joined in a federal case, which was heard by Judge Higginbotham (*Philadelphia World Hockey Club v. Philadelphia Hockey Club, Inc.*, 351 F. Supp. 462 (E.D. Pa. 1972)). This was the first antitrust case filed involving hockey. In his decision, Judge Higginbotham enjoined the NHL from attempting to enforce the reserve clause in its contracts. The argument that the business rules structure of the NHL was needed to preserve the noble game of hockey got the following reaction:

"Despite the thousands of words uttered on this record by all parties about the glory of the sport of hockey and the grandeur of its superstars, the basic factors here are not the sheer exhilaration from observing the speeding puck, but rather the desire to maximize the available buck."

Judge Higginbotham went on to rule that the NHL was engaged in interstate commerce, that its reserve clause had a long history within the NHL of being interpreted as a perpetual option, and that the reserve clause had never been the subject of bona fide good faith collective bargaining. Among other things, he pointed out that the NHL had awarded an expansion franchise in 1971 to Long Island even before an owner was selected, and that this occurred only after the NHL had learned that the WHA was attempting to establish a team in Long Island. Moreover, when the WHA had tried to negotiate a contract with the Nassau Coliseum, the only practical choice in Long Island, it had been turned down by William Shea, the administrator of the facility, who also was a board member of the NHL Los Angeles Kings.

In February 1974, the WHA and NHL settled their legal differences out of court under an agreement approved by Judge Higginbotham. The WHA received $1.75 million in cash plus the promise of 15 NHL-WHA exhibition games. In addition, the two leagues agreed to recognize each other's reserve clauses, and the NHL agreed to permit the WHA to use its arenas.

In October 1975, an agreement was reached between the NHL and the union under which the NHL version of the option clause was accepted by the players, with compensation for free agency to be chosen by an arbitrator, the agreement extending through 1980. A merger between the NHL and the WHA was agreed to by both parties in March 1979, and union agreement was obtained in June 1979, with an extension of the existing labor contract until 1984, under the same option-compensation terms, but with increased fringe benefits for players.

An interesting case dealing with the labor exemption from the antitrust laws came up in 1979, involving Dale McCourt, who had signed a three-year contract with Detroit in 1977 (*McCourt v. California Sports, Inc.*, 600 F.2d 1193 (1979)). At the end of the 1977/78 season, Rogie Vachon, goalie for the L.A. Kings, opted for free agency, and ended up signing with Detroit. Detroit and L.A. couldn't agree upon compensation, and the case went to the arbitrator, who awarded the Kings McCourt's contract.

McCourt objected to being traded, and sued under the antitrust laws to have the trade voided. The defense offered by the NHL was that its player reservation system had been agreed to in collective bargaining with the NHLPA and hence was exempt from the antitrust laws. The trial court granted an injunction against the trade, holding instead that the NHL reserve system violated the antitrust laws. The appeals court reversed in a split decision, holding that the reservation system satisfied the three essential features of the *Mackey* test, including good faith arm's-length bargaining between the parties. The NHL might have decided to let sleeping dogs lie, because the case became moot when L.A. decided to agree to compensation other than McCourt, who agreed to drop a further appeal of the case, and remained with the Red Wings.

In 1984, the compensation rules were changed to make them similar to the NFL rules, with compensation based on the salary of the player being signed. In 1986, the collective bargaining agreement was extended for another five years, retaining the basic elements of the compensation scheme.

Summary

Briefly, as of early 1992, the situation concerning the player reservation systems was as follows. In baseball, something approaching free agency was in place, coupled with salary arbitration, under a collective bargaining agreement signed in 1990, extending the basic approach that has now been followed since 1976. In hockey, bargaining continued concerning extension of the agreement in force until 1991, which restricted player movement by a compensation scheme similar to that in place in the NFL. In the NBA, players were guaranteed 53 percent of gross league revenues and there was free agency, but salary caps apply to all teams. In the NFL, most players were subject to compensation requirements, with something over one-third of the players being free agents ("Plan B free agents"). The NFLPA had decertified itself and was following a strategy of attempting to eliminate the player reservation system through an antitrust suit in the courts. The critical issue in the NFLA case was whether the labor exemption from antitrust achieved by owners through earlier collective bargaining continues when a union has decertified itself and collective bargaining has ceased. Finally, in both baseball and the NFL, owners were discussing a move toward revenue sharing and salary caps, following the lead of the NBA.

Chapter 6

Why Do Pro Athletes Make So Much Money?

No rational person can view what's going on in baseball and not have concerns.

—**Fay Vincent**
Commissioner of Baseball

It will take a club to go belly up in order to stop this madness.
—**Dave Dombrowski**
Montreal Expos General Manager

HUGH DUFFY played in the major leagues from 1888 through 1906. In 1894, while with Boston, he led the National League in batting (.438), hits (236), home runs (18), and runs batted in (145). The following year, he became baseball's first famous holdout. The owners, Boston's legendary, penny-pinching "Triumvir," finally capitulated, agreeing to a $12.50 per month increase in Duffy's salary. However, Duffy was required to assume the duties of team captain, including responsibility for team equipment. In 1895, Duffy's raise evaporated when the team lost equipment worth more than his salary increase.

Contrary to a generally held perception that players were pretty sedentary in the "good old days," Duffy was one of many baseball stars of his era who jumped their contracts whenever rival leagues appeared to challenge existing leagues. Duffy jumped from the Chicago NL team to the Chicago Players League entry in 1890, spent a year in the American Association, and then returned to the National League. In 1901, he left the Boston NL team to join Milwaukee of the American League before ending his career as manager of the Phillies in 1906.

In *The Hustler's Handbook*, Bill Veeck tells of coming across the long-lost accounting records of Charles Comiskey's 1919 "Black Sox," after Veeck had bought the White Sox in 1959. He discovered that Comiskey was every bit as tight-fisted as the Triumvir, leading Veeck to refer to Comiskey as the "cheapest skate in town." In the end, Comiskey's closeness with a buck was his team's undoing. For example, "Shoeless Joe" Jackson, a 10-year veteran with the second-highest lifetime batting average in the history of baseball, hit .354 in 1918 and earned $6,000 ($46,000 in 1991 dollars) in 1919. Eddie Cicotte, with 13 years in the majors, won 29 games in 1919 and was paid $7,000 ($55,000 in 1991 dollars). Buck Weaver, a .300-hitting third baseman in 1919, earned the same amount as Jackson. These salary figures, modest even for the times, applied to one of the best young players in the league (Weaver), along with two players (Jackson and Cicotte) who would have been lead-pipe cinches for the Hall of Fame had it not been for the 1919 Black Sox scandal. All three were banned from baseball for life for their involvement in the conspiracy to throw the 1919 World Series. Cicotte turned out to be the leader of the conspiracy, Jackson was a reluctant fellow traveler, and Weaver went to his grave claiming that he had nothing to do with the plot.

Anecdotal evidence like this suggests that in the distant past, salaries in professional sports, while far above blue-collar wage levels, were still moderate. For a more recent period, complete salary information for all baseball teams over the years 1952 through 1956 were compiled in the late 1950s during a congressional investigation into the antitrust status of pro sports. These team salary figures are show in Table 6.1. Entries are given in 1991 dollars for comparison purposes.

Even in the early 1950s, baseball salaries averaged only in the $67,000 to $74,000 range (in 1991 dollars), or around the $14,000 mark in current (early 1950s) dollars. The minimum wage in baseball in 1954 was a mere $6,000 ($30,100 in 1991 dollars). Table 6.1 provides some solace for the long-suffering Pittsburgh fans of the 1950s, since those Pirate players got paid pretty much what they deserved. On the other hand, it is surprising to find that the Yankees were winning all those pennants under the management of Casey Stengel with payrolls generally less than the amount Cleveland paid its players. The data in Table 6.1 lend additional support to the common perception that players' salaries back in the "good old days" generally were not outrageously high.

My, how times have changed. In the spring of 1991, at the age of 28, Boston Red Sox pitcher Roger Clemens became the highest-paid player in baseball history, with a four-year contract, beginning in 1992, worth $21.5 million. His package totaled $400,000 more than Doubleday and Co. paid for the New York Mets in 1980, a record price in its day. By

Table 6.1
Average Baseball Salaries by Team, 1952–1956 (1991 dollars)

Team	Average Salary per Player				
	1952	1953	1954	1955	1956
NATIONAL LEAGUE					
Brooklyn	73,065	78,096	88,891	83,968	93,984
Chicago	53,751	82,051	72,884	61,233	56,450
Cincinnati	52,014	49,850	47,717	55,423	60,830
Boston/Milwaukee	61,977	59,282	75,049	87,606	87,414
New York	88,495	85,905	72,180	86,494	78,950
Philadelphia	64,737	67,852	70,267	72,803	81,439
Pittsburgh	60,700	42,040	45,502	44,561	49,481
St. Louis	80,729	79,414	80,183	70,529	80,692
Avg. (1991 dollars)	66,934	68,061	69,084	70,327	73,618
Avg. (current dollars)	13,100	13,421	13,725	13,290	14,789
AMERICAN LEAGUE					
Boston	80,525	79,820	74,596	71,792	77,606
Chicago	58,707	70,489	82,146	87,000	87,214
Cleveland	90,539	95,287	90,804	114,585	92,191
Detroit	74,700	68,004	61,006	61,435	72,031
New York	82,722	85,500	95,082	79,977	87,462
Philadelphia/					
Kansas City	59,831	60,093	51,694	57,747	59,984
St. Louis/Baltimore	53,401	61,817	57,130	54,716	55,653
Washington	58,401	60,600	60,502	58,101	48,684
Avg. (1991 dollars)	69,884	72,701	71,620	73,169	72,603
Avg. (current dollars)	13,678	14,336	14,229	14,483	14,585

December 1991, Bobby Bonilla had signed with the Mets for even more than Clemens—$29 million over five years—and in early 1992 Ryne Sandberg's package totaled around $30 million for four years! In the NBA in 1991, Patrick Ewing fought a losing battle with the Knicks to extricate himself from a contract paying a mere $14.2 million (plus bonuses) for four years. Even in the NFL and the NHL, traditionally the lowest-paying leagues, million-dollar-per-year contracts have become commonplace.

In this chapter, we try to answer the burning question: How can it possibly be that pro athletes like Clemens, Bonilla, Sandberg, and Ewing make so much money? This takes us into the workings of the player market under free agency and under a reserve clause system, and the relationship between salaries and ticket prices is also discussed. The main focus of the chapter is on major league baseball, and on modeling the process that determines salaries in that sport. We identify the variables that are the best predictors of baseball salaries in the free agency markets of the late 1980s and early 1990s. Among other things, this approach can be used to provide evidence of owner collusion in the 1986 baseball free agent market. It also can be used to estimate the value of free agency to players in the late 1980s; in turn, these estimates imply that salary increases in the recent past reflect demand-side forces operating in the salary market, rather than supply-side forces.

Finally, the salary distribution in pro sports is examined. In baseball, it turns out that salaries have become less equally distributed over time, and dramatically so following the demise of the reserve clause. In a comparison across sports, what limited data there are suggest that major league baseball has the most unequal distribution of salaries of the four major sports, followed by NBA basketball, and then the NFL, with the NHL having the most equal salary distribution.

Pro Athletes as Entertainers

Figure 6.1 documents the rise in average salaries in the four pro team sports over the past few years, in real (1991 dollars) terms. Prior to the appearance of player unions in the 1970s, salary information was avail-

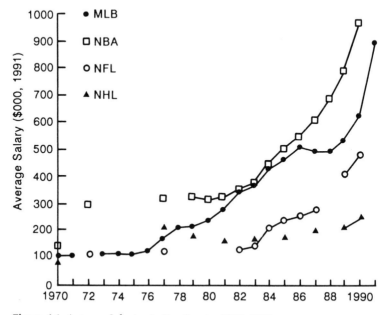

Figure 6.1 Average Salaries in Pro Sports, 1970–1991

able only to owners, except for scattered data collected during congressional hearings, so detailed comparisons with earlier periods are not possible. Unlike unions in most industries, players' unions do not negotiate "standard wage" policies binding on most or all members. Instead, individual player salaries are determined by direct negotiation between the player and the team owner. Unions do bargain for league-wide minimum salaries, so the changes over time in minimum salaries reflect in part changes in the bargaining power of unions. Figure 6.2 shows the rise in minimum salaries over roughly the same time period for baseball and basketball (again, in 1991 dollars), the two sports where data are sufficient to allow comparisons.

Returning to Figure 6.1, the graph charts an explosive growth in player salaries in both baseball and basketball over the past 15 years or so, to the point where the average salary in major league baseball in 1991 was $851,000. Interestingly, there was a lull in the rise of baseball salaries (but not in basketball) over the 1986 through 1989 period. Since the owners were found guilty in 1989 of colluding to restrict the movement of free agents in 1986 and 1987, this lull should come as no surprise.

While average salary levels are much lower for football and hockey, football (and, to a lesser extent, hockey) also showed marked increases in real salary levels in the 1980s, despite the restrictions on player mobility (free agency) for NFL football relative to baseball and basketball. Thus, in rounding up the usual suspects to explain the real growth in

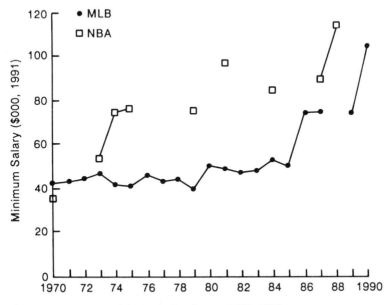

Figure 6.2 Minimum Salaries in Pro Sports, 1970–1990

player compensation in all sports, free agency is not the only candidate. Other factors must be at work as well, including the impressive increase in demand for pro team sports tickets, and the striking increase in value of pro sports television rights for all pro team sports, as noted in Chapter 1.

But the common perception of fans is that pro athletes are wildly overpaid, and that free agency is the culprit. Every red-blooded American boy wants to grow up to be a major leaguer in some sport, and most red-blooded American adult males would toss their careers in a minute if they thought they had a chance to make it in the pros. One example of this sports idolatry can be found in the vastly overinflated assessments that high school athletes make about their chances of turning pro, and, in turn, the similar mistaken perceptions that possess college athletes. Given that many fans would pay for the privilege of playing in the majors (and some actually do pay for the major league experience at adult major league baseball fantasy camps), fans find it a little difficult to accept the fact that pro athletes demand and get salaries in the six- or seven-figure range.

One way to add some perspective to the rise in real salaries for pro athletes is to look at the compensation paid to other entertainers. Perhaps Norby Walters put it best during his 1988 trial for signing college athletes to pro contracts prior to expiration of their college eligibility: "No difference. A sports star is a rock star. They're all the same" (quoted in Telander 1989, 41). Walters' insight is right on the mark—star pro athletes are entertainment stars every bit as much as movie and rock stars. The same factors are at work determining the sizes of the big incomes in sports as in other areas of entertainment. These factors are demand by the public for tickets to see stars, the rarity of skilled and/or charismatic individuals with star qualities (in the economist's jargon, an inelastic supply of talent), and the bargaining power of stars relative to that of the promoters who hire them (team owners in the case of pro sports). In explaining the rise in salaries for sports stars, both increases in the demand for their output and changes in their bargaining power (for example, free agency's replacing a reserve system) are relevant.

By way of comparison, Table 6.2 lists reported compensation for some prominent movie stars, from press reports in 1990 and 1991. Movie star's salaries compare more than favorably with those earned by pro sports stars. In another entertainment area, Janet Jackson reportedly received $15 million to sign with Virgin Records in 1991. The first album with her new label will earn her $5 million, while albums two and three will up the ante to $6 million and $7 million, respectively. In the same way that incentive clauses boost the pay of pro athletes, performance

Table 6.2
Movie Star Compensation, 1990–1991 (dollars)

Name	Film	Compensation
Sylvester Stallone	*Rocky V*	20 million
Jack Nicholson	*Batman*	11 million
Arnold Schwarzenegger	*Total Recall*	10 million
Tom Cruise	*Days of Thunder*	8 million
Bruce Willis	*Die Hard II*	7 million
Meryl Streep	Per picture	5 million
Cher	"	3–5 million
Sally Field	"	3–5 million
Jane Fonda	"	3–5 million
Michelle Pfeiffer	"	3–5 million
Sigourney Weaver	"	3–5 million

Source: New York Times, various issues, 1990, 1991.

clauses in her contract will make it possible for Janet Jackson to earn in the neighborhood of $10 million for each of the first three records she produces.

In an interesting analogy to the elimination of the reserve clause in baseball, movie entertainers' earnings skyrocketed with the breakdown of the "contract player" mode of operation in place in the motion picture industry until the 1950s. Studio owners of that era, much as sports team owners today, argued vigorously that the runaway growth in star salaries spelled disaster for their industry. True to predictions, the earnings of movie stars did go up dramatically, but the U.S. motion picture industry remains quite healthy even up to the present time, and is one of the few American industries that has retained its competitive edge in an international setting.

It is interesting that the public perception of the importance of rising salaries for entertainers is so different between movie stars and pro athletes. That star salaries in pop music or the movies cause little public concern is borne out by where news on salaries can be found. For example, the news of Janet Jackson's contract was found *inside* the entertainment section of the newspaper. If the level of discussion about salaries in movies and in popular music is a murmur, then it is a high-pitched scream in pro sports. Roger Clemens clearly is not in the same salary league with fellow entertainment stars Sylvester Stallone, Jack Nicholson, or Janet Jackson, but the behavior of baseball salaries generates statements like the ones of Commissioner Vincent and Mr. Dombrowski that opened this chapter, and opinions like those of Deputy (Baseball) Commissioner Steve Greenberg: "The current system is a prescription for disaster. But whether the disaster is just around the corner or will take place ten years from now, I don't know" (*Sporting News*, December 31, 1990).

To fans, the answer to why pro sports are different from other entertainment endeavors is obvious. Other mass entertainment media do not bring philosophers to their defense, lead presidents of the United States to throw out first pitches, or give poets pause to reflect. Whatever the reason, pro team sports are viewed differently from the other mass entertainment industries by almost everyone—fans, sportswriters, players, and owners. But there are some fundamental economic facts of life that apply across the board to all labor markets, including the market for rock stars and pro sports players.

The Workings of the Player Market

The market for any labor service, such as the market for the services of pro athletes, follows the good old law of supply and demand and operates on the basis of bids and offers by teams and players. Looking at things from the point of view of any team, we can calculate the *most* that a profit-oriented team would offer a player; it is the amount that the player would add to the team's revenue if he were signed. In the jargon of economists, as noted earlier, this is the player's *marginal revenue product*, which we will refer to as his *MRP*. The player's MRP is the most a team would pay a player because paying a player more than this would decrease team profits; on the other hand, signing a player for anything less than his MRP means that adding the player increases profits for the team.

When George Steinbrenner was running the Yankees, he was asked once how he decided how much to pay a player. He said, "It depends on how many fannies he puts in the seats." That was George's way of saying it depends on the player's MRP. A recent example illustrates the point. In May of 1991, the California Angels signed pitcher Fernando Valenzuela (just released by the L.A. Dodgers) for a $300,000 base salary, plus incentives that could have added up to $1 million for his total 1991 compensation. Alas for Fernando, his 1991 season was short, but his debut appearance in Anaheim drew 49,977 fans. The Angels' front office estimated that 25,000 of those tickets were sold because Valenzuela, rather than some other Angel pitcher, was on the mound. Even if all of these fans purchased $3 general admission tickets, $75,000 is a hefty offset (25 percent) of his base salary for just one appearance!

From the player's point of view, the least he would be willing to accept as a salary offer to sign with a team is what he could earn in his next-best employment opportunity (taking into account locational and other non-monetary considerations). We hesitate to push our luck, but economists refer to this next-highest employment value as the player's *reservation wage*. If a team offers a player less than his reservation wage, the player would simply reject the offer and remain employed in his next-best opportunity.

The player's MRP and reservation wage give the maximum and minimum limits on the salary that a player can be expected to earn. Just where the player's salary will end up within these limits depends on a number of considerations. Union activities have an impact, especially on players whose reservation wage would have been below the league-wide minimum salary resulting from collective bargaining. The most important consideration is the bargaining power of the player relative to that of the owner. Generally, the more close substitutes there are (that is, the easier he is to replace), the more bargaining power the team has, and the salary will be closer to the player's reservation wage than to his MRP. The more unique are the skills and drawing power of the player (that is, the tougher he is to replace), the more bargaining power the player has, and the closer the salary will be to the player's MRP.

Just how far apart the reservation wage and MRP limits on a player's salary will be depends critically on the negotiating rights for players and owners, built into the player market by the rules of the sport. At one extreme is complete free agency, where the ability of players and owners to negotiate with whomever they choose is unrestricted. At the other extreme is the reserve clause system that operated in baseball until 1976. Under the reserve clause, as we have seen in the previous chapter, a player can negotiate only with the team owning his contract. Generally speaking, the more freedom there is for players and owners to negotiate, the closer the minimum (reservation wage) and maximum (MRP) limits on a player's salary will be. However, there can be substantial remaining bargaining room even under unrestricted free agency.

Suppose first that there is unrestricted free agency, with players and owners free to negotiate with whomever they choose. Under such circumstances, if we ignore locational and other non-monetary considerations, each player will end up signing with the team to which he is most valuable (the team for which the player has the highest MRP). He will be paid a salary that lies between his MRP with that team, and his MRP with the team to which he is second most valuable (the team to which he has the second-highest MRP). The reason for this is that the team to which the player is most valuable can outbid any other team for the player's services, and still increase its profits by hiring him. But the team can sign the player only if it offers him at least as much as the player can earn elsewhere (the player's reservation wage), and the most the player can earn elsewhere is clearly his MRP with the team to which he is second most valuable. In a market with completely unrestricted free agency, if we ignore non-monetary considerations, the grand conclusion is that the highest salary offered to the player will capture at least his *second*-highest value in the league, and can be up to (but not exceeding) his *highest* value in the league.

Under a reserve clause system, the team owning a player's contract has exclusive negotiating rights to the player. Similarly, the college draft gives the team holding a player's draft rights exclusive rights to negotiate with him (in baseball, for up to six years, and longer in football and hockey). Instead of a competitive market for the player's services, under a reserve clause system, there is only one bidder for the player's services. The highest salary the team holding the player's contract would be willing to pay the player still is the MRP of the player for that team; but under the reserve clause, there is no competitive pressure on the owner of the contract. As a result, the player's reservation wage is not bid up to his second-highest MRP in the league. Instead, the player's reservation wage under a reserve clause system is what the player can earn *outside* of the league, or the league minimum salary, whichever is higher.

Needless to say, for most athletes, the reservation wage calculated in this way lies far below the player's value to *any* team in the league. Under the reserve clause system, a player's wage will end up some place between his reservation wage and his MRP with the team owning his contract. The reserve clause system lowers the value of the player's reservation wage by eliminating competing offers by other teams, and, unless the player happens to be under contract with the team in the league to which he is most valuable, the upper bargaining limit has been reduced as well. Predictably, the overall effect of a reserve clause system is to lower player salaries relative to what they would earn under free agency.

Put another way, a reserve clause system acts to direct more of the revenue that a player produces to the team owner than to the player. The effect of unrestricted free agency on a league that previously was under a reserve clause system, as in the case of baseball since 1976, would be a bidding up of player salaries to the point where most of the revenue that is linked to the performance of the team ends up in player salaries. Under a reserve clause system, the team can capture a significant fraction of the revenue linked to a team's performance, as well as revenue that is not so linked.

For both players and owners, the issue of free agency is critical to their economic well-being. While claims that free agency will destroy pro sports thus far are clearly exaggerated, the division of the monopoly rents created by pro sports certainly is at stake. It should come as no surprise, then, that free agency is the central issue in pro team sports collective bargaining. A secondary collective bargaining concern is the league minimum salary, which under a reserve clause system becomes the reservation wage for most players. Under free agency, the league minimum salary is no longer relevant to regulars, but it remains an important bargaining element for other players not yet eligible for free agency.

The point of all this is that the sports labor market has the same fundamental driving forces as any other labor market, that is, the value produced by an employee and his or her bargaining power, with the wage rate ending up somewhere between the reservation wage and the player's MRP, and with the player's MRP depending upon the demand by the public for the sport. Interestingly, what goes on in the player market is often portrayed in the press in exactly the opposite fashion, as though it were changes in player salaries that controlled ticket prices and TV revenues.

Ticket Price and Player Salaries

Owners of sports teams understandably are concerned about escalating salaries for players. After all, they have to pay the bills. But when owners and league commissioners express their opinions about the level of player salaries in public, they like to come on in their self-appointed role of protectors of the fans. Owners are fond of pointing out that if player salaries increase, they (the owners) will be forced to raise ticket prices, or turn to pay-per-view alternatives, in order to obtain the revenues to pay those salaries. The owners' line would have it that putting a brake on salary increases really is in the interest of fans, who prefer low ticket prices to high ones. This argument seems to be very effective, because fans typically side with the owners in salary disputes with players and in labor negotiations with player unions. The general sentiment was summed up by Carl Barger, president of the Pittsburgh Pirates, commenting on Cy Young Award winner Doug Drabeck's $3.5 million arbitration award: "Wouldn't it be tragic if it reached the point where you couldn't afford to win?" (Sporting News, March 4, 1991).

While the owners get effective mileage from this line, it makes very little economic sense. With some rare classic exceptions, such as Phil Wrigley and Tom Yawkey, owners of sports teams are in the business to make money, or at least not lose money. Nobody has to force an owner to raise ticket prices if he or she is fielding a successful team with lots of popular support and a sold-out stadium. Put another way, even if player costs did not rise, one would expect that ticket prices and TV contract values would rise in the face of increasing fan demand. On the other hand, if the team already is having trouble selling tickets, only sheer folly would dictate raising ticket prices.

Given a team's roster of players, the simple economic fact of life is that the ticket pricing decision by a profit-oriented owner is completely independent of the salaries paid to those players. Profit-oriented ticket-pricing decisions depend solely on the demand by fans for tickets to the team's games. The demand for the inputs used to produce the games, including players, is derived from this profit-oriented decision, not the other way around. Ticket prices rise when fan demand rises, which in turn increases player MRPs, which spills over into higher salaries for players.

Nowhere is this logic more clearly evident than in the case of baseball in the period just after the beginning of free agency. Free agency acted immediately to raise player salaries, as indicated earlier in Figure 6.1. But fans would not pay more to watch the same players just because they started earning more. The initial effect of free agency was to lower team profits with little impact on ticket prices. Table 6.3 gives ticket prices (in 1991 dollars) around the relevant years, 1971–1990. With few exceptions, ticket prices *fell* in real terms during the very first years of free agency! Indeed, only the Boston Red Sox and New York Yankees had ticket prices in excess of their 1971 levels as late as 1980, four years after free agency. Thus, salaries rose, but ticket prices did not. Ticket prices prior to free agency were already set by owners at levels representing their best guesses as to what would maximize revenue for their teams. Free agency shifted the bargaining power in the direction of players, and player salaries went up. But changes in player salaries per se had no effect on the demand for tickets and no effect on ticket prices.

Tables 6.4 and 6.5 show baseball ticket prices and player salaries by team during the free agency era of the 1980s. This has been a period of rising demand by the public for the major pro team sports. Rising demand led to increases in both ticket prices and TV contract revenues. In turn, the increased demand for pro sports tickets and TV coverage acted to increase the value of skilled players to teams, that is, their MRPs rose. Then, the bargaining process translated the increased value of player skills into higher player salaries. Salaries continued to grow through the 1980s for all pro sports, spurred on by the growth in team revenues. Under free agency, as in baseball and basketball, more of the increased revenue goes to players than under a reserve clause system, such as that in football and hockey. But salaries go up in either case

Table 6.3
Baseball Ticket Prices before and after Free Agency,
Various Years, 1971–1980 (1991 dollars)

Team	1971	1975	1976	1977	1978	1979	1980
NATIONAL LEAGUE							
Atlanta	9.06	9.66	9.14	8.58	7.97	7.16	6.31
Chicago	9.60	7.20	7.81	8.33	8.47	7.94	7.99
Cincinnati	11.10	9.76	9.23	8.67	9.10	8.17	7.90
Houston	11.37	9.99	9.45	9.12	8.68	8.26	8.05
Los Angeles	—	7.55	9.07	8.51	8.22	7.39	6.51
Montreal	10.16	8.51	8.04	7.55	9.20	8.26	9.50
New York	10.53	8.10	7.66	8.18	7.60	6.92	7.44
Philadelphia	11.13	8.58	8.83	8.29	7.70	6.92	7.44
Pittsburgh	10.16	8.71	8.23	8.18	9.22	8.28	7.64
St. Louis	10.00	8.46	8.45	9.23	8.97	8.06	8.04
San Diego	8.73	5.76	6.07	6.23	5.79	6.23	5.49
San Francisco	13.37	9.04	8.54	8.87	8.24	7.40	7.87
AMERICAN LEAGUE							
Baltimore	9.36	6.52	6.16	5.97	6.67	6.99	6.54
Boston	7.76	8.96	8.95	9.52	9.28	8.34	8.04
California	11.70	7.90	7.47	7.95	7.10	6.77	5.96
Chicago	8.66	7.07	6.66	6.70	6.94	7.16	7.10
Cleveland	11.00	8.18	7.73	7.91	9.20	8.37	7.39
Detroit	9.19	7.70	7.28	7.51	9.12	8.19	7.81
Kansas City	9.56	10.49	9.92	9.32	9.45	8.49	7.46
Milwaukee	10.83	8.05	7.61	7.64	8.47	7.61	8.07
Minnesota	9.66	7.88	7.45	8.62	7.64	8.47	7.61
New York	9.39	8.98	10.64	11.17	11.32	10.82	10.12
Oakland	9.49	8.68	8.88	8.33	7.75	6.96	6.13
Seattle	—	—	—	8.45	7.85	7.42	6.61
Texas	—	8.20	7.76	8.33	8.16	7.33	7.90
Toronto	—	—	—	8.94	8.31	7.91	6.97

Source: Data provided by Roger Noll, Stanford University.
Note: Values are averages of ticket prices for types of seats, weighted by the proportion of each type of seat.

when demand for the sport increases, and, contrary to the argument of owners, they are the effect and not the cause of higher ticket prices.

It might be that the mistaken perception about the link between player salaries and ticket prices comes from a confusion of two different sources of salary escalation. If a team's salary bill rises because the team has acquired more expensive talent, then the owner can and undoubtedly will raise ticket prices, not because he or she is

Table 6.4
Baseball Ticket Prices in the Free Agency Era, 1981–1988 (1991 dollars)

Team	1981	1982	1983	1984	1985	1986	1987	1988
NATIONAL LEAGUE								
Atlanta	7.43	6.37	7.16	7.28	7.03	6.91	6.66	6.40
Chicago	7.24	6.82	7.35	7.39	8.58	8.43	8.13	7.81
Cincinnati	7.81	7.35	8.01	7.68	7.79	7.65	7.38	7.08
Houston	6.85	7.45	7.19	6.89	7.92	7.77	7.50	7.20
Los Angeles	7.08	7.60	6.91	6.62	6.39	6.28	6.05	5.81
Montreal	8.61	9.20	9.45	9.06	8.56	8.40	8.10	7.78
New York	6.61	6.23	7.79	7.47	8.47	8.31	8.02	7.70
Philadelphia	7.19	6.78	7.60	7.28	7.49	7.35	7.09	6.81
Pittsburgh	7.39	6.96	6.62	7.71	7.45	7.31	7.06	6.78
St. Louis	8.03	7.77	8.17	7.83	8.25	8.10	7.82	7.51
San Diego	6.57	6.19	6.81	7.19	7.22	7.09	6.84	6.57
San Francisco	7.13	6.72	7.97	7.64	7.37	7.24	6.98	6.71
AMERICAN LEAGUE								
Baltimore	7.48	7.98	7.74	7.42	7.16	7.03	6.78	6.51
Boston	8.03	7.56	7.33	8.97	8.91	8.75	8.44	8.10
California	6.26	6.38	7.06	6.76	6.53	6.41	6.19	5.94
Chicago	7.30	6.13	7.41	7.52	7.26	7.13	6.88	6.60
Cleveland	7.12	6.71	7.56	7.25	6.95	6.82	6.58	6.32
Detroit	8.45	8.53	9.11	8.73	8.43	8.28	7.99	7.67
Kansas City	7.13	6.72	7.95	7.62	7.36	7.23	6.97	6.70
Milwaukee	8.03	7.56	8.63	8.28	7.99	7.84	7.57	7.27
Minnesota	7.97	10.17	9.57	7.82	7.55	7.41	7.15	6.87
New York	9.18	9.84	10.51	10.07	10.58	10.39	10.02	9.63
Oakland	7.05	6.72	6.51	7.18	7.97	7.82	7.54	7.24
Seattle	6.76	7.02	6.89	7.25	7.49	7.35	7.09	6.81
Texas	7.45	7.02	8.14	7.43	7.68	7.54	7.27	6.98
Toronto	7.05	6.64	6.80	7.65	8.81	8.65	8.34	8.01

Source: As in table 6.3.

paying more in salaries, but because he or she is fielding a more attractive team. That was certainly the case with the Yankees in the early days of free agency, as shown in Table 6.3. But looking at the league as a whole, the same group of players was around right after free agency as before, so for an average team, the quality of players didn't change. Consequently, there was no way that the average owner could pass on to fans the increase in salaries that came with free agency; the salary cost increase came directly out of profits, instead.

Table 6.5
Average Salaries by Team, Baseball, 1983–1991 (thousands of 1991 dollars)

Team	1983	1984	1985	1986	1987	1988	1989	1990	1991
NATIONAL LEAGUE									
Atlanta	473	525	681	812	576	440	367	455	701
Chicago	366	550	521	373	595	540	460	523	1,073
Cincinnati	325	351	424	493	413	349	429	571	928
Houston	496	499	461	536	532	624	613	746	465
Los Angeles	392	412	534	614	482	656	750	672	1,041
Montreal	480	480	397	387	364	393	600	568	697
New York	416	369	490	590	660	693	938	768	1,253
Philadelphia	601	523	503	454	542	575	326	402	717
Pittsburgh	428	431	494	370	192	351	437	590	923
St. Louis	353	379	486	428	481	598	608	635	794
San Diego	356	406	504	591	439	469	565	688	779
San Francisco	337	368	403	352	467	462	612	616	1,142
AMERICAN LEAGUE									
Baltimore	415	469	551	555	584	486	355	301	542
Boston	360	388	486	730	604	698	729	744	1,260
California	530	562	546	650	531	478	637	682	1,096
Chicago	396	583	439	401	411	259	332	414	573
Cleveland	329	208	277	333	338	350	372	520	695
Detroit	359	484	512	577	638	701	544	730	1,106
Kansas City	421	379	464	596	662	598	630	750	1,172
Milwaukee	479	502	542	439	377	441	389	633	904
Minnesota	133	224	325	451	593	511	561	541	930
New York	630	598	688	763	646	823	614	761	1,062
Oakland	363	500	443	415	495	486	777	670	1,397
Seattle	162	220	214	232	261	278	320	353	576
Texas	246	322	324	300	280	276	409	539	738
Toronto	290	385	486	524	593	554	649	762	888

Sources: Data for 1983–1987 are from Paul Staudohar, *The Sports Industry and Collective Bargaining* (Ithaca, N.Y.: ILR Press, 1989), 32. The remaining data are from *Sporting News*, various issues.

The Winner's Curse

Things are not quite as simple as we have been making them, of course—general managers and scouts really do earn the money they are paid. It is no easy task to predict how a player will perform next season, what his contribution to the team will be, and the size of the crowds the team will draw. Correctly evaluating the MRP of a player is a skill that earns successful general managers like Andy McPhail of the Twins salaries in the high six-figure range.

We do not pretend to any such skills. Instead, we assume that the market for players "works" in the sense that, on average, bids by skilled general managers and offers by skilled player agents lead to a situation in which players get paid pretty much according to what we have outlined, that is, what they would be worth in their second-best employment in the league.

Well, actually, they may get a little more than that, and maybe even more than their MRPs to the teams that sign them. There is a well-known phenomenon in bidding theory known as "the winner's curse," which might be operative in the player markets of the free agency period. It is a little easier to explain this in the context of a sealed-bid auction, so let's start with that.

In a sealed-bid auction, say, for league TV rights, the prospective bidders (the networks and cable systems) each evaluate the revenue potential of the TV rights and then, at a specified time, each in effect submits a dollar bid in a sealed envelope. The "lucky" winner is the individual submitting the highest bid. "Lucky" is in quotes, because, by definition, the winning bidder ends up paying more for the right to televise games, and occasionally much more, than any other bidder was willing to offer. Given that all bidders had access to pretty much the same information about the potential market for TV, this suggests that the winner might well have made a mistake in overvaluing the revenue potential of the contract. This is "the winner's curse"—winning in a sealed-bid auction means the winner might very well have bid too much, and maybe far too much, for the property. In particular, a measure of how much the winner has overbid is the difference between the winner's bid and the second-highest bid. In the jargon of the field, this difference is what is "left on the table."

The recent experience of CBS in connection with its baseball TV contract is convincing evidence of existence of the "winner's curse." It now is pretty much generally accepted that CBS dramatically overbid for the television contract it received from major league baseball.

The free agent market in baseball is not as formal as a sealed-bid auction, but there are problems for a general manager in determining how much a player will be worth to his team and in guessing how much other teams will be willing to offer the player. Ideally, a general manager would like to pay any player just $1 more than the player's best offer anywhere else, but this option is only available in cases where the team has "right of first refusal," that is, the right to match any outside offer.

With lots of teams out there operating in the free agent market (and assuming no collusion), there will be vigorous competitive bidding for players. Clearly, teams underestimating the MRPs of free agents will typically not be the teams signing them; instead, there is better chance that the "winners" in the free agent market will be teams overestimating player MRPs, and these are the teams stuck with the "winner's curse." And, in turn, the presence of the winner's curse means that players get paid on average even more than their value in their second-best employment opportunities in the league. This cannot be too surprising. Sportswriters, each year, are fond of rubbing owners' noses in the winner's curse by pointing out how overpaid many (some would say most) free agents are, relative to their subsequent performance.

Salary Determination in Baseball

Assuming that the baseball player market operates to generate salary offers that correlate roughly with player MRPs, we can identify factors that can be said to "determine" baseball player salaries in the sense that these factors are highly correlated with market-determined salary levels, and thus do a good job of predicting the level of baseball player salaries. For each of several time periods, a simple equation is used to estimate the salary of any player based on his playing time, on-field performance, age-experience relationship, and player category (for example, rookie, hopeful, veteran). The equation can be thought of as estimating the player's MRP in that time period. The equation is a "best fit" model of salary determination in the sense that (1) it explains a large portion of the total variation in player salaries, and (2) adding other factors to the equation would not significantly improve its predictive power. Models such as those specified below are used both by players and by owners in justifying their positions on salary demands in the baseball salary arbitration process.

Our player salary model is based on an extensive data set, covering salaries in 1965–1974, 1976–1977, and 1986–1990. For the reserve clause period (1965–1974), salaries are from a player sample that is dramatically different from those used in past studies. The data were collected by agents of the Internal Revenue Service and employees of the American League office, as evidence in a tax case involving the Milwaukee Brewers (*Allan Selig v. United States*, 565 F. Supp 524 (1983), 740 F.2d 572 (1984); see Chapter 3 for details). The data cover the salaries of all major league players who were traded or sold in baseball between 1965 and 1974 in transactions that involved American League players. Rich Hill at Central Michigan University provided the immediate free agency period data (1976–1977), and Phil Porter at the University of South Florida shared his 1986 data set. The remainder of the salary data came from published reports in the *New York Times*, the *Sporting News*, and the *San Francisco Chronicle*.

Table 6.6 lists the players with the top 26 salaries in the 1991 season, and traces their earnings (in 1991 dollars) back to 1986. All players listed in the table earned $3.2 million or more in 1991; free agent eligibility is indicated by an asterisk. Even in real terms, all but three of these mega-stars more than doubled their salaries between 1986 and

Table 6.6
Salary Histories for Top 1991 Earners, Baseball, 1986–1991
(thousands of 1991 dollars)

Player	1991	1990	1989	1988	1987	1986
Boddicker, Mike	3,167	705	1,501	973[a]	954	1,035
Canseco, Jose	3,500	2,098[a]	1,747	372	197	86
Clark, Will	3,750[a]	2,375	1,228	366	143	74
Darwin, Danny	3,250	1,383	890	870	852	754
Davis, Eric	3,600	2,192	1,698[a]	1,029	358	111
Davis, Glenn	3,275	2,072	1,185[a]	389	256	148
Davis, Mark	3,625	2,218	655	595	495[a]	432
Dawson, Andre	3,300	2,192	2,293	2,117	596	1,293
Drabek, Doug	3,350[a]	1,148	355	183	101	74
Henderson, Rickey	3,250	2,349	2,315	2,026	1,990	1,940
Hershiser, Orel	3,167	2,053	3,021[a]	1,259	954	1,235
Langston, Mark	3,550	1,879	1,529[a]	939	441	299
Martinez, Dennis	3,333	1,537	803	841	992	692
Mattingly, Don	3,420	2,610	2,402	2,289[a]	2,354	1,699
McGee, Willie	3,562	1,566	1,529	1,373	834	618
Mitchell, Kevin	3,750[a]	2,201	611	272	149	74
Molitor, Paul	3,233	2,540	1,911	1,602	1,502	1,433
Puckett, Kirby	3,167	2,819	2,238[a]	1,248	435	315
Raines, Tim	3,500	2,275	2,299	1,907	—	1,872[a]
Ryan, Nolan	3,300	1,462	2,020	1,145	1,192	1,390
Stewart, Dave	3,500	1,148	1,174	687	596	494
Strawberry, Darryl	3,800	1,931	1,578	1,511[a]	1,454	1,167
Viola, Frank	3,167	2,053	3,021	1,545	989[a]	833
Welch, Bob	3,450	1,392	1,237	1,074	999	919
Winfield, Dave	3,300	2,242	2,139	2,242	2,218	2,306
Yount, Robin	3,200	3,341	1,256	1,316	1,192	1,174

Sources: Data for 1986 were provided by Phil Porter. Later data are from the *New York Times, Sporting News,* and the *San Francisco Chronicle,* various issues.

[a]The player's sixth full major league year (40 at-bats or 30 innings pitched). For older players, free agency occurred as follows: Darwin, 1984; Dawson, 1981; Henderson, 1984; Martinez, 1982; Molitor, 1983; Ryan, 1976; Welch, 1983; Winfield, 1978; Yount, 1979.

1991. Indeed, for the younger players, the increases, even in real terms, are staggering. For example, Will Clark and Kevin Mitchell of the San Francisco Giants earned six-year increases in the 5,000 percent (50 times!) range, while Jose Canseco of the Oakland A's and Doug Drabek of the Pittsburgh Pirates had to settle for increases in the 4,000 percent range. In addition, and in keeping with our earlier discussion of the impact of free agency, dramatic increases typically occur on or near the year of eligibility for free agency.

In explaining salary histories such as those in Table 6.6, the estimating model we use is built upon the pioneering work in the area by Scully (1974b), although some of the variables Scully used have since been found to carry little weight, and the final model used here represents an improvement over his original attempts. The variables used to explain salaries are of four basic types: playing time, on-field performance, age and experience, and a few used to distinguish types of players (pitchers and hitters, rookies and regulars, and major league hopefuls).

Playing time for hitters is measured by the player's lifetime share of total team at-bats, while the variable that captures the playing time of pitchers is their lifetime share of total team innings pitched. The idea behind these playing time variables is that the best judge of the quality of a player is the manager of the player's team. Managers try to get as much use out of the best players as possible. This argues that playing time is a good measure to use as a proxy for the contribution a player makes to the success of a team. It gives explicit recognition to the manager's decision as to who will play for the team on a day-to-day basis.

Left as it is, the playing time variable for pitchers overstates the value of starters relative to relievers. To capture this difference, a pitcher's proportion of games started out of all appearances is used. Further, for all players, recent playing time (departure from lifetime average) may be used as an adjustment in the salary determination process. For variables that measure playing time, a substantial change from career averages can occur because of injuries that may have a bearing on a player's long-run abilities. Poor players may get more playing time in a given season because of an injury to a regular in the starting lineup, or a starting regular may be out of the lineup temporarily because of an injury that is not permanently disabling.

On-field performance is captured by power indexes. For hitters, slugging average (total bases from base hits, divided by number of at-bats) provides the index, while power pitching (strikeout to walk ratio) works best for pitchers. It might be thought that other on-field performance variables should be included, as well as assessments made after a player's on-field performance has occurred (for example, Cy Young, Fireman of the Year, MVP, and batting title awards). But it turns out that once playing time and the power index are in the equation, any other measures of on-field performance are so highly correlated with them that they provide no significant increases in the predictive power of the equation.

The estimating equation also makes allowance for the age and experience of players, for rookies, "star quality" players, and "hopefuls" (players with less than five years on a major league roster and less than 40 at-bats in any season, or less than 30 innings pitched in any season for pitchers).

Finally, in estimating salaries, the introduction of free agency represents the major change in the entire salary process. This dramatic structural change suggests that the salary process during the reserve clause period (1965–1974 in our data set), the transition period (1976–1977), and the free agency period (1986–1990 in our data set) are quite different. Thus in each period, we would expect to find different estimating equations relating performance and other variables to salaries. The approach adopted here to test this hypothesis involves estimating the salaries of free agents separately from those of other players, and then using a simple, widely accepted statistical test to decide whether or not the salary equation generates different results for free agents than for other players.

Taking this approach, it can be concluded that the salary process during the reserve clause period differs significantly from the process operating during the transition period and the free agency period. Within the transition period (1976–1977), the data reveal that the salary process for free agents was different from that for other players in 1976, but not in 1977. In the 1986–1990 period of free agency, the salary determination process is different for free agents than for other players in all years from 1987 through 1990, but not for 1986, a year in which collusion by owners occurred. Finally, the salary process differs from year to year during the 1986–1990 period, except for non-free agents in 1987 and 1988. It is unclear whether this volatility is due to collective bargaining gains by free agents or the shifting nature of the demand for baseball, or both.

Salary Estimation Equations

The salary estimation equations appear in the appendix to this chapter (p. 369). The estimation equations are log linear in form (alternatively, salary is taken to be a product of factors, each raised to a power estimated from the data set), but the specifics are of less importance than the general features of the approach.

In the estimating equations, playing time and performance (power index) variables perform as expected (more playing time or higher performance leads to a higher salary). Young players get paid less simply because they are young, but the impact was much stronger in the reserve clause period than afterward. On the other hand, rookies and hopefuls typically received a salary increment relative to other players with the same performance and playing time stats. Most important, the clearest result from the equations is that the impact of playing time and performance (and the other determinants of salary) has been rising over time, reflecting the rising average level of salaries (in 1991 dollars) from the reserve clause period to the present. For non-free agents in the 1986–1990 period, playing time elasticities (percent change in salary per 1 percent change in playing time) are up nearly 100 percent for hitters and 50 percent for pitchers, relative to the reserve clause period. Performance elasticities are up only slightly for non-free agent hitters, but up 100 percent for non-free agent pitchers.

For free agents, playing time elasticities haven't changed much for hitters as between the reserve clause era and recent years, but they are up 100 percent for pitchers. Performance elasticities for free agents have simply exploded, rising by 300 to 400 percent for hitters and 200 to 300 percent for pitchers. What this means is that for free agents, a 1 percent increase in the slugging average for a hitter produces a three to four times higher percentage increase in salary in 1990 as it did, say, in 1975. Again, this raises the question of whether this general growth in the overall levels of salary determinants is due to free agency, or due to the rise in demand for baseball.

A natural question to raise is how well the salary estimation model performs as a predictor of player salaries. Table 6.7 lists the salaries for a sample of players in each of three time periods (reserve clause, transition, free agency), converts these to 1991 dollars, and then compares these salaries to the salaries predicted by the salary estimation equations. The total variation in salaries that is explained by the estimation equation for the relevant years is given (81 percent for 1969, 80 percent for 1976, and 53 percent for 1990). This "goodness of fit" statistic is an important indicator of the believability of the estimates.

Turning to the difference between actual and estimated salaries, the differences are all positive, suggesting that these highly paid players were all overpaid in each year, whether during a reserve clause or free agency period. But the salary model we are using estimates a player's MRP solely on the basis of his contribution to a team's success on the field. The other important element of a player's MRP, his fan attraction, is difficult to incorporate into salary estimation equations. Star or superstar players attract fans to games not only on the basis of how

Table 6.7
Predicted and Actual Salaries, Selected Players, Reserve Clause,
Transition, and Free Agency Periods

Player	Actual Salary (dollars)	Salary (1991 dollars)	Predicted Salary (1991 dollars)	% Difference
RESERVE CLAUSE PERIOD[a]				
Adair, Ken	44,000	164,560	95,439	72
Alou, Felipe	60,000	224,400	173,899	29
Chance, Dean	55,000	205,700	197,395	4
Davis, Tommy	69,000	258,060	135,458	91
Dillman, Bill	50,000	187,000	30,853	506
Ellsworth, Dick	50,000	187,000	136,798	37
Flood, Curt	90,000	336,600	165,621	103
Harrelson, Ken	50,000	187,000	110,728	69
Pascual, Camillo	51,000	190,740	175,943	8
Pinson, Vada	60,500	226,270	186,871	21
TRANSITION PERIOD: 1976[b]				
Brock, Lou	185,000	445,850	282,255	58
Holtzman, Ken	165,000	397,650	329,035	21
Jackson, Reggie	185,000	445,850	283,569	57
Messersmith, Andy	200,000	482,000	346,877	39
Montanez, Willie	156,000	375,960	187,643	100
Morgan, Joe	200,000	482,000	238,011	103
Murcer, Bobby	160,000	385,600	233,678	65
Palmer, Jim	177,500	427,775	369,719	16
Ryan, Nolan	170,000	409,700	252,510	62
Tiant, Luis	160,000	385,600	242,855	59
FREE AGENCY PERIOD: 1990[c]				
Bell, George	2,035,000	2,136,750	1,724,622	24
Gooden, Dwight	1,916,667	2,012,500	1,183,565	70
Hayes, Von	2,000,000	2,100,000	1,181,912	78
Higuera, Ted	2,125,000	2,231,250	795,035	181
Parrish, Lance	1,991,667	2,091,250	1,117,814	87
Puckett, Kirby	2,700,000	2,835,000	1,946,532	46
Scott, Mike	2,187,500	2,296,875	939,221	145
Sutcliffe, Rick	1,925,000	2,021,250	1,290,305	57
Valenzuela, Fernando	2,200,000	2,310,000	675,858	242
Yount, Robin	3,200,000	3,360,000	1,792,034	87

[a]Explained variation: 81%.
[b]Explained variation: 80%.
[c]Explained variation: 53%.

much they add to a team's won-lost record, but also because of their own distinctive appeal as charismatic individuals. Bill Veeck used to argue that baseball and the other sports are really selling "dreams," and not just pennant races. Owners and players alike are aware of this, so star drawing power is reflected in player salaries, as indicated by the data in Table 6.7.

Some of the other larger differences are explained by contract inflexibilities not captured by the equations. For example, Bill Dillman was a pitcher of great promise (Baltimore's sixth pick in the very first draft in 1965) signed to a multi-year contract, who managed to pitch in only 50 games in two disappointing major league years. As another example, in 1990, the impending end of Fernando Valenzuela's career was becoming apparent in his performance, but because of his multi-year contract, his salary remained well in excess of his revealed ability. Table 6.7 provides some evidence for the reliability of the salary estimation equations, and their limitations as well.

Table 6.8 illustrates the use of the salary estimation equations in a different way, by displaying the variation in predicted salaries over time. Fifteen players were chosen to represent a range of salaries in

Table 6.8
Predicted Salary Comparisons, Selected Players, 1990
(thousands of 1991 dollars)

		Predicted Salary			% Change	
Name	Salary in 1990	1969	1976	1990	1969–1976	1976–1990
Bell, George	2,124	147	272	1,697	84	524
Crim, Chuck	626	81	170	949	110	458
Dascenzo, Doug	117	33	40	166	21	313
Downs, Kelly	463	52	49	384	−6	686
Eckersley, Dennis	1,649	135	89	714	−35	705
Farr, Steve	809	66	76	511	14	576
Gedman, Rich	960	95	131	582	38	344
Hennerman, Mike	350	70	110	649	56	491
Lansford, Carney	1,383	168	263	1,295	57	392
Rohde, Dave	104	22	15	36	−33	142
Smith, Dwight (Cubs)	188	74	116	811	57	602
Stewart, Dave	1,148	122	215	1,648	75	666
Venable, Max	245	54	68	244	24	261
Vizquet, Omar	141	54	73	865	36	1,078
Whiten, Mark	104	19	14	56	−28	296

1990, and the estimating equations for 1969, 1976, and 1990 were used to predict their salaries in 1969, 1976, and 1990 on the basis of their performance in 1990. The results in Table 6.8 show how these players' salaries would have changed over time (with constant performance) as between the reserve clause, transition, and free agency periods. The unweighted average percentage increase in salary between 1969 and 1976 was 31 percent, and the unweighted average percent increase between 1976 and 1990 was 502 percent. For this group of 15 players, the average salaries (in 1991 dollars) predicted by the estimation equations are as follows: for 1969, $79,000; for 1976, $113,000; for 1990, $707,000. Thus, on average in this group, a player would have earned almost $600,000 more in 1990 than in 1976, given the same performance on the field, in dollars of constant purchasing power. Looking at how a given group of players would have been treated in the reserve clause, transition, and free agency periods serves to point out how free agency combined with a rising demand for baseball has impacted baseball salaries throughout the entire salary distribution.

The most interesting finding shown in Table 6.8 is how large the predicted increases in salary have been since the 1976–1977 transition period. Intuitively, it seems likely that the effects of free agency per se would be concentrated in the early years, following the changeover from the reserve clause, as owners and players learned how the new system works. Once free agency had been absorbed into the salary negotiation process, any further increases in salaries would have occurred only as player MRPs rose, say, in response to an increase in demand for baseball by fans. (An important qualification to this, of course, is the period of collusion by owners.) In any case, this strongly suggests that increases in salaries in recent years, 10 or more years after the introduction of free agency, reflect primarily the impact of increased demand for baseball rather than any lingering effects from the introduction of free agency. One way to test this is to look at changes over time in the value of free agency to players.

The Value of Free Agency to Players

The value of free agency to any player is the difference between what the player earns under free agency and what the player would have been paid as a non-free agent. We are interested in seeing how this has changed over time. The period chosen for calculating the value of free agency is the 1986–1990 free agent period. In order to make the comparison, players who were free agents during this period are also treated as if they never achieved free agency. The value of free agency for a player is, then, the difference between a player's estimated value as a free agent, and his estimated value as a non-free agent.

For 1986, the salary estimation model for free agents could not be distinguished statistically from the model for non-free agents—that is, on average, given the same performance and playing time characteristics, the salary earned by a player was the same whether he was a free agent in 1986 or was a non-free agent. Thus, for 1986, on average, the value of free agency to players was zero. This simply corroborates all of the other evidence of collusion in the 1986 free agent market, for example, lack of salary offers by other teams for free agents of any given team, lack of movement of free agent players from team to team, and the flattening out of the rise in average salaries shown in Figure 6.1.

For 1987 through 1990, the value of free agency was calculated by taking a sample of players in each year. The players chosen for the sample were those that occupied the deciles (10 percent, 20 percent, . . . 90 percent, 99 percent) of the salary distribution for each year. Even though the particular players occupying each decile might be different in each year, they represent 10 percent increments in the salary distribution for that year. Interestingly, with the exception of 2 of the 40 observations, all of the players had achieved free agent eligibility (in their sixth major league season or more). Thus, while estimating free agent salaries would be required for non-free agents, for this sample we calculate the value of free agency as the difference between actual observed salary and estimated non-free agent salary.

Average values for free agency are reported here in two ways in order to portray how the value of free agency has changed over the sample period and how the value of free agency varies for deciles of the salary distribution. First, we turn to an analysis of how the value of free agency changed over time during 1986–1990. The value of free agency is calculated for each year, 1987 through 1990, as follows. For each year, we calculate the average difference between actual salary and estimated non-free agent salary, using an unweighted average of the 10 decile observations. This is an estimate of the value of free agency for each year. We then divide the estimated value of free agency for each year by the average actual salary for the year, again using an unweighted average of the 10 decile observations. The ratio tells us how much, percentage-wise, free agency added to average salaries for the year.

The results are as follows:

1986 Free agency added nothing to average salaries.
1987 Free agency added 28 percent to average salaries.
1988 Free agency added 59 percent to average salaries.
1989 Free agency added 22 percent to average salaries.

1990 Free agency added 23 percent to average salaries.

This pattern of the value of free agency yields two important conclusions. First, the approximate doubling of the value of free agency in 1988 shows that the salary determination process captured the discounted present value of the record-setting television contract set to begin in 1989. But, despite the large increases in average salaries that occurred in 1989 and 1990, free agency added no more percentagwise to average salaries in these years than it had in 1987. Instead, what was going on was that salaries of both free and non-free agents were increasing, more or less proportionately, as would be expected in as period of rising demand for baseball.

The fact that there was no differential percentage increase in free agent salaries relative to non-free agent salaries is evidence supporting the conclusion that what occurred in the late 1980s and early 1990s was a demand-driven escalation of player salaries, rather than an escalation arising from free agency per se. Since free agents and non-free agents are close substitutes for each other, absent other exogenous changes, salaries of the two types of players would be expected to move together, with free agent salaries incorporating a premium that reflects their superior bargaining power.

Next, we look at the value of free agency across deciles in the salary distribution. The data in Table 6.9 show that the value of free agency typically rises with player salaries. But the largest increases occur as players move from the 20th to the 30th and from the 80th to the 90th salary deciles. The move from the 20th to the 30th decile probably reflects the initial attainment of free agent eligibility (younger players reaching the six-year free agency threshold), while the move from the 80th to the 90th represents the leap in the value of free agency as a player joins the ranks of the true giants of the current game. While none of this should come as any surprise, it is important to note that while the large jumps at these two important points in the salary distribution are similar percentagewise, the value of free agency at the 90th decile is nearly 2.5 times the value of free agency at the 30th decile. As documented in the next section of this chapter, there is nothing at all equal about the distribution of salaries in professional baseball.

The upshot of all this is that, while baseball salaries have been rising, there is no indication that the value of free agency to players has been increasing, at least in the late 1980s and early 1990s. This means that there is no apparent independent effect of free agency present in the salary figures. Instead, the increase in baseball salaries following collusion in 1986 can be explained simply by the increase in gate receipts and television revenue that occurred over that period.

Table 6.9
The Estimated Value of Free Agency, 1987–1990
(thousands of 1991 dollars)

Decile	Average Value[a]	Percent Change[b]
99th	941,347	+ 14.3
90th	823,866	+ 66.8
80th	494,017	+ 6.0
70th	465,884	+ 18.2
60th	394,273	+ 17.3
50th	336,196	− 3.8
40th	349,641	+ 5.8
30th	330,413	+ 78.7
20th	184,922	− 3.5
10th	191,613	

[a]Calculated as the average of the estimated values of free agency for the players occupying the stated decile over the period 1987–1990. The estimated value of free agency is actual salary minus estimated non-free-agent salary.
[b]Percentage change from next lower decile.

The Salary Distribution in Sports

Finally, we want to look into the question of the degree of inequality in the salary distribution in sports, and how this has been affected by free agency. In particular, are superstars the most favored beneficiaries of free agency, so that the salary distribution becomes more unequal under free agency, or does free agency spread the benefits of competitive markets around more or less equally? Which sports leagues have the most equal salary distributions?

We begin by looking at baseball, the sport with a salary data set covering years in the reserve clause era, the transition period, and the free agency period. The tool we use to address the characteristics of the salary distribution is the Lorenz curve (see also the discussion of competitive balance and the Lorenz curve in Chapter 7). Figures 6.3 and 6.4 show the Lorenz curves in baseball for 1974 and 1990, respectively, as representative of the reserve clause and free agency periods. On the horizontal axis is the cumulative percentage of players (the cumulative distribution of salary earners arrayed from lowest to highest salary), and on the vertical axis is the cumulative percentage of salary income. We plot the Lorenz curve by associating with each cumulative percentage of players the cumulative percentage of total salary income for the

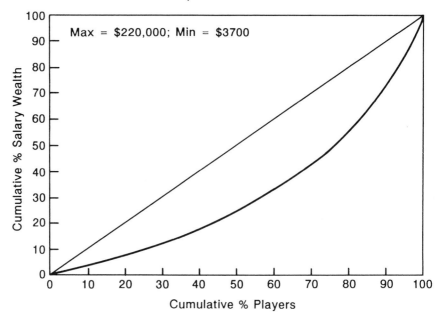

Figure 6.3 Baseball Salary Lorenz Curve, 1974

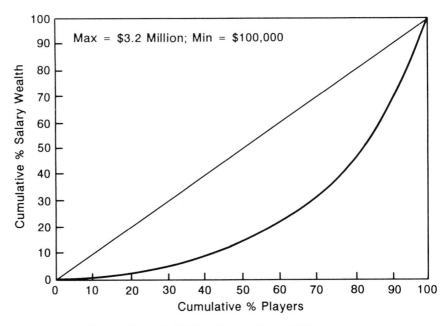

Figure 6.4 Baseball Salary Lorenz Curve, 1990

league that they earn. A Lorenz curve in the form of a straight line from the lower-left corner to the upper-right corner would represent a completely equal distribution of income, that is, a situation in which every player receives the same salary. Inequality in the income distribution shows up as a "bulge" in the Lorenz curve.

The graphs indicate that baseball salaries are not equally distributed; both Lorenz curves bulge. In order to determine the degree of inequality in a Lorenz curve, one can calculate the area of the "bulge" relative to the total area below the line of income equality. This is called the Gini coefficient. The larger the Gini coefficient, the more unequal is the salary distribution; a Gini coefficient of 1 would represent complete inequality (one person earns all of the salary), and a Gini coefficient of 0 would represent complete equality of the salary distribution. Table 6.10

Table 6.10
Gini Coefficients, Baseball 1965–1974, 1976–1977, 1986–1991

Year	Gini Coefficient	Percent Change from Previous Year
1965	.363	—
1966	.327	− 9.9
1967	.350	+ 7.0
1968	.338	− 3.4
1969	.347	+ 2.7
1970	.328	− 5.5
1971	.350	+ 6.7
1972	.370	+ 5.7
1973	.369	− 0.3
1974	.395	+ 7.0
Avg. reserve clause years	.354	
1976	.373	− 2.8[a]
1977	.457	+22.5
Avg. transition years	.415	
1986	.488	+ 0.8[b]
1987	.504	+ 3.3
1988	.494	− 2.0
1989	.529	+ 5.0
1990	.508	− 4.0
1991	.539	+ 6.1
Avg. free agency years	.510	

[a]On an annual average basis over the two years between 1974 and 1976.
[b]On an annual average basis over the nine years between 1977 and 1986.

reports Gini coefficients for baseball for the three periods, reserve clause, transition, and free agency. The average Gini coefficient during the 1965–1974 reserve clause era was .354; during the 1976–1977 transition period, it rose to an average of .415; and over the 1986–1991 period, the average Gini coefficient was .510. A recent undergraduate text (Byrns and Stone 1992, 808–811) reports that for the U.S. population, the Gini coefficients for income distribution in 1986 were .389 for families and .443 for unrelated singles (both values are high; those for other industrialized countries tend to cluster around .300 to .350). The clear conclusion is that income inequality in the rest of the U.S. economy, although high relative to other countries, pales in comparison to the inequality in recent years in baseball salaries.

It is also clear that baseball salaries have become less equally distributed over time, and skewed toward the top of the salary scale, with a noticeable jump between the reserve clause and free agency periods—a 22 percent increase in the Gini coefficient between 1976 and 1977. Overall, from the baseball salary data, we can conclude that while all players benefited from free agency, a disproportionate share of the benefits went to the top players, who were the big gainers from free agency. Players at the lower end of the distribution, still held captive by united mobility for their first six years, lost ground relative to their star teammates.

Table 6.11 provides a comparison between baseball and the other sports, over a three-year period for which data were available, 1988 through 1990. One of the striking things about this comparison is that the level of salary inequality in hockey was far less than the inequality in baseball salaries that were observable *during the reserve clause period.* Football salary inequality approximated the inequality in baseball just before free agency became the rule, and basketball inequality was only a bit higher than the inequality in baseball just before the advent

Table 6.11
Salary Inequality across Professional Sports Leagues (Gini Coefficient)

	1988	1989	1990
Baseball	.494	.529	.508
NFL	.411	—	—
NBA	—	.427	—
NHL[a]	—	—	.284

[a]Salaries of some players for Canadian teams, reported in Canadian dollars, were adjusted at the rate of $1 Canadian = U.S. $0.86 (the June 1, 1990, quote in the *Wall Street Journal*).

of free agency. This pattern is consistent with a ranking of the sports in terms of the degree of free agency (labor mobility) enjoyed by players in the sport. Baseball has the highest degree of player mobility, followed by basketball. Football is still struggling for most of the fruits of free agency, and hockey enjoys nearly none, still stifled under its own version of the Rozelle rule. In turn, the degree of free agency reflects the relative strengths of the players' unions in the various sports, with the Major League Players' Association the strongest union, and the National Hockey Players' Association the weakest.

Chapter 7

Competitive Balance in
Sports Leagues

BETWEEN 1946 and 1949, the best team in professional football was the Cleveland Browns of the All American Football Conference. The Browns won the AAFC championship four years in a row—every championship in the entire history of the AAFC—and had regular season records (won-lost-tied) of 12–2–0 (1946), 12–1–1 (1947), 14–0–0 (1948), and 9–1–2 (1949). These were the teams of Otto Graham, Dante Lavelli, and Marion Motley, all at their best, and coach Paul Brown was at the peak of his career as well. In 1946, the first year of the AAFC, Cleveland drew just under 400,000 for its seven home games, an average of 57,000 per game, outdrawing every other team in the AAFC, and outdrawing every team in the long-established NFL except for the New York Giants. By 1949, the Browns were drawing under 30,000 a game except for the one game matching them with their only close rival in the league, the San Francisco 49ers, featuring Frankie Albert and Norm Standlee.

The Browns and the AAFC ran into problems because of a lack of competitive balance within the league. In 1946, Dan Topping's New York Yankees won the Eastern division crown of the AAFC with a record of 10–3–1, a full seven games better than the second-place Brooklyn Dodgers (3–10–1), and the Browns won the Western title with a three-game lead over the 49ers. (By way of comparison, the NFL has never had a season in which the final lead in a division was greater than four and one-half games, and less than 10 percent of the time has a final lead in the NFL been as much as three games.) The Miami Seahawks (3–11–0) pulled out of the AAFC after the 1946 season, after averaging only 7,000 per game in attendance, to be replaced by the Baltimore Colts.

Things were a little better in 1947, when the Yankees ended up only two and one-half games ahead of the Buffalo Bills, and the Browns were again three games ahead of the 49ers. But the Colts (2–11–1) were so outmanned on the playing field that the league acted to bolster the Baltimore squad by allowing the team to draft players from other teams in the league.

The Brooklyn Dodgers (2–12–0) and the Chicago Rockets (1–13–0) were the weak teams in 1948. Average attendance at Brooklyn games fell to under 10,000 in 1948, and the Dodgers dropped out, to merge with the New York Yankees. By 1948, the AAFC had become in effect a two-tiered league, with the Browns and the 49ers in a class of their own. In 1949, the two-tiered structure continued, and the Los Angeles Dons (4–8–0) ran into problems at the gate, when their NFL rival, the Los Angeles Rams, won the Western division title. That spelled the end of the AAFC, which merged with the NFL in December 1949, with the Browns, the 49ers, and the Colts moving to the NFL—and the Browns then went on to win the NFL championship in 1950, and won two more titles in the next five years.

It is not only rival leagues, such as the AAFC, that have run into problems because of a lack of competitive balance. Back around 1910, after baseball's Washington Senators had suffered through some pretty bad years, someone coined the famous saying, "Washington—first in war, first in peace, and last in the American League." Baseball fans could certainly identify with this because in the first 10 years of operation of the American League—then an eight-team league—the Senators compiled a record of one sixth-place finish, five seventh-place finishes, and four eighth-place finishes. And all during this period, needless to say, the Senators were the poorest-drawing team in the league. Ban Johnson, president of the American League, made heroic efforts to find some way to build up the Senators. His help finally paid off when Clark Griffith moved to the Senators as manager and part owner in 1912, and almost immediately turned the team around to make it a pennant contender.

During the 1930s and 1940s, there were three perennially weak teams in the American League—the Philadelphia Athletics, the St. Louis Browns, and, once again, the Washington Senators. Over the 20-year period between 1932 and 1951, the Athletics were in the second division 16 times and were last 10 times, including one stretch (1940–1946) of six last-place finishes in seven years; the Browns were in the second division for 17 years, and were last five times; and the Senators spent 13 years in the second division, two of them in last place. It is no surprise that the first franchises in the American League to move following World War II were these three teams—St. Louis going to Baltimore in 1954, Philadelphia moving to Kansas City in 1955, and Washington moving to Minnesota in 1961.

Actually, the American League has had problems with woefully weak franchises over most of its history. During the World War I period, the problem club was the Philadelphia Athletics. In 1915, Connie Mack sold off the star players from a team that had won four of the previous five pennants, because he wasn't willing to match the salary offers that were coming from the newly formed Federal League. The Athletics dropped into the cellar for the next seven years, from 1915 through 1921. Then it was the turn of the Boston Red Sox. Harry Frazee, who bought the pennant-winning Boston Red Sox in 1916, ran into money problems financing his Broadway shows, and solved them by selling star players (including Carl Mays in 1919, and Babe Ruth in 1920) to the New York Yankees, for cash and for loan advances. Frazee finally sold what was left of the Red Sox franchise in 1923. The Sox ended up in last place in 1922, 1923, 1925, 1926, 1927, 1928, 1929, 1930, and 1932. Mercifully for Sox fans, Tom Yawkey stepped in to buy the team in 1933, and the Red Sox have been one of the stronger franchises in baseball since that time.

The other side of the coin for the American League, of course, has been the dominance of the league since the 1920s by one team—the New York Yankees. The Yankees entered the league in 1903, when Frank Farrell and "Big Bill" Devery bought the Baltimore Orioles AL franchise for $18,000 and moved the team to New York. The team had only middling success in its early years, and it was sold in 1914 to Jacob Ruppert and Colonel Tillinghast Huston. The Yankee dynasty began with those player purchases of 1919 and 1920 from Harry Frazee. The first Yankee pennant was in 1921, and between then and 1964, when CBS bought the team from Dan Topping and Del Webb, the Yankees won 29 of 43 league championships. Following an 0-for-9 run under CBS ownership, the George Steinbrenner-controlled Yankees returned to form, winning four of the next eight AL pennants, before the long dry stretch of the 1980s.

There is a fascinating tension between the need for competitive balance within a league to maintain fan interest throughout the league, and the yearning of owners and fans alike for truly memorable dominant teams, like the 1927 Yankees, the 1931 Athletics, the 1962 Packers, the 1965 Celtics, the 1967 76ers, the 1972 Lakers, or the 1973 Dolphins—the teams that fans and sportswriters talk about for years afterwards. The 1927 Yankees had that "murderers row" of Babe Ruth (.356), Lou Gehrig (.373), Bob Meusel (.337), and Earle Combs (.356), and pitchers like Waite Hoyt (22–7), and Herb Pennock (19–8). The Yankees tore up the league in 1927, winning 110 games and losing 44, ending the season 19 games ahead of a very good Philadelphia Athletics team. Yet, while attendance at New York increased from 1,027,000 in 1926 to

1,164,000 in 1927, the runaway race caused attendance for the American League as a whole to drop by 300,000, from 4,913,000 to 4,613,000.

The record of the 1931 Philadelphia Athletics is even more striking. The Athletics featured Hall of Famers Jimmy Foxx, Al Simmons, Mickey Cochrane, Jimmy Dykes, and Lefty Gomez, and won their third straight American League pennant in 1931 by 13 games over the Yankees. Not only did attendance in the league fall some 800,000 from 1930 levels—understandable given the deepening Depression—but the Athletics themselves lost 100,000 in attendance, drawing only 627,000. In the face of this, Athletics owner Connie Mack made the decision to once again sell off his best players to other, wealthier owners. Tom Yawkey picked up Foxx and Gomez for his Red Sox, Cochrane went to the Tigers, and Simmons ended up with the White Sox. The Athletics never recovered from Mack's player sales during their remaining years in Philadelphia. Eventually the team was sold and moved to Kansas City and then to Oakland, where Charlie Finley's teams of the early 1970s brought back memories of Mack's pennant winners. And when the fans refused to come out to watch the Athletics in Oakland, Finley followed Connie Mack's lead by deciding to sell his team, player by player, to the highest bidders, leading to a bitter confrontation with Commissioner Bowie Kuhn (see *Charles O. Finley v. Bowie Kuhn*, 569 F.2d 1193 (6th Cir. 1978)), and to a revision of the laws of baseball concerning player sales.

One of the key ingredients of the demand by fans for team sports is the excitement generated because of the uncertainty of outcome of league games. For every fan who is a purist who simply enjoys watching athletes with outstanding ability perform regardless of the outcome, there are many more who go to watch their team win, and particularly to watch their team win a close game over a challenging opponent. In order to maintain fan interest, a sports league has to ensure that teams do not get too strong or too weak relative to one another so that uncertainty of outcome is preserved. If a league becomes too unbalanced, with too much playing talent concentrated in one or two teams, fan interest at the weaker franchises dries up and ultimately fan interest even at the strong franchises dries up as well.

Preservation of competitive balance is a legitimate problem for sports leagues, and deserves serious attention. Moreover, from the time that the player reservation system was introduced into baseball in the 1870s, owners have used the need for competitive balance among teams to justify restrictions on the rights of players to sell their services in a freely competitive labor market. This chapter reviews the actual performance of the major sports leagues with respect to competitive balance over their histories, and examines the arguments that owners have made to justify the reserve or option clause of player contracts. We will summarize what microeconomics has to say about such arguments, what the actual experience of baseball and basketball under free agency has been since the 1970s, and how this squares with the claims of owners and with the conclusions of microeconomic theory.

Measures of Competitive Balance

Competitive balance within a league is actually a catchall term that refers to a number of different aspects of competition on the playing field, but, in essence, there is more competitive balance within a league when there is more uncertainty of outcome in league games and pennant races.

In what follows, various kinds of data relevant to competitive balance are presented. Our primary emphasis, however, is on the dispersion ("spread") of W/L percentages in a league and the concentration of championships and high W/L percentages among league teams. A league in which team W/L percentages are bunched together around .500 displays more competitive balance than does a league in which team W/L percentages are widely dispersed; and the more concentrated is the winning of championships and high W/L percentages among a few teams, the less competitive balance there is in a league.

The basic approach we take follows that suggested by Noll (1988) and applied by Scully (1989). They argue convincingly that a natural way to measure the degree of competitive balance in a league is to compare the actual performance of a league to the performance that would have occurred if the league had the maximum degree of competitive balance in the sense that all teams were equal in playing strengths. The less the deviation of actual league performance from that of the ideal league, the greater is the degree of competitive balance. That's what we will do here—compare the actual performance of leagues with the performance that would have occurred if all teams were equal in playing strengths. We begin by looking at the dispersion (spread) of W/L percentages in a league.

Dispersion of W/L Percentages

The simplest measure of dispersion of W/L percentages in a league is the range, that is, the difference between the highest and the lowest W/L percentages in a league for the season. In what follows, we will present historical data on the range as one measure of competitive balance in a league. The main advantages of the range are that it is easy to understand and easy to calculate; the disadvantage is that the range only takes into account the two extreme (highest and lowest) W/L percentages for the league season, and ignores intermediate W/L percentages.

A better measure of dispersion of W/L percentages for a league is the standard deviation of the distribution of W/L percentages, which is calculated as follows: for each team, calculate the difference between the team's W/L percentage for the season and the league average (.500). Square the difference for each team. Add these figures for all teams in the league, and then divide the total by the number of teams in the league. Take the square root, and you have the standard deviation of the league W/L percentages for that season.

The standard deviation can be a very informative measure of the spread of a distribution. For example, if the W/L percentages for a league are distributed as the normal (bell-shaped) distribution, then approximately two-thirds of the W/L percentages will lie within one standard deviation of the league average, approximately 95 percent will lie within two standard deviations, and approximately 99 percent will lie within three standard deviations of the league average.

Using the Noll-Scully approach, we can evaluate the degree of competitive balance in a league by comparing the realized values of the standard deviation of the W/L percentages for a league to an idealized measure, namely, the standard deviation of W/L percentages for a league in which every team is of equal playing strength. That is, the idealized measure applies to a league in which, for each team, the probability of winning any game is one-half. The value of the idealized standard deviation depends on the number of games in a team's league schedule. If a team plays N league games in a season, then the idealized value of the standard deviation for the season-long W/L percentage is simply equal to $(.5)/\sqrt{N}$. For example, a league composed of teams of equal playing strengths and playing a 16-game schedule (as in the case of the NFL) would have a standard deviation of $(.5)/4 = .125$. A league composed of teams of equal playing strengths playing an 81-game schedule (roughly the NBA and NHL schedules) would have a standard deviation of $(.5)/9 = .055$. The more games in a league schedule, the lower the idealized standard deviation for the league.

It also is known that the distribution of W/L percentages for a league with teams of equal playing strengths conforms closely to the normal distribution. Thus, for a league comprising of equal playing strengths, roughly two-thirds of the W/L percentages will lie within one standard deviation of the league average (.500). For a league with a 16-game schedule and all teams of equal playing strengths, we have seen that the standard deviation would be $(.5)/4 = .125$. Thus roughly two-thirds of the W/L percentages will lie between .375 and .625; for a comparable league with an 81-game schedule, where the standard deviation would be $(.5)/9 = .055$, roughly two-thirds will lie between .445 and .551.

In Table 7.1, historical data are shown for the average range of the W/L percentages of the major pro team sports leagues, decade by decade, from 1901 through 1990, along with historical data on actual and idealized average annual standard deviations of W/L percentages, again on a decade-by-decade basis.

The final section of the table provides a measure of the degree of competitive balance for each league in each decade, using the following ratio: actual average annual standard deviation divided by the idealized standard deviation. The idealized standard deviation is that which would hold if all teams were of equal playing strength. The closer is the ratio of actual to idealized standard deviation to 1, the more competitive balance there is in the league.

Table 7.1 covers the period from 1901, the first year of operation of the AL, through 1990, and hence it covers the complete playing histories up to 1990 of all present-day major leagues except for the NL, which began play in 1876. Table 7.1 shows the expected result that the more games there are in a league season, the smaller the range tends to be, with baseball having an average annual range only about one-third that of NFL football. What is of interest in this respect is that NBA basketball and NHL hockey have roughly the same number of games per season, but the NBA has a significantly larger average range per season than that of the NHL, except for the decade of the 1970s. Finally, while both the AL and the NL show trends toward a lower range over time, none of the other leagues displays any discernible trends so far as the range is concerned.

Much the same comments apply to the actual standard deviation data, except that the downward trend for baseball (signaling a move toward more competitive balance) also is matched by a similar declining trend for the NFL, while neither the NBA nor the NHL shows any perceptible trend. The idealized standard deviation measures reflect increases over time in the number of league games scheduled per team, for example, baseball's moving from a 154-game schedule to its 162-game schedule after expansion (AL in 1961, NL in 1962), and NFL football's moving from a 12-game schedule in the 1950s to a 14-game schedule, and then to a 16-game schedule after 1976. Similar changes have occurred in the other leagues.

The final section of the table provides the competitive balance measures for all leagues in the form of the ratio of the actual average standard deviation to the idealized standard deviation. This section of the table also indicates the statistical significance levels associated with

Table 7.1
Competitive Balance in Team Sports Leagues: Average Dispersion of W/L Percentage

	1901–1909	1910–1919	1920–1929	1930–1939	1940–1949	1950–1959	1960–1969	1970–1979	1980–1990	Avg.
Average Range of W/L Percentage										
AL	300	328	284	331	269	284	246	256	238	280
NL	364	284	257	275	290	241	266	240	210	269
NBA					554	369	489	495	558	484
NFL			936	739	795	672	769	748	738	769
NHL		479	423	346	343	344	331	513	409	391
Average Standard Deviation of W/L Percentage										
AL	97	102	90	105	88	97	83	76	65	88
NL	123	89	87	89	96	80	82	68	65	85
NBA					161	119	147	131	150	139
NFL			299	240	261	210	222	208	191	232
NHL		190	142	110	115	113	112	142	107	123
Idealized Standard Deviation of W/L Percentage[a]										
AL	40	40	40	40	40	40	39	39	39	40
NL	40	40	40	40	40	40	39	39	39	40
NBA					66	59	56	55	55	57
NFL			163	150	151	144	135	132	125	140
NHL		111	88	72	68	60	59	56	56	63
Ratio: Actual Standard Deviation/Idealized Standard Deviation										
AL	2.43**	2.55**	2.25**	2.62**	2.20*	2.43**	2.13*	1.95*	1.67*	2.20**
NL	3.08**	2.22*	2.18*	2.22*	2.40**	2.00*	2.56**	1.74*	1.67*	2.12**
NBA					2.44**	2.02	2.62**	2.36*	2.73**	2.43**
NFL			1.83**	1.60**	1.73*	1.46*	1.64**	1.58*	1.53*	1.66**
NHL		1.71	1.61	1.53	1.69	1.88*	1.90**	2.54**	1.91**	1.95**

Sources: Hollander 1977; Hollander and Bock, 1970; Riffenburgh 1986; Reichler 1964; and league guides for later years.
[a]Assuming all teams of equal strength.
*Significant at the .05 level.
**Significant at the .01 level.

each observation, using a *t*-test. If there were perfect competitive balance in a league (equal playing strengths), the ratio for that league would be 1. In fact, values of the ratio vary between a high of 3.08 (NL, 1901–1909) and a low of 1.48 (NFL, 1950–1959). A general observation is that for all leagues, the ratio values shown differ significantly from the ideal value of 1, both for the overall averages over the histories of the various leagues, and for most decade-by-decade cases as well. Thus all of the leagues in almost all time periods display a significant variation from the equal playing strengths ideal, so on the basis of the dispersion measure alone, none of the leagues have come close to attaining the goal of equality in competitive balance among teams.

On the basis of the ratios shown, the NFL shows up as the league with the most competitive balance, while the NBA is the league with the least competitive balance. Within baseball, the NL has an overall average ratio that is less than that of the AL (more competitive balance), but the difference is not significant. Beginning in the late 1950s and early 1960s, there has been a clear downward trend in the ratios for both baseball leagues, that is, a discernible trend toward more competitive balance in both leagues. (See also the discussion in Scully (1989).) In part, this reflects the beneficial effects of franchise moves in the 1950s of perennial second-division AL teams into more profitable new markets, along with the moves of the Braves, the Dodgers, and the Giants. A second factor acting to equalize competitive balance was the introduction of a reverse-order-of-finish rookie free agent draft in 1964. One other factor favorable to competitive balance has been the virtual disappearance of sales of star players for cash since the 1950s. Acting in the opposite direction (to decrease competitive balance) was expansion by the AL in 1961 and by the NL in 1962. Expansion by the AL (and not the NL) in the 1970s might help to account for the higher value of the ratio for the AL in that decade. The historically low values of the ratios for the two baseball leagues in the 1980s occurred, of course, during a period when there was collusion among owners in the veteran free agent market, and might not continue into the 1990s.

As noted earlier in connection with the range, a somewhat surprising feature of Table 7.1 is that NHL hockey shows up as having notably more competitive balance over its history than does the NBA (with the sole exception of the 1970s). The NHL-NBA comparison is surprising because the NHL and the NBA have many similarities, including especially the 100–0 gate split between the home and visiting team, roughly the same schedule length, and the same season of the year for league play, often in the same arenas. A likely explanation for the marked difference in competitive balance is the history of the two leagues with respect to expansion, contraction, and movement of league franchises.

The history of the NBA has been hectic, as was noted in Chapter 2. During the 1946–1949 period, six of the original 11 members of the BAA (Basketball Association of America) dropped out of the league, the league added one team (Baltimore) from the American Basketball League, plus 10 teamss from the National Basketball League, and changed its name in 1949 to the National Basketball Association. The 1950s began with a winnowing out of the smaller NBL teams (Anderson, Sheboygan, Waterloo) and Denver, followed by the loss of Indianapolis and Baltimore midway in the decade, and various franchise moves (Rochester to Cincinnati, Fort Wayne to Detroit, Tri Cities to Milwaukee and then to St. Louis). During the 1960s, when the Celtics owned the league (8 of 10 titles), the NBA did battle with the ABA, added six new franchises (Chicago, Chicago once again, Seattle, San Diego, Milwaukee, Phoenix), and had more franchise moves (Philadelphia to San Francisco, Syracuse to Philadelphia, Minneapolis to Los Angeles, St. Louis to Atlanta, Chicago to Baltimore).

In the 1970s, it was more of the same. Buffalo, Cleveland, Portland, and New Orleans were added as expansion franchises; the Nets, San Antonio, Denver, and Indiana were taken in as part of the ABA-NBA merger agreement; and there were more moves (San Francisco to Oakland, Cincinnati to Kansas City-Omaha, Baltimore to Washington, San Diego to Houston, Buffalo to San Diego, New Orleans to Utah, the Nets from New York to New Jersey). Given this history, the 1980s were positively placid—there have been only five more expansion teams (Dallas, Charlotte, Miami, Minnesota, Orlando), and a mere two moves of existing franchises (Kansas City to Sacramento, and San Diego to Los Angeles).

The NHL has had only two comparably tumultuous decades—the 1920s, when Montreal (Maroons), Boston, Pittsburgh, New York (Rangers and Americans), Chicago, and Detroit came into the league, and the 1970s, when the league absorbed the six expansion franchises of 1967 (Philadelphia, Los Angeles, St. Louis, Minnesota, Pittsburgh, and Oakland); added Buffalo, Vancouver, the Islanders, Atlanta, Washington, and Kansas City as six more expansion franchises; and in addition took in Edmonton, Winnipeg, Hartford, and Quebec from the defunct WHA. Franchise moves in the 1970s were from California to Cleveland (which then merged with Minnesota), and Kansas City to Colorado.

Looking at Table 7.1, the decade of the 1970s shows up as an outlier for the NHL, with a value for the ratio of actual to idealized standard deviation that looks like the ratios for the NBA over its history. (See the discussion of franchise turnovers in Chapter 2.) The 1920s do not show up as a blip for the NHL, presumably because the expansion of that decade took the unusual form of the NHL's buying up the Patrick brothers' Pacific Coast Hockey League, which had been the NHL's postseason competitor for the Stanley Cup. Veteran players from PCHL teams were allocated to the incoming expansion teams, which generally performed more like old-line teams than like expansion teams. The evidence for the NHL in the 1970s suggests that it might well be the case that once the NBA settles down to a more or less stable lifestyle, with settled franchises, the NBA competitive balance measure might begin to look more like the measure for the NHL.

In connection with this, it might be of interest to look a little closer at the effect of league expansion on competitive balance. For the first few years of their history, expansion teams are manned primarily by players acquired in the expansion draft, which pretty much ensures very weak teams with low W/L records. Thus, periods of league expansion tend to be periods of highly dispersed W/L percentages. Table 7.2 gives the W/L histories of expansion teams in the various leagues since 1960.

If we look simply at average W/L percentages over the first five years in the league, the worst league from the point of view of an expansion franchise is the NFL, where the average expansion team had a first-year W/L percentage of only .151, and where the five-year average W/L percentage for expansion teams was .322. On the other hand, baseball has the worst record in terms of average number of years for an expansion franchise to reach a .500 W/L percentage (8 years); and the NFL has the best record (5.5 years), followed closely by the NBA (5.6 years). In the first two years of operation, expansion teams in all leagues can expect to post W/L records of less than .400, and only in the NBA does the average W/L percentage for expansion teams reach .500 within five years. The extremely weak W/L records of expansion teams are matched by unusually strong W/L records for existing teams during a period of expansion, both of which act to increase the dispersion of W/L percentages for a league.

Historical Distributions
of League W/L Percentages

Another way to look at the issue of competitive balance so far as the spread of W/L percentages is concerned is to compare the actual distribution of W/L percentages for a league over its history with the idealized distribution based on the equal playing strengths assumption. Figures 7.1 through 7.5 show the actual and idealized frequency distributions of W/L percentages for the AL, NL, NBA, NFL, and NHL over their entire league histories (1901–1990). The actual frequency distribution is

Table 7.2
First Five-Year Records of Expansion Teams, 1960–1989

	W/L Record by Years in League					Five-Year W/L Avg.	Years to Reach .500
	1	2	3	4	5		
BASEBALL							
N.Y. Mets (1962)	.250	.315	.327	.309	.410	.322	8
Houston (1962)	.400	.407	.407	.401	.444	.412	8
Washington (1961)	.379	.373	.346	.383	.432	.383	9
California (1961)	.435	.531	.435	.506	.463	.474	2
San Diego (1969)	.321	.389	.379	.379	.370	.368	10
Montreal (1969)	.321	.451	.441	.481	.488	.436	11
Kansas City (1969)	.426	.401	.528	.494	.543	.478	3
Seattle/Milwaukee (1969)	.395	.401	.429	.417	.457	.420	10
Seattle (1977)	.395	.350	.414	.364	.404	.385	15
Toronto (1977)	.335	.366	.327	.414	.349	.358	7
Average	.365	.398	.403	.415	.436	.404	8.2
NATIONAL FOOTBALL LEAGUE							
Dallas (1960)	.000	.308	.385	.286	.385	.273	6
Minnesota (1961)	.214	.154	.385	.615	.500	.374	4
Miami (1966)	.214	.286	.385	.231	.714	.366	5
Atlanta (1966)	.214	.077	.143	.429	.333	.239	6
New Orleans (1967)	.214	.308	.357	.154	.333	.273	13
Cincinnati (1968)	.214	.308	.571	.286	.571	.390	3
Seattle (1976)	.143	.357	.563	.563	.250	.375	3
Tampa Bay (1976)	.000	.143	.313	.625	.344	.285	4
Average	.151	.243	.388	.399	.429	.322	5.5
NATIONAL BASKETBALL ASSOCIATION							
Chicago/Baltimore/Washington (1961)	.225	.313	.388	.463	.475	.373	8
Chicago (1966)	.407	.354	.402	.476	.622	.452	5
Seattle (1967)	.280	.366	.439	.463	.573	.424	5
San Diego/Houston (1967)	.183	.451	.329	.488	.415	.373	8
Milwaukee (1968)	.329	.683	.805	.768	.732	.663	2
Phoenix (1968)	.195	.476	.585	.598	.463	.463	3
Cleveland (1970)	.183	.280	.390	.354	.488	.339	6
Portland (1970)	.354	.220	.256	.329	.463	.324	7
Buffalo/San Diego/Los Angeles (1970)	.268	.268	.256	.512	.598	.380	4
New Orleans/Utah (1974)	.280	.463	.427	.476	.317	.393	10
Dallas (1980)	.183	.341	.463	.524	.537	.410	4
Miami (1988)	.244	.232	.293				
Charlotte (1988)	.183	.240	.317				
Orlando (1989)	.220	.378					

(continued)

Table 7.2 (cont.)
First Five-Year Records of Expansion Teams, 1960–1989

	W/L Record by Years in League					Five-Year W/L Avg.	Years to Reach .500
	1	2	3	4	5		
Minnesota (1989)	.268	.354					
Average	.254	.360	.411	.496	.516	.417	5.6
NATIONAL HOCKEY LEAGUE							
Oakland/California/Cleveland (1967)	.318	.454	.382	.288	.385	.365	11[a]
Los Angeles (1967)	.486	.382	.250	.404	.314	.367	7
Minnesota (1967)	.466	.336	.395	.462	.551	.442	5
Philadelphia (1967)	.493	.401	.382	.486	.423	.447	6
Pittsburgh (1967)	.453	.336	.421	.397	.423	.429	8
St. Louis (1967)	.473	.579	.566	.558	.429	.521	2
Buffalo (1970)	.404	.327	.564	.487	.706	.498	3
Vancouver (1970)	.359	.308	.340	.378	.538	.385	5
Atlanta/Calgary (1972)	.417	.474	.519	.513	.500	.485	3
N.Y. Islanders (1972)	.192	.359	.550	.631	.663	.479	3
Kansas City/Colorado/ New Jersey (1974)	.256	.225	.338	.369	.263	.290	14
Washington (1975)	.200	.388	.300	.394	.419	.341	8
Average	.376	.381	.417	.447	.468	.420	6.3

Sources: As in table 7.1.
[a]Team did not reach .500 before merging with Minnesota in 1977.

the solid curve, and the idealized distribution is the dotted curve. As was noted earlier, the idealized distribution is closely approximated by the bell-shaped normal curve, with roughly two-thirds of the W/L percentages lying within one standard deviation of .500, roughly 95 percent lying within two standard deviations, and roughly 99 percent lying within three standard deviations. Note that the dotted (idealized) curves for the baseball leagues are much more concentrated about .500 than those for basketball and hockey, and the curve for the NFL is the flattest of the dotted curves. This reflects the difference in the number of games in a league season for these different sports—the more games in a season, the smaller is the standard deviation and hence the less spread out is the W/L distribution under the equal playing strengths assumption.

For all leagues, the actual frequency distributions are more spread out than the idealized distributions—for all leagues, the actual W/L percentages are more dispersed than they would be if all teams were of equal

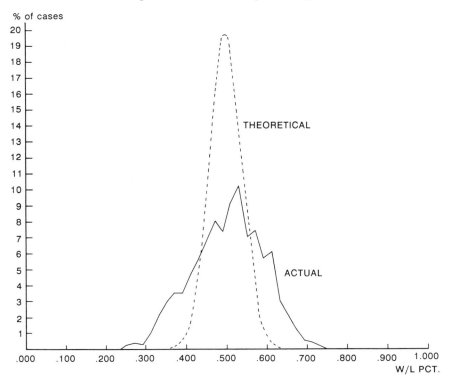

Figure 7.1 Frequency Distribution, W/L Percentage, American League, 1901–1990

playing strength. This is another indication that all of the leagues depart from the ideal of equality of competitive balance among teams.

We can rank the various leagues in terms of their degree of competitive balance by calculating the "excess tail frequencies" of their W/L distributions. In other words, we look at the difference between the percentage of cases that actually lie in the tails of the W/L distribution and the percentage of cases that would lie in the tails if all teams were of equal playing strengths. This is the "excess tail frequency." The larger value is the "excess tail frequency," the less competitive balance in the league. In Table 7.3, we calculate the excess tail frequencies for the various leagues, using for our tails the two- and three-standard-deviation limits.

Table 7.3 reinforces the conclusions from Table 7.1. The league showing the most competitive balance is the NFL, while the league with the least competitive balance is the NBA, with the NHL, AL, and NL lying between these extremes. Moreover, even in the case of the NFL, there is a substantial difference between the actual and idealized distributions, as indicated, for example, by the excess tail frequencies in the

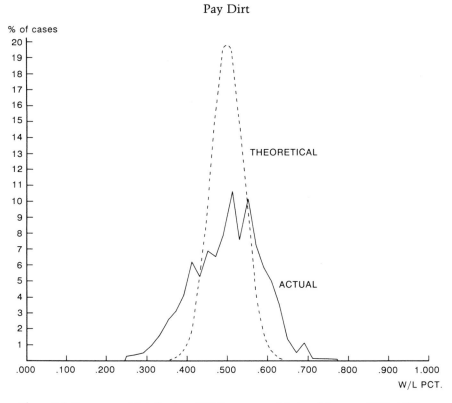

Figure 7.2 Frequency Distribution, W/L Percentage, National League, 1901–1990

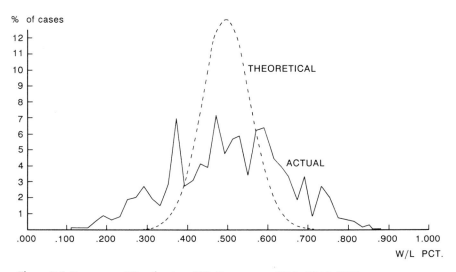

Figure 7.3 Frequency Distribution, W/L Percentage, NBA, 1946–1990

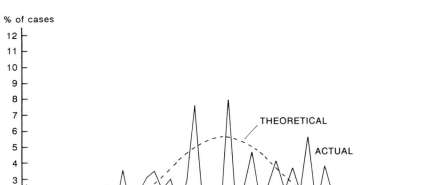

Figure 7.4 Frequency Distribution, W/L Percentage, NFL, 1920–1990

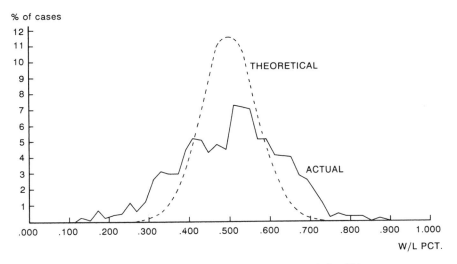

Figure 7.5 Frequency Distribution, W/L Percentage, NHL, 1917–1990

two-standard-deviation case. Thus, once again, when we use this measure, all leagues exhibit significant departures from the equal competitive balance ideal.

Concentration of League Championships

Under the equal playing strengths assumption, over a sufficiently long period of time we would find that league championships would be

Table 7.3
Excess Tail Frequencies by League (percent)

League and Tail Limits	Actual Frequency	Idealized Frequency	Excess Frequency
TWO STANDARD-DEVIATION TAILS			
AL (under .420, over .580)	38.1	4.6	33.5
NL (under .420, over .580)	37.0	4.6	32.4
NHL (under .374, over .626)	32.4	4.6	28.3
NBA (under .386, over .614)	55.5	4.6	50.9
NFL (under .220, over .780)	24.9	4.6	20.3
THREE STANDARD DEVIATION TAILS			
AL (under .380, over .620)	19.0	0.3	18.7
NL (under .380, over .620)	16.3	0.3	16.0
NHL (under .311, over .689)	13.1	0.3	12.8
NBA (under .329, over .671)	32.4	0.3	32.1
NFL (under .080, over .920)	5.9	0.3	5.6

shared on a more or less equal basis among all teams, that most teams would have winning seasons about half the time, and that most team lifetime W/L percentages would be close to .500. One of the clearest indications that leagues differ significantly from the ideal of equal playing strengths is the fact that for every league, one or more successful teams can be identified that win a disproportionate share of championships, that consistently have winning seasons, and that have lifetime W/L percentages far above .500. Every league has its dominant teams—the Yankees in the AL, the Dodgers in the NL, the Celtics and Lakers in the NBA, the Canadiens and Oilers in the NHL, and the Raiders, the Cowboys, and the Dolphins in the NFL. Thus there is concentration of playing strengths in all leagues, but is there some way to determine which leagues show more concentration of playing strengths in a few favored teams—and hence less competitive balance—than other leagues?

The approach to be followed here uses once again the Lorenz curve, the device used in Chapter 6 to measure the degree of inequality of income in the salary distributions of the various sports. In our treatment here, we will be looking at the extent of inequality in the winning of league championships.

Table 7.4 lists the most successful teams in each of the five leagues, where success is measured in terms of number of league championships won per year a team is in the league. The table, which covers the period 1901–1990, shows that the most successful team in terms of championships won per year in the league was the Edmonton Oilers, with five

Table 7.4
Titles per Year Won by Most Successful Teams, All Leagues,
Teams with at Least 10 Years in League, 1901–1990

Team	Titles	Years in League	Titles/Year
AMERICAN LEAGUE			
New York	33	88	.38
Oakland	6	23	.26
Philadelphia	9	54	.17
Baltimore	6	37	.16
Boston	10	90	.11
Detroit	9	90	.10
K.C. Royals	2	22	.09
Minnesota	2	30	.07
Chicago	5	90	.06
Milwaukee	1	21	.05
NATIONAL LEAGUE			
Los Angeles	9	33	.27
N.Y. Giants	15	57	.26
St. Louis	15	90	.17
Brooklyn	9	57	.16
Milwaukee	2	15	.15
Chicago	10	90	.11
N.Y. Mets	3	29	.10
Pittsburgh	9	90	.10
Cincinnati	9	90	.10
San Francisco	2	33	.06
NATIONAL BASKETBALL ASSOCIATION			
Minneapolis	5	12	.42
Boston	16	44	.36
L.A. Lakers	6	31	.19
Philadelphia Warriors	2	16	.13
St. Louis	1	13	.08
Philadelphia 76ers	2	28	.07
Syracuse	1	14	.07
Detroit	2	33	.06
Golden State	1	20	.05
NATIONAL HOCKEY LEAGUE			
Edmonton	5	11	.46
Montreal Canadiens	23	73	.32
Ottawa	4	16	.25
N.Y. Islanders	4	18	.22
Toronto	13	73	.18

(continued)

Table 7.4 (cont.)
Titles per Year Won by Most Successful Teams, All Leagues,
Teams with at Least 10 Years in League, 1901–1990

Team	Titles	Years in League	Titles/Year
Montreal Maroons	2	14	.14
Detroit	7	64	.11
Calgary	1	10	.10
Philadelphia Flyers	2	23	.09
Boston	5	66	.08
NATIONAL FOOTBALL LEAGUE			
Oakland	2	12	.17
Green Bay	11	70	.16
Chicago Bears	9	71	.13
Cleveland Browns	4	41	.10
San Francisco	4	41	.10
Miami	2	21	.10
N.Y. Giants	6	65	.09
Baltimore	3	38	.08
Washington	4	54	.07
Pittsburgh	4	58	.07
Detroit	4	58	.07

Sources: As in table 7.1.

Stanley Cups in just 11 years, four of them won with the team featuring Wayne Gretzky. The second most successful team is the Minneapolis Lakers of the late 1940s and early 1950s—the lineup featuring George Mikan, Jim Pollard, Vern Mikkelson, Dugie Martin, and Bob Harrison—who pulled down five NBA titles in 12 seasons. These are, of course, short-run success stories. As expected, the best long-term record is that of the Yankees, followed closely by the Celtics, and then the Canadiens. The L.A. Dodgers are next in line, llowed by the Oakland Athletics and the old-time New York Giants of John McGraw, Mel Ott, Carl Hubbell, and Bill Terry.

In the NFL, it is the Oakland Raiders with the best short-run titles/year record, and the Green Bay Packers and Chicago Bears with the best long-run records, but they rank far down the line from the leading teams in the other leagues. Still, there were periods in the past when the Packers and the Bears dominated the NFL almost as conclusively as the Celtics and Lakers have dominated the NBA in recent years. The record of championships for those two teams by decades in the NFL looks like this:

	1920s	1930s	1940s	1950s	1960s	1970s	1980s
Green Bay	1	4	1	0	5	0	0
Chicago Bears	1	2	4	0	1	0	1

The Packers won three championships in a row in 1929, 1930, and 1931, with the lineup featuring the inimitable and incorrigible Johnny Blood; rebuilt the team into the great lineups of the late 1930s with Don Hutson, Arnie Herber, and later Cecil Isbell, to win a couple more; and then came back in the 1960s under Vince Lombardi to take another three in a row—1965, 1966, and 1967, after winning in 1961 and 1962. The Bears had the powerhouse team of the 1930s with Bronko Nagurski at fullback, and then dominated the league in the early to mid-1940s, when they revolutionized football with the T-formation with the man in motion run by Sid Luckman at quarterback.

The data from Table 7.4 are used to construct Lorenz curves for each of the five leagues, as shown in Figure 7.6. Along the vertical axis, we plot the cumulative percentage of league championships, and along the horizontal axis, we plot the cumulative percentage of team years in the league. For each league, the Lorenz curve is plotted by beginning with the most successful teams in the league (in terms of championships won per year in the league) and working down to less and less successful teams.

If league championships were shared equally by all league teams, in the sense that each team had the same frequency of league championships per year in the league, then the Lorenz curve for that league would be a straight line from the lower left-hand corner to the upper right-hand corner. This is shown as the diagonal line labeled "equal competitive balance" in Figure 7.6.

The actual Lorenz curves for the leagues "bulge" upward from the diagonal line. The further the actual curve above the diagonal line, that is, the larger the "bulge," the more concentrated is the winning of championships. Briefly, the league exhibiting the most concentration of championships and hence the least competitive balance is the NBA. The NBA curve lies above the curves for all other leagues everywhere on the graph. The NHL and AL are the next most concentrated leagues so far as championships are concerned, with the NHL curve bulging out above the AL curve for all but a few stretches. Both of these leagues exhibit more concentration of championships than does the NFL, with a Lorenz curve that lies below the AL and NHL (and NBA) curves everywhere in the diagram. Interestingly, the league with the least amount of concentration of league championships is the NL, with a Lorenz curve that lies inside that for the NFL, al-

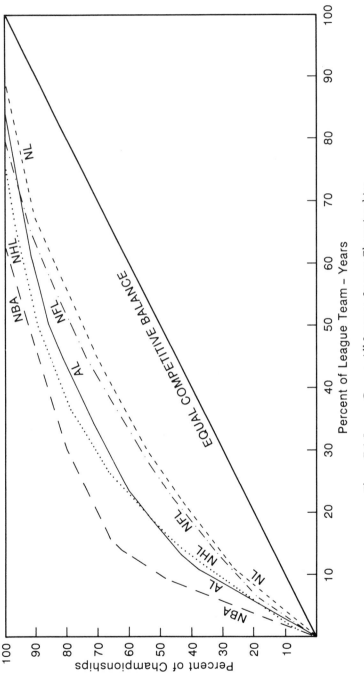

Figure 7.6 Lorenz Curves, All Leagues, League Championships

though the difference between the NL and NFL is small, over the entire range of league team years.

The leagues may also be ranked in terms of Gini coefficients (see Chapter 6), that is, in terms of the area under a Lorenz curve and above the equal competitive balance line. The larger the Gini coefficient, the bigger the "bulge," and hence the less competitive balance. Gini coefficients for the concentration of league championships are as follows: NBA, .419; NHL, .386; AL, .377; NFL, .350; NL, .334. The NBA has the least competitive balance and the NL the most, in terms of concentration of championships.

Lifetime Team W/L Percentages and Competitive Balance

In a league where all teams were of equal playing strength, the lifetime team W/L percentages would be bunched closely around the league average of .500. In contrast, actual lifetime W/L performance records of teams differ significantly from this ideal. Table 7.5 lists the lifetime W/L percentages for the most successful teams (in terms of W/L percentages) in each of the five major sports leagues, and also gives relative frequencies of winning seasons for each team. Data cover the period through the 1990 (or 1990/91) season.

Among all teams with more than 10 years in a league, the best lifetime W/L record is held by the Oakland Raiders, who compiled a .699 W/L record in their 12 years in the NFL, and had winning seasons in 11 of the 12 years they were in Oakland. The Dolphins have the next best lifetime W/L record, at .682, with 19 winning seasons in 21 NFL campaigns. Then come the Los Angeles Lakers, who have had winning seasons 87 percent of the time over the 31 years since the team was moved from Minneapolis, and have compiled a .638 lifetime W/L record, just nosing out the Celtics, at .630.

Ranking far down the list of lifetime W/L records are the leading baseball teams—the Yankees, with a lifetime W/L record of .567, with 70 winning seasons in the 88 years they have been in the AL. The NL's best record is still held by the old Milwaukee Braves, who never had a losing season in their 13 years in the league, compiling a .563 W/L record.

In trying to make comparisons among the various successful teams in the different sports, we need to take into account the differences in schedules of the various leagues, and the number of years that a team has been in a league. In particular, the longer is the league schedule,

Table 7.5
Lifetime W/L Percentages of Most Successful Teams, All Leagues,
Teams with at Least 10 Years in League, 1901–1990

Team	Lifetime W/L %	Years in League	Winning Seasons (%)
AMERICAN LEAGUE			
New York	.567	88	80
Baltimore	.535	37	70
Oakland	.523	23	65
K.C. Royals	.521	22	68
Detroit	.518	90	67
Boston	.510	90	63
Cleveland	.509	90	56
Minnesota	.501	30	53
NATIONAL LEAGUE			
Milwaukee Braves	.563	13	100
Los Angeles	.545	33	76
N.Y. Giants	.545	57	75
Pittsburgh	.523	90	67
San Francisco	.517	33	70
St. Louis	.515	90	62
Chicago	.509	90	49
Cincinnati	.504	90	53
NATIONAL BASKETBALL LEAGUE			
L.A. Lakers	.638	31	87
Boston	.630	44	84
Milwaukee	.610	22	77
Philadelphia 76ers	.582	28	79
Syracuse	.571	14	71
Minneapolis	.550	12	58
St. Louis	.550	13	62
Denver	.538	14	71
Washington	.520	17	47
NATIONAL HOCKEY LEAGUE			
Edmonton	.607	11	82
Montreal Canadiens	.597	73	88
Philadelphia Flyers	.582	23	74
Calgary	.578	10	80
Buffalo	.559	20	80
N.Y. Islanders	.559	18	78
Ottawa	.558	16	69
Boston	.551	66	68
N.Y. Rangers	.522	64	53

(*continued*)

Table 7.5 (cont.)
Lifetime W/L Percentages of Most Successful Teams, All Leagues,
Teams with at Least 10 Years in League, 1901–1990

Team	Lifetime W/L %	Years in League	Winning Seasons (%)
NATIONAL FOOTBALL LEAGUE			
Oakland	.699	12	92
Miami	.682	21	90
Chicago Bears	.624	71	72
Cleveland Browns	.612	41	81
Dallas Cowboys	.579	31	68
L.A. Rams	.576	45	71
N.Y. Giants	.560	66	67
Denver	.554	21	71
Green Bay	.552	70	66
Minnesota	.546	30	67

Sources: As in table 7.1.

and the more years a team has been in a league, the more significant is a high lifetime W/L percentage for a team.

Once again, we are going to use the ideal of a league composed of teams with equal playing strength as a device to compare the winning percentages of teams shown. We have already seen that in a league with teams of equal strength, the standard deviation of the distribution of W/L percentages for a season is given by $(.5)/\sqrt{N}$, where N is the number of games during the season. The more games in a league season, the smaller is this idealized standard deviation, that is, the more bunched up are the team W/L percentages around .500 for teams assumed to be of equal playing strength. Because of this, under the equal playing strengths assumption, it is less likely that a team's W/L percentage will be, say, at .550 or above, if a league plays a 162-game schedule, as in baseball, than if it plays an 80-game schedule, as in the NHL.

When we calculate the lifetime W/L percentage for a team that been in a league T years, what we do is to add up the team's W/L percentage in each of the T years, and then divide by T. Suppose that the team were playing in a league where all teams were of equal playing strength. Then the lifetime W/L percentage for a team is simply the sample mean of a sample of size T drawn from a population of W/L percentages with mean .500 and standard deviation $(.5)/\sqrt{N}$. From elementary statistics, we know that, for any T sufficiently large, the sample mean will be distributed approximately as the normal distribution, with a mean of .500 and with a standard deviation equal to the population standard deviation divided by $\sqrt{T}$.

This gives us a way to evaluate the lifetime W/L percentages of teams. For each team, we know T, and we know the average league schedule N over the period in which the team was in the league. Thus we can calculate for each team, how many standard deviations above .500 the observed lifetime W/L percentage lies, assuming equal playing strengths. This becomes a measure of the "achievement" of a team, which can be used to rank teams within a league, and between leagues. Tables 7.6 through 7.10 provide a ranking of teams in the five leagues, and Table 7.11 identifies the prize "overachievers" and "underachievers" in the history of major league pro team sports.

When we adjust for the length of the season and for the number of years a team has been in a league, the New York Yankees end up as the team with the best lifetime record, 15.6 standard deviations above the mean, under the equal playing strengths assumption. If there actually were equal playing strengths in the AL, the probability that a team

Table 7.6

Lifetime W/L Percentages Ranked by Achievement Measure, American League, Teams with at Least 10 Years in League, 1901–1990

Team	Years in League	Lifetime W/L %	Standard Deviations above .500[a]
New York	88	.567	15.6
Baltimore	37	.537	5.6
Detroit	90	.518	4.3
Oakland	23	.523	2.8
K.C. Royals	22	.521	2.5
Boston	90	.510	2.4
Cleveland	90	.509	2.1
Minnesota	30	.501	0.1
Chicago	90	.496	−1.0
Milwaukee	21	.485	−1.7
Toronto	14	.480	−1.9
Texas	19	.472	−3.0
Philadelphia	54	.478	−4.11
Washington II	11	.418	−6.8
Washington I	60	.464	−6.9
Seattle	14	.423	−7.2
K.C. Athletics	13	.404	−8.6
St. Louis Browns	52	.434	−12.0

Sources: As in table 7.1.

[a]Under equal playing strengths assumption.

Table 7.7

Lifetime W/L Percentages Ranked by Achievement Measure, National League, Teams with at Least 10 Years in League, 1901–1990

Team	Years in League	Lifetime W/L %	Standard Deviations above .500[a]
N.Y. Giants	57	.545	8.5
Los Angeles	33	.546	6.6
Milwaukee	13	.563	5.7
Pittsburgh	90	.522	5.2
St. Louis	90	.515	3.6
San Francisco	33	.517	2.4
Chicago	90	.509	2.1
Brooklyn	57	.510	1.9
Cincinnati	90	.504	1.0
Montreal	22	.488	−1.4
Houston	29	.484	−2.2
N.Y. Mets	29	.466	−4.6
Atlanta	25	.462	−4.8
San Diego	22	.443	−6.7
Boston	52	.429	−12.9

Sources: As in table 7.1.
[a]Based on equal playing strengths assumption.

would end up with a record like the Yankees would be roughly comparable to the probability of coming up with the winning ticket to LOTTO America once or maybe two weeks in a row. The Celtics rank a close second, followed by the Lakers and the Canadiens. A surprising fifth place is held by the Milwaukee Bucks, ranking ahead of the NL New York Giants (1901–1957), the Philadelphia 76ers, the Bears, the Boston Bruins, and then the Philadelphia Flyers, with the L.A. Dodgers, Miami, Edmonton, the old Milwaukee Braves, and the Baltimore Orioles completing the top-15 list.

The list of all-time losers (underachievers) is headed by a trio of baseball teams—the Boston Braves, the St. Louis Browns, and the Kansas City Athletics, all long since gone to other towns. Cleveland and New Jersey from the NBA come next, followed by two hockey teams—Vancouver and the now defunct New York Americans. Then there is a matched pair from baseball—the original Washington Senators and the second Washington team, both of which have moved on. The list is completed with San Diego (NL), Tampa Bay, the Chicago Cardinals (another team that moved), the New Orleans Saints, the Pittsburgh Penguins, and the Detroit Pistons.

Table 7.8
Lifetime W/L Percentages Ranked by Achievement Measure, National Football
League, Teams with at Least 10 Years in League, 1920–1990

Team	Years in League	Lifetime W/L %	Standard Deviations above .500[a]
Chicago Bears	71	.624	7.5
Miami	21	.682	6.5
Cleveland Browns	41	.612	5.4
Oakland	12	.699	5.2
L.A. Rams	45	.576	3.7
N.Y. Giants	66	.560	3.5
Dallas Cowboys	31	.579	3.3
Green Bay	70	.552	3.1
Washington	54	.546	2.4
Denver	21	.554	1.9
Minnesota	30	.546	1.9
San Francisco	41	.530	1.4
Cincinnati	21	.533	1.2
Baltimore	32	.523	1.0
Seattle	15	.486	−0.4
St. Louis	28	.486	−0.5
New England	21	.464	−1.3
Detroit	57	.470	−1.6
Kansas City	21	.449	−1.8
San Diego	21	.444	−2.0
Pittsburgh	58	.458	−2.3
N.Y. Jets	21	.427	−2.6
Buffalo	21	.425	−2.6
Brooklyn	15	.381	−3.1
Philadelphia	58	.440	−3.3
Houston	21	.400	−3.5
Atlanta	25	.377	−4.6
New Orleans	24	.366	−5.0
Chicago Cardinals	40	.368	−5.6
Tampa Bay	15	.304	−6.1

Sources: As in table 7.1.
[a]Under equal playing strengths assumption.

Tables 7.6 through 7.10 give us one more way to rank leagues in terms of competitive balance, by comparing the fraction of teams in each league for which the lifetime W/L record lies close to .500. Table 7.12 provides this comparison among leagues. The larger the fraction of teams with lifetime W/L percentages near .500, the more turnover occurs. Here the NBA comes out as the league with the best competitive

Table 7.9

Lifetime W/L Percentages Ranked by Achievement Measure, National Basketball
Association, Teams with at Least 10 Years in League, 1946–1990

Team	Years in League	Lifetime W/L %	Standard Deviations above .500[a]
Boston	44	.630	15.4
L.A. Lakers	31	.638	13.7
Milwaukee Bucks	23	.609	9.2
Philadelphia 76ers	28	.582	7.7
Syracuse	14	.571	4.7
St. Louis	13	.550	3.2
Minneapolis	12	.550	3.0
Portland	21	.524	1.9
San Antonio	15	.521	1.4
Phoenix	23	.517	1.4
Denver	15	.519	1.3
Washington	18	.514	1.0
Atlanta	23	.509	0.8
N.Y. Knicks	44	.505	0.6
Philadelphia Warriors	16	.506	0.4
Utah	12	.494	−0.4
Baltimore	10	.493	−0.4
Chicago Bulls	25	.497	−0.6
Seattle	24	.492	−0.7
Houston	20	.487	−1.0
Dallas	11	.480	−1.2
Golden State	20	.481	−1.5
Kansas City-Omaha	13	.463	−2.3
Cincinnati	15	.458	−2.9
Detroit	34	.452	−4.9
Indiana	15	.410	−6.1
New Jersey	14	.392	−7.1
Cleveland	21	.409	−7.3

Sources: As in table 7.1.
[a]Under equal playing strengths assumption.

balance record, with over half the teams with lifetime W/L records within two standard deviations of the mean, using the idealized standard deviation measure. Clearly, what has been happening is that the Celtics, Lakers, Bucks and 76ers have had very good teams year after year, but most of the rest of the league go from good to bad seasons and back on a year-to-year basis.

The worst leagues shown in Table 7.12 are the baseball leagues,

Table 7.10

Lifetime W/L Percentages Ranked by Achievement Measure, National Hockey
League, Teams with at Least 10 Years in League, 1917–1990

Team	Years in League	Lifetime W/L %	Standard Deviations above .500[a]
Montreal Canadiens	74	.596	13.1
Boston	67	.552	7.1
Philadelphia Flyers	24	.578	6.7
Edmonton	12	.598	6.0
Calgary	11	.582	4.9
Buffalo	21	.556	4.6
Ottawa	16	.558	4.1
N.Y. Islanders	19	.549	3.8
N.Y. Rangers	65	.522	3.0
Toronto	74	.508	1.1
Montreal Maroons	14	.507	0.5
Detroit	65	.496	−0.5
St. Louis	24	.488	−1.0
Winnipeg	11	.461	−2.3
Quebec	11	.452	−2.8
Washington	17	.461	−2.9
Chicago	65	.478	−3.0
Los Angeles	24	.464	−3.1
Hartford	12	.448	−3.2
Minnesota	24	.447	−4.6
Pittsburgh	24	.443	−4.9
N.Y. Americans	17	.407	−6.8
Vancouver	21	.413	−7.1

Sources: As in table 7.1.

[a]Under equal playing strengths assumption.

where teams like the St. Louis Browns and Boston Braves made lifetime
careers out of being in the second division. Inability to move franchises
in baseball until the 1950s played an important role in those failures,
but there is also the case of the hapless Kansas City Athletics to consider. Overall, Table 7.12 provides further evidence of the limited
amount of competitive balance that has characterized the major pro
team sports leagues over their histories.

The Reserve Clause and Competitive Balance

One obvious conclusion from our extended look at historical data on
competitive balance in the five major team sports leagues is that none

Table 7.11
Top Overachievers and Underachievers Ranked by Achievement Measure,
All Sports Leagues

	Top Overachievers			*Top Underachievers*	
	Team	*Standard Deviations over .500*[a]		*Team*	*Standard Deviations over .500*[a]
1.	N.Y. Yankees	15.6	1.	Boston Braves	−12.9
2.	Boston Celtics	15.4	2.	St. Louis Browns	−12.0
3.	L.A. Lakers	13.7	3.	K.C. Athletics	−8.6
4.	Montreal Canadiens	13.1	4.	Cleveland (NBA)	−7.3
5.	Milwaukee Bucks	9.2	5.	Vancouver Canucks	−7.1
6.	N.Y. Giants (NL)	8.5	5.	N.J. Nets	−7.1
7.	Philadelaphia 76ers	7.7	6.	Washington Senators I	−6.9
8.	Chicago Bears	7.5	7.	Washington Senators II	−6.8
9.	Boston Bruins	7.1	7.	N.Y. Americans (NHL)	−6.8
10.	Philadelphia Flyers	6.7	8.	San Diego (NL)	−6.7
11.	L.A. Dodgers	6.6	9.	Tampa Bay Buccaneers	−6.1
12.	Miami Dolphins	6.5	10.	Chicago Cardinals	−5.6
13.	Edmonton Oilers	6.0	11.	New Orleans Saints	−5.0
14.	Milwaukee Braves	5.7	12.	Pittsburgh Penguins	−4.9
15.	Baltimore Orioles	5.6	12.	Detroit Pistons	−4.9

Sources: As in table 7.1.
[a]Under equal playing strengths assumption.

Table 7.12
Percentage of Teams with Lifetime W/L Percentages Lying within Specified
Standard Deviation Limits of .500 by League

League	*Within ± 1 SD*	*Within ± 2 SDs*	*Within ± 3 SDs*	*Outside ± 3 SDs*
AL	10.5	26.3	52.6	47.4
NL	6.3	18.8	37.5	62.5
NBA	34.6	57.7	69.2	30.8
NFL	13.3	36.7	50.0	50.0
NHL	13.0	17.4	39.1	60.9

Sources: As in table 7.1. (Based on equal playing strengths assumption.)

of the leagues comes close to achieving the ideal of equal playing strengths. There is ample evidence of long-term competitive imbalance in each league, despite the league rules that are supposedly designed to equalize team strengths. On the other hand, with all their flaws, the leagues have not only survived but have flourished, with growth in numbers of teams, in geographic coverage, in attendance and public interest, and in profitability.

Owners of sports teams, league commissioners, and most sports-writers argue that an important reason for this success is that the leagues have attained at least an acceptable level of competitive balance. They further argue that this acceptable level of competitive balance is due in no small part to the restrictions that have been imposed by owners on the player market in sports. These restrictions are the ones discussed in Chapter 5: the reserve or option clause in player contracts, combined with other devices—the college draft, the waiver system—that act to equalize access to players by teams. Owners continue to claim that if the reserve-option clause is eliminated, with players free to sell their services to the highest bidder, competitive balance within the league will be severely damaged. Wealthy owners with teams in the best markets will sign up the star players, and the resulting imbalance will lead first to the destruction of the weak teams and finally to the destruction of the league itself.

Free agency has now been a part of the labor picture in baseball and basketball since 1976, and we will want to see how the actual results from these free agency experiments square with the claims of the owners. But before doing this, we will take an excursion into the microeconomic theory of competitive balance; that is, we will examine the structure of profit incentives that operates in a team sports league and see what effects this structure has on competitive balance in a league. The arguments we will present follow closely those first developed in a seminal paper by Rottenberg (1956). Later extensions, including an explicit modeling and analysis of team sports leagues using a Nash equilibrium framework, appear in El Hodiri and Quirk (1974).

It will be easier to follow the economic argument if it presented graphically. In order to do this, we will look at the special case of a two-team league in which one team, team A, is located in a strong-drawing area, and the second team, team B, is located in a weak-drawing area. We should emphasize that the essence of the basic economic argument we will make extends to the case of a league with an arbitrary number of teams; it is only the graphics that restrict us to the two-team case.

We will assume that the revenue that any team earns from its home games depends on only two things: the underlying drawing potential of its franchise area, and the playing strength of the team relative to that of the other teams in the league, that is, how successful the team is on the playing field. In particular, we assume that revenue from the home games of any team varies positively with the W/L percentage of the team.

Market Equilibrium under Free Agency

We consider first the profit incentives at work in a league in which there is an unrestricted competitive labor market, with players free to sell their services to the highest bidder. For simplicity, we first consider the case where all of a team's revenues come from its own home games, that is, the case of a 100–0 gate split, as is the case in the NBA and NHL. After going through this case, we will examine what happens when there is a sharing of gate and TV revenues, as in baseball and the NFL.

Figure 7.7 shows the revenue curves for the two teams: team A, located in the strong-drawing area, and team B, located in the weak-drawing area. Revenue for each team is plotted against the team's W/L percentage, with revenue increasing as the W/L percentage increases, and with the revenue of team A higher than that of team B for any given W/L percentage.

In the upper panel of Figure 7.8, we have graphed the marginal revenue, *MR*, curves for teams A and B. For any value of the W/L percentage,

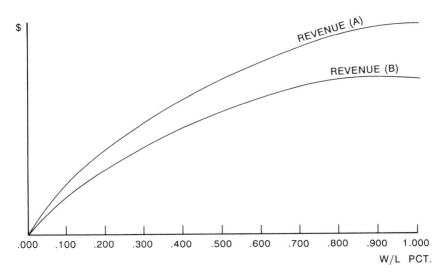

Figure 7.7 Revenue Curves, Teams A and B

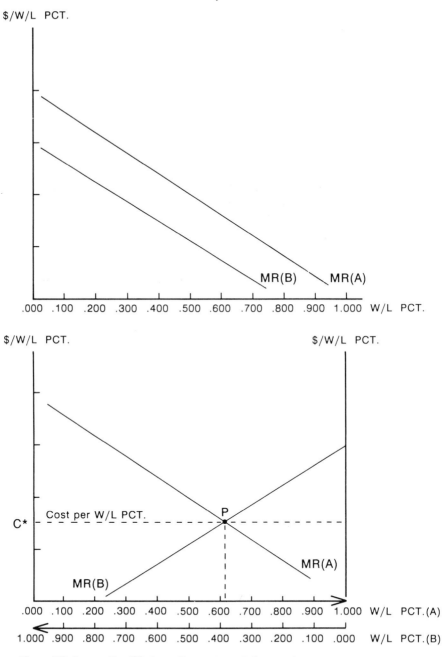

Figure 7.8 League Equilibrium: Competitive Labor Market

the MR curve for a team tells us the increase in revenue for the team that occurs if the team increases its W/L percentage by one point. MR is positive, but it falls as the W/L percentage increases—each additional W/L percentage increases revenue, by smaller and smaller increments. Again we have the MR curve for the stronger-drawing team, team A, lying above the MR curve for the weak-drawing team, team B, for every W/L percentage—winning another game adds more to revenue in the strong-drawing area than it does in the weak-drawing area, for the same W/L percentage.

The lower panel of Figure 7.8 plots the two MR curves on a diagram where the W/L percentage for team A reads from left to right, and the W/L percentage for team B reads from right to left, so that the MR curve for team B is now an upward sloping curve. We consider the case where there is unrestricted free agency and both owners act to maximize profits for their teams. The result will be a bidding up of player salaries and bonuses to the point where an additional W/L percentage point will cost each team C^* dollars, as indicated along the vertical axis, with team A ending up with a W/L percentage of roughly .615, and team B with a W/L percentage of roughly .385; that is, market equilibrium under unrestricted free agency will occur at the point P where the two MR curves cross.

Why is this? First, with unrestricted free agency, both teams will face the same market cost per unit of playing strength, and hence the same cost (C^*) to increase the team's W/L percentage by one point. Profit maximization implies that each team will add playing strength (W/L percentage points) to the point where the added revenue to the team from an additional W/L percentage point (MR) equals the increase in cost (C^*) to attain that. Thus when each team is maximizing profits and the player market is cleared, both teams end up with the same value of MR, which in turn is equal to C^*. Moreover, the W/L percentages chosen by the two teams also clearly must satisfy the condition that when we add the two W/L percentages up, they add up to unity. The only point in the lower diagram where these conditions are satisfied is P; hence, the point P defines an equilibrium for the league under unrestricted free agency.

What happens when we introduce gate and TV revenue sharing into the picture? Figure 7.9 shows the impact of sharing rules in the case of a 60–40 home-visitor sharing arrangement, as in the gate-sharing rules of the NFL. In general, consider a sharing arrangement under which the home team receives a percent of gate and TV revenues, and the visitor receives $(1 - a)$ percent, where a is some number between .5 and 1. Let $R(A)$ denote gate and TV revenue at A, and let $R(B)$ denote gate and TV revenue at B. $R^*(A)$ is revenue to team A under the gate-sharing

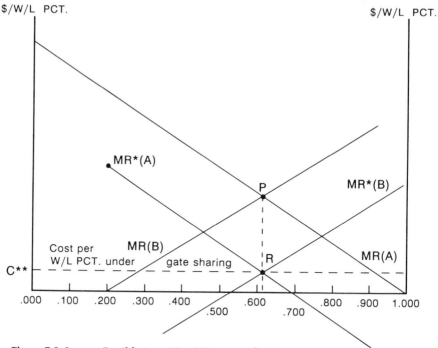

Figure 7.9 League Equilibrium: 60–40 Revenue Sharing

arrangement, and $R^*(B)$ is revenue to team B under gate-sharing. Then we have

$$R^*(A) = aR(A) + (1 - a)R(B),$$

and

$$R^*(B) = aR(B) + (1 - a)R(A).$$

Under gate sharing, marginal revenue for team A, $MR^*(A)$, is the increase in revenue to team A when its W/L percentage increases by one point. Note that in our two-team league, an increase of one point in team A's W/L percentage means that team B's W/L percentage must decrease by one point; and similarly for team B's marginal revenue, $MR^*(B)$. Thus

$$MR^*(A) = aMR(A) - (1 - a)MR(B),$$

and

$$MR^*(B) = aMR(B) - (1 - a)MR(A).$$

In Figure 7.9, $MR^*(A)$ and $MR^*(B)$ are graphed for the case of a 60–40 gate and TV split, with the two curves crossing at the point R, directly below P. At a league equilibrium with profit maximization, $MR^*(A) = MR^*(B) =$ cost per W/L percentage point, with the W/L percentages for the two teams summing to unity. But from the expressions for $MR^*(A)$ and $MR^*(B)$ above, it can be seen that $MR^*(A) = MR^*(B)$ if and only if $MR(A) = MR(B)$. This means that introducing gate sharing leads to the same condition that held earlier; gate sharing has no effect on the distribution of playing strengths between the two clubs. Once again, as shown in Figure 7.9, team A ends up with a W/L percentage of .615 and team B ends up with .385.

So long as teams take into account in their decisionmaking the effects not only on their home gate receipts and TV revenues, but also on their revenues as a visiting team, then the W/L percentages under profit maximization and a free competitive labor market are the same whatever are the sharing rules. And what determines the W/L percentages and hence the degree of imbalance in playing strengths among teams is the disparity in team MR curves based on home gate and TV revenues only, and not the $(1 - a)$ percent of receipts that is given to the visiting team.

The fact that the two MR^* curves cross in Figure 7.9 at the point R below the crossing of the MR curves at P has some important implications. What this says is that at a league equilibrium under gate sharing, increasing a team's W/L percentage by one point is less valuable to the team than when there is no gate sharing. One reason for this is that the increase in home game revenues that results from adding a W/L percentage point is offset in part by the decrease in revenues that a team earns on the road, because its opponent will draw less with a lower W/L percentage. But if a one-point increase in the W/L percentage is worth less to teams under gate sharing, this means in turn that the salaries and bonuses that teams are willing to pay players will be less under gate sharing than when there is no gate sharing. From the point of view of profits, winning is less important under gate sharing than it is when a team's revenues come only from its home game receipts. In Figure 7.9, the market-clearing cost per W/L percentage point is C^{**}, less than C^*, the cost per W/L percentage point when there is no gate sharing. In fact, with 60–40 gate sharing as in Figure 7.9, C^{**} is only about 20 percent as large as C^*.

There is one important caveat to the conclusion that gate sharing has no effect on the degree of competitive balance in a league. Gate sharing shifts income from strong-drawing teams to weak-drawing teams, and, as we have seen, it reduces the market-clearing cost of players to teams, so it shifts income from players to owners. In the absence of gate sharing, it might be the case that some weak-drawing teams could find themselves losing money. An example is the Green Bay Packers, a small-town team that has survived in large part because of NFL gate and TV revenue sharing (and it also helps that the team is organized as a nonprofit community enterprise). So gate sharing does play a potentially important role in enabling weak-drawing franchises to survive, even though it does not affect the distribution of playing strengths among league teams that survive.

As expected, the league equilibrium under unrestricted free agency involves an imbalance of playing strengths; the strong drawing team, team A, ends up with a better team (a .615 W/L percentage in Figure 7.8 or 7.9) than the weak-drawing team (a .385 W/L percentage). This is the element of truth in the argument by owners—given that franchises are located in areas with differing drawing potential, profit incentives operating in a free competitive labor market will lead to a situation in which, on average, strong-drawing areas have strong teams, and weak drawing areas have weak teams.

However, this is still a far cry from a situation in which competitive imbalance is so extreme that only the strong-drawing team can survive, or that the league is doomed to extinction. As we have already seen, all five team sports leagues have long histories characterized by a considerable degree of competitive imbalance, even when operating under restrictions on player mobility, and they have survived. In fact, one conclusion that comes out of our analysis is that there is a limit to how many star players even a strong-drawing team would want to hire under unrestricted free agency, because, beyond the point P in Figure 7.8 where MR equals C^*, each increase in the W/L percentage adds more to the team's cost than it does to the team's revenue (MR) so that profits fall if the team attempts to increase its W/L percentage beyond the point P. This is the built-in limit on competitive imbalance in a league operating under unrestricted free agency, arising simply from profit incentives.

Market Equilibrium under a Player Reservation System

But does the degree of competitive imbalance that occurs under free agency as pictured in Figure 7.8 exceed the acceptable level of competitive balance that leagues have attained historically under their player reservation systems? In fact, what we will show is that the profit incentives associated with a player reservation system lead to precisely the same outcome in terms of W/L percentages for teams as under unrestricted free agency so long as teams are free to sell players for cash to one another.

Figure 7.10 presents the case where a player reservation system is in place, but teams are free to buy and sell players among themselves. Once again, for simplicity, we look at the case where there is no revenue sharing, but the conclusions we reach hold as well in the revenue-sharing case. In Figure 7.10, suppose that the operation of the free agent draft and waiver rules produces a situation in which, initially, teams A and B have the same playing strength (both teams have W/L percentages equal to .500). Note that at a W/L percentage of .500 for each team, $MR(A) = MR''$ is greater than $MR(B) = MR'$. This means that an additional W/L percentage point is worth more to team A than to team B. Team A would be willing to pay anything up to MR'' for an additional W/L percentage point, and team B should be willing to sell the players to provide that at any price more than MR'. Both teams are more profitable, if team B sells players to team A.

This situation continues to exist so long as players are distributed between the two teams so that $MR(A)$ is greater than $MR(B)$. With each owner acting to maximize his or her team's profits, player sales for cash will continue between the two teams until all profitable opportunites have been exhausted. These opportunities are exhausted only when $MR(A)$ is brought into equality with $MR(B)$, which occurs at the point

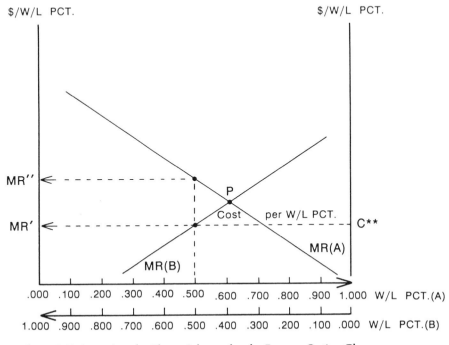

Figure 7.10 Incentives for Player Sales under the Reserve-Option Clause

P. What we can conclude, then, is that so long as there are no restrictions on the sale of players for cash in a league, profit incentives will generate precisely the same distribution of playing strengths in a league under a player reservation system as under unrestricted free agency. In effect, if profit incentives are fully exploited under a reservation system, player sales will completely offset any equalizing effects of such devices as the free agent draft or the waiver system. With unrestricted sales of players for cash among the owners of a league, a player reservation system has no effect at all on competitive balance in a league, which will be the same under a reservation system as it is under unrestricted free agency, given profit-maximizing behavior by team owners. This can be viewed as an application of the Coase theorem, which states that the allocation of resources in a society is independent of the assignment of property rights in the society, except for income effects (see Coase 1960).

Revenue sharing under a reservation system with unrestricted player sales moves the *MR* curves of the team down, but does not change the equilibrium W/L percentages of team A or team B. The closer the league sharing rules are to equal sharing, the less important winning is to the profitability of a team, just as in the case of unrestricted free agency. Revenue sharing under a reservation system thus also has the effect of reducing salaries and bonuses paid to players, again as in the case of unrestricted free agency.

Qualifications

There are some caveats to the conclusion that the distribution of playing strengths among teams is the same under unrestricted free agency as under a player reservation system with unrestricted sales of players. The player reservation system, including the college or rookie free agent draft, performs somewhat the same functions that revenue sharing does, in that it lowers salaries and bonuses paid to players (by restricting their bargaining rights), and it redistributes income from strong- to weak-drawing teams through the cash that is received by weak-drawing teams in their player sales to strong-drawing teams. Under unrestricted free agency, some weak-drawing teams might go under without the subsidies they receive from their sales of players. An example in point is the St. Louis Browns in the early post-World War II years, when the team was kept afloat almost exclusively by sales of players to other teams. If a change were to be made in a league from a player reservation system to free agency, it might be necessary to introduce more equal revenue sharing (that is, subsidization of weak-drawing teams by strong-drawing teams) if all teams were to remain profitable after the change.

A second caveat is that team owners are not always concerned only with the profits that they can earn from their teams. There have been well known instances of "sportsmen owners" in the history of baseball, as noted earlier, including especially Phil Wrigley, who insisted on playing daytime baseball in Wrigley Park during his years of ownership of the team, despite the sacrifice of profits involved. Tom Yawkey invested large sums during the 1930s and 1940s in players for the Red Sox, to buy a winner for Boston. Recently, Eddie DeBartolo, Jr., the wealthy owner of the 49ers, has been in the spotlight, because of his lavish spending on salaries and other expenses, which resulted in four Super Bowl championships between 1982 and 1990. Dabscheck (1975), Schofield (1982), Sloane (1971), and Vamplew (1982) have presented convincing evidence that in English, Scottish, and Australian football and cricket, the profit maximization model is inapplicable, and certainly some of their comments can be taken to apply to American sports as well. Davenport (1969) emphasizes the incentive to win as motivation for owners, above and beyond profit considerations. Brower (1977), Cairnes, Jennett, and Sloane (1986), Daly and Moore (1981), and Neale (1964) all raise questions concerning aspects of the profit maximization model of team ownership.

There is no question but that owners are typically highly competitive individuals who enjoy winning intensely. There also is no question but that owners also prefer to make more profits than less. Profit maximization is of course an idealized concept that is only approximated in practice. As was pointed out in the discussion of franchise prices in Chapter 2, however, professional team sports has become such an expensive business to enter that even wealthy owners must take the bottom line seriously. Ultimately, the proof is in the pudding—either the profit-oriented model produces good predictive results or it doesn't. We will look at some of these results below.

Sales of Players for Cash—
Qualifications to the Theory

One final qualification to our theoretical conclusions is that leagues have formal and informal restrictions on the sale of players for cash. In June 1976, Charles O. Finley announced the sale of three of his Oakland A's players—Joe Rudi, Rollie Fingers, and Vida Blue. Rudi and Fingers were to be sold to the Red Sox for a combined total of $2 million, and

Blue was to go to the Yankees for $1.5 million. This was during an era when an outstanding Oakland team wasn't drawing all that well:

	Oakland AL West Standing		Oakland Attendance	
			No.	AL (12-team) Rank
1970	second	(89–73 .549)	778,355	9
1971	first	(101–60 .627)	914,993	7
1972	first[a]	(93–62 .600)	921,323	5
1973	first[a]	(94–68 .580)	1,000,763	8
1974	first[a]	(90–72 .556)	845,683	11
1975	first	(98–64 .605)	1,075,518	6
1976	second	(87–74 .540)	780,593	11

[a]Won World Series.

Charlie Finley might have been one of the world's greatest insurance salesmen, but he seemed to have had no flair at all for establishing rapport with the fans of his sports teams, the Athletics (in Kansas City or Oakland), the NHL California Golden Seals, and the ABA Memphis Tams. In Oakland, Finley was understandably frustrated with a situation in which his team was winning big and couldn't draw. It was widely believed that the Bay Area could only support one baseball team (San Francisco was drawing badly at the time as well). Finley made attempts to find a buyer to move the A's, but several were reportedly scared off by the threat of an antitrust suit by the city of Oakland. It was in these circumstances that Finley decided to sell his star players, as Connie Mack had done 45 years earlier.

Three days after Finley announced the player sale, Bowie Kuhn, then the commissioner of baseball, issued an order disapproving the sale "as inconsistent with the best interest of baseball, the integrity of the game, and the maintenance of public confidence in it." This was the first case in baseball history of a player sale that was disapproved when no other baseball rule was violated. Finley sued, and lost in the trial court, where it was ruled that the owners had vested almost unlimited powers in the Commissioner to determine that actions were "not in the best interest of baseball," so long as procedural due process strictures were followed. The appeals court affirmed the ruling of the trial court (*Finley v. Kuhn*, 569 F.2d 527 (1978)). The player sales were revoked, and Finley sold the team several years thereafter to new owners who agreed to keep the team in Oakland. Since that time, it is understood that the Commissioner will review all sales of players for cash, above some threshold amount.

Baseball has a history of famous sales of players for cash, dating back to the sensational sale of "King" Kelly to Boston by Chicago for $10,000 after the 1886 World Series. These include, of course, the sale of Babe Ruth by the Red Sox to the Yankees in 1920, Clark Griffith's sale of his son-in-law, Joe Cronin, to the Red Sox in 1935, the $150,000 paid by the Cubs for the Cardinals' sore-armed Dizzy Dean in 1938, and Connie Mack's dismantling of his two Philadelphia championship teams. Branch Rickey made a career of selling players for cash during his years with the Cardinals, and later with the Dodgers, after developing the farm system as a source of talent for his clubs.

Accurate data on the extent of player sales for cash in baseball and the other sports do not exist. However, in the 1952 report of the Celler Committee, data are presented on player acquisition costs for major league teams for six years—1929, 1933, 1939, 1943, 1946, and 1950. Assuming that these years are typical for the period 1920–1950, and adjusting for assumed interleague sales, the relation between player sales and profits of teams appears in Table 7.13.

These data indicate that player sales were an important element in business operations for most teams during this period, and that, generally speaking, the flow of players was from weak drawing, low-profit, small-city teams to strong-drawing, big-profit, big-city teams, as the theory suggests. The teams with the largest purchases of players were the Giants, the Cubs, the Yankees, and, of course, Tom Yawkey's Red Sox. Rickey's Cardinals and Dodgers were sellers of players, as expected, but, excluding these, it was the weak teams—the Browns, the Braves, the Phillies, the Athletics—who were the big sellers of players.

Other data indicate that an estimated 90 percent of the profits of the Cardinals over the 1920–1950 period came from player sales, and the Browns earned $1.3 million from sales between 1947 and 1951, an amount in excess of total profits for the club over the 1920–1950 period.

In recent years, sales of players for cash in baseball have been rare events. The rarity of sales over his term in office might have led Commissioner Kuhn to refer to the Finley sale in somewhat overblown fashion as "unparalleled in the history of the game" and an act that "threatened so seriously to unbalance the competitive balance of baseball" in his decision. At least one sportswriter has claimed that the "Oakland sales . . . [were] reversing a 'no sale' policy which went unwritten among major league owners for the last twenty years [prior to 1976]" (quoted in Daly and Moore 1981).

Several factors were at work in the post-World War II period to limit or eliminate cash sales of players in all pro sports leagues. Under Bill

Table 7.13
Hypothetical Intraleague Player Purchases, Baseball, 1920–1950
(thousands of dollars)

Team	Profits	Hypothetical Net Intraleague Player Purchases
AMERICAN LEAGUE		
New York	8,497	1,585
Detroit	4,702	660
Cleveland	3,670	750
Washington	2,746	−650
Chicago	1,347	−880
Philadelphia	1,091	−1,445
St. Louis	1,088	−2,330
Boston	−2,075	2,295
NATIONAL LEAGUE		
St. Louis	5,962	−3,390
Brooklyn	3,944	−825
Pittsburgh	3,213	690
Chicago	2,920	1,835
New York	2,892	2,930
Cincinnati	1,571	−85
Philadelphia	−13	−630
Boston	−295	−535

Source: El Hodiri and Quirk 1974, 53.
Note: Negative purchases are sales.

Veeck's tax shelter, invented in 1949 (see Chapter 3), there are incentives to overvalue player contracts at the time of purchase of a team. This made it very inconvenient to have comparative data available for perusal by the IRS and the courts on actual cash sales in the player market as a basis for lowering player valuations. Since every owner will be a seller of his team at some point in time, this provided incentives for all owners to avoid cash sales.

Okner (1974b) has pointed out a second factor, namely, the capital gains tax. When a player is sold for cash, the team is charged a capital gains tax on the difference between the sale price of the player and his depreciated book value. In making roster adjustments, a team can avoid the capital gains tax by trading players for players rather than selling players for cash and then using the cash to buy another player. An even more efficient way of making trades is by using draft choices, which give the team receiving a draft choice the option of choosing the kind of player it most needs. This alternative has been available to NFL teams since 1936, and became an option for baseball teams after the rookie free agent draft was introduced in 1964.

Many of the cash sales in the pre-World War II days were by cash-strapped owners barely hanging on in marginal markets. In the post-World War II days, an alternative was available, namely, moving the franchise to a new location, and many teams took advantage of this. Together with the Veeck tax shelter, this meant that sales of teams and moves of teams have replaced sales of players in the more recent period.

In the early days of the NFL, the amounts of money involved were a lot less, but there were some famous sales comparable to those in baseball. One of the first sales occurred in 1922, when the Bears bought Ed Healy from the Rock Island Independents for $100. Four years later, George Halas paid $3,500 for the Cardinals' Paddy Driscoll. In 1949, Halas sold Bobby Layne to Ted Collins' Yanks team for $50,000, and lived to regret it, never really finding an adequate replacement for Sid Luckman at quarterback for the Bears. The era of cash sales in the NFL seems to have ended sometime in the 1950s. The only sale of a player for cash since that time that comes to mind is the purchase of an over-the-hill Johnny Unitas from the Colts by the Chargers in 1973. It appears that there has been a gentlemen's agreement in the NFL, at least since that time, not to engage in sales of players for cash.

A league operating under a reverse-order-of-finish draft, and one in which the only player transactions allowed were trades of players for players, would generate equal competitive balance among league teams. However, trading players for draft choices acts as a close substitute for cash sales, and has similar effects in fostering competitive imbalance in a league. Draft choices are valuable to owners because the team has certain built-in advantages in bargaining with draftees, whio usually have very limited financial resources and limited knowledge of the player market as well. This provides teams with the opportunity to sign rookie players at salaries closer to their reservation wages than in the case of veteran players so that, on average, draft choices generate extra profits for owners and, in that sense, produce payoffs similar to those from cash sales. The long-term gentlemen's agreement in the NFL to avoid cash sales of players has played a role in the NFL's record as the league with the most competitive balance, but the active market in draft choices in the league offsets this in part. The league's scheduling policy (strong teams against strong teams, and weak teams against weak teams) has been another important factor for competitive balance in the NFL since the policy began in 1977.

Free Agency in Baseball and Basketball—
Empirical Results

If microeconomic theory does not offer any grounds for arguing the case for retention of the reserve-option clause to preserve competitive balance in team sports leagues, there still remain the actual results from operation of something approaching free competitive labor markets in baseball and basketball since the mid-1970s. If the owners' position is valid, we should see some evidence of a significant decline in competitive balance in the AL, NL, and NBA, resulting from the introduction of free agency in those leagues. In contrast, the results based on microeconomic theory argue that free agency will not have any effect on the degree of competitive balance. We will use the various measures of competitive balance that have been introduced earlier to provide before-and-after comparisons for each of the leagues. We begin with baseball.

Free agency began in baseball in 1976, following decisions by an arbitrator that any player playing out his option for one year became a free agent. While there have been various modifications of this in the labor contracts that have been negotiated since that time, still the period from 1976 represents a significant break from the pre-1976 period, when a strict interpretation of the reserve clause was enforced in baseball.

In Table 7.14, a comparison is made between the 14-year period preceding free agency (1963–1976) and the 14-year period following free agency (1977–1990), by use of the four measures of competitive balance discussed earlier. For the AL, the average range is slightly larger in the the post-free agency period (249 versus 241), but there are basically no changes in the average standard deviation, excess tail frequencies, or concentration of pennant winners. In particular, the Gini coefficient of concentration of pennant winners drops from .400 in the pre-free agency period to .392 in the post-free agency period, a slight increase in competitive balance. For all practical purposes, the two periods are indistinguishable. For the NL, all measures of competitive balance show moves in the direction of more competitive balance under free agency, with the Gini coefficient of concentration of pennant winners falling from .415 in the pre-free agency period to .372 in the post-free agency period, again, an increase in competitive balance. More to the point, running a t-test on the difference between the average standard deviation in the pre-free agency period and that in the post-free agency period leads to the conclusion that there is no significant difference either for the AL or NL. It would be difficult indeed to argue with the conclusion that the experience of baseball since 1976 looks almost exactly like the prediction of microeconomic theory, that is, no change in competitive bal-

Table 7.14
Competitive Balance: Baseball, Pre- and Post-Free Agency

	Pre-Free Agency (1963–1976)		Post-Free Agency (1977–1990)	
AVERAGE RANGE OF W/L PERCENTAGE				
AL	241		249	
NL	251		211	
AVERAGE STANDARD DEVIATION OF W/L PERCENTAGE				
AL	71		70	
NL	66		64	
EXCESS TAIL FREQUENCIES				
AL				
Outside two standard deviations	24.4		23.5	
Outside three standard deviations	11.4		10.9	
NL				
Outside two standard deviations	23.1		21.0	
Outside three standard deviations	12.5		6.9	
CONCENTRATION OF PENNANT WINNERS				
AL	Bal	4	NY, Oak	3
	NY, Oak	3	Bal, KC	2
	Bos	2	Bos, Det,	
	Det, Min	1	Mil, Min	1
NL	Cin, LA	4	LA	4
	StL	3	StL	3
	NY	2	Phi	2
	Pit	1	Cin, NY, Pit,	
			SD, SF	1

Sources: As in table 7.1.

ance due to free agency, and bears no resemblance at all to the forecasts of owners that free agency would have a devastating deleterious effect on competitive balance.

Turning to basketball, there are many more problems present in making comparisons over time than in the case of baseball. League expansion and contraction, the battle between the ABA and NBA, and important innovations in labor-management agreements, such as the salary cap, are among the factors that can affect an evaluation of free agency in NBA basketball. As Noll (1989) points out, basketball effectively operated as a monopsony (monopoly on the demand side of the labor market) from 1950 to 1966, when the ABA entered the picture, introducing competitive elements into the labor market in basketball. Those competitive elements have been continued by the free agency agreements that have been concluded between the players and owners since the NBA-ABA merger in 1976. Thus a natural breaking point in evaluating the effect of a competitive labor market on competitive balance in NBA basketball is 1966. Table 7.15 presents the four measures of competitive balance for the NBA for the 1950–1966 period and the 1967–1990 period.

The average range is about 25 percent higher in the "mostly competitive" period (1967–1990) that it was in the "mostly monopsonistic" period (1950–1966). Unquestionably, this reflects the effects of more or less continuous expansion all during the "mostly competitive" period, because, as we have seen earlier, NBA expansion teams tend to be woefully weak during the first few years of operation, which directly impacts the range, of course. The standard deviation of the W/L percentage also increased during the "mostly competitive" period, but by a much more modest amount. The t-test yields no significant difference between the average standard deviation in the two periods. The same applies to the ratio of the actual average standard deviation to the ideal-

Table 7.15
Competitive Balance: NBA Basketball, "Mostly Monopsony" Period and "Mostly Competitive" Period

	Mostly Monopsony (1951–1966)		Mostly Competitive (1967–1990)	
Average range of W/L percentage	418		526	
Average standard deviation of W/L percentages	131		142	
Idealized standard deviation	55		55	
Ratio: actual/idealized	2.30		2.58	
Excess tail frequencies				
Outside two standard deviations	42.4		42.4	
Outside three standard deviations	24.7		24.2	
Concentration of championships	Bos	9 (53%)	Bos	7 (29%)
	Mpls	3 (18%)	LA	6 (25%)
	Phil	2 (12%)	Det, NY	2 (8%)
	Roch, StL,		GSt, Mil,	
	Syr	1 (17%)	Phil,	
			Port,	
			Sea,	
			Wash	1 25%

Sources: As in table 7.1.

ized standard deviation, that is, there is no significant difference at either the 1 percent or 5 percent level of confidence between the ratios in the two periods. Excess tail frequencies are almost identical between the two periods. So far as concentration of championship winners is concerned, the dominance of Boston (53 percent) in the 1950–1966 period has been replaced by the dominance of Boston and the Lakers (combined 54 percent) in the post-1966 period. Once again, there is no indication of a noticeable shift in the concentration of league champions between the two periods. The Gini coefficient of concentration of league champions drops from .648 in the "mostly monopsonistic" period to .592 in the "mostly competitive" period, an increase in competitive balance.

Figures 7.11, 7.12, and 7.13 plot "before" and "after" distributions of W/L percentages for the AL, NL, and NBA. The pre-free agency distributions are the solid curves, and the post-free agency distributions are the dotted curves. It is clear that none of the distributions show any significant differences between pre- and post-free agency.

Revenue Sharing and a Salary Cap

It also is of interest to see what the impact is on competitive balance and on player income of an NBA-style labor agreement in which players are guaranteed a certain percent of gross league revenues, and salary caps (maximum payroll limits) are imposed on teams. In Figure 7.14, the implications of an NBA-style contract in a two-team league can be seen.

In the figure, C^* represents the cost per W/L percentage point (a proxy for average player salary) under unrestricted free agency. As we have seen, under unrestricted free agency with profit-maximizing teams, team A, located in the strong-drawing market, ends up with a stronger team (higher W/L percentage) than team B, located in the weak-drawing market.

When owners agree to revenue sharing and salary caps, presumably the reason they do so is because they feel that this arrangement will enable them to reduce their player costs to below those that would prevail under unrestricted free agency. In Figure 7.14, the average salary under revenue sharing and a salary cap is shown as C^{**}, below C^*.

In an NBA-style plan, there is supposed to be unrestricted bidding for players by teams, subject only to the constraint that no team's total payroll can exceed the salary cap. If all teams end up spending an amount equal to the salary cap, then, assuming all teams have equally astute general managers and coaches, the league would end up with all teams' having roughly the same playing strength. In Figure 7.14, teams A and B would end up at the point P, with W/L percentages of .500 each,

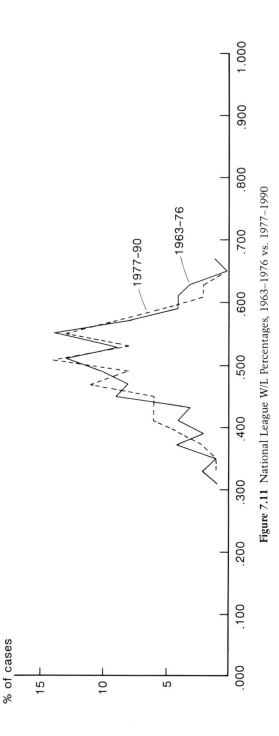

Figure 7.11 National League W/L Percentages, 1963–1976 vs. 1977–1990

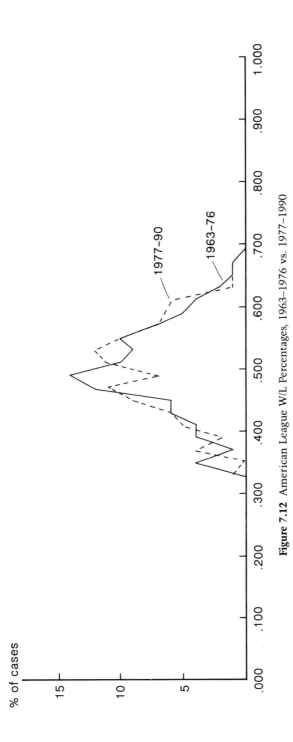

Figure 7.12 American League W/L Percentages, 1963–1976 vs. 1977–1990

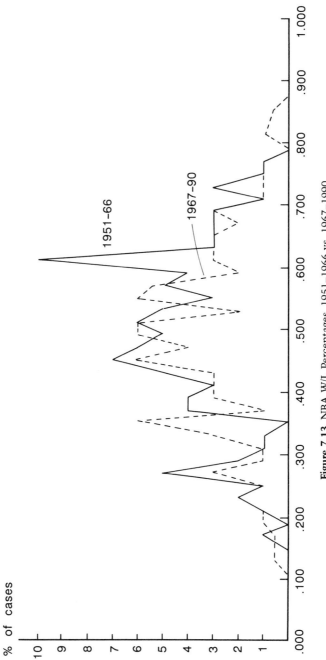

% of cases

1951–66

1967–90

Figure 7.13 NBA W/L Percentages, 1951–1966 vs. 1967–1990

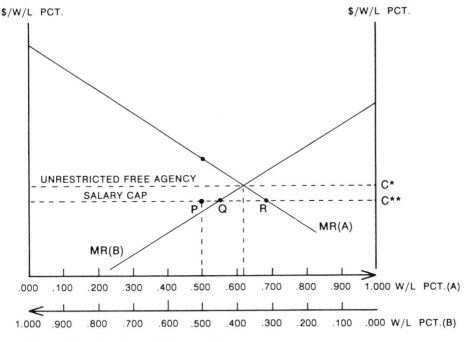

Figure 7.14 Salary Cap and Revenue Sharing

and spending the same amount on players. The salary cap will have solved the competitive balance problem.

There are some potential difficulties with this, however. To begin with, given a cost per W/L percentage point (player salary) of C^{**}, team A, the team in the strong-drawing area, maximizes its profits not at P, but at R, where $MR(A) = C^{**}$. If team A were free to hire talent, not subject to the salary cap, it could increase its profits by hiring more talent. Team B, the team in the weak-drawing area, increases its profits by hiring *less* playing talent than at P, that is, by moving to Q, where $MR(B) = C^{**}$. In the NBA scheme, the negative incentives for teams in the weak-drawing areas are taken care of, in part at least, by imposing a salary (payroll) minimum as well as a salary cap, forcing such teams to spend more than can be justified in terms of profit incentives.

In any case, by introducing a salary cap, the league has also introduced a nontrivial enforcement problem for itself—monitoring the big-city teams to make sure they don't spend more than the cap, and making sure that small-city teams spend at least the salary minimum. There have been a number of disputes already concerning violations of the salary cap by big-city teams, and this has occurred during a period when grandfathering rules have worked to mitigate the impact of the cap on big-city teams. The enforcement problems are only going to get harder as the older players retire and the full impact of the salary cap rules begins to hit the dominant teams in the league. Moreover, because the salary minimum might actually push some small-city teams into the red, this leads to a need for subsidization of such teams by the rest of the leaguea, which is also a part of the NBA scheme.

One further problem with the salary cap should be pointed out. When, as in Figure 7.14, the effect of the salary cap and of revenue sharing is to change the allocation of players from that achieved under unrestricted free agency, this also has the effect of reducing total league revenue. It is easy to see this in the figure. Suppose both teams spend the salary cap, and end up with W/L percentages of .500. Given W/L percentages of .500, team A has a higher *MR* from adding a W/L percentage point than does team B. This means that increasing team A's W/L percentage by one point (decreasing team B's W/L percentage by a point), increases total league revenue, since team A gains more in revenue than team B loses. The fact that total league revenue is less under a salary cap than under unrestricted free agency should not be a matter of indifference to players, since their total (guaranteed) income is set at a fixed fraction of total league revenues.

An enforceable salary cap applied equally to all teams leads to competitive balance in a league. However, because the cap is not consistent with profit incentives for teams, there are enforcement problems for big-city teams, who have incentives to spend more than the cap, and for small-city teams, who have incentives to spend less than the cap. A cap acts to reduce the average salary of players relative to what they would earn under unrestricted free agency, and also acts to reduce total league revenues relative to what they would be under unrestricted free agency.

Finally, because players share in gross league revenues, this creates incentives for the league to shift revenues from the league to other entities. For example, if other NBA teams follow the Celtics' lead in purchasing their own TV stations, this can be used as a device for lowering team (and league) revenues through artifically low TV payments to the team, shifting revenue to the station. This lowers payments to players and increases income for owners, representing a potential enforcement problem for players. The ability of creative lawyers and accountants to find such shifting devices should not be underestimated.

Conclusions

Briefly, what we have seen in this chapter is that each of the five major team sports leagues operates with a significant degree of competitive imbalance, however this is measured. In most respects, the NFL comes off as the league with the most competitive balance, although even this falls far short of the ideal of equal playing strengths; and the NBA is the league with the least competitive balance. Over the past 20 or 30 years, there has been a trend toward more competitive balance in both baseball leagues, both absolutely and relative to the NFL, NBA, and NHL. The argument of owners that the reserve-option clause is needed for competitive balance is offered no support at all by microeconomic theory. Instead, that theory asserts that there will be the same degee of competitive balance in a league with a reserve-option clause and unrestricted sales of players as there would be in a league with a free competitive labor market. The evidence from free agency in baseball and basketball is consistent with microeconomic theory and not with the claims of owners—there are no indications that introducing competitive labor markets into baseball and basketball has had any measurable impact on competitive balance in those leagues.

Chapter 8

Rival Leagues
and League Expansion:
Baseball, Basketball,
and Hockey

IN 1991, the five major pro team sports leagues—the AL, NL, NBA, NFL, and NHL—comprised 103 franchises, located in 39 U.S. and 7 Canadian cities. In each of the sports of baseball, basketball, football, and hockey, the leagues held monopoly positions (if we treat the AL and NL as a single entity). Dr. Pangloss, Voltaire's addlepated expert in "metaphysico-theologo-cosmolonigology," argued with all possible vigor in *Candide* that "things cannot be otherwise than they are," and it must be admitted that sometimes, and maybe more often than sometimes, economists sound more like Dr. Pangloss than they are willing to admit.

In particular, economists have a tendency to regard any and all observed features of markets as equilibrium configurations due to the more less benign workings of economic incentives and the good old law of supply and demand. This naturally raises the question as to whether there are good economic reasons for believing that the cities that have franchises have them because, in terms of economic rationality, the franchise locations "cannot be otherwise than they are." And it also raises the question as to whether sports leagues "naturally" tend to become monopolies. Finally, there is the question as to when market incentives might be expected to lead to the emergence of a rival league, and what the probable course of any resulting "war" between leagues will be. All of these are interrelated aspects of the pro team sports industry, of course, but our main interest in this chapter is with entry into

---

294

the team sports industry by a rival league, competing with an existing monopoly league, and the role of rival leagues in expansion in pro team sports. We take up rival leagues in baseball, basketball, and hockey in this chapter; football is treated separately in the next chapter.

Rival leagues are not an everyday phenomenon in sports, but there have been a number of them over the period since the National League began operations in 1876. There have been six rival baseball leagues: the American Association (1883–1891), the Union Association (1884), the Players League (1890), the American League (1901–1902), the Federal League (1914–1915), and the Continental League (stillborn in 1960), if we treat the post-World War II Mexican League as an overblown minor league, rather than a rival league. There have been seven rival football leagues: the American Football League I (1926), the AFL II (1936–1937), the AFL III (1940–1941), the All American Football Conference (1946–1949), the AFL IV (1960–1969), the World Football League (1974–1975), and the U.S. Football League (1983–1985). There have been two rival basketball leagues since the organization of the NBA in 1949, the American Basketball League (1960–1961) and the American Basketball Association (1967–1976), and one rival hockey league, the World Hockey Association (1972–1979).

Outcomes of entry have ranged from highly profitable permanent success (American League, AFL IV) through profitability for some owners in the rival league (American Association, All American Football Conference) to unmitigated failure (World Football League, USFL). We want to explore the economic benefits that rival leagues, successful or not, provide for fans and for players and the reasons why some rival leagues failed and others succeeded. We begin by summarizing the location of franchises in the major pro sports leagues as of 1991, and the links between those locations and rival leagues of the past and possible rival leagues of the future.

Franchise Locations, 1991

Table 8.1 identifies the metropolitan areas in which sports franchises in the major team sports leagues were located as of 1991. Franchise locations are shown for the AL, NL, NHL, NBA, and NFL. The expansion of leagues over the decades of the 1960s, 1970s, and 1980s has pretty well blanketed the country with franchises, and the location of franchises corresponds rather closely with the population sizes of cities. The cities of New York and Los Angeles, with metropolitan area populations exceeding 10 million, are blessed with nine and seven franchises, respectively. Chicago and San Francisco-Oakland rate five franchises

Table 8.1
Franchise Locations in Professional Team Sports, 1991

Metropolitan Statistical Area	Population, 1988 (thousands)	No. of Major League Teams					
		AL	NL	NBA	NFL	NHL	Total
New York City	18,120	1	1	2	2	3	9
Los Angeles	13,770	1	1	2	2	1	7
Chicago	8,181	1	1	1	1	1	5
San Francisco	6,042	1	1	1	1	1	5
Philadelphia	5,963		1	1	1	1	4
Detroit	4,620	1		1	1	1	4
Boston	4,110	1		1	1	1	4
Dallas	3,776	1		1	1		3
Washington, D.C.	3,734			1	1	1	3
Houston	3,642		1	1	1		3
Miami	3,000			1	1		2
Cleveland	2,769	1		1	1		3
Atlanta	2,737		1	1	1		3
St. Louis	2,467		1			1	2
Seattle	2,421	1		1	1		3
Minneapolis-St. Paul	2,388	1		1	1	1	4
San Diego	2,370		1		1		2
Baltimore	2,342	1					1
Pittsburgh	2,284		1		1	1	3
Phoenix	2,030			1	1		2
Tampa	1,995				1		1
Denver	1,858			1	1		2
Cincinnati	1,728		1		1		2
Kansas City	1,575	1			1		2
Milwaukee	1,572	1		1	0.5		2.5
Portland	1,414			1			1
Sacramento	1,385			1			1
Norfolk	1,380						0
Columbus	1,344						0
San Antonio	1,323			1			1
New Orleans	1,307				1		1
Indianapolis	1,237			1	1		2
Buffalo	1,176				1	1	2
Providence	1,125						0
Charlotte	1,112			1			1
Hartford	1,068					1	1
Salt Lake City	1,085			1			1
Orlando	971			1			1
Green Bay	88				0.5		0.5

(continued)

Table 8.1 (cont.)
Franchise Locations in Professional Team Sports, 1991

Metropolitan Statistical Area	Population, 1988 (thousands)	No. of Major League Teams					
		AL	NL	NBA	NFL	NHL	Total
CANADA							
Toronto	3,427	1				1	2
Montreal	2,921		1			1	2
Vancouver	1,380					1	2
Edmonton	785					1	1
Calgary	671					1	1
Winnipeg	625					1	1
Quebec	603					1	1
Total		14	12	27	28	22	103

Sources: 1990 *World Almanac;* league guides.

each. Cities in the 4 million to 6 million bracket have four franchises each, and cities in the 2 million to 4 million bracket have three each, with a few exceptions—only two each in Miami, St. Louis, and San Diego, only one in Baltimore, and four in the Twin Cities. Cities with populations between 1.5 and 2 million, have two franchises each, and then, as we get to the marginal cities with populations between 1 and 1.5 million, one franchise is average, and two is exceptional (as in the cases of Indianapolis and Buffalo).

While there were no rival leagues in existence in 1991, the role of rival leagues from the past in this listing of franchises is impressive. As we shall see, a full 40 of the 103 franchises operating in major league pro sports in 1991 began life as members of rival leagues, and another 7 or 8 were created in direct response to the threats posed by rival leagues. Thus, almost half the existing major league pro sports franchises came into existence because of rival leagues.

If we look at Table 8.1 from the point of view of the prospects of setting up a successful future rival league, a critical feature is the number of league franchises in the megalopolis markets of New York, Los Angeles, and, to a lesser extent, Chicago. These are the markets with the greatest potential for excess profits, especially given the dominating importance of TV revenues in the income of sports teams, and it is essential for rival leagues to establish a base in these markets. The second factor is the existence of gaps in coverage of the various sports. Entry into the big-city markets is difficult, expensive, and time consuming, while the best bets for instant success in the rival leagues are in smaller cities that have been bypassed in the current allocation of franchises. As expansion franchises are added in the 1990s to the various sports, predictably the gaps in Table 8.1 will be filled.

Expansion over the 1960s through the 1980s has done a pretty good job of spreading franchises around so as to make it difficult for a new league to make it off the ground. But even as we speak, there are rumors of new leagues being formed, of a new baseball league to threaten the majors, and of a new football league being organized by the same group that put together the USFL. The recent escalation of franchise values in the existing leagues has increased the potential payoff from success in getting a new league off the ground, and individuals with money and an affinity for risk taking may once again be exploring the possibilities of challenging the existing leagues.

The Economics of Expansion and Rival Leagues

In principle, there doesn't appear to be any reason why two or more independent and competing major leagues couldn't exist simultaneously in a sport. Competition between the leagues would eliminate most monopoly rents, to be sure, so team owners would earn no more than normal profits, and income would be redistributed to players and to TV networks and other outside interests, but in principle, a competitive pro team sports industry seems feasible.

Historically, things haven't worked out that way. When rival leagues come onto the scene in a sport, it is exceptional for them to survive as independent entities for more than a few years—either they fall by the wayside drenched in red ink, or an agreement is reached with the dominant league, which takes in one or more members of the rival league, reestablishing its monopoly position in the sport. The monopoly rents to be derived from an amalgamated league are so large, and the losses suffered in an interleague war are so devastating, that there are strong incentives to eliminate competition between leagues.

Thus, based on the historical record, the "normal" situation in pro team sports is the case of a monopoly league, which is where we will begin our theorizing. With a monopoly league in place, a natural question to ask is, Which locations will be incorporated into the league?

It is instructive to look first at an unrealistic but simple case, namely, the case of a league operated as a syndicate, in which all league members share equally in league profits. (An attempt to organize the NL in this way at the turn of the century was narrowly defeated, but no existing leagues are organized in this fashion.) Given an existing league membership of, say, N members, when will an $(N + 1)$st member be admitted to the league? It might seem as though this $(N + 1)$st member would have to bring along at least as much additional profit as the average team is currently earning (total league profits divided by N), because otherwise the existing league members would lose money by admitting the outsider, who, as a member, will share equally with the original members.

But this ignores the possibility of charging the outsider an entry fee. Assuming that admitting an outsider would increase total league profits, the existing members can charge the outsider an admission fee that transfers to existing members essentially all of the present value of the added profits that the outsider brings in. Thus, on net balance, the outsider, as a member sharing in league profits, ends up earning only slightly above zero (excess) profits, net of its entry fee. The outsider is better off—it is earning something rather than nothing—and existing league members are better off, since they have captured essentially all of the extra profits that the outsider brings in. Thus we conclude that if a league is organized as a syndicate on a profit-maximizing basis, it will rationally expand into all locations that add to total league profits in the sport, in the process siphoning off all excess profits that outsiders bring in.

One qualification of this conclusion is that in an era in which teams play in publicly owned stadiums, there are obvious strategic advantages for league members in having cities available that lack league teams but are capable of supporting a team. Profits associated with the threat value of such locations have to be included in the league's expansion decisions.

Of course, if the existing league makes a mistake and permits enough potentially profitable outside locations to exist without teams in a sport so that they could form a rival league, then the outsiders might be able to avoid the siphoning-off phenomenon. In a successful rival league, in principle, the outsiders could retain most of the profits they bring to the sport; in practice, for a successful rival league, as has been noted, an even better alternative is to amalgamate with the existing league, to share monopoly profits.

The actual situation in sports leagues is a little more complicated than this. Leagues are not operated as syndicates; instead, members are granted exclusive territorial franchises, and earn profits based on their exploitation of these monopoly rights. The consequence is that league decisions are not made on the basis of maximizing total league profits, but rather on the basis of individual team profit maximization, and the two do not necessarily always coincide with each other. In addition, traditionally, league constitutions have required either unanimous agreement of existing members for approving admission of a new member or something approaching consensus (a three-fourths majority is common). Up to the 1980s, all leagues had provisions giving veto power to members on expansion into their own territories, but, under recent court decisions, those rules have now been replaced by a three-fourths majority vote as well (see *L.A. Memorial Coliseum Commission v. NFL*, 468 F. Supp. 154 (C.D. Cal. 1979), 726 F.2d 1381 (9th Cir. 1984), 791 F.2d 1356 (9th Cir. 1986); *National Basketball Association v. SDC Basketball Club*, 815 F.2d 562 (9th Cir. 1987); and *San Francisco Seals v. National Hockey League*, 379 F. Supp. 867 (C.D. Cal. 1975), 556 F.2d 682 (9th Cir. 1977)). As a practical matter, expansion, especially into an existing territory, can be blocked by one or at most a few league members.

The other important institutional fact of life is that league franchises are granted on the basis of geography rather than on drawing power. For example, in the NFL, each member team is granted an exclusive right to NFL football within a 75-mile radius of the home field of the team. (An exception is made for Green Bay, which plays half its games in Milwaukee, and for two-team cities.) Thus, Chicago and Kansas City have the same square miles of territorial rights, but the Bears have roughly a five to one advantage over the Chiefs in terms of population. To compensate in part for the disparity in drawing potential among league teams, baseball and football have gate sharing (60–40 home-away shares in football, roughly 80–20 sharing in baseball), and all sports leagues have equal sharing of national TV revenues. In effect, these sharing rules are devices by which strong-drawing, big-city teams subsidize weak-drawing, small-city member teams.

The economics of sports literature (see, e.g., Rottenberg 1956; El Hodiri and Quirk 1971) has pointed out that one consequence of the disparity in drawing potential among league teams is that there will be a tendency for teams located in the strong drawing areas to field, on average, stronger teams than those located in weak drawing areas. (See also the discussion in Chapter 7.) Another consequence of allocating franchises on the basis of square miles is that teams located in the best-drawing areas will tend to earn higher profits than those of the average league team. Excess profits encourage entry into the favored market by outsiders. Because of the veto power a league team exercises over entry into its territory by other league teams, expansion of a league that involves adding additional teams to the best marketing areas is difficult to accomplish. On the other hand, when expansion into the best markets is thwarted, this encourages the formation of a rival league, composed of one or more teams in the best markets, and other teams in more marginal locations, with the objective of forcing entry into the industry, and ultimately, entry into the existing league.

Balancing of the costs and benefits of expansion can be a complicated matter for the members of an existing league. Still, expansion into new markets is relatively straightforward for a league to deal with, since the costs and benefits of expansion are spread more or less evenly among all league members.

In contrast, if a new team is placed in the territory of an existing team, then the existing team at that location is exposed to differential costs not borne by the other teams in the league. The monopoly position of the existing team is eliminated. There will be competition with the new team for fans, for local TV contracts, and for stadium access, all of which act to lower profits for the existing team. In fact, since the original team presumably would have acted so as to maximize profits subject to the demand for the sport at its location, it is to be expected that total profits at the location (summed over both teams) will fall after entry. (Some limited evidence for this is provided by profit data for baseball over the 1920–1956 period, from the Cellar Committee and Kefauver Committee reports. The Yankees, with an AL monopoly in New York, captured 47 percent of AL profits over the period, while the Dodgers and the Giants combined earned 42 percent of NL profits.) This suggests that it would be difficult indeed to arrive at a negotiated agreement within the league under which an entering team buys its way into an already occupied big-city location by compensating the original team for the present value of the profits the original team will lose because of entry.

Thus, given the traditional veto power of existing teams over entry into their territories (or the modified veto power under the three-fourths rule), the only way that internal expansion into an existing league territory can be accomplished is if the rest of the league subsidizes the team whose territory is invaded. Since the territories that invite entry are the highly profitable big-city markets, this would mean that league expansion into those markets would involve subsidization of rich teams by poor teams.

Adding another team at a big-city location might well increase profits for small-city league teams, even when total profits captured by the teams in the big city fall, because of league-wide benefits from more teams in the big cities, for example, higher national TV revenues. But even when it is in the long term interests of the small-city teams that expansion take place in big-city markets, there are the usual free-rider problems with putting together a coalition to accomplish this, along with the equity problems of having the poor subsidize the rich.

The inability to solve these short-term "burden sharing" problems can create an environment in which a rival league is formed to force entry into the best market areas, where existing teams are earning excess profits, leading to an interleague war. This can occur even when total profits for the existing league would be higher under league-sponsored expansion into the best markets. Successful entry by a rival league forces the existing league to seek a solution to its burden-sharing problem, or, failing this, to put pressure on the teams in the best markets to arrive at a negotiated settlement with members of the rival league. Side payments to teams whose territory is invaded often occur in the case of successful entry by a rival league. On the other hand, members of the rival league might overestimate the threat they pose to the existing league, and entry might be unsuccessful, in which case the high-profit teams in the best markets continue to maintain their market monopolies, and continue to act as magnets attracting possible entry of other leagues.

One other aspect of entry and interleague wars should be mentioned. This is the economic infeasibility of side payments by the existing league to preclude entry by a rival league, in contrast to the feasibility of side payments ("bribes") by the rival league to the existing league to permit entry into an amalgamated league. The appendix to this chapter examines this and other aspects of entry in a simple formal model (see p. 374).

Entry into a monopolized industry provides benefits for consumers of the industry's product, by increasing output of the product and lowering its price. Rival leagues perform these functions in professional team sports. In *The Wealth of Nations*, Adam Smith talked about the "invisible hand" of competition that directed the self-interest-motivated actions of businessmen to the good of the society as a whole. Burt Klein, of Caltech and the Rand Corporation, used to talk about the "hidden foot" of competition, with entering rivals kicking the bejesus out of monopolists who are exploiting the public or who have become fat and complacent. Rival leagues provide the market feedback that seems to be needed on a regular basis, to put some fear of God into the dominant monopoly leagues, and to force leagues into economically desirable expansion.

Everything that has been said thus far of course is simply theoretical, and we need to look at the actual history of rival leagues to see how things work out in practice. We begin our discussion by looking at the history of rival leagues in baseball.

Rival Leagues and Organized Baseball

Baseball Before the Turn of the Century

The National League, organized in 1876, is the oldest existing professional team sports league in the United States. The original lineup of the NL closely matched the list of the largest cities in the country: New York (1), Philadelphia (2), St. Louis (3), Chicago (4), Boston (6), Cincinnati (7), Louisville (13), Hartford (27) (the number in parentheses is the population rank of the city in the country as of 1870). The only cities in the top ten missing from the NL's original list were Baltimore (5), New Orleans (8), San Francisco (9), and Buffalo (10). Transportation problems naturally led to the exclusion of New Orleans and San Francisco, while Baltimore and Buffalo's times were still to come as sports centers. Table 8.2 gives the franchise history of the NL between 1876 and 1882, the date of emergence of the first rival league in baseball.

New York (Brooklyn) and Philadelphia were bounced from the league in its first season after they refused to play scheduled games in western cities, such as Chicago and Cincinnati. Louisville dropped out after the 1877 season because of a gambling scandal involving four of its star players, and St. Louis dropped out at the same time because those players were to form the nucleus of the St. Louis team in 1878. Other teams dropped out because of attendance and other problems. By 1882, the NL had become a league of small- and medium-city teams: Chicago (3), Boston (6), Cleveland (10), Buffalo (12), Detroit (17), Providence (19), Worcester (26), Troy (no rank) (figures in parentheses indicate population rank in 1880 census).

The NL had managed its affairs so that by 1882, 7 of the 10 largest

Table 8.2
National League Franchise Histories, 1876–1882

1876	1877	1878	1879	1880	1881	1882
NY (1)	NY (1)					
Phi (2)						
StL (3)	StL (3)					
Chi (4)	Chi (4)	Chi (4)	Chi (4)	Chi (4)	Chi (4)	Chi (4)
Bos (6)	Bos (6)	Bos (6)	Bos (6)	Bos (6)	Bos (6)	Bos (6)
Cin (7)	Cin (7)	Cin (7)	Cin (7)	Cin (7)	Cin (7)	Cin (7)
Lou (13)	Lou (13)		Buf (10)	Buf (10)	Buf (10)	Buf (10)
Hart (27)			Cle (14)	Cle (14)	Cle (14)	Cle (14)
		Mlw (18)			Det (17)	Det (17)
		Prv (20)	Prv (20)	Prv (20)	Prv (20)	Prv (20)
		Ind (24)	Syr (25)			
				Wrc (26)	Wrc (26)	Wrc (26)
			Troy (nr)	Troy (nr)	Troy (nr)	Troy (nr)

Sources: U.S. Department of Commerce 1975; Seymour 1960.

Note: Number in parentheses is city's population rank in 1880 census; nr = not ranked.

U.S. cities did not have an NL team, and this situation was made to order for entry of a rival league. Actually, there were even more factors working in that direction. The NL had opted to clean up its image by banning Sunday baseball, and the league also banned beer at baseball games. It should come as no surprise to followers of the "Tastes great"-"Less filling" controversy that a number of the backers of a new rival league, the American Association, were brewers, headed by the legendary Chris Von Der Ahe of St. Louis, and by Harry Vonderhorst of Baltimore. The owner of the Philadelphia AA team was brewer Billy Sharsig of Philadelphia, and among the owners of the Louisville Eclipse AA team was the treasurer of the local Kent Malting Company. The AA—the American Association and definitely not Alcoholics Anonymous—announced that beer and liquor would be available at its parks, and that there would be Sunday ball as well. To sweeten things even more, the AA decided on an admission charge of 25 cents, in contrast to the NL's "50-cent baseball."

The AA moved into markets that the NL had abandoned, and began operations in 1882 with the following lineup: Philadelphia (2), St. Louis (5), Baltimore (6), Cincinnati (7), Pittsburgh (11), and Louisville (15) (numbers in parentheses are 1880 population rankings). A bidding war developed between the AA and NL, with each league ignoring the other's reserve list. Despite the bidding war, newpaper accounts at the time indicate that all AA teams showed a profit for the 1882 season, with one team earning $15,000. In contrast to the usual interleague war, it was the existing league, the NL, that was losing money and eager to end the war. The weak franchise lineup of the NL and its stadium rules put the NL in a poor bargaining position. Peace was declared after the first year of the AA-NL war, with the two leagues signing a National Agreement under which they agreed to honor each other's reserve lists, putting an end to the brief period of high player salaries. In 1883, the AA moved into New York (1) and Columbus (28), to complete its eight-team lineup. The 1883 season was reportedly highly profitable for the AA, and for the NL as well.

The peace treaty between the AA and the NL held (with some occasional spats) for the next nine years, a period that was also marked by the emergence of two other short-lived rival leagues—the Union Association of 1884, and the Players League of 1890. Both of these leagues had the stated objective of fighting the restrictions on player mobility imposed by the reservation system, which certainly made them popular with players. But it must be admitted to the cynical that in 1884, there was another simpler explanation for the entry of the Union Association—baseball was a profitable business—and the same applied in 1890 as well.

Table 8.3 summarizes the way in which baseball franchises were distributed among cities during the lifetime of the AA, 1882 through 1891. Competition from the AA caused the NL to drop its smallest members, Troy and Worcester, in 1883, in favor of a return to New York City, with the Giants, under owner John Day, and to Philadelphia, under owner Alfred J. Reach. (In one of the interesting sidelights on the AA-NL situation, Day also owned the New York Metropolitans (the "Mets") of the AA. The waiver rule came into baseball because of Day. He decided to switch some of his Met players to his Giants roster, and the resulting protests by AA owners led to the formulation of a rule under which a player could not be sold to a team outside the league unless all league teams had turned down a chance to purchase the player at the predetermined waiver price.) New York and Philadelphia were the only two cities where the two leagues came into direct confrontation with one another.

In 1884, promoter James Jackson organized the Union Association, which sponsored teams in Philadelphia (2), Chicago (3), Boston (4), St. Louis (5), Baltimore (6), Cincinnati (7), Washington (13), and Altoona, Pa. (no rank), competing with the AA or NL in seven of their member cities. In a move designed to combat the UA, the AA expanded to 12 teams for the 1884 season only, by adding Washington, Toledo, Indianapolis, and Brooklyn. The financial backer of the new league was Henry Lucas, owner of the St. Louis UA franchise. The league had attendance and financial problems, and a classic competitive imbalance problem. In mid-season, Altoona moved to Kansas City, Philadelphia moved to Wilmington and then to Milwaukee, and Chicago moved first to Pittsburgh and then to St. Paul. And the competitive balance problem was truly classic—Lucas's St. Louis team won the league pennant with a W/L record of .850, by far the highest W/L percentage in major league baseball in all the years since the NL was first formed.

The effects of the rival league were felt throughout baseball. Most AA teams lost money in 1884, and the AA expansion team in Washington was moved to Richmond in mid-season. Reportedly, the UA franchises in Kansas City and Washington made money ($6,000 or $7,000 each), but the other UA teams lost money, most around $15,000. The UA disbanded after the 1884 season. Once the UA had disbanded, the AA dropped four teams—Richmond, Toledo, Columbus, and Indianapolis—to revert to an eight-team league. When the Union Association went broke, Henry Lucas bought the Cleveland NL franchise for $2,500, and moved it to St. Louis, where he paid Chris Von Der Ahe of the AA $5,000 for territorial invasion, and became a member of the NL, the league he had been fighting just weeks before.

With the exit of the Union Association, a stability of sorts reigned in

Table 8.3
Baseball Franchises Ranked by City's 1890 Population, 1882–1900
(number of franchises)

City	1882			1883			1884				1885		
	NL	AA	Total	NL	AA	Total	NL	AA	UA	Total	NL	AA	Total
New York City	0	0	0	1	1	2	1	2	0	3	1	2	3
Chicago	1	0	1	1	0	1	1	0	1	2	1	0	1
Philadelphia	0	1	1	1	1	2	1	1	1	3	1	1	2
St. Louis	0	1	1	0	1	1	0	1	1	2	1	1	2
Boston	1	0	1	1	0	1	1	0	1	2	1	0	1
Baltimore	0	1	1	0	1	1	0	1	1	2	0	1	1
San Francisco	0	0	0	0	0	0	0	0	0	0	0	0	0
Minneapolis-St. Paul	0	0	0	0	0	0	0	0	1	1	0	0	0
Cincinnati	0	1	1	0	1	1	0	1	1	2	0	1	1
Cleveland	1	0	1	1	0	1	1	0	0	1	0	0	0
Buffalo	1	0	1	1	0	1	1	0	0	1	1	0	1
New Orleans	0	0	0	0	0	0	0	0	0	0	0	0	0
Pittsburgh	0	1	1	0	1	1	0	1	1	2	0	1	1
Detroit	1	0	1	1	0	1	1	0	0	1	1	0	1
Milwaukee	0	0	0	0	0	0	0	0	1	1	0	0	0
Washington	0	0	0	0	0	0	0	1	1	2	0	0	0
Newark	0	0	0	0	0	0	0	0	0	0	0	0	0
Jersey City	0	0	0	0	0	0	0	0	0	0	0	0	0
Louisville	0	1	1	0	1	1	0	1	0	1	0	1	1
Kansas City	0	0	0	0	0	0	0	0	1	1	0	0	0
Rochester	0	0	0	0	0	0	0	0	0	0	0	0	0
Providence	1	0	1	1	0	1	1	0	0	1	1	0	1
Denver	0	0	0	0	0	0	0	0	0	0	0	0	0
Indianapolis	0	0	0	0	0	0	0	1	0	1	0	0	0
Albany	0	0	0	0	0	0	0	0	0	0	0	0	0
Syracuse	0	0	0	0	0	0	0	0	0	0	0	0	0
Columbus	0	0	0	0	1	1	0	1	0	1	0	0	0
New Haven	0	0	0	0	0	0	0	0	0	0	0	0	0
Worcester	1	0	1	0	0	0	0	0	0	0	0	0	0
Toledo	0	0	0	0	0	0	0	0	0	0	0	0	0
OTHER													
Troy	1	0	1	0	0	0							
Richmond	0	0	0	0	0	0	0	1	0	1	0	0	0
Altoona		0	0	0	0	0	0	0	1	1	0	0	0
Wilmington	0	0	0	0	0	0	0	0	1	1			
Total	8	6	14	8	8	16	8	12	8	34	8	8	16

Sources: As in table 8.2.

Notes: Washington (AA) moved to Richmond in midseason, 1984. In the UA (1884), in midseason, Altoona moved to Kansas City, Philadelphia moved to Wilmington, Wilmington moved to Milwaukee, Chicago moved to Pittsburgh, and Pittsburgh moved to St. Paul.

Table 8.3 (cont.)

1886			1887			1888			1889			1890				1891			1892–
NL	AA	Total	NL	AA	Total	NL	AA	Total	NL	AA	Total	NL	AA	PL	Total	NL	AA	Total	NL
1	2	3	1	2	3	1	1	2	1	1	2	2	1	2	5	2	0	2	2
1	0	1	1	0	1	1	0	1	1	0	1	1	0	1	2	1	0	1	1
1	1	2	1	1	2	1	1	2	1	1	2	1	1	1	3	1	1	2	1
1	1	2	0	1	1	0	1	1	0	1	1	0	1	0	1	0	1	1	1
1	0	1	1	0	1	1	0	1	1	0	1	1	0	1	2	1	1	2	1
0	1	1	0	1	1	0	1	1	0	1	1	0	1	0	1	0	1	1	1
0	0	0	0	0	0	0	0	0	0	0	0	0	0	0	0	0	0	0	0
0	0	0	0	0	0	0	0	0	0	0	0	0	0	0	0	0	0	0	0
0	1	1	0	1	1	0	1	1	0	1	1	1	0	0	1	1	1	2	1
0	0	0	0	1	1	0	1	1	1	0	1	1	0	1	2	1	0	1	1
0	0	0	0	0	0	0	0	0	0	0	0	0	0	1	1	0	0	0	0
0	0	0	0	0	0	0	0	0	0	0	0	0	0	0	0	0	0	0	0
0	1	1	1	0	1	1	0	1	1	0	1	1	0	1	2	1	0	1	1
1	0	1	1	0	1	1	0	1	0	0	0	0	0	0	0	0	0	0	0
0	0	0	0	0	0	0	0	0	0	0	0	0	0	0	0	0	1	1	0
1	0	1	1	0	1	1	0	1	1	0	1	0	0	0	0	0	1	1	1
0	0	0	0	0	0	0	0	0	0	0	0	0	0	0	0	0	0	0	0
0	0	0	0	0	0	0	0	0	0	0	0	0	0	0	0	0	0	0	0
0	1	1	0	1	1	0	1	1	0	1	1	0	1	0	1	0	1	1	1
1	0	1	0	0	0	0	1	1	0	1	1	0	0	0	0	0	0	0	0
0	0	0	0	0	0	0	0	0	0	0	0	0	1	0	1	0	0	0	0
0	0	0	0	0	0	0	0	0	0	0	0	0	0	0	0	0	0	0	0
0	0	0	0	0	0	0	0	0	0	0	0	0	0	0	0	0	0	0	0
0	0	0	1	0	1	1	0	1	1	0	1	0	0	0	0	0	0	0	0
0	0	0	0	0	0	0	0	0	0	0	0	0	0	0	0	0	0	0	0
0	0	0	0	0	0	0	0	0	0	0	0	0	1	0	1	0	0	0	0
0	0	0	0	0	0	0	0	0	0	1	1	0	1	0	1	0	1	1	0
0	0	0	0	0	0	0	0	0	0	0	0	0	0	0	0	0	0	0	0
0	0	0	0	0	0	0	0	0	0	0	0	0	0	0	0	0	0	0	0
0	0	0	0	0	0	0	0	0	0	0	0	0	1	0	1	0	0	0	0
8	8	16	8	8	16	8	8	16	8	8	16	8	9	18	25	8	9	17	12

baseball for the next five years. By the 1886 season, all teams in the AA (except the Mets) were profitable again, and the same was true of the NL. There were some notable transactions during the period of stability. After the 1885 season, the Detroit NL team bought the Buffalo NL team (the Bisons) for $7,000, to acquire Dan Brouthers and several other star Bison players, and Buffalo left the league. At about the same time, Arthur Soden, owner of the Boston NL team, bought the Providence NL club for $6,600, to acquire star pitcher Hoss Radbourn, and Providence's major league history came to an end.

In 1886, Cleveland and Pittsburgh switched places, Cleveland moving from the NL to the AA, and Pittsburgh from the AA to the NL. There was a fight among AA members after the 1889 season, with Cincinnati and Brooklyn moving from the AA to the NL, and Kansas City and Baltimore dropping out of the AA.

Generally, the period of the late 1880s was a profitable time for most NL and AA teams. The era of peaceful coexistence between the NL and AL lasted until 1890, when yet another rival league came on the scene. This was the Player's League, organized as a league of profit-sharing teams by the charismatic player John Montgomery Ward, and fielding teams competing directly with the AA and/or NL in New York (1), Brooklyn (1), Chicago (2), Philadelphia (3), Boston (5), Cleveland (10), and Pittsburgh (13). The PL also fielded a team in Buffalo (11). The PL was so popular among players that it was able to recruit the best players from the NL and AA for its teams, and, consequently, the PL outdrew the NL and AA teams in almost every city. The best guess of one baseball historian (Dellinger 1989) is that the PL outdrew the NL by 200,000, but that the total attendance at PL and NL games combined was less than NL attendance in 1889, and that the AA ran a bad third behind the other two leagues. All contemporary accounts indicate that teams in all leagues—NL, PL, and AA—lost large amounts of money in the 1890 season, with the NL reportedly losing $500,000 in aggregate, and with another $500,000 of losses accruing to owners in the AA and PL.

At the end of the 1890 season, because of the losses, and despite the fact that the PL had become the leading baseball league in attendance, PL owners decided to negotiate the dissolution of their league, with owners from the NL and AA. At the joint meeting of the leagues, the players on PL teams, who had a strong stake in the continued operation of the league, were denied a voice in the proceedings. An agreement was reached among the owners, which provided compensation for the PL owners in return for their agreement to dissolve the PL. The New York PL team, owned by Edwin McAlpin, received $15,000 for its player contracts, which were sold to the New York Giants. The Pittsburgh PL team merged with the Pittsburgh NL team, and Al Spalding, owner of the Chicago NL team, bought the Chicago PL team for $18,000. The Brooklyn NL and PL teams merged, the Boston PL team moved to the AA for the 1891 season, and the Philadelphia PL owners, the Wagner brothers, became owners of the Philadelphia AA team. Cleveland owner Al Johnson became the owner of a new Cincinnati franchise in the AA.

By 1890, the AA had five of its nine teams in small cities—Louisville (19), Rochester (21), Syracuse (26), Columbus (27), and Toledo (30), while the NL had once again become a big-city league: New York (1), Chicago (2), Philadelphia (3), Boston (4), Cincinnati (9), Cleveland (10), and Pittsburgh (13). The AA franchises in Toledo, Rochester, Syracuse, Cincinnati, and Brooklyn all went under after the 1890 season, and a resumption of the war with the NL in 1891, over a signing of two star AA player by NL teams, spelled the end of the road for the AA.

The end came after the 1891 season, when an agreement was reached between the AA and the NL under which the four strongest AA franchises—St. Louis, Baltimore, Washington, and Louisville—moved to the NL, which became a 12-team league. NL owners then paid $131,000 to purchase the player contracts and other assets of the remaining AA teams, which went out of existence. The NL operated as a 12-team monopoly league from the 1892 season through the 1899 one.

In hindsight, the collapse of the AA can be blamed on bad league management, which lost the league the leading position in big city markets it had attained in the mid-1880s. There was internal bickering among league members, a weak and ineffective league office, and a problem of competitive balance. The AA was dominated by Chris von der Ahe and his St. Louis Browns, managed by Charles Comiskey, who won league pennants in 1885, 1886, 1887, and 1888. What ultimately sank the AA was a rule that had been incorporated into the National Agreement of 1883, which permitted teams to move freely between the AA and the NL. There were ongoing disputes about player contracts, and about officiating, which led to teams leaving the AA. By 1891, the AA had lost Brooklyn, Pittsburgh, Cincinnati, and Cleveland to the NL, costing the AA important big-city markets. In the mid-1880s, the AA had more big-city teams, higher attendance, and higher profits than the NL, but its advantages steadily eroded from then on. By the time of the PL war, the situation had almost completely reversed itself, with the AA becoming a league of small to medium-size towns, and with most teams losing money or only marginally profitable.

While the AA as a league went under after the 1891 season, it is of interest that eight of the twelve teams forming the monopoly NL league from 1892 on were originally AA members—Brooklyn, Pittsburgh, Cincinnati, Cleveland, St. Louis, Baltimore, Washington, and Louisville. Beyond this, AA teams were generally profitable during most of the 10-year history of the league. Thus, from the point of view of the economic interests of the owners of the AA, the AA is rightly to be considered a successful rival league. Moreover, over the period between 1882 and 1899, the AA had the effect of increasing the number of cities with major league baseball teams.

Once the monopoly NL was formed and the AA had gone out of existence, scattered reports from *Sporting News* indicate that most NL teams were profitable during the decade of the 1890s, with some exceptions. In 1892, *Sporting News* reported that Baltimore had lost $18,000, New York had lost $30,000, and Philadelphia had lost $12,000. But in 1894, Baltimore made an estimated $40,000, Pittsburgh made $17,000, and New York made $40,000. In 1895 and 1896, *Sporting News* reported that all teams made money, ranging from $6,000 for Louisville to $75,000 for Boston and Chicago.

Despite its monopoly status, the NL still had important unresolved problems. Especially damaging to public confidence in the league was joint ownership of teams supposedly competing with one another on the playing field. In 1898, Harry Vonderhorst and Ned Hanlon, owners of the NL Baltimore club, purchased a controlling interest in the Brooklyn NL team. They transferred the best players on the Orioles to Brooklyn, with the result that Brooklyn won the 1899 pennant after having finished in 10th place in 1898. At about the same time, Cleveland was owned by Frank De Hass Robison and his brother, Matthew Stanley Robison. In 1899, they bought the St. Louis NL team, and moved Cleveland's best players to St. Louis. St. Louis improved from 12th place in 1898 to 5th place in 1899, and Cleveland dropped from 5th to 12th. Cleveland was denuded of talent, and the team posted the worst W/L record in the entire history of the NL: 20 wins and 134 losses, for a .129 W/L percentage. (By way of comparison, the Mets posted a record of 40–120, with a .250 W/L percentage in that horrendous opening year of 1962.) Cleveland fans were so turned off by the player raid that Cleveland played 53 of its last 77 home games on the road during the 1899 season. Louisville and Pittsburgh were both owned by Barney Dreyfuss in 1899. Moreover, half a dozen NL owners had a financial interest in the New York franchise, dating back to some rescue work that had been done during the PL war of 1890.

After 1899, the NL decided to solve its problems of joint ownership and weak franchises by lopping off four teams—Baltimore, Cleveland, Washington, and Louisville, with the owners paid $110,000 in aggregate for their franchises and player contracts. The NL played the 1900 season with the eight-team lineup that represented the league for the next 53 years: New York (1), Brooklyn (1), Chicago (2), Philadelphia (3), St. Louis (4), Boston (5), Cincinnati (11), Pittsburgh (12) (1900 population rankings).

Eliminating Baltimore, Louisville, and Cleveland eliminated the most glaring joint ownership problems of the NL, but an even less appealing alternative for fans came under consideration at the behest of Andrew Freedman, the owner of the New York Giants. After the 1900 season, Freedman pushed his proposal for organizing the NL as a syndicate, with all teams to be owned in common under a profit-sharing arrangement. The NL split right down the middle on this, with Boston, Cincinnati, and St. Louis supporting the Giants, and Brooklyn, Philadelphia, Chicago, and Pittsburgh in opposition. The ongoing dispute led to the famous league meeting in 1901 where there were 25 ballots for league president, all ending in a 4-4 tie. After the Freedman four had left the room, the teams in opposition held a rump session, elected Chicago owner A. J. Spalding as president, and spirited away the league books to be held in a secret hiding place until a court injunction mandated their return to the league office. This intraleague battle makes the 1989 NFL squabble about a new commissioner look like a tempest in a teapot.

The American League-National League War 1901–1902

Back to 1900. As the syndication controversy was going on, along came yet another rival league to challenge the NL, the American League, organized by Ban Johnson. Johnson's league began operations in 1900 as a member in good standing of organized baseball, honoring the reserve clause in NL player contracts. At its meeting after the 1900 season, the NL rejected Johnson's request to exempt the American League from its minor league player drafting rules, and Johnson and his backers, particularly financier Charles Somers, decided to pull out of the National Agreement and operate as an "outlaw" major league. The AL began operations in the 1901 season with teams in Chicago (2), Philadelphia (3), Boston (4), Cleveland (5), Baltimore (6), Milwaukee (14), Detroit (15), and Washington (16) (1900 census), taking over three of the four cities abandoned by the NL, and competing directly with the NL in Chicago, Philadelphia, and Boston. In 1902, Milwaukee moved to St. Louis (4), and in 1903, Baltimore moved to New York (1), both new teams competing directly with existing NL teams.

The AL waged all-out war with the NL in the player market, ignoring the reserve clause in NL contracts. In its first season as an outlaw league, 113 of the 182 players in the AL were signed away from NL teams. The AL was spectacularly successful. In the 1901 season, the NL outdrew the AL, 1.9 million to 1.7 million, but the Chicago and Boston AL teams far outdrew their NL competitors. In 1902, the AL outdrew the NL, 2.2 million to 1.7 million, and AL teams in Chicago, Philadelphia, Boston, and St. Louis outdrew their in-town NL rivals by an average of almost 40 percent. In 1903, there was unconditional surrender on the part of the NL, and the AL was accepted by the NL as a major league on equal footing with it, with no compensation demanded or offered. The AL rates as the most successful rival league in the history of team sports in the United States.

The success of the AL can be attributed in part to the NL's public relations problem concerning syndication. But much more critical was the fact that the big cities of the East were willing and able to support more major league teams than the NL provided. Fans in Baltimore, Cleveland, and Washington had been left without teams when the NL was cut from 12 to 8 teams in 1900, and were natural markets for the new league. And in the big-city markets of Chicago, Boston, Philadelphia, and St. Louis, the NL had created one-team monopolies in cities that had profitably supported two or more teams as recently as the late 1880s or early 1890s, when the AA was in operation. To add to this, eastern cities of the country were experiencing a population boom, fueled by unprecedented levels of immigration, and concentrated in the blue-collar occupations, where baseball was most popular. It was scarcely the time for cutting back on the coverage of the league, and yet that is just what the NL did.

Finally, Murphy's law was in operation, too. The worst thing that could have happened to the NL was to have a runaway pennant race while the AL-NL war was on. As it turned out, in 1902, the Pittsburgh Pirates featuring Honus Wagner won the pennant by 27 games—the biggest winning margin in NL history—while the AL had a four-team race going into the final weeks of the season, with the Athletics finally winning by five games.

Beyond the economic factors that favored the entry of the AL, there was solid leadership and financing for the league, with Ban Johnson as organizer and CEO, and with Charles Somers to supply the funds. It is one of the great ironies of the short-lived AL-NL war that syndication of the NL was one of the issues that led to the defeat of the NL, and yet in practice, the AL was more highly syndicated than the NL. Somers assisted in financing at least half of the AL teams, usually in collaboration with Johnson, and Johnson also required that each team deposit a majority of its stock with the league office to preclude possible sellouts to NL owners. Johnson and his close associate, Charles Comiskey, had personal knowledge of the mistakes that had been made by the AA with respect to movement of teams between leagues, and they were not going to permit the AL to be whipsawed in this fashion by the NL.

In any case, within two years it was the NL that was on the ropes, and it was the junior league that hammered out the terms of an agreement under which the new league maintained its identity, maintained its franchise rights, and also maintained ownership of the player contracts that had originally been bid away from NL teams.

The Federal League War, 1914–1915

Baseball had a decade of peace after the conclusion of the AL-NL war, and then, in 1914, one final challenge occurred to major league baseball in the form of the Federal League. The incentive in this case was certainly the box office success of masjor league baseball.

Between 1901 and 1913, total baseball attendance increased roughly 4.5 percent per year (a doubling time of 15 years), so that by 1913, the average team in the NL was drawing about 350,000 per year, and the average AL team was drawing about 450,000 per year. This looked like a profitable opportunity for entry to John Powers, an entrepreneur who organized the Columbian League in 1913, with a six-team membership consisting of Chicago (2), St. Louis (4), Cleveland (6), Pittsburgh (8), Indianapolis (22), and Covington, Kentucky (no rank) (1910 census). Before the 1913 season began, the name of the league was changed to Federal League, and during the season, Covington moved to Kansas City (20). The league played the 1913 season with free agents only, honoring the reserve clause in AL and NL contracts.

Late in the 1913 season, Powers was voted out of office, to be replaced by his co-owner of the Chicago franchise, James Gilmore. After the season, the Federal League owners, led by Phil Ball of St. Louis, and Robert Ward of Brooklyn, made the decision to operate as an "outlaw" major league, signing players from AL and NL teams, and competing with organized baseball in the major population centers of the country. The FL dropped Cleveland, and added Brooklyn, Baltimore, and Buffalo, to line up for the 1914 season with teams in Brooklyn (1), Chicago (2), St. Louis (4), Baltimore (7), Pittsburgh (8), Buffalo (11), Kansas City (20), and Indianapolis (22), filling in the gaps left by the AL and NL in the two large eastern cities left without teams, Baltimore and Buffalo, and competing directly with the AL and NL in Brooklyn, Chicago, St. Louis, and Pittsburgh.

The FL ignored the reserve clause of AL and NL contracts, and for the 1914 season, signed 80 players who had been on AL or NL rosters in the 1913 or 1914 season. The pace of signings from the AL or NL slowed considerably in 1915 with only 16 more players moving from the majors to the FL. Table 8.4 identifies the losses suffered by each major league team in 1914 and 1915, due to the FL raids. Interestingly, the NL was the big loser from the raids, and among NL teams, Cincinnati and Philadelphia lost the most players. Among the big names who made the move to the FL were Chief Bender and Eddie Plank, the aces of Connie Mack's Philadelphia Athletics' pitching staff, Mordecai "Three Finger" Brown of the Reds, "Prince Hal" Chase of the White Sox, "Slick" Hartley of the Giants, "Dutch" Knabe of the Phillies, the Senators' Frank La Porte, Bill McKechnie of the Yankees, Dan Murphy of the A's, John Quinn and Bill Rariden of the Braves, Brooklyn's "Big Ed" Reulbach, the Senators' "Germany" Schaefer, and the Cubs' Joe Tinker of Tinker to Evers to Chance fame.

The desertion of Bender and Plank to the Federal League panicked Connie Mack so much that he sold off his best players to other AL teams in 1915, which, unfortunately for him, turned out to be the last

Table 8.4
Player Losses to the Federal League by Major League Teams, 1914 and 1915

Team	Player Losses			League Finish		
	1914	*1915*	*Total*	*1913*	*1914*	*1915*
NATIONAL LEAGUE						
New York	4	2	6	1	2	8
Philadelphia	10	1	11	2	6	1
Chicago	3	—	3	3	4	4
Pittsburgh	5	—	5	4	7	5
Boston	7	2	9	5	1	2
Brooklyn	6	2	8	6	5	3
Cincinnati	13	1	14	7	8	7
Total	52	10	62			
AMERICAN LEAGUE						
Philadelphia	2	2	4	1	1	8
Washington	2	1	3	2	3	4
Cleveland	3	—	3	3	8	7
Boston	6	2	8	4	2	1
Chicago	4	—	4	5	6	3
Detroit	2	1	3	6	4	2
New York	4	—	4	7	6	5
St. Louis	5	—	5	8	5	6
Total	28	6	34			
Grand total	80	16	96			

Source: As in table 8.2.

year of operation of the FL. Mack's A's dropped from first to last place in the AL, going from a W/L percentage of .651 in 1914 to .283 in 1915, certainly the steepest drop in one year in all of baseball history. If Mack had simply waited just one year, he could have avoided that long period of cellar teams for the Athletics, and the history of baseball might have been quite different.

Table 8.5 gives the breakdown of player rosters for FL teams during the 1914 and 1915 seasons. Of the 205 players who appeared on FL rosters during the 1914 season, only 75 did not have some major league experience, and only 69 of the 207 players appearing on 1915 rosters did not have major league experience. The major league caliber of FL teams is indicated by the distribution of major league experience shown in the table, and by the number of players who moved to major league rosters after the FL went out of existence, as shown by the next to last column in the table.

Among the players who began their careers in the FL were pitcher Howard Ehmke, later of Detroit and the Athletics, Max Flack of the Cubs and Cards, and John Tobin of the Browns. The most sought-after player in the league was star outfielder and slugger Benny Kauff, who moved to the New York Giants when the FL folded.

Reliable estimates of attendance for FL teams do not exist; again, as with most rival leagues, there was a considerable amount of puffery in estimates published by league teams or by the league itself. What is known with some assurance is that the FL had a substantial impact on attendance at AL and NL games—NL attendance dropped 1.1 million from 1913 to 1914, from 2.8 million to 1.7 million; and AL attendance dropped by 800,000, from 3.5 million to 2.7 million. At the end of the 1914 season, the FL league office announced league-wide attendance of 1.6 million. In contrast, in November 1914, the *Brooklyn Times* reported a confidential estimate of FL attendance for 1914, prepared by the National Commission (the governing board of organized baseball). Comparisons of this estimate with actual attendance for AL and NL teams in 1914 are shown in Table 8.6.

The National Commission also estimated that the FL had lost $1.1 million in aggregate during the 1914 season. The FL denied the published report, claiming that Chicago had made between $20,000 and $25,000, Baltimore had made $18,000, and Buffalo and Indianapolis had made $6,000 each, while Pittsburgh had lost between $5,000 and $10,000, Kansas City had lost $12,000, St. Louis had lost $45,000, and Brooklyn had lost $60,000, for a league-wide loss of about $77,000.

Whatever the true state of affairs (and the National Commission's guess was certainly closer to the truth than the figures given out by the FL), when the 1914 season had been completed, the FL announced that

Table 8.5
Federal League Player Rosters by Previous Major League Experience, 1914–1915

FL Standing	No. on Roster	1913 Status			Major League Experience (years)				ML 1916–
		AL	NL	Other	0	1	2	3+	
1914									
1. Indianapolis	25	5	3	17	11	6	2	6	7
2. Chicago	26	2	7	17	13	6	—	7	13
3. Baltimore	27	—	12	15	9	2	4	12	7
4. Buffalo	28	2	—	26	7	6	3	12	8
5. Brooklyn	30	3	6	21	11	5	5	9	9
6. Kansas City	23	4	2	17	10	5	4	4	5
7. Pittsburgh	32	2	9	21	10	4	5	13	7
8. St. Louis	24	2	10	12	6	7	1	10	10
Total	205	25	50	130	75	38	21	71	66

FL Standing	No. on Roster	1914 Status				Major League Experience (years)				ML 1916–
		AL	NL	FL	Other	0	1	2	3+	
1915										
1. Chicago	26	—	1	18	7	13	4	1	8	16
2. St. Louis	25	1	1	19	4	3	7	2	13	13
3. Pittsburgh	31	—	2	22	7	8	5	1	17	12
4. Kansas City	21	1	—	18	2	7	5	4	5	7
5. Newark	27	2	1	17	7	9	7	3	8	10
6. Buffalo	24	1	—	20	3	6	5	3	10	10
7. Brooklyn	37	1	4	26	6	14	4	6	13	15
8. Baltimore	36	1	—	24	11	17	3	3	13	14
Total	207	7	9	144	47	69	35	23	80	89

Source: Hy Turkin and S. C. Thompson, *The Official Encyclopedia of Baseball,* 7th ed. (London A. S. Barnes and Co., 1974).

Note: Totals exclude double counting because players were on the roster of more than one team during a season.

it would continue operations in 1915. Harry Sinclair, later to become notorious because of the Teapot Dome scandal in the Harding administration, bought up the Indianapolis club, and moved it to Newark as the Newark Peppers, but the rest of the league remained in place. In January 1915, the FL filed an antitrust suit against organized baseball. Among the facts alleged to back up the FL suit was the refusal of Western Union

Table 8.6
Attendance, AL, NL, and FL, 1914

	AL	NL	FL (est.)
Chicago	469,290	202,516	200,729
New York	359,447	364,313	—
Brooklyn	—	122,671	77,101
Philadelphia	346,641	138,474	—
Boston	481,225	382,913	—
St. Louis	244,714	256,099	47,586
Detroit	416,225	—	—
Pittsburgh	—	136,620	63,482
Cincinnati	—	100,791	—
Washington	243,888	—	—
Cleveland	185,997	—	—
Indianapolis	—	—	136,186
Baltimore	—	—	124,672
Kansas City	—	—	65,346
Buffalo	—	—	71,101

Source: Brooklyn Times, November 15, 1914.

to carry FL scores on its tickers, undoubtedly in response to pressure by organized baseball. There were also calls for an antitrust investigation of baseball in Congress in 1914. The FL continued to make bids for players under reserve to AL and NL teams, but, as noted earlier, only a handful of additional players made the move from organized baseball to the FL before the 1915 season.

Whatever else can be said about the Federal League, it certainly provided exciting pennant races. In 1914, Indianapolis won the FL pennant with a record of 88 wins and 65 losses, for a W/L percentage of .575. Chicago was one and a half games out, at .565, and Baltimore was four games out, at .549. In 1915, the FL put on what is arguably the most exciting pennant race in the history of major league baseball. The 1915 season ended up with the following standings:

	W	L	%	Games Behind
Chicago	86	66	.566	—
St. Louis	87	67	.565	—
Pittsburgh	86	67	.562	1/2
Kansas City	81	72	.533	5 1/2
Newark	80	72	.526	6
Buffalo	74	78	.487	12
Brooklyn	70	82	.461	16
Baltimore	47	107	.305	40

Five of the eight teams in the league had a chance at winning the pennant going into the last 10 days of the season. The pennant-winning percentage of .566 is the third lowest in the history of baseball, being surpassed only by the .564 winning percentage of the 1959 Dodgers, and the .562 percentage of the 1983 Dodgers and the 1974 Orioles. The only serious contender for a race keeping much of the league in the chase up to the last minute is the 1964 NL race, which ended with St. Louis's winning the pennant (93–69, .574), followed one game back by a two-way tie for second place between Cincinnati and Philadelphia (92–70, .568), followed two more games back by San Francisco (90–72, .556), and another two back, Milwaukee (88–74, .543).

The FL had supplied all the excitement that could be demanded so far as pennant races are concerned. And how did the FL do at the box office? *Sporting Life* provided estimates of profits (and losses) in baseball for the 1915 season in its issue of October 30, 1915, reporting the following estimates:

NL	Pittsburgh: − $50,000		Boston: small profit
	Brooklyn: + $25,000 to $50,000		St Louis: − $10,000 to $25,000
	Cincinnati: − $50,000		Chicago: break-even
	Philadelphia: break-even		New York: + $100,000
AL	Boston: + $50,000 to $75,000		Cleveland: − $50,000 to $100,000
	Detroit: + $75,000		St. Louis: no information
	Chicago: break-even		Philadelphia: no information
	Washington: − $25,000 to $50,000		New York: − $75,000 to $100,000
FL	Brooklyn: − $100,000		Chicago: small profit
	Buffalo: − $10,000 to $25,000		Baltimore: − $100,000 plus
	Pittsburgh: + $2,000		Newark: break-even
	Kansas City: + $75,000[a]		St. Louis: + $50,000

[a]Later audited published profits for Kansas City were reported as − $35,332.13, from *Sporting Life*, November 6, 1915.

In December 1915, *Sporting Life* revised its estimate of FL losses over the 1914–1915 seasons upward, to $2 million, of which $800,000 represented losses by Robert Ward, the Brooklyn owner, and his brothers, and $600,000 were losses of Edward Gwimmer and C. B. Comstock, owners of the Pittsburgh franchise. The losses suffered by all the leagues combined with two other events to bring about an end to the FL war—the death of Robert Ward late in 1915, and the decision of Harry Sinclair to begin construction of a baseball park in New York City to house his Newark team. Ward was the most energetic supporter of the Federal League among its owners, and was also the owner most willing and able to absorb losses to keep the league afloat. The losses suffered by the Yankees made them especially vulnerable to the threat posed by a move of the Newark FL franchise into New York. With Ward dead, an agreement was reached under which the FL was to drop its antitrust suit against organized baseball, and to go out of existence.

The terms of the agreement were these: Charles Weeghman, owner of the Chicago FL Whales, was allowed to buy the Chicago Cubs for $500,000, with the NL kicking in $50,000 of the purchase price. Phil Ball, owner of the St. Louis FL Terriers, was allowed to buy the St. Louis Browns for $525,000; whether there was a sweetener of $50,000 by the AL is not known. The heirs of Robert Ward, owners of the Brooklyn FL Tip Tops, were given $20,000 per year for 20 years. Edward Gwimmer and C. B. Comstock, owners of the Pittsburgh Rebels, were given $50,000 in cash and the option to purchase an unspecified major league team within a month, an option that was not exercised. Harry Sinclair, owner of the Newark Peppers, was given $10,000 per year for 10 years as well as control of the player contracts of several players, including Benny Kauff. Kansas City and Buffalo had gone bankrupt after the 1915 season, and might have been given some unspecified sum, perhaps $50,000. The owner of the Baltimore Terrapins, Carroll Rasin, was offered $50,000, together with the Baltimore franchise in the International League.

Among the FL owners, only Rasin rejected the proposed agreement. He decided to continue to press the FL antitrust suit (now a suit by the Baltimore FL club), with results as discussed in Chapter 3. This is the end of the story of the FL, and of the story of rival leagues in baseball, as of 1991.

Postscript

Well, not quite. Just after World War II, the Mexican League created a brief panic among major league owners when a few major league players jumped their reserve clause contracts to play for one season in the "outlaw" Mexican League. And there was a movement at about the same time by owners of the Pacific Coast League franchises to create a new major league consisting of Los Angeles, San Francisco, Oakland, San Diego, Hollywood, Seattle, Portland, and Sacramento, operating within the rules structure of organized baseball. The majors had simply ignored the shift in population to the West and Southwest that was taking place between 1900 and 1950, together with the development of fast, reliable, and safe air transportation to the major cities of those regions. The Celler Committee hearings of the early 1950s into the antitrust status of baseball focused on the reluctance of the major leagues to expand into the West, and might have helped to trigger the wave of franchise moves in that direction in the 1950s.

The franchise moves of Brooklyn and New York after the 1957 season again opened up a lucrative big-city market for possible invasion by a rival league. Immediately after the Dodgers and the Giants moved, the rival Continental League was formed (on paper) by Branch Rickey and William Shea in 1958 as a vehicle to put pressure on organized baseball to create an expansion franchise in New York. Franchises in the proposed Continental League were to be located in New York, the Twin Cities, Denver, Houston, Toronto, Buffalo, Atlanta, and Dallas. The league was stillborn because of an agreement reached between the major leagues and the Continental League under which the majors agreed to add teams in New York, Houston, the Twin Cities, and Los Angeles. Having accomplished its main goal when the Mets were created, the Continental League folded its tents and stole softly into the night.

Tallying up the impact of rival leagues on expansion in major league baseball, the record is as follows: Of the 26 big league teams operating in 1991, 12 originated as members of rival leagues: NL members Los Angeles (Brooklyn), Pittsburgh, Cincinnati, and St. Louis from the American Association; and AL members Boston, New York (Baltimore), Oakland (Philadelphia), Detroit, Cleveland, Minnesota (Washington), Chicago, and Baltimore (Milwaukee/St. Louis) from the original AL rival league of 1901–1902.

Rival Leagues in Basketball

Of all the major professional team sports, basketball is the one sport where a dominant monopoly league did not develop until quite late in its history—not until after World War II, in fact. There is not much documentation of the early history of professional basketball. About the time of World War I, the original Celtics from New York organized as an independent pro basketball team. For years thereafter, the Celtics were the best team in the sport, touring the East and Midwest playing local pro and semi-pro teams. In the early to mid 1920s, the Celtics played with a Hall of Fame lineup of Joe Lapchick, Nat Holman, Pete Barry, Dutch Dehnert, and Johnny Beckman.

In 1924, the first American Basketball League was organized, by Joe Carr according to some accounts, and by George Marshall according to others. The league was in existence for seven years, 1925–1931, and Carr served as its president during this time, while also serving as president of the NFL. Marshall was with the league as an owner for just one year, reportedly losing $65,000, although this figure sounds overstated given the probable costs of operating a basketball team in the 1920s.

The original lineup of the ABL had a football flavor, with Marshall owning the Washington team (although this was eight years before Marshall became an NFL owner), George Halas being the owner of the Chicago Bruins entry, and with Carr the league president. The other teams in the league for the initial 1925/26 season were the Cleveland Rosenblooms, owned by businessman Max Rosenbloom; a Fort Wayne team owned by the Fort Wayne Chamber of Commerce; the Brooklyn Arcadians, owned by Harry Heilmann, the old Red Sox outfielder; the Buffalo Germans, owned by Allie Heerdt; the Boston and Detroit teams; and the Rochester Centrals, owned by Johnny Murphy.

Cleveland won the first ABL title, but the best team in pro basketball, the Celtics, was not in the league. In 1926/27, Buffalo was dropped, and the ABA added a Baltimore team (the Orioles) and the first version of the Philadelphia Warriors, this one owned by Jules Aronson. A few weeks into the season, the Celtics, owned by Jim Furey, joined the league, replacing Brooklyn. The Celts ended up winning the 1926/27 ABL championship. And they won again in 1927/28, dominating the league, which consisted of the Detroit Cardinals, the Rochester Centrals, the (New York) Celtics, the Cleveland Rosenblooms, the Chicago Bruins, the Visitation Triangles, the Brooklyn Jewels, and Fort Wayne. Before the 1928/29 season, the ABL owners got together and decided to solve their competitive balance problems by breaking up the Celtics. But three ex-Celtics (Lapchick, Dehnert and Barry) ended up with Cleveland, and Cleveland won the 1929/30 title, beating Fort Wayne in the championship series. Cleveland also won the 1930/31 title, and the Depression, together with competitive imbalance problems, sank the ABL after that season.

A new version of the ABL was put together in 1934, concentrated in the New York-Philadelphia area. The original list of teams in the second ABL included the Brooklyn Jewels, the Trenton Moose, the Bronx Americans, the Union City Reds, the South Philadelphia Hebrew Association (SPHAs), owned by Eddie Gottlieb, and the Brooklyn Visitations. The Visitations won the first title of the new ABL in a playoff with the Jewels. A year later, a new version of the Celtics was added, named Kate Smith's Celtics, and owned by Smith and Ted Collins, her manager. In 1936, it was the SPHAs playing the Jersey Reds in the championship round, and again in 1937. In 1938, the New York Whirlwinds, the Troy Celtics, and a Wilkes-Barre team joined the league, which had a revolving set of teams. In 1939, Kingston won the ABL title, and in 1940 it was the SPHAs and the Washington Brewers fighting for the championship. World War II cut ABL league membership down—in 1941, the league consisted of Wilmington, the SPHAs, Trenton, and Washington. In 1942, Washington was out, with Camden, Harrisburg, and Baltimore in; and in 1943, the SPHAs once again met Trenton for the ABL championship.

The ABL went out of existence after the 1946/47 season, with the entry of a new rival league, the Basketball Association of America, organized by a group of arena owners, all of whom either had NHL teams or minor league hockey teams. The arena owners were looking for an attraction to fill their buildings on the nights that the hockey team was not home. What attracted them was the crowds that were being drawn in the early post-war years by the Madison Square Garden college basketball doubleheaders, which later ran into problems because of game-throwing scandals. But years before the BAA was organized, there was another pro basketball league in operation, the National Basketball League, with its lineup of teams concentrated in the Midwest. The NBL began operations in 1937, with two Akron teams (one from Firestone and one from Goodyear), the Pittsburgh Pirates, the Buffalo Bisons, Warren (Ohio), Columbus, the Oshkosh All Stars, the Whiting (Indiana) Caesar All Americans, the GE of Fort Wayne, the Indianapolis Kautskys, Cincinnati, and the Kankakee Gallagher Trojans. Over the years, teams were added and dropped out—at one time or another, Cleveland, Sheboygan Redskins, Hammond, Chicago, Detroit, Toledo, and Rochester all played in the NBL.

In 1946, the NBL consisted of Rochester, Fort Wayne, Toledo, Syracuse, Tri Cities (Davenport, Rock Island, Moline), Youngstown, Oshkosh, Indianapolis, Chicago, Sheboygan, Anderson, and Detroit. The BAA began operations in 1946 with a lineup of New York (1), Chicago (2), Philadelphia (3), Detroit (4), Cleveland (6), St. Louis (8), Boston (10), Pittsburgh (11), and Toronto, while the NBL had just Chicago (2) and Detroit (4) from the big-city list. The BAA owners, most whom controlled the only large-capacity arenas in their cities, effectively had monopoly control over entry into the BAA list of cities. On the other hand, the NBL had the players.

After the 1947/48 season, the four strongest franchises in the NBL—Minneapolis Lakers, Rochester Royals, Fort Wayne Pistons, and Indianapolis Olympics—moved to the BAA. The NBL broke up after the 1948/49 season, when six more of its teams—Anderson, Syracuse, Tri Cities, Sheboygan, Waterloo, and Denver—moved to the BAA, which was now renamed the NBA, and fielded 17 teams for the 1949/50 season. By 1954, the NBA was down to only eight teams—New York Knicks (1), Philadelphia Warriors (4), Boston Celtics (6), Minneapolis Lakers (13), Milwaukee Hawks (17), and the smaller-city Syracuse Nationals, Rochester Royals, and Fort Wayne Pistons—and the league played with only eight teams for the next seven seasons. Milwaukee moved to St. Louis (9) in 1955, Rochester moved to Cincinnati (18), and Fort Wayne moved to

Detroit (5) in 1957, and the Lakers made their move to Los Angeles (3) in 1960.

In 1961, Abe Saperstein, of Harlem Globe Trotter fame, organized a new version of the American Basketball League. In the first year of the ABL, the league consisted of the Washington Tapers (moved to Long Island as the Long Island Tapers in midseason), George Steinbrenner's Cleveland Pipers, the San Francisco Saints, the Chicago Majors (owned by Saperstein), the Hawaii Chiefs, the Kansas City Steers, Los Angeles, and the Pittsburgh Rens (named after the great black basketball team of the 1930s, the Renaissance). The Los Angeles entry faced the newly relocated Los Angeles Lakers, and disbanded before the end of the season. Steinbrenner's Pipers featured the local favorite, Jerry Lucas, who had starred on Ohio State's national championship team, and the Pipers won the 1961/62 ABL title handily. Steinbrenner was responsible for an important breakthrough with the Pipers as well—the hiring of John McLendon, the first black coach to be hired by any major league pro sports team. It will come as no surprise to Steinbrenner fans of all colors and creeds that McLendon was fired midway through the season. The ABL as a whole had problems at the gate; Saperstein reported that the ABL lost about $1 million during the season, with no team in the black.

After the first ABL season, there were newspaper reports that the ABL was going to disband, and this led to negotiations between Steinbrenner and the NBA aimed at bringing the Pipers into the NBA as an expansion team. The proposed fee was $200,000 plus a $40,000 indemnity to the Cincinnati Royals, who owned the NBA draft rights to Lucas. The negotiations ended when Saperstein threatened an antitrust suit, and the ABL went on with a six-team lineup for the 1962/63 season—the Philadelphia Tapers (moved from Long Island), Pittsburgh, Kansas City, and Cleveland, plus Long Beach (moved from Hawaii) and Oakland (moved from Chicago). The league folded on January 1, 1963, with league-wide losses for the 1962/63 season estimated at $250,000.

While the ABL had signed a few players who had also been drafted by the NBA, the league did not constitute a serious threat to the NBA. But in 1967, another rival league—the American Basketball Association—was formed that did have the financial backing and the players to cause problems for the NBA. The ABA was organized by Gary Davidson and Dennis Murphy. Davidson went on to create both the World Football League, and the World Hockey Association; thus, at one point in the 1970s, there were three rival leagues in operation, all originating from Davidson's Santa Ana (California) law office.

The ABA played nine seasons (1967/68 through 1975/76) before merging with the NBA. The franchise history of the ABA is shown in Table

8.7. The period when the ABA was operating was also a period of expansion for the NBA. Table 8.8 provides a rundown of the location of NBA and ABA franchises by year during the lifespan of the ABA. The table shows that the ABA began operations as a textbook rival league, locating teams in the megalopolis centers of New York and Los Angeles, and filling in the gaps in coverage of the NBA in medium-size cities—Pittsburgh, Houston, the Twin Cities, and Dallas. The ABA also located a team in Oakland, competing in the Bay Area market wih the San Francisco Warriors, and it added teams in the relatively small cities of Denver, Indianapolis, New Orleans, and Louisville. As time went on, the NBA expanded its original list of 12 teams to 18 teams in the 1975/76 season, basically going from a top-20 (population-wise) league to a top-30 league. The smallest city in the NBA in 1975 was Phoenix, 29th on the list of cities.

The ABA started out in 1967/68 with 11 teams and began the 1975/76 season with just 8 teams. The league got squeezed out of its larger city markets, with Los Angeles moving to Utah, Oakland moving to Washington and then to Norfolk, Pittsburgh going out of business, Dallas moving to San Antonio, and the Twin Cities moving to Miami, and then going out of business.

The attendance history of ABA franchises, shown in Table 8.9, pro-

Table 8.7

Franchise History of American Basketball Association, 1967/68–1975/76

1967/68	1968/69	1969/70	1970/71	1971/72	1972/73	1973/74	1974/75	1975/76	1976/77 (NBA)
Pitt	Minn	Pitt	Pitt	Pitt	Out	Out	Out	Out	Out
Minn	Miami	Miami	Miami	Miami	Out	Out	Out	Out	Out
Ind	Ind	Ind	Ind	Ind	Ind	Ind	Ind	Ind	Ind
Ky	Ky	Ky	Ky	Ky	Ky	Ky	Ky	Ky	Out
NJ	NY	NY	NY	NY	NY	NY	NY	NY	NY
NwO	NwO	NwO	Memp	Memp	Memp	Memp	Memp	Bal/out	Out
Dall	Dall	Dall	Dall	Dall	Dall	SnAnt	SnAnt	SnAnt	SnAnt
Hous	Hous	Caro	Caro	Caro	Caro	Caro	StL	StL	Out
Anah	LA	LA	Utah	Utah	Utah	Utah	Utah	Utah	Out
Oak	Oak	Wash	Va	Va	Va	Va	Va	Va	Out
Denv	Denv	Denv	Denv	Denv	Denv	Denv	Denv	Denv	Denv

						Expansion Team			
			SD	SD	SD	Out	Out	Out	

Sources: Sporting News, ABA league guides.

Table 8.8

Franchise Locations by 1970 Population Rank, ABA and NBA, 1967/68–1976/77
(number of franchises)

Rank and City	1967/68 N	A	1968/69 N	A	1969/70 N	A	1970/71 N	A	1971/72 N	A	1972/73 N	A	1973/74 N	A	1974/75 N	A	1975/76 N	A	1976/77– N
1. New York	1	1	1	1	1	1	1	1	1	1	1	1	1	1	1	1	1	1	2
2. Los Angeles	1	1	1	1	1	1	1	0	1	0	1	0	1	0	1	0	1	0	1
3. Chicago	1	0	1	0	1	0	1	0	1	0	1	0	1	0	1	0	1	0	1
4. Philadelphia	1	0	1	0	1	0	1	0	1	0	1	0	1	0	1	0	1	0	1
5. Detroit	1	0	1	0	1	0	1	0	1	0	1	0	1	0	1	0	1	0	1
6. San Francisco	1	1	1	1	1	0	1	0	1	0	1	0	1	0	1	0	1	0	1
7. Washington	0	0	0	0	0	1	0	0	0	0	0	0	0	1	0	1	0	1	1
8. Boston	1	0	1	0	1	0	1	0	1	0	1	0	1	0	1	0	1	0	1
9. Pittsburgh	0	1	0	0	0	1	0	1	0	1	0	0	0	0	0	0	0	0	0
10. St. Louis	1	0	0	0	0	0	0	0	0	0	0	0	0	0	0	1	0	1	0
11. Baltimore	1	0	1	0	1	0	1	0	1	0	0	0	0	0	0	0	0	1	0
12. Cleveland	0	0	0	0	0	0	1	0	1	0	1	0	1	0	1	0	1	0	1
13. Houston	0	1	0	1	0	0	0	0	1	0	1	0	1	0	1	0	1	0	1
14. Minneapolis-St. Paul	0	1	0	1	0	0	0	0	0	0	0	0	0	0	0	0	0	0	0
15. Dallas	0	1	0	1	0	1	0	1	0	1	0	0	0	0	0	0	0	0	0
16. Seattle	1	0	1	0	1	0	1	0	1	0	1	0	1	0	1	0	1	0	1
17. Milwaukee	0	0	1	0	1	0	1	0	1	0	1	0	1	0	1	0	1	0	1
18. Atlanta	0	0	1	0	1	0	1	0	1	0	1	0	1	0	1	0	1	0	1
19. Cincinnati	1	0	1	0	1	0	1	0	1	0	0	0	0	0	0	0	0	0	0
20. San Diego	1	0	1	0	1	0	1	0	0	0	0	1	0	1	0	1	0	0	0
21. Buffalo	0	0	0	0	0	0	1	0	1	0	1	0	1	0	1	0	1	0	1
22. Miami	0	0	0	1	0	1	0	1	0	1	0	0	0	0	0	0	0	0	0
23. Kansas City	0	0	0	0	0	0	0	0	0	0	1	0	1	0	1	0	1	0	1
24. Denver	0	1	0	1	0	1	0	1	0	1	0	1	0	1	0	1	0	1	1
25. Indianapolis	0	1	0	1	0	1	0	1	0	1	0	1	0	1	0	1	0	1	1
26. New Orleans	0	1	0	1	0	1	0	0	0	0	0	0	0	0	0	1	0	1	1
27. Tampa	0	0	0	0	0	0	0	0	0	0	0	0	0	0	0	0	0	0	0
28. Portland	0	0	0	0	0	0	1	0	1	0	1	0	1	0	1	0	1	0	1
29. Phoenix	0	0	0	0	1	0	1	0	1	0	1	0	1	0	1	0	1	0	1
30. Columbus	0	0	0	0	0	0	0	0	0	0	0	0	0	0	0	0	0	0	0
33. San Antonio	0	0	0	0	0	0	0	0	0	0	0	0	0	1	0	1	0	1	1
34. Louisville	0	1	0	1	0	1	0	1	0	1	0	1	0	1	0	1	0	1	0
37. Memphis	0	0	0	0	0	0	0	1	0	1	0	1	0	1	0	1	0	0	0
42. Norfolk	0	0	0	0	0	0	0	1	0	1	0	1	0	1	0	1	0	1	0
53. Salt Lake City	0	0	0	0	0	0	0	1	0	1	0	1	0	1	0	1	0	1	0
70. Charlotte	0	0	0	0	0	1	0	1	0	1	0	1	0	1	0	0	0	0	0

Sources: Bureau of the Census, *Statistical Abstract of the United States, 1980* (Washington, D.C.: U.S. Government Printing Office, 1980); *American Basketball Guide,* 1967–1976 (St. Louis: *Sporting News,* annual).

Note: N = NBA; A = ABA.

vides an introduction to the problems that beset the league. In the first years of the ABA, the weakest teams (in terms of attendance) included the big-city teams of New York, Los Angeles, and Houston; in fact, the only team with a decent attendance record was the Indiana Pacers. The superstar of the early years of the ABA was Rick Barry, who spent almost as much time in the law courts as on the basketball court after signing up with at least two teams, San Francisco and Oakland, simultaneously. Later on, Julius Erving, the incomparable "Doctor J," made a major difference in the drawing appeal first of Virginia and later of New York, and the North Carolina phenom, David Thompson, was instrumental in turning a weak-drawing team in Denver into a major league attraction. The winnowing out of weak franchises, coupled with brief honeymoon periods after franchise moves, accounts for much of the upward trend in per-game attendance for the ABA.

Table 8.9
Per-Game Attendance, ABA, 1968/69–1975/76

Team	1968/69	1969/70	1970/71	1971/72	1972/73	1973/74	1974/75	1975/76
Minnesota	2,183	—	—	—	—	—	—	—
Pittsburgh	—	2,009	2,714	2,215	—	—	—	—
Miami	3,197	2,724	4,020	2,108	—	—	—	—
Indiana	6,090	7,787	8,236	8,524	8,180	7,373	8,585	7,879
Kentucky	4,157	3,834	7,375	8,811	7,113	8,201	8,727	6,935
New York	1,094	3,504	4,636	6,689	6,735	8,923	9,135	7,755
New Orleans	2,834	2,599	—	—	—	—	—	—
Memphis	—	—	3,199	4,441	3,476	2,331	3,879	—
Dallas/	2,861	3,709	3,436	3,205	2,395	—	—	—
San Antonio	—	—	—	—	—	6,119	7,906	8,028
Houston/	820	—	—	—	—	—	—	—
Carolina/	—	6,088	5,579	5,077	6,811	5,889	—	—
St. Louis	—	—	—	—	—	—	4,618	3,779
Los Angeles	2,281	1,461	—	—	—	—	—	—
Utah	—	—	6,106	7,998	7,156	6,727	8,501	6,097[a]
Oakland/	2,867	—	—	—	—	—	—	—
Washington	—	2,032	—	—	—	—	—	—
Virginia	—	—	4,309	6,124	6,095	3,313	4,581	4,613
Denver	4,294	6,320	3,982	4,117	4,964	4,069	6,707	12,652
San Diego	—	—	—	—	2,247	1,843	2,581	2,375[a]
ABA avg.	2,981	3,948	4,924	5,331	5,554	5,485	6,591	7,264
NBA avg.	6,483	7,563	7,647	8,060	8,396	8,479	9,339	10,179

Sources: ABA game summaries in Sporting News; 1967/68 data not available.
[a]Franchise abandoned in midseason.

The ABA began its last season, 1975/76, with nine teams, but one, the Baltimore Claws, went under before the season started. During the season, the league lost the San Diego Sails and the Utah Stars, and the Virginia Squires went broke before the season was finished. The St. Louis Spirits franchise was taken over by a group that was going to move the team to Salt Lake City as the Utah Rockies. This left the ABA wih only six teams—New York Nets, Denver, Indiana, San Antonio, Kentucky, and the Utah Rockies. On June 17, 1976, an agreement was announced between the ABA and the NBA under which New York, Denver, Indiana, and San Antonio moved into the NBA. The terms of the agreement provided that each team would pay the NBA an expansion fee of $3.2 million. In addition, the Nets agreed to pay the New York Knicks $4 million for invading their territory. And the four teams going into the NBA also agreed to split the cost of paying Kentucky and Utah $3.2 million each, as compensation for folding the ABA.

Thus the cost to Denver, Indianapolis, and San Antonio was roughly $4.8 million each, and the cost to the Nets was $8.8 million, to move to the NBA, with the player contract rights of the team to be protected. By way of comparison, in 1974, the expansion fee charged to the New Orleans Jazz was $6.15 million, but of course New Orleans ended up with a weaker group of players than those owned by the ABA teams. In 1980, Dallas came into the NBA as an expansion team for a $12 million fee. Estimates at the time of the merger were that the ABA lost roughly $40 million during its nine-year history, which averages out to about $4 million per team. By the time of the ABA-NBA merger, all of the original owners of ABA teams were gone, having lost substantial sums. There were a few fortunate individuals who bought into ABA teams shortly before the merger, and in the process acquired NBA franchises for less than their market value. But generally speaking, the ABA was not an example of a "successful" rival league.

The payoff from rival leagues in terms of the NBA is in the form of 9 of the current 27-team NBA lineup. These are Philadelphia (Syracuse), Atlanta (Tri Cities), Los Angeles (Minneapolis), Sacramento (Rochester), and Detroit (Fort Wayne), from the National Basketball League; and New Jersey, San Antonio, Denver, and Indiana, from the ABA.

Rival Leagues in Hockey

The National Hockey League began operations in 1917 as a four-team league—the Montreal Canadiens, the Toronto Arenas, the Ottawa Senators, and the Montreal Wanderers. The Wanderers left the league midway in the season, after its rink burned down, and in 1918/19, the NHL again operated as a three-team league. Beginning in the 1917/18 season, the NHL scheduled Stanley Cup playoffs with the Pacific Coast Hockey League, consisting of Calgary, Edmonton, Saskatoon, and Regina. Another league, the Western Canada Hockey League, was formed in 1921, and the Stanley Cup playoffs became a round robin among the three leagues until 1924, when the PCHL went out of business. A non-NHL team, Victoria of the WCHL, won the Stanley Cup, beating the Canadiens, in the magic year of 1925.

In 1924, the NHL expanded into the United States, adding the Boston Bruins to a lineup consisting of Hamilton, Toronto, the Montreal Canadiens, Ottawa, and the Montreal Maroons. Hamilton moved to New York as the New York Americans for the 1925/26 season. After the season was over, the NHL bought the PCHL for $258,000 and distributed the player contracts among four new expansion teams—the New York Rangers, Chicago Blackhawks, Detroit Cougars, and Pittsburgh Pirates.

The Depression laid a number of NHL franchises low, and by 1942, the NHL was back down to six teams—the Montreal Canadiens, Detroit Red Wings, Toronto Maple Leafs, Chicago Blackhawks, Boston Bruins, and New York Rangers. The NHL lineup stayed this way for 26 years, through the 1966/67 season. In 1967, the NHL added six expansion teams—Los Angeles Kings, Philadelphia Flyers, St. Louis Blues, Minnesota North Stars, Pittsburgh Penguins, and Oakland Seals—for an expansion fee of $2 million each. The Buffalo Sabres and Vancouver Canucks were added in 1970, for a $6 million fee, and the Atlanta Flames came into the league in 1972, again for $6 million.

In the face of all this expansion, it might be thought that the prospects for a rival league in hockey were not all that favorable, but nonetheless, in 1972, a rival hockey league came onto the scene, the World Hockey Association, organized by Gary Davidson and Dennis Murphy. The WHA played for seven seasons, 1972–1979, with franchise histories as shown in Table 8.10. Of the 16 different franchises that made up the WHA during its history, 4 survived to become members of the NHL from 1979 on, 10 went broke before 1979, and 2 (Birmingham and Cincinnati) survived to the end of the WHA and were compensated for not joining the NHL.

It is clear from Table 8.10 that the WHA game plan was to locate franchises in the medium-size Canadian cities lacking NHL franchises (Winnipeg, Edmonton, Ottawa, and Quebec) and in the largest U.S. markets (New York, Los Angeles, Chicago, Philadelphia, and Boston), where it was in direct competition with the NHL. In addition, WHA franchises were located in a couple of smaller U.S. cities—Houston and Cleveland—where there was no NHL competition, and one, St. Paul, where there was NHL competition just across the river. WHA franchises in

Table 8.10

Franchise Histories, World Hockey Association, 1972/73–1978/79

1972/73	1973/74	1974/75	1975/76	1976/77	1977/78	1978/79	1979/80–
New England	New England	New England	New England	New England	New England	New England	NHL
Philadelphia	Vancouver	Vancouver	Calgary	Calgary	Out	Out	Out
New York	New York	New Jersey	San Diego	San Diego	San Diego	Out	Out
Cleveland	Cleveland	Cleveland	Cleveland	Out	Out	Out	Out
Quebec	Quebec	Quebec	Quebec	Quebec	Quebec	Quebec	NHL
Ottawa	Toronto	Toronto	Toronto	Birmingham	Birmingham	Birmingham	Out
Chicago	Chicago	Chicago	Out	Out	Out	Out	Out
Minnesota	Minnesota	Minnesota	Minnesota/out	Minnesota/out	Out	Out	Out
Alberta	Edmonton	Edmonton	Edmonton	Edmonton	Edmonton	Edmonton	NHL
Winnipeg	Winnipeg	Winnipeg	Winnipeg	Winnipeg	Winnipeg	Winnipeg	NHL
Los Angeles	Los Angeles	Michigan/Baltimore	Out	Out	Out	Out	Out
Houston	Houston	Houston	Houston	Houston	Houston	Out	Out
Expansion Teams							
		Indianapolis	Indianapolis	Indianapolis	Indianapolis	Indianapolis/out	Out
		Phoenix	Phoenix	Phoenix	Out	Out	Out
			Denver/Ottawa	Out	Out	Out	Out
			Cincinnati	Cincinnati	Cincinnati	Cincinnati	Out

Source: Pro and Amateur Hockey Guide, 1972–1979 (St. Louis: Sporting News, annual).
Notes: Minnesota disbanded in midseason in 1975/76 and in 1976/77; Indianapolis disbanded in midseason in 1978/79, and Ottawa disbanded in midseason in 1975/76.

the large U.S. markets found it impossible to compete with their in-town NHL rivals, so all of the franchises eventually moved. Attempts to break into the big-city Canadian market, through moves to Toronto and Vancouver, also failed. The survivors of the WHA-NHL war were the medium-size Canadian teams—the Winnipeg Jets, Quebec Nordiques, and Edmonton Oilers—along with the Hartford Whalers.

One problem that the WHA faced in breaking into the hockey market was the control over players exercised by the NHL. Professional hockey, especially in the 1970s, was organized on the model of organized baseball, with an elaborate system of minor leagues and ties to amateur hockey associations. As a practical matter, essentially every decent hockey player in Canada or the United States over the age of 18 was under contract, directly or indirectly, to the NHL. The consequence was that WHA teams went after players under NHL reserve contracts, and the first years of the WHA-NHL war involved a lot of court cases. The WHA ended up signing some star players from the NHL, including Bobby Hull, Gary Cheevers, J. C. Tremblay, Derek Sanderson, John McKenzie, and Gordy Howe. A survey of NHL players signed by the WHA in 1972 indicated that the average salary paid was $53,000, as compared to an average salary of $31,000 per NHL player for the 1971/72 season; thus the WHA might have accounted for something like a 65 percent increase in player salaries in the first year.

Of the 246 players signed by the WHA for the 1972/73 season, 76 had played under NHL contracts in the previous season, 35 were amateurs, and the remainder were minor league players. The minor leaguers were under contract to teams owned or controlled by NHL teams; thus roughly 85 percent of the players making up the rosters of WHA teams in the first year of play had been under reserve clause contracts in the previous season. The fact that 50 of the WHA players signed had been NHL regulars in the previous season gives some indication of the impact of the WHA on the quality player market for NHL teams.

Table 8.11 gives the attendance records of WHA teams. The one striking success story from the point of view of attendance is that of the Edmonton Oilers, reflecting the drawing power of Wayne Gretzky, of course. The New England (Hartford) franchise survived because it became a community team, owned and supported by leading Hartford businesspeople. Winnipeg's story is similar; after the first few years of operation, the team became a city-subsidized enterprise, and to some extent the same was true of the Minnesota Fighting Saints. The Fighting Saints established a record of sorts by having a franchise disbanded two years in a row in midseason. The team also exhibited an admirable disregard for the the idea that sports is a very serious business, by making one of their draft choices in the first WHA draft a 35-year-old ex-

Table 8.11
Per-Game Attendance, WHA, 1972/73–1978/79

Team	1972/73	1973/74	1974/75	1975/76	1976/77	1977/78	1978/79
New England	6,575	5,976	7,921	9,205	8,980	8,578	7,028
Philadelphia/	4,414	—	—	—	—	—	—
Vancouver/	—	9,149	7,656	—	—	—	—
Calgary	—	—	—	4,948	4,313	—	—
New York/	5,868	4,618	—	—	—	—	—
New Jersey/	—	1,946	—	—	—	—	—
San Diego	—	—	6,090	6,248	5,974	—	—
Cleveland	5,220	6,215	6,931	6,228	—	—	—
Quebec	6,884	7,887	10,450	9,372	8,952	8,814	8,835
Ottawa/	3,214	—	—	—	—	—	—
Toronto/	—	3,968	10,454	9,033	—	—	—
Birmingham	—	—	—	—	8,347	8,476	6,271
Chicago	4,631	4,946	3,167	—	—	—	—
Minnesota	5,860	6,682	8,063	8,396[a]	6,211[a]	—	—
Alberta/	3,573	—	—	—	—	—	—
Edmonton	—	4,322	10,699	7,756	8,651	10,235	11,255
Winnipeg	6,060	6,488	8,639	8,826	8,478	9,470	8,731
Los Angeles	6,003	5,219	—	—	—	—	—
Michigan/	—	—	2,938	—	—	—	—
Baltimore	—	—	3,593	—	—	—	—
Houston	4,688	6,571	6,796	9,217	8,868	7,324	—
EXPANSION TEAMS							
Indianapolis	—	—	7,975	10,190	9,258	6,915	6,370[a]
Phoenix	—	—	7,452	6,602	6,893	—	—
Denver/	—	—	—	3,645	—	—	—
Ottawa	—	—	—	8,906[a]	—	—	—
Cincinnati	—	—	—	7,894	8,009	7,156	7,028
WHA avg.	5,247	5,849	7,528	7,822	7,794	8,267	8,108
NHL avg.	13,743	13,848	13,224	12,644	11,894	11,842	11,408

Source: Game summaries in *Sporting News.*
[a]Franchise abandoned in midseason.

Olympic hockey player named Wendell Anderson. At the time, Anderson was holding down a job as governor of the state of Minnesota, and he reluctantly concluded that he would be unable to suit up with the Saints.

The regional nature of the demand for hockey is indicated by the difference in attendance figures for Canadian and U.S. cities. Quebec, Winnipeg, and Edmonton rather consistently outdrew the league average over the history of the WHA. Houston found that even with a lineup containing Gordy Howe and his kids, it still couldn't make a go of hockey in Texas.

When the WHA was first formed, the announced policy of the league was to survive as an independent hockey league. By the end of the 1977/78 season, it was clear that this was an unachievable objective. In May 1978, WHA owners approved an amendment to the WHA constitution to permit individual teams to leave the league to join the NHL. Over the next year, there were discussions between WHA and NHL owners about merging the leagues, and about admissions of individual WHA teams. As in the biblical story, three times the WHA applied for a kind of merger, and thrice the NHL turned the WHA down.

The last rejection occurred in March 1979, as the WHA was completing its last season. Outraged fans in Winnipeg, Quebec, and Edmonton announced a boycott of Molson beer after the Montreal Canadiens, owned by Molson, voted against admitting those teams. In Quebec City, there was a bomb threat against the local Molson brewery, and in Winnipeg, someone fired a bullet through the front door of the Molson brewery. One week later, the NHL reconsidered its vote, agreeing to admit the Winnipeg Jets, Quebec Nordiques, Edmonton Oilers, and Hartford Whalers as NHL members, and also agreeing to allow Edmonton to retain title to Wayne Gretzky, something that had been a major stumbling block in the earlier discussions. Each of the WHA teams going into the NHL had to pay a $6 million entrance fee; in addition, the teams paid $1.5 million each (a total of $6 million) as compensation to the Cincinnati and Birmingham teams, which had survived the 1978/79 season, but which did not move into the NHL.

Thus the surviving WHA teams paid $7.5 million each to join the NHL. In addition, it has been estimated that the typical WHA team lost roughly $1 million per year during the seven years of the WHA-NHL war, although of course more of such losses were suffered by teams that went out of business than by the survivors. Once again, as in the case of the ABA, it appears that, in hindsight, the decision to invest in a WHA franchise was not a money-making one. One exception, however, is Peter Pocklington, who bought into the Edmonton franchise late in the WHA-NHL war, avoiding most of the earlier losses and in effect obtaining an NHL franchise for a bargain price.

The impact of the WHA on the 1991 list of 22 NHL teams includes the four teams that came into the NHL in 1979. It also includes the New York Islanders, a franchise that was created by the NHL in a direct attempt to forestall a WHA franchise in Long Island. Thus 5 of the 22 teams in the NHL are in operation because of the one rival hockey league in the history of the sport.

1. Chris von der Ahe, one of the founders of the American Association (1882–1891), and owner of the AA St. Louis Browns. His team, starring player-manager Charles Comiskey, won four straight AA pennants (1885–1888). National Baseball Library, Cooperstown, N.Y.

John M. Ward, Capt. New York B. B. Club.

Newsboy   **NEW YORK.**

2. John Montgomery Ward, during his playing days with the NL New York Giants. Ward organized the Players League (1890) as a rival league to the NL and AA, but he later became an NL owner (Boston Braves), and ended his career in baseball as lawyer for the NL. National Baseball Library, Cooperstown, N.Y.

3. The "Old Roman," Charles Comiskey, Chicago White Sox owner (*left*), with Ban Johnson, longtime president of the AL (*right*). These two were co-founders of the AL and close friends during the early years of the league, but they became implacable and irreconcilable enemies later on. National Baseball Library, Cooperstown, N.Y.

4. Judge Kenesaw Mountain Landis, showing the pitching form that earned him a regular job of throwing out the first ball to start a new baseball season. National Baseball Library, Cooperstown, N.Y.

5. Colonel Jacob Ruppert, owner of the New York Yankees (*center*), with Miller Huggins, Yankee manager (*left*), and Frank Chance, Boston Red Sox manager (*right*), at the opening of Yankee Stadium in 1923. National Baseball Library, Cooperstown, N.Y.

6. Red Grange (*right*), with his manager, C. C. "Cash and Carry" Pyle (*center*), arriving in New York in September 1926 for the premiere showing of his first (and possibly his last) film. The two stayed in town for the rest of the year as co-owners of the AFL New York Yankees. UPI/ Bettman

7. Babe Ruth (*left*) and Yankee owner Jacob Ruppert (*right*) in 1930 at the signing of the first "mega-contract" in baseball. Ruth was paid the then incredible sum of $80,000 for the 1930-1931 seasons. National Baseball Library, Cooperstown, N.Y.

8. Stan Kostka, hard-driving fullback for Bernie Bierman's 1934 national champion Minnesota Gophers. The bidding war for Kotska in the 1935 NFL preseason led to the creation of the NFL college draft the next year. University of Minnesota Archives

9. The young, irrepressible Bill Veeck in 1943, during his salad days, as the happy-go-lucky owner of the minor league Milwaukee Brewers. Judge Landis seems to be looking down disapprovingly from the picture on the wall, and with good reason! National Baseball Library, Cooperstown, N.Y.

10. Ben Lindheimer (*center*), the financial angel of the All American Football Conference (1946–1949) and owner of the AAFC L.A. Dons, with Dons coach Dud DeGroot (*left*), and Dons general manager Harry M. Thayer (*right*). Department of Special Collections, University Research Library, UCLA

11. That's Branch Rickey, president of the Brooklyn Dodgers, at bat in a 1949 photo taken at the annual baseball writers' outing, with Burt Shotton, Dodger manager, catching, and Leo Durocher, manager of the hated N.Y. Giants, calling the balls and strikes. National Baseball Library, Cooperstown, N.Y.

12. Walter O'Malley, longtime owner of the Dodgers, with his ever-present cigar in place, going over the day's receipts in his office in the spanking new Dodger Stadium in Los Angeles. Department of Special Collections, University Research Library, UCLA

13. "Papa Bear" George Halas, the patriarch of the NFL, at a Bears-Rams game in the early 1960s, during his final stint as coach of the Bears. Department of Special Collections, University Research Library, UCLA

14. Red Auerbach (*right*), the legendary coach of the Boston Celtics, talking things over with Fred Schaus (*left*), then coach of the Los Angeles Lakers. This photograph was taken in the early 1960s when Auerbach's Celtics were midway in their string of nine successive NBA titles. Department of Special Collections, University Research Library, UCLA

15. The unbelievably young, wide-eyed, and innocent-looking Pete Rozelle, in the early 1960s, when he was learning the ropes in his new job as commissioner of the NFL. Players and even some owners would learn that appearance could be deceiving. Department of Special Collections, University Research Library, UCLA

16. Al Davis, managing general partner of the Oakland Raiders (which later moved to Los Angeles), during the AFL-NFL war of the 1960s. Davis ranks as the most successful as well as the most controversial owner in the history of the NFL. Department of Special Collections, University Research Library, UCLA

17. Gary Davidson (*left*), the first president of the American Basketball Association, with George Mikan (*center*), the first commissioner of the ABA, at the February 1967 news conference in New York, where the league was unveiled to the public. UPI/Bettman

18. Marvin Miller, director of the Major League Players Association, in 1972, when he was negotiating the first labor agreement in baseball, which included salary arbitration. Miller ws the most successful labor leader in the history of pro team sports, and literally revolutionized the economics of baseball. National Baseball Library, Cooperstown, N.Y.

19. Ed Garvey, the longtime director of the NFL Players Association, in the familiar role of carrying a picket sign at yet another NFL player strike, this one being the pre-season strike of 1974. UPI/Bettman

20. George Steinbrenner (*right*), the stormy owner of the Yankees, with another popular favorite of the public and the media, Roy Cohn of Senator Joe McCarthy fame, at a 1978 victory celebration for the Yankees. UPI/Bettman

Chapter 9

Rival Leagues:
The Great Football Wars

THE NFL has a long history of dealing with rival leagues, dating back to 1926, when the NFL engaged in an interleague war with the first American Football League. The story of the NFL's off and on again battles with rival leagues given here follows closely the account given in Quirk and Saposnik (1992).

The NFL began its existence as the American Professional Football Association, organized in 1920 by George Halas and several other owner-players of Midwest pro football teams. The first president of the APFA was Jim Thorpe, then in the twilight of his career, playing for the Canton Bulldogs. In 1922, the league was reorganized as the National Football League, with Joe Carr, the owner of the Columbus Panhandles, elected president of the league, a position he held into the late 1930s.

In its earliest years, the NFL was a strange organization, consisting of a large number of small-town teams from the Midwest and a few big-city teams, with only a couple of clearly profitable teams—the Chicago Bears and the Frankford Yellowjackets among them—and, from Halas's recollections, the Bears were lucky to end up with $1,000 in profits for a season, in the early 1920s. There are major data problems with the early history of the NFL; league records are almost nonexistent, and newspaper reports, even in league cities, are sketchy at best. League-wide attendance records date only from 1934, and reliable attendance data for most teams are available only from the 1960s on.

Reorganization of the APFA in 1922 into the NLF reflected unhappiness of many owners with the loose arrangements of the APFA. League schedules were haphazard and subject to change at a moment's notice, collecting the visitor's share was an adventure in many league cities, and territorial rights were somewhat nebulous. For example, George Halas moved his Decatur Staleys into Chicago after the 1920 season as the Chicago Staleys (later the Chicago Bears) at a time when two other

APFA teams were located in Chicago—the Racine (Street) Cardinals (later the Chicago Cardinals), and the Chicago Tigers—without paying any compensation to either of these teams.

Things changed in the NFL under Joe Carr, who acted to establish enforceable territorial rights for franchise owners. In 1925, the Pottsville Maroons won the NFL championship, and then played an unauthorized exhibition game in Philadelphia against a team of ex-Notre Dame players (including the Four Horsemen) on a date when the NFL Frankford Yellowjackets of Philadelphia were playing a home game. Pottsville ignored several warnings from Carr. Because of its violation of Frankford's territorial rights, Pottsville had its 1925 NFL championship stripped from it (the Chicago Cardinals were awarded the title), and Pottsville also lost its NFL franchise.

Based on scattered newspaper reports collected by Joe Horrigan of the Pro Football Hall of Fame, Table 9.1 gives estimates of per-game home and away attendance for a number of NFL teams in the period 1922–1924.

Football salaries in the early years of the NFL ran from $75 to $100 per game, and the average ticket price was $1 or less. The standard game contract provided for a guaranteed payment to the visiting team ($1,000 or thereabouts in the early 1920s) against a visitor's cut of 40 percent of the gate, after deducting 15 percent for rental and field maintenance. The typical NFL roster was about 15 players. Add in some transportation expenses and stadium rentals, and it is clear from the attendance data in Table 9.1 that most teams in the NFL were hobby enterprises in the early years. The situation hadn't changed all that much by 1926, when the first AFL came on the scene. It was not the profitability of the NFL that led to the entry of a new league, but the drawing power of a single individual, the Galloping Ghost, old number 77 from the Fighting Illini, Red Grange.

AFL I, 1926

Just a week or so before the Pottsville incident, Halas had signed Red Grange to a contract with the Bears, one day after Grange had completed his college eligibility. Grange was arguably the most charismatic football player in the history of the sport, and was a box office sensation. The Bears played two league and six exhibition games in 11 days following the Grange signing, including one game at the Polo Grounds against the New York Giants that drew 64,300 fans, an NFL record that held for 20 years. This was at a time when the typical NFL game was drawing around 5,000 (the Bears averaged around 10,000 at Wrigley

Table 9.1
Estimated NFL Attendance per Game, 1922–1924

Team	1922 Home	1922 Away	1923 Home	1923 Away	1924 Home	1924 Away
Akron	2,500	3,500	—	4,500	5,000	4,100
Buffalo	—	—	3,500	—	4,300	—
Canton	2,750	7,000	5,000	12,600	—	—
Chicago Bears	7,000	4,800	6,700	4,500	9,800	5,000
Chicago Cardinals	4,600	2,500	4,500	13,,500	4,200	12,000
Cleveland	—	—	17,000	3,500	4,000	8,500
Columbus	—	3,200	15,000	—	2,750	—
Dayton	3,000	3,000	—	3,500	4,000	3,600
Duluth	—	—	3,000	5,000	2,600	2,600
Evansville	—	—	—	—	—	—
Green Bay	4,000	4,250	3,250	4,500	3,500	4,200
Hammond	—	2,000	—	2,600	—	2,800
Kansas City	—	—	—	—	3,000	2,800
Kenosha	—	—	—	—	600	—
Louisville	1,200	2,750	2,000	—	—	—
Milwaukee	6,600	2,750	3,150	4,300	3,000	3,600
Minneapolis	4,000	3,000	1,200	3,000	—	2,750
Oorang	—	5,700	—	2,300	—	—
Racine	3,700	5,500	4,300	3,600	2,800	5,800
Rochester	—	—	—	2,500	1,200	2,500
Rock Island	4,100	8,000	3,000	6,000	3,700	7,250
St. Louis	—	—	2,150	2,800	—	—
Toledo	3,200	5,000	5,000	5,000	—	—

Sources: Estimates based on two or three games per team for which attendance data were published in local newspapers; data collected by Joe Horrigan, curator of the NFL Hall of Fame.

Field). After the NFL season, Grange and the Bears went on an exhibition tour around the country, playing local pro teams and drawing large crowds. Grange and his manager, C. C. "Cash and Carry" Pyle, had arranged a contract with the Bears under which they ended up making over $250,000 during and after the 1925 season.

In 1926, Grange and Pyle offered the Bears a deal under which Grange would sign for a share of the gate at Bears games, along with a one-third interest in the team. Halas and Dutch Sternaman, co-owners of the Bears, rejected the offer. Grange and Pyle then obtained a lease on Yankee Stadium, and petitioned the NFL for a New York franchise. According to newspaper accounts at the time, 19 of the 20 NFL owners were in favor of the Grange-Pyle petition, because of the gate attraction Grange represented. The dissenting owner was, of course, Tim Mara, owner of the New York Giants. Under NFL rules, Mara had veto power over entry into his territory, and he exercised the veto. Grange and Pyle responded by forming the first rival league in pro football, the original American Football League.

Table 9.2 lists the teams in the NFL and AFL I, in order of the population rank of their cities in the 1920 census. (Both the Los Angeles teams featured West Coast players, but were based in Chicago, and played all of their games on the road. Pottsville, which had been expelled from the NFL after the 1925 season, was enticed back into the league for 1926 to preclude a move by the AFL to recruit Pottsville as a member.)

Basically, AFL I decided to compete directly with the NFL in the largest city markets, and to "fill the gaps" in the medium-size-city markets that were accessible with existing transportation systems. In contrast, the NFL remained a hodge-podge of large- and medium-size-city teams, together with a number of small town teams.

The *New York Times* reported scattered attendance data for New York teams for 1926. Per-game attendance was 19,083 for the AFL New York Yankees, 6,667 for the AFL Brooklyn Horsemen, 12,833 for the

Table 9.2
NFL and AFL I, 1926

NFL	AFL I
New York Giants (1)	New York Yankees (1)
Brooklyn Lions (1)	Brooklyn Horsemen (1)
Chicago Bears (2)	Chicago Bulls (2)
Chicago Cardinals (2)	
Frankford Yellow Jackets (3)	Philadelphia Quakers (3)
Detroit Panthers (4)	
	Cleveland Panthers (4)
	Boston Bulldogs (7)
Buffalo Rangers (11)	
Milwaukee Badgers (14)	
	Newark Bears (16)
Kansas City Cowboys (19)	
OTHERS: Pottsville, Akron, Canton, Los Angeles, Duluth, Hartford, Dayton, Racine, Green Bay, Hammond, Louisville, Providence, Columbus	Others: Rock Island, Los Angeles

Source: Official Encyclopedia of Football.
Note: Numbers in parentheses are population ranks in 1920 census.

NFL New York Giants, and 8,600 for the NFL Brooklyn Lions. The Giants allowed the Brooklyn NFL team to play in New York under a special arrangement, financial details unknown. In an unusual move, the AFL Horsemen merged with the NFL Lions midway through the season, with the Horsemen dropping out of the AFL.

In head-to-head competition between the Yankees and the Giants, the Yankees outdrew the Giants every Sunday almost two to one, until the last game of the season, when the Yankees drew only 2,500 fans, with Grange on the bench with an injury. In part because of Grange's injury, the Yankees were beaten out for the AFL title by the Philadelphia Quakers, the only other AFL team to survive the entire 1926 season—every other AFL team went bankrupt before the season ended. According to the *Official NFL Encyclopedia*, the Yankees lost $100,000 during 1926, while the Giants lost $40,000. An indication of the AFL's problems is given by the fact that a week after the NFL season ended, the Giants, who had tied for sixth in the regular NFL season with an 8–4–1 record, hosted the AFL champion, the Philadelphia Quakers, at a game at the Polo Grounds, which the Giants won, 31–0, drawing only 5,000 fans.

The AFL disbanded after the 1926 season, but the NFL then agreed to admit Grange and the Yankees as an expansion team for the 1927 season. The agreement involved an unknown payment to Mara and the Giants, together with a proviso that the Yankees had to play 13 of their 16 games on the road. Grange was injured once again early in the 1927 season, and the Yankees ended up 7–8–1, and went out of business after the 1927 season. Grange was out of football in 1928 with his injury, and then returned to the Bears for the remainder of his pro career, retiring after the 1934 season.

One important consequence of the NFL-AFL I war was the decision taken by Carr and the dominant teams of the league to convert the NFL into a big-city league, eliminating almost all of the small-town members. Horrigan (1983) reports that under the Carr plan, selected small-town franchise owners were given the choice of dropping out of the league or suspending their franchises. Retiring from the league meant that the team would get its pro rata share of the NFL treasury, and the affected franchise would be sold by July 7, 1928 or canceled. The effect of the change was to pare the league down to 12 teams for the 1927 season.

It appears clear that the first football war arose on the NFL side because of the veto power exercised by the Giants, combined with the inability of the NFL to find a way to compensate the Giants for the losses they would suffer from expansion into their territory by the Grange-led Yankees. On the AFL side, Grange's drawing power in New York was the catalyst for the league, but there was a miscalculation as to the ability of one man, Red Grange, to carry an entire league. If Grange had not been injured, the Yankees might have broken even for the season, but the other teams (excluding the Quakers) were so marginal that they went broke even before Grange was injured. The weakness of the AFL ended the war before large costs were incurred by NFL teams, but the AFL war brought home to NFL owners the potential for problems with their underfinanced small-town members, and certainly played a critical role in the restructuring of the NFL into a big-city league.

AFL II, 1936–1937; and AFL III, 1940–1941

Divisional play was adopted by the NFL beginning with the 1934 season. By 1936, when the next rival league, AFL II, came onto the scene, the NFL had a nine-team league. Table 9.3 lists the teams in the NFL and AFL II in 1936; the numbers in parentheses indicate city population rank according to the 1930 census.

Once again, the rival league placed teams in direct competition with the NFL in New York City, and added competition in Boston and Pittsburgh, with Cleveland filling in a medium-size-city gap in the NFL. The new league used almost exclusively newly recruited ex-collegians, but there were a few ex-NFL players signed, including Michigan star Harry Newman, who was also a co-owner of the AFL Brooklyn team, and Sid Gillman. The most famous NFL player to move to AFL II was Ken Strong, a Hall of Famer for the Giants, who was suspended by the NFL for five

Table 9.3
NFL and AFL II, 1936

NFL	AFL II
New York Giants (1)	New York Yankees (1)
Brooklyn Dodgers (1)	Brooklyn Tigers (1)
Chicago Bears (2)	
Chicago Cardinals (2)	
Philadelphia Eagles (3)	
Detroit Lions (4)	
	Cleveland Rams (6)
Boston Redskins (9)	Boston Shamrocks (9)
Pittsburgh Pirates (11)	Pittsburgh Americans (11)
Green Bay Packers (nr)	Rochester Braves (23)

Source: As in table 9.2.
Note: Numbers in parentheses are population ranks in 1930 census.

years for jumping to AFL II, and who actually didn't move back on the Giants roster until the 1939 season.

Maher and Gill (1981) collected data on attendance for AFL II teams in their *The Second AFL Fact Book, 1936–37*. In Table 9.4, their data are compared with per-game attendance for NFL teams, based on reports from the *New York Times*.

In head-to-head confrontations, the AFL teams were not in the same ballpark with the NFL, except for the Yankees and Shamrocks in 1936. While the box office figures indicate that every team in AFL II lost money (with the possible exception of the Bulldogs), AFL II did have an impact on the NFL. As noted in earlier chapters, after the 1936 season, the NFL took in the Cleveland Rams as an expansion team for a fee of $10,000, and George Marshall moved his Boston Redskins team to Washington.

AFL II replaced the Cleveland Rams in 1937 with the Los Angeles Bulldogs, a powerhouse team that had beaten the Philadelphia Eagles in an exhibition game during the 1936 season. Unfortunately, the Bulldogs were so much better than the rest of the AFL (ending with a record of 9–0–0), that no other team in the league had a winning record in 1937, and the lack of competitive balance certainly had something to do with the fact that the league expired after the 1937 season.

It might be asked why the owners of teams in AFL II didn't file an anti-trust suit against the NFL for recruiting the Rams after the 1936 season. As noted in Chapter 8, this was the strategy employed by the ABL in 1961 when the NBA began negotiating with the Cleveland Pipers for an expan-

Table 9.4
Average Per-Game Attendance, NFL and AFL II, 1936 and 1937

NFL	1936	1937	AFL II	1936	1937
N.Y. Giants	23,192	35,563	N.Y. Yankees	17,280	2,500
Brooklyn Dodgers	15,143	18,300	Brooklyn Tigers	4,700	6,000
Chicago Bears	21,447	27,393	Cleveland Rams	10,000	—
Chicago Cardinals	6,500	8,618	Rochester Braves	2,600	—
Philadelphia Eagles	14,623	11,921	Cincinnati Bengals	—	7,417
Detroit Lions	18,000	20,800	Los Angeles Bulldogs	—	13,200
Boston Redskins	8,571	—	Boston Shamrocks	7,800	4,875
Washington Redskins	—	20,200			
Pittsburgh Pirates	18,700	14,159	Pittsburgh Americans	2,500	5,000
Green Bay Packers	11,100	15,442			
Cleveland Rams	—	11,000			
League avg.	15,111	17,510		8,384	8,075

Sources: Game summaries in the *New York Times;* Maher and Gill 1981.

sion franchise. But the ABL suit occurred only after *Radovich v. NFL*, 352 U.S. 445 (1957), which established that the NFL (and, by implication, the NBA) did not share the immunity from antitrust prosecution that baseball enjoys. In 1936, the best legal opinion probably was that all sports were covered by the baseball exemption. Moreover, even if a suit had been filed, the outcome in *American Football League v. National Football League*, 205 F. Supp. 60 (C.D. Md. 1962), 323 F.2d 124 (4th Cir. 1963) (discussed below), suggests that success in the courts for AFL II would have been questionable.

AFL III operated during the 1940 and 1941 seasons, with a matchup against the NFL, as shown in Table 9.5. The population rankings in parentheses are according to the 1940 census.

Except for the New York entry, AFL III avoided direct competition with NFL teams, and ended up in several marginal markets as a consequence. The six-team league of 1940 dwindled to a four-team league in 1941, and was treated in both years by the *New York Times* as a minor league. The scattered attendance data reported by the *Times* are shown in Table 9.6. The *Times* actually gave more coverage to the minor league American Football Association than it gave to AFL III.

The surge in attendance for the New York AFL III entry in 1941 resulted from the midseason signings by new owner William Cox of two big-name ex-college stars: Tom Harmon, Michigan's Heisman Trophy winner in 1940, and John Kimbrough of Texas A & M, the runner-up for the Trophy in 1940. Kimbrough stayed with the Americans for the rest of the season, but Harmon played only one game, and then returned to Ann Arbor to his

Table 9.5
NFL and AFL III, 1940 and 1941

NFL	AFL III
N.Y. Giants (1)	N.Y. Yankees/Americans (1)
Brooklyn Dodgers (1)	
Chicago Bears (2)	
Chicago Cardinals (2)	
Philadelphia Eagles (3)	
Detroit Lions (4)	
Cleveland Rams (5)	Boston Bears (10) (1940 only)
Pittsburgh Steelers (11)	Milwaukee Chiefs (14)
Washington Redskins (13)	Buffalo Indians (15) (1940 only)
Green Bay Packers (nr)	Cincinnati Bengals (18)
	Columbus Bullies (27)

Source: As in table 9.2.
Note: Numbers in parentheses are population ranks in 1940 census.

Table 9.6
Average Per-Game Attendance, NFL and AFL III, 1940 and 1941

NFL	1940	1941	AFL III	1940	1941
N.Y. Giants	35,377	35,674	N.Y. Yankees	5,652	
Brooklyn Dodgers	24,351	19,991	N.Y. Americans		14,936
Chicago Bears	29,074	29,424	Boston Bears	7,625	—
Chicago Cardinals	15,714	16,229	Milwaukee Chiefs	5,000	—
Philadelphia Eagles	17,210	22,509	Buffalo Indians	10,055	—
Detroit Lions	22,993	23,752	Cincinnati Bengals	—	—
Cleveland Rams	16,750	15,242	Columbus Bullies	—	6,661
Pittsburgh Steelers	19,247	17,678			
Washington Redskins	32,240	33,498			
Green Bay Packers	17,752	17,121			

Source: Game summaries in the *New York Times.*

regular job as a radio sports announcer. It was the one move of the AFL to attain major league status, and it wasn't enough—average per-game attendance of the Americans was below that of any NFL team, and the other AFL III franchises were clearly submarginal.

While AFL II led to expansion of the NFL into Cleveland and the move of the Boston NFL franchise to Washington, the league did not constitute a credible threat to the NFL. Homer Marshman, owner of the Cleveland Rams, obtained an NFL expansion franchise for $10,000, which he sold four years later to Dan Reeves for $125,000. Other owners of AFL II teams (except possibly for the Bulldogs) certainly lost money in the enterprise. AFL III was, in fact, a minor league parading as a major league, and had no impact on the NFL at all. In hindsight, AFL II and AFL III were mistakes on the part of the owner-investors in these leagues, overestimating the profit potential of the pro football market.

AAFC, 1946–1949

A league that did pose a credible threat to the NFL was the All American Football Conference, which was in existence for four seasons, 1946 through 1949. The story behind the league goes like this. In 1941, Don Ameche headed a syndicate of Los Angeles investors that petitioned the NFL for an expansion franchise for Buffalo, with the understanding that at some time in the future, the Buffalo team would be moved to Los Angeles. In *Halas by Halas*, George Halas recounts that he voted against the bid by the Ameche group, because "I had promised Charles Bidwill [owner of the Cardinals] that I would back him when Los Angeles opened" (Halas 1979, 205). Thus Bidwill was keeping his options open for the Cardinals, who were barely hanging on in Chicago, and the votes by Bidwill and Halas took care of the Ameche bid.

During the war years, preliminary meetings were held involving various investors concerning organization of a new pro league, with Ben Lindheimer, a Los Angeles financier, the major investor in the project. In 1945, a major development occurred that solidifed support for the league. Dan Topping, owner of the NFL Brooklyn Dodgers, had just purchased the AL New York Yankees, in a deal that involved co-partners Del Webb and Larry McPhail. Topping wanted to move his NFL Brooklyn team into Yankee Stadium, but this would involve an infringement of the New York Giants' territory, and required approval from Tim Mara, owner of the Giants. Mara turned Topping down, apparently fearing competition just across the river from the Polo Grounds. Topping then talked to the Lindheimer group, and reportedly was offered $100,000 to move his team from the NFL to the AAFC.

Topping announced the move of his team, which was a major boost to the credibility of the AAFC. Upon the news of formation of the league, including a franchise in Cleveland with Paul Brown as coach, Dan Reeves went before NFL owners to request permission to move the 1945 league champion Rams to Los Angeles; after agreeing to pay transportation costs for visiting teams to the West Coast, he was allowed to move the team. Thus, as it turned out, the 1941 vote by Halas and Bidwill didn't accomplish anything for the Cardinals at all, but it did get the NFL involved in a major interleague war.

The confrontation between the NFL and AAFC in 1946 is shown in Table 9.7. Once again, the rival league took on the NFL in its big-city markets. The only large cities in the country missing from this lineup were Baltimore (8), St. Louis (9), and Minneapolis-St. Paul (10). In the AAFC roster, the oddball entry was Miami, which had a 1940 SMSA population of 172,000, as compared, say, to Buffalo's 576,000. Miami was really out of place; the team didn't draw flies in the 1946 season, and was replaced by the Baltimore Colts in 1947.

As is the case with most of the rival football leagues, the AAFC used only minimal numbers of ex-NFL players, preferring to stock up with newly graduated ex-collegians, and with ex-servicemen. Of the 625 different players who appeared on AAFC rosters between 1946 and 1949, only 132 (21.1 percent) had any NFL experience, and these were almost exclusively players who had previously been cut by their NFL teams, or had been inactive because of war service. The AAFC developed its own superstars—Otto Graham, Marion Motley, Frankie Albert, Buddy Young—to

Table 9.7
NFL and AAFC, 1946

NFL	AAFC
New York Giants (1)	New York Yankees (1)
	Brooklyn Dodgers (1)
Chicago Bears (2)	Chicago Rockets (2)
Chicago Cardinals (2)	
Philadelphia Eagles (3)	
Detroit Lions (4)	
Los Angeles Rams (5)	Los Angeles Dons (5)
	San Francisco 49ers (6)
	Cleveland Browns (7)
Boston Yanks (11)	
Pittsburgh Steelers (12)	
Washington Redskins (13)	
	Buffalo Bills (15)
Green Bay Packers (nr)	Miami Seahawks (nr)

Sources: As in table 9.2.
Note: Numbers in parentheses are population ranks in 1940 census.

compete with the NFL's Sammy Baugh, Sid Luckman, and Steve Van Buren.

The AAFC more than held its own against the NFL in per-game attendance, as the data in Table 9.8 show. In 1946, the NFL outdrew the AAFC, 1.7 million to 1.4 million, and had about a 27 percent edge in per-game attendance, 31,943 to 24,589. But in the next three years, the AAFC outdrew the NFL on a per-game basis; and in 1947 and 1948, the AAFC actually outdrew the NFL in total attendance. In head-to-head confrontations, the AAFC Yankees outdrew the NFL Giants in 1947, 1948, and 1949, while the AAFC Dons outdrew the NFL Rams in 1947 and 1948, and then were buried when the Rams won the NFL West title in 1949. The Chicago Hornets (originally the Rockets) found themselves unable to compete with the well-established Chicago Bears, the strongest-drawing team in the NFL. Morevoer, the Hornets were unfortunate enough to be playing during one of the few periods in the history of the Chicago Cardinals when that team was also a powerhouse, featuring the "Dream Backfield" of Paul Christman, Charlie Trippi, Marshall Goldberg, and Pat Harder. The Cardinals won the NFL championship in 1947, and then won the Western division title in 1948, before losing a close game, 7–0, to the Eagles for the 1948 NFL championship.

The Cleveland Browns dominated the AAFC on the playing field, and at the box office, as noted in earlier chapters. By the end of the 1949 sea-

Table 9.8
Average Per-Game Attendance, NFL and AAFC, 1946–1949

	1946	1947	1948	1949	4–Yr Avg
NATIONAL FOOTBALL LEAGUE					
New York Giants	58,407	31,696	23,221	23,915	34,310
New York Bulldogs	—	—	11,906	8,001	9,954
Chicago Bears	42,291	38,924	44,438	43,824	42,369
Chicago Cardinals	33,744	35,260	30,203	28,740	31,989
Philadelphia Eagles	26,951	36,655	26,202	27,843	29,413
Detroit Lions	24,730	25,889	18,794	20,121	22,384
Los Angeles Rams	42,820	36,109	32,401	51,555	40,721
Boston Yanks	18,819	20,910	—	—	19,864
Pittsburgh Steelers	29,937	34,654	28,709	24,461	29,440
Washington Redskins	33,567	35,811	32,586	27,852	32,454
Green Bay Packers	22,679	27,737	22,552	17,472	22,610
Avg.	31,493	30,624	27,101	25,086	28,576
ALL-AMERICAN FOOTBALL CONFERENCE					
New York Yankees	27,734	37,916	23,320	24,161	28,283
Brooklyn Dodgers	13,953	11,017	10,356	—	11,775
Chicago Hornets	27,946	19,801	14,783	17,847	20,094
Los Angeles Dons	19,899	43,454	40,050	22,096	31,374
San Francisco 49ers	26,028	35,218	40,883	47,697	37,456
Cleveland Browns	57,138	55,848	45,517	31,580	47,500
Buffalo Bills	16,851	31,001	25,171	26,638	24,915
Miami Seahawks	7,164	—	—	—	7,164
Baltimore Colts	—	28,297	29,244	25,027	27,523
Avg.	24,589	32,819	28,691	26,513	28,153

Sources: AAFC attendance figures are from Grosshandler (1985) and are the official AAFC league attendance figures. NFL attendance figures were compiled from game reports n the *New York Times* and *Los Angeles Times.*

Note: From comments by George Halas (1979), it appears that attendance figures for the L.A. Rams were overstated by as much as 50,000 for certain seasons, and the Bears attendance is also overstated for certain seasons.

son, to all appearances, the AAFC was more than holding its own against the NFL. There were problems, however. The Chicago Hornets were on the verge of bankruptcy. More important was the L.A. situation, where the Rams had outdrawn the Dons, 309,327 to 132,574. The Dons' problems were compounded when Ben Lindheimer suffered a severe heart attack midway through the 1949 season, and was under medical advice to avoid high-stress situations. This helped to precipitate a merger meeting between the two leagues.

While the final merger agreement was highly favorable to the NFL, actually both leagues were eager to bring an end to the war. According to one observer (Vass 1971), the AAFC lost $5 million between 1946 and 1949, and the NFL lost $3 million, with the only profitable teams during the war being the Browns, the Bears, and the Redskins. Other teams were unable to meet the rising cost of signing college players because of the bidding war. For example, Oates (1953) reports that the L.A. Rams lost $161,000 in 1946, $201,500 in 1947, $253,000 in 1948, and $169,000 in 1949. The 1949 loss occurred during a year in which the Rams set a team record for attendance. Despite their impressive attendance records in 1947 and 1948, the L.A. Dons lost a reported $1.7 million over the four-year war, according to Vass (1971).

The agreement ending the AAFC-NFL war was announced on December 8, 1949. Under the agreement, Cleveland, San Francisco, and Baltimore moved from the AAFC to the NFL. The New York Yankees AAFC team was purchased by Ted Collins, owner of the NFL New York Bulldogs, with the Bulldogs' franchise being canceled. The Colts paid $150,000 to George Marshall for invading the territory of the Redskins. James Breuil, owner of the Buffalo Bills, received a 25 percent interest in the Cleveland Browns, and the Bills team was merged with the Browns. The NFL paid an unknown amount to James C. Thompson, owner of the Chicago Hornets, and the Hornets' franchise was canceled. The New York Giants team was allowed to choose six players from the Yankees' roster as compensation for the invasion of the Giants' territory. Lindheimer was offered the chance to become a part-owner of the Rams, but turned this down because of his health problems.

Following the merger, the Browns immediately became the dominant team in the NFL, and have continued to be one of the most successful franchises in sports. The Colts franchise went under a year after the merger, only to be resuscitated when the team's successor, the Dallas Texans, went bankrupt midway through its first season (1951). Once the Colts found Johnny Unitas, that franchise became the most exciting team in the NFL, and a financial success as well. One loser from the merger was the unfortunate Ted Collins, who threw in the towel and disbanded his Yankee team after the 1951 season. Collins managed to own three of the worst-drawing NFL teams in modern history—the Boston Yanks (1944–1947), the New York Bulldogs (1948–1949), and the New York Yanks (1950–1951)—and lost well over $1 million in the process.

What is significant about the merger is that the Dons and the Hornets, who competed directly against existing NFL teams, did not survive the merger, and the Yankees replaced an existing NFL team, so that the merger eliminated the most important direct threats to NFL teams posed by the AAFC. The 49ers and the Browns infringed on no NFL territory, and the Colts paid a bundle to invade the territory of the Redskins.

Once the merger and the shakedown aftermath were accomplished, the NFL experienced a rare period of franchise stability between 1952 and 1960, with no rival leagues around. Oates (1955) reports that the Rams became profitable almost immediately after the merger, breaking even in 1950, and then showing profits of $10,000 in 1951, $150,000 in 1952, $200,000 in 1953, and $250,000 in 1954. The three AAFC teams taken into the NFL survived and ultimately became profitable. While it is possible that if Lindheimer had not had health problems, the AAFC might have achieved a complete merger of the two leagues, à la AFL IV, it is doubtful because of the territorial rights problems in the three biggest cities in the NFL.

AFL IV

In 1960, the fifth and most successful rival league, AFL IV, came on the scene. Between 1950 and 1960, average per-game attendance at NFL games had increased 60 percent, from 25,356 to 40,106, while the number of teams in the league had dropped from 13 to 12. During the 1950s, there had been some discussion of expansion within the NFL, but financial problems for certain franchises (especially the Cardinals and Redskins) and lack of competitive balance had held up any action. George Halas and Art Rooney were the main advocates of expansion, with George Marshall and the Wolfners (owners of the Cardinals) the leaders of the opposition. Under NFL rules at the time, expansion required unanimous agreement by all NFl owners, giving Marshall or the Wolfners veto power over expansion.

By 1959, court records indicate that a majority of NFL owners were in favor of expansion into Houston, Dallas, and Miami, along with either Minneapolis or Buffalo, with expansion to occur between 1960 and 1965. Earlier on, Clint Murchison had tried to buy San Francisco, Washington, and then the Cardinals, to move a team to Dallas, but failed. In 1957, Lamar Hunt had applied to the NFL for an expansion franchise for Dallas and was turned down; in 1958, the Houston Sports Association had applied for a franchise for Houston, and Max Winter, H. P. Skoglund, and Bill Boyer had applied for a franchise for Minneapolis, and both requests had been turned down. NFL Commissioner Bert Bell suggested to each of three applicants that they should buy the Chicago Cardinals and move the team, but negotiations failed in each case.

In 1959, Hunt tried one more time to get an expansion franchise for Dallas, but was informed by Bell that there would be no expansion for the 1960 season. At that point, Hunt began to organize a rival league, AFL IV. After getting commitments for AFL teams in Houston and Denver, in early August of 1959, Hunt announced the formation of the AFL. In October 1959, the NFL conducted a straw vote, in which all NFL owners except for Marshall voted to add two teams in 1960, of which one would be in Dallas, to compete directly with Hunt's AFL Dallas team. In early November of 1959, Hunt talked with Halas about an NFL expansion taking in the six owners he had lined up for the AFL, but Halas informed him that the NFL would limit expansion to four teams, and would not accept Denver.

On November 22, 1959, the AFL held its organizational meeting in Minneapolis, with Winter, Skoglund, and Boyer representing the Minnesota entry in the AFL. The Minnesota owners were also continuing to conduct sub rosa negotiations with Halas and the NFL about an expansion franchise. The day of the meeting, the *Minneapolis Star-Journal* printed a wire received from Halas in which he reported that 11 of the 12 owners in the NFL (all except Marshall) had agreed to a proposal to take in Minnesota as an expansion franchise. The news almost broke up the AFL meeting, and led to an announcement by the Metropolitan Stadium Commission of Minnesota that it would withhold approval of a contract for an AFL team until the situation with respect to an NFL team was cleared up. Winter, Skoglund, and Boyer pulled out of the AFL a few weeks later, and the Minnesota AFL franchise was assigned instead to Oakland.

In early January, 1960, the NFL bylaws were amended to require only a 10/12 vote to approve league expansion, while retaining a unanimous vote requirement for adding a team within an existing team's territory. There was one last stumbling block. One member of the Murchison group had acquired the copyright to the Redskins' marching song, "Hail to the Redskins." Near the end of January, that copyright was assigned to George Marshall; following this there was a unanimous vote of NFL owners to admit Dallas as an expansion franchise in 1960 and Minnesota in 1961. The Cardinals also were given approval for a move to St. Louis for the 1960 season. The AFL began operations in the 1960 season, and filed an antitrust suit against the NFL for the actions taken by the NFL with respect to Dallas and Minnesota (*American Football League v. National Football League*, 205 F. Supp. 60 (C.D. Md. 1962), 323 F.2d 124 (4th Cir. 1963)).

The lineups of the two leagues at the beginning of the AFL IV-NFL war are shown in Table 9.9. The smaller number in parentheses indicates the city's population rank, and the larger is the city's population in thousands, both according to the 1960 census.

AFL IV was unusual in that the league was originally organized to place teams in a few medium-size cities—Dallas, Houston, and the Twin Cities—rather than being oriented toward entry into the New York-Chicago-

Table 9.9
NFL and AFL IV, 1960

NFL	AFL IV
New York Giants (1) (16,174)	New York Titans (1) (16,174)
Los Angeles Rams (2) (7,751)	Los Angeles Chargers (2) (7,751)
Chicago Bears (3) (6,934)	
Philadelphia Eagles (4) (5,130)	
Detroit Lions (5) (4,223)	
San Francisco 49ers (6) (3,723)	Oakland Raiders (6) (3,723)
	Boston Patriots (7) (3,357)
Cleveland Browns (8) (2,732)	
Pittsburgh Steelers (9) (2,574)	
Washington Redskins (10) (2,214)	
St. Louis Cardinals (11) (2,161)	
Baltimore Colts (12) (1,820)	
Dallas Cowboys (13) (1,715)	Dallas Texans (13) (1,715)
	Houston Oilers (15) (1,570)
	Buffalo Bills (17) (1,306)
	Denver Broncos (24) (934)
Green Bay Packers (nr)	

Source: As in table 9.2.
Note: First number in parentheses is population rank of SMSA in 1960 census, and second number in parentheses is actual SMSA population (in thousands) in 1960 census.

Los Angeles markets. Once it was decided to operate a rival league, though, it became critical to enter the big-city markets partly because of television considerations, so AFL teams were located in New York and Los Angeles. The L.A. franchise ran into difficulties in its first year, and moved to San Diego the next year. Lamar Hunt's Dallas franchise was successful on the playing field but it was clear after a couple of years that Dallas couldn't support two teams, and the AFL Dallas team moved to Kansas City after the 1962 season. The AFL New York Titans also ran into difficulties, which were resolved when owner Harry Wismer sold out, and when Joe Namath was drafted.

A relevant fact concerning AFL IV is that this was the first rival league where TV income played a critical role in the survival of the league. There was an unusual situation with respect to TV in 1960, when AFL IV began operations. The NFL was under a court- ordered injunction (see *United States v. NFL*, 116 F. Supp. 310 (1953), 196 F. Supp. 445 (1961)) prohibiting it from signing a league-wide contract with any TV network. This was at a time when organized baseball had signed "Game of the Week" network contracts, and when the AFL had signed a contract with ABC paying roughly $2 million per year ($250,000 per team per year) for the first five years of league play. NFL teams operated in 1960 and 1961 under local TV contracts, with income levels ranging in 1960 from $105,000 (Green Bay) to $340,000 (New York), and in 1961 from $120,000 (Green Bay) to $370,000 (New York), averaging about 15 percent more per team than the AFL. In 1962, Congress passed an act exempting league-wide TV agreements in sports from the antitrust laws, and the NFL then signed a contract with CBS and NBC under which each NFL team received $337,000 for 1962. By 1969, TV income had risen to $1.6 million per team in the NFL and $900,000 per team in the AFL.

The antitrust suit filed by the AFL was heard in 1962, with the district court ruling that "the evidence established that [the NFL] did not have monopoly power, and had not undertaken an expansion into new cities with specific intent to destroy [the AFL] as a competitor." It reached this ruling despite the testimony of George Marshall that "[t]he only reason for expansion I have heard from the other owners is that we would destroy the new league." The court ruled that Marshall's statement was not true, because the NFL owners had stated many different reasons for expansion. The court concluded, "The test of monopoly power in this case . . . is whether the NFL had sufficient power to prevent the formation or successful operation of a new league. It is not sufficient that they might have had the power to exclude a new league from a particular city or group of cities unless that power . . . would have effectively prevented the formation or operation of a new league." On appeal, Judge Haynsworth wrote the unanimous opinion of the appeals court that upheld the decision of the district court.

Generally, the AFL was a well-financed league, and TV income provided a buffer against low attendance. While actual attendance of the AFL never posed the threat to the NFL that the AAFC did, still attendance was rather impressive, as indicated in Table 9.10.

In 1966, the AFL added Miami as an expansion team, and the NFL added Atlanta, with Cincinnati to enter the AFL in 1967 and New Orleans coming into the NFL in 1967. Up until the 1966 season, the two leagues had pretty much avoided competition in the market for veteran players. In fact, of the 1,318 players who appeared on AFL rosters between 1960 and 1969, only 217 (16.5 percent) had previous NFL experience. As was the case with the AAFC, the players with NFL experience had almost all been cut by their NFL teams, so there were few contract disputes between the two leagues.

Then, before the 1966 season, the Houston Oilers signed Mike Ditka of the Bears to a contract for the 1967 season, including a $50,000 signing bonus. In a much more threatening development, the AFL reached pre-

Table 9.10
Attendance, NFL and AFL IV, 1960–1969

Year	Total Attendance		Per-Game Attendance	
	AFL	NFL	AFL	NFL
1960	926,156	3,128,296	16,358	40,106
1961	1,002,657	3,986,159	17,904	40,675
1962	1,147,302	4,003,421	20,487	40,851
1963	1,242,741	4,163,643	22,174	42,486
1964	1,447,875	4,563,049	25,855	46,562
1965	1,782,384	4,634,021	31,899	47,296
1966	2,160,369	5,337,044	34,291	50,829
1967	2,295,697	5,938,924	36,439	53,026
1968	2,635,004	5,882,213	37,643	52,521
1969	2,843,373	6,096,127	40,619	54,430

Source: NFL Guide, 1991.

liminary agreement for an expansion franchise for Chicago with a local businessman, a Mr. Nussbaum, posing a direct threat to the Bears, who were having an only so-so season. These might have been the incidents that convinced Halas to bring his considerable influence to bear to end the war. In any case, an agreement was reached in 1966 between the two leagues providing for an interleague championship game beginning after the 1966 season, and for full amalgamation beginning in 1970, after the existing league TV contracts had expired.

Under the merger agreement, all teams in the AFL became members of the NFL, with equal sharing of TV revenues. The AFL agreed to pay the NFL $18 million over a 20-year time span (with present value under $10 million, given the interest rates of the time), with the bulk of the money to be paid to the San Francisco 49ers and New York Giants, whose territory was to be invaded. In addition, the AFL agreed to turn over to the NFL the $7.5 million it was to receive for the Cincinnati Bengals, and the AFL agreed to stock the Bengals with players in the expansion draft. The present value of the compensation involved in the agreement per AFL team was roughly $2 million, as compared to an NFL expansion franchise price of $8 million or more. The merger agreement was given final approval by the two leagues in October, 1966, after Congress had passed a law exempting the merger agreement from the antitrust laws.

From almost every point of view, the AFL had achieved a stunning success. The NFL could have avoided the interleague war that took place if it had been willing to expand into Dallas, Houston, and the Twin Cities in the late 1950s, rather than delaying expansion as long as it did. The hang-up on expansion was the veto power exerted by George Marshall, whose Redskins had been hurt badly at the gate by the Colts from the last previous expansion, and by the Wolfners, who presumably opposed expansion because it would eliminate potential candidates for a move by the Cardinals. While the war arose because of the desire for franchises in Dallas, Houston, and the Twin Cities, it ended with rival franchises installed in New York and the Bay area, and with side payments to the owners of NFL franchises in these territories.

WFL, 1974–1975

The next rival league to be faced by the NFL was the World Football League, organized in 1973 by Gary Davidson, creator of the American Basketball Association and the World Hockey Association. The WFL played an ambitious 20-game per team schedule, beginning play in late July, to get a head start on the NFL. The league played a full 1974 schedule, and then disbanded midway through the 1975 season. The WFL faced a 26-team NFL, with the matchups at the beginning of the 1974 season as shown in Table 9.11.

By 1974, the only cities from the top-30 list not sporting an NFL franchise were Seattle (16), Indianapolis (25), Tampa (27), Portland (28), Phoenix (29), and Columbus (30). (By 1991, the NFL had added Seattle, Indianapolis, Tampa Bay, and Phoenix to its list, while dropping Baltimore, Oakland, and St. Louis.) The WFL opted to go head to head with the NFL in the five biggest markets in the country (and in Houston as well), but half the franchises in the WFL were in cities with SMSA populations of less than 1 million. Memphis had an SMSA population of 770,000, and Orlando, home of the Florida Blazers, had a 1970 SMSA population of only 428,000.

By 1974, the NFL TV contract was paying about $2.2 million per team. The WFL had a one-year TV contract that paid $130,000 per team, and then the league lost its network contract for the 1975 season. The WFL ran into major problems in its big-city markets, which helped to scuttle the TV contract. During the 1974 season, the New York Stars team was moved to Charlotte as the Charlotte Hornets, and the Detroit team went out of business midway through the season. The Chicago Fire went bankrupt after the 1974 season and was taken over by the league. The team was sold, renamed Chicago Wind, and went out of business after the first few games of the 1975 season. The Southern California Sun and Philadelphia Bell franchises stayed in place during the one-and-one-half year history of the WFL, but the Houston Texans made it only midway through

Table 9.11
NFL and WFL, 1974

NFL	WFL
New York Giants (1)	New York Stars (1)
New York Jets (1)	
Los Angeles Rams (2)	Southern California Sun (2)
Chicago Bears (3)	Chicago Fire (3)
Philadelphia Eagles (4)	Philadelphia Bell (4)
Detroit Lions (5)	Detroit Wheels (5)
San Francisco 49ers (6)	
Oakland Raiders (6)	
Washington Redskins (7)	
New England Patriots (8)	
Pittsburgh Steelers (9)	
St. Louis Cardinals (10)	
Baltimore Colts (11)	
Cleveland Browns (12)	
Houston Oilers (13)	Houston Texans (13)
Minnesota Vikings (14)	
Dallas Cowboys (15)	
Atlanta Falcons (18)	
Cincinnati Bengals (19)	
San Diego Chargers (20)	
Buffalo Bills (21)	
Miami Dolphins (22)	
Kansas City Chiefs (23)	
Denver Broncos (24)	
	Portland Storm (25)
New Orleans Saints (26)	
Green Bay Packers (174)/Milwaukee[a] (17)	Memphis Southmen (37)
	Birmingham Americans (39)
	Hawaiians (48)
	Jacksonville Sharks (60)
	Florida Blazers (66)

Sources: As in table 9.2.
Note: Numbers in parentheses are population ranks in 1970 census.
[a]The Packers played half of their games in Milwaukee.

the 1974 season before being moved to Shreveport as the Shreveport Steamer.

The attendance figures reported to *Sporting News* and other publications, which undoubtedly overstated actual paid attendance at WFL games are shown in Table 9.12. On the basis of the attendance data, it will

Table 9.12
Average Per-Game Attendance, NFL and WFL, 1974 and 1975

NFL	1974	1975	WFL	1974	1975
N.Y. Giants	45,686	51,261	New York	10,735	—
N.Y. Jets	49,562	51,586			
Los Angeles	70,542	62,396	Southern California	25,806	13,450
Chicago	41,374	46,267	Chicago	28,571	3,470
Philadelphia	60,030	61,234	Philadelphia	19,879	3,107
Detroit	45,328	72,919	Detroit	10,233	—
San Francisco	49,564	43,201			
Oakland	49,895	49,397			
Cleveland	60,017	55,023			
Washington	53,919	53,790			
Baltimore	34,029	46,253			
Pittsburgh	46,494	48,756			
Houston	33,915	45,037	Houston	18,742	—
Dallas	53,348	57,364			
Minnesota	47,063	46,188			
New England	56,072	56,709			
Atlanta	37,858	40,723			
St. Louis	46,078	45,680			
San Diego	36,876	32,959			
Cincinnati	52,624	51,415			
Miami	65,395	64,762	Florida	15,691	—
Buffalo	78,161	73,444			
Kansas City	58,974	60,562			
Denver	50,326	48,680			
New Orleans	56,051	45,682			
			San Antonio	—	13,548
			Portland	14,536	8,298
			Jacksonville	32,809	12,984
			Memphis	20,440	19,696
			Hawaiians	13,031	15,363
			Charlotte	22,129	10,924
			Birmingham	41,486	25,700
			Shreveport	19,859	15,059
Green Bay	50,162	49,907			
League avg.	56,244	56,116		21,667	14,111

Sources: Game summaries in *Sporting News;* and *NFL Guide, 1991.*

come as no surprise that the turnover rate of WFL franchises was breath-taking. Five teams were sold three times in the two years between the organization of the WFL and the time the league disbanded. One team was sold twice, and four other teams were sold once. The only two teams not sold during the two-year history of the WFL were the Detroit Wheels and the Memphis Southmen. Pretty clearly, the WFL was a case of a league organized to make money, if at all, from franchise sales, located in many cities only marginally able to support major league pro football, and wtih owners who didn't have the capital to ride out early losses. The inability to develop popular teams in New York, Los Angeles, and Chicago effectively eliminated national TV as a revenue source, and the league was doomed.

USFL, 1983–1985

The last of the rival leagues was organized in 1982 by Donald Dixon, with a novel twist, namely, football during the spring rather than the fall. The USFL played three seasons, 1983, 1984, and 1985, before disbanding. Franchises in the league moved and changed hands at a pace that even outdid what went on in the WFL. Table 9.13 gives the matchup between the NFL and the changing USFL over the period between 1983 and 1985.

Over the three-year history of the USFL, two teams were sold five times, one was sold four times, four more were sold twice, and five were sold once. What Table 9.13 shows is that the USFL began operations with a lineup of teams mainly in big-city markets, competing with the NFL (in the off-season) in 10 of the 13 USFL cities. In 1984, there was some slippage toward smaller cities, but the losses of Philadelphia and Boston were offset by the new teams in Houston and Pittsburgh and the move into Baltimore. The year 1985 saw the abandonment of Chicago, Detroit, Washington, and Pittsburgh, with 8 of the 13 USFL teams now located in small to medium-size cities. By 1985, only six USFL teams were located in NFL cities.

What turned out to be a disastrous mistake for the USFL was the decision to expand in the second year of operation, by adding five new franchises. Of the new franchises, Pittsburgh and Oklahoma lasted only one year, and San Antonio was a very weak-drawing team. Just one or two really weak franchises can cause major problems for a league, and the USFL had managed its affairs so that it was almost guaranteed to have half a dozen or more marginal franchises. The reported attendance record of the USFL is shown in Table 9.14.

Using a 30,000 attendance figure as a generous break-even minimum, the only USFL teams to average at or over this between 1983 and 1985

Table 9.13
NFL and USFL, 1983–1985

NFL	USFL 1983	USFL 1984	USFL 1985
N.Y. Giants (1)	N.J. Generals (1)	Same	Same
N.Y. Jets (1)			
L.A. Rams (2)	L.A. Express (2)	Same	Same
L.A. Raiders (2)			
Chicago Bears (3)	Chicago Blitz (3)	Same	Out
San Francisco 49ers (4)	Oakland Invaders (4)	Same	Same
Philadelphia Eagles (5)	Philadelphia Stars (5)	Out	Out
Detroit Lions (6)	Michigan Panthers (6)	Same	Out
New England Patriots (7)	Boston Breakers (7)	Out	Out
Dallas Cowboys (8)			
Houston Oilers (9)		Houston Gamblers	Same
Washington Redskins (10)	Washington Federals (10)	Same	Out
Miami Dolphins (11)			
Cleveland Browns (12)			
Atlanta Browns (12)			
St. Louis Cardinals (14)			
Pittsburgh Steelers (15)		Pittsburgh Maulers (15)	Out
Minnesota Vikings (16)			
Seattle Seahawks (17)			
Baltimore Colts (18)[a]		Baltimore Stars (18)	Same

(continued)

Table 9.13 (cont.)
NFL and USFL, 1983–1985

NFL	USFL 1983	USFL 1984	USFL 1985
San Diego Chargers (19)			
Tampa Bay Buccaneers (20)	Tampa Bay Bandits (20)	Same	Same
	Arizona Wranglers (21)	Same	Same
Denver Broncos (22)	Denver Gold (22)	Same	Same
Cincinnati Bengals (23)			
Kansas City Chiefs (25)			
New Orleans Saints (27)		New Orleans Breakers (27)	Portland Breakers (26)
		San Antonio Gunslingers (31)	Out
Buffalo Bills (33)			
		Memphis Showboat (41)	Same
	Birmingham Stallions (44)	Same	Same
			Orlando (46)
		Jacksonville Bulls (47)	Same
		Oklahoma Outlaws (52)	Out
Green Bay (Milwaukee [24]) [nr]			

Sources: As in table 9.2.
Note: Numbers in parentheses are population ranks in 1980 census.
[a]Moved to Indianapolis in 1984.

Table 9.14
Average Per-Game Attendance, NFL and USFL, 1983–1985

	1983	1984	1985
NATIONAL FOOTBALL LEAGUE			
New York Giants	64,937	72,993	72,550
New York Jets	51,510	64,323	67,729
Los Angeles Rams	52,791	54,455	56,242
Los Angeles Raiders	46,047	64,065	63,725
Chicago Bears	52,346	57,772	60,777
San Francisco 49ers	54,386	58,357	58,813
Philadelphia Eagles	55,711	57,375	60,753
Detroit Lions	69,199	57,155	63,077
New England Patriots	46,370	49,032	54,834
Dallas Cowboys	63,224	60,068	59,763
Houston Oilers	40,180	40,441	41,180
Washington Redskins	52,064	52,688	53,033
Miami Dolphins	60,992	65,609	67,869
Cleveland Browns	70,564	57,304	63,425
Atlanta Falcons	41,670	39,044	34,017
St. Louis Cardinals	38,702	46,519	40,669
Pittsburgh Steelers	57,846	55,945	54,512
Minnesota Vikings	58,113	55,550	56,713
Seattle Seahawks	60,754	61,707	59,605
Baltimore/Indianapolis Colts	37,440	60,163	58,974
San Diego Chargers	46,243	51,243	51,953
Tampa Bay Buccaneers	49,802	45,732	38,753
Denver Broncos	74,061	73,154	73,688
Cincinnati Bengals	49,686	48,756	53,073
Kansas City Chiefs	46,599	46,415	44,770
New Orleans Saints	66,235	59,086	48,599
Buffalo Bills	59,987	44,937	37,893
Avg.	54,436	55,461	55,258
U.S. FOOTBALL LEAGUE			
New Jersey Generals	33,821	30,466	41,268
Los Angeles Express	19,901	15,361	8,414
Chicago Blitz	18,090	7,455	—
Oakland Invaders	30,622	24,867	17,509
Philadelphia Stars	19,692	—	—
Baltimore Stars	—	28,352	14,210
Michigan Panthers	22,250	32,457	—
Boston Breakers	12,735	—	—
New Orleans Breakers	—	30,558	—
Portland Breakers	—	—	19,975
Houston Gamblers	—	28,151	18,971

(continued)

Table 9.14 (cont.)
Average Per-Game Attendance, NFL and USFL, 1983–1985

	1983	1984	1985
Washington Federals	13,848	7,694	—
Orlando Renegades	—	—	25,607
Pittsburgh Maulers	—	22,858	—
Tampa Bay Bandits	39,896	46,148	45,220
Arizona Wranglers	25,781	25,568	17,982
Denver Gold	41,736	33,953	14,466
San Antonio Gunslingers	—	15,444	11,554
Memphis Showboat	—	27,599	30,941
Birmingham Stallions	22,046	36,850	31,598
Jacksonville Bulls	—	46,730	44,329
Oklahoma Outlaws	—	19,815	—
Avg.	24,960	26,892	24,423

Source: Game summaries in *Sporting News.*

were Donald Trump's New Jersey Generals (featuring Herschel Walker), Tampa Bay, Denver, and Jacksonville. The league also suffered from the disparity between NFL and USFL TV income. In 1983, the USFL operated under contracts with ABC and ESPN that brought in $16.5 million ($1.4 million per team), while the NFL had $316 million in TV income ($11.12 million per team). In 1984, per-team TV income was $800,000 per USFL team, and $15.5 million per NFL team. In 1985, USFL TV contracts called for a league-wide income of $38 million (roughly $2.1 million per team), with each NFL team receiving $17 million. However, actual payments to USFL teams were much less than the contract amount, because of markets that were lost when big-city USFL teams went out of business.

Following a decline in attendance and franchise losses in 1985, a controversial decision was made at the behest of Donald Trump, to move to a fall schedule in 1986. This led to the abandonment of several franchises, and the league effectively went out of busines after the 1985 season. The formal disbanding of the USFL followed the resolution of the league's antitrust suit against the NFL. The league went down in history as the "$1 league," when $1 was assessed as the damages suffered by the league from the antitrust violations of the NFL (see *United States Football League v. National Football League*, 644 F. Supp. 1040 (S.D.N.Y. 1986)). Byrne (1986) gives a detailed account of the trials and tribulations of the USFL, from an insider's point of view.

Summary

There are a number of lessons to be learned from this extended look at the history of rival leagues in pro team sports. The most obvious is that getting involved in a rival league is a very risky business. Since 1960, five rival leagues have been organized—AFL IV, ABL, ABA, WFL, WHA, and USFL—and only AFL IV was a financial success for its investors.

The rival leagues that did succeed—the AA, AL, and AFL IV—did so because of gross mistakes by the dominant league in the sport. The NL effectively abandoned its big-city markets between 1876 and 1882, leaving the door open for the AA; and then it opened the door again in 1900 by cutting back to an 8-team league, in a sport that had profitably supported as many as 16 teams in the late 1880s. The NFL ignored the population shift to the West and Southwest in the post-war years, and was handcuffed in its expansion policies by the veto power exercised by just one or two teams. Organized baseball avoided a league war at about the same time by coming to an agreement with the CL over the same basic issue. The reason that successful rival leagues require gross mistakes, not simply fine-tuning mistakes, by the dominant league is clear. A rival league succeeds only when enough of the market potential in a sport is left unexploited to support a league roster of eight or more teams; and a dominant league that leaves this much market potential unexploited is making a gross mistake indeed.

The combination of monopoly profits in big-city markets and veto power over league expansion into such markets was the critical factor in the AFL I-NFL war and, to a lesser extent, in the AAFC-NFL war. In the AFL IV-NFL war and in the AAFC-NFL war, vetos of league expansion by the Chicago Cardinals, to save potential markets for a franchise move, were percipitating factors in entry of the rival league.

The positive gain to the public from rival leagues is the impetus that rival leagues provide to expansion of the dominant league, at a pace faster than monopoly profit considerations dictate. Rival leagues also bring market feedback forces to bear on the dominant league, which act to force the league to correct mistakes in its siting of franchises and other such business or marketing mistakes. In fact, even the threat of a rival league, as in the case of the Continental League, can have such desirable consequences for the general public.

Especially in the current, TV-dominated environment, it is critical to the success of a rival league that a base be established in one or more of the megalopolis centers of the country. A strong-drawing, big-city base supports the entire league, through gate- and TV-sharing subsidies of small city teams. It was the failure to establish this base that doomed the rival leagues following AFL IV. Los Angeles seems to be a particularly hard market for a rival league to crack; there hasn't been a strong-drawing rival league franchise in L.A. since the AAFC Dons in the late 1940s. The city has seen the Anaheim Amigos, Los Angeles Sharks, Southern California Sun, Los Angeles Chargers, Los Angeles Stars, and Los Angeles Express come and go without any discernible interest. The record in Chicago is every bit as dismal for rival leagues. New York has been somewhat more hospitable—the Nets and the New Jersey Generals both were relatively decently drawing teams, and, of course, the Jets made it, after a struggle.

Expansion, in part forced on the dominant leagues by rival leagues, has left only a few gaps of coverage in medium size cities, but there is still unexploited profit potential in megalopolis markets. Given the problems the TV networks have been experiencing dealing with monopoly leagues, it is a little surprising that more efforts haven't been made by TV interests to correct this by helping in the financing of rival leagues. This is a natural future development for the industry.

To recap the role of rival leagues in the development of pro team sports over its history, the following teams entered sports originally as members of rival leagues:

BASEBALL. NL—Los Angeles (Brooklyn), Pittsburgh, St. Louis, Cincinnati (from AA); AL—Oakland (Philadelphia), Boston, New York (Baltimore), Cleveland, Detroit, Chicago, Minnesota (Washington), Baltimore (Milwaukee/St. Louis) (from AL 1901/02). Moreover, New York (Mets), Houston, California (Los Angeles), and Texas (Washington) were created because of pressure by the Continental League.

FOOTBALL. L.A. Rams (Cleveland) (from AFL II); Cleveland, San Francisco, and Baltimore (from AAFC); and New England (Boston), Buffalo, Kansas City (Dallas), Denver, Houston, San Diego (Los Angeles), New York Jets, Los Angeles Raiders (Oakland), Miami, and Cincinnati (from AFL IV). In addition, Minnesota and Dallas entered the league in a direct response to plans for AFL IV franchises in those cities.

BASKETBALL. Philadelphia (Syracuse), Atlanta (Tri-Cities), Los Angeles (Minneapolis), Sacramento (Rochester), and Detroit (Fort Wayne) (from NBL); New Jersey, San Antonio, Indiana, and Denver (from ABA).

HOCKEY. Hartford (New England), Quebec, Winnipeg, and Edmonton (from WHA); and New York Islanders franchise created to counter a proposed WHA franchise in Long Island.

Finally, given the problems with fielding economically viable rival leagues, it would be of interest to look at the possibility of antitrust action aimed at breaking up the existing monopoly leagues, as in the Standard Oil case of the early 1900s. The best possible solution to abuse of monopoly power is not regulation, with all of its top-down bureaucratic problems, but creating a competitive market with two or three independent leagues, with roughly equal drawing potential, all with bases in the megalopolis markets. In contrast, government actions in the past thirty years have been directed toward encouraging mergers, in football (AFL-NFL), basketball (ABA-NBA), and hockey (WHA-NHL), treating a monopoly league as a foregone long-term situation in professional team sports.

Postscript

A S THIS BOOK was going through the final stages of page proofs in mid-July 1992, the *McNeil v. NFL* antitrust trial was under way in Minneapolis, potentially the most important lawsuit in the history of the NFL. The central economic issues in the trial were free agency for NFL players and its consequences for operation of the league, including competitive balance and the profitability of NFL teams. Data collected for this book on franchise prices (Chapter 2), on measures of competitive balance (Chapter 7), and on the impact of free agency on competitive balance in baseball and basketball (Chapter 7) were introduced in the trial and became part of the trial record.

There have been some interesting disclosures at the trial. The NFL revealed that there is a league rule prohibiting the sale of players for cash that has been in force since at least the time of the introduction of the Rozelle Rule in the early 1960s (see Chapter 5). Testimony for the players by expert witness Roger Noll showed that there have been a number of instances of "unbalanced trades" since that time, in which high-salaried players have been traded by teams in weak markets for low-salaried players on the rosters of teams in strong drawing markets. These "unbalanced trades" act along with trades of draft choices for players to offset the equalizing effects of the NFL ban on sales of players for cash (see Chapter 7).

The most interesting disclosures at the trial related to the profitability of NFL teams. NFL owners argued that even under the restricted labor market of the late 1980s, with the option clause and the Rozelle Rule in full force, a number of NFL teams were barely breaking even or were actually losing money. The owners claimed that imposing free agency on the NFL would then have disastrous consequences, especially for marginally profitable teams. To buttress this argument, the NFL provided data on the profitability of individual teams over the 1986–1989 period. A summary of this data appeared in the *New York Times*, July 9, 1992.

The NFL data showed that 9 of the 28 NFL teams lost money in 1986, 16 showed losses in 1987, 13 in 1988, and 12 in 1989. San Francisco, Dallas, Cleveland, New England, Kansas City, the Jets and the Giants, and the Raiders, all lost money in each of the four years. Teams that made money all four years were Philadelphia, New Orleans, Cincinnati, Pittsburgh, Chicago, Indianapolis, Tampa Bay, Miami, and Minnesota. The data also showed that the average operating profit per NFL team in 1991 was just over $6 million. (These data exclude player contract amortization (see Chapter 3) and interest expenses.) This is to be contrasted with the *Financial World* estimates summarized in Chapter 1, indicating an average profit per NFL team of around $9 million.

One of the striking aspects of the profit data was the lack of correlation between profitability and W/L performance for NFL teams. Gate and TV revenue sharing in the NFL have acted to minimize the profit incentives for owners to field winning teams, as compared to the other major pro team sports leagues. A more important factor in profitability appears to be the kind of stadium contract under which a team operates. Tampa Bay, Indianapolis, and New Orleans all have highly favorable stadium contracts and all are profitable; New England, the Jets and the Giants all have relatively unfavorable stadium contracts and all of these teams showed losses over the 1986–1989 period. (See the discussion in Chapter 4.)

Testimony at the trial by Roger Noll also served to cast some doubt about the meaningfulness of the profit data itself. He pointed out that Norman Braman, owner of the Eagles, had paid himself a salary in excess of $7 million during one year of the 1986–1989 period, and there were published reports of large salary payments to family members of owners of the Bears, the Falcons, and other teams. It becomes a subtle matter indeed to try to determine the true "economic profit" earned by the owner of a sports team under these circumstances. One thing was sure—profits of teams were not *over*estimated in the data supplied by the NFL.

This brings to mind the old story about the accounting profession. Ask a mathematician what $2 + 2$ is, and you can expect to get an elegant and convincing proof that $2 + 2 = 4$. Ask a statistician, and he or she might provide you with an interval estimate, say 3.5 to 4.5, within which you can be 95 percent confident that the answer will lie. But ask any competent accountant what $2 + 2$ is, and you will get the standard answer: "What would you like it to be?"

Thus it is rational to take the data supplied by the NFL as to its own profitability with the proverbial grain of salt. This is especially true given the prices that NFL teams are selling for these days, as seen in the data presented in Chapter 2. The first indication that the bloom is off the rose for NFL owners will be a fall in franchise prices, as investors revise their profit expectations in a downward direction. The franchise market provides the best information as to the prospective future profitability of NFL teams, especially given the ambiguous nature of management costs as reported in the NFL income statements.

Finally, it should be pointed out that even if free agency were to put certain NFL teams into the red, as argued by the owners, that in and of itself is not a valid economic reason for rejecting free agency. A free enterprise system does not provide profits for all firms, but only for those firms that do an efficient job of supplying a product that consumers desire. Inefficient firms *should* lose money—there are no profit guarantees in a market economy. The experience of baseball and basketball, summarized in Chapter 7, indicates that free agency can be absorbed in a sport without calamitous effects to competitive balance or profitability, and this applies as well to the NFL as to the other sports leagues.

Appendix to Chapter 3

Calculating the Value of the Contract Depreciation Tax Shelter for Sports Teams

WE LOOK at the theoretical value of the contract depreciation tax shelter, under some simplifying assumptions about the franchise market and the behavior of team owners. In all that follows, it is assumed that teams are operated as limited partnerships. In all cases, it is assumed that the market price of a team is equal to the present value of the after-tax net cash flow from the team.

The notation used in the derivations below is the following:

$M(t)$ = market price of team at time t

$m(t)$ = net before tax cash flow from team operations at time t

$m(t)$ = $m(O) \cdot e^{\rho t}$, where ρ is the rate of growth of the net before-tax cash flow of the team

α = percent of $M(t)$ assigned to player contracts

a = number of years for contract writeoffs

β = marginal personal income tax rate

γ = capital gains tax rate

i = interest rate (rate at which the market discounts future after-tax income of the team)

The basic market relationship that is assumed is that the current market price of the team correctly reflects the future after-tax earnings from the team, and correctly anticipates the after-tax proceeds from re-sale of the team, under the assumption that the present structure of tax rates, and the present treatment of the tax shelter by the IRS, will con-tinue to hold into the indefinite future.

We want to look at three different scenarios. First, we calculate the value of the team in the absence of the contract writeoff tax shelter, assuming ownership in perpetuity. Second, we calculate the value of the team with the contract writeoff tax shelter, but assuming that the present owner will hold the team indefinitely into the future. Third, we calculate the value of the team under the assumption that each succeed-ing owner holds the team only long enough to make full use of the tax shelter before selling the team to the next owner.

A. Value of Team with No Tax Writeoffs, with Ownership in Perpetuity

Assuming that the market places a value on the team that correctly reflects (only) the future after-tax earnings of the team, with no contract writeoff tax shelter available, then the market value of the team is cal-culated from the present value formula, as below. If we denote the value of the team at time t without tax shelter as $M_1(t)$,

$$M_1(t) = \int_t^\infty (1-\beta)m(s)e^{-i(s-t)}ds,$$

or,

$$M_1(t) = \frac{(1-\beta)}{(i-s)} m(O)e^{\rho t}.$$

B. Value of the Team with Tax Shelter, But Perpetual Ownership for Individual Purchasing the Team

The second scenario considered is one in which the team is purchased by a new owner, who takes advantage of the tax shelter over the writeoff period (a years), but then holds the team into the indefinite future. The value of the team to the new owner is designated by $M_2(t)$, and is calcu-lated from the present value formula as follows:

$$M_2(t) = \int_t^{t+a} \left\{ m(s) - \beta[m(s) - \frac{\alpha}{a} M_2(t)] \right\} e^{-i(s-t)}ds + M_1(t+a)e^{-ia}$$

Thus, during the first a years of ownership, the new owner receives not only the cash flow from operations, $m(s)$, but also the tax savings on outside income generated by the book losses of the team. After a

years of contract writeoffs, the team reverts to the non-tax shelter situation, with a value of $M_1(t + a)e^{-ia}$ (discounting back to time (t), using the value for $M_1(t + a)$, as calculated from the formula above.

Solving, we obtain:

$$M_2(t) = M_1(t)\left\{(ai)\middle/[ai + \alpha\beta(e^{-ia} - 1)]\right\}$$

C. Resale of Team after Contract Writeoffs Are Over

Finally, we consider the case in which the current market price of the team correctly reflects a situation in which the current and each succeeding owner holds the team for a years to take advantage of tax sheltering, and then sells the team to the next owner, who does the same. We assume that each succeeding owner has sufficient outside income to take full advantage of the tax shelter.

In this case, we denote the value of the team by $M_3(t)$, which is calculated from the present value formula as follows:

$$M_3(t) = \int_t^{t+a} \left\{ m(s) - \beta[m(s) - \frac{\alpha}{a} M_3(t)] \right\} e^{-i(s-t)}ds$$
$$+ \left\{ M_3(t+a) - (\theta\beta + (1-\theta)\gamma)[M_3(t+a) - (1-\alpha)M_3(t)] \right\} e^{-ia},$$

where θ is the fraction of excess depreciation that is recaptured by the IRS at the time of sale.

Here, the after-tax earnings during the first a years of ownership are calculated as in part B above. At the end of a years, the team is sold for the price $M_3(t + a)$, and the old owner receives that price less the taxes (capital gains and/or depreciation recapture at normal income tax rates) on the difference between the sales price and the book of the team (the basis).

It is easy to verify that

$$M_3(t + a) = M_3(t)e^{\rho a},$$

that is, that the market value of the team rises at the same rate that the net cash flow from operations rises. Let

$$k = \theta\beta + (1-\theta)\gamma.$$

Solving the present value formula, we obtain

$$M_3(t) = M_1(t)\left\{ \frac{(ai)(1 - e^{(\rho - i)a})}{ai - \beta\alpha(1 - e^{-ia}) - ai(1 - k)e^{(\rho + i)a} - ai(1 - \alpha)ke^{-ia}} \right\}$$

Appendix to Chapter 6

Salary Estimation and Elasticity Calculation

I N THIS APPENDIX, a simple "how to" presentation of the approach to salary estimation is adopted. Readers with a higher pain threshold are referred to Fort (1992) for the complete statement of the method, plus empirical results for the entire reserve clause period.

According to the theory, profit maximizers pay (at most) a player's marginal revenue product (MRP). Thus, salary at time t depends upon MRP considerations up to time $t - 1$, that is, to the end of "last season" (approximately September 30).

The seminal work of Gerald Scully (1974b) provides the benchmark model for analysis of baseball salaries. The major explanatory variables include a measure of playing time, on-field performance, age, and experience. The playing time, performance, and experience variables are meant to capture the marginal productivity of the player, one of the components in the player's MRP.

Another important element in the salary process is the difference between stars and others. The idea is that star MRPs are dramatically different from the MRP of other players because of their special impact on forthcoming revenues (local television, ticket sales, concessions). Thus, there may be a non-linear relationship between pay and performance. In Scully's (1974b) original work, a log-log structure was used, with the nice characteristic that estimated coefficients are elasticities but with the shortcoming that elasticities do not vary across playing time and performance levels. In a more recent work, Scully (1989) related the logarithm of salary to untransformed performance variables so that the elasticities do vary with the independent variables. The work in this book used a particular log-log framework that allows the elasticities to vary.

Attempts at widening the repertoire of performance variables have all reached the same conclusion: the variables are so highly correlated that once a few are included, more variables provide little added explanation. Typically, playing time seems to provide most of the explanation since a rational team manager will give more playing time to the players who contribute most to the team.

Despite this, a few areas of improvement in the specification of the salary process seem important (Fort and Noll 1984). The first is distinguishing different types of hitters and pitchers. Playing time gives undue weight to starting pitchers. Correcting for starting appearances should isolate this effect. At the lower end of the talent and/or experience spectrum, "rookies" and "hopefuls" are different from other players. While coefficient estimates will be sensitive to the way these players are identified, special identification of these players will keep them from being lost in the shuffle because of low levels of on-field performance, age, and experience. An additional category consists of players who did not play in the major leagues in the previous year.

A second improvement involves unfolding the intracacies of the relationship between age and experience. There is no reason to suspect that age enters the process linearly (or linearly in logarithms), since age has pronounced effects early and late in a player's career, but not in the middle years. Furthermore, age and experience typically are closely related. Experience is thought to improve performance, especially early in a player's career; for two players of equal age, better performance is expected of the player with more experience.

To handle non-linearity, age is used in deviation-from-mean form, separating players of above and below average ages. In addition, the squares of these deviations from the mean age are included. To untangle the age-experience relationship, experience is represented by the residual of a regression of experience on age; the regression results for all years except 1976–77 are in Fort (1992). Residual experience captures the independent impact of experience that is not explained by age.

A third improvement treats recent playing time separately from career playing time. A substantial change from career playing time can occur because of injuries that may have bearing on a player's long-run abilities. Poor players may get more playing time in a given season as a result of an injury to a regular in the starting lineup, or a starting regular may be out of the lineup temporarily because of an injury that is not permanently disabling.

Finally, in the analysis of baseball salaries, no structural change has been more important than the demise of the reserve clause. Obtaining free agency had the same effect, eventually, upon MLB salaries that the demise of the "contract player" mode of operations had upon the salaries of movie stars. In order to investigate the impact of free agency, the salary equation is estimated separately for each year and a standard statistical test of pooling across the sample years is employed. The results are discussed in the text.

Table 6A shows the results of estimating the salary equation for 1968, 1977, and 1990 salaries. The 1968 sample uses all available salary observations and represents the reserve clause period. The other samples use a randomly selected subsample of 200 players for each year and represent the transition and free agency periods, respectively. A complete description of the derivation of all explanatory variables appears in Fort (1992). While only three years are shown here, the regressions for the remaining sample years also were performed with similar results. The model results compare favorably with Scully's (1974b, 1989) previous work, although interesting quantitative differences do occur.

A quantitative examination of the MLB salary process requires that elasticities be computed. Because zero is a possible value for some variables for some players, most of the variables are transformed by adding one. Let S = salary, X = an independent variable of interest, and b = the estimated coefficient for X. Starting from $\log S = b \log (X + 1)$ and applying the exponential function to both sides, one finds that

$$S = (X + 1)^b.$$

Taking the partial derivative with respect to X, multiplying both sides by X/S, and recalling that $S = (X \times 1)^b$, we obtain

$$\epsilon = b \left(\frac{X}{X + 1} \right).$$

Elasticities vary with levels of the continuous independent variables. For the dummy variables, the coefficients are interpreted directly in percentage change terms and are constant.

In Table 6B, elasticities for the modern data are shown. Each entry in the table, by the definition of elasticity, represents the percentage change in salary resulting fom 1 percent change in the variable of interest. For example, a 1 percent change in lifetime slugging average for a high-level slugger in 1990 increases salary by 1.8 percent (about $72,000 for a $4 million player). The high (H), medium (M), and low (L) ranges of independent variables chosen for calculating playing time and performance elasticities run the entire gamut of ability from reserved to regulars. Table 6B forms the basis of the discussion of salary determinants appearing in the text.

Playing time elasticities calculated for the reserve clause period (1965–1974) are comparable to Scully's (1974b) findings for his 1968–1969 sample of hitters and pitchers. However, Scully's *performance* elasticities are much higher. For the free agency period shown in Table 6B, elasticities are in the same ball park with Scully's (1989) later analysis, but typically larger here.

Table 6A
Salary Regressions, 1968, 1977, and 1990

Variable	1968		1977		1990	
Share of team at-bats	11.1	(2.04)*	14.0	(2.00)*	19.1	(1.77)*
Slugging average	1.13	(.853)	4.75	(.786)*	2.52	(.750)*
Recent at-bats increase	8.63	(3.68)*	1.85	(2.59)	7.90	(3.05)*
Recent at-bats decrease	−5.85	(3.87)*	−11.2	(3.78)*	−564	(5.20)
Share of team innings pitched	11.0	(2.46)*	12.3	(2.02)*	15.2	(2.20)*
Strikeout-to-walk ratio	.331	(.242)	1.47	(.230)*	.983	(.232)*
Games-started ratio	−.769	(.347)*	−.921	(.278)*	−.694	(.266)*
Recent innings increase	−.476	(3.64)	12.8	(2.72)*	1.93	(2.60)
Recent innings decrease	−2.37	(3.39)	.579	(3.03)	−3.80	(3.15)
Older than the mean	−.046	(.152)	.438	(2.16)	.380	(.201)*
Square of "Older"	.095	(.065)	−.158	(.089)*	−.089	(.084)
Younger than the mean	.324	(.177)*	.255	(.263)	−.028	(.255)
Square of "Younger"	−.282	(.091)*	−.226	(.131)*	−.264	(.111)*
Experienced beyond age	.238	(.062)*	.117	(.074)	.113	(.076)
Experienced below age	−.107	(.071)	−.075	(.073)	−.435	(.080)*
Hopeful	.249	(.220)	1.34	(.217)*	1.45	(.256)*
Rookie	.640	(.240)*	.045	(.149)	−.376	(.232)*
Did not play last year	.020	(.120)	−.043	(.123)	−142	(.190)
Pitcher	.080	(.114)	−.047	(.124)	.273	(.152)*
Constant	9.93	(.242)*	9.35	(.245)*	11.0	(.242)*
R^2	.828		.811		.865	
Adjusted R^2	.797		.792		.850	
Degrees of freedom	105		180		180	
Residual sum of squares	8.59		22.9		29.2	

Note: Standard errors are in parentheses.
*Significant at the .05 level (two-tailed test for the constant and one-tailed test for the remaining coefficient estimates.

Table 6B
Salary Determinants for Free Agents, 1986–1990

	1986			1987–1988			1989			1990		
	H	M	L	H	M	L	H	M	L	H	M	L
HITTERS												
AB	1.5	1.0	.40	1.8	1.2	.48	1.7	1.1	.68	1.3	.82	.34
Slug	.36	.24	.12	1.1	.84	.50				1.8	1.6	1.3
AB+				.27	.18	0.0				.27	.09	0.0
AB−	−.40	−.21	0.0				−.55	−.37	0.0			
PITCHERS												
IP	2.2	1.2	.28	2.0	1.5	.80				2.0	1.5	.79
SW	.55	.50	.43	.59	.55	.48	.80	.73	.64	−.67	−.61	.54
GS	−.29	−.21	−.09	−.70	−.48	−.11				−.72	−.52	−.19
IP+				.28	.17	.06						
IP−	−1.5	−.40	0.0									
AGE AND EXPERIENCE												
Old^2	−.34	−.30	−.19	−.22	−.22	.00						
Young												
Less experienced	−.38	−.31	−.05				−.18	−.14	−.07			
OTHER VARIABLES												
Pitchers											$19	
Constant		$109,098			$40,135			$29,733			$29,733	

Notes: H = one standard deviation above the mean, M = the mean level, and L = one standard deviation below the mean. AB = share of team at-bats (+ and − designate recent increases and decreases), Slug = slugging average, IP = share of team innings pitched (+ and − designate recent increases and decreases), SW = strikeout-to-walk ratio, and GS = games-started ratio. The rest are self-explanatory. Elasticities are calculated only for variables that were statistically significant (.05 level of confidence).

Appendix to Chapter 8

League Wars

FORMALLY, let S be the set of possible locations for teams. Given a monopoly league, sites $1, \ldots, T$ can support two (or more) teams, while sites $T + 1, \ldots, S$ can support at most one team.

Let L_e denote the existing league and L_c denote the rival league. Although in reality gates and TV revenue are not shared equally among teams, the case of syndication—where all teams share equally in total league profits—presents a nice foil to the more complicated realistic case.

Assume syndication and let $P_e(L_e, L_c)$ denote aggregate profit accruing to the existing league, and let $P_c(L_e, L_c)$ denote aggregate profit accruing to the rival league. Both profit figures are net of side payments made by either group.

Under what conditions will a war erupt between L_e and L_c? A war is assumed to be costly to both leagues in the sense that

$$P_e(L_e, \phi) > P_e(L_e, L_c),$$

and

$$P_c(L_e, \phi) \equiv 0 > P_c(L_e, L_c),$$

where ϕ denotes the absence of a league.

Clearly,

$$(1) \quad P_c(L_e \cup L_c, \phi) > P_c(L_e, \phi)$$

is a necessary condition for L_c to engage in a war; that is, members of L_c must earn positive profits under an amalgamated league situation (in which L_e and L_c are treated as separate syndicates in the same league). Similarly, for a war to arise, L_e must lose from amalgamation; that is,

$$(2) \quad P_e(L_e, \phi) > P_e(L_e \cup L_c, \phi).$$

However, if

$$P_c(L_e \cup L_c, \phi) > [P_e(L_e, \phi) - P_e(L_e \cup L_c, \phi)],$$

L_c can bribe L_e to accept amalgamation, averting war. If

$$P_c(L_e U L_c, \phi) < [P_e(L_e, \phi) - P_e(L_e U L_c, \phi)],$$

in principle, L_e can bribe L_c to disband. The problem with this course of action is that it does not eliminate the threat of entry from leagues other than L_c; in fact, it provides an incentive for other rival leagues to spring up, constituting a constant threat to L_e. In view of this, L_e does not have the incentive to bribe L_c not to enter. Whether L_c will in fact enter depends, then, on the assessment by L_c of the short-term staying power of the two leagues and the chances of winning the resulting war.

The actual situation in sports leagues, such as the NFL, that are not syndicated and in which teams within a league have differing incentives is more complicated. In particular, conflicts can develop between big-city and small-city teams.

Let $P_{es}(L_e, L_c)$ denote profits earned by the team in the existing league at site s, and $P_{cs}(L_e, L_c)$ denote the profits earned by the rival league team at site s, both exclusive of side payments. Under exclusive territorial rights each league would assign only one team to each site. Then,

$$P_e(L_e, L_c) = \sum_{s=1}^{s} P_{es}(L_e, L_c),$$

and

$$P_c(L_e, L_c) = \sum_{s=1}^{s} P_{cs}(L_e, L_c),$$

Under monopoly conditions, given exclusive territorial rights, L_e would maximize profits by expanding to the point where there were n teams in the league, located at the first n sites in S (which were numbered in descending order of market size), where

$$P_{en}(L_e^n, \phi) \geq \sum_{s=1}^{n-1} P_{es}(L_e^{n-1}, \phi) - \sum_{s=1}^{n-1} P_{es}(L_e^n, \phi),$$

$$P_{e,n+1}(L_e^{n+1}, \phi) < \sum_{s=1}^{n} P_{es}(L_e^n, \phi) - \sum_{s=1}^{n} P_{es}(L_e^{n+1}, \phi),$$

and

$$P_{e,n-1}(L_e^{n-1}, \phi) < \sum_{s=1}^{n} P_{es}(L_e^n, \phi) - \sum_{s=1}^{n-2} P_{es}(L_e^{n-1}, \phi)$$

where L_e^n is a vector with 1's in the first n components, corresponding to the first n sites, ranked in terms of drawing power.

If $n \geq T$, League L_e will have at least one team at each of the T leading sites. League L_c will locate its teams at the best remaining sites. In particular we assume that L_c will place certain of its teams in the T "two-team" cities.

If a league L_e operated simply as a syndicate, a team in L_e would exercise its exclusive territorial rights to veto the entry of a new member of L_e into its site only if such entry would reduce total profits to the league. However, in the actual situation in practice, teams within a league such as the NFL have much stronger incentives to exercise their veto power: all that is required is that entry of a team into a site already occupied by a team reduce the profits of the latter team.

Under the assumption that profits are maximized at each site if there is only one team at each site, if each team has veto power, L_c will engage in war only if

$$(1') \quad P_{cs}(L_e ULc, \phi) > P_{cs}(L_e, \phi) \text{ for all } s \epsilon L_c.$$

Similarly, for war to arise, some team in L_e must lose from amalgamation; that is,

$$(2') \quad P_{es}(L_e, \phi) > P_{es}(L_e s ULc, \phi) \text{ for some } s \epsilon L_e.$$

Condition $(2')$ is clearly satisfied under the "monopoly pays" assumption if L_e already has a team at site s.

Once again, war can be avoided by appropriate side payments. Specifically if

$$\sum_{s=1}^{s} P_{cs}(L_e ULc, \phi) > \sum_{s=1}^{s} P_{es}(L_e, \phi) - \sum_{s=1}^{s} P_{es}(L_e ULc, \phi),$$

the winner (in L_c and L_e) can compensate the losers, with amalgamation taking place and war averted. But the "monopoly pays" assumption implies that

$$P_{cs}(L_e ULc, \phi) + P_{es}(L_e ULc, \phi) < P_{es}(L_e, \phi) \text{ for } s = 1, \ldots, T,$$

the "big city" sites.

Thus, any compensation would entail the weak-drawing teams bribing the strong-drawing teams, which would create difficult burden sharing and potential free rider problems—each small-city team would attempt to make its case that equity considerations should shift the compensation burden to other, wealthier, teams.

Finally, as before, if

$$\sum_{s=1}^{s} P_{cs}(L_e ULc, \phi) < \sum_{s=1}^{s} P_{es}(L_e, \phi) - \sum_{s=1}^{s} P_{es}(L_e ULc, \phi),$$

then teams in L_e can, in principle, bribe teams in L_c to disband. But, again, this does not eliminate entry threats from other leagues, and it makes L_e vulnerable to blackmail.

Data Supplement

THE FOLLOWING pages represent a first attempt at establishing a data base for the economic history of major league pro team sports. The first section of the supplement provides ownership histories of teams in all the major leagues in baseball, football, basketball, and hockey over the league histories. There are some gaps in coverage, especially in the early years of the leagues, so there is certainly more work to be done in this area. Sources for team histories appear in the bibliography, and are so numerous that they will not be identified here. The basic source, of course, was the *New York Times*, supplemented by anything else that was available, including especially material available at the Baseball Hall of Fame, the Pro Football Hall of Fame, the Basketball Hall of Fame, and the Hockey Hall of Fame.

The second section provides information on attendance by team over selected periods, for selected leagues. Baseball attendance data by team are taken from standard official encyclopedia sources. Baseball is the only sport where there is complete coverage of attendance data, but only for the period since 1901. No attempt has been made here to extend the available data back in time earlier than 1901. For the other sports, team attendance data are available from league publications or encyclopedias only for very recent periods. The data presented here are based on league publications and on team media guides, supplemented in some cases by game summaries from the *New York Times*, *Sporting News*, and the *Los Angeles Times*. There is a good deal of additional work needed in extending the attendance data presented here backwards in time, and some gaps even in the relatively recent past. In particular, the NHL does not publish team attendance data, and most NHL team media guides have traditionally not contained attendance data, except for the class of expansion franchises, beginning in 1967.

Finally, some summary data on radio and TV income are included in this section. With the exception of baseball team data for 1990 and 1991 (which are from the *Los Angeles Times*, Febuary 23, 1992, C3), all the data presented come from *Broadcasting*, which has been publishing estimates of league (and in some cases, team) radio and TV revenues since the 1950s. (Note: *Broadcasting* does not publish local radio and TV revenue data for hockey teams.).

Ownership Histories

Baseball

Early National League (1876–1900)

Baltimore (1892–1899)
(see also under American Association)

1892 Team moves from AA in AA-NL merger. Owner: Harry Vonder-horst.
1899 Owner: Vonderhost 40 percent, Ned Hanlon 10 percent, Ferdinand Abel 40 percent, Charles Ebbets 10 percent. This group of owners also owns like percentages of Brooklyn NL club, after purchase of shares owned by Charles Byrne, who dies in late 1898.
1900 Franchise canceled when NL reduces to eight teams. NL pays $30,000 to owners and gives them right to sell players on Baltimore roster (most good players had already been transferred to Brooklyn in 1899 season).

Brooklyn (1890–)
(see also under American Association)

1890 Team moves from AA to NL after 1889 season. Owners: Charles Byrne, Ferdinand Abel, and —— Doyle.
1899 After Byrne dies, shares are bought by syndicate, with Harry Vonderhorst owning 40 percent, Ned Hanlon owning 10 percent, Charles Ebbets owning 10 percent, and Ferdinand Abel owning 40 percent.

Boston (1876–)

1876 Original franchise in NL. Owner: Nathaniel Apollonio.
1877 Team purchased by syndicate headed by Arthur Soden, James Billings, William Conant ("The Triumvir"), and 17 other minority stockholders.

378

Buffalo (1879–1885)

1879 Expansion franchise in NL. Owner unknown.
1886 Detroit owner Fred Stearns buys Buffalo team for $7,000 to acquire Dan Brouthers, Hardy Richardson, Davy Rowe, and Deacon White. Franchise is canceled before 1886 season.

Chicago (1876–)

1876 Original franchise in NL. Owner: William Hulbert.
1877 Hulbert dies; A. J. Spalding becomes majority owner, and James Hart becomes minority owner.

Cincinnati (1890–)

1890 Team moves from AA to NL after 1890 season. Owner: Aaron Stern.
1890 After 1890 season, Stern sells team to a syndicate of PL owners for $40,000 (Al Johnson, Charles Prince, J. Earl Wagner), but NL negates sale and arranges sale instead to John T. Brush.

Cleveland (1879–1884)
(see St. Louis Maroons under National League)

1879 Expansion franchise in NL. Owner: C. H. Bulkley.
1885 Team sold before 1885 season to Henry Lucas for $2,500, who moves franchise to St. Louis as St. Louis Maroons. There were court cases concerning the fact that the team had already sold all its players to the Brooklyn AA club, but Lucas does not get the players when he buys the franchise.

Cleveland Spiders (1889–1899)

1889 Expansion team in NL. Owners: Matthew Stanley Robison and Frank De Haas Robison.
1900 Franchise canceled after 1899 season when NL reduces to eight teams for the 1900 season. The Robisons receive $25,000 for franchise and players; most good players had already been transferred to St. Louis before the 1899 season.

Detroit (1881–1888)

1881 Expansion franchise in NL. Owner: W. G. Thompson.
1886 Owner: Fred Stearns.
1888 Franchise is canceled before 1889 season.

Hartford (1876–1877)

1876 Original franchise in NL. Owner: Morgan Bulkley.
1877 Team plays games during 1877 season in Brooklyn, and franchise is canceled after 1877 season.

Indianapolis (1878–1878)

1878 Expansion franchise in NL. Owner unknown. Franchise is canceled after 1878 season.

Indianapolis (1887–1889)

1887 Expansion team in NL. Owners: John T. Brush, A. J. Treat, and G. W. Burnham.
1889 Franchise canceled after 1889 season.

Kansas City (1886–1886)

1886 Expansion franchise in NL. Owner unknown.
1887 Franchise and players are purchased by the NL for $6,000, and franchise is canceled before 1887 season.

Louisville (1876–1877)

1876 Original franchise in NL. Owner: Walter Haldeman.
1877 Franchise canceled after 1877 because of evidence that four players on the Louisville team threw games during 1876 season.

Louisville (1892–1899)
(see also under American Association)

1892 Team moves from AA to NL in AA-NL merger. Owners: Zack Phelps and Jim Hart.
1898 Owner is Barney Dreyfuss, who buys Pittsburgh NL franchise this year and transfers most Louisville players there for the 1899 season.
1900 Franchise is canceled when NL cuts to eight teams, with NL paying Dreyfuss $10,000 for franchise and players.

Milwaukee (1878–1878)

1878 Expansion franchise in NL. Owner unknown. Franchise is canceled after 1878 season.

New York (1876–1876)

1876 Original franchise in NL; team plays in Brooklyn. Owner: William Cammeyer. Franchise is canceled after 1876 season, when team refuses to complete playing schedule by traveling to western cities.

New York (1883–)

1883 Expansion team in NL. Owner: John Day.
1890 Team runs into financial trouble; Day borrows $60,000 from Arthur Soden (Boston), and sells shares to John T. Brush (Cincinnati), Ferdinand Abel (Brooklyn), A. J. Spalding (Chicago), and Edward B. Talcott.
1891 Team merges with New York PL club owned by Edwin McAlpin, with McAlpin being paid $15,000 for his players and franchise.
1892 Edward Talcott takes over majority interest in club from Day.
1895 Team is sold to Andrew Freedman.

Philadelphia (1876–1876)

1876 Original franchise in NL. Owner: B. W. Thompson. Franchise is canceled after 1876 season, when team refuses to complete its NL schedule by playing games in western cities.

Philadelphia (1883–)

1883 Expansion team in NL. Owners: A. J. Reach and John I. Rogers.

Pittsburgh (1887–)
(see also under American Association)

1887 Team moves from AA to NL. Owner: —— Nimick.
1891 Owner: J. Palmer O'Neill.
1894 Owner: William C. Temple.
1899 Barney Dreyfuss, owner of Louisville NL team, and William Kerr become equal co-owners of Pittsburgh, and Dreyfuss moves most good players from Louisville to Pittsburgh.
1900 Dreyfuss buys out Kerr for unknown price.

Providence (1878–1885)

1878 Expansion team in NL. Owner: Henry Root.
1885 Boston NL team buys team for $6,600 to acquire Hoss Radbourne and Con Dailey, and franchise is canceled.

St. Louis (1876–1877)

1876 Original franchise in NL. Owner: Charles Fowle.
1877 Franchise canceled after 1877 season.

St. Louis (1885–1886)

1885 Cleveland NL franchise moved to St. Louis, with Chris von der Ahe being paid between $2,500 and $5,000 for invading his AA territory. Owner: Henry Lucas.
1887 Franchise and players purchased by NL for $12,000 and franchise canceled before 1887 season.

St. Louis (1892–)
(see also under American Association)

1892 Team moves from AA to NL in AA-NL merger; owner Chris von der Ahe.
1899 Matthew S. and Frank De Haas Robison, owners of Cleveland NL team, buy team for $40,000, and transfer most good players on Cleveland roster to St. Louis for 1899 season.

Syracuse (1879–1882)

1879 Expansion franchise in NL. Owner unknown.
1882 Franchise is canceled after 1882 season.

Troy (1879–1882)

1879 Expansion franchise in NL. Owner unknown.
1882 Franchise is canceled after 1882 season.

Washington (1886–1889)

1886 Expansion franchise in NL. Owners: Robert and Walter Hewitt.
1889 Franchise is canceled after 1889 season.

Washington (1892–1899)
(see also under American Association)

1892 Team moves from AA to NL in AA-NL merger. Owner: J. Earl Wagner.
1900 Franchise is canceled after 1899 season, when NL cuts back to

eight teams. Owner is paid $46,500 for franchise and players, less $7,500 already received from sale of some players to Boston.

Worcester (1880–1882)

1880 Expansion franchise in NL. Owner unknown.
1882 Franchise canceled after 1882 season.

American Association (1882–1891)

League organized in 1881 by Chris von der Ahe, Billy Sharsig, and J. H. Pank. League merged with NL after 1891 season.

Baltimore (1882–1891)

1882 Original franchise in AA. Owner: Harry Vonderhorst.
1892 Team moves to NL in AA-NL merger.

Boston (1891–1891)
(see also under Players League)

1891 Team moves into AA from PL in PL-AA-NL agreement. Owner: Charles Prince.
1891 Franchise canceled, with unknown payment to Prince, in AA-NL merger.

Brooklyn (1884–1889)
(see also under National League)

1884 Expansion franchise in AA. Owners: Ferdinand Abel, Charles Byrne, R. I. Byrne, and Joseph Doyle.
1889 Team moves from AA to NL after 1889 season.

Cincinnati (1882–1889)
(see also under National League)

1882 Original franchise in AA. Owners: Justus Thorner, Colonel Harris, and O. P. Caylor.
1886 Team sold to Aaron Stern.
1889 Team moves to NL after 1889 season.

Cincinnati (1891–1891)
(see also Milwaukee under American Association)

1891 Expansion franchise in AA. Owner: Al Johnson. Johnson's franchise in AA revoked after NL pays him $30,000 for his shares in Cincinnati NL club. New club installed in Cincinnati by AA. Owner: Chris von der Ahe. Midway through season, von der Ahe sells franchise and players back to AA for $12,000, and team is moved to Milwaukee for remainder of 1991 season.

Cleveland (1887–1888)

1887 Expansion team in AA. Owner unknown.
1888 Franchise canceled after 1888 season. Whether this is the same team that moved to NL for 1889 season is unknown.

Columbus (1883–1884)

1883 Expansion franchise in AA. Owner unknown.
1884 Franchise canceled after 1884 season.

Columbus (1889–1891)

1889 Expansion franchise in AA. Owner unknown.
1891 Franchise canceled for unknown payment in AA-NL merger after 1891 season.

Indianapolis (1884–1884)

1884 Expansion franchise in AA. Owner unknown.
1884 Franchise canceled after 1884 season.

Kansas City (1888–1889)

1888 Expansion franchise in AA. Owner unknown. During season, team is sold to George Kitchum.
1889 Franchise is canceled after 1889 season.

Louisville (1882–1891)
(see also under National League)

1882 Original franchise in AA. Owner: J. H. Pank.
1886 Team sold to Zack Phelps and Jim Hart.
1891 Team moves to NL in AA-NL merger.

Milwaukee (1891–1891)
(see also Cincinnati under American Association)

1891   Cincinnati AA team moved to Milwaukee midway through 1891 season. Owner unknown. Franchise canceled for unknown payment in AA-NL merger.

New York (1883–1887)

1883   Expansion team in AA. Owner: John Day.
1885   Team sold to Erastus Wiman for $25,000, and moved to Staten Island.
1887   Franchise and players sold to owners of the Brooklyn AA team for unknown price, with players moving to Brooklyn and franchise canceled after 1887 season.

Philadelphia (1882–1890)

1882   Original franchise in AA. Owners: Bill Sharsig, Lew Simmons, and Charlie Mason.
1890   Team expelled from AA after 1890 season for not paying bills due to league and league members.

Philadelphia (1891–1891)

1891   Expansion team in AA. Philadelphia PL team moves to AA as part of the PL-AA-NL agreement after 1890 season. Owner: J. Earl Wagner. Franchise canceled with unknown payment in AA-NL merger after 1891 season.

Pittsburgh (1882–1886)
(see also under National League)

1882   Original franchise in NL. Owner: —— Nimick.
1886   Team moves from AA to NL after 1886 season.

Richmond (1884–1884)
(see also Washington under American Association)

1884   Washington AA team moves to Richmond midway through 1884 season. Owner unknown. Franchise canceled after 1884 season.

Rochester (1890–1890)

1890 Expansion franchise in AA. Owner: Henry Brinker. Franchise bought by AA after 1890 season and canceled. Toledo, Rochester, and Syracuse shared $24,000 payment by AA.

St. Louis (1882–1891)

1882 Original franchise in AA. Owner: Chris von der Ahe.
1891 Team moves into NL as part of AA-NL merger after 1891 season.

Syracuse (1890–1890)

1890 Expansion franchise in AA. Owner unknown. Franchise bought by AA after 1890 season and canceled. Toledo, Syracuse, and Rochester share $24,000 league payment.

Toledo (1890–1890)

1890 Expansion franchise in AA. Owner unknown. Franchise bought by AA after 1890 season and canceled. Toledo, Syracuse, and Rochester share $24,000 league payment.

Washington (1884–1884)
(also see Richmond under American Association)

1884 Expansion team in AA. Owner unknown. Team moves to Richmond midway through 1884 season.

Washington (1891–1891)

1891 Expansion team in AA. Owner unknown. After 1891 season, team moves to NL in AA-NL merger, and team is sold to J. Earl Wagner.

Union Association (1884)

Altoona

Original franchise in UA. Owners: officials of the Pennsylvania Railroad. In midseason, the franchise was moved to Kansas City.

386

Baltimore

Original franchise in UA. Owner: A. H. Henderson.

Boston

Original franchise in UA. Owner: syndicate headed by George Wright.

Chicago

Original franchise in UA. Owner: A. H. Henderson. Franchise moved to Pittsburgh in midseason.

Cincinnati

Original franchise in UA. Owner: syndicate including Justus Thorner.

Kansas City

Altoona franchise moves to Kansas City in midseason. Owner unknown.

Milwaukee

Wilmington franchise moves to Milwaukee in midseason. Owner unknown.

Philadelphia

Original franchise in UA. Owner unknown. Franchise moves to Wilmington in midseason.

Pittsburgh

Chicago franchise moves to Pittsburgh in midseason, and then moved to St. Paul. Owner unknown.

St. Louis

Original franchise in UA. Owner: Henry Lucas. Minority owners: Ellis Wainwright and Adolphus Busch.

St. Paul

Chicago/Pittsburgh franchise moves to St. Paul in midseason. Owner unknown.

Washington

Original franchise in UA. Owner: William Warren White.

Wilmington

Philadelphia franchise moves to Wilmington in midseason. Owner unknown.

Players League (1890)

Organized by John Montgomery Ward, played only 1890 season, then merged with AA and NL after 1890 season. No franchise moves during 1890 season.

Boston

Owner: Charles Prince. Team moves to AA in 1891 as part of PL-AA-NL agreement.

Brooklyn

Owners: Wendell Goodwin, John Walles, and Edward Linton. Owners obtain a 20 percent share of Brooklyn NL team as part of PL-AA-NL agreement.

Buffalo

Owners: Jack Rowe and Deacon White.

Chicago

Owner: John Addison. After 1890 season, owner sells players to A. J. Spalding, owner of Chicago NL team, for $18,000.

Cleveland

Owner: Al Johnson. After 1890 season Johnson is part of a syndicate (other members: Charles Prince, J. Earl Wagner), which purchases control of the Cincinnati NL club after the PL-AA-NL agreement, with Johnson being given all the syndicate shares when Prince and Wagner obtain an AA franchise. NL revokes the sale, leading to lawsuits, which are not settled until 1901.

New York

Owner: Edwin McAlpin. Under PL-AA-NL agreement, McAlpin sells his players to New York NL team for $15,000.

Philadelphia

Owner: J. Earl Wagner, with his brothers minority owners. Under PL-AA-NL agreement, Wagner becomes owner of new Philadelphia team in AA.

Pittsburgh

Owner unknown.

Federal League (1914–1915)

The Federal League operated as a minor league in 1913, and then became an outlaw major league in 1914 and 1915. The league disbanded after the 1915 season under an agreement with the AL and NL.

Baltimore

1914 Expansion franchise in FL. Owners: Ned Hanlon and —— Schleunes.
1915 Team sold to Carroll Rasin. Rasin was offered $50,000 and ownership of the Baltimore franchise in the International League as part of the FL-NL-AL agreement, but Rasin rejected the agreement and sued under the Sherman Act, ultimately losing his suit.

Brooklyn

1914 Expansion team in FL. Owners: Robert Ward and brother.
1915 Ward dies. Under FL-NL-AL agreement, his brother and his heirs get $20,000 per year for 20 years.

Buffalo

1914 Expansion team in FL. Owner: Walter Mullen.
1915 Team sold to Laurens Eeros, Howard Forman, and O. E. Foster for unknown price. Team goes bankrupt after 1915 season, and was given unknown sum in FL-AL-NL agreement.

Chicago

1913 Original member of FL. Owners: J. T. Powers and James Gilmore.
1914 Team sold to Charles Weegham for unknown price.
1915 As part of FL-AL-NL agreement, Weegham allowed to buy the Chicago NL team for $500,000, with NL giving him $50,000 of purchase price.

Cleveland

1913 Orginal member of FL. Owner M. F. Bramley. Team is dropped from FL after 1913 season.

Covington

1913 Original member of FL. Owners: C. E. Clark and J. Spinney. Midway through 1913 season, team moved to Kansas City.

Indianapolis

1913 Original member of FL. Owners: James A. Ross and J. E. Krause.
1914 After 1914 season, team is sold to Harry Sinclair and P. J. White, and team is moved to Newark.

Kansas City

1913 Covington team moved to Kansas City midway through 1913 season, and was sold to C. C. Madison, H. Wright, and F. Turner.
1915 Team sold to Charles Baird and C. H. Mann. Team goes bankrupt after 1915 season, and is given unknown amount in FL-AL-NL agreement.

Newark

1914 After 1914 season, Indianapolis team moved to Newark. Owners: Harry Sinclair and P. J. White.

1915 As part of FL-AL-NL agreement, Sinclair and White are given $10,000 per year for 10 years and are allowed to sell several player contracts owned by Newark.

Pittsburgh

1913 Original franchise in FL. Owner: M. Henderson.
1915 Team sold to Edward Gwynner and C. B. Comstock for unknown price. As part of the FL-AL-NL agreement, Gwymmer and Comstock are given $50,000 in cash plus the option to purchase an unspecified major league team within a month, an option that was not exercised.

St. Louis

1913 Original franchise in FL. Owners: Phil Ball, O. Stifel, Eugene Handlan, and E. A. Steininger.
1915 As part of FL-AL-NL agreement, Ball was allowed to buy the St. Louis AL team for $525,000; whether the AL kicked in $50,000, as with the purchase of the Cubs by Weegham, is not known.

National League (1901–1991)

Atlanta Braves

1900 Boston Nationals owned by the "Triumvir," a syndicate of Arthur Soden, William Conant, and J. R. Billings, who have owned team since 1877.
1904 Billings sells his share in team to Conant and Soden for unknown price.
1906 Majority interest in team and park sold to John Harris, George Dovey, and John Dovey for $75,000. Playing manager Fred Tenney has $12,000 interest in team. Nickname changed to Doves.
1907 Tenney is fired as manager; he offers his shares for $15,000 but there are no takers. Tenney continues as part-owner of Boston while playing for the New York Giants.
1910 Doveys sell their stock to Harris, who sells club to a syndicate headed by William Hepburn Russell. Syndicate includes Louis G. Page, George Page, Frederic Murphy, and James Phelan. Team sells for $114,000 (including $13,000 paid to Tenney for his stock). Team now known as the Boston Rustlers.
1911 Russell dies. Ed Hanlon offers $169,000 for team, to move it to Baltimore, but is refused. Team sold to James Gaffney, John Montgom-

ery Ward, and John Carroll for $187,000 with Gaffney putting up most of the money. Team is renamed the Boston Braves.

1912 Ward sells his interest to Gaffney in midseason for unknown price.

1916 Team sold to a syndicate headed by Percy Haughton, and including Miller, Roe, Hagan, Louis A. Frothingham, David Walsh, Stallings, and Hapgood, for unknown price ("a lot more than $187,000").

1919 George Washington Grant buys team for $400,000 (price does not include park, Braves Field, which cost $600,000 to build in 1915).

1923 Team sold to a syndicate headed by Judge Emil Fuchs, and including Christy Mathewson, Charles Levine, and James McDonough. Price of team is $500,000.

1925 Mathewson dies. Fuchs buys up his interest at unknown price. Albert Powell attempts to take over club, acquires 45 percent of stock and then gives up attempt, selling his 45 percent to James Giblen for $175,000.

1927 Charles Adams and Bruce Wetmore buy Giblen's stock for unknown price.

1934 Fuchs and team are in financial trouble. National League guarantees park rental and loans club money.

1935 Fuchs goes broke. Adams acquires control of 65 percent of team as collateral on loans, and then turns over control of team to a group headed by Leo Goulston, and including Oscar Horton, who give Adams a claim of $325,000 against the team.

1941 Team is again in financial trouble. Adams's interest and control of the team is acquired by a syndicate headed by Bob Quinn, for a price of $750,000. Syndicate includes Max Meyer, Dr. William Wrang, J. W. Powdrell, Richard Hevessy, Frank McCourt, Daniel Marr, Casey Stengel, Guido Rugo, Joseph Maney, and Lou Perini.

1944 Syndicate headed by Perini and his brothers (who hold 50 percent interest), and including Rugo and Maney, buys control of the team (not including park) for $750,000.

1946 Perini buys out minority stockholders (other than Rugo and Maney) for unknown price, and syndicate acquires 100 percent control of team.

1949 Team buys Braves stadium for $350,000.

1951 Rugo sells out to Perini and Maney for unknown price. Club is valued at $3.5 million by tax assessors.

1952 Perini and his brothers acquire 100 percent control of team for unknown price.

1953 Braves move to Milwaukee, and team is renamed Milwaukee Braves. No change in ownership.

1962 Milwaukee Braves sold to a syndicate headed by William Bartholomay and Donald Reynolds, for $6.2 million.

1966 Team moves to Atlanta and is renamed Atlanta Braves. No change in ownership.

1976 Ted Turner buys the team for $11 million.

Boston Braves (see Atlanta Braves)

Brooklyn Dodgers (see Los Angeles Dodgers)

Chicago Cubs

1900 Team is owned by Jim Hart.

1905 Charles Murphy heads a syndicate, bankrolled by Charles P. Taft, that buys Cubs for $105,000.

1915 As part of settlement of the *Federal League* case, Charles Weegham is permitted to buy the Cubs for $500,000, with the National League putting up $50,000 of purchase price. The Weegham syndicate includes William Wrigley.

1918 William Wrigley acquires controlling interest in team for unknown price.

1932 William Wrigley dies. His son, Phil Wrigley, takes over the team.

1977 Phil Wrigley dies. By this time, Wrigley owns 8,015 of the 10,000 outstanding shares of team. Ownership is passed on to his son, Bill Wrigley, with his daughter a minority stockholder.

1981 Team sold for $20.5 million (including Wrigley Field) to the Tribune Company, which acquires all outstanding stock. Cubs had lost $1.7 million in 1980.

Cincinnati Reds

1900 Team owned by John T. Brush.

1902 Team is sold for $146,000 to a syndicate headed by Julius and Max Fleischman. Syndicate includes George Cox and August Herrmann.

1913 For tax purposes, franchise and players valued at $450,000.

1915 Tax assessment of field and land owned by team is set at $371,000.

1919 Campbell Johnson McDiarmid becomes large minority stockholder at unknown price.

1929 Sidney Weil buys control of team, spending $640,000 for 53 percent of shares (implicit value of team is $1.2 million). Minority interest (4 percent) is held by Lon Widrig.

1933 Weil goes broke, and team is taken over by the Central Trust Company, which held Weil's notes.

1934 Team is sold to a syndicate headed by Powell Crosley, at unknown price.

1961 Crosley dies. By this time, Crosley has acquired 98 percent interst in team. Team is left to the Crosley Foundation.

1962 Crosley Foundation sells its 98 percent interest in team to a syndicate headed by Bill DeWitt, for $4,625,000.

1966 DeWitt group sells its shares to "617, Inc.," a syndicate headed by Francis Dale. No single owner owns more than 15 percent of team. Syndicate includes Louis Nippert, David Gamble, Ray and Barry Buse, Jim and Bill Williams, William Hackett, John Sawyer, A. E. Knowlton, and Andrew Hoppie.

1984 Majority control of team sold to Marge Schott for unknown price.

Colorado Rockies

1991 Expansion franchise for 1993 season awarded to Colorado Baseball Partnership syndicate, headed by John Antonucci, and including Stephen Ehrhart, Michael Monus, and Coors Brewery. Expansion fee is $95 million. Team will play in Mile High Stadium for two years while new stadium, Coors Field, is being built.

Florida Marlins

1991 Expansion franchise for 1993 season awarded to South Florida Big League Baseball, Inc., a syndicate headed by H. Wayne Huizenga. Expansion fee is $95 million. Team will play in Joe Robbie Stadium.

Houston Astros

1960 Expansion team for 1961 season. Expansion fee is $1.8 million. Owner is Houston Sports Association, headed by Craig Culinan, and including Roy Hofheinz, Bob Smith, Bud Adams (10 percent), and George Kirksey. Team known as Houston Colts.

1963 Hofheinz acquires all other shares in Houston Sports Association at unknown price and becomes sole owner of club.

1964 Astrodome opens. Houston Sports Association acquires a 40-year lease on Astrodome. Team renamed the Houston Astros.

1976 Hofheinz goes broke. Astros are taken over and operated by the two main creditors of Hofheinz: GE Credit Corporation, and Ford Motor Credit Corporation.

1979 Astros (including the Astrodome lease) are sold for $19 million to a syndicate headed by John McMullen, and including David LeFevre, Jack Trotter, and Herb Neyland.

1992 Team is reportedly on the market.

Los Angeles Dodgers

1900 Owners of team are Harry Vonderhorst, Charles Ebbets, and Ferdinand Abel.

1902 Abel sells his shares to Ebbets for unknown price, and then Vonderhorst sells his shares as well. Ebbets now controls 90 percent of team, with Ned Hanlon, team manager, owning 10 percent.

1903 Hanlon sells his shares to Ebbets for unknown price.

1912 Ebbets sells 50 percent of team to Ed and Steve McKeever for $100,000 to obtain the funding needed to finish construction of Ebbets Field.

1925 Ebbets dies, leaving his 50 percent ownership to his wife and children. A week later, Ed McKeever dies, leaving his 25 percent to his family.

1938 Team is near bankruptcy. Larry McPhail is brought in as president. Steve McKeever dies, leaving his 25 percent interest to his daughter, Mrs. Jim Mulvey.

1942 Team is free of debt after four profitable years under McPhail. McPhail resigns as president to go into the army, and is replaced by Branch Rickey. Team hires Walter O'Malley as lawyer.

1944 Ed McKeever stock is put up for sale by heirs. Branch Rickey, Walter O'Malley, and John Smith buy the 25 percent interest for $347,000.

1945 Rickey, O'Malley, and Smith buy 50 percent Ebbets interest from Ebbets heirs for $750,000, to obtain 75 percent control of team. Remaining 25 percent is owned by Mrs. Jim Mulvey.

1950 John Smith dies. Rickey sells his 25 percent to O'Malley and Smith's widow for $1,025,000, after getting an offer of $1 million from William Zeckendorf. Rickey is out as president, replaced by O'Malley. Later in the year, O'Malley acquires part of Smith's widow's holding for an unknown price, to obtain a 67 percent interest in team. Mrs. Jim Mulvey dies, leaving her 25 percent to her daughter, Ann Branca, and son, Bud Mulvey.

1958 Dodgers move to Los Angeles and are renamed the Los Angeles Dodgers. Ebbets Field is sold to Marvin Kratter for $3 million.

1962 Dodger Stadium opens.

1970 Peter O'Malley is appointed president of Dodgers.
1979 Walter O'Malley dies. His stock is left to his son, Peter O'Malley.

Milwaukee Braves (see Atlanta Braves)

Montreal Expos

1968 Expansion team for 1969 season. Expansion fee is $12.5 million. Owner of team is a syndicate headed by John McHale and Charles Bronfman, with five other minority partners, including Hugh Hallward.
1990 Team sold for $86 million to a syndicate headed by Charles Brochu, including a food chain and a credit union, plus investments by the city of Montreal ($12.9 million) and the province of Quebec ($15.5 million).

New York Giants (see San Francisco Giants)

New York Mets

1960 Expansion team for 1961 season. Expansion fee is $1.8 million. Owner is a syndicate headed by Joan Payson, and including Donald Grant, Dwight Davis, G. H. Walker, and William Simpson.
1975 Joan Payson dies. Eighty percent of stock in team is held by the Payson estate, and is left to her husband and children. Daughter Lorinda de Roulet is team president.
1980 Team is sold to a syndicate headed by Doubleday and Co., and including John O. Pickett and Fred Wilpon. Price of team is $21 million.
1986 Nelson Doubleday and Fred Wilpon buy Doubleday and Co.'s 95 percent interest in team for $95 million.

Philadelphia Phillies

1990 Team is owned by John Rodgers.
1903 Team sold for $200,000 to a syndicate headed by James Potter, and including Barney Dreyfuss and August Herrmann (owners of Pittsburgh and Cincinnati).
1905 Control of team is sold to a syndicate of Israel Durham, James McNichol, and Clarence Wolf, with Billy Murray buying up Dreyfuss's minority interest, all at unknown prices. Durham dies in midseason.
1909 Team sold to a syndicate headed by Horace Fogel, backed by Charles P. Taft, and including Charles Murphy, owner of the Cubs. Team price is $350,000.

1913 Team sold at unknown price to syndicate headed by William Locke, and including William Baker, Walter and Morris Clothier, Harrison Caner, Thomas Murphy, Frederick Chandler, and Chester Ray. Locke dies in midseason, and Baker buys Locke's interest at unknown price and takes control of team.

1930 Baker dies and leaves stock to wife and to the club secretary, Mrs. May Mallon Nugent.

1933 Mrs. Baker dies and leaves her stock to Mrs. Nugent and Mrs. Nugent's son, Gerald P. Nugent, who take control of tema.

1943 Team is bankrupt. National League takes over team for $325,000. Team is sold for $230,000 to a syndicate of 11 individuals headed by William Cox. Judge Landis then throws Cox out of baseball for betting on games. Bob Carpenter buys the team from the Cox syndicate for $400,000.

1973 Team is taken over by Carpenter's son, Rudy Carpenter.

1981 Team is sold for $31,175,000 to a syndicate headed by Bill Giles, with major investor Taft Broadcasting Co. of Cincinnati.

Pittsburgh Pirates

1900 Barney Dreyfuss and William Kerr, Owners of Louisville NL team, buy the Pittsburgh franchise when Louisville franchise is canceled, and move Louisville players to Pittsburgh.

1901 Dreyfuss buys out Kerr for $70,000.

1932 Dreyfuss dies. Team is left to his widow, but team is operated by Dreyfuss's son-in-law, William Benswanger.

1946 Dreyfuss heirs sell their 90 percent of the team for $2,250,000 to a syndicate headed by Frank McKinney (40 percent), and including Bing Crosby (15 percent), John Galbreath (20 percent), Tom Johnson (15 percent), and —— Margiotti (19 percent).

1950 Galbreath and Johnson buy out McKinney for $750,000 and then buy out Margiotti for $200,000.

1983 Warner Communications buys 49 percent of Pirates for unknown price; remaining 51 percent is held by Galbreath.

1985 Galbreath and Warner sell 99 percent of team for $22 million to a public-private syndicate including the city of Pittsburgh, Westinghouse, Alcoa, and three individuals.

St. Louis Cardinals

1900 Owner is Frank De Haas Robison and his brother, Stanley Robison.

1905 Frank De Haas Robison dies, and his brother takes over team.

1911 Stanley Robision dies. His niece, Mrs. Schuleyer Britton, takes over team.

1917 Cardinals are bankrupt. Team (including Robison Field) is sold for $375,000 to a syndicate headed by James C. Jones. Branch Rickey is hired as president, and is sued by Phil Ball for leaving his management job with the St. Louis Browns.

1920 Cardinals are in financial trouble again. Team sells Federal park and grounds for $275,000, and begins a rental arrangement at Sportsman's Park, owned by the Browns. Sam Breadon lends the team $18,000, and acquires 72 percent of the stock in the team. Rickey obtains an 18 percent interest. One other minority stockholder is Rogers Hornby.

1925 Rickey is fired as Cardinals manager and sells his 20 percent interest in team to Hornsby and Breadon for $250,000.

1935 Breadon tries to sell the Cardinals for $1.1 million, but there are no takers. Breadon tries to move the team to Detroit, but the move is vetoed by the Tigers.

1947 Fred Saigh and Bob Hannegan buy the team for $4.1 million. Assets of the team include $2 million in cash.

1949 Saigh buys out Hannegan for $1.5 million. Saigh now controls 90 percent of the team.

1953 Team sold for $3.75 million to a subsidiary of Anheuser Busch. Saigh had been offered $4 million by a group that planned to move the team to Milwaukee, but Saigh turned down the offer.

1980 Report in press that Anheuser Busch offered to sell the team to Apex Oil for $23.5 million. Later in the year, Anheuser Busch acquires control of the corporation that owns Busch Stadium.

1988 Gussie Busch dies.

San Diego Padres

1968 Expansion team for 1969 season. Expansion fee of $12.5 million. Owner is a syndicate headed by C. Arnholdt Smith, and including Buzzy Bavazi.

1973 Smith is indicted for tax evasion. Group headed by Joseph Danzansky offers $12 million for team to move it to Washington, D.C., but deal falls through.

1974 Team sold to Ray Kroc for $12 million.

1980 Kroc announces that the team lost $2.7 million in 1980.

1984 Kroc dies. Team is taken over by his widow, Joan Kroc.

1987 Sale of team to George Argyros is announced, but bid for team is withdrawn.

1990 Team is on the market for a reported $100 million. In March

1990, team is sold for $75 million to a syndicate headed by Tom Warner, and including (Leon Parma, Ernest Rady, Malin Burnham, Bob Payne, Russell Goldsmith, Arthur Engel, Jackson Goodall, Arthur Rivkin, and Scott Wolfe.

San Francisco Giants

1900 Andrew Freedman is owner of the Giants.
1903 After selling the Reds, John T. Brush buys the Giants for $125,000.
1912 Brush dies, Giants are left to his widow and two daughters. Harry Hempstead, husband of daughter Eleanor, takes over operation of team.
1919 Brush heirs sell their interest in the Giants (1,362 shares of 2,200 outstanding) for $1,092,000, to a three-man syndicate: Charles Stoneham, Francis McQuade, and John McGraw. Implicit price of team, including the Polo Grounds, is $1.8 million.
1928 Stoneham fires McQuade as team treasurer and buys up his shares for unknown price.
1934 McGraw dies. His shares are sold to Stoneham for unknown price.
1936 Charles Stoneham dies. Team is left to his son, Horace Stoneham.
1958 Joan Payson, minority stockholder in Giants, offers to buy the team to keep it in New York, but Stoneham moves the team to San Francisco. Team is renamed San Francisco Giants.
1976 LaBatt's Breweries offers $13.5 million for team, which price includes $5 million to pay compensation to city of San Francisco, to move team to Toronto. Offer of $8.5 million for owners of Giants is matched by Bob Lurie (51 percent) and Bud Herseth (49 percent), and team is sold to the Lurie-Herseth syndicate, which keeps the team in San Francisco.
1977 Group headed by Emil Bernard and Rocky Aoki obtain an option to buy Herseth's shares for $5 million, in order to move the team to Washington, D.C. Lurie exercises his right of first refusal to match the offer and buys out Herseth for $5 million, with team staying in San Francisco.

American League (1901–1991)

Baltimore Orioles I (see New York Yankees)

Baltimore Orioles II
1901 Milwaukee Brewers original AL franchise. Owner: Henry Killilea.

1902 Killilea sells Milwaukee team for $50,000 to a syndicate headed by Robert Leed Hedges, and including Ralph Orthwein and R. Gardner. Team is moved to St. Louis for the 1902 season and renamed St. Louis Browns.

1915 Phil Ball buys team for $525,000 as part of the Federal League settlement.

1933 Ball dies, leaving team to family.

1936 Ball estate sells team for $325,000 to a syndicate headed by Don Barnes, and including Bill DeWitt and Anthony Buford. Price does not include Sportsmans Park.

1945 Richard Muckerman buys team from Barnes syndicate for $1,443,000, and also buys Sportsmans' Park for $500,000.

1949 DeWitt brothers buy 56 percent of the team (including stadium) for $1 million.

1951 Syndicate headed by Bill Veeck pays $1.4 million for DeWitt brothers' 58 percent share of team and stadium; then syndicate buys an additional 21 percent of the shares for $350,000.

1953 Veeck bid to move team to Baltimore rejected by AL for second time. Veeck group sells its 79 percent share of the team to a Baltimore syndicate headed by Clarence Miles for $2,475,000 and sells the stadium to the Cardinals for $850,000. Cardinals also pay $300,000 of moving expenses for team. Team move to Baltimore is approved by the AL. Team is renamed Baltimore Orioles.

1965 Team is sold to Jerry Hoffberger for unknown price.

1978 Hoffberger reports talks with prospective buyers. Asking price for team is $12 million.

1979 Hoffberger sells 80 percent interest in team to Edward B. Williams for $10.5 million, retaining 20 percent. Implicit value of team is $13 million.

1988 Edward B. Williams dies. Team is sold by Williams' heirs for $70 million, to a syndicate headed by Eli Jacobs, and including Sargent Shriver, Robert Shriver, and Larry Luchino.

Boston Red Sox

1901 Boston Puritans (also known as Pilgrims) original AL team. Owner is a syndicate headed by Charles Somers and Ban Johnson.

1903 Somers sells out his interest to Henry Killilea for unknown price.

1904 Team sold by Johnson and Killilea for unknown price to Charles Taylor and his son, John Taylor.

1907 Name changed to Boston Red Sox.

1912 John Taylor sells 50 percent of team to Jim McAleer and Robert

McRoy for $150,000. Fenway Park opens, under ownership of the Taylors.

1913 McAleer and McRoy sell their 50 percent share of team to Joseph Lannin for $200,000. The Taylors retain their 50 percent of team and ownership of Fenway Park.

1916 By this time, Lannin has acquired 100 percent control of team and ownership of Fenway Park, for a total investment of $600,000. Team and park are sold for $1 million to Harry Frazee and Hugh Ward.

1923 Team is sold for $1,150,000 to a syndicate headed by Bob Quinn and including Palmer Winslow.

1926 Winslow dies. Majority owners are Quinn and Winslow's widow.

1933 Team is bankrupt and is sold to Tom Yawkey for $350,000. Yawkey also buys Fenway Park for $400,000.

1976 Yawkey dies. Trustees take over operation of team.

1978 Team sold to syndicate with general partners Jean Yawkey (widow of Tom Yawkey), Haywood Sullivan, and Buddy LeRoux. General partners own 47 percent of team. Price is $15 million plus $5.5 million for Fenway Park and land. There are nine limited partners, owning 53 percent of syndicate.

1987 Buddy LeRoux sells out his interest to Jean Yawkey and Haywood Sullivan for unknown price, after an unsucessful attempt by LeRoux to take over control of the team from the other two partners. A panel is set up to value team for a proposed buyout of the 53 percent held by limited partners. Team and park valued at $150 million.

1992 Mrs. Yawkey dies.

California Angels

1960 Expansion franchise as the Los Angeles Angels, for 1961 season. Expansion fee $2.1 million. Owner is a syndicate headed by Gene Autry, and including Bob Reynolds and Paul O'Bryan.

1965 Team moves to Anaheim, and is renamed California Angels. No ownership change.

Chicago White Sox

1900 Original AL franchise. Owner: Charles Comiskey.

1931 Charles Comiskey dies, leaves team to his son, Lou Comiskey.

1939 Lou Comiskey dies, leaves 50 percent to his widow, and 50 percent to his children, Dorothy, Charles, and Grace.

1956 Grace Comiskey dies. Will and earlier bequests result in 54 percent of team's being owned by her daughter, Dorothy Rigney, and 46 percent by her son, Charles.

1959 Dorothy Rigney sells her 54 percent of team for $2.7 million to a syndicate headed by Bill Veeck, with Charles Comiskey retaining his 46 percent. The Veeck syndicate is organized as the CBC Corporation; Veeck has 30 percent of the shares, Hank Greenberg 40 percent, Arthur Allyn 24 percent, and John Allyn 6 percent.

1961 Arthur Allyn buys out Veeck and Greenberg for $2.94 million, so that Arthur Allyn owns 54 percent of team. Implicit price of team is $7.8 million.

1969 Between 1961 and 1969 (date unknown), Charles Comiskey sells his shares to Arthur Allyn for unknown price. Arthur Allyn then sells team to John Allyn for unknown price.

1975 John Allyn sells 80 percent of team for $8.55 million to a syndicate headed by Bill Veeck, with Allyn retaining a 20 percent interest in the team. Implicit price of team is $10.7 million.

1980 Edward DeBartolo, Sr., makes bid for team of $20 million, but AL rejects the bid.

1981 Team is sold for $20 million to a syndicate headed by Jerry Reinsdorf and including Eddie Einhorn.

1982 White Sox sell Comiskey Park for $12.5 million.

Cleveland Indians

1900 Original AL franchise, Cleveland Blues. Owners: Charles Somers and Jack Kilfoyl.

1901 Name of team changed to Cleveland Bronchos.

1903 Name of team changed to Cleveland Naps, after Napoleon Lajoie.

1910 Kilfoyl sells out to Somers for unknown price. Name changed to Cleveland Indians.

1916 Somers goes broke and sells team for $500,000 to syndicate headed by James C. Dunn, and including Pat McCarthy, John Burns, and Tom Walsh.

1922 Dunn dies; team is left to his widow.

1927 Dunn's widow, now Mrs. George Pross, sells team for $1 million to syndicate headed by Alva Bradley, and including John Sherwin, Charles Bradley, Percy Morgan, Newton Baker, Joseph Hostetter, and O. P. and M. J. Van Swearingen.

1932 Van Swearingens sell their original $250,000 investment (25 percent of team) for $125,000 to a group headed by Alva Bradley, and including E. G. Crawford, I. F. Freiberger, and W. G. Bernet. Morgan sells his original $200,000 investment (20 percent) to George Martin and George Tomlinson for unknown price.

1946 Team sold by Bradley group for $1.6 million to syndicate headed by Bill Veeck, and including Lester Armour, Phil Clark, Phil Swift, Arthur Allyn, Newton Frye, Sidney Schiff, Harry Grabiner, Robert Goldstein, W. Crozier Smith, J. J. Klein, Ralph Perkins, Jack Harris, Richard Downing, and Herman Radner.

1948 Hank Greenberg buys 67 percent of syndicate for unknown price.

1949 Veeck group sells team for $2.5 million to a syndicate headed by Ellis Ryan.

1956 Team sold for $3.96 million to syndicate headed by William Daley, and including Shaughnessy and Greenberg.

1966 Daley group sells team to Stauffer for $8 million.

1972 Team sold to syndicate headed by Nick Mileti for $9.75 million to $10.8 million, with Mileti owning less than 10 percent.

1973 Gabe Paul sells his 7 percent interest in team to Ansor for $500,000.

1975 Team reportedly loses $500,000.

1977 Team sold for unknown price to syndicate headed by Steve O'Neill and including Gabe Paul.

1980 Proposed bid for 63 percent of team by Neil Papiano and James Nederlander for $10 million, with O'Neill and Paul to retain minority interests, but deal falls through.

1983 Steve O'Neill dies. Patrick O'Neill, trustee of estate, announces that majority interest in the club is for sale.

1984 Sale of team for $41 million to David LeFevre is announced, but deal is canceled because of threatened suits by minority stockholders.

1986 Team is sold to Richard and David Jacobs for unknown price.

Detroit Tigers

1901 Original AL franchise. Owner: James Burns. Minority owner: George Stallings.

1902 Team sold for unknown price to Samuel Angus.

1903 Control of team sold to William Hoover Yawkey for $50,000, with Frank Navin having $5,000 interest and Ed Barrow $2,500 interest.

1907 Yawkey gives Navin an additional 40 percent interest in team.

1912 Navin acquires sole control of team, which is valued for tax purposes at $650,000.

1920 Navin sells 25 percent of team to Walter O. Briggs and 25 percent to John Kelsey, at a total price of $500,000. Later in the year, Kelsey dies, and Briggs buys up his interest at unknown price.

1935 Navin dies, and Briggs buys his shares (50 percent) for $1 million.

1952 Briggs dies. Team is operated by his son, Spike Briggs.

1956 Briggs estate sells team for $5.5 million to a syndicate headed by

John Fetzer, and including Fred Knorr, Carl Lee, and Kenyon Brown. A syndicate headed by Bill Veeck had earlier bid $5.2 million for the team, and upped its bid to $5.6 million after the Fetzer bid came in.

1960 Fetzer buys out Kenyon Brown's interest at unknown price.

1961 Fred Knorr dies. Fetzer buys up his and all remaining interest in team for an unknown price, and becomes sole owner of team.

1983 Fetzer sells team to Tom Monaghan for $53 million.

1992 Team reportedly is on the market.

Kansas City Athletics (see Oakland Athletics)

Kansas City Royals

1968 Expansion team for 1969 season. Expansion fee of $5.55 million. Owner: Ewing Kaufman.

1983 Kaufman sells 49 percent interest in team to Aaron Fogelman for $11 million, with a purchase option agreement under which Fogelman can purchase Kaufman's shares when he wishes, at a price of $11 million.

1988 Kaufman sells an additional 1 percent of shares to Fogelman.

1990 Kaufman announces that he will repurchase Fogelman shares early in 1991.

Milwaukee Brewers I (see Baltimore Orioles)

Milwaukee Brewers II

1968 Seattle Pilots expansion franchise in AL for 1969 season. Expansion fee of $5.3 million, plus forgoing team share of national TV contract for three years, plus 2 percent of team gate receipts to be given to league for three years. Owner is syndicate headed by Dewey Soriano, financed by majority stockholder William Daley.

1970 Team goes bankrupt. Group headed by James Douglas and Eddie Carlson offers $11.5 million for team, to keep it in Seattle, but AL turns down deal because of financing. Team is sold for $10.8 million to a syndicate headed by Bud Selig and including Ed Fitzgerald. Team is moved to Milwaukee and renamed Milwaukee Brewers.

Minnesota Twins

1900 Original franchise in AL of Washington Senators (also known as Washington Nationals). Owned by syndicate headed by Ban Johnson (51 percent), and including Fred Postal and Tom Loftus.

1903   Johnson buys out Postal for $15,000.

1904   Controlling interest in team sold for unknown price to syndicate headed by Thomas Noyes, and including Wilton Lambert, William Dwyer, W. H. Rapley, Benjamin Minor, Henry Blair, Corcoran Thom, and E. J. Walsh.

1912   Noyes dies. Benjamin Minor takes over operation of team. Clark Griffith is hired as manager, and buys 10 percent interest in team for $27,000.

1919   Griffith and William Richardson buy 40 percent each for $145,000 each, giving Griffith a 50 percent interest in team.

1950   John Jachym buys Richardson's estate's 40 percent. Later in the year, Jachym sells out to H. Gabriel Murphy. Both transactions at unknown price.

1955   Clark Griffith dies, leaves his 50 percent interest to his nephew, Calvin Griffith.

1961   Team moves to Minnesota and is renamed the Minnesota Tiwns.

1984   Team is sold to Carl Pohlad for between $32 million and $38 million, mainly in deferred payments. Pohlad acquires all stock, Griffith and Murphy shares combined.

New York Yankees

1901   Baltimore Orioles original AL franchise. Owners: Harry Goldman, S. Mahon, and Sidney Frank.

1903   Frank Farrell (75 percent) and Big Bill Devery head a syndicate that buys team for $18,000 and moves team to New York. Team renamed the New York Highlanders.

1913   Team moves to Polo Grounds as tenants of the Giants, and is renamed the New York Yankees.

1914   Colonel Tillinghast Huston (50 percent) and Jacob Ruppert (50 percent) buy team for $460,000.

1922   Ruppert buys out Huston for $1.5 million.

1923   Yankee Stadium opens; construction cost is $2.5 million.

1939   Ruppert dies. His shares (86.9 percent) are divided equally among his nieces and a friend (Mrs. James Holleran, Mrs. J. Basil Maguire, and Miss Helen Wyant). Minority stockholders include Ed Barrow (10 percent).

1945   Ruppert heirs sell their 86.9 percent interest in the team to a syndicate of Dan Topping, Del Webb, and Larry McPhail, for $2.5 million. Syndicate then buys Ed Barrow's 10 percent interest for $300,000. Total price of $2.8 million includes Yankee Stadium.

1948   Topping and Webb buy out McPhail's one-third interest for $2.2 million.

1953 Topping and Webb sell Yankee Stadium and Blues Stadium in Kansas City to Arnold Johnson for $6.5 million, under a 20-year lease-back arrangement at an annual rent of $180,000 per year. Leaseback includes option to renew for an additional 40 years.

1955 Johnson sells the land under Yankee Stadium to the Knights of Columbus for an unknown price, and then sells the stadium itself to John Cox, who donates it to Rice University.

1964 Topping and Webb sell 80 percent of team to CBS for $11.2 million.

1965 Webb sells his remaining 10 percent to CBS for $1.4 million.

1967 Topping sells his remaining 10 percent to CBS for an unknown price (probably $1.4 million); $1.35 million is paid to modernize Yankee Stadium.

1973 New York City buys Yankee Stadium and begins refurbishment, at a final cost of between $106 million and $125 million. George Steinbrenner heads a 16-man syndicate that buys the Yankees from CBS for $10 million. Syndicate includes Mike Burke, Joseph Iglehart, and Marvin Warner.

1976 Joseph Iglehart and Marvin Warner sell their interest to George Steinbrenner at an unknown price. Steinbrenner now has majority control of team.

1989 *Wall Street Journal* estimates value of team at $250 million.

1990 Commissioner Vincent removes Steinbrenner from control (but not ownership) of team.

Oakland Athletics

1901 Philadelphia Athletics original franchise in AL (also known as the Philadelphia White Elephants). Owner is a syndicate consisting of Connie Mack (25 percent), Ben Shibe (50 percent), and Frank Hough and Sam Jones (25 percent), with much of the financing being supplied by Charles Somers.

1913 Mack buys out Hough and Jones to become an equal partner with Shibe.

1922 Shibe dies. His shares are left to his sons, Tom and John Shibe.

1946 Connie Mack give 10 percent interest in club each to sons Connie Jr., Earle, and Roy.

1950 Earle and Roy Mack buy out Connie Jr., and other minority interests (Shibe heirs and McFarlands). They acquire 60 percent of team for $1.75 million (includes Connie Mack Stadium).

1954 Connie Mack, Earl Mack, and Roy Mack get $6.7 million for the team, plus $1.2 for Connie Mack Stadium, from Arnold Johnson, who moves the team to Kansas City, and renames it the Kansas City Athletics.

1955 Johnson sells Blues Stadium in Kansas City to city for $650,000 under a leaseback arrangement.

1960 Johnson dies. Estate sells 52 percent of stock in team to Charlie Finley for $1,975,000. Later Finley buys the remaining 48 percent of team for about $1.8 million, to acquire 100 percent control of team.

1967 Team moves to Oakland for 1968 season and is renamed the Oakland Athletics.

1977 Finley asks $12.5 million for team. Offer of $10 million by Alan Steelman terminated. Marvin Davis offers $12 million for team to move it to Denver, but offer is withdrawn because of the possibility that Oakland will sue to keep team.

1980 Team is sold for $12.7 million to Walter Haas, Jr., his son, Wally Haas, and his son-in-law, Roy Eisenhardt.

Philadelphia Athletics (see Oakland Athletics)

St. Louis Browns (see Baltimore Orioles)

Seattle Mariners

1976 Expansion franchise in AL. Expansion fee $6.25 million. Owner syndicate includes Danny Kaye, Lester Smith, Stan Golub, and Walter Schoenfeld.

1981 George Argyros buys 80 percent interest in team for $10.4 million, with each of the above four owners retaining a 5 percent interest in the team.

1983 Argyros buys remaining 20 percent of team for unknown price.

1989 Team is sold for $80 million to Jeff Smulyan and Michael Browning. Team ownership is set up so that Emmis Broadcasting (owned by Smulyan) owns 50 percent, Smulyan owns 10 percent, Browning owns 10 percent, and Morgan Stanley and Co. owns 25 percent, with the remainder owned by some Emmis executives.

1992 Team is sold for $100 million to a syndicate headed by Hiroshi Yamanchi, head of Nintendo of America (60%); syndicate includes Christopher Larson (22%), John McCaw (9%), Frank Shrontz, and John Ellis (less than 1%). Sale followed a long and acrimonious debate among AL owners concerning ownership by a non-American (and non-Canadian).

Seattle Pilots (see Milwaukee Brewers II)

Texas Rangers

1960 Washington Senators expansion franchise. Expansion fee $2.1 million. Owner is syndicate headed by Quesada.
1963 Quesada, Lemon, and Johnson sell to another syndicate headed by Johnson and Quesada for $5 million.
1965 Johnson and Quesada buy up remaining 40 percent of shares from other members of syndicate for $2 million.
1969 Johnson dies. Johnson's estate and Quesada sell 90 percent of team to Bob Short for $9.4 million.
1971 Team moves to Arlington, Texas, and is renamed the Texas Rangers. Short sells his 90 percent interest to a syndicate headed by Brad Corbett for $10 million. Short retains a 14 percent interest in the new syndicate.
1980 Rangers sold to a syndicate headed by Eddie Chiles (58 percent) for an unknown price.
1985 Gaylord Broadcasting buys one-third of team for an unknown price. Offer is first rejected by AL, and then accepted.
1986 Gaylord Broadcasting makes bid for team, but it is rejected by AL.
1988 Offer for team by Edward Gaylord and Gaylord Broadcasting. The two offer $46.4 million for Chiles's 58 percent interest in team, but bid is rejected by AL.
1989 Chiles sells his share of team to a syndicate headed by George Bush, Jr. (son of president), and including Ed "Rusty" Rose, Richard Rainwater, and Bill DeWitt, Jr. Price is $46 million, for implicit price of team of $80 million.
1990 City of Arlington sells Arlington Stadium to team for $17.8 million.

Toronto Blue Jays

1976 Expansion franchise. Expansion fee $7 million. Owners: Labatt's Breweries (45 percent), Howard Webster (45 percent), and Canadian Imperial Bank of Commerce (10 percent).
1991 Webster estate sells its 45 percent to Labatt's Breweries for $67.5 million Canadian (U.S. $60.3 million).

Washington Senators I (see Minnesota Twins)

Washington Senators II (see Texas Rangers)

Football

National Football League

Akron Indians

1920 Original member of APFA, Akron Pros. Owners: Frank Neid and Art Ranney.
1922 Original member of NFL.
1923 Akron Pros change name to Akron Indians. Owner: Frank Neid.
1927 Team suspends operations for 1927 season.
1928 Franchise canceled before 1928 season.

Akron Pros (see Akron Indians)

Atlanta Falcons

1965 Expansion franchise, fee $8.5 million. Owners: Rankin Smith, plus minority owners.

Baltimore Colts (see Indianapolis Colts)

Boston Braves (see Washington Redskins)

Boston Bulldogs

1923 Pottsville Maroons organized as independent pro team.
1925 Pottsville Maroons expansion team in NFL. Owner: J.G. Striegel. Team wins championship in 1925 season, but then plays unauthorized exhibition game in Philadelphia, and has championship and league franchise stripped from it by NFL.
1926 Pottsville readmitted to NFL for 1926 season, to keep team from jumping to AFL.
1929 Pottsville Maroons franchise moved to Boston for 1929 season, name changed to Boston Bulldogs.
1930 Franchise canceled before 1930 season.

Boston Patriots (see New England Patriots)

Boston Redskins (see Washington Redskins)

Boston Yanks (see New York Bulldogs)

Brooklyn Dodgers (see Brooklyn Tigers)

Brooklyn Lions

1926 Expansion team in NFL. Owner unknown.
1927 Team suspends operations for 1927 season, with ownership of team transferred to Tim Mara of New York Giants. Mara permits the New York Yankees I to operate under this franchise for the 1927 and 1928 seasons.
1929 Franchise canceled before the 1929 season.

Brooklyn Tigers

1920 Dayton Triangles original member of APFA. Owner: Carl Storck.
1922 Dayton Triangles original member of NFL.
1930 Dayton Triangles go broke after 1929 season.
1931 Dwyer and John Depler buy the defunct Dayton Triangle's franchise for unknown price and move it to Brooklyn as the Brooklyn Dodgers.
1932 Team is sold to Chris Cagle and Shipwreck Kelly for unknown price.
1933 Cagle sells his interest to Dan Topping for unknown price.
1934 Sonja Henie marries Dan Topping and buys 25 percent of team from him, Kelly retains 50 percent interest in team.
1939 Topping buys out Kelly at unknown price.
1944 Brooklyn Dodgers' name changed to Brooklyn Tigers. Owner: Dan Topping.
1945 Team is merged with Boston Yanks; Topping and Ted Collins are co-owners.
1946 Brooklyn franchise canceled when Dan Topping announces he is moving to AAFC.

Buffalo All Americans (see Buffalo Rangers)

Buffalo Bills

1959 Original member of AFL, fee of $25,000. Owner: Ralph C. Wilson.
1970 Team joins NFL in 1970 season in AFL-NFL merger.

Buffalo Bisons (see Buffalo Rangers)

Buffalo Rangers

1920 Buffalo All Americans original member of APFA. Owner: Frank McNeil.
1922 Buffalo All Americans original member of NFL.
1924 Buffalo All Americans are sold. Name is changed to Buffalo Bisons. Price unknown. New owners: Walter Patterson and T. F. Hughitt.
1926 Name changed to Buffalo Rangers.
1928 Team suspends operations for 1928 season.
1929 Team resumes play for 1929 season.
1930 Franchise canceled before 1930 season.

Canton Bulldogs

1920 Original member of APFA. Owner: Ralph Hayes.
1922 Original member of NFL. Team sold to Canton Athletic Co. before 1923 season for unknown price.
1924 Franchise sold to Sam Deutsch (owner of Cleveland Indians NFL) for $1,200. Deutsch moves players to Cleveland. Franchise is inactive for 1924 season.
1925 Franchise sold to Canton Professional Football Company, headed by Pete Henry, for $3,000. Team resumes play for 1925 season.
1927 Franchise is canceled before 1927 season.

Chicago Bears

1919 Team organized as Decatur Staleys. Owner: A. E. Staley.
1920 Decatur Staleys original member of APFA.
1921 Team moves to Chicago as Chicago Staleys. Co-owners: George Halas and Dutch Sternaman.
1922 Chicago Staleys' name changed to Chicago Bears. Original franchise of NFL. Owners: George Halas and Dutch Sternaman. Offer of $35,000 for team refused by Halas.
1931 Halas buys out Sternaman for $38,000, by refinancing, selling 50

percent of team for $40,000: Ralph Brizzolara, $5,000; Jim McMillen, $5,000; Charlie Bidwill, $5,000 (possibly a loan); Mrs. Trafton (mother of George Trafton), $20,000; Halas's mother $5,000. In *Halas by Halas* it is reported that "some years later, Mrs. Trafton sold out (to Halas) for $40,000."

1954   McMillen sells out to Halas for $40,000.

1976   Offer for Bears at reported figure of $22 million.

1981   Financial reorganization of team, with 50.65 percent of stock assigned to Halas's heirs, Halas retaining 49.35 percent. Team valued for tax purposes at $8 million.

1983   George Halas dies. Team is left to daughter, Virginia McCaskey, and family, including son, Michael McCaskey.

1990   Twenty percent of Bears sold for unknown price to Andrew J. McKenna and Patrick G. Ryan, "for the financial well-being of the team." Tax case involving Halas's estate was settled a few weeks earlier.

Chicago Cardinals (see Phoenix Cardinals)

Chicago Staleys (see Chicago Bears)

Chicago Tigers

1920   Original member of APFA. Owner unknown. Team folds after 1920 season after losing game with Chicago Cardinals for the pro championship of Chicago.

Cincinnati Bengals

1967   AFL expansion team, with fee of $7.5 million. Owners: Paul Brown and others.

1970   Team joins NFL in AFL-NFL merger.

1991   Paul Brown dies.

Cincinnati Celts

1921   Expansion team of APFA. Owner unknown.

1922   Franchise canceled before 1922 season.

Cincinnati Reds (see St. Louis Gunners)

Cleveland Browns

1946 Original member of AAFC. Owner: Arthur "Mickey" McBride.

1950 Team joins NFL in AAFC-NFL merger; as part of merger agreement, James Brueil acquires 25 percent interest in club as payment for players from his Buffalo Bills AAFC team, acquired by Browns in merger.

1953 Team is sold for $600,000 to David Jones, Ellis Ryan, Saul Silberman, and Homer Marshman.

1955 Silberman sells his 7 percent to partners for unknown price.

1961 Arthur Modell and R. J. Schaefer head a syndicate that purchases all shares in team for $3,925,000. Modell and Schaefer have 25 percent each, with Schaefer's shares in an irrevocable trust voted by Modell. Remaining 50 percent of shares are sold to eight minority partners; the largest share is 28 percent to Robert Gries, Sr.

1965 Modell buys out Schaefer for $1.5 million, by having the Browns borrow $3 million and pay this out in dividends.

1971 Modell ups his share to 53 percent at an unknown price, while Gries and others have 47 percent.

1980 Estimate by bank that buyout of minority 47 percent would cost $9.5 million.

1982 Offer by Modell of $661,000 to Richard Cole for his 4.3 percent of Browns stock.

Cleveland Bulldogs

1923 Cleveland Indians expansion team of NFL. Owner: Sam Deutsch.

1924 Cleveland Indians owner Sam Deutsch buys Canton franchise, transfers most players to Cleveland, and renames team Cleveland Bulldogs.

1926 Team suspends operations for 1926 season. Most players jump to Cleveland AFL team.

1927 Team suspends operations for 1927 season.

1928 Team suspends operations for 1928 season. Franchise and players, including Benny Friedman, sold to Detroit Wolverines.

Cleveland Indians (see Cleveland Bulldogs)

Cleveland Rams (see Los Angeles Rams)

Cleveland Tigers

1920 Original member of APFA. Owner: Jimmy O'Donnell.
1922 Franchise canceled before 1922 season.

Columbus Panhandles (see Columbus Tigers)

Columbus Tigers

1919 Columbus Panhandles founded as independent pro team by Joseph Carr.
1920 Original member of APFA. Owner: Joseph Carr.
1922 Original member of NFL; owner Carr becomes first NFL president.
1923 Columbus Panhandles' name changed to Columbus Tigers. Owner: Joseph Carr.
1927 Team suspends operations for 1927 season.
1928 Franchise canceled before 1928 season.

Dallas Cowboys

1960 NFL expansion franchise, fee $600,000 (team assigns $50,000 to franchise and $550,000 to player contracts). Owners: Clint Murchison and Bedford Wynne. Murchison has 90 percent of team, but this is split 50–50 with his brother, who is silent partner.
1971 Team moves out of Cotton Bowl into Texas Stadium ($30 million construction cost).
1984 Team sold to a syndicate headed by H. R. "Bum" Bright, for $60 million plus $26 million for the team's operating lease to Texas Stadium plus other team-owned real estate. Bright owns 17 percent of team, two others own 15 percent each, one 10 percent, one 5 percent, and there are six other junior partners owning a total of 35 percent, while Tex Schramm owns 3 percent.
1988 Team (excluding $30 million in deferred liabilities) sold for $95 million and stadium lease sold for $45 million to syndicate headed by Jerrold Jones (53 percent), and including Sam, Charles, and Evan Wyly, Russell Glass, and Tex Schramm (3 percent).

Dallas Texans I

1946 New York Yankees original franchise in AAFC when NFL Brooklyn Tigers move to AAFC as the Yankees; players for NFL Brooklyn

Tigers team become players for Yankees. Owner: Dan Topping, who was reportedly paid $100,000 to make the move from the NFL to the AAFC.
1947 Larry McPhail and Del Webb become co-owners with Topping for unknown price.
1948 McPhail sells out to Topping and Webb for unknown price.
1950 As part of AAFC-NFL merger, team is sold for unknown price to Ted Collins, who gives up his New York Bulldogs franchise. New York Giants NFL obtain rights to six players of their choice from Yankee roster as part of merger agreement. Team continues to operate as New York Yankees.
1952 Yankees lose $1 million in 1951 season. Franchise returned to NFL by Collins, who receives $100,000 from NFL for player contracts. Franchise is then purchased from NFL for $300,000 by a group of Dallas businessmen headed by Giles and Connell Miller. Team is renamed the Dallas Texans. Team loses $250,000 in first five games of season, team goes broke midway in 1952 season, and NFL operates franchise until end of season. Franchise is canceled after the 1952 season.

Dallas Texans II (see Kansas City Chiefs)

Dayton Triangles (see Brooklyn Tigers)

Decatur Staleys (see Chicago Bears)

Denver Broncos

1959 Original member of AFL, $25,000 fee. Owner: Rocky Mountain Empire Sports Corporation, headed by Howsam brothers.
1961 Team is sold to a group headed by Calvin Kunz and Gerald Phipps.
1965 Cox Broadcasting Co. offers $4 million for team to move it to Atlanta. Offer is refused. Gerald and Allan Phipps buy out remaining (58 percent) of stockholders for $1.5 million.
1970 Team joins NFL as part of AFL-NFL merger.
1981 Team sold to Edgar F. Kaiser for unknown price.
1984 Team sold to a syndicate headed by Pat Bowlen for $70.5 million.

Detroit Heralds

1920 Original member of APFA. Owner unknown. Team disbanded after 1920 season.

Detroit Lions

1930 Portsmouth Spartans expansion team in NFL; owner is Portsmouth NFL Corporation, which issues 250 shares at $100 each. Stockholders include Harry Snider (91 shares), with 67 shares held by Harold Griffen, Harry Doerr, and Homer Selby.

1931 Team loses $16,000.

1934 Team goes broke after 1933 season. George A. Richardson buys the franchise for $15,000 (plus $6,500 to pay off outstanding debts) and moves team to Detroit. Team is renamed the Detroit Lions.

1940 Richards is fined $5,000 by NFL for tampering, and sells Lions for $225,000 to a syndicate headed by Fred Mandel.

1948 Team is sold to a five man group headed by D. Lyle Fife and Edwin J. Anderson for $185,000.

1963 W. Clay Ford heads a syndicate that buys the Lions for $6 million.

1964 Ford buys out his partners (implicit price of team is $6.5 million), to become sole owner of the Lions.

Detroit Panthers I

1921 Expansion team in APFA. Owner unknown.

1922 Franchise canceled before 1922 season.

Detroit Panthers II (see Detroit Wolverines)

Detroit Wolverines

1925 Detroit Panthers II expansion team in NFL. Owner: Jimmy Conzelman.

1927 Team suspends operations for 1927 season.

1928 Cleveland Indians NFL franchise and players purchased by group of 20 Detroit businessmen for $10,000, to acquire rights to Benny Friedman. Detroit Panthers franchise reactivated, and name changed to Detroit Wolverines. Team makes $7,000 in 1928 season after signing Friedman.

1929 Franchise sold to Tim Mara for unknown price. Mara buys team to acquire rights to Friedman for New York Giants, and franchise is inactive after purchase, presumably canceled.

Duluth Eskimos (see Washington Redskins)

416

Duluth Kellys (see Washington Redskins)

Evansville Crimson Giants

1921 Expansion team in APFA. Owner: Frank Fausch.
1922 Original member of NFL.
1923 Franchise canceled before 1923 season.

Frankford Yellow Jackets (see Philadelphia Eagles)

Green Bay Packers

1919 Earl "Curly" Lambeau and George Calhoun organize the Packers as an independent team.
1921 Expansion team in APFA. Owners: Curly Lambeau and J. E. Clair.
1922 Franchise revoked by NFL because of use of college players by Packers during 1921 season. Lambeau buys a new franchise in NFL for $250 for initial (1922) NFL season.
1923 Lambeau and team go broke after 1923 season. A group of Green Bay businessmen make a $2,500 loan to the team and set up the Green Bay Football Corporation to operate the team, a nonprofit corporation with all dividends to be given to the local American Legion. Franchise is taken over by the corporation; stock in corporation is sold on a tie-in basis to season tickets for Green Bay games.
1933 Bleachers in the Packers' stadium collapse, and the mutual insurance company covering the stadium fails, so the Packers go into receivership to satisfy outstanding claims. Team is operated by the court until 1937.
1937 Lee Joannes, president of club, raises enough money to satisfy the claims of creditors. Receivership is ended and team is reorganized on same nonprofit basis, with a new corporate name, Green Bay Packers, Inc.
1950 Battle betwen Lambeau and the board of directors concerning Lambeau's attempt to convert the team into a for-profit enterprise, with a syndicate headed by Lambeau ready to buy the team. Instead, the board retains its nonprofit status and solves its financial problems by selling more no-dividend stock ($125,000 worth) to Green Bay citizens.

Hammond Pros

1920 Original member of APFA. Owner: A. A. "Doc" Young.
1922 Original member of NFL.

1927 Team suspends operations for 1927 season.
1928 Franchise canceled before 1928 season.

Hartford Blues

1926 Expansion franchise in NFL. Owner unknown.
1927 Team suspends operations for 1927 season.
1928 Franchise canceled before 1928 season.

Houston Oilers

1959 Original franchise in AFL, $25,000 fee. Owner: K. S. "Bud" Adams.
1970 Team joins the NFL as part of AFL-NFL merger.

Indianapolis Colts

1947 Baltimore Colts replace Miami Seahawks in AAFC; owner Bob Rodenberg.
1948 Rodenberg pulls out, and team is taken over by a group of 15 Baltimore businessmen, headed by Robert C. Embry. Group pays $180,000 for team.
1949 Majority interest in team sold to Abraham Watner for unknown price.
1950 Team enters NFL in AAFC-NFL merger, after payment of $150,000 to George Marshall for invading his territory.
1951 Team loses $106,000 in 1950 season. Franchise returned to NFL before 1951 season by Watner, who receives $50,000 from sale of Colt players to other NFL teams.
1952 Minority stockholders sue NFL concerning sale of franchise to NFL by Watner. NFL agrees to return franchise to Baltimore if 15,000 1953 season tickets are sold. Tickets are sold, and Colts are organized as new franchise, but awarded the players and draft rights of the defunct Dallas Texans I; owners are Carroll Rosenbloom (51 percent), and others, including William Hilgenberg, Zanvyl Krieger, Tom Mullan, and Bruce Livie.
1964 Between 1953 and 1964, Rosenbloom buys additional 18 percent of stock at unknown prices. In 1964, Rosenbloom pays $1 million for remaining 31 percent of shares to become sole owner of Colts.
1972 Robert Irsay becomes owner by purchasing the Los Angeles Rams for $19 million and then trading the Rams for the Colts; trade includes a side payment from Rosenbloom to Irsay of between $3 million and $4 million.
1984 Colts move to Indianapolis, and name is changed to Indianapolis Colts; owner remains Robert Irsay.

Kansas City Blues (see Kansas City Cowboys)

Kansas City Chiefs

1959   Dallas Texans II original franchise of AFL. Fee $25,000. Owner: Lamar Hunt.
1963   Team moves to Kansas City, renamed Kansas City Chiefs; owner is still Lamar Hunt.
1970   Team joins NFL as part of AFL-NFL merger.

Kansas City Cowboys

1924   Kansas City Blues expansion team of NFL. Owner: Roy Andrews.
1925   Name changed to Kansas City Cowboys.
1927   Team disbands, sells players, and relinquishes franchise to NFL before 1927 season.

Kenosha Maroons

1922   Toledo Maroons original franchise of NFL. Owner: Bill Hartley.
1924   Toledo Maroons franchise transferred to Kenosha, name changed to Kenosha Maroons. Owner unknown.
1925   Franchise canceled before 1925 season.

Los Angeles Buccaneers

1926   Expansion team of NFL, located in Chicago, but plays all games on the road. Owner unknown.
1927   Team suspends operations for 1927 season.
1928   Franchise canceled before 1928 season.

Los Angeles Chargers (see San Diego Chargers)

Los Angeles Raiders

1959   Oakland Raiders original franchise in AFL, replacing proposed Minnesota franchise; $25,000 fee. Owner is an eight-man syndicate headed by Chet Soda and Wayne Valley, and including Ed McGah and Robert Osborne.
1961   McGah, Valley, and Osborne buy out other partners for unknown price.
1962   Osborne sells out to Valley and McGah for unknown price.

1963 Raiders are reorganized with Al Davis as managing general partner, and with 24 limited partners headed by Wayne Valley and Ed Mc-Gah; Davis receives 10 percent interest in Raiders for $18,000.

1970 Team joins NFL as part of AFL-NFL merger.

1972 Ed McGah (45 percent of voting rights) and Al Davis (10 percent of voting rights) sign a contract giving Davis absolute control over team, including voting rights for Raiders at NFL meetings. Wayne Valley sues to void contract.

1976 Valley sells his shares to team at unknown price after losing court battle with Davis over control of the Raiders.

1982 Raiders win antitrust case with NFL. Team moves to Los Angeles and is renamed Los Angeles Raiders.

Los Angeles Rams

1936 Cleveland Rams member of AFL II; owner is Homer Marshman, with minority owners Thomas Lipscombe, Dan Hanna, John Pott, Eddie Bruck, and Leonard Firestone.

1937 Team becomes expansion franchise in NFL. Expansion fee $10,000.

1941 Team sold to syndicate headed by Dan Reeves and Fred Levy for $125,000.

1943 Team suspends operations for season.

1944 Team resumes NFL play.

1945 Team wins NFL championship, loses $50,000 for season. Total losses 1941–1945 = $82,000.

1946 Cleveland Rams move to Los Angeles; team renamed Los Angeles Rams. Owner: Dan Reeves. Team loses $161,000.

1947 Reeves brings in Fred Levy, Ed Pauley, Harold Pauley, and Hal Seley as partners for $1 each, to share losses of Rams. Ownership distribution: Reeves, 37.5 percent; Ed Pauley, 27.5 percent; Harold Pauley, 10 percent; Fred Levy and Julius Krug, 25 percent. Team losses in 1947 = $253,300.

1950 Los Angeles Dons merge with Rams as part of AAFC-NFL merger agreement. Financial details unknown. Reportedly, Ben Lindheimer, Dons owner, was offered 25 percent of Rams (gratis) and refused because of health problems.

1953 Harold Pauley dies, with Bob Hope buying his shares at unknown price.

1955 Ownership split at this time: Reeves, 33 percent; Ed Pauley, 30.5 percent; Seley, 13.9 percent; Levy, 11.1 percent; Hope, 11.1 percent.

1962 Sealed-bid auction for Rams among Reeves, Pauley, Levy, Seley, and Hope. Reeves comes up with top bid (value of Rams = $7.1 million). Reeves sets up new corporation to raise $4.8 million to pay off other partners, with Reeves owning 51 percent of stock, and with 11 minority stockholders in new corporation.

1971 Reeves dies.

1972 Robert Irsay buys up all the stock in the Rams from the Reeves estate and others for $19 million. He then exchanges the Rams for the Colts with Carroll Rosenbloom, with Rosenbloom making a side payment of between $3 million and $4 million.

1979 Carroll Rosenbloom drowns. His will leaves 70 percent of the team to his widow, Georgia, 15 percent to his three children from his first marriage, and 15 percent to his two children from his second marriage.

1980 Rams move to Anaheim. Financial reorganization under which widow Georgia Frontierre buys up 30 percent of minority shares at an unknown price, to become sole owner of Rams.

Louisville Brecks (see Louisville Colonels)

Louisville Colonels

1921 Louisville Brecks expansion team APFA. Owner: Breckenridge Co., Louisville (owned by Aaron Hertzman).

1922 Louisville Brecks original franchise in NFL.

1924 Team suspends operations for 1924 season.

1925 Team suspends operations for 1925 season.

1926 Louisville Brecks changes name to Louisville Colonels; based in Chicago; resumes play for 1926 season.

1927 Team suspends operations for 1927 season.

1928 Franchise canceled before 1928 season.

Miami Dolphins

1965 Expansion franchise in AFL. Expansion fee $7.5 million. Owners: Joe Robbie and Danny Thomas Enterprises as general partners, and a number of limited partners, including Martin Decker, Joseph O'Neill, George Hamid, Sr., and George Hamid, Jr.

1966 Willard Kleland buys out Decker and the Hamids. Danny Thomas sells out to Kleland, with Robbie retaining operational control. Prices for these transactions unknown.

1968 Kleland and Robbie each have 50 percent of team, and Kleland attempts to take over control of team. Case goes to NFL. Rozelle rules that Robbie is the NFL's choice for majority owner, and orders Kleland to sell out his interest within 90 days.

1969 Syndicate consisting of J. Early Smalley, Wilbur Robinson, Frank Callahan, James MacLamore, and Harper Sibley buys out Kleland's 50 percent, with Robbie retaining 50 percent of team.

1970 Don Shula brought in as coach and given 10 percent of team, with Robbie having an option to buy back these shares at any time after five years, at 10 percent of the market value of the team less $750,000. Team joins the NFL as part of AFL-NFL merger.

1988 Joe Robbie Stadium opens; cost $100 million. By this time, Joe Robbie has acquired a majority interest in team.

1990 Joe Robbie dies, with his majority interest left to his widow and children. Timothy Robbie, Daniel Robbie, and sister Janet Robbie are assigned as trustees to manage the Dolphins. They sell 50 percent of the stadium and 15 percent of the Dolphins to W. Wayne Huizenga. In July 1990, trustees fire their brother J. Michael Robbie, from his job as vice president of the Dolphins.

Milwaukee Badgers

1922 Original franchise of NFL. Owners: Joe T. Plunkett, and Ambrose McGurk.

1923 McGurk becomes sole owner at unknown price.

1927 Team suspends operations for 1927 season.

1928 Franchise canceled before 1928 season.

Minneapolis Marines

1905 Team organized as independent pro football team.

1921 Expansion franchise in APFA. Owner: Johnny Dunn.

1922 Original franchise in NFL.

1925 Team suspends operations for 1925 season.

1926 Team suspends operations for 1926 season.

1927 Team suspends operations for 1927 season.

1928 Franchise canceled before 1928 season.

Minneapolis Red Jackets

1929 Expansion franchise in NFL. Fee $2,500. Owners: Johnny Dunn and Val Ness.

1930 Midway through 1930 season, team combines with Frankford Yellow Jackets to finish the season.

1931 Team suspends operations for 1931 season; players move to Frankford Yellow Jackets.

1932 Franchise canceled before 1932 season.

Minnesota Vikings

1959 Max Winter, H. P. Skoglund, and Bill Boyer head a syndicate requesting AFL franchise. They pull out of AFL to accept an expansion franchise in NFL for 1961 season.

1960 Expansion franchise in NFL. Expansion fee $600,000. Owner: Minnesota Vikings, Inc., with shareholders Max Winter (20 percent), Bill Boyer (20 percent), Ole Haugsrud (10 percent), H. P. Skoglund (20 percent), and Bernard Ritter, for North West Publishing, owner of the *St. Paul Dispatch* (30 percent). Each owner gets the same share of nonvoting stock as shares of voting stock shown.

1972 Boyer dies; shares left to his widow.

1975 Haugsrud shares sold to Minnesota Vikings, Inc., for unknown price and then canceled.

1977 North West Publishing taken over; takeover agreement requires divestiture of Vikings stock. Stock is sold to Minnesota Vikings, Inc., for $3 million (implicit value of team is $15 million), and shares are canceled. Owners of Minnesota Vikings at this point are Winter, Skoglund, and Mrs. Boyer, each with one-third of the voting shares. Nonvoting shares are more widely distributed.

1985 Winter sells his one-third voting interest and 46 percent equity interest (share of voting and nonvoting stocks) to Carl Pohlad and Irwin Jacobs for $25 million. Suit brought by Skoglund estate and Mrs. Boyer to enforce an earlier agreement involving right of first refusal by other owners in the disposition of Winter's voting shares.

1987 Minnesota Supreme Court rules in favor of Pohlad and Jacobs, and sale of Winter's stock takes place. Pohlad and Jacobs have a majority of total shares outstanding (and one-third of voting shares) and bring suit to change the voting rules so that nonvoting stock will have voting rights.

1989 Pohlad and Jacobs lose suit re voting rights. Boyer and Skoglund interests retain two-thirds voting control of Vikings. Boyer and Skoglund interests sell their shares to a new group headed by Mike Lynn, and including Jack Steele, John Skoglund, Roger Headrick, Jaye Dyer, Wheelock Whitney, Phil Maas, and Carol Sperry. This group has two-thirds of voting shares and 49 percent of all stock in team; Jacobs and Pohlad have one-third of voting shares and 51 percent of all stock.

1991 NFL Commissioner Tagliabue attempts to settle ownership dispute between Lynn group and Pohlad and Jacobs, with no success. Vikings owners are informed that they will have to settle their dispute to meet NFL rule that one individual must control at least 60 percent of the team. Pohlad and Jacobs sell their 51 percent for $52 million to the Lynn group in December 1991.

1992 Lynn sells his 10 percent to other owners at an unknown price.

Muncie Flyers

1920 Original franchise in APFA. Owner unknown.

1922 Franchise canceled before 1922 season.

Newark Tornadoes (see Washington Redskins)

New England Patriots

1959 Boston Patriots original franchise in AFL. Fee $25,000. Owner is a 10-man syndicate headed by Billy Sullivan; each member of syndicate holds 10 percent interest in team.

1960 Team loses $350,000 in first season.

1961 Team issues nonvoting stock for sale to public; team has 100,000 voting shares (held by members of 10-man syndicate) and 139,000 nonvoting shares.

1970 Real estate trust formed to finance $6 million stadium (Schaefer Stadium) in Foxboro, Mass.

1971 Schaefer Stadium opens. Team moves to Foxboro and changes name first to Bay State Patriots and then to New England Patriots.

1973 By 1973, Billy Sullivan has 23.7 percent of voting shares, and Mary Sullivan (cousin of Billy) has 12.5 percent; other owners are David McConnell and Robert Wetenhall (a total of 34 percent), Bob and Dan Marr (14 percent), and George Sargent Trust (14 percent).

1975 Billy Sullivan buys out Sargent Trust, the Marrs, and McConnell for $5.3 million cash and Wetenhall for a $1.7 million note due in 1982.

1976 Law is passed in Massachusetts permitting a buyout of minority stockholders on approval of 51 percent of total (voting and nonvoting) shares. Sullivan uses this law to buy out public nonvoting shares for $1.5 million.

1982 Patriots buy Schaefer Stadium for $6.4 million and rename stadium Sullivan Stadium.

1988 Following losses on Jackson Family tour and court case by minority stockholders concerning 1976 buyout, Patriots are sold for $85 million to Victor Kiam (51 percent) and Fran Murray (49 percent). Purchase price is $65 million for team, but new owners take over $20 million in deferred salaries and other deferred costs. Purchase price does not include Sullivan Stadium. Court instead requires public bids for stadium, which is sold separately from team when Kiam bid is beaten by a bid of $25 million by Robert Kraft and Steve Karp.

1991 Kiam is reported to be in the process of trying to raise $38 million to buy out Murray; under terms of original purchase agreement, if Murray is not paid by October 10, 1991, he has the right to assume control of the team for purposes of selling it.

1992 Deadline for buying out Murray is extended to March 15. Kiam sells his 51 percent interest in the team to James Busch Orthwein of St. Louis at unknown price.

New Orleans Saints

1966 Expansion franchise in NFL. Expansion fee $8 million. Owner: John Mecom, Jr.

1985 Team sold to Tom Benson for $70.2 million; deal includes a renegotiated Superdome contract and a $15 million loan guarantee by the state of Louisiana.

New York Bulldogs

1944 Boston Yanks expansion franchise in NFL. Owner: Ted Collins.

1945 Brooklyn Tigers merge with team for 1945 season, with half of games played in Boston and half in Brooklyn. Team name is shortened to Yanks. Co-owners for the year are Ted Collins and Dan Topping.

1946 Brooklyn franchise canceled by NFL when Topping moves team to AAFC. Boston Yankees resume original name. Owner is still Ted Collins.

1949 Team moves to New York and is renamed New York Bulldogs. Owner is still Ted Collins.

1950 Bulldog franchise relinquished to league, when Ted Collins buys the New York AAFC team from Dan Topping and Del Webb as part of AAFC-NFL merger agreement.

New York Giants I

1921 Expansion franchise in APFA. Owners: Billy Gibson and Charlie Brickley.

1922 Franchise canceled before 1922 season.

New York Giants II

1925   Expansion franchise in NFL; reportedly, franchise is purchased for $500 (or $2,500) from Jimmy Jernail (possibly Jernail is owner of defunct 1921 Giants franchise). Owners: Tim Mara and Billy Gibson.
1928   Giants lose $54,000.
1929   Tim Mara buys Detroit Wolverines franchise to obtain Benny Friedman. Giants make $8,500.
1930   Team makes $23,000. Control of Giants turned over to sons of Tim Mara: Jack Mara and Wellington Mara, Jack as president. This happens after Tim Mara is sued by Billy Gibson over control of team; suit is apparently settled out of court, with Gibson selling out to Mara.
1931   Team makes $35,000.
1959   Tim Mara dies, leaves 50 percent of team to Jack Mara and 50 percent to Wellington Mara.
1965   Jack Mara dies, leaves his 50 percent to his son, Tim Mara, and his daughters; Wellington takes over as president of Giants.
1976   Team moves to the Meadowlands in East Rutherford, N.J.
1991   Fifty percent of team owned by Tim Mara, Helen Nugent, and Maura Concannon (Jack Mara's heirs) is sold to Laurence Tisch for $75 million; Wellington Mara retains 50 percent interest.

New York Jets

1959   New York Titans original franchise in AFL, $25,000 fee. Owner: Harry Wismer.
1962   Wismer sells 30 percent of team to Royal Raidle for $500,000.
1963   At end of season, Titans go broke and AFL takes over team. Team is sold for $1 million to a five-man syndicate: David "Sonny" Werblin (25 percent), Townsend Martin, Donald Lillis, Leon Hess (25 percent), and Phililp Iselin. Team is renamed New York Jets.
1968   Werblin sells his interest to Leon Hess and Philip Iselin for $1,638,000. Hess now has 33 percent, and Iselin has 16 percent. Lillis dies two months after transaction.
1970   Team joins NFL as part of AFL-NFL merger.
1976   Iselin dies. Hess buys out Iselin's widow's shares and becomes 50 percent owner, at unknown price.
1984   Between 1976 and 1984, Hess has acquired all the outstanding shares in Jets, at unknown prices, and is sole owner. Final sale occurs in 1984, when Helen Dillon sells her 25 percent share in team to Hess.
1984   Jets move to the Meadowlands.

New York Titans (see New York Jets)

New York Yankees I

1926 Original franchise in AFL I. Owners: C. C. Pyle and Red Grange.
1927 Expansion franchise in NFL; given permission by Tim Mara to operate in New York City under the Brooklyn Lions franchise Mara acquired in 1927.
1929 Team goes broke before 1929 season.

New York Yankees II (see Dallas Texans I)

Oakland Raiders (see Los Angeles Raiders)

Oorang Indians

1922 Original franchise in NFL. Owner: Walter Lingo, who owns the Oorang dog kennels in LaRue, Ohio. Team plays its home games in Marion.
1924 Team suspends operations for the 1924 season, and then goes out of business.

Orange Tornadoes (see Washington Redskins)

Philadelphia Eagles

1924 Frankford Yellow Jackets expansion team in NFL. Team is located in Philadelphia; founder and part-owner is Charles (Sherry) O'Brien, head of the Frankford Athletic Association.
1930 Midway through season, team combines with Minneapolis Red Jackets, with Minneapolis players moving to Frankford team for 1931 season.
1931 Team goes broke midway through 1931 season, and NFL takes over franchise.
1933 Franchise purchased from NFL by Bert Bell and Lud Wray for $2,800. Team is renamed the Philadelphia Eagles.
1936 Bell becomes sole owner by buying out Wray for $4,000, after Eagles lose $80,000 in first three years of operation.
1940 After the 1940 season, Art Rooney buys half-interest in Eagles from Bell for unknown price.
1941 Before the 1941 season, Rooney and Bell trade the Eagles franchise to W. A. "Alex" Thompson for the Pittsburgh Steeler franchise. No cash changes hands.

1943   Eagles merge for one year with Steelers as the Steagles. Joint owners for the year are Rooney, Bell, and Thompson.

1944   Merger with Pittsburgh ends; Eagles field own team for 1944 season.

1948   Eagles lose $80,000 in winning NFL championship.

1949   Thompson sells Eagles for $250,000 to a syndicate of 100 Philadelphia businessmen, headed by James P. Clark.

1962   Clark dies.

1963   Syndicate sells team for $5,505,500 to a three-man group: Jerry Wolman (51 percent) and Foreman and Ed Snider (49 percent).

1967   Snider sells out to Wolman for unknown price. Group headed by Norman Raab offers $14.5 million for team.

1969   Wolman goes bankrupt. Eagles sold for $16,155,000 to a syndicate headed by Leonard Tose (50 percent), and including Herb Barness (29 percent), Solomon Katz, John Firestone, and John Connelly.

1976   Firestone sells his 5.1 percent interest to Tose for unknown price.

1977   Barness offers $21.5 million for team.

1978   Barness sells his 29 percent of shares for $3 million to Tose.

1979   Wally Leventhal sells his 6 percent interest to Tose for $1 million.

1983   Ed Snider offers $52 million for team.

1985   Norman Braman buys Eagles for between $65 million and $70 million.

Phoenix Cardinals

1899   Team organized on South Side of Chicago as independent pro team. First named Morgan Athletic Club, then Chicago Normals, and finally Racine (Avenue) Cardinals. Owner: Chris O'Brien.

1920   Original franchise in APFA. During season, team changes name to Chicago Cardinals. Owner: Chris O'Brien.

1929   Team sold to David Jones for $12,500, under an agreement with George Halas that he will absorb 40 percent of any losses in first year, and will take none of the profits.

1932   Team sold to Charles Bidwill for $50,000.

1944   Team merges with Steelers for 1944 season as Carpitts. Co-owners: Bidwill, Bert Bell, and Art Rooney.

1947   Charles Bidwill dies, and team is left to his wife, Violet, who owns 90 percent of shares; remaining 10 percent is owned by Joseph Griesedieck.

1949   Violet Bidwill marries Walter Wolfner, who takes over operation of team.

1960 Team moves to St. Louis, and is renamed St. Louis Cardinals. Owners are still Violet Wolfner (90 percent) and Joseph Griesedieck (10 percent).

1962 Violet Wolfner dies. Her will leaves her share of the team to her two sons, William Bidwill (45 percent) and Charles Bidwill (45 percent). William Wolfner, her widower, challenges the will in court, but it is upheld.

1972 Bill Bidwill buys out his brother for $6.5 million.

1988 Team moves to Phoenix and is renamed the Phoenix Cardinals. Owner is still Bill Bidwill.

Pittsburgh Pirates (see Pittsburgh Steelers)

Pittsburgh Steelers

1933 Pittsburgh Pirates expansion team in NFL. Expansion fee $2,500. Owners: Art Rooney and A. McCool. Rooney estimates operating costs for season are $125,000.

1940 After 1940 season, Pirates sold for $165,000 to Alex Thompson of East-West Sports Club. Team is renamed the Pittsburgh Steelers.

1941 Before 1941 season, Thompson trades franchises with Philadelphia Eagles owners Bert Bell and Art Rooney. No money changes hands.

1943 Pittsburgh and Philadelphia merge for 1943 season as Steagles. Co-owners: Bell, Thompson, and Rooney.

1944 Pittsburgh and Chicago Cardinals merge for 1944 season as Car-pitts. Bidwill, Bell, and Rooney are still co-owners.

1988 Art Rooney dies, and his son, Dan Rooney, takes over the team.

Portsmouth Spartans (see Detroit Lions)

Pottsville Maroons (see Boston Bulldogs)

Providence Steam Roller

1925 Expansion franchise in NFL. Owner unknown.

1932 Team suspends operations for 1932 season.

1933 Franchise canceled before 1933 season.

Racine Cardinals (see Phoenix Cardinals)

Racine Legion (see Racine Tornadoes)

Racine Tornadoes

1922 Racine Legion original franchise in NFL. Owner: George "Babe" Ruetz.
1923 Team sold for unknown price to William Horlick.
1925 Franchise canceled before 1925 season.
1926 Racine Legion francise reactivated for 1926 season; name changed to Racine Tornadoes. Owner unknown.
1927 Franchise canceled before 1927 season.

Rochester Jeffersons

1920 Original franchise in APFA. Owner: Leo Lyons.
1922 Original franchise in NFL.
1926 Team suspends operations for 1926 season.
1927 Team suspends operations for 1927 season.
1928 Franchise canceled before 1928 season.

Rock Island Independents

1920 Original franchise in APFA. Owner: Walter Flannigan.
1922 Original franchise in NFL.
1926 Team moves to AFL for 1926 season.
1927 Team applies for readmission to NFL when AFL folds, but request is turned down.

St. Louis All Stars

1923 Expansion team in NFL. Owner: Ollie Kraehe.
1924 Franchise canceled before 1924 season.

St. Louis Cardinals (see Phoenix Cardinals)

St. Louis Gunners

1933 Cincinnati Reds expansion team in NFL. Owner unknown.
1934 Cincinnati Reds go broke midway through the 1934 season. Franchise is purchased from NFL for between $20,000 and $30,000 by the St. Louis Gunners, an independent pro team. Owner: Edward Butler.

Gunners play the last three games of the Reds schedule for the 1934 season.

1935   Franchise canceled before 1935 season.

San Diego Chargers

1959   Los Angeles Chargers original franchise in AFL; $25,000 fee. Owners: Barron Hilton and Conrad Hilton.

1960   Team loses $900,000 in first year.

1961   Team moves to San Diego and is renamed San Diego Chargers. No change in owners.

1963   One-third interest in Chargers sold for unknown price to John Mabee, George Fernicano, Kenneth Swanson, James Copley, and M. L. Bengston.

1966   Team sold for $10 million to a syndicate headed by Gene Klein (20 percent) and Sam Schulman (20 percent) as general partners, with 19 limited partners, including Barron Hilton (20 percent), Conrad Hilton (10 percent), Gene Wyman, Pierre Salinger, Frank Rothman, and John DeLorean.

1970   Team moves to NFL as part of AFL-NFL merger agreement.

1972   Klein buys out Schulman (and Schulman buys out Klein's interest in NBA Seattle Supersonics) at unknown price.

1973   Klein ups his interest in Chargers to 56 percent at unknown price; Hiltons still own 30 percent of team.

1976   Klein increases his share to 63 percent at unknown price.

1982   Alex Spanos, minority partner, buys 10 percent of team from Barron Hilton for $4 million, and acquires right of first refusal when Klein sells the team.

1984   Spanos buys out Klein for $50 million (implicit value of team is $80 million), and becomes majority owner of team.

San Francisco 49ers

1946   Original franchise in AAFC. Owner: Anthony Morabito, with two minority owners.

1947   Morabito buys out minority partners for $100,000, and sets up a 75–25 partnership with his brother, Vic Morabito. Team's estimated losses are $250,000 per year.

1950   Team joins the NFL as a part of AAFC-NFL merger.

1957   Anthony Morabito dies of heart attack at Bears game. His interest is left to his widow. Vic Morabito takes over operation of team.

1964   Vic Morabito dies of heart attack. Widows Josephine and Jane

Morabito control 90 percent of team, with Franklin Mieuli having 10 percent interest.

1976 Mieuli announces that he and Joe Alioto will buy control of the team, but deal falls through.

1977 Edward DeBartolo, Jr., buys 80 percent interest in team from Morabito widows for $18.2 million; rest of shares owned by widows and Mieuli.

Seattle Seahawks

1974 Expansion franchise in NFL. Expansion fee $16 million. Owner is family group headed by Lloyd W. Nordstrom, plus minority partners Herman Sarkowsky, David Skinner, Howard Wright, M. Lamont Bean, and Lynn P. Himmelman.

1976 Lloyd Nordstrom dies; stock (51 percent) held by family-owned group.

1988 Nordstrom family buys out five minority stockholders (49 percent) for $35 million. Team then sold to Ken Behring (75 percent) and Ken Hoffman (25 percent) for $80 million. New owners also take over existing deferred-salary and other liabilities of $17 million.

Staten Island Stapletons

1929 Tim Mara, owner of Giants, permits Staten Island Stapletons to play in New York area. Owners: Bill Baline and Doug Wycoff.

1933 Team suspends operations for 1933 season.

1934 Franchise canceled before 1934 season.

Tampa Bay Buccaneers

1974 Expansion franchise in NFL. Expansion fee $16 million. Owner is a syndicate headed by Hugh Culverhouse.

1976 Marvin Warner reportedly buys "a major share" of team for unknown price, but Culverhouse syndicate still has majority control.

Toledo Maroons (see Kenosha Maroons)

Tonawanda Kardex

1921 Expansion team in APFA. Owner unknown.

1922 Franchise canceled before 1922 season.

Washington Redskins

1923 Duluth Kellys expansion team in NFL. Expansion fee $1,000 (probably not paid). Owners: Gebert and Scanlon.

1926 Team sold to Ole Haugsrud for $1. Team name changed to Duluth Eskimos. Haugsrud signs Ernie Nevers and team plays a 29-game schedule (2 home and 27 road); season ends in mid-February. Team shows a $4,000 profit for year.

1927 Eskimos make $1,000.

1928 Team suspends operations for 1928 season.

1929 Franchise sold to Edwin Simandl for $2,000. Franchise is moved to Orange, New Jersey; team is renamed Orange Tornadoes. Haugsrud receives a commitment from NFL of first bidding rights on any new franchise granted in Minnesota, and exercises this in 1960, when the Vikings came into the NFL.

1930 After 1929 season, team moves to Newark and is renamed the Newark Tornadoes. Owner remains Edwin Simandl. On November 17, Simandl announces that all remaining games are canceled because of lack of public support. Team goes broke.

1931 Franchise returned to NFL, which puts it up for highest bidder. No bids are received before 1931 season, so franchise is suspended for one year.

1932 Expansion franchise is purchased from NFL for unknown price (possibly $7,500) by a syndicate headed by George Marshall, and including Vincent Bendix, Jay O'Brien, and M. Dorland Doyle, who jointly put up $30,000 to buy franchise and operate team for one year. Ole Haugsrud says this is the old Duluth Eskimos-Orange-Newark franchise, but NFL records do not identify this specifically as that franchise. Franchise is moved to Boston, and team is renamed the Boston Braves.

1933 Boston Braves lose $46,000 in 1933 season. Bendix and O'Brien pull out, and Marshall takes over majority control of team, with minority partners Woolworth Donohue, Doyle, and Eddie Reeves. Name is changed to Boston Redskins.

1937 Team is moved to Washington and renamed Washington Redskins. No change in ownership.

1950s By this time, Marshall has acquired control of roughly 90 percent of team. He sells 25 percent of shares to Harry Wismer for unknown price.

1960 Wismer sells his 25 percent share to Jack Kent Cooke for $350,000, and uses the proceeds to buy New York Titans franchise in AFL.

1962 Edward B. Williams buys 50 shares of Pro Football, Inc., the Redskins' corporate shell. At this time, Marshall owns 520 shares, Cooke owns 250, Leo Dorsey owns 130, Milton King owns 120, and Williams owns 50.

1969 Vince Lombardi becomes coach and part-owner of unknown number of shares. Marshall dies and leaves his stock to a foundation, disinheriting his children. Court battle occurs concerning will.

1970 Lombardi dies.

1972 Pro Football, Inc., purchases 260 shares from the Marshall estate for $3 million, to pay off claims of the Marshall children. Shares are retired after purchase.

1974 Pro Football, Inc., purchases the remaining 260 shares held by the Marshall estate, for retirement. Purchase price is $5,720,000.

1979 Edward B. Williams sells shares to Pro Football, Inc., for unknown price when he buys the Baltimore Orioles.

1988 At this time, Jack Kent Cooke is sole owner of the Redskins. *Sports Inc.* reports that Cooke has paid $15 million since 1960 for the shares he acquired.

Washington Senators

1921 Expansion team of APFA. Owner unknown.

1922 Franchise canceled before 1922 season.

American Football League I (1926)

Organized by C. C. Pyle and Red Grange. Operated for 1926 season only.

Boston Bulldogs

Owner: Robert K. McKirby.

Brooklyn Horsemen

Owner: Humbert J. Fugasy. In mid-November, team merges with Brooklyn Lions of NFL and leaves AFL.

Chicago Bulls

Owner: Joey Sternaman.

Cleveland Panthers

Owner: General C. X. Zimmerman. Team folds midway through season.

Los Angeles Wildcats

Operated out of Rock Island, Illinois. Owner: George Wilson.

Newark Bears

Owner: W. Coughlin. Team folds midway through season.

New York Yankees

Owners: C. C. Pyle and Red Grange.

Philadelphia Quakers

Owner: L. S. Conway.

American Football League II (1936–1937)

Boston Shamrocks (1936, 1937)

Owner: Bill Scully.

Brooklyn Tigers (1936) (see Rochester Tigers)

Cincinnati Bengals (1937)

Expansion franchise, 1937 season. Owner unknown.

Cleveland Rams (1936)
(see also Cleveland Rams under National Football League)

Owner: Homer Marshman. Team moves into NFL as expansion team in 1937 season.

Los Angeles Bulldogs (1937)

Expansion team, 1937 season. Owner: Pro Sports Enterprises, Inc., a subsidiary of the Los Angeles City American Legion.

New York Yankees (1936, 1937)

Owner: James Bush.

Pittsburgh Americans (1936, 1937)

Owner unknown.

Rochester Braves (1936) (see Syracuse Braves)

Rochester Tigers (1936, 1937)

Team began 1936 season as Brooklyn Tigers, played one game in Brooklyn, and then moved to Rochester for remainder of season as Rochester Tigers. Owners: Mike Palm and Harry Newman.

Syracuse Braves (1936)

Team began 1936 season as Rochester Braves, and moved to Syracuse as Syracuse Braves when Brooklyn Tigers moved to Rochester. Team went out of business after 1936 season. Owner unknown.

American Football League III (1940–1941)

Boston Bears (1940)

Owner: Sheldon Fairbanks.

Buffalo Indians/Tigers (1940, 1941)

Original owner unknown. After 1940 season, team sold to "unnamed Scranton coal magnate" (Gill and Maher 1984).

Cincinnati Bengals (1940,1941)

Owner unknown.

Columbus Bullies (1940, 1941)

Original owner: J. Fred Schmidt. After 1940 season, team sold to Chris Carter and Dean Van Camp.

Milwaukee Chiefs (1940)

Owner: George Harris. In midseason, team goes broke and is taken over by league.

New York Americans (1941)

Original franchise in AFL in 1940 as New York Yankees. Owner: Douglas Hertz. In 1941, the franchise was revoked by AFL and taken away from Hertz. The team was then sold to William Cox for an unknown price, and its name was changed to New York Yankees.

New York Yankees (1941) (see New York Americans)

All American Football Conference (1946–1949)

Baltimore Colts (see Indianapolis Colts under National Football League)

Brooklyn Dodgers

1946   Original franchise in AAFC. Owner: William Cox.
1948   Team goes broke after 1947 season. Team taken over by Brooklyn NL team. Team loses $750,000 in 1948, and baseball Dodgers pull out.
1949   Team merges with New York Yankees. Owners: Dan Topping and Del Webb.

Buffalo Bills

1946   Original franchise in AAFC as Buffalo Bisons. Owner: James Breuil.
1949   Name changed to Buffalo Bills.
1949   Breuil gets 25 percent interest in Cleveland Browns under AAFC-NFL agreement. Bills franchise canceled, with Bills' players going to Browns.

Buffalo Bisons (see Buffalo Bills)

Chicago Hornets

1946 Original franchise in AAFC as Chicago Rockets. Owner: John Keeshin.
1947 Team sold for unknown price to a syndicate headed by Jim Crowley.
1948 Team sold to a syndicate headed by R. Edward Garn.
1949 Team sold to James C. Thompson for unknown price, and name changed to Chicago Hornets. Team disbanded after AAFC-NFL merger; owner obtains unknown compensation.

Chicago Rockets (see Chicago Hornets)

Cleveland Browns (see Cleveland Browns under National Football League)

Los Angeles Dons

1946 Original franchise in AAFC. Majority owner is Ben Lindheimer; minority owner and president is Don Ameche; other minority owners include Louis B. Mayer, Bing Crosby, Bob Hope, Pat O'Brien, Leo Spitz, Dan Rice, Norman Church, and Lloyd Wright.
1949 Team merges with Los Angeles Rams as part of AAFC-NFL merger. Financial details unknown.

Miami Seahawks

1946 Original franchise in AAFC. Owner: Harvey Hester.
1947 Team pulls out of AAFC after first season, to be replaced by Baltimore Colts.

New York Yankees (see New York Yankees II under National Football League)

San Francisco 49ers (see San Francisco 49ers under National Football League)

World Football League (1974–1975)

League played a full 1974 season and half of the 1975 season before going out of business. Original entry fee into league was $75,000 plus an escrow payment of $545,000 to league to cover claims and contingencies.

Birmingham Americans (see Birmingham Vulcans)

Birmingham Vulcans

1974 Original member of WFL as Birmingham Americans. Owners: Bill Putnam and Carol Stallworth.
1975 Team sold to Ferd Weil for unknown price; name changed to Birmingham Vulcans. Team disbands when WFL folds.

Boston Bulldogs (see Charlotte Hornets)

Charlotte Hornets

1974 Original franchise in WFL as Boston Bulldogs. Owner: Howard Baldwin. Before 1974 season, team sold to Bob Schmertz, who moved the team to New York as the New York Stars. Team begins 1974 season as New York Stars, but in midseason, team is sold to a syndicate headed by Upton Bell, who moves the team to Charlotte and renames the team the Charlotte Hornets..
1975 Team disbanded when WFL folds.

Chicago Fire (see Chicago Wind)

Chicago Wind

1974 Original franchise in WFL as Chicago Fire. Owner: Nick Mileti. Before 1974 season opens, team is sold for unknown price to Tom Origer. Team loses $800,000 in 1974 season, and Origer pulls out, with WFL taking over team.
1975 Team sold to Eugene Pullano, and renamed Chicago Wind. Team folds in early September of 1975.

Detroit Wheels

1974 Original franchise in WFL. Owner is a 34-man syndicate headed by Louis Lee. Team goes bankrupt in September 1974. WFL operates team for one month and then disbands team.

Florida Blazers (see San Antonio Wings)

Honolulu Hawaiians

1974 Original franchise in WFL. Owners: Chris Hemmeter, Danny Rogers, Sam Battistone.
1975 Team sold to Edward Sultan for unknown price. Team disbanded when WFL folds.

Houston Texans (see Shreveport Steamer)

Jacksonville Express

1974 Original franchise in WFL as Jacksonville Sharks. Owner: Francis Monaco. Team goes broke in September 1974, and WFL takes over franchise.
1975 Team sold by WFL to Earl Knabb for unknown price, and renamed Jacksonville Express. Team disbanded when WFL folds.

Jacksonville Sharks (see Jacksonville Express)

Memphis Grizzlies

1974 Memphis Southmen original franchise in WFL. Owner is John Bassett; minority owners include Charlie Rich and Isaac Hayes.
Team was originally planned for Toronto as Toronto Northmen, but moved to Memphis because of objections by the CFL.
1975 Team renamed Memphis Grizzlies. Team disbanded when WFL folds.

Memphis Southmen (see Memphis Grizzlies)

New York Star (see Charlotte Hornets)

Philadelphia Bell

1974 Original franchise in WFL. This franchise was assigned to Gary Davidson as his fee for organizing the WFL, and was sold by him to Ken Bogdanoff for an unknown price. Bogdanoff sold the team to John B. Kelly, Jr., for an unknown price, who then sold it to John Bosaco for an unknown price, all of these transactions occurring before the initial 1974 season of WFL.

1975 Team disbanded when WFL folds.

Portland Storm

1974 Original franchise in WFL. Owner: Frank Gelkes. Team originally planned for New York, but sold by Gelkes to Robert Harris and moved to Portland, before the 1974 season. WFL takes over franchise in December 1974.

1975 Team sold by WFL to Richard Bayless for unknown price. Team disbanded when WFL folds.

San Antonio Wings

1974 Original franchise in WFL as Washington Capitals, later Washington Ambassadors, later Washington-Baltimore Ambassadors. Owner: E. Joseph Wheeler. Franchise planned for Washington, D.C., but owner cannot get stadium contract. Team moved to Norfolk and then sold to syndicate headed by Ronnie Loud, who moves the team to Orlando before the 1974 season and renames it the Florida Blazers. WFL takes over franchise in December 1974.

1975 Team sold to Norm Bevan for unknown price, moved to San Antonio, and renamed San Antonio Wings. Team disbanded when WFL folds.

Shreveport Steamer

1974 Original franchise in WFL as Houston Texans. Owner: Steve Arnold. Team was originally planned for Memphis, but moved to Houston before 1974 season. Midway through 1974 season, team moved to Shreveport and renamed Shreveport Steamer.

1975 Team sold to John B. Atkins for unknown price. Team disbanded when WFL folds.

Southern California Sun

1974 Original franchise in WFL. Owners: Larry Hatfield and Al Lapin.

1975 Team sold to Sam Battistone for unknown price. Team disbanded when WFL folds.

Toronto Northmen (see Memphis Grizzlies)

Washington Ambassadors (see San Antonio Wings)

Washington Capitals (see San Antonio Wings)

Washington-Baltimore Ambassadors (see San Antonio Wings)

U.S. Football League (1983–1985)

No entry fee into league for original teams, but each team was required to post a $1.5 million letter of credit with the league office, and to agree to spend at least $6 million on operating expenses during the first two years of league operation.

Arizona Wranglers

1982 Original franchise in USFL, destined for Los Angeles. Owner: Alex Spanos. Spanos pulls out when he buys the San Diego Chargers of NFL, and Jim Joseph takes over team. Before the initial 1983 season, team is moved to Phoenix and named the Arizona Wranglers.
1983 After the 1983 season, Joseph sells the franchise location to Ted Dietrich and George Allen for $7 million. Dietrich and Allen move their team (the Chicago Blitz) to Phoenix, they rename the team the Arizona Wranglers, and the Phoenix team moves to Chicago.
1984 After the 1984 season, the Oklahoma team merges with Phoenix, and William Tatham, Sr., and William Tatham, Jr., take over the franchise for an unknown price.
1986 Team disbands when USFL folds.

Baltimore Stars

1982 Original franchise in USFL as Philadelphia Stars. Owner: Myles Tannenbaum.
1984 Philadelphia Stars move to Baltimore, renamed Baltimore Stars. Owner: Myles Tannenbaum.
1985 Team sold to Steve Ross for $3 million.
1986 Team disbands when USFL folds.

Birmingham Stallions

1982 Original franchise in USFL. Owner: Marvin L. Warner.
1985 Warner goes bankrupt when his mortgage guarantee company

fails. Midway through the 1985 season, the city of Birmingham makes a $1 million loan to keep the franchise afloat.
1986 Team disbands when USFL folds.

Boston Breakers (see Portland Breakers)

Chicago Blitz

1982 Original franchise in USFL. Owners: Ted Dietrich and George Allen.
1983 After 1983 season, Dietrich and Allen move Blitz players to Phoenix, move Wrangler players to Chicago, and sell Chicago franchise to Dr. James F. Hoffman for $7 million.
1984 Before 1984 season begins, Hoffman drops out, and the team is taken over by a 17-man syndicate. Midway through the 1984 season, Eddie Einhorn becomes owner for unknown price, and decides not to field a team in 1985, but has the option to field a team in 1986.
1986 Team disbands when USFL folds.

Denver Gold

1982 Original franchise in USFL. Owner: Ron Blanding.
1984 Midway through 1984 season, team sold to Doug Spedding for $10 million.
1985 After 1985 season, team folds and merges with Jacksonville.

Houston Gamblers

1982 Franchise assigned to Donald Dixon (creator of USFL), to be located in Washington, D.C., but franchise is not active in 1983 season.
1983 Dixon sells the franchise for $4,750,000 to Jerry Argovitz and Bernard Lerner, who move the franchise to Houston.
1984 Midway through 1984 season, Lerner sells out his interest to Jay Roulier for $3.3 million. After 1984 season, Roulier trades his interest in Houston to USFL for ownership of L.A. Express, with his interest in Houston valued at $3.5 million.
1985 Trade is reversed, with Roulier out of L.A. Express, and back as part-owner of Houston. After 1985 season, Roulier goes broke, and USFL takes over his interest in Houston. Later in the year, Donald Trump buys the Gamblers franchise for unknown price, and merges the team with New Jersey.

Jacksonville Bulls

1983 Expansion franchise in USFL awarded after 1983 season. Expansion fee $6 million. Owner: Fred Bullard.

1985 After 1985 season, Bullard offers public sale of stock in team, offering price of $12.5 million for 49 percent interest in team.

Actual public bids for stock total $80,000, so stock offering is withdrawn. After 1985 season, Denver merges with Jacksonville.

1986 Team disbands when USFL folds.

Los Angeles Express

1982 Original franchise in USFL to be located in San Diego. Owners: Bill Daniels and Alan Harmon. Before 1983 season, team is moved to Los Angeles and named Los Angeles Express.

1984 Team sold to William Oldenberg for unknown price. Oldenberg pulls out after 1984 season, and USFL takes over team. USFL then sells the team to Jay Roulier in transfer deal, where the league takes his interest in Houston, which is valued at $3.5 million.

1985 USFL takes over Express from Roulier, who returns as part-owner of Houston. Team goes out of business at end of 1985 season.

Memphis Showboat

1983 Expansion franchise in USFL awarded after 1983 season. Expansion fee $6 million. Owner: Logan Young.

1984 Before 1984 season, Young runs out of money, and team is taken over by Billy Dunavant for unknown price.

1986 Team disbands when USFL folds.

Miami Renegades (see Orlando Renegades)

Michigan Panthers

1982 Original franchise in USFL. Owner is A. Alfred Taubman; minority owner is Peter Spivak.

1984 After 1984 season, team folds and is merged with Oakland.

New Jersey Generals

1982 Original franchise in USFL. Owner: Donald Trump. Before 1983 season, team is sold for unknown price to J. Walter Duncan, with minority stockholder Chuck Fairbanks.

1983 After 1983 season, team is sold back to Donald Trump for $9 million (to be paid over several years, with present value of payments estimated at $4 to $5 million).
1986 Team disbands when USFL folds.

New Orleans Breakers (see Portland Breakers)

Oakland Invaders

1982 Original franchise in USFL. Owners: Tad Taube and Jim Joseph. Before initial 1983 season, Joseph pulls out.
1985 After 1985 season, team folds.

Oklahoma Outlaws

1983 Expansion franchise awarded to San Diego after 1983 season. Expansion fee $6 million. Owners: William Tatham, Sr., and William Tatham, Jr. When the city of San Diego denies the team use of Jack Murphy Stadium, the team moves to Tulsa for the 1984 season as the Oklahoma Outlaws.
1984 Team merges with Arizona Wranglers, with Tathams taking over merged team at unknown price.
1986 Team disbands when USFL folds.

Orlando Renegades

1982 Original franchise in USFL as Washington Federals. Owner: Berl Bernard.
1984 After 1984 season, team is sold for unknown price to Sherwood Weiser, to be moved to Miami as the Miami Renegades. When the league announces a move to a fall schedule for 1986, the team is sold for an unknown price to Donald Dizney, who moves the team to Orlando as the Orlando Renegades for the 1985 season.
1986 Team disbands when USFL folds.

Philadelphia Stars (see Baltimore Stars)

Pittsburgh Maulers

1983 Expansion franchise in USFL awarded after 1983 season. Expansion fee $6 million. Owner: Edward DeBartolo, Sr.
1984 After 1984 season, team folds.

Portland Breakers

1982 Original franchise in USFL as Boston Breakers. Owner is George Matthews; minority owner is Randy Vataha.
1983 After the 1983 season, team sold to Joe Canizaro for unknown price and moved to New Orleans as the New Orleans Breakers.
1984 After the 1984 season, Casnizaro moves the team from New Orleans to Portland and renames it Portland Breakers.
1985 After 1985 season, team folds.

San Antonio Gunslingers

1983 Expansion franchise in USFL awarded after 1983 season. Expansion fee $6 million. Owner: Clinton Manges.
1985 Team disbands after 1985 season when Manges misses player salary payments.

Tampa Bay Bandits

1982 Original franchise in USFL. Owner is John Bassett; minority owner is Steve Arky.
1985 After 1985 season, Bassett pulls out, and team is taken over by Arky. One month after the end of the 1985 season, Arky commits suicide, and team is taken over by Lee Scarfone and Tony Cunningham for unknown price.
1986 Team disbands when USFL folds.

Washington Federals (see Orlando Renegades)

Basketball

National Basketball Association
(includes Basketball Association of America)

Anderson Packers

1949 Joins NBA from NBL when NBL and BAA merge. Owner unknown.
1950 Franchise canceled before 1950 season.

Atlanta Hawks

1949 Tri Cities Blackhawks join NBA from NBL when NBL and BAA merge. Owners: Ben Kerner, B. W. Grafton, and Leo Ferris.

1950 Kerner buys out his partners for unknown price.

1951 Team moves to Milwaukee, renamed Milwaukee Hawks.

1955 Team moves to St. Louis, renamed St. Louis Hawks.

1968 St. Louis Hawks sold by Kerner for $3.5 million to syndicate headed by Tom Cousins and Terry Saunders, and including Robert Chambers, John Wilcox, William Holstein, R. Ledbetter, C. Loudermilk, Dillard Munford, Herman Russell, and Paul Duke. Team moves to Atlanta, renamed Atlanta Hawks.

1972 Saunders sells out to other members of syndicate at unknown price.

1973 Other owners sell out to Tom Cousins and John Wilcox at unknown price.

1975 Fifty-one percent control of Hawks sold to syndicate headed by Simon Selig, and including his wife and his son, Stephen Selig; Cousins and Wilcox continue as minority partners.

1977 Ted Turner buys 55 percent interest in team for $4 million.

1982 Team reportedly lost $2 million in 1981/82 season.

Baltimore Bullets I

1947 Expansion team in BAA. Owner unknown.

1949 Joins NBA from BAA when BAA and NBL merge.

1954 Team disbanded midway through 1954–55 season.

Baltimore Bullets II (see Washington Bullets)

Boston Celtics

1946 Original franchise in BAA. Owner: Boston Garden Corporation (Walter Brown, president).

1949 Team joins NBA from BAA when NBL and BAA merge.

1951 Boston Garden Corporation sells team to Brown for $2,500; Brown sells half-interest to Lou Pieri for $50,000.

1964 Brown dies; team is owned jointly by Pieri and Brown's widow.

1965 Team sold for $3 million to Ruppert Knickerbocker, headed by Marvin Kratter and Jack Waldron.

1968 Team sold to Ballantine Brewing Co. for $6 million.

1969 Ballantine Brewing taken over by Investors Funding Co.

1970 Team sold to Transnational Communications for $6 million.

1972 Transnational goes broke, and team reverts to Ballantine Brewing.

1972 Team sold to Bob Schmertz for $4 million.

1975 Schmertz sued by Irv Levin and Harold Lipton on claim to prior agreement by Schmertz to share ownership. Schmertz loses case. Schmertz indicted for bribery of New Jersey officials. Schmertz sells 50 percent of team to Levin and Lipton for $2 million. Schmertz dies, and Levin and Lipton buy out remaining Schmertz interest from Schmertz's heirs for unknown price.

1978 Levin and Lipton swap ownership of Celtics for ownership of Buffalo Braves. Under the agreement, Levin and Lipton retain rights to several starting Celtics players. New Celtics owner is John Y. Brown, with Harry Mangurian minority owner.

1979 Mangurian acquires sole ownership of Celtics for unknown price.

1983 Mangurian sells team for $15 million to Allen H. Cohen, Don F. Gaston, and Paul DuPee. Cohen disposes of his minority interest in the New Jersey Nets.

1986 Celtics stock offered to the public. Forty percent interest sold in the form of 2.6 million shares; offering price $18.50 per share. Implicit value of team is $120.5 million. Celtics stock is now traded on New York Stock Exchange.

Buffalo Braves (see Los Angeles Clippers)

Capital Bullets (see Washington Bullets)

Charlotte Hornets

1988 Expansion team in NBA. Expansion fee $32.5 million. Owner is syndicate headed by George Shinn (51 percent) and including Cy Bahakel (35 percent). Shinn paid $8.7 million for his share, and Bahakel paid $6 million for his (remainder is bank loans). Deal included a buyout clause, with Shinn having option to buy out Bahakel after one year.

1989 Shinn exercises his buyout option. Bahakel goes to court to prevent buyout, but court rules in favor of Shinn, who buys out Bahakel.

Chicago Bulls

1966 Expansion franchise in NBA. Expansion fee $1.25 million. Owner is syndicate headed by Dick Klein, and including Elmer Rice,

Harold Myer, Dan Cearle, Newton Fry, Gregston Barter, and Lamar Hunt.

1972   Team sold for $5.1 million to new corporation, headed by Arthur Wirtz, and including James Cooke, Albert Adelman, Lester Crown, E. Ginsberg, Lamar Hunt, P. Klutznick, J. Kovier, Arnold Meyer, and George Steinbrenner. This offer was accepted after a previous offer of $4.3 million had been accepted from Marvin Fishman. Fishman then could not exercise his offer because of the refusal of Arthur Wirtz to allow Fishman to use Chicago Stadium for the team. Fishman sues Wirtz for antitrust violations.

1983   Arthur Wirtz dies, and his son, William Wirtz, takes over team.

1984   Fishman is awarded a $17 million judgment in antitrust case.

1985   Syndicate headed by Jerry Reinsdorf buys 56 percent of Bulls for $9.2 million, purchasing the 26 percent interest of William Wirtz, the 10 percent interest of George Steinbrenner, and other interests. Lester Crown, Jonathon Kovier, and Lamar Hunt (11 percent) remain as minority stockholders.

Chicago Packers (see Washington Bullets)

Chicago Stags

1946   Original franchise in BAA. Owner: Chicago Stadium Corporation, John A. Sbarbaro, president, James D. Norris, Jr., and Arthur Wirtz joint owners.

1949   Team joins NBA from BAA in merger of BAA and NBL.

1950   Franchise canceled before 1950 season.

Chicago Zephyrs (see Washington Bullets)

Cincinnati Royals (see Sacramento Kings)

Cleveland Cavaliers

1970   Expansion franchise in NBA. Expansion fee $3.7 million. Owner: syndicate headed by Nick Mileti (20 percent) and including Louis Mitchell.

1980   Mileti sells his 20 percent interest for $1.4 million to Louis Mitchell, who owned 12 percent before purchase. Ted Stepien then buys a controlling interest in team for unknown price.

1982 Stepien claims team lost $7 million over three years since he acquired ownership.

1983 Stepien sells team to Gordon and George Gund for unknown price.

Cleveland Rebels

1946 Original franchise in BAA. Owner unknown.

1947 Franchise canceled before 1947 season.

Dallas Mavericks

1980 Expansion team in NBA. Expansion fee $12 million. Owner: syndicate headed by Donald Carter, and including Norman Sonjus and M. Douglas Adkins.

Denver Nuggets I

1949 Joins NBA from NBL in merger of BAA and NBL. Owner unknown.

1950 Franchise canceled before 1950 season.

Denver Nuggets II

1967 Denver Rockets original franchise in ABA. Fee $30,000. Owner: syndicate headed by J. J. Trindle.

1972 Team sold for unknown price to syndicate headed by Fred Goldberg, and including J. W. Ringsby and Alex Hannum. Name is changed to Denver Nuggets.

1974 Thirty-three percent of team sold for unknown price to a syndicate headed by Gary Antonoff, and including Carl Scheer, Myron Miller, William Newland, David Hoffman, O. Wesley Box, and Stephen Grossman.

1975 Remaining 67 percent of team sold to Antonoff syndicate.

1976 Team joins NBA when ABA disbands; fee $3.2 million to NBA plus $1.6 million compensation to ABA teams not joining NBA.

1982 Team sold for unknown price to Red McCombs.

1985 Team is sold by McCombs for $19 million to Sidney Shlenker and Allen Becker. Shlenker sells his minority interest in the Houston Rockets.

1989 Team is sold for $54 million to a syndicate headed by Bertram Lee and Peter Bynoe, funded by majority owner Robert Wussler. Lee and Bynoe have 37.5 percent of team, as managing partners, with Wussler owning 62.5 percent of team.

1991 Peter Bynoe and Comsat Video buy out others for reported $70 million.

Denver Rockets (see Denver Nuggets II)

Detroit Falcons

1946 Original franchise in NBA. Owner: Detroit Olympic Stadium Corporation.
1947 Franchise canceled before 1947/48 season.

Detroit Pistons

1948 Fort Wayne Pistons jump from NBL to BAA. Owner: Fred Zollner.
1949 Team joins NBA from BAA in merger of BAA and NBL.
1957 Team moves to Detroit. Name changed to Detroit Pistons. Owner is still Fred Zollner.
1974 Zollner sells team for $8.1 million to syndicate headed by William N. Davidson (51 percent) and including Herbert Tyner.

Fort Wayne Pistons (see Detroit Pistons)

Golden State Warriors

1946 Philadelphia Warriors original franchise in BAA. Owners: Pete Tyrell and Eddie Gottlieb.
1949 Team joins NBA from BAA in merger of BAA and NBL.
1952 Team sold for unknown price to syndicate headed by Eddie Gottlieb.
1962 Team sold for $850,000 to a syndicate headed by Franklin Mieuli, and including Matty Simmons and Leonard Mogul. Team is moved to San Francisco and renamed the San Francisco Warriors.
1971 Team moves to Oakland, renamed the Golden State Warriors; no change in ownership.
1986 Mieuli sells control of team to a syndicate headed by Jim Fitzgerald (former owner of Milwaukee Bucks) and including Dan Finnane for unknown price.

Houston Rockets

1967 San Diego Rockets expansion franchise in NBA. Expansion fee $1.75 million. Owner: syndicate headed by Robert Breitbard.

1971 Team sold for $5.6 million to Texas Sport Investment, headed by Billy Goldberg and Wayne Puddlestein. Team moved to Houston, renamed Houston Rockets.

1972 Team sold for unknown price to Texas Pro Sports, Inc., headed by Ray Patterson, Irving Kaplan minority interest.

1973 Kaplan buys 55 percent interest in team for $1.1 million.

1979 George Maloof acquires control of Rockets for unknown price.

1982 Team sold for $11 million to Charlie Thomas and Sidney Shlenker.

1985 Sidney Shlenker sells his minority interest in team when he acquires control of Denver Nuggets; Charlie Thomas now has majority control of team.

Indiana Pacers

1967 Original franchise in ABA. Fee $30,000. Owner: three-man syndicate headed by Charles DeVoe.

1974 Owners are John Weissart and Dick Tinkham. Team asks for financial help from league.

1975 Team sold for $650,000 to a six-man group headed by Tom Binford, and including Bill Bindley, Bob Wilds, and Jim Walker.

1976 Team joins NBA when ABA disbands. Fee is $3.2 million to NBA plus $1.6 million in compensation to ABA teams not moving to NBA.

1977 Forty percent of team reportedly up for sale.

1979 Team is sold for unknown price to syndicate headed by Sam Nassi.

1983 Sam Nassi and Frank Mariani sell team for unknown price to Melvin and Herbert Simon.

Indianapolis Jets (see Indianapolis Olympians)

Indianapolis Olympians

1948 Indianapolis Jets jump from NBL to BAA. Owner unknown.

1949 Team sold for unknown price to Alex Groza, Ralph Beard, Wallace Jones, and Cliff Barker. Name changed to Indianapolis Olympians. Team joins NBA from BAA in merger of NBL and BAA.

1951 Owners, all Kentucky players in college, are implicated in game-throwing scandal from their college days.

1954 Team goes bankrupt, franchise is canceled before 1954 season.

Kansas City-Omaha Kings (see Sacramento Kings)

Los Angeles Clippers

1970   Buffalo Braves expansion franchise in NBA. Expansion fee $3.7 million. Owner: syndicate headed by Philip Ryan and including Peter Crotty. Before initial 1970/71 season begins, syndicate sells out to Paul Snyder for unknown price.

1976   Snyder gives Irving Cowan an option to buy the team for $6.1 million. Cowan intends to move team to Hollywood, Florida. Deal falls through when city gets injunction against move.

1977   Team sold to John Y. Brown for unknown price.

1978   Irv Levin and Harold Lipton trade the Boston Celtics for the Buffalo Braves, taking several Celtics players with them. Team is moved to San Diego before the 1978/79 season. Name changed to San Diego Clippers.

1981   Team sold to a syndicate headed by Donald Sterling for $13.5 million.

1984   Team moves to Los Angeles, renamed Los Angeles Clippers. No change in ownership.

1988   Clippers pay $6 million to NBA for invading territory of Lakers, after NBA suit against Clippers.

Los Angeles Lakers

1947   Ben Berger and Morris Chalfen buy the Detroit Gems of the NBL for $15,000, and move the team to Minneapolis as the Minneapolis Lakers. Later, Max Winter comes in as one-third owner and manager of team.

1948   Team jumps from NBL to BAA. Same owners.

1949   Team joins NBA from BAA in merger of BAA and NBL.

1954   George Mikan buys Winter's one-third share of team for unknown price and becomes general manager.

1956   Ben Berger buys up Mikan's one-third; ownership is now Berger two-thirds, Chalfen one-third.

1957   Berger and Chalfen get offer of $150,000 for team from Milton Fischman and Marty Marion, who plan to move the team to Kansas City. *Minneapolis Star* mounts campaign to keep team in town; 117 businesses and individuals contribute $200,000 to a fund, of which $150,000 is price of team, and $50,000 working capital. Group buys the team from Berger and Chalfen. Group is headed by Bob Short.

1958   Short becomes 80 percent owner of team, buying out others in community group, "paying as little as 10 cents on the dollar." The Lakers are placed on financial probation by the NBA: if they don't average $6,600 in gate receipts per game, NBA has option of buying team for $150,000 and moving it elsewhere.

1960 Lakers move to Los Angeles. Name changed to Los Angeles Lakers. Owner Bob Short.

1965 Team sold to Jack Kent Cooke for $5 million.

1967 Los Angeles Forum opens. Construction cost $16.5 million.

1979 Team sold to Jerry Buss as part of a deal in which Buss buys the L.A. Kings, the L.A. Lakers, the Forum, and some Nevada real estate from Cooke for $67.5 million.

Miami Heat

1988 Expansion franchise in NBA. Expansion fee $32.5 million. Owner: syndicate headed by Ted Arison and Lewis Schaffel, and including Billy Cunningham and Zev Bufman.

Milwaukee Bucks

1968 Expansion franchise in NBA. Expansion fee $2 million. Owner: syndicate headed by Marvin Fishman and Wesley Pavalon.

1977 Team sold to Jim Fitzgerald for unknown price.

1985 Team sold to Herbert Kohl for $16.5 million.

Milwaukee Hawks (see Atlanta Hawks)

Minneapolis Lakers (see Los Angeles Lakers)

Minnesota Timberwolves

1989 Expansion franchise in NBA. Expansion fee $32.5 million. Owners Marv Wolfenson and Harvey Ratner.

New Jersey Americans (see New Jersey Nets)

New Jersey Nets

1967 New Jersey Americans original franchise in ABA. Fee $30,000. Owner: Arthur Brown.

1968 Team moved to Long Island, renamed New York Nets.

1969 Team sold for $1.1 million to Roy Boe.

1976 Team joins NBA when ABA disbands. Fee is $3.2 million to NBA plus $4 million to Knicks for invading their territory plus $1.6 million compensation to ABA teams not moving to NBA.

1978 Roy Boe goes bankrupt, and team is sold for unknown price to a syndicate headed by Joseph Taub and Alan Cohen.

1985 Joseph Taub sells his 40 percent interest for unknown price to his partners, Jerry Cohen, Alan Aufzien, David Gerstein, and Bernie Mann.

New Orleans Jazz (see Utah Jazz)

New York Knicks

1946 Original franchise in BAA. Owner: Madison Square Garden Corporation.

1949 Team joins NBA from BAA in merger of BAA and NBL.

New York Nets (see New Jersey Nets)

Orlando Magic

1989 Expansion team in NBA. Expansion fee $32.5 million. Owners: Jim and Bob Hewitt and Bill DuPont.

1991 Team sold for reported $85 million to Rich DeVos and his family (wife, three sons, and son-in-law).

Philadelphia 76ers

1949 Syracuse Nationals of NBL join NBA in merger of BAA and NBL. Owner: Leo Ferris.

1956 Team sold to Jack Egan for unknown price.

1963 Team sold for $500,000 to syndicate headed by Irv Kosloff and including Ike Richman. Team is moved to Philadelphia and renamed Philadelphia 76ers.

1976 Team is sold for unknown price to F. Eugene Dixon.

1981 Team is sold for $12 million to Harold Katz.

Philadelphia Warriors (see Golden State Warriors)

Phoenix Suns

1968 Expansion team of NBA. Expansion fee $2 million. Owner is syndicate headed by Richard Bloch, and including Carl Eller, Donald Pitt.

1987 Team sold for between $44.5 million and $52 million (*Sports Inc* estimates price at $55 million) to syndicate headed by Jerry Colangelo.

Pittsburgh Ironmen

1946 Original franchise in BAA. Owner unknown.
1947 Franchise canceled before 1947–48 season.

Portland Trail Blazers

1970 Expansion franchise in NBA. Expansion fee $3.7 million. Owner: syndicate headed by Herman Sarkowsky, and includes Bob Schmertz and Larry Weinberg.
1972 Schmertz sells out to Sarkowsky for unknown price when he buys Boston Celtics.
1973 Larry Weinberg and F. R. Backer buy 25 percent of team from Sarkowsky at unknown price.
1975 Weinberg becomes principal owner by buying out Sarkowsky at unknown price.
1988 Larry Weinberg sells the team for $70 million to Paul Allen.

Providence Steamrollers

1946 Original franchise in BAA. Owner unknown.
1949 Franchise canceled before 1949/50 season.

Rochester Royals (see Sacramento Kings)

Sacramento Kings

1948 Rochester Royals jump from NBL to BAA. Owners: Jack and Lester Harrison.
1949 Team joins NBA in merger of BAA and NBL.
1957 Team moves to Cincinnati, renamed Cincinnati Royals. No change in ownership.
1958 Team sold to Frank E. Woods and others for $225,000.
1961 Team sold for unknown price to Carl Rich.
1969 Team sold for unknown price to syndicate headed by Max Jacobs.
1972 Team sold for unknown price to Missouri Valley Sports, Inc., a syndicate including Frank Armanees, Clay Blair, Ray Evans, Herb Jacobson, Leon Karosen, Bob Margolin, John Muir, Paul Rosenberg, Truman Sloane, and Leonard Strauss. Team is moved to Kansas City-Omaha, and renamed Kansas City-Omaha Kings.
1982 Team sold for unknown price to syndicate including Frank and

Greg Lukenbill, Joseph Benvenuti, Robert A. Cook, Frank McCormack, and Stephen Cippa.

1984 Team moves to Sacramento, renamed Sacramento Kings.

1992 53 percent of team and ARCO arena sold for reported $140 million to syndicate headed by Jim Thomas.

St. Louis Bombers

1946 Original franchise in BAA. Owner: Arthur Wirtz.

1949 Team joins NBA in merger of BAA and NBL.

1950 Franchise canceled before 1950/51 season.

St. Louis Hawks (see Atlanta Hawks)

San Antonio Spurs

1967 Dallas Chaparrals original franchise in ABA. Fee $30,000. Owners: Gary Davidson, August Speth, John Klug, and James Peters. Team is sold before first ABA season for unknown price to syndicate headed by John Geary.

1970 Name changed to Texas Chaparrals for 1970/71 season, and then changed back to Dallas Chaparrals.

1973 Team sold for unknown price to syndicate headed by Angelo Drossos and including Red McCombs. Team moves to San Antonio, renamed San Antonio Spurs.

1976 Team joins NBA when ABA disbands. Fee is $3.2 million to NBA plus $1.6 million for compensation of ABA teams not moving to NBA.

1988 Team sold for $47 million to minority owner Red McCombs. McCombs, who had owned 35 percent of the team, pays $30.5 million to Drossos and other shareholders to obtain sole ownership of team.

San Diego Clippers (see Los Angeles Clippers)

San Diego Rockets (see Houston Rockets)

San Francisco Warriors (see Golden State Warriors)

Seattle SuperSonics

1967 Expansion franchise of NBA. Expansion fee $1.75 million. Owner is a syndicate headed by Sam Schulman and Gene Klein.

1972 Klein sells his interest to Schulman for unknown price (and Schulman sells his interest in NFL San Diego Chargers to Klein for unknown price).

1984 Schulman claims losses of $1 million in 1982/83, $2 million in 1981/82. Team is purchased for $21 million by Ackerly Communications, Inc. (owned by Barry Ackerly).

Sheboygan Redskins

1949 Team joins NBA from NBL in merger of NBL and BAA. Owner unknown.

1950 Franchise canceled before 1950/51 season.

Syracuse Nationals (see Philadelphia 76ers)

Toronto Huskies

1946 Original franchise in BAA. Owner unknown.

1947 Franchise canceled before 1947 season.

Tri-Cities Blackhawks (see Atlanta Hawks)

Utah Jazz

1974 New Orleans Jazz expansion team in NBA. Expansion fee $6.15 million. Owner: syndicate headed by Fred Rosenfield, and including Sam Battistone, Sheldon Beychak, Andrew Martin, Fred Miller, and Jerrold Rabin.

1979 Team moved to Salt Lake City, renamed Utah Jazz. Sam Battistone has controlling interest in team.

1985 Larry Miller buys 50 percent of team for unknown price.

1987 Bid by Minneapolis group to buy team and move it to Minneapolis averted when Miller buys remaining 50 percent of shares for unknown price and keeps team in Salt Lake City.

Washington Bullets

1961 Chicago Packers expansion franchise in NBA. Fee unknown. Owner: syndicate headed by Dave Trager, and including Max Winter.

1962 Team name changed to Chicago Zephyrs.

1963 Team moved to Baltimore; name changed to Baltimore Bullets. No change in ownership.

1964 Team sold for $1.1 million to syndicate headed by Abe Pollin, and including Earl Foreman and Arnold Heft.
1968 Pollin buys out other partners for unknown price.
1973 Team moves to Washington, D.C.; name changed to Capital Bullets.
1974 Name changed to Washington Bullets. Owner remains Abe Pollin.

Washington Capitols

1946 Original franchise in BAA. Owner: Art Uline.
1949 Team joins NBA in merger of BAA and NBL.
1951 Team folds in midseason, and franchise is canceled.

Waterloo Hawks

1949 Team joins NBA from NBL in merger of NBL and BAA. Owner unknown.
1950 Franchise canceled before 1950 season.

American Basketball Association

Anaheim Amigos (see Utah Stars)

Carolina Cougars (see St. Louis Spirits)

Dallas Chaparrals (see San Antonio Spurs under National Basketball Association)

Denver Nuggets (see Denver Nuggets under National Basketball Association)

Houston Mavericks (see St. Louis Spirits)

Indiana Pacers (see Indiana Pacers under National Basketball Association)

Kentucky Colonels

1967 Original franchise in ABA. Fee $30,000. Owners: Mamie and Joseph Gregory.

1973 Team sold for unknown price to David Jones, Stuart Jay, Wendell Cherry, Bill DeWitt, and Mike Storen.

1973 Team sold to Ellie and John Y. Brown for $2 million.

1976 Team goes out of business when ABA is absorbed by NBA, but Browns receive $2.8 million compensation from four teams moving to NBA.

Los Angeles Stars (see Utah Stars)

Memphis Pros (see Memphis Sounds)

Memphis Sounds

1967 New Orleans Buccaneers original franchise in ABA. Fee $30,000. Owners: Maurice Stern and Charles G. Smithers.

1970 Team sold for unknown price to P. L. Blake, moved to Memphis, and renamed Memphis Pros.

1972 Team sold to Charlie Finley for unknown price. Name changed to Memphis Tams.

1974 ABA buys team from Finley for $1.1 million, and then resells team for unknown price to Mike Soren, who changes name to Memphis Sounds.

1975 Team goes broke, and ABA takes over operation. ABA announces a move of franchise to Baltimore, but the team goes out of business before the end of the 1975/76 season.

1977 Finley sues the ABA and the four remaining ABA teams; as of 1977, he was still owed $1 million of ABA purchase price from 1974.

Memphis Tams (see Memphis Sounds)

Miami Floridians

1967 Minnesota Muskies original franchise in ABA. Fee $30,000. Owners: L. P. Shields and F. Jefferson.

1968 Team moved to Miami, name changed to Miami Floridians.

1972 Team goes out of business before 1972/73 season.

Minnesota Muskies (see Miami Floridians)

Minnesota Pipers (see Pittsburgh Condors)

New Jersey Americans (see New Jersey Nets under National Basketball Association)

New Jersey Nets (see New Jersey Nets under National Basketball Association)

New Orleans Buccaneers (see Memphis Sounds)

New York Nets (see New Jersey Nets under National Basketball Association)

Oakland Oaks (see Virginia Squires)

Pittsburgh Condors

1967 Pittsburgh Pipers original franchise in ABA. Fee $30,000. Owner: Gabe Rubin.
1968 Team moved to Minnesota, renamed Minnesota Pipers.
1969 Team returns to Pittsburgh, renamed Pittsburgh Pipers.
1970 Team sold for unknown price to Metro Sports, headed by H. Abrams. Renamed Pittsburgh Condors.
1971 Team goes broke, and franchise is canceled before 1971/72 season.

Pittsburgh Pipers (see Pittsburgh Condors)

St. Louis Spirits

1967 Houston Mavericks original franchise in ABA. Fee $30,000. Owners: William Witmore, Charles Frazier, Bud Adams, and T. S. Morrow.
1969 Team sold for unknown price to James Gardiner. Team moves to Charlotte, renamed Charlotte Cougars.
1971 Team sold for unknown price to Tedd Munchak.
1973 Team sold for $2.2 million to a syndicate headed by Harry Welt-

man, including Donald Schupak and Daniel and Ozzie Stins, and is moved to St. Louis, renamed St. Louis Spirits.

1975 Team announces a move to Salt Lake City, but goes out of business before 1975/76 season.

San Antonio Spurs (see San Antonio Spurs under National Basketball Association)

San Diego Conquistadors (see San Diego Sails)

San Diego Sails

1972 San Diego Conquistadors expansion team in ABA. Expansion fee $1 million. Owner: Leonard Bloom.

1975 Team sold for $2 million to Frank Goldberg, and renamed San Diego Sails. Team folds after 11 games of the 1975/76 season.

Texas Chaparrals (see San Antonio Spurs under National Basketball Association)

Utah Stars

1967 Anaheim Amigos original franchise in ABA. Fee $30,000. Owners: Art Kim and J. Ackerman.

1968 Team sold to Jim Kirst for $450,000. Team moved to Los Angeles and renamed Los Angeles Stars.

1970 Team sold for $850,000 to Bill Daniels, moved to Salt Lake City, and renamed the Utah Stars.

1974 Team sold to a syndicate headed by James A. Collier for unknown price.

1975 Team goes out of business midway through 1975/76 season.

Virginia Squires

1967 Oakland Oaks original franchise in ABA. Fee $30,000. Owners: Pat Boone, Ken Davidson, and Dennis Murphy.

1969 Team sold for $2 million to Earl Foreman. Team is moved to Washington, D.C., and renamed Washington Capitols.

1970 Team moved to Norfolk, and renamed Virginia Squires. No change in ownership.

1974 Foreman sells team for unknown price to ABA, which in turn sells team to a syndicate headed by John Bernhardt and Van Cunningham, for unknown price.

1976 Team goes out of business before 1976 season.

Washington Capitols (see Virginia Squires)

Hockey

National Hockey League

Atlanta Flames (see Calgary Flames)

Boston Bruins

1924 Expansion franchise in NHL. Expansion fee $15,000. Owner: Charles Adams.

1928 Boston Garden opens, owned by Tex Rickard.

1933 Rickard dies. Garden sold for unknown price to Major Dibley and Dick Dynn.

1934 Garden sold for unknown price to Henry Lapham.

1936 Garden sold for unknown price to Weston Adams and Art Ross.

1951 Team and Boston Garden sold to Boston Garden Arena Co. (Walter Brown, president) for $187,000. Largest stockholder is Weston Adams (40 percent).

1963 Walter Brown dies. Garden and team bought by Weston Adams for unknown price.

1973 Storer Broadcasting buys Garden and team for unknown price.

1975 Garden and team sold for unknown price to SportsSystems of Buffalo (owned by Max Jacobs, Charles Jacobs, and Louis Jacobs).

1976 Garden refurbished.

1981 Garden and team are now owned by Delaware North Co. which is owned by Irwin Jacobs, heir to the Jacobs brothers' property.

1985 Syndicate headed by James Brennan and Godfrey Wood reportedly makes a bid of $50 million for Bruins and Boston Garden, but deal falls through.

Brooklyn Americans

1917 Quebec Bulldogs original franchise in NHL, but team does not operate in 1917/18 or 1918/19 season. Owner: Michael Quinn.

1919 Quebec begins play in NHL.

1920 Team sold for $5,000 to Percy Thompson. Team is moved to Hamilton before 1920 season, renamed Hamilton Tigers.

1925 Team sold for $75,000 to Bill Dwyer and moved to New York, renamed New York Americans.

1938 Team goes broke, and NHL takes over team from Dwyer and operates it under the management of Red Dutton.

1941 Team name changed to Brooklyn Americans. Owner: Red Dutton, subsidized by NHL.

1942 Team goes broke; franchise canceled before 1942/43 season.

Buffalo Sabres

1970 Expansion franchise in NHL. Expansion fee $6 million. Owner: Niagara Frontier Hockey (owned by Seymour Knox and Northrup Knox).

Calgary Flames

1972 Atlanta Flames expansion franchise in NHL. Expansion fee $6 million. Owners: William Putnam and Dillard Munford.

1973 John Wilcox buys up Putnam interest for unknown price.

1976 R. Charles Loudermilk buys controlling interest in team for unknown price.

1977 Tom Cousins buys team for unknown price.

1980 Cousins says that team lost $2 million in 1979/80 season. Team is sold for unknown price to a syndicate headed by Nelson Skalbania, and including Norman Green, Harley Hotchkiss, Ralph Scarfield, B. J. Seaman, and D. K. Seaman. Team is moved to Calgary, renamed Calgary Flames.

1991 Norman Green sells his interest for unknown price to other members of the Skalbania syndicate when he buys Minnesota North Stars.

California Seals (see Cleveland Barons)

Chicago Blackhawks

1926 Expansion franchise in NHL. Expansion fee $12,000. Owner: Major Frederic McLaughlin. McLaughlin purchased the Portland Rosebuds of the Pacific Coast Hockey League and transferred the team to Chicago, where it is known as the Chicago Blackhawks.

1929 Chicago Stadium open. Construction cost $7 million. Owner: Paddy Harmon.

1935 Stadium sold to James D. Norris, Jr., and Arthur Wirtz for $300,000 (debt outstanding on stadium unknown).

1944 McLaughlin dies, leaving team to son William McLaughlin.

1945 William Tobin heads a syndicate that buys team from McLaughlin for unknown price. Financial backers of syndicate are James D. Norris, Sr., James D. Norris, Jr., and Arthur Wirtz, but this is kept secret until 1954.

1966 James Norris, Jr., dies; Arthur Wirtz takes over the team and stadium as sole owner.

1983 Arthur Wirtz dies. Son William Wirtz takes over control of the team and stadium.

Cleveland

1952 Cleveland applies for an expansion franchise at a fee of $425,000. NHL turns down application when financial problems arise.

Cleveland Barons

1967 Oakland Seals expansion franchise in NHL. Expansion fee $2 million. Owners: Barry Van Gerbig and George Fleharty.

1968 Labatt Breweries offers to buy the team and move it to Vancouver, but deal falls through.

1969 Team sold for $4.5 million to Transnational Corporation. Owners: Whitey Ford, Dick Lynch, and Pat Sumner (80 percent), with minority interest held by Seymour and Northrup Knox (20 percent).

1970 Team is in default of debts, is sold for $4.5 million to Charles Finley, and is renamed California Seals.

1974 Team sold by Finley to NHL for a price between $4.5 million and $6 million.

1975 NHL sells team for unknown price to Mel Swig.

1976 California Golden Seals move from Oakland to Cleveland, renamed the Cleveland Barons. Owner: Mel Swig.

1977 Team goes broke again, and is sold for $5.3 million, which just covers the debts of the team, to George Gund; minority owner is Sanford Greenberg.

1978 Team loses $3 million in 1977/78 season, and wishes to relocate. Team merges with Minnesota North Stars; Cleveland Barons go out of existence. (see Minnesota North Stars under National Hockey League for details)

Colorado Rockies (see New Jersey Devils)

Detroit Cougars (see Detroit Red Wings)

Detroit Falcons (see Detroit Red Wings)

Detroit Red Wings

1926 Detroit Cougars expansion team in NHL. Expansion fee $12,000. Owner: a syndicate headed by Charles Hughes, and including members of the Fisher, Ford, Kresge, and Scripps families, which pays $25,000 for the Victoria Cougars of the Pacific Coast Hockey League and moves team to Detroit, renamed the Detroit Cougars.

1927 Detroit Olympia Stadium opens. Construction cost $2.15 million.

1930 Name of team changed to Detroit Falcons.

1933 Team is on verge of bankruptcy. Team is sold for $100,000 to James D. Norris, Sr., James D. Norris, Jr., and Arthur Wirtz. Team is renamed the Detroit Red Wings. Trio also buys Olympic Stadium for $250,000.

1952 James D. Norris, Sr., dies. Team and Olympic Stadium are left to James D. Norris, Jr., and Arthur Wirtz. Children of James D. Norris, Jr.—Bruce Norris, Marguerite Riker, and Eleanor Kneible—buy out the Norris-Wirtz interest for unknown price. Marguerite Riker becomes president of team.

1955 Bruce Norris takes over team.

1979 Olympic Stadium closes. Team moves to publicly owned Joe Louis Arena.

1982 Team sold for unknown price to Michael Illitch, who also is the operator of Joe Louis Arena for the city of Detroit.

Edmonton Oilers

1972 Original franchise in WHA. Fee $25,000. Owners: Charles Allard and Zane Feldman.

1976 Team sold for unknown price to Peter Pocklington and Nelson Skalbania.

1977 Skalbania sells his half of team to Peter Pocklington for unknown price, when Skalbania buys the WHA Indianapolis Racers.

1979 Team joins NHL when WHA disbands. Fee is $6 million to NHL, plus $1.5 million compensation to WHA teams that did not move to NHL.

Hamilton Tigers (see Brooklyn Americans)

Hartford Whalers

1972 New England Whalers original franchise in WHA. Fee $25,000. Owner: syndicate headed by Bob Schmertz.

1974 Team moves to Hartford after being purchased for unknown price by a group of local firms: Aetna Life, Howard L. Baldwin, Bank of Boston—Connecticut, William E. Barnes, CIGNA Assets, John Coburn, CBT Corporation, Connecticut Light and Power, Connecticut Mutual Life, Allbert Ford, Greater Hartford Chamber of Commerce, Hartford Attractions, Inc., Hartford Courant Co., Hartford Federal Savings and Loan, Hartford Fire Insurance, Hartford National Corporation, Hartford Steam Boiler, Heublein, Inc., Peter Leonard, Bob Schmertz, Society for Savings, Travelers, United Technologies Corporation, Sanford Weil.

1975 Bob Schmertz dies.

1977 Hartford Federal S & L pulls out.

1979 Team renamed Hartford Whalers, and enters the NHL in WHA-NHL agreement. Fee to NHL is $6 million plus $1.5 million in compensation to WHA teams not moving to NHL. Barnes, Coburn, Ford, Leonard, Society for Savings, and Weil pull out of consortium.

1987 Team makes $500,000 in 1986/87 season.

1988 Team makes $2 million in 1987/88 season. Team is sold for $31 million to Donald Conrad and Richard Gordon. 37.5 percent of team is owned by Colonial Realty Co.

1992 Colonial Realty goes bankrupt. NHL announces it might rescind 1988 sale of Whalers because of false information provided at time of 1988 sale.

Kansas City Scouts (see New Jersey Devils)

Los Angeles Kings

1967 Expansion franchise in NHL. Expansion fee $2 million. Owner: Jack Kent Cooke.

1979 Kings, Lakers, and Forum plus Nevada real estate sold by King to Jerry Buss for $67.5 million.

1988 Buss sells 51 percent interest in Kings for $20 million to Bruce McNall.

Minnesota North Stars

1967 Expansion franchise in NHL. Expansion fee $2 million. Owner is a syndicate headed by Walter Bush, Jr., and including Gordon Ritz, and Robert McNulty. A majority of the stock is owned by members of the Weyerhauser family.

1978 Team has lost $3 million between 1973 and 1978. Team merges with Cleveland Barons. No name change. New owners are George and Gordon Gund; minority owner is Sanford Greenberg. Under merger agreement, the new owners will pay $1.1 million to Charlie Finley, an amount owed him since the NHL bought the California Seals in 1974, and they will also pay the NHL the outstanding debts owed to the league (amount unknown) by Mel Swig when he was owner of the team.

1990 North Stars sold for $31.5 million to Howard Baldwin and Morris Belzberg. Deal involves the Gunds' obtaining an expansion franchise in San Jose for 1991/92, and in addition, the Gunds are allowed to pick 11 skaters and 2 goalies from the North Star list of players with less than 50 games in NHL, plus 6 amateur prospects drafted by Minnesota who haven't yet signed contracts. The Gunds will also collect the North Stars' share of the expansion fees for the San Jose club and the other expansion teams coming into the NHL in 1992/93, estimated at around $6.7 million, for a total out-of-pocket cost to Baldwin and Belzberg of $38.2 million. Gunds claim to have lost $7 million in the 1988/89 season. Later in 1990, Baldwin and Belzberg sell 51 percent of North Stars to Norman Green, retaining 49 percent for themselves. Sale price is 51 percent of $31.5 million. In August 1990, Baldwin sells his 24.5 percent to Green for a reported $4.25 million, and in October, Belzberg sells his 24.5 percent for another $4.25 million, to make Green sole owner of Minnesota.

Montreal Canadiens

1909 Team formed by Ambrose O'Brien.

1910 Team sold to George Kennedy for $7,500.

1917 Original franchise in NHL. Owner: George Kennedy.

1921 Kennedy dies. Team is sold for $11,000 to Louis Letourneau, Joe Catterinich, and Leo Dandurand.

1924 Montreal Forum opens.

1935 Dandurand now owns team. He sells team for $165,000 to Canadian Arena Co., owned by Ernest Savard, Louis Gelinas, and Maurice Forget, who also own the Montreal Maroons.

1940 Control of Canadian Arena Co. sold for unknown price to Senator Donat Raymond.

1957 Sixty percent control of Canadian Arena Co. is sold to Hartland Molson and his brother, Thomas Molson, owners of Molson Breweries, for between $4 and $5 million. Price includes both the Montreal Forum and the Canadians.

1968 Control of Canadian Arena Co. is sold to three cousins, Peter, J. David, and Bill Molson.

1968 Forum refurbished at a cost of $10.5 million.

1971 Control of team and Forum is sold for $15.4 million to Placements Rondelle Ltd., owned by Edward and Peter Bronfman, and Baton Broadcasting Ltd. John Bassett is the major owner of Baton Broadcasting. Syndicate acquires 700,000 of the outstanding 1,025,000 shares of Canadian Arena Co.

1978 Team sold to Molson Breweries for unknown price.

1988 Team announces loss for season of $686,778.

1989 Team announces loss for season of $139,569.

Montreal Maroons

1924 Expansion franchise in NHL. Expansion fee $15,000. Owners: Thomas Strachan and Donat Raymond, owners of Montreal Forum. Team comes in as soon as Forum opens. Construction cost $1.5 million.

1938 Franchise voluntarily suspended for one year due to financial problems. Team asks to move to St. Louis but is turned down by NHL.

1939 Franchise canceled before 1939/1940 season.

Montreal Wanderers

1917 Original franchise in NHL. Owner: Samuel Lichtenhein.

1918 Team goes out of business when its rink burns down during the 1917/18 season.

New England Whalers (see Hartford Whalers)

New Jersey Devils

1974 Kansas City Scouts expansion franchise in NHL. Expansion fee $6 million. Owner: E. G. Thompson.

1976 Team sold to syndicate headed by Jack Vickers, and including Bud Palmer and Peter Gilbert. Team moved to Denver, renamed Colorado Rockies.

1978 Arthur Imperatore buys team for unknown price to move team to New Jersey, but NHL turns down move.

1981 Peter Gilbert buys team for unknown price. Team then sold for unknown price to John McMullen and John C. Whitehead, and moved to New Jersey for 1982/83 season, renamed New Jersey Devils.

New York Americans (see Brooklyn Americans)

New York Islanders

1972 Expansion franchise in NHL. Expansion fee $6 million to NHL plus $5 million indemnity to New York Rangers. Owner: Roy L. M. Boe.
1979 Boe goes broke, and team is sold for unknown price to a syndicate headed by John Pickett, who was a minority stockholder in the Boe syndicate.
1991 Team reportedly on the market for an asking price of $55 million.

New York Rangers

1925 Madison Square Garden opens. Construction cost $6 million.
1926 Expansion team in NHL. Fee $12,000, plus $25,000 for players acquired from Western Canada League. Owner: Madison Square Garden Corporation.
1967 New Madison Square Garden opens.

Oakland Seals (see Cleveland Barons)

Ottawa Senators I (see St. Louis Eagles)

Ottawa Senators II

1991 Expansion franchise in NHL, to join league for 1992/93 season. Expansion fee $45 million. Owner: Bruce Firestone.

Philadelphia Quakers

1925 Pittsburgh Pirates expansion team in NHL. Expansion fee $12,000, plus $25,000 for players from Western Canada League. Owner: Odie Cleghorn.
1930 By now, owner of team is Benny Leonard. Team goes broke, moves to Philadelphia, and is renamed Philadelphia Quakers. Owner is still Benny Leonard.

1931 Team voluntarily suspends operations for one year due to financial problems (lost $100,000 in 1930/31 season).

1931 Franchise canceled before 1932/33 season.

Philadelphia Flyers

1967 Expansion franchise in NHL. Expansion fee $2 million. Owner: Ed Snider.

Pittsburgh Penguins

1967 Expansion franchise in NHL. Expansion fee $2 million. Owner: syndicate headed by Jack McGregor and W. Russell Byers, with 31 minority partners, including Art Rooney.

1968 Eighty percent control of team sold for unknown price to Donald Parsons.

1971 Team goes broke; NHL takes over franchise. Team sold for $7 million to a group of Pittsburgh businessmen, including Thayer Potter, Peter Bloch, and Peter Burchfield.

1975 Team goes broke again and is sold by NHL for $3.8 million to a group headed by Al Savill.

1978 Team sold for unknown price to Edward DeBartolo, Sr.

1991 Edward DeBartolo sells team for unknown price to a syndicate headed by Howard Baldwin, includes Morris Wielzberg and Thomas Ruta.

Pittsburgh Pirates (see Philadelphia Quakers)

Quebec Bulldogs (see Brooklyn Americans)

Quebec Nordiques

1972 Original member of WHA. Fee $25,000. Owners: Jean Lesage and Paul Racine. This franchise was awarded to Gary Davidson for organizing the WHA, and was originally intended for San Francisco. Davidson sold the franchise to Lesage and Racine for $215,000 before the first WHA season, and they moved the team to Quebec.

1979 Team joins NHL as part of WHA-NHL agreement. Fee is $6 million to the NHL, plus $1.5 million to pay compensation to WHA teams not moving to NHL.

1988 Team lost $500,000 in 1987/88 season. Team is owned by Carling O'Keefe Brewery. Team is sold for between $15 million and $18 million to a syndicate headed by Michael Aubut, and including the Quebec Federation of Labor, Metro-Richeleau, Diashowa Canada, Le Capitale, and Autil, Inc.

St. Louis Blues

1967 Expansion franchise in NHL. Expansion fee $2 million, plus $4.5 million to buy St. Louis Arena from Arthur Wirtz. Owners: Sidney Salmon and son Sidney Salmon II.
1977 Team and stadium sold to Ralston Purina for unknown price, when team is near bankruptcy.
1983 Team sold by Ralston Purina for unknown price to syndicate headed by Harry Ornest, after NHL rejects several bids that would have involved move of franchise (one a move to Saskatoon in a bid by Batoni-Hunter Enterprises).
1986 Team sold for unknown price to Michael Shanahan.

St. Louis Eagles

1917 Ottawa Eagles original franchise in NHL. Owner: Tommy Gorman.
1924 Controlling interest in team sold for unknown price to T. Franklin Ahern.
1931 Team voluntarily suspends operations for one year due to financial problems.
1932 Team resumes play.
1934 Ottawa franchise moved to St. Louis; team renamed St. Louis Eagles. Owner unknown.
1935 Team goes broke. NHL buys out owner for unknown price and distributes players among existing teams.

San Jose Sharks

1990 Expansion franchise for 1991/92 season. Expansion fee $45 million. Owners: George and Gordon Gund. (see Minnesota North Stars for details)

Tampa Bay Lightning

1991 Expansion franchise in NHL for 1992/93 season. Expansion fee $45 million. Owner is a syndicate headed by Phil Esposito, and including George Steinbrenner and four Japanese bankers, Link International.

Late in 1991, Japanese members of the syndicate buy out the other members; implicit price of team is $50 million.

Toronto Arenas (see Toronto Maple Leafs)

Toronto Maple Leafs

1917   Toronto Arenas original franchise in NHL. Majority owner is Charlie Querrie; minority owners are J. P. Bickell, N. L. Nathanson, and Paul Ciceri.
1919   Name of team changed to Toronto St. Patricks.
1926   Team sold for $160,000 to a syndicate headed by Major Conn Smythe. Name of team changed to Toronto Maple Leafs.
1930   Team issues $200,000 in stock to pay to complete Maple Leaf Garden. Construction cost $1.2 million. Gardens opens for 1931/32 season.
1961   Majority control of team and Garden sold by Smythe to son C. Stafford Smythe, Harold Ballard, and John Bassett for $2 million.
1970   Smythe and Ballard buy out Bassett for unknown price.
1972   Stafford Smythe dies, and Ballard assumes control of team.
1989   Harold Ballard announces that he is buying the 24 percent of shares in H. E. Ballard Ltd, the holding company owning the Maple Leafs, from his son Harold Ballard, Jr., paying $25 million.

Toronto St. Patricks (see Toronto Maple Leafs)

Vancouver Canucks

1970   Expansion franchise in NHL. Expansion fee $6 million. Owner: Medicore Investment Co., firm controlled by Tom Scallen and Lyman Walters.
1971   Medicore fails to repay $3.5 million debt, and team is in financial distress. New public company is formed, Northwest Sports Enterprises, which sells shares publicly; Scallen in majority control.
1974   Scallen sent to prison. Team sold for $8.5 million to Western Broadcast Sales Corporation, Frank Griffiths principal shareholder.

Washington Capitals

1975   Expansion franchise in NHL. Expansion fee $6 million. Owner: Abe Pollin.

Winnipeg Jets

1972 Original franchise in WHA. Fee $25,000. Owners: Ben Haskin and Saul Simken.
1974 Team is up for sale after losing $250,000 in first season.
1976 Team is owned by Hockey Ventures, Inc., with seven shareholders—Winnipeg businessmen plus Bobby Hull (12 percent).
1978 Team purchased by Bob Graham and Barry Shenkarow for unknown price.
1979 Team joins NHL. Fee includes $6 million to NHL, plus $1.5 million to pay compensation to WHA teams not moving to NHL.
1986 Shekarow buys out Graham for unknown price.

World Hockey Association (1972–1979)

Estimated losses for league per year were approximately $12 million, or roughly $1 million per team.

*Alberta Oilers (see Edmonton Oilers
under National Hockey League)*

Baltimore Blades

1972 Original franchise in WHA as Los Angeles Sharks. Fee $25,000. Owner: syndicate headed by Dennis Murphy. Team goes bankrupt during initial year and is taken over by Dr. Rhoades. Team is then bought for unknown price by Leonard Bloom.
1974 Team is sold for $2.5 million to Metro Sports Association, a syndicate headed by Charles Nolton and Peter Shagena. Team is moved to Detroit and renamed the Michigan Stags.
1975 Midway through the 1974/75 season, the Stags go broke and the team is taken over by the WHA, which moves the team to Baltimore, to finish the season as the Baltimore Blades. The WHA seeks a group to take over the team, but no group is found, and the franchise is canceled before the 1975/76 season.

Birmingham Bulls

1972 Original franchise in WHA as Ottawa Nationals. Fee $25,000. Owners: Doug Michel and Martin Fishman. Team is sold to N. Trbovitch and John Craig Eaton for unknown price.

1973 John Bassett buys the team for $1.8 million and moves the team to Toronto, renaming it the Toronto Toros.

1976 Team moved to Birmingham, renamed the Birmingham Bulls. No ownership change.

1979 Franchise canceled after the 1978/79 season.

Calgary Cowboys

1972 Original franchise in WHA as Miami Screaming Eagles. Fee $25,000. Owner: Herb Martin. Before initial 1972/73 season, team is sold for $210,000 to James Cooper (minority interest Bernard Brown) and moved to Philadelphia as the Philadelphia Blazers.

1972 Cooper sells out to Brown for $125,000, and Brown becomes the sole owner of the Blazers.

1973 Team sold for $1.9 million to Jim Pattison, who moves team to Vancouver, renaming it the Vancouver Blazers. Later in the year, team is sold again, to Neonex International Ltd., for unknown price.

1975 Team moved to Calgary, renamed the Calgary Cowboys.

1977 Team goes bankrupt, and franchise is canceled before 1977/78 season.

Chicago Cougars

1972 Original franchise in WHA. Fee $25,000. Owners: Jordan and Walter Kaiser.

1974 Team is sold for unknown price to Cougar Hockey Organization, Inc., owned by Jordan and Walter Kaiser. Later in the year, team is sold for $2 million to a syndicate headed by Pat Stapleton, Ralph Backstrom, and Dave Dryden.

1975 Team goes broke and franchise is canceled before 1975/76 season.

Cincinnati Stingers

1975 Expansion franchise in WHA. Fee $2 million. Owners: Brian Heekin and Bill DeWitt.

1979 After 1978/79 season, franchise is canceled.

Cleveland Crusaders

1972 Original franchise in WHA. Fee $25,000. Owner: Nick Mileti.

1976 Owner is Jay Moore. Team goes broke, and a tentative sale is made to Florida Pro Sports (Bill Putnam, head) to move team to Florida. Sale falls through, and franchise is canceled before 1976/77 season.

Denver Spurs (see Ottawa Civics)

Edmonton Oilers (see Edmonton Oilers under National Hockey League)

Hartford Whalers (see Hartford Whalers under National Hockey League)

Houston Aeros

1972 Original franchise in WHA. Fee $25,000. Majority owner is Paul Deneau; minority owner is Jim Smith.
1974 Team sold to Irving Kaplan for unknown price.
1975 Kaplan files for bankruptcy, and team is taken over by a group headed by George Bolin and Walter Fondren.
1977 Team goes broke and is taken over by Kenneth Schnitzer.
1978 Team is sold for unknown price by Schnitzer to the Winnipeg Jets, and the franchise is canceled before the 1978/79 season.

Indianapolis Racers

1974 Expansion franchise in WHA. Expansion fee $2 million. Owners: John Weissart and Dick Tinkhaur.
1975 During 1974/75 season, team goes bankrupt and is taken over by Paul Deneau for unknown price.
1977 Team bought for $1 million by Nelson Skalbania.
1978 Team folds midway through 1978/79 season.

Los Angeles Sharks (see Baltimore Blades)

Michigan Stags (see Baltimore Blades)

Minnesota Fighting Saints

1972 Original franchise in WHA. Fee $25,000. Owners: Lou Kaplan, John Finley, Fred Grothe, Hal Greenwood, and Lenny Vanelli.

1974 Team sold for unknown price to syndicate headed by Wayne Belisle, and including Andy Williams and Henry Mancini.

1975 Team reports losses of $1.26 million in 1973/74, $1.42 million in 1972/73, and $2.3 million in 1974/75.

1976 Team pulls out of league midway through 1975/76 season and announces it is bankrupt. Owner Jock Irvine says team has $1.5 million in outstanding debts. Team is sold for $1 to Frank Marzitgelli, E. E. Parranto, Lou Kaplan, Pat O'Halloran, John Finley, and Len Vanelli.

1977 Team is back in league for 1976/77 season with new owners Nick Mileti and Jay P. Moore, but drops out midway through season, and franchise is canceled.

New England Whalers (see Hartford Whalers under National Hockey League)

New Jersey Knights (see San Diego Mariners)

New York Golden Blades (see San Diego Mariners)

New York Raiders (see San Diego Mariners)

Ottawa Civics

1975 Expansion franchise in WHA as Denver Spurs. Fee is $2 million. Owner: Ivan Mullenix.

1976 Midway through 1975/76 season, team moves to Ottawa and is renamed the Ottawa Civics. No change in ownership. Mullenix reports losses of $2 million during half-season stay in Denver. Franchise canceled at end of 1975/76 season.

Ottawa Nationals (see Birmingham Bulls)

Philadelphia Blazers (see Calgary Cowboys)

Phoenix Roadrunners

1974 Expansion team in WHA. Expansion fee is $2 million. Owner is syndicate headed by Bert Gaetz, and including Karl Eller, L. G. Hooker, H. J. Louis, Stephen Craig, and Jim Wells.

1977 Franchise canceled before 1977/78 season.

Quebec Nordiques (see Quebec Nordiques under National Hockey League)

San Diego Mariners

1972 Original franchise in WHA as New York Raiders. Fee $25,000. Owners: Neil Shayne and Norman Dachs. Before initial season, Dachs sells out to Dick Wood and Sy Siegel.

1973 Team goes broke in first season. WHA takes over team and sells it for $1.5 million to a syndicate headed by L. Madison. Team is renamed the New York Golden Blades.

1974 Midway through 1973/74 season, team goes broke again, and WHA takes over team again. WHA sells team for $800,000 to D. Richard and Seymour Siegel, who move the team to Cherry Hill, New Jersey, renaming it the New Jersey Knights. Midway through 1974/75 season, team goes broke yet again, and is sold to Joe Schwartz and Peter Graham for $2 million. The team is moved to San Diego and renamed the San Diego Mariners.

1975 Before the 1975/76 season, the team is sold again, for $2.75 million, to a ten-man syndicate headed by Sam Hartman.

1976 Team goes broke and is taken over by Ray Kroc. Team loses $1.4 million in 1976/77 season.

1977 Team goes broke after the 1976/77 season, and franchise is canceled.

Toronto Toros (see Birmingham Bulls)

Vancouver Blazers (see Calgary Cowboys)

Winnipeg Jets (see Winnipeg Jets under National Hockey League)

Attendance Records

Baseball

National League

Year	Bs/Mi/At	Brkn/LA	Chicago	Cincin	NY/SF	Phil
[**Bold** indicates the last year before a franchise moves to a new facility.]						
1901	146,502	198,200	205,071	205,728	298,650	234,937
1902	116,960	199,868	263,700	217,300	302,875	112,066
1903	143,155	224,670	386,205	351,680	579,530	151,729
1904	140,694	214,600	439,100	391,915	609,826	140,771
1905	150,003	227,924	509,900	313,927	552,700	317,932
1906	143,280	277,400	654,300	330,056	402,850	294,680
1907	203,221	312,500	422,550	317,500	538,350	341,216
1908	253,750	275,600	665,325	399,999	910,000	420,660
1909	195,198	321,300	633,480	424,643	783,700	303,177
1910	149,027	279,321	526,152	380,622	511,785	296,597
1911	96,000	269,000	576,000	300,000	675,000	416,000
1912	121,000	243,000	514,000	344,000	638,000	250,000
1913	208,000	347,000	419,000	258,000	630,000	470,000
1914	382,913	122,671	202,516	100,791	364,313	138,714
1915	376,253	297,766	217,058	218,878	391,850	449,898
1916	313,495	447,747	453,685	255,846	552,056	515,365
1917	174,253	221,619	300,218	269,056	500,264	354,428
1918	84,938	83,831	337,256	163,009	256,618	122,266
1919	167,401	360,721	424,430	532,501	708,857	240,424
1920	162,483	808,722	480,783	568,107	929,609	330,998
1921	318,627	613,245	410,107	311,227	973,477	273,961
1922	167,965	498,865	542,283	493,754	945,809	232,471
1923	227,802	564,666	703,705	575,063	820,780	228,168
1924	177,478	818,883	716,922	473,707	844,068	299,818
1925	313,528	659,435	622,610	464,920	778,993	304,905
1926	303,598	650,819	885,063	672,987	700,362	240,600
1927	288,685	637,230	1,159,168	442,164	858,190	305,420
1928	227,001	664,863	1,143,740	490,490	916,191	182,168
1929	372,351	731,886	1,485,166	295,040	868,806	281,200

479

Year	Bs/Mi/At	Brkn/LA	Chicago	Cincin	NY/SF	Phil
1930	464,835	1,097,329	1,463,624	386,727	868,714	299,007
1931	515,005	753,133	1,086,422	263,316	812,163	284,849
1932	507,606	681,827	1,086,422	359,950	484,868	268,914
1933	517,803	526,815	594,112	216,281	604,471	156,421
1934	303,205	434,188	707,525	206,773	730,851	169,885
1935	232,754	470,517	692,604	448,247	748,748	205,470
1936	340,585	489,618	699,370	466,345	837,952	249,219
1937	385,339	482,481	895,020	411,221	926,887	212,790
1938	341,159	663,087	951,640	706,756	799,633	166,111
1939	285,994	955,668	726,663	981,443	702,457	277,973
1940	241,616	975,978	534,878	850,180	747,852	207,177
1941	263,680	1,214,910	545,159	643,513	763,098	231,401
1942	285,332	1,037,765	590,872	427,031	779,621	230,183
1943	271,289	661,739	508,247	379,122	466,095	466,975
1944	208,691	605,905	640,110	409,567	674,483	369,586
1945	374,178	1,059,220	1,036,386	290,070	1,016,468	285,057
1946	969,673	1,796,824	1,324,970	715,751	1,219,873	1,045,247
1947	1,277,361	1,807,526	1,364,039	899,975	1,600,793	907,332
1948	1,455,439	1,398,967	1,398,967	823,386	1,459,268	767,429
1949	1,081,795	1,633,747	1,143,139	707,782	1,218,446	819,698
1950	944,391	1,185,896	1,165,944	538,794	1,008,878	1,217,035
1951	487,475	1,282,628	894,415	588,268	1,059,539	937,568
1952	**281,278**	1,088,704	1,024,826	604,197	964,940	755,417
1953	1,826,397	1,163,419	763,183	548,086	811,518	853,644
1954	2,131,388	1,020,531	748,183	704,167	1,155,067	738,001
1955	2,005,836	1,033,589	875,800	693,662	824,112	922,886
1956	2,046,331	1,213,562	720,118	1,125,928	629,179	934,798
1957	2,215,404	**1,028,256**	670,622	1,070,850	**652,932**	1,146,230
1958	1,971,101	1,845,556	979,904	788,582	1,272,625	931,110
1959	1,749,112	2,071,045	858,255	801,255	1,422,130	802,815
1960	1,497,799	2,253,887	809,770	663,486	1,795,356	862,205
1961	1,100,781	1,813,465	673,067	1,123,240	1,391,221	584,039
1962	766,921	2,755,184	766,921	982,095	1,592,594	762,034
1963	773,018	2,538,602	979,551	858,805	1,571,316	907,141
1964	910,991	2,228,751	751,647	862,466	1,504,364	1,425,891
1965	**555,584**	2,553,577	641,361	1,047,824	1,546,075	1,155,376
1966	1,539,801	2,671,029	635,891	742,958	1,657,192	1,108,201
1967	1,389,222	1,664,362	977,226	958,300	1,242,480	828,888
1968	1,126,540	1,581,093	1,043,409	733,354	837,220	664,546
1969	1,458,320	1,784,527	1,674,993	987,991	873,603	519,414
1970	1,078,848	1,697,142	1,642,705	1,803,568	740,720	708,247
1971	1,006,320	2,046,594	1,653,007	1,501,122	1,106,048	1,511,223
1972	752,973	1,860,858	1,299,163	1,611,459	647,744	1,343,329

Year	Bs/Mi/At	Brkn/LA	Chicago	Cincin	NY/SF	Phil
1973	800,655	2,136,192	1,351,705	2,017,601	834,193	1,475,934
1974	981,085	2,632,474	1,015,378	2,164,307	519,987	1,808,648
1975	534,672	2,539,349	1,034,819	2,315,603	522,919	1,909,233
1976	818,179	2,386,301	1,026,217	2,629,708	626,868	2,480,150
1977	872,464	2,955,087	1,439,834	2,519,670	700,056	2,700,070
1978	904,494	3,347,845	1,525,311	2,523,497	1,740,477	2,538,389
1979	769,465	2,860,954	1,648,587	2,356,923	1,456,402	2,775,011
1980	1,048,411	3,249,287	1,206,776	2,022,450	1,096,115	2,651,650
1981	535,418	2,381,292	565,637	1,093,730	632,274	1,638,752
1982	1,801,985	3,608,881	1,249,278	1,326,528	1,200,948	2,376,394
1983	2,110,935	3,510,313	1,479,717	1,190,419	1,215,530	2,128,339
1984	1,724,892	3,134,824	2,107,655	1,275,887	1,001,545	2,062,693
1985	1,350,137	3,264,593	2,161,534	1,834,619	818,697	1,830,350
1986	1,387,181	3,023,208	1,859,102	1,692,432	1,528,748	1,933,335
1987	1,217,402	2,797,409	2,035,130	2,185,202	1,917,168	2,100,110
1988	848,039	2,980,262	2,089,034	2,072,528	1,758,297	1,990,041
1989	948,930	2,944,653	2,491,942	1,979,320	2,059,701	1,861,985
1990	980,129	3,002,396	2,243,791	2,400,892	1,975,528	1,992,484
1991	2,140,217	3,348,170	2,314,250	2,372,377	1,737,478	2,050,012

Year	Pitt	St L	NY Mets	Hous	San Diego	Montreal	NL Total
1901	251,955	379,988					1,920,031
1902	243,826	226,417					1,683,012
1903	326,855	266,538					2,390,362
1904	340,615	386,750					2,664,271
1905	369,124	292,800					2,734,310
1906	394,877	283,770					2,781,213
1907	319,506	185,377					2,640,220
1908	382,444	205,129					3,512,108
1909	534,950	299,982					3,496,420
1910	436,586	355,668					3,494,544
1911	432,000	447,000					3,231,768
1912	384,000	241,000					2,735,759
1913	296,000	203,000					2,831,531
1914	136,620	256,099					1,707,397
1915	225,743	252,666					2,430,142
1916	289,132	224,308					3,051,634
1917	192,807	288,491					2,361,136
1918	213,610	110,599					1,372,127
1919	276,810	167,059					2,878,203

Year	Pitt	St L	NY Mets	Hous	San Diego	Montreal	NL Total
1920	429,037	326,836					4,036,575
1921	701,567	384,773					3,986,984
1922	523,675	536,998					3,941,820
1923	611,082	338,551					4,069,817
1924	736,883	272,885					4,340,644
1925	804,354	404,959					4,353,704
1926	798,542	668,428					4,920,399
1927	869,720	749,340					5,309,917
1928	495,070	761,574					4,881,097
1929	491,377	399,887					4,925,713
1930	357,795	508,501					5,446,532
1931	260,392	608,535					4,583,815
1932	287,262	279,219					3,841,334
1933	288,747	256,171					3,162,821
1934	322,622	325,056					3,200,105
1935	352,885	506,084					3,657,309
1936	372,524	448,078					3,903,691
1937	459,679	430,811					4,204,228
1938	641,033	291,418					4,560,837
1939	376,734	400,145					4,707,177
1940	507,934	324,078					4,389,683
1941	482,241	633,645					4,777,647
1942	448,897	553,552					4,353,353
1943	498,740	517,135					3,769,342
1944	604,278	461,968					3,974,588
1945	604,694	594,630					5,260,703
1946	749,962	1,061,807					8,902,107
1947	1,283,531	1,247,913					10,388,470
1948	1,517,021	1,111,440					9,770,743
1949	1,449,435	1,430,676					9,484,718
1950	1,166,267	1,093,411					8,320,616
1951	988,590	1,013,429					7,244,002
1952	686,673	913,113					6,339,148
1953	572,757	880,242					7,419,721
1954	475,494	1,039,689					8,013,519
1955	469,397	849,130					7,674,412
1956	949,878	1,029,773					8,649,567
1957	850,732	1,183,575					8,819,601
1958	1,311,988	1,063,730					10,164,596
1959	1,359,917	929,953					9,994,525
1960	1,705,828	1,096,632					10,684,963
1961	1,199,618	855,615					8,731,502
1962	1,099,648	953,895	922,530	924,456			11,360,159
1963	783,648	1,176,546	1,080,104	719,502			11,382,227

Year	Pitt	St L	NY Mets	Hous	San Diego	Montreal	NL Total
1964	759,496	1,143,294	1,732,597	725,773			12,045,190
1965	909,279	1,241,201	1,768,389	2,151,407			13,581,136
1966	1,196,618	1,712,980	1,932,693	1,872,108			15,015,471
1967	907,102	2,090,145	1,565,492	1,348,303			12,971,430
1968	693,485	2,011,167	1,781,657	1,312,887			11,785,358
1969	769,369	1,682,783	2,175,363	1,442,995	512,970	1,212,608	15,094,946
1970	1,341,947	1,629,736	2,697,479	1,253,444	643,679	1,424,683	16,662,198
1971	1,501,132	1,604,671	2,266,680	1,262,589	557,513	1,106,043	17,324,857
1972	1,427,460	1,196,894	2,134,185	1,469,247	664,273	1,142,145	15,529,730
1973	1,319,913	1,246,863	1,912,390	1,394,004	611,826	1,246,863	16,676,272
1974	1,110,552	1,838,413	1,722,209	1,090,728	1,075,399	1,019,134	16,978,314
1975	1,270,018	1,695,270	1,730,566	868,002	1,281,747	908,292	16,600,490
1976	1,025,945	1,207,079	1,468,754	886,146	1,458,478	646,704	16,660,529
1977	1,237,349	1,659,287	1,066,825	1,109,560	1,376,269	1,433,757	19,070,228
1978	964,106	1,278,815	1,007,328	1,126,145	1,670,107	1,427,007	20,106,921
1979	1,435,454	1,672,156	788,905	1,900,312	1,456,967	2,102,473	21,178,419
1980	1,646,757	1,385,147	1,192,073	2,278,217	1,139,026	2,208,175	21,124,084
1981	541,789	1,010,247	704,244	1,312,282	519,161	1,534,564	12,478,390
1982	1,024,106	2,111,906	1,323,036	1,558,555	1,607,516	2,319,292	21,507,425
1983	1,225,916	2,317,914	1,112,774	1,351,962	1,539,815	2,320,651	21,549,285
1984	773,500	2,037,448	1,842,695	1,229,862	1,983,904	1,606,531	20,781,436
1985	735,900	2,637,563	2,761,601	1,184,314	2,210,352	1,502,494	22,292,154
1986	1,000,917	2,471,974	2,767,601	1,734,276	1,805,716	1,128,981	22,333,471
1987	1,161,193	3,072,122	3,043,129	1,909,902	1,454,061	1,859,324	24,734,155
1988	1,866,713	2,892,799	3,055,445	1,933,505	1,506,896	1,478,659	24,472,218
1989	1,374,141	3,080,980	2,918,710	1,834,908	2,009,031	1,783,533	25,287,834
1990	2,049,908	2,573,225	2,732,745	1,310,927	1,856,396	1,373,087	24,491,508
1991	2,065,302	2,448,699	2,284,484	1,196,152	1,804,289	934,742	24,696,172

American League

Year	Boston	Chicago	Cleveland	Detroit	Balt/NY	Ph/KC/Oak	Milw/StL/Bal	Wash/Min
1901	289,448	354,350	131,380	259,430	141,952	206,329	**139,034**	161,661
1902	348,898	337,898	275,395	189,469	**174,607**	420,078	272,283	188,158
1903	379,338	286,183	311,280	224,253	211,808	422,473	380,405	128,878
1904	623,295	557,123	264,749	177,796	438,919	512,294	318,108	131,744
1905	468,828	687,419	316,306	193,384	309,100	554,576	339,112	252,027
1906	410,209	585,202	325,733	174,043	434,700	489,129	389,157	129,903

Year	Boston	Chicago	Cleve-land	Detroit	Balt/NY	Ph/KC/Oak	Milw/StL/Bal	Wash/Min
1907	436,777	666,307	382,046	297,079	352,020	625,581	419,025	221,929
1908	473,048	636,096	422,262	436,199	305,500	433,062	617,947	274,252
1909	668,965	478,400	354,627	490,490	501,000	674,915	366,274	205,199
1910	584,619	552,084	293,456	391,925	355,857	588,905	249,889	269,881
1911	503,961	583,208	406,296	484,988	302,444	605,749	207,984	244,884
1912	597,096	602,241	336,844	402,870	242,194	517,653	214,070	350,663
1913	437,194	644,501	541,000	398,502	357,551	571,896	250,330	325,831
1914	481,359	468,290	185,997	416,225	359,447	346,641	244,714	243,888
1915	539,885	539,461	159,285	476,105	256,035	146,223	150,358	167,332
1916	436,397	679,923	492,106	615,772	469,211	184,771	335,740	177,265
1917	387,856	684,521	477,298	457,289	330,294	221,432	210,486	89,682
1918	249,533	195,081	295,515	203,719	282,047	177,926	122,076	182,122
1919	417,291	627,186	538,135	643,805	619,164	225,209	349,350	234,096
1920	402,445	833,492	912,832	579,650	1,289,422	287,888	419,311	359,260
1921	279,273	543,650	748,705	661,527	1,230,696	344,430	355,978	456,069
1922	259,184	602,860	528,145	661,206	1,026,134	425,356	712,918	458,552
1923	229,668	573,778	558,856	911,377	1,007,066	534,122	430,296	357,406
1924	448,556	696,658	481,905	1,015,136	1,053,533	531,992	533,349	584,310
1925	267,782	832,231	419,005	820,766	697,267	869,703	462,898	817,199
1926	185,155	710,339	627,426	711,914	1,027,675	714,508	283,980	551,580
1927	305,275	614,423	373,138	773,716	1,164,017	605,529	247,879	528,976
1928	396,920	494,152	375,907	474,323	1,072,132	689,752	339,497	378,501
1929	364,620	426,795	536,210	869,318	960,148	839,176	280,697	355,506
1930	444,045	406,123	528,657	649,450	1,169,230	721,663	152,088	614,474
1931	350,975	403,550	483,027	434,056	912,437	627,464	179,126	492,657
1932	182,150	233,198	468,953	397,157	962,320	405,500	112,558	371,396
1933	268,715	397,789	387,936	320,972	728,014	297,138	88,113	437,533
1934	610,640	236,559	391,338	919,161	854,682	305,847	115,305	330,074
1935	558,568	470,281	397,615	1,034,929	657,508	233,173	80,922	255,011
1936	626,895	440,810	500,849	875,948	976,913	285,173	93,267	379,799
1937	559,659	589,245	564,849	1,072,276	998,148	430,738	123,121	397,799
1938	646,459	338,278	652,002	799,557	970,916	385,357	130,417	522,694
1939	573,070	594,104	563,926	836,279	859,785	395,022	109,159	339,257
1940	716,234	660,336	903,576	1,112,693	988,975	432,145	239,591	381,241
1941	718,497	677,077	745,948	684,915	964,722	528,984	176,240	415,663
1942	730,340	425,734	459,447	580,087	922,011	423,787	255,617	403,493
1943	358,275	508,962	438,894	606,287	618,330	376,735	214,392	574,694
1944	506,975	563,539	475,272	923,176	789,995	505,322	508,644	525,235
1945	603,794	675,981	558,182	1,280,341	881,845	462,631	482,986	652,660
1946	1,416,944	983,403	1,057,289	1,722,790	2,265,512	621,793	526,435	1,027,216
1947	1,427,315	876,948	1,521,978	1,398,093	2,178,937	911,566	320,474	850,758
1948	1,558,798	777,844	2,620,627	1,743,035	2,373,901	945,076	335,564	795,254
1949	1,596,650	937,151	2,233,771	1,821,204	2,283,676	816,514	270,936	770,745

484

Year	Boston	Chicago	Cleve-land	Detroit	Balt/NY	Ph/KC/Oak	Milw/StL/Bal	Wash/Min
1950	1,344,080	781,330	1,726,464	1,951,474	2,081,380	309,805	247,131	699,697
1951	1,312,282	1,328,234	1,704,984	1,132,641	1,950,107	465,469	293,790	695,167
1952	1,115,750	1,231,675	1,444,607	1,026,846	1,629,665	627,106	518,796	699,457
1953	1,026,133	1,191,313	1,069,176	884,658	1,531,811	362,113	**297,238**	595,594
1954	931,127	1,231,629	1,335,472	1,079,847	1,475,171	**304,660**	1,060,910	503,542
1955	1,203,200	1,175,684	1,221,780	1,181,838	1,490,138	1,392,054	852,139	425,238
1956	1,137,158	1,000,090	865,467	1,051,182	1,491,784	1,015,154	901,201	431,647
1957	1,181,097	1,135,668	722,256	1,272,346	1,497,134	901,167	1,029,581	457,079
1958	1,077,047	797,451	663,805	1,098,924	1,428,438	925,090	829,991	475,288
1959	984,102	1,423,144	1,497,976	1,221,221	1,552,030	963,683	891,926	615,372
1960	1,129,866	1,655,460	950,985	1,167,669	1,167,349	774,944	1,187,849	**743,404**
1961	859,916	1,151,999	735,547	1,605,500	1,748,836	683,549	950,819	1,256,722
1962	733,080	1,131,562	716,076	1,207,891	1,493,574	635,675	790,254	1,433,116
1963	942,642	1,158,848	562,507	821,973	1,308,920	762,364	774,254	1,406,652
1964	883,276	1,250,053	653,478	816,139	1,305,638	642,278	1,116,215	1,207,514
1965	652,201	1,130,519	934,786	1,029,645	1,213,552	528,344	781,649	1,463,258
1966	811,172	990,359	903,359	1,124,293	1,124,648	773,929	1,203,366	1,259,374
1967	1,727,832	985,634	662,980	1,447,143	1,259,514	**726,639**	955,053	1,438,547
1968	1,940,788	803,775	857,994	2,031,847	1,185,666	837,466	943,977	1,143,257
1969	1,833,246	589,546	617,970	1,577,481	1,067,966	778,232	1,062,094	1,349,328
1970	1,595,278	495,355	729,752	1,501,293	1,136,879	778,355	1,057,069	1,261,887
1971	1,678,732	833,891	591,361	1,591,073	1,070,771	914,993	1,023,037	940,858
1972	1,441,718	1,177,318	626,354	1,892,386	966,328	921,323	899,950	797,901
1973	1,481,002	1,302,527	615,107	1,724,146	1,252,103	1,000,763	958,667	907,499
1974	1,556,411	1,149,596	1,114,262	1,243,080	1,273,075	845,693	962,572	662,401
1975	1,748,587	750,802	977,039	1,058,836	1,288,048	1,075,518	1,002,157	737,156
1976	1,895,846	914,945	948,776	1,467,020	2,012,434	780,593	1,058,609	715,394
1977	2,074,549	1,657,135	900,365	1,359,856	2,103,092	495,599	1,195,769	1,162,727
1978	2,074,549	1,657,135	900,365	1,359,856	2,103,092	526,999	1,051,724	787,878
1979	2,353,114	1,280,702	1,011,644	1,630,929	2,537,765	306,763	1,681,009	1,070,521
1980	1,956,092	1,200,365	1,033,827	1,785,293	2,627,417	842,259	1,797,438	769,206
1981	1,060,379	946,651	661,395	1,149,144	1,614,353	1,304,052	1,024,247	469,090
1982	1,950,124	1,567,787	1,044,021	1,636,058	2,041,219	1,735,489	1,613,031	921,186
1983	1,782,285	2,132,821	768,941	1,829,636	2,257,016	1,294,941	2,042,071	858,939
1984	1,661,618	2,136,988	734,079	2,704,784	1,821,815	1,353,281	2,045,784	1,598,692
1985	1,786,633	1,669,888	655,181	2,286,609	2,214,587	1,334,599	2,132,387	1,651,814
1986	2,147,641	1,424,313	1,417,805	1,899,437	2,268,030	1,314,646	1,973,176	1,255,453
1987	2,231,551	1,208,060	1,077,898	2,061,830	2,427,672	1,678,921	1,835,692	2,081,976
1988	2,464,851	1,115,749	1,411,610	2,081,162	2,633,701	2,287,335	1,660,738	3,030,672
1989	2,510,012	1,045,651	1,285,542	1,543,656	2,170,485	2,667,225	2,535,208	2,277,438
1990	2,528,986	2,002,357	1,225,240	1,495,785	2,006,436	2,900,217	2,415,189	1,751,584
1991	2,562,435	2,934,154	1,051,863	1,641,661	1,863,733	2,713,493	2,552,753	2,293,842

Year	LA/Cal	Wash/ Texas	Sea/Milw	KC II	Sea II	Toronto	AL Total
1901							1,683,584
1902							2,206,454
1903							2,344,888
1904							3,024,028
1905							3,120,752
1906							2,938,076
1907							3,398,764
1908							3,611,366
1909							3,739,570
1910							3,270,689
1911							3,339,514
1912							3,263,631
1913							3,526,805
1914							2,747,591
1915							2,434,684
1916							3,451,885
1917							2,858,858
1918							1,707,999
1919							3,654,236
1920							5,084,300
1921							4,620,328
1922							4,874,355
1923							4,602,589
1924							5,255,439
1925							5,186,851
1926							4,912,583
1927							4,612,951
1928							4,221,188
1929							4,662,470
1930							4,685,730
1931							3,883,292
1932							3,133,232
1933							2,926,210
1934							3,763,606
1935							3,688,007
1936							4,178,922
1937							4,735,835
1938							4,445,684
1939							4,270,602
1940							5,433,791
1941							4,911,956
1942							4,200,216

Year	LA/Cal	Wash/ Texas	Sea/Milw	KC II	Sea II	Toronto	AL Total
1943							3,696,569
1944							4,798,158
1945							5,580,420
1946							9,621,182
1947							9,486,069
1948							11,150,099
1949							10,730,647
1950							9,142,361
1951							8,882,674
1952							8,293,896
1953							6,964,076
1954							7,922,364
1955							8,942,971
1956							7,893,683
1957							8,196,218
1958							7,296,034
1959							9,149,454
1960							9,226,526
1961	603,510	597,497					10,163,016
1962	1,144,063	729,775					10,015,056
1963	821,015	535,604					9,094,847
1964	760,439	600,106					9,235,151
1965	**566,727**	560,083					8,860,764
1966	1,400,321	576,260					10,166,738
1967	1,317,713	770,868					11,336,923
1968	1,025,956	546,661					11,317,387
1969	758,388	918,106	**677,944**	902,414			12,130,819
1970	1,077,741	824,789	933,607	693,047			12,085,135
1971	926,373	**655,156**	731,531	910,784			11,868,560
1972	744,190	662,974	600,440	707,656			11,438,538
1973	1,058,206	686,085	1,092,158	1,345,341			13,439,181
1974	917,269	1,193,902	955,741	1,173,292			13,047,294
1975	1,058,836	1,127,924	1,213,357	1,151,836			13,189,423
1976	1,006,774	1,164,982	1,012,164	1,680,265			14,657,802
1977	1,432,633	1,250,722	1,114,938	1,852,603	1,338,511	1,701,052	19,639,551
1978	1,755,386	1,447,963	1,601,906	2,255,493	877,440	1,562,585	20,529,965
1979	2,523,845	1,519,671	1,918,343	2,261,845	844,447	1,431,651	22,371,979
1980	2,297,327	1,198,175	1,857,408	2,288,714	836,204	1,400,327	21,890,052
1981	1,441,545	850,076	850,076	1,279,403	636,276	755,083	14,065,986
1982	2,807,360	1,154,432	1,978,896	2,284,463	1,070,404	1,275,978	23,080,449
1983	2,555,016	1,363,469	2,397,131	1,963,875	813,537	1,930,415	23,991,053
1984	2,402,997	1,102,471	1,608,509	1,810,018	870,372	2,110,009	23,961,427
1985	2,567,427	1,112,497	1,360,265	2,162,717	1,128,696	2,468,925	24,532,225

Year	LA/Cal	Wash/ Texas	Sea/Milw	KC II	Sea II	Toronto	AL Total
1986	2,655,872	1,692,002	1,265,041	2,320,794	1,029,045	2,455,477	25,172,732
1987	2,696,299	1,763,053	1,909,244	2,392,471	1,134,255	2,778,429	27,277,351
1988	2,340,925	1,581,901	1,923,328	2,350,181	1,022,398	2,595,175	28,499,726
1989	2,647,291	2,043,993	1,970,735	2,477,700	1,289,443	3,375,883	29,849,262
1990	2,555,688	2,057,911	1,752,900	2,244,956	1,509,727	3,885,284	30,332,260
1991	2,416,236	2,297,720	1,478,729	2,161,537	2,147,905	4,001,527	32,117,588

Football

National Football League

Year	Detroit	Gr Bay	Cle/LA Rams	Chi B	Cle Br (AA 46–49)	Mia/Bal (AA 46–49)

[**Bold** indicates the last year before a franchise moves to a new facility.]

Year	Detroit	Gr Bay	Cle/LA Rams	Chi B	Cle Br (AA 46–49)	Mia/Bal (AA 46–49)
1934	105,000	n.a.		107,500		
1935	82,200	n.a.		97,000		
1936	109,000	66,600		108,680		
1937	114,673	91,000	n.a.	137,000		
1938	198,251	85,000	45,000	128,000		
1939	181,561	109,446	96,998	132,430		
1940	127,939	107,000	83,752	145,371		
1941	119,214	102,726	66,000	176,546		
1942	100,508	86,250	n.a.	160,424		
1943	153,749	81,675	Out	124,614		
1944	117,907	90,000	n.a.	141,000		
1945	123,325	112,699	**75,000**	143,064		
1946	123,651	113,396	214,101	253,748	399,962	**50,171**
1947	155,335	166,423	n.a.	233,544	392,760	199,661
1948	112,762	135,312	194,308	266,628	318,619	206,109
1949	104,057	104,832	309,329	262,946	189,604	152,381
1950	151,600	118,621	n.a.	265,568	200,319	98,217
1951	237,181	105,969	279,057	230,196	231,414	Out
1952	288,080	n.a.	318,662	236,341	240,204	Out
1953	315,549	126,716	328,466	221,807	274,671	169,975
1954	326,040	118,668	326,586	243,283	183,476	164,238
1955	311,372	153,241	396,954	258,686	251,444	236,826

Year	Detroit	Gr Bay	Cle/LA Rams	Chi B	Cle Br (AA 46–49)	Mia/Bal (AA 46–49)
1956	330,966	138,402	367,168	280,936	221,648	238,471
1957	334,477	161,103	445,776	273,701	324,165	279,888
1958	321,727	167,626	502,084	270,000	370,781	321,849
1959	308,090	189,998	444,476	270,000	338,380	343,373
1960	306,110	204,221	370,341	278,843	337,972	342,858
1961	345,113	290,111	335,942	n.a.	426,886	391,812
1962	357,595	292,404	291,004	n.a.	422,043	391,659
1963	346,247	307,418	296,122	334,550	487,430	403,835
1964	366,293	312,370	384,346	326,691	549,334	474,352
1965	362,769	348,334	282,333	321,283	557,283	416,361
1966	358,181	349,442	348,432	327,527	544,250	418,143
1967	368,443	352,586	421,217	320,550	544,807	418,143
1968	359,430	352,080	455,891	319,113	527,107	418,292
1969	383,627	348,105	498,693	315,198	578,360	414,918
1970	401,200	369,104	499,427	321,437	567,377	415,351
1971	380,926	269,005	507,168	385,343	541,505	407,911
1972	380,213	368,019	507,229	389,907	528,591	395,006
1973	324,663	355,277	519,175	318,625	475,867	354,009
1974	317,294	351,134	493,797	289,619	420,122	238,204
1975	510,436	349,349	436,770	323,868	385,161	323,769
1976	478,796	381,791	441,986	351,812	471,960	361,738
1977	457,494	362,576	375,098	336,500	478,180	354,295
1978	498,862	432,937	427,103	385,976	510,046	363,900
1979	520,589	426,611	423,760	417,078	593,821	299,452
1980	621,353	435,521	500,403	464,897	619,683	304,775
1981	603,679	433,077	493,964	436,564	601,725	286,456
1982	352,481	196,905	258,421	183,626	247,314	107,646
1983	553,595	429,387	422,329	418,771	564,513	**299,526**
1984	457,238	422,062	435,637	462,172	458,433	481,306
1985	504,613	401,930	449,938	486,212	507,403	471,788
1986	432,429	407,305	474,282	495,484	583,739	442,534
1987	190,768	379,033	331,491	459,192	492,939	436,867
1988	296,607	413,255	435,749	494,093	615,545	468,369
1989	392,296	443,335	470,770	488,976	613,415	467,446
1990	521,597	441,792	479,356	481,018	568,093	440,681
1991	491,502	424,916	412,683	491,778	571,752	434,008

Year	Chi C/ SL/Ph	Pitt	NYG	Phil	SF (AA 46–49)	Bos/ Wash
1934	31,200	71,671	151,500	n.a.		116,060
1935	n.a.	60,000	155,000	n.a.		89,000
1936	n.a.	74,842	162,000	n.a.		**68,000**
1937	26,000	87,269	226,000	72,000		121,000

Year	Chi C/ SL/Ph	Pitt	NYG	Phil	SF (AA 46–49)	Bos/ Wash
1938	n.a.	n.a.	231,208	n.a.		n.a.
1939	35,000	56,386	233,427	129,000		n.a.
1940	79,000	56,000	247,642	56,000		193,439
1941	n.a.	81,209	249,718	135,051		201,000
1942	66,691	86,417	156,538	47,990		195,483
1943	47,854	54,000	245,388	83,288		213,622
1944	n.a.	n.a.	245,062	135,528		212,700
1945	38,000	95,765	281,633	161,633		208,728
1946	n.a.	179,622	409,851	161,707	163,588	201,401
1947	176,309	207,925	190,173	219,920	210,808	214,863
1948	181,217	172,252	139,326	155,566	276,611	195,513
1949	171,764	152,767	143,589	167,059	267,514	167,144
1950	145,314	157,943	176,010	208,515	150,208	153,540
1951	105,776	n.a.	174,076	120,341	180,657	n.a.
1952	131,769	n.a.	203,090	123,248	215,159	145,753
1953	120,804	n.a.	n.a.	148,223	194,503	144,886
1954	125,665	184,177	190,447	158,170	251,439	126,090
1955	151,071	176,877	163,847	183,081	265,403	156,461
1956	99,444	170,267	280,727	147,586	247,758	142,841
1957	n.a.	n.a.	290,667	129,754	370,074[a]	n.a.
1958	121,126	140,592	n.a.	174,532	315,076	160,145
1959	160,438	159,826	389,603	224,518	316,167	170,759
1960	140,019	173,099	357,649	286,301	297,516	n.a.
1961	138,557	157,873	423,949	412,328	357,007	208,492
1962	128,574	177,037	439,456	422,096	295,310	n.a.
1963	164,823	243,010	441,017	418,963	225,050	317,550
1964	166,075	241,900	440,517	420,061	233,066	342,886
1965	213,862	n.a.	439,813	400,564	267,046	n.a.
1966	317,166	246,331	439,905	408,619	249,887	347,994
1967	316,923	271,522	440,043	424,868	253,286	353,159
1968	318,409	235,051	440,115	412,579	237,297	354,535
1969	329,538	284,060	440,318	424,606	242,110	352,860
1970	332,123	323,387	440,333	407,353	311,771	352,904
1971	346,740	323,812	439,856	457,506	313,968	371,287
1972	319,604	340,543	438,869	460,040	422,067	371,273
1973	326,849	377,351	461,299	414,441	376,282	369,875
1974	322,549	325,457	319,803	420,211	346,948	377,432
1975	319,759	341,295	358,830	428,640	302,409	376,529
1976	340,611	330,620	479,223	392,921	352,001	364,008
1977	333,851	348,486	464,362	368,747	298,983	379,733
1978	361,720	380,319	544,737	501,956	323,178	426,211
1979	376,771	391,931	557,530	550,611	354,470	427,651
1980	373,573	426,106	553,256	557,325	373,055	407,699
1981	384,375	421,234	552,626	548,171	435,182	412,276

National Football League

Year	Chi C/ SL/Ph	Pitt	NYG	Phil	SF (AA 46–49)	Bos/ Wash
1982	163,901	209,890	350,694	297,595	274,837	205,530
1983	309,612	462,767	519,494	445,684	435,088	416,512
1984	372,154	447,558	583,945	458,997	466,859	421,500
1985	325,353	436,069	580,399	486,022	470,506	424,266
1986	284,280	414,937	594,443	466,659	470,339	434,854
1987	**194,748**	353,402	432,433	429,950	394,675	341,317
1988	472,937	396,044	565,482	510,776	480,039	426,737
1989	345,198	383,494	596,319	494,552	483,426	418,749
1990	347,652	434,769	599,570	520,358	506,176	427,246
1991	326,345	406,936	609,967	513,196	478,570	438,226

Year		Brklyn		Cin/ StL		Bos/ NYB
1934		80,500		39,500		
1935		88,000				
1936		106,000				
1937		91,000				
1938		125,352				
1939		126,285				
1940		146,111				
1941		119,946				
1942		106,198				
1943		69,962				
1944		73,784				71,464
1945		Out				**n.a.**
1946						112,874
1947						**125,460**
1948						71,436
1949						48,006

Year	Dallas	Minn	Atlanta	New Or	Tampa B	Seattle
1960	128,500					
1961	172,000	242,102				
1962	152,446	226,102				
1963	188,727	230,743				
1964	268,661	274,026				
1965	388,912	321,119				
1966	473,373	315,119	395,679			
1967	460,476	304,901	384,891	528,242		
1968	460,476	304,901	384,891	528,242		
1969	443,352	342,570	375,044	521,133		
1970	411,531	335,300	491,590	483,234		

Year	Dallas	Minn	Atlanta	New Or	Tampa B	Seattle
1971	455,774	344,720	410,090	550,578		
1972	446,990	344,623	410,432	467,686		
1973	410,788	329,322	347,589	451,566		
1974	373,435	329,438	265,006	392,354		
1975	401,549	323,303	285,064	319,772		
1976	410,478	325,745	263,522	359,631	295,981	421,216
1977	432,885	321,571	349,284	334,502	366,458	406,502
1978	498,865	354,724	434,334	457,607	503,799	480,720
1979	508,965	360,781	407,658	495,260	545,980	487,881
1980	477,378	367,299	442,457	384,815	522,785	468,416
1981	511,541	361,210	419,281	440,708	531,936	453,275
1982	269,981	285,824	217,651	255,726	329,297	260,888
1983	505,793	464,902	333,359	529,878	398,414	486,036
1984	480,545	444,399	312,351	472,685	365,856	493,657
1985	478,104	453,701	272,133	388,795	310,027	476,842
1986	469,806	463,555	389,922	463,611	320,646	492,921
1987	344,406	403,095	189,815	420,873	303,676	421,956
1988	393,219	463,081	267,813	531,156	388,257	494,103
1989	418,346	463,496	320,551	488,998	439,685	481,233
1990	575,432	452,064	394,853	536,438	455,776	465,881
1991	501,901	416,762	402,931	540,916	371,800	466,880

Year	Oak/LA	Miami	New Eng	NYJ	SDiego	Buff
1960	69,122		118,260	114,628	109,656	111,860
1961	53,582		115,610	106,619	195,014	133,408
1962	76,953		150,626	36,161	153,908	195,436
1963	122,048		169,870	103,550	191,491	242,763
1964	128,156		199,652	298,972	169,656	297,566
1965	136,427		143,098	384,144	202,402	306,675
1966	253,508	182,431	190,138	415,768	185,712	299,127
1967	276,498	202,849	138,861	437,036	277,311	280,461
1968	328,705	214,098	127,267	433,760	303,188	251,796
1969	371,714	242,815	149,412	440,422	324,178	286,648
1970	381,714	440,139	245,537	439,688	315,549	277,966
1971	382,755	484,379	411,109	441,099	347,530	274,441
1972	379,522	557,881	426,993	424,051	366,035	313,677
1973	375,897	442,482	405,456	309,873	306,079	531,270
1974	349,264	457,768	392,507	346,933	258,135	547,126
1975	345,782	453,335	396,963	361,102	230,714	514,111
1976	357,153	358,127	369,219	329,643	259,739	384,933
1977	363,867	339,698	405,350	314,062	307,826	286,413
1978	404,895	465,251	475,081	400,704	378,623	377,482
1979	423,838	456,251	475,081	400,704	378,623	451,140

Year	Oak/LA	Miami	New Eng	NYJ	SDiego	Buff
1980	375,614	384,829	458,283	396,642	409,530	585,649
1981	368,560	489,292	414,561	429,036	411,661	601,138
1982	185,138	238,951	149,051	182,349	200,249	302,360
1983	368,376	487,939	370,958	412,081	369,944	479,892
1984	512,520	524,874	392,257	514,591	409,942	359,499
1985	509,798	542,951	438,672	541,832	415,626	303,145
1986	516,205	467,288	482,572	524,688	414,611	531,813
1987	350,409	394,672	374,302	352,895	371,676	437,187
1988	421,002	469,277	438,627	483,037	347,400	622,793
1989	396,962	447,663	375,779	429,465	376,434	619,714
1990	468,933	510,359	311,623	466,519	393,748	621,549
1991	507,781	476,858	308,442	495,562	442,908	635,889

Year	Cincin	Denver	Houston	Dall/ KC	AFL Total	NFL Total
1934						492,684
1935						638,178
1936						816,007
1937						936,039
1938						937,197
1939						1,071,200
1940						1,063,025
1941						1,108,615
1942						887,920
1943						969,128
1944						1,019,649
1945						1,270,401
1946						1,732,135
1947						1,837,437
1948						1,525,243
1949						1,391,735
1950						1,977,753
1951						1,913,019
1952						2,052,126
1953						2,164,585
1954						2,190,571
1955						2,521,836
1956						2,551,263
1957						2,836,318
1958						3,006,124
1959						3,140,000
1960		91,333	190,819	171,500	926,156	3,128,296
1961		74,508	197,016	123,000	1,002,657	3,986,159

Year	Cincin	Denver	Houston	Dall/ KC	AFL Total	NFL Total
1962		178,485	257,208	155,409	1,147,302	4,003,421
1963		132,218	187,011	150,567	1,208,697	4,163,643
1964		118,259	191,444	126,881	1,447,875	4,563,049
1965		219,786	260,999	150,449	1,782,384	4,634,021
1966		192,198	214,831	259,071	2,160,369	5,337,044
1967		231,801	254,616	315,006	2,295,697	5,938,924
1968	180,362	281,374	460,628	338,911	2,635,004	5,882,213
1969	191,091	326,851	309,420	345,519	2,843,373	6,096,127
1970	407,757	355,739	294,479	354,480		9,533,333
1971	414,859	358,428	289,954	351,705		10,076,035
1972	397,557	361,414	285,851	509,291		10,445,827
1973	399,366	357,067	219,337	459,249		10,730,933
1974	368,368	352,282	237,403	412,819		10,236,322
1975	359,902	340,763	315,256	423,935		10,213,193
1976	362,908	434,463	288,402	378,011		11,070,543
1977	321,586	523,243	314,090	357,393		11,018,632
1978	355,451	596,937	382,814	342,863		12,771,800
1979	329,946	597,503	395,996	450,743		13,182,039
1980	358,621	593,094	400,156	410,486		13,392,230
1981	422,430	598,402	364,259	506,634		13,606,990
1982	216,233	369,555	200,344	123,042		7,367,438
1983	397,486	592,493	321,440	372,794		13,277,222
1984	390,047	585,233	323,529	371,317		13,398,112
1985	424,582	589,500	329,445	358,158		13,345,047
1986	433,081	589,037	303,786	385,335		13,588,551
1987	376,249	498,715	259,875	282,018		11,406,166
1988	441,586	597,680	365,981	406,249		13,539,848
1989	440,906	588,144	451,027	487,056		13,625,662
1990	473,238	560,703	449,275	560,193		14,266,240
1991	422,592	583,821	482,726	595,144		13,841,459

Note: NFL total includes no-shows, while team totals for later years exclude no-shows.

[a]Includes playoff game.

Basketball

National Basketball Association

Year	Boston	Tr C/ Mil/St L Atlanta	Chicago	Clev	Dallas	Ft W/ Det
46/47	108,240					
47/48	90,264					
48/49	144,275					n.a.
49/50	110,552	n.a.				n.a.
50/51	197,888	n.a.				n.a.
51/52	160,167	n.a.				n.a.
52/53	161,808	n.a.				n.a.
53/54	156,912	n.a.				n.a.
54/55	175,675	n.a.				n.a.
55/56	209,645	n.a.				n.a.
56/57	262,918	n.a.				n.a.
57/58	240,943	n.a.				134,411
58/59	244,642	n.a.				119,351
59/60	209,274	n.a.				178,007
60/61	201,564	n.a.				164,230
61/62	191,855	n.a.				143,081
62/63	262,581	n.a.				144,150
63/64	223,347	n.a.				100,386
64/65	246,529	n.a.				121,239
65/66	246,189	n.a.				120,013
66/67	322,690	n.a.	171,793			193,782
67/68	320,788	n.a.	131,165			224,164
68/69	322,130	n.a.	151,608			201,433
69/70	277,632	n.a.	333,668			167,648
70/71	313,768	n.a.	414,857	144,252		283,913
71/72	346,701	n.a.	435,282	214,119		188,763
72/73	423,234	n.a.	424,944	186,477		212,094
73/74	355,261	n.a.	334,183	164,520		300,565
74/75	452,421	n.a.	438,860	334,582		307,180
75/76	484,039	n.a.	258,406	519,010		251,352
76/77	453,672	n.a.	476,636	570,445		303,792
77/78	437,937	304,050	548,844	454,961		223,382
78/79	407,926	329,064	368,968	325,616		389,936
79/80	565,105	449,843	363,605	322,788		333,233
80/81	536,883	362,702	389,718	224,489	319,347	228,349

Year	Boston	Tr C/ Mil/St L Atlanta	Chicago	Clev	Dallas	Ft W/ Det
81/82	582,160	309,899	369,611	236,523	402,918	406,317
82/83	582,160	292,690	301,050	160,537	474,373	522,063
83/84	565,820	292,059	260,950	208,095	591,444	652,865
84/85	565,820	299,794	487,370	323,984	667,673	691,540
85/86	565,820	377,678	469,226	390,842	693,052	695,239
86/87	565,820	549,652	650,718	447,125	696,333	908,240
87/88	565,820	583,073	740,842	504,847	695,592	1,066,505
88/89	565,820	644,291	772,925	730,925	695,065	879,614
89/90	565,820	573,731	791,372	695,710	695,418	879,614
90/91	611,537	529,671	757,745	623,906	683,927	879,614

Year	Den	Phil/SF/ Golden St	Hous	Ind	Roch/ Cin/ KC/Sac	Mpls/ LA Lakers
46/47		129,142				
47/48		109,095				
48/49		94,847			n.a.	n.a.
49/50		63,270			n.a.	n.a.
50/51		105,108			n.a.	n.a.
51/52		96,578			n.a.	n.a.
52/53		56,882			n.a.	n.a.
53/54		113,088			n.a.	n.a.
54/55		123,438			n.a.	n.a.
55/56		169,929			n.a.	n.a.
56/57		158,004			n.a.	n.a.
57/58		156,988			n.a.	n.a.
58/59		153,566			n.a.	n.a.
59/60		226,412			n.a.	n.a.
60/61		196,223			n.a.	151,344
61/62		161,795			n.a.	190,321
62/63		101,218			n.a.	285,462
63/64		132,678			n.a.	322,331
64/65		76,963			n.a.	392,004
65/66		124,160			n.a.	426,467
66/67		216,352			n.a.	435,008
67/68	161,007	185,322	188,865	201,522	n.a.	421,326
68/69	167,806	194,683	248,217	228,678	n.a.	483,262
69/70	257,505	189,642	232,684	319,261	n.a.	536,513
70/71	173,849	195,935	264,206	327,487	n.a.	566,108
71/72	172,120	200,917	203,599	355,985	n.a.	668,340
72/73	203,468	244,504	189,773	347,817	261,860	664,872

Year	Den	Phil/SF/ Golden St	Hous	Ind	Roch/ Cin/ KC/Sac	Mpls/ LA Lakers
73/74	173,539	265,095	158,059	318,307	232,692	603,145
74/75	281,890	360,740	187,457	361,359	308,906	474,287
75/76	545,523	490,846	261,518	325,050	272,675	524,976
76/77	703,133	479,328	347,920	432,726	330,526	501,434
77/78	657,673	474,715	384,905	501,759	315,722	534,017
78/79	603,356	427,252	434,400	367,160	442,354	482,611
79/80	527,208	344,483	413,572	433,402	375,387	582,882
80/81	423,287	413,480	385,354	409,839	336,585	538,537
81/82	475,688	401,646	480,128	318,062	280,564	605,367
82/83	496,307	341,243	307,131	197,364	340,359	648,244
83/84	462,397	337,817	435,852	421,202	370,270	622,398
84/85	448,464	300,580	569,018	437,677	262,812	613,826
85/86	531,814	401,279	604,644	460,969	423,653	689,905
86/87	494,943	423,997	660,175	520,007	423,653	681,707
87/88	520,913	465,348	681,051	502,319	423,653	714,477
88/89	555,498	587,820	680,728	468,912	677,197	717,349
89/90	519,404	616,025	649,697	528,275	697,574	712,498
90/91	438,103	616,025	613,230	475,291	697,574	697,203

Year	Milw	NY Knicks	Syr/ Phil	Phoen	Portl	Dall/ San Ant
46/47		82,001				
47/48		174,641				
48/49		211,284				
49/50		186,882	n.a.			
50/51		151,742	n.a.			
51/52		140,746	n.a.			
52/53		195,240	n.a.			
53/54		221,079	n.a.			
54/55		214,125	n.a.			
55/56		246,756	n.a.			
56/57		266,998	n.a.			
57/58		247,632	n.a.			
58/59		317,924	n.a.			
59/60		335,578	n.a.			
60/61		326,895	n.a.			
61/62		265,153	n.a.			
62/63		302,775	n.a.			
63/64		293,704	108,271			
64/65		322,870	108,729			
65/66		369,812	145,372			

Attendance Records

Year	Milw	NY Knicks	Syr/ Phil	Phoen	Portl	Dall/ San Ant
66/67		410,057	246,275			
67/68		534,568	304,631			n.a.
68/69	212,362	569,153	361,161	160,565		n.a.
69/70	360,650	761,226	311,976	281,821		154,862
70/71	378,106	763,487	336,815	332,945	245,383	143,906
71/72	372,439	785,298	326,493	342,922	279,506	130,525
72/73	372,951	790,031	182,921	342,117	333,480	n.a.
73/74	373,191	784,433	171,159	284,324	327,495	258,434
74/75	403,201	760,786	296,721	253,103	441,506	329,844
75/76	426,784	672,745	509,699	295,293	413,992	336,083
76/77	396,947	644,811	632,949	411,294	499,302	376,136
77/78	435,057	626,815	644,456	470,009	519,306	373,707
78/79	443,926	545,715	506,485	465,010	519,306	488,207
79/80	446,972	508,597	479,727	480,659	519,306	468,657
80/81	448,366	546,441	469,355	482.693	519,306	440,553
81/82	443,288	444,189	506,847	487,215	519,306	434,234
82/83	425,572	438,823	646,788	465,603	519,306	399,462
83/84	414,250	495,944	588,139	445,703	519,306	375,900
84/85	422,924	457,317	572,569	493,446	519,306	364,398
85/86	443,064	592,486	513,459	455,969	519,306	336,407
86/87	450,987	538,058	587,748	471,172	519,306	328,368
87/88	452,057	586,752	513,113	461,293	519,306	346,960
88/89	700,984	746,851	558,292	511,076	528,244	459,514
89/90	659,602	730,432	574,710	578,661	528,244	603,660
90/91	676,687	654,962	634,210	589,591	528,244	651,965

Year	Sea	Chi/ Wash	Nw O/ Utah	Buff/SD LA Clip	NJ
46/47					
47/48					
48/49					
49/50					
50/51					
51/52					
52/53					
53/54					
54/55					
55/56					
56/57					
57/58					
58/59					
59/60					

Year	Sea	Chi/ Wash	Nw O/ Utah	Buff/SD LA Clip	NJ
60/61					
61/62		n.a.			
62/63		n.a.			
63/64		195,783			
64/65		187,124			
65/66		170,194			
66/67		144,568			
67/68	202,263	180,348			n.a.
68/69	210,232	285,406			43,195
69/70	278,444	225,371			154,678
70/71	372,612	248,507		204,053	210,043
71/72	444,302	272,039		350,852	390,579
72/73	387,382	263,660		321,710	300,081
73/74	491,856	414,202		427,270	478,449
74/75	524,692	383,775	203,141	467,267	415,312
75/76	557,304	440,837	513,276	418,696	406,426
76/77	532,196	467,745	444,138	319,398	284,059
77/78	504,668	446,539	527,353	252,457	199,090
78/79	747,243	524,356	353,905	311,789	198,990
79/80	890,713	466,823	320,649	325,012	257,418
80/81	675,097	375,360	311,140	217,341	302,061
81/82	750,059	369,807	318,266	178,103	568,861
82/83	574,986	368,601	355,819	158,883	530,808
83/84	446,970	324,701	407,818	228,710	512,441
84/85	303,342	383,188	373,790	384,119	501,976
85/86	329,296	373,802	477,842	341,614	482,854
86/87	356,362	485,352	491,382	316,140	452,704
87/88	492,312	433,376	503,969	359,674	476,054
88/89	529,733	402,377	517,256	450,623	519,601
89/90	502,014	474,166	509,519	486,621	497,838
90/91	510,166	487,097	514,751	522,104	489,915

Year	Charl	Miami	Orl	Minn	Total NBA
46/47					n.a.
47/48					n.a.
48/49					n.a.
50/51					n.a.
51/52					n.a.
52/53					1,126,698
53/54					981,606
54/55					900,016
55/56					1,101,897

Attendance Records

Year	Charl	Miami	Orl	Minn	Total NBA
56/57					1,199,217
57/58					1,167,462
58/59					1,249,028
59/60					1,296,973
60/61					1,455,866
61/62					1,433,878
62/63					1,657,737
63/64					1,795,665
64/65					1,804,759
65/66					2,022,436
66/67					2,552,930
67/68					2,935,879
68/69					3,721,532
69/70					4,341,028
70/71					5,330,393
71/72					5,618,497
72/73					5,852,081
73/74					5,910,023
74/75					6,892,378
75/76					7,512,249
76/77					9,898,521
77/78					9,874,155
78/79					9,761,377
79/80					9,937,575
80/81					9,449,340
81/82					9,964,919
82/83					9,637,614
83/84					10,014,543
84/85					10,506,355
85/86					11,214,888
86/87					12,065,351
87/88					12,654,374
88/89	950,064	612,754			15,464,994
89/90	979,941	615,328	617,468	1,072,572	17,368,659
90/91	980,141	615,328	617,668	779,470	16,876,125

Hockey

National Hockey League, 1960–1991

Year	Atl/Cal	Van	Buf	Mon	Tor	NY Ran
[**Bold** indicates the last year before a franchise moves to a new facility.]						
60/61				n.a.	n.a.	n.a.
61/62				n.a.	n.a.	n.a.
62/63				n.a.	n.a.	n.a.
63/64				488,663	494,634	435,531
64/65				495,582	502,730	415,748
65/66				508,060	521,062	428,664
66/67				524,805	551,801	472,248
67/68				n.a.	n.a.	n.a.
68/69				n.a.	n.a.	n.a.
69/70				n.a.	n.a.	n.a.
70/71		n.a.	379,121	n.a.	n.a.	n.a.
71/72		n.a.	597,622	n.a.	n.a.	n.a.
72/73	488,106	n.a.	609,570	n.a.	n.a.	n.a.
73/74	552,314	613,420	618,973	649,742	636,463	671,716
74/75	537,761	627,213	635,159	647,552	650,602	692,633
75/76	478,500	n.a.	657,320	n.a.	n.a.	n.a.
76/77	490,356	n.a.	657,320	n.a.	n.a.	n.a.
77/78	420,026	n.a.	657,320	n.a.	n.a.	n.a.
78/79	457,640	n.a.	657,320	n.a.	n.a.	n.a.
79/80	**400,961**	n.a.	657,320	n.a.	n.a.	n.a.
80/81	288,679	n.a.	657,320	n.a.	n.a.	n.a.
81/82	289,258	n.a.	619,400	n.a.	n.a.	n.a.
82/83	289,680	n.a.	515,766	n.a.	n.a.	n.a.
83/84	666,960	n.a.	566,562	n.a.	n.a.	n.a.
84/85	667,320	n.a.	613,441	n.a.	n.a.	n.a.
85/86	670,480	n.a.	587,635	n.a.	n.a.	n.a.
86/87	671,920	n.a.	527,241	n.a.	n.a.	n.a.
87/88	755,252	n.a.	571,088	n.a.	n.a.	n.a.
88/89	778,324	548,000	572,648	n.a.	641,800	n.a.
89/90	794,444	606,630	634,692	n.a.	648,400	n.a.
90/91	796,946	601,560	626,171	n.a.	649,720	n.a.

Year	Boston	Wash	St Louis	Pitt	Phil	Minn
60/61	n.a.					
61/62	n.a.					
62/63	n.a.					
63/64	368,002					
64/65	389,986					
65/66	405,454					
66/67	444,715					
67/68	n.a.		329,201	274,049	288,747	438,891
68/69	n.a.		548,565	228,285	425,443	490,940
69/70	n.a.		622,798	265,936	508,132	544,061
70/71	n.a.		711,287	377,182	551,113	565,616
71/72	n.a.		716,657	375,711	560,796	597,461
72/73	585,117		725,458	436,601	626,468	595,290
73/74	578,874		702,375	396,197	663,273	589,752
74/75	585,514	400,171	723,037	448,975	683,080	543,460
75/76	570,287	393,412	692,838	458,198	683,080	386,229
76/77	469,823	432,252	585,955	401,580	683,080	363,325
77/78	494,744	434,864	425,323	421,933	683,080	346,631
78/79	519,444	397,007	405,200	457,209	683,080	428,899
79/80	494,633	442,491	490,355	426,156	683,080	523,733
80/81	446,903	472,013	584,124	413,407	683,080	567,199
81/82	480,989	455,086	577,301	451,965	681,744	608,797
82/83	530,870	495,050	504,460	336,300	673,880	579,403
83/84	543,534	473,479	519,472	273,550	665,445	574,206
84/85	530,297	560,309	535,865	400,711	678,036	539,218
85/86	497,277	599,894	489,193	503,020	687,342	528,622
86/87	485,159	611,561	529,613	598,614	688,497	540,460
87/88	548,301	638,212	580,212	606,638	696,180	457,617
88/89	563,730	680,506	605,537	629,345	696,202	391,787
89/90	572,571	690,023	632,525	640,700	696,268	454,147
90/91	573,607	664,338	686,304	637,072	693,674	313,520

Year	LA	Cal/Clev	Det	NY Isl	Chi	KC/Co/NJ
60/61			401,744		n.a.	
61/62			379,614		n.a.	
62/63			404,792		n.a.	
63/64			426,677		581,593	
64/65			462,370		601,452	
65/66			457,898		630,913	
66/67			480,795		621,260	
67/68	297,394	183,507	475,695		n.a.	
68/69	334,482	172,481	496,067		n.a.	
69/70	321,163	236,555	536,458		n.a.	

Year	LA	Cal/Clev	Det	NY Isl	Chi	KC/Co/NJ
70/71	359,638	208,953	509,314		n.a.	
71/72	338,399	237,542	519,005		n.a.	
72/73	424,456	208,803	544,590		n.a.	
73/74	433,424	191,782	509,689	450,691	617,147	
74/75	504,817	246,897	498,445	506,929	593,100	294,222
75/76	494,613	**277,977**	437,002	590,476	n.a.	**n.a.**
76/77	497,424	247,758	387,318	598,551	n.a.	n.a.
77/78	471,856	n.a.	547,372	618,435	n.a.	n.a.
78/79	399,696		587,638	529,615	n.a.	n.a.
79/80	417,747		604,177	585,749	n.a.	n.a.
80/81	442,400		533,019	598,304	n.a.	n.a.
81/82	430,062		499,846	603,444	n.a.	**n.a.**
82/83	464,670		519,144	605,997	n.a.	n.a.
83/84	419,725		669,705	624,586	n.a.	n.a.
84/85	486,624		696,577	631,000	677,093	n.a.
85/86	409,240		681,072	632,305	668,554	n.a.
86/87	425,769		750,225	594,382	672,127	n.a.
87/88	466,677		785,532	582,871	673,399	n.a.
88/89	595,000		788,102	557,004	646,400	n.a.
89/90	659,694		781,679	524,685	719,382	n.a.
90/91	628,028		786,548	481,508	716,854	525,934

Year	NE/Hart	Que	Edm	Win	NHL Total
60/61					2,317,142
61/62					2,435,424
62/63					2,590,574
63/64					2,732,642
64/65					2,822,635
65/66					2,941,164
66/67					3,084,759
67/68					4,938,043
68/69					5,550,613
69/70					5,992,065
70/71					7,257,677
71/72					7,609,368
72/73					8,575,651
73/74					8,640,978
74/75					9,521,536
75/76					9,103,761
76/77					8,563,890
77/78					8,526,564
78/79					7,758,053
79/80	394,228	429,672	n.a.	531,836	10,533,623

Year	NE/Hart	Que	Edm	Win	NHL Total
80/81	461,008	489,096	n.a.	530,588	10,726,198
81/82	456,510	604,817	n.a.	535,951	10,710,894
82/83	427,819	602,318	n.a.	517,413	11,020,610
83/84	459,525	599,420	n.a.	494,942	11,359,386
84/85	481,059	594,712	n.a.	519,148	11,633,730
85/86	510,753	591,376	n.a.	489,747	11,621,000
86/87	569,219	593,289	691,889	581,717	11,855,880
87/88	582,969	597,707	678,270	533,929	12,117,512
88/89	556,823	581,795	673,802	558,234	12,417,969
89/90	548,025	603,193	680,334	574,401	12,579,651
90/91	497,224	568,000	673,723	517,246	13,365,475

Additional data on Detroit, 1926–1960

26/27	48,000	38/39	203,302	50/51	409,575
27/28	142,000	39/40	159,916	51/52	418,578
28/29	167,966	40/41	219,913	52/53	430,834
29/30	176,500	41/42	183,880	53/54	413,516
30/31	201,066	42/43	271,337	54/55	407,252
31/32	164,232	43/44	285,644	55/56	422,678
32/33	209,481	44/45	275,821	56/57	451,147
33/34	239,963	45/46	328,397	57/58	372,061
34/35	158,896	46/47	388,300	58/59	387,555
35/36	210,272	47/48	394,199	59/60	421,563
36/37	271,559	48/49	402,153		
37/38	224,057	49/50	442,443		

Radio and Television Income

Baseball

Major Leagues (thousands of dollars)

Year	Network	AL Local	NL Local	Total Local	Grand Total
1962	4,000	6,550	6,225	12,775	16,775
1963	5,200	6,550	6,450	13,000	18,200
1964	7,000	6,775	7,550	14,325	21,325
1965	9,700	7,440	8,530	15,970	25,670
1966	9,750	7,815	9,520	17,335	27,085
1967	11,800	7,530	9,595	17,125	28,925
1968	12,700	9,040	9,300	18,340	31,040
1969	15,500	10,540	11,150	21,690	37,190
1970	16,240	10,550	11,300	21,850	38,090
1971	18,000	10,540	11,910	22,450	40,540
1972	18,000	10,575	12,510	23,085	41,085
1973	18,000	10,825	13,580	24,405	42,405
1974	18,000	10,825	14,420	25,245	42,245
1975	18,000	11,500	14,700	26,200	44,200
1976	23,000	12,600	14,300	26,700	49,700
1977	23,000	14,800	14,100	28,900	51,900
1978	23,000	15,300	14,000	29,300	52,300
1979	23,000	15,600	15,900	31,500	54,500
1980	41,000	20,100	18,900	39,000	80,000
1981	41,000	22,400	25,700	48,100	89,100
1982	53,000	30,000	34,600	64,600	117,600
1983	59,000	48,300	46,400	94,700	153,700
1984	163,000	54,000	51,400	105,400	268,400
1985	161,500	59,800	56,000	115,800	277,300
1986	181,500	74,000	66,100	140,100	321,600
1987	196,500	81,500	72,900	154,400	350,900
1988	206,500	83,800	73,800	157,600	364,100
1989	246,500			232,000	478,500
1990	362,500			250,000	612,500
1991	367,500			252,500	615,000

Local Radio and Television—American League Teams (thousands of dollars)

Year	Bal	Bos	Cle	Det	NY	Cal	Chi	KC/Oak	Minn	Wa/Tx
	[**Bold** indicates the last year before a franchise moves to a new facility.]									
1962	600	600	700	625	1,200	775	850	300	600	300
1963	600	600	700	625	1,200	775	850	300	600	300
1964	700	600	700	650	1,200	825	900	300	600	300
1965	700	690	700	1,200	1,200	850	900	300	600	300
1966	700	690	700	1,200	1,500	900	900	300	575	300
1967	700	690	750	1,200	1,250	900	950	**165**	600	325
1968	700	689	750	1,000	1,500	950	1,400	1,100	600	350
1969	750	690	750	1,000	1,500	950	1,400	1,100	650	350
1970	775	700	800	1,100	1,500	1,000	1,400	1,000	700	325
1971	775	700	800	1,200	1,500	1,000	1,400	1,000	700	**466**
1972	775	700	800	1,200	1,300	1,000	1,000	1,000	850	700
1973	775	1,000	800	1,000	1,300	1,000	1,050	1,000	950	700
1974	775	1,000	800	1,000	1,300	1,000	1,000	1,000	1,000	700
1975	800	1,500	800	1,200	1,300	1,000	1,200	1,000	1,000	700
1976	800	2,000	900	1,200	1,200	1,000	1,800	1,000	1,000	700
1977	800	2,000	900	1,200	1,300	1,000	1,800	1,000	1,100	700
1978	800	2,400	900	1,300	1,300	1,000	1,800	1,000	1,100	700
1979	1,000	2,500	900	1,300	1,300	1,000	1,800	1,000	1,100	700
1980	1,000	2,600	1,100	1,400	3,000	1,000	2,000	1,000	1,300	800
1981	1,100	2,700	1,300	1,500	4,000	1,000	900	1,200	1,200	800
1982	1,800	2,700	2,000	1,700	6,500	1,100	2,000	1,300	1,300	2,800
1983	3,000	3,200	3,400	2,000	11,500	4,000	3,400	1,400	1,300	5,500
1984	3,500	4,000	3,400	3,700	11,700	4,000	4,000	2,000	1,500	5,500
1985	4,000	4,200	3,400	4,000	14,000	4,200	4,000	2,500	3,500	6,000
1986	6,000	4,600	3,000	4,400	15,500	4,200	8,300	3,000	3,600	6,000
1987	6,300	6,500	3,000	5,000	17,500	4,200	9,300	3,000	4,000	6,000
1988	6,300	6,600	3,000	6,000	16,500	4,400	9,300	3,200	4,200	6,100
1989					(no data available)					
1990	8,500	20,100	6,000	8,300	45,400	10,000	10,200	7,200	5,600	10,600
1991	8,500	20,100	6,000	8,300	45,400	10,000	10,200	7,200	5,600	10,600

Year	Sea/Mil	Tor	KC	Sea II
1969	**750**		650	
1970	600		650	
1971	600		650	
1972	600		650	
1973	600		650	

Year	Sea/ Mil	Tor	KC	Sea II
1974	600		650	
1975	600		400	
1976	600		400	
1977	600	1,200	400	800
1978	600	1,200	400	800
1979	600	1,200	400	800
1980	600	3,000	500	800
1981	800	4,000	1,000	900
1982	800	4,000	1,000	1,000
1983	2,700	4,400	1,300	1,200
1984	2,700	5,000	1,800	1,200
1985	2,200	7,000	2,400	1,600
1986	3,500	7,800	2,000	2,100
1987	3,600	7,800	2,000	2,200
1988	3,600	7,800	3,100	3,700
1989	3,600	7,800	3,100	3,700
1989		(no data available)		
1990	5,000	14,000	5,000	3,000
1991	5,000	14,000	5,000	3,000

Local Radio and Television—National League Teams (thousands of dollars)

Year	Chi	Mont	NYM	Phil	Pitt	StL
	[**Bold** indicates the last year before a franchise moves to a new facility.]					
1962	500		1,000	650	350	425
1963	500		1,000	650	350	425
1964	550		1,000	650	450	450
1965	550		1,200	1,300	450	500
1966	550		1,200	1,300	450	550
1967	550		1,275	1,300	450	550
1968	1,000		1,200	1,300	450	550
1969	1,000	450	1,350	1,350	450	600
1970	1,000	450	1,250	1,350	450	600
1971	1,000	500	1,250	1,500	450	600
1972	1,000	600	1,250	1,500	450	800
1973	1,200	800	1,250	1,600	1,000	800
1974	1,200	950	1,500	1,600	1,200	800
1975	1,200	1,000	1,500	1,600	1,200	1,000

Year	Chi	Mont	NYM	Phil	Pitt	StL
1976	1,200	1,100	1,600	1,700	1,200	1,000
1977	1,200	1,200	1,500	1,700	1,200	1,000
1978	1,500	1,200	1,500	1,200	1,200	1,000
1979	1,500	1,200	1,500	3,000	1,200	1,000
1980	1,800	1,400	1,500	3,500	1,800	1,500
1981	1,900	6,300	1,500	4,000	1,800	1,500
1982	2,000	8,100	4,200	6,500	1,800	1,500
1983	3,000	7,300	10,500	7,000	2,200	1,700
1984	3,600	7,500	10,900	8,000	3,000	2,600
1985	3,600	7,500	12,100	8,500	3,000	3,100
1986	4,300	8,000	14,500	9,100	3,000	4,600
1987	4,300	7,000	16,500	9,500	4,000	5,100
1988	4,300	7,000	17,000	10,000	5,000	6,000
1989			(no data available)			
1990	10,200	6,000	24,300	21,000	6,000	13,400
1991	10,200	6,000	24,300	21,000	6,000	13,400

Year	Milw/ Atl	Cin	Hou	LA	SD	SF
1962	375	525	500	1,000		900
1963	475	550	600	1,000		900
1964	400	550	1,600	1,000		900
1965	**210**	550	1,770	1,000		1,000
1966	1,200	500	1,770	1,000		1,000
1967	1,200	500	1,770	1,000		1,000
1968	1,000	500	1,300	1,000		1,000
1969	1,000	600	1,300	1,800	700	1,100
1970	1,000	600	1,000	1,800	700	1,100
1971	1,000	1,000	1,000	1,800	710	1,100
1972	1,000	1,300	1,000	1,800	710	1,100
1973	1,000	1,300	1,000	1,800	710	1,100
1974	1,000	1,560	1,000	1,800	710	1,100
1975	1,000	1,600	1,000	1,800	710	1,100
1976	1,000	1,000	1,000	1,800	710	1,100
1977	1,000	1,000	1,000	1,800	710	1,100
1978	1,000	1,000	1,000	1,800	710	900
1979	1,000	1,000	1,000	1,800	800	900
1980	1,500	1,200	1,000	1,800	1,000	900
1981	1,500	1,600	1,100	2,400	1,100	1,000
1982	1,600	1,900	2,000	2,800	1,200	1,000
1983	2,000	2,100	3,100	3,100	2,400	2,000
1984	2,100	2,300	3,100	3,500	2,400	2,400
1985	3,100	2,300	3,200	4,000	2,800	2,800

Year	Milw/ Atl	Cin	Hou	LA	SD	SF
1986	3,500	5,500	3,400	4,600	2,800	2,800
1987	4,000	6,800	3,600	5,000	4,200	2,900
1988	4,000	4,200	4,000	5,000	4,300	3,000
1989			(no data available)			
1990	6,000	7,800	10,200	15,700	8,000	9,300
1991	6,000	7,800	10,200	15,700	8,000	9,300

Football

Breakdown by Leagues (thousands of dollars)

Year	League	Total	CBS	NBC	ABC	Local	Cable
1960	NFL	3,100				3,100	
	AFL	1,616			1,616		
1961	NFL	3,510				3,150	
	AFL	1,805			1,805		
1962	NFL	4,714	4,485	229			
	AFL	2,064			2,064		
1963	NFL	5,819	4,815	1,001			
	AFL	1,945			1,945		
1964	NFL	16,200	16,125	75			
	AFL	2,600			2,600		
1965	NFL	16,750	16,750				
	AFL	8,400		8,400			
1966	NFL	21,850	21,850				
	AFL	8,900		8,900			
1967	NFL	25,700	25,700				
	AFL	8,900		8,900			
1968	NFL	25,200	25,200				
	AFL	8,900		8,900			
1969	NFL	25,700	25,700				
	AFL	9,000		9,000			
1970	NFL	49,435	21,000	17,500	8,500	2,435	
1971	NFL	49,541	22,500	16,000	8,500	2,541	
1972	NFL	49,947	21,000	17,500	8,500	2,947	
1973	NFL	50,403	22,500	16,000	8,560	3,403	
1974	NFL	57,682	22,000	19,600	13,000	3,082	
	WFL						1,582

Year	League	Total	CBS	NBC	ABC	Local	Cable
1975	NFL	58,228	25,000	16,600	13,000	3,628	
	WFL						160
1976	NFL	59,000	22,000	19,600	13,000	4,400	
1977	NFL	58,400	26,000	16,600	11,500	4,300	
1978	NFL	166,100	51,000	51,000	59,700	4,400	
1979	NFL	166,600	57,000	45,000	59,700	4,900	
1980	NFL	167,000	51,000	51,000	59,700	5,300	
1981	NFL	169,400	57,000	45,000	59,700	7,700	
1982	NFL	211,200	72,000	63,000	65,000	11,200	
1983	NFL	316,400	108,000	94,000	98,000	16,400	
1984	NFL	433,800	150,000	130,000	135,000	18,800	
	USFL	14,500		(ABC, ESPN)			
1985	NFL	475,000	150,000	140,000	160,000	25,000	
	USFL	34,000		(ABC, ESPN)			
1986	NFL		(strike year, unknown TV revenues)				
1987	NFL	509,000	150,000	120,000	160,000	33,000	46,000
1988	NFL	512,400	156,000	143,000	135,000	38,400	51,000
1989	NFL	571,000	194,000	146,000	135,000	40,000	56,000
1990	NFL	948,000	265,000	188,000	231,200	42,000	222,400
1991	NFL	940,000	265,000	188,000	225,000	40,000	222,000

Breakdown by Teams, Prior to 1962 Contracts (thousands of dollars)

AFL	1960	1961	NFL	1960	1961
Boston	200	223	Baltimore	220	235
Buffalo	203	225	Chicago	300	320
Dallas	210	234	Cleveland	250	280
Denver	196	217	Dallas	180	195
Houston	215	240	Detroit	250	270
Oakland	194	216	Green Bay	105	120
New York	200	225	Los Angeles	300	310
L.A./San Diego	198	225	Minnesota	—	160
			New York	340	370
			Philadelphia	210	250
			Pittsburgh	235	250
			San Francisco	250	270
			St. Louis	170	190
			Washington	290	290

Basketball

National Basketball Association
(thousands of dollars)

64/65	ABC	1,500					
65/66	ABC	1,500					
66/67	ABC	1,500					
67/68	ABC	1,500					
68/69	ABC	1,500					
69/70	ABC	5,500					
70/71	ABC	5,500					
71/72	ABC	5,500					
72/73	CBS	8,800					
73/74	CBS	8,800					
74/75	CBS	8,800					
75/76	CBS	8,800					
76/77	CBS	10,500					
77/78	CBS	10,500					
78/79	CBS	18,500					
79/80	CBS	18,500					
80/81	CBS	18,500					
81/82	CBS	18,500					
82/83	CBS	22,000	Cable	3,000			
83/84	CBS	22,000	Cable	3,000			
84/85	CBS	22,000	Cable	3,000			
85/86	CBS	22,000	Cable	3,000			
86/87	CBS	43,000	TNT	13,000			
87/88	CBS	43,000	TNT	23,000			
88/89	CBS	47,500	TNT	27,000	Local	85,000	
89/90	NBC	150,000	TNT	68,800	Local	n.a.	
90/91	NBC	150,000	TNT	68,800	Local	104,000	
91/92	NBC	150,000	TNT	68,800	Local	104,000	

Note: Network and cable contracts only, prior to 1988/89.

Bibliography

Books and Articles

Acocella, Bart. Nick Acocella. and Donald Dewey. 1985. *The All-Time, All Star Baseball Book.* New York: Avon Books.

Adler, Bill. 1986. *Baseball Wit.* New York: Crown Publishers.

Allen, Lee. 1948. *The Cincinnati Reds.* New York: G. P. Putnam Sons.

———. 1960. *100 Years of Baseball.* New York: Bartholomew House.

———. 1961. *The National League Story.* New York: Hill and Wang.

———. 1964. *The Giants and the Dodgers.* New York: G. P. Putnam Sons.

Alm, Richard. 1983. "Sports Stadiums: Is the U.S. Overdoing It?" *Business Week,* December 5, 110–112.

Andreano, Ralph. 1965. *No Joy in Mudville.* Cambridge. Mass.: Schenkman Publishing.

Anonymous. 1980a. "The Spartans Live On (in Detroit)." *Coffin Corner* 2 (October).

———. 1980b. "Ken Haycraft Remembers the Way It Was." *Coffin Corner* 2 (December).

———. 1981. "NFL Competitors. 1926–1975." *Coffin Corner* 3 (September).

———. 1983. "Suddenly Everyone Wants to Build a Superdome." *Business Week,* December 5, 110–112.

Ashenfleter, Orley. 1987. "Arbitrator Behavior." *American Economic Review* 77 (May): 342–345.

AudArena Stadium 1990 International Guide. 1990. Nashville.

Axtheim, Peter. 1970. *The City Game.* New York: Harper and Row.

Baade, Robert. 1987. *Is There an Economic Rationale for Subsidizing Sports Stadiums?* Chicago: Heartland Institute.

Baker, L. H. 1945. *Football: Facts and Figures.* New York: Farrar and Rinehart.

Bassett, Gilbert. 1981. "Point Spreads versus Odds." *Journal of Political Economy* 89 (August): 752–768.

Bavazi, Buzzy (with John Strege). 1987. *Off the Record.* Chicago: Contemporary Books.

Benson, Michael. 1989. *Ballparks of North America.* Jefferson. N.C.: McFarland and Company.

Bergmann, T. J., and J. B. Dworkin. 1978. "Collective Bargaining v. the Rozelle Rule: An Analysis of Labor-Management Relations in Professional Football." *Akron Business and Economic Review* 9 (Summer): 34–40.

Berry, Henry. 1975. *The Boston Red Sox.* New York: Macmillan.

Bird, P. 1982. "The Demand for League Football." *Applied Economics* 14 (1): 637–649.

Bisheff, Steve. 1973. *The Los Angeles Rams.* New York: Macmillan.

Blum, M. 1976. "Valuing Intangibles: What Are the Choices for Valuing Professional Sports Teams?" *Journal of Taxation* 45 (November): 286–303.

Braunewalt, Bob. 1975. "All Those AFLs: NFL Competitors. 1935–1941." *Coffin Corner* 1 (April).

Bronsteen, Peter. 1988. "Of Monopsony, Regulation and Competition: The Impact of Bargaining Structure on Baseball Salaries." Analysis Group, Inc., Princeton, N.J., May. Mimeo.

Brower, N. 1977. "Professional Sports Team Ownership: Fun, Profit, and Ideology of the Power Elite." *International Review of Sport Sociology* 4 (December): 79–98.

Bruggink, Thomas, and David Rose. 1990. "Financial Restraints in the Free Agent Labor Market for Major League Baseball: The Players Look at Strike Three." *Southern Economic Journal,* April, 1029–43.

Burman, George (editor). 1974. *Conference on the Economics of Professional Sports.* Washington, D.C.: NFLPA.

Byrne, Jim. 1986. *The $1 League: The Rise and Fall of the USFL.* New York: Prentice Hall.

Byrns, Ralph T., and Gerald W. Stone, Jr. 1992. *Economics.* 5th ed. New York: Harper Collins.

Cairnes, J., N. Jennett, and P. J. Sloane. 1986. "The Economics of Professional Team Sports: A Survey of Theory and Evidence." *Journal of Economic Studies,* no. 1: 1–80.

Canes, Michael. 1974. "The Social Benefits of Restrictions on Team Quality." In *Government and the Sports Business,* edited by Roger Noll, 81–114. Washington, D.C.: Brookings.

Carroll, Bob. 1985. "1922: Birth. Rebirth. and Resuscitation." In *Professional Football Researchers Association Annual.*

Cassing, James, and Richard Douglas. 1980. "Implications of the Auction Mechanism in Baseball's Free Agent Draft." *Southern Economic Journal* 47 (July): 110–121.

Chelius, J. R., and J. Dworkin. 1980. "An Economic Analysis of Final Offer Arbitration as Conflict Resolution Device." *Journal of Conflict Resolution* 24 (June): 293–310.

Clary, Jack. 1974. *Washington Redskins*. New York: Macmillan.

Coakley, Jay. 1978. *Sport in Society*. St. Louis: C.V. Mosby.

Coase, Ronald. 1960. "The Problem of Social Cost." *Journal of Law and Economics* 3 (October): 1–44.

Cobb, Ty (with Al Stump). 1961. *My Life in Baseball—The True Record*. Garden City, N.J.: Doubleday.

Cope, Myron. 1970. *The Game That Was*. Cleveland: World Publishing.

Cottle, Rex, and R. Lawson. 1981. "Leisure as Work: A Case in Professional Sports." *Atlantic Economic Journal* 9 (September): 50–59.

Craig, Peter. 1950. *Organized Baseball—An Industry Study of a $100 Million Spectator Sport*. Oberlin: Oberlin College Library.

Creamer, Robert. 1991. *Baseball in '41*. New York: Viking.

Curran, Bob. 1969. *Pro Football's Rag Days*. Englewood Cliffs, N.J.: Prentice Hall.

Cymrot, D. 1983. "Migration Trends and Earnings of Free Agents in Major League Baseball, 1976–1979." *Economic Inquiry* 21 (1): 545–556.

Cymrot, D., and James Dunlevy. 1987. "Are Free Agents Perspicacious Peregrinators?" *Review of Economics and Statistics* 69 (February): 50–58.

Dabscheck, Braham. 1975. "The Wage Determination Process for Sportsmen." *Economic Record*, March, 52–65.

Daley, Arthur. 1963. *Pro Football's Hall of Fame*. Chicago: Quadrangle Books.

Daly, Dan, and Bob O'Donnell. 1990. *Pro Football Chronicle*. New York: Macmillan, Collier Books.

Daly, George, and William Moore. 1981. "Externalities, Property Rights, and the Allocation of Resources in Major League Baseball." *Economic Inquiry* 19 (January): 77–95.

Danzig, Allison. 1971. *Oh How They Played The Game*. New York: Macmillan.

Danzig, Allison, and Joe Reichler. 1959. *The History of Baseball*. Englewood Cliffs, N.J.: Prentice Hall.

Davenport, David. 1969. "Collusive Competition in Major League Baseball: Its Theory and Institutional Development." *American Economist* 13 (Fall): 6–30.

Davidson, Gary (with Bill Libby). 1974. *Breaking the Game Wide Open*. New York: Athaneum.

Davis, Lance. 1974. "Self Regulation in Baseball, 1909–1971." in *Government and the Sports Business*, edited by Roger Noll, 349–386. Washington, D.C.: Brookings.

Davis, Lance, and James Quirk. 1974. "The Ownership and Valuation of

Professional Sports Franchises." California Institute of Technology. Mimeo.

——. 1975. "Tax Writeoffs and the Value of Sports Teams." In *Management Science Applications to Leisure Time Activities*, edited by Shaul Ladany, 262–275. Amsterdam: North Holland.

DeBrock, Lawrence, and Alvin Roth. 1981. "Strike Two: Labor-Management Negotiations in Major League Baseball." *Bell Journal of Economics* 12 (Autumn): 413–425.

Dellinger, Harold. 1989. "Rival Leagues." In *Total Baseball*, edited by John Thorn and Pete Palmer, 563–581. New York: Warner Books.

Demmert, H. 1973. *The Economics of Professional Team Sports.* Lexington, MA: Lexington Books.

Dickey, Glenn. 1980. *The History of the American League.* New York: Stein and Day.

——. 1982. *The History of Professional Basketball.* New York: Stein and Day.

Dietrich, Phil. n.d. *The Suncheaters: The Story of the Akron Awnings, 1923–1941.* Akron: privately printed.

Dolan, Robert, and Robert Schmidt. 1985. "Assessing the Competitive Effects of Baseball's Reentry Draft." *American Economist* 29 (Spring): 21–31.

Drahozel, Christopher. 1986. "The Impact of Free Agency on the Distribution of Playing Talent in Major League Baseball." *Journal of Economics and Business* 38 (May): 113–122.

Durso, Joseph. 1972. *Yankee Stadium: 50 Years of Drama.* Boston: Houghton Mifflin.

Dworkin, J. 1981. *Owners versus Players: Baseball and Collective Bargaining.* Boston: Auburn Books.

Edwards, Harry. 1973. *The Sociology of Sports.* Homewood, Ill.: Dorsey Press.

El Hodiri, Mohamed, and James Quirk. 1975. "Stadium Capacities and Attendance in Professional Sport." In *Management Science Applications to Leisure Time Activities*, edited by Shaul Ladany, 246–262. Amsterdam: North Holland.

——. 1971. "An Economic Model of a Professional Sports League." *Journal of Political Economy* 79 (March/April): 1302–1319.

——. 1974. "The Economic Theory of a Professional Sports League." in *Government and the Sports Business*, edited by Roger Noll, 33–80. Washington, D.C.: Brookings.

Enright, Jim. 1975. *The Chicago Cubs.* New York: Macmillan.

Eskenazi, Gerald. 1976. *There Were Giants in Those Days.* New York: Grossett and Dunlap.

——. 1988. *Bill Veeck: A Baseball Legend.* New York: McGraw Hill.

Falls, Joe. 1975. *The Detroit Tigers.* New York: Macmillan.

Fitzgerald, Ed. 1955. *The American League.* New York: Grossett and Dunlap.

Fort, Rodney. 1992. "Pay and Performance: Is the Field of Dreams Barren?" In *Diamonds Are Forever,* edited by Paul Sommers. Washington, D.C.: Brookings Institution.

Fort, Rodney, and Roger Noll. 1984. "Pay and Performance in Baseball: Modeling Regulars, Reserves, and Expansion." Division of Humanities and Social Science Working Paper 527, California Institute of Technology.

Fractor, David. 1979. "The Economic Impact on Major League Baseball of Recent Changes in the Reserve Clause." University of Oregon. October. Mimeo.

Frank, Allan. 1986. "How to Play Ball in Pittsburgh." *Forbes Magazine,* February 24, 40–42.

Gallico, Paul. 1945. *Farewell to Sports.* New York: Alfred A. Knopf.

Gallner, Sheldon. 1974. *Pro Sports: The Contract Game.* New York: Charles Scribner's Sons.

Gibbs, Curtis. 1976. "NFL Highlights: Public Policy and the Player Reserve System." University of California, Berkeley. Mimeo.

Gill, Bob. 1984a. "The St. Louis Gunners." In *Professional Football Researchers Association Annual, 1984.*

———. 1984b. "The Bulldogs: L.A. Hits the Big Time." In *Professional Football Researchers Association Annual, 1984.*

Gill, Bob, and Tod Maher. 1984. *The Unofficial 1940–41 American Football League Guide.* Professional Football Researchers Association.

Gilroy, T., and P. Madden. 1977. "Labor Relations in Professional Sports." *Labor Law Journal* 27 (December): 768–776.

Glick, J. 1983. "Professional Sports Franchise Movements and the Sherman Act: When and Where Teams Should Be Able to Move." *Santa Clara Law Review* 23 (Winter): 55–94.

Goldstein, M. 1983. "Arbitration of Grievance and Salary Disputes in Professional Baseball: Evolution of a System of Private Law." *Cornell Law Review* 23 (Winter): 1049–1074.

Graham, Frank. 1952. *The New York Giants.* New York: G. P. Putnam Sons.

Grasmann, Peter. 1986. "The Economics of Professional Team Sports: Some Additional Considerations." University of California, Berkeley. Mimeo.

Grauer, Myron. 1983. "Recognition of the National Football League as a Single Entity under Section 1 of the Sherman Act: Implications of the Consumer Welfare Model." *Michigan Law Review* 82 (October): 1–59.

Greenberg, Jay, Frank Orr, and Gary Ronberg. 1981. *NHL: The World of Professional Hockey.* New York: Rutledge Press.

Gregory, Paul. 1979. *The Baseball Player—An Economic Study.* Washington, D.C.: Public Affairs Press.

Grosshandler, Stan. 1985. "AAFC." *Coffin Corner* 11 (July).

Gwartney, James, and Charles Haworth. 1974. "Employer Costs and Discrimination: The Case of Baseball." *Journal of Political Economy* 82 (July/August): 873–881.

Halas, George (with Gwen Morgan and Arthur Veysey). 1979. *Halas by Halas.* New York: McGraw Hill.

Halberstram, David. 1981. *The Breaks of the Game.* New York: Alfred A. Knopf.

Harris, David. 1986. *The League: The Rise and Decline of the NFL.* New York: Bantam Books.

Harris, Merv. 1972. *The Fabulous Lakers.* New York: Associated Features.

Hill, Bob, and Randall Baron. 1987. *The Amazing Baseball Book: The First 100 Years.* Louisville: Devyn Press.

Hill, James. 1985. "The Threat of Free Agency and Exploitation in Professional Baseball: 1976–1979." *Quarterly Review of Economics and Business* 25 (Winter): 68–82.

Hill, James, and William Spellman. 1983. "Professional Baseball: The Reserve Clause and Salary Structure." *Industrial Relations* 22 (Winter): 1–19.

Hoch, Paul. 1972. *Rip Off the Big Game: The Exploitation of the Power Elite.* Garden City, N.Y.: Doubleday.

Hochberg, Philip. 1974. "Congress Kicks Field Goal: The Legislative Attack in the 93rd Congress on Sports Broadcasting Practices." *Federal Communications Bar Journal* 27(3): 27–80.

Hollander, Zander (editor). 1977. *The Pro Basketball Encyclopedia.* Los Angeles: Corwin Books.

Hollander, Zander, and Hal Bock. 1970. *The Complete Encyclopedia of Hockey.* Englewood Cliffs, N.J.: Prentice-Hall.

Holohan, William. 1978. "The Long Run Effects of Abolishing the Player Reserve System." *Journal of Legal Studies* 129 (January): 129–137.

Honig, Donald. 1981. *The New York Yankees.* New York: Crown Publishers.

Horowitz, Ira. 1974. "Sports Broadcasting." In *Government and the Sports Business,* edited by Roger Noll, 275–324. Washington, D.C.: Brookings.

Horrigan, Joe. 1983. "NFL Transactions." *Coffin Corner* 9 (July).

Hunt, Joseph, and Kenneth Lewis. 1976. "Dominance, Recontracting, and the Reserve Clause: Major League Baseball." *American Economic Review* 66 (December): 936–943.

James, Bill. 1986. *The Bill James Historical Baseball Abstract.* New York: Villard Books.

Jarrett, William. 1989. *Timetables of Sports History: Football.* New York: Facts on File.

Johnson, Arthur. 1979. "Congress and Professional Sports: 1951–1978." *Annals of the American Academy of Political and Social Science* 445 (September): 102–115.

———. 1983."Municipal Administration and the Sports Franchise Relocation Issue." *Public Administration Review,* (November/December): 519–528.

———. 1985. "The Sports Franchise Relocation Issue and Public Policy Responses." in *Government and Sport: The Public Policy Issues,* edited by Arthur Johnson and James Frey, 219–247 Totowa, N.J.: Rowan and Allanheld.

Johnson, Arthur, and James Frey (editors). 1985. *Government and Sport: The Public Policy Issues.* Totowa, N.J.: Rowan and Allanheld.

Jones, J. C. 1969. "The Economics of the National Hockey League." *Canadian Journal of Economics* 2(1).

Jones, Michael (editor). 1980. *Issues in Professional Sports.* Durham, N.H.: University of New Hampshire Press.

Kaese, Harold. 1948. *The Boston Braves.* New York: G. P. Putnam Sons.

Kariher, Harry. 1973. *Who's Who in Hockey.* New Rochelle, N.J.: Arlington House.

Karst, Gene, and Martin Jones. 1973. *Who's Who in Professional Baseball.* New Rochelle, N.J.: Arlington House.

Kidd, Bruce, and Brian McFarlane. 1972. *The Death of Hockey.* Toronto: New Press.

Klein, Gene, and David Fisher. 1987. *First Down and a Billion.* New York: William Morrow.

Klobuchar, Jim. 1977. *Will the Vikings Ever Win the Super Bowl?* New York: Harper and Sons.

Koppett, Leonard. 1968. *24 Seconds to Shoot.* New York: Macmillan.

Kowet, Don. 1977. *The Rich Who Own Sports.* New York: Random House.

Kramer, Jerry. 1968. *Instant Replay.* Cleveland: World Publishing.

Krautmann, Anthony. 1990. "Shirking or Stochastic Productivity in Major League Baseball?" *Southern Economic Review,* April, 961–968.

Kuhn, Bowie. 1987. *Hardball: The Education of a Baseball Commissioner.* New York: Time Books.

Kuklick, Bruce. 1991. *To Every Thing a Season*. Princeton, N.J.: Princeton University Press.

Kurlantzick, Lewis. 1983. "Thoughts on Professional Sports and the Antitrust Laws: Los Angeles Memorial Coliseum v. National Football League." *Connecticut Law Review* 15 (Winter): 183–208.

Ladany, Shaul (editor). 1975. *Management Science Applications to Leisure-Time Occupations*. Amsterdam: North Holland.

Lautier, Jack. 1987. *Fifteen Years of Whalers Hockey*. Hartford: Hartford Whalers Hockey Club.

Lazaroff, D. 1984. "The Antitrust Implications of Franchise Relocation Restrictions in Professional Sports." *Fordham Law Review* 53 (November): 157–220.

Lehn, Kenneth. 1982. "Property Rights. Risk Sharing. and Player Disability in Major League Baseball." *Journal of Law and Economics* 25 (October): 343–366.

———. 1984. "Information Asymmetries in Baseball's Free Agent Market." *Economic Inquiry* 22 (Spring): 37–44.

Leuthner, Stuart. 1988. *Iron Men*, New York: Doubleday.

Lewis, Franklin. 1949. *The Cleveland Indians*. New York: G. P. Putnam Sons.

Lewis, Robert. 1977. *The Harry B. Truman Sports Complex: Rocky Road to the Big Leagues*. Kansas City: privately printed.

Lieb, Fred. 1947. *The Boston Red Sox*. New York: G. P. Putnam Sons.

———. 1977. *Baseball as I Have Known It*. New York: Grossett and Dunlap.

Lieb, Fred, and Stan Baumgartner. 1953. *The Philadelphia Phillies*. New York: G. P. Putnam Sons.

Linn, Ed. 1982. *Steinbrenner's Yankees*. New York: Rinehart and Winston.

Lipsyte, Robert. 1975. *Sportsworld*. New York: Quadrangle.

Lowell, Cym. 1973. "Collective Bargaining and the Professional Team Sports Industry." *Law and Contemporary Problems* 38 (Winter-Spring): 3–41.

Lowry, Philip. 1990. *Green Gridirons*. Professional Football Researchers Association.

Loy, J., and G. S. Kenyon (editors). 1969. *Sport, Culture, and Society*. New York: Macmillan.

Machol, Robert, Shaul Ladany, and D. Morrison (editors). 1976. *Management Science in Sports*. Amsterdam: North Holland.

Mack, Connie. 1950. *My 66 Years in the Big Leagues*. Philadelphia: John C. Winston.

Madura, Jeff. 1981a. "A Note on Risk Averse Baseball Contracts." *Atlantic Economic Journal* 9 (July): 67.

———. 1981b. "Collective Bargaining Modifications in the Professional Basketball Industry." *Atlantic Economic Journal* 9 (September): 117.

———. 1982. "The Theory of the Firm and Labor Portfolio Choices in Professional Team Sports." *Business Economics,* (September): 11–18.

Maher, Tod, and Bob Gill. 1981. *The Second American Football League Fact Book, 1936–37.* Professional Football Researchers Association.

Mann, Arthur. 1957. *Branch Rickey: American in Action.* Boston: Houghton Mifflin.

Markman, Joseph. 1976. "A Note on Discrimination by Race in Professional Basketball." *American Economist* 20 (Spring): 65–67.

Matthews, Stafford. 1989. "Taxation of Sports Franchises." Mimeo.

McFarlane, Brian. 1973. *The Story of the National Hockey League.* New York: Charles Scribner's Sons.

———. 1976. *60 Years of Hockey.* Toronto: Pagurian Press.

McKenna, M. (editor). 1980. *Sport: Money, Morality, and the Media.* Sydney: University of South Wales Press.

Markham, J., and P. Teplitz. 1981. *Baseball Economics and Public Policy.* Lexington, Mass.: Lexington Books.

Mehl, Ernst. 1961. *The Kansas City Athletics.* New York: Henry Holt.

Mendell, Ronald. 1973. *Who's Who in Basketball.* New Rochelle. N.J.: Arlington House.

Mendell, Ronald, and Timothy Phares. 1974. *Who's Who in Football.* New Rochelle. N.J.: Arlington House.

Merchant, Larry. 1973. *The National Football League Lottery.* New York: Holt, Rinehart, and Winston.

Meserole, Mike (editor). 1990. *Information Please Sports Almanac.* Boston: Houghton Mifflin.

Miller, Marvin. 1991. *A Whole Different Ball Game.* New York: Birch Lane Press.

Mona, Dave (editor). 1982. *The Hubert H. Humphrey Metrodome Souvenir Book.* Minneapolis: MSP Publications.

Morris, John. 1973. "In the Wake of the Flood." *Law and Contemporary Problems* 38 (Winter-Spring): 85–98.

National Football League. Annual. *Official NFL Record Manual.* New York: NFL.

Neale, Walter. 1964. "The Peculiar Economics of Professional Sports." *Quarterly Journal of Economics* 78 (February): 1–14.

Neft, David, Richard M. Cohen, and Robert Carroll. 1982. *The Sports Encyclopedia: Pro Football.* Volume 2, *The Modern Era (1960 to present).* New York: St. Martin's Press.

——. 1987. *The Sports Encyclopedia: Pro Football*. Volume 1, *The Early Years (1892–1959)*. Sports Products.

Nelson, Paul. 1980. "Professional Sports and the Non-Statutory Labor Exemption to Federal Antitrust Law." *University of Toledo Law Review* 11 (Spring): 633–653.

Noll, Roger (editor). 1974a. *Government and the Sports Business*. Washington, D.C.: Brookings.

——. 1974b. "Attendance and Price Setting." In *Government and the Sports Business*, edited by Roger Noll, 115–158. Washington, D.C.: Brookings.

——. 1974c. "Alternatives in Sports Policy." In *Government and the Sports Business*, edited by Roger Noll, 411–428. Washington, D.C.: Brookings.

——. 1985. "The Economic Viability of Professional Baseball: Report to the Major League Players' Association." Mimeo.

——. 1987. "The Economics of Sports Leagues." Stanford University Studies in Industrial Economics.

——. 1988. "Professional Basketball." Stanford University Studies in Industrial Economics Paper no. 144.

Oates, Bob. 1955. *The Los Angeles Rams*. Los Angeles: Murray and Gee.

Okkonen, Mark. 1989. *The Federal League of 1914–15: Baseball's Third Major League*. N.p.: Society for American Baseball Research.

Okner, Benjamin. 1974a. "Subsidies of Stadiums and Arenas." In *Government and the Sports Business*, edited by Roger Noll, 325–348. Washington, D.C.: Brookings.

——. 1974b. "Taxation and Sports Enterprises." In *Government and the Sports Business*, edited by Roger Noll, 159–184. Washington, D.C.: Brookings.

Olderman, Murray. 1963. *Nelson's 20th Century Encyclopedia of Baseball*. New York: Thomas Nelson Sons.

Parrott, Harold. 1976. *The Lords of Baseball*. New York: Praeger Publishers.

Pascal, Anthony, and Leonard Rapping. 1970. "Racial Discrimination in Organized Baseball." Rand. RM-6227-RC, December.

Paul, William. 1974. *The Grey Flannel Football*. Philadelphia: J. B. Lippincott.

Peterson, R. W. 1970. *Only the Ball Was White*. Englewood Cliffs, N.J.: Prentice-Hall.

Polner, Murray. 1982. *Branch Rickey: A Biography*. New York: Atheneum.

Porter, Philip, and Gerald Scully. 1982. "Measuring Managerial Efficiency: The Case of Baseball." *Southern Economic Journal* 48 (January): 642–650.

Bibliography

Powers, John. 1979. *The Short Season: A Boston Celtics Diary. 1977–78.* New York: Harper and Row.

Quirk, James. 1973. "An Economic Analysis of Team Movements in Professional Sports." *Law and Contemporary Problems* 38 (Winter-Spring): 42–66.

———. 1980. "The Reserve Clause: Recent Developments." In *Issues in Professional Sports*, edited by Michael Jones. 107–134 Durham, N.H.: University of New Hampshire Press.

———. 1984. *Minnesota Football: The Golden Years 1932–1941.* Minneapolis: privately printed.

———. 1987. "Economic Analysis of the Feasibility of a Domed Stadium in St. Louis." *St. Louis Post Dispatch*, January 17.

———. 1988. "Sport." In *New Palgrave Dictionary of Economics.* New York: Macmillan.

Quirk, James, and Rubin Saposnik. 1992. "The Great Football Wars." In *Advances in the Economics of Sports*, edited by Gerald Scully, New York: JAI Press. Forthcoming.

Quirk, James, and Katsuaki Terasawa. 1986. "Sample Selection and Cost Underestimation Bias in Pioneer Projects." *Land Economics* 62 (May): 192–200.

Reichler, Joe. 1964. *Ronald Encyclopedia of Baseball.* 2d ed. New York: Ronald Press.

Riffenbrugh, Beau. 1986. *The Official NFL Encyclopedia.* New York: New American Library.

Ritter, Lawrence. 1984. *The Glory of Their Times.* New York: William Morrow.

Roberts, Howard. 1953. *The Story of Pro Football.* New York: Rand McNally.

Ronberg, Gary. 1984. *The Illustrated Hockey Encyclopedia.* New York: Balsam Press.

Rosen, Sherman. 1981. "The Economics of Superstars." *American Economic Review* 71 (December): 845–898.

Rosenthal, Harold. 1981. *Fifty Faces of Football.* New York: Atheneum.

Rosentraub, Mark, and Samuel Nunn. 1978. "Suburban City Investment in Professional Sports." *American Behavioral Scientist* 21 (January/February): 393–414.

Ross, Gary. 1975. "The Determination of Bonuses in Professional Sports." *American Economist* 18 (Fall): 43–46.

Rottenberg, Simon. 1956. "The Baseball Players' Labor Market." *Journal of Political Economy* 64 (June): 253–256.

Sahadi, Lou. 1972. *Miracle in Miami.* Chicago: Henry Regnery.

———. 1983. *The Redskins.* New York: William Morrow.

Salzberg, Charles. 1987. *From Set Shot to Slam Dunk*. New York: E. P. Dutton.

Scahill, E. 1985. "The Determinants of Average Salary in Professional Football." *Atlantic Economic Journal* 13 (March): 103.

Schofield, J. A. 1982. "The Development of First Class Cricket in England: An Economic Analysis." *Journal of Industrial Economics* 30 (June): 337–360.

Scott, Frank, James Long, and Ken Scomppi. 1985. "Salary vs. Marginal Revenue Product under Monopsony and Competition—The Case of Professional Basketball." *Atlantic Economic Journal* 13 (March): 50–59.

Scully, Gerald. 1973. "Economic Discrimination in Professional Sports." *Law and Contemporary Problems* 38 (Winter-Spring): 67–84.

———. 1974a. "Discrimination: The Case of Baseball." In *Government and the Sports Business*, edited by Roger Noll, 221–274 Washington, D.C.: Brookings.

———. 1974b. "Pay and Performance in Major League Baseball." *American Economic Review* 64 (December): 915–930.

———. 1989. *The Business of Major League Baseball*. Chicago: University of Chicago Press.

Seymour, Harold. 1960. *Baseball: The Early Years*. New York: Oxford University Press.

———. 1971. *Baseball: The Golden Age*. New York: Oxford University Press.

Shannon, Bill, and George Kalinsky. 1975. *The Ballparks*. New York: Hawthorn Books.

Shaw, Gary. 1972. *Meat on the Hoof*. New York: St. Martins Press.

Sloane, Peter. 1971. "The Economics of Professional Football: The Football Club as Utility Maximizer." *Scottish Journal of Political Economy* (June): 121–145.

Smith, Myron. 1986. *Baseball, A Comprehensive Bibliography*. Jefferson, N.C.: McFarland.

Sobel, L. 1977. *Professional Sports and the Law*. New York: Law-Arts Publishers.

Spink, J. G. Taylor. 1947. *Judge Landis and 25 Years of Baseball*. New York: Thomas Y. Crowell.

Sporting News Baseball Guide. Annual. St. Louis: Sporting News.

Sporting News Pro Basketball Guide. Annual. St. Louis: Sporting News.

Sporting News Pro Football Guide. Annual. St. Louis: Sporting News.

Sporting News Pro Hockey Guide. Annual. St. Louis: Sporting News.

Bibliography

Standohar, Paul. 1989. *The Sports Industry and Collective Bargaining.* Ithaca, N.Y.: ILR Press.

Staudohar, N. 1988. "The Football Strike of 1987: The Question of Free Agency." *Monthly Labor Review,* August, 26–31.

Stern, Leon (editor). 1975. *The Sporting Set.* New York: Arno Press.

Stockfish, Jack. 1967. "The Interest Rate Applicable to Government Investment Projects." *Journal of Economic History* 26 (March): 133–43.

Strahler, Steven. 1987. "Michael McCasky Manages the Monsters of the Midway." *MBA,* January, 53–57.

Styer, Robert. 1970. *The Encyclopedia of Hockey.* Cranbury, N.J.: A. S. Barnes.

Telander, Rick. 1989. *The Hundred Yard Lie.* New York: Simon and Schuster.

Thorn, John, and Peter Palmer (editors). 1989. *Total Baseball.* New York: Warner Books.

Thornley, Stew. 1989. *Basketball's Original Dynasty: The History of the Lakers.* Minneapolis: Nodin Press.

Torinus, John. 1982. *The Packer Legend.* Neshkoro. WI: Laranmark Press.

Treat, Roger. 1977. *The Encyclopedia of Football.* 15th ed. Cranbury, N.J.: A. S. Barnes.

Tullius, John. 1986. *I'd Rather Be a Yankee.* New York: Macmillan.

Turkin, Hy, and S. C. Thompson. 1972. *The Official Encyclopedia of Baseball.* 6th ed. Cranbury, N.J.: A. S. Barnes.

Uberstein, Gary. 1988. *The Law of Professional and Amateur Sports.* New York: Clark Boardman.

U.S. Department of Commerce, Bureau of the Census. 1975. *Historical Statistics of the United States.* Washington, D.C.: U.S. Government Printing Office.

———. 1990. *Statistical Abstract of the United States.* Washington, D.C.: U.S. Government Printing Office.

Vamplew, Wray. 1982. "The Economics of a Sports Industry: Scottish Gate-Money Football, 1890–1914." *Economic History Review* 48 (November): 549–567.

Vass, George. 1971. *George Halas and the Chicago Bears.* Chicago: Henry Regnery.

Veeck, Bill (with Ed Linn). 1962. *Veeck as in Wreck.* New York: Ballantine Books.

———. 1965. *The Hustler's Handbook.* New York: G. P. Putnam Sons.

Voigt, David. 1983. *American Baseball.* 4 vols. University Park, Pa.: Pennsylvania State University Press.

White, Michael. 1986. "Self-Interest, Redistribution and the National

Football League Players' Association." *Economic Inquiry* 24 (October): 669–680.

Whitman, Robert. 1984. *Jim Thorpe and the Oorang Indians.* Defiance, Ohio: Hubbard.

Whitney, James. 1988. "Winning Games vs. Winning Championships: The Economics of Fan Interest and Team Performance." *Economic Inquiry* 26 (October): 703–724.

Whittingham, Richard. 1984. *What a Game They Played.* New York: Harper and Row.

Wien, Sandra. 1973. "The Case for Equality in Athletics." *Cleveland State Law Review* 22 (Fall): 570–584.

Windhausen, John. 1987. *Sports Encyclopedia: North America.* Gulf Breeze, FL: Academia International Press.

Wiseman, N. 1977. "The Economics of Football." *Lloyds Bank Review* 123 (January): 29–43.

Zech, Charles. 1981. "An Empirical Estimation of a Production Function: The Case of Major League Baseball." *American Economist* 25 (Fall): 19–23.

Zimbalist, Andrew. 1991. "Salaries and Performance in Major League Baseball: An Appraisal of the Scully Model." Smith College. Mimeo.

Congressional Hearings

Amendments to the Communications Act of 1934, Senate Committee on Commerce, Science, and Transportation, 96th Congress, 1st session, May, June 1979, S261–6, Y4.C73/7:96–45/part f3.

Annual Report of the Federal Communications Commission on the Effects of Public Law 93–107, The Sports Antiblackout Law, General Accounting Office, Annual, 1973–1978, S262–17, Yr.C73/7:Sp6/ 1978.

The Antitrust Laws and Organized Professional Team Sports, Including Consideration of the Proposed Merger of the American and National Basketball Associations, House Committee on the Judiciary, 92d Congress, 2d session, July, August, September 1972, H521–3, Y4.J89/1:92–38.

Antitrust Policy and Professional Sports, House Committee on the Judiciary, 97th Congress, 1st and 2d sessions, February, July, September, and December 1982, H5321–35, Y4.J89/1:97/114.

Blackout of Sporting Events on Television, Senate Committee on Commerce, 92d session, October 1972, S261–66, Y4.C73/ 2:92–78.

Bibliography

Broadcasting and Televising Baseball Games, Senate Committee on Interstate and Foreign Commerce, 83d Congress, 1st session, May 1953, S1052–3, Y4.In8/3:B29.

Cable Copyright and Signal Carriage Act of 1982, Senate Committee on the Judiciary, 97th Congress, 2d session, December 1982, S261–19, Y4.C73/7:97–140.

Cable Copyright Protection, House Committee on Energy and Commerce, 97th Congress, 2d session, June 1982, H361–111, Y4.En2/3:97–148.

Cable TV Regulation, Senate Committee on Commerce. Science. and Transportation, 97th Congress, April 1982, S261–59, Y4.C73/7:97–97/part 2.

Collegiate Student-Athlete Protection Act of 1983, Senate Committee on the Judiciary, 98th Congress, 1st session, March, May 1983, S921–80, Y4.J89/2:S.hrg.98–378.

The Communications Act of 1979, Volume II, Part 1, House Committee on Interstate and Foreign Commerce, 96th Congress, 1st session, May, June 1979, H501–86, Y4.In8/4:96–123.

Comprehensive Tax Reform, Part 4, House Committee on Ways and Means, 99th Congress, 1st session, May, June, July 1985, H781–20, Y4.W36:99–44.

Copyright/Cable TV, House Committee on the Judiciary, 97th Congress, 1st and 2d sessions, May, June, July, December 1981, March 1982, H521–39, Y4.J89/1:97/44/parts 1 and 2.

Copyright Law Revision—CATV, Senate Committee on the Judiciary, 89th Congress, 2d session, August 1966, S1766–5, Y4.J89/2:C79/3.

Copyright Issues: Cable Television and Performance Rights, House Committee on the Judiciary, 96th Congress, 1st session, November 1979, H521–12, Y4.J89/1:96/28.

Copyright Royalty Fees for Cable Systems, House Committee on the Judiciary, 98th Congress, 1st session, October 1983. February 1984, H531–56, Y4.J89/1:98/102.

Federal Sports Act of 1972, Senate Committee on Commerce. 92d Congress, 2d session, June 1972, S261–17, Y4.C73/2:92–96.

Final Meetings of the House Select Committee on Professional Sports, 94th Congress, 2d session, December 1976, January 1977, Y4.Sp6:Sp6/1977.

Inquiry into Professional Sports, House Select Committee on Professional Sports, 94th Congress, 2d session, June, July, August, September 1976, H961–2,3, Y4.Sp6:Sp6/parts 1 and 2.

Labor Reform Act of 1977, Senate Committee on Human Resources. 95th Congress, 1st session, October, November 1977, S411–23, Y4.H88:L11/part 2.

Labor Relations in Professional Sports, House Committee on Education and Labor, 92d Congress, 2d session, March 1972, H341–24, Y4.Ed8/1:Sp6.

Organized Professional Team Sports, House Committee on the Judiciary, 85th Congress, 1st session, June, July, August 1957, H1619–4, H1620–1, H1634–3, Y4.J89/1:85/8/parts 1, 2, and 3.

Organized Professional Team Sports, Senate Committee on the Judiciary, 86th Congress, 1st session, July 1959, S1350–2, Y4.J89/2:Sp6/959.

Organized Team Sports, Senate Committee on the Judiciary. 85th Congress, 2d session, July 1958, S1292–3, Y4.J89/2:sp6.

Oversight Hearings on NFL Labor-Management Dispute, House Committee on Education and Labor, 94th Congress, 1st session, September 1975, H341–18, Y4.Ed8/1:N21f/3.

Proceedings of the Congressional Copyright and Technology Symposium, Senate Committee on the Judiciary, 99th Congress, 1st session, July 1985, Y4.J89/ss2:prt.s99–71.

Professional Baseball, Senate Committee on the Judiciary, 92d Congress, 1st session, September 1971, S521–48, Y4.J89/2:B29/2/parts 1 and 2.

Professional Football League Merger, House Committee on the Judiciary, 89th Congress, 2d session, October 1966, H2234–5, Y4.J89/1:89/22.

Professional Sports, House Committee on Energy and Commerce, 97th Congress, 1st session, April, July 1985, H361–6, Y4.En2/3:99–36.

Professional Sports and the Law, Study by the House Select Committee on Professional Sports, 94th Congress, 2d session, August 1976, H962–4, Y4.Sp6:L41.

Professional Sports Antitrust Bill—1964, Senate Committee on the Judiciary, 88th Congress, 2d session, January, February 1964, S1630–1, Y4.J89/2:Sp6/964.

Professional Sports Antitrust Bill—1965, Senate Committee on the Judiciary, 89th Congress, 1st session, February 1965, S1700–1, Y4.J89/2:Sp6/965.

Professional Sports Antitrust Immunity, Senate Committee on the Judiciary, 97th Congress, 2d session, August, September 1982, S521–48, Y4.J89/2:J-97–134.

Professional Sports Antitrust Immunity, Senate Committee on the Judiciary, 99th Congress, 1st session, February, March, June 1985, S521–37, Y4.J89/2:S.hrg.99–496.

Professional Sports Blackouts, House Committee on Interstate and Foreign Commerce, 93d Congress, 1st session, July, August, September 1973, H501–52, Y4.In8/4:93–40.

Bibliography

Professional Sports Community Protection Act of 1985, Senate Committee on Commerce, Science, and Transportation, 99th Congress, 1st session, February 1985, S261–25, Y4.C73/7:S.hrg.99–36.

Professional Sports Team Community Protection Act, Senate Committee on Commerce, Science and Transportation, 98th Congress, 2d session, April, May 1984, S261–58, Y4.C73/7:S.hrg.98s-855.

Professional Sports Team Community Protection Act, House Committee on Energy and Commerce, 98th Congress, 2d session, June 1984, H361–41, Y4.En2/3:98–171.

Regulation of Community Antenna Television, House Committee on Interstate and Foreign Commerce, 89th Congress, 2d session, March, April 1966, H2172–6, Y4.In8/4:89–34.

Rights of Professional Athletes, House Committee on the Judiciary, 94th Congress, 1st session, October 1975, H521–16, Y4.J89/1:94–59.

Sports Anti-Blackout Legislation Oversight, House Committee on Interstate and Foreign Commerce, 95th Congress, 2d session, April 1978, H501–63, Y4.In8/4:95–185.

Sports Broadcasting Act of 1975, House Committee on Interstate and Foreign Commerce, 94th Congress, 1st session, September, October 1975, H501–7, Y4.In8/4:94–47.

Study of Monopoly Power, Part 6, *Organized Baseball*, House Committee on the Judiciary, 82d Congress, 1st session, July, August, October 1951, H1365–3, Y4.J89/1:82/1/pt.6.

Subjecting Professional Baseball Clubs to the Antitrust Laws, Senate Committee on the Judiciary, 83d Congress, 1st session, March, April, May 1954, S1102–2, Y4.J89/2:B29.

Tax Reform Act of 1975, Senate Committee on Finance, 94th Congress, 2d session, March, April 1976, S361–26, Y4.F149:T19/46/part 2.

Telecasting of Professional Sports Contests, House Committee on the Judiciary, 87th Congress, 1st session, August 1961, H1885–3, Y4.J89/1:87/13.

Television Blackout of Sporting Events, Senate Committee on Commerce, 94th Congress, 1st session, November 1975, S261–39, Y4.C73/2:94–56.

Index of Names

Index of Names

533

Index of Names

Index of Names

Index of Court Cases